A Sociology of Educating

Also available from Continuum

Psychology and the Teacher 8th Edition, Dennis Child

Teaching Thinking 3rd Edition, Robert Fisher

When Teaching Becomes Learning 2nd Edition, Eric Sotto

Analysing Underachievement in Schools, Emma Smith

Education and Community, Dianne Gereluk

Philosophy of Education, Richard Pring

A Sociology of Educating

5th EDITION

**Roland Meighan
and Clive Harber**

with contributions by

Len Barton, Iram Siraj-Blatchford and
Stephen Walker

continuum

Continuum International Publishing Group

The Tower Building   80 Maiden Lane
11 York Road   Suite 704
London SE1 7NX   New York NY 10038

www.continuumbooks.com

First published in the United Kingdom by Cassell, 1981.
Reprinted 1986, 1997, 2004.

First published in the United States by Holt, Rinehart and Winston Ltd, 1981.
Reprinted 1986.

Fifth edition published by Continuum, 2007.

Reprinted 2009, 2010 (twice)

British Library Cataloguing-in-Publication Data
A catalogue record for this book is available from the British Library.

ISBN: 9780826481283 (paperback)
       9780826481290 (hardcover)

Library of Congress Cataloging-in-Publication Data
A catalog record for this book is available from the Library of Congress.

Typeset by YHT Ltd, London
Printed and bound in Great Britain

Mixed Sources
Product group from well-managed
forests and other controlled sources
www.fsc.org Cert no. TT-COC-002769
© 1996 Forest Stewardship Council

Contents

Part Six SIGNPOSTS TO THE NEXT LEARNING SYSTEM

Acknowledgements

Many of the people who have contributed to this book cannot be adequately acknowledged. They include pupils, students, colleagues, friends and writers who have contributed ideas, comments or reactions that have become part of our consciousness or woven into our teaching and writing. Although we cannot name them all, we recognize our considerable debt to them all. Among those we can name are Len Barton, Christine Brown, Gerald Cortis, Lynn Davies, Janet Meighan, Frank Reeves, Mike Roberts, Richard Szreter and Stephen Walker. Special thanks are due to John Siraj-Blatchford for his comments and support during the preparation of the manuscript for the third edition. Inadequacies in the work, however, remain the writers' sole responsibility. The authors and publisher would like to thank the following for permission to use material in this book:

British Journal of Educational Psychology
Department of Education and Skills
Education Otherwise
Educational Review
Grant MacIntyre
Heinemann
Sophia and Frances Howard
Journal of Curriculum Studies
New Science Publications
Open University Press
Oxford University Press
Penguin Books
Peter Davies Ltd
Punch
Ivan Reid
Routledge and Kegan Paul
Anthony Rudolf
Social Science Teacher
Times Educational Supplement

Preface to the 5th Edition

I was delighted when Clive Harber agreed to join me as co-author of the 5th Edition of this book after Iram Siraj-Blatchford had decided she had to withdraw for personal and family reasons. It meant a renewal of a previous successful partnership, as I worked with Clive at the University of Birmingham in the 1980s.

Clive Harber has distinguished himself in the field of International Education and Education in Developing Countries. He was Head of the School of Education at the University of Birmingham until August 2006 and Head of the School of Education at the University of Natal before that. But he is not afraid of taking a radical position, as his book, *Schooling as Violence* (2004), gives witness. His experience of teaching courses and supervising research on International Education, plus his experience of working in South Africa, while conducting research in various countries throughout Africa and elsewhere, adds a fresh, new dimension to this book. There are now many more comparative and international passages, illustrations and references in the book. Specifically, his analysis of schooling internationally as, paradoxically, both currently contributing to authoritarianism and violence on the one hand, and peace and democracy on the other, has added a fresh aspect to the book.

A Sociology of Educating, has become regarded as a classic text, ranking alongside works such as Waller's *Sociology of Teaching* (first published in 1932), according to feedback we have received. Moreover, regular users of the book frequently request that we leave the main text alone as far as possible, using the 'Signposts', 'Discussion and Activities' and 'Further Reading' as the main vehicles for updating – especially as many have devised their own notes for students on recent developments in the subject matter, research and readings.

Nevertheless, a long-standing problem is that the general principles outlined in this book are subject to many local variations in practice and in legal stipulation. There are variations across Europe, within the British Isles among England, Wales, Scotland, Northern Ireland and the Republic of Ireland, and in other countries across the globe. If we take the single example of home-based education, there are variations in legal requirements, expectations and practice from country to country. But this problem did not prevent Polish academics from organizing a translation of the text into Polish. They argued that they could explain to their students the nature of the variations that occurred within Polish education.

We continue to use website references sparingly, knowing that current-day students are usually computer literate and so are their tutors, and well able to do any necessary searches for contemporary material.

Inevitably, statistics in a textbook refer to a particular time and situation. Readers will need to use their computer skills to assess changes and current positions by using the Internet. A start can be made by readers in the UK by visiting www.dfes.gov.uk, www.statistics.gov.uk and www.statsed.co.uk.

This 5th Edition comes with a new chapter, entitled 'The Discourses of Education', written by Stephen Walker, which appears at the end of Part Four. As Walker notes, 'Discourses, then, are central to both the formation of the individual in society and they provide the rules for the conduct and interactions of any individual in all social situations and encounters.' Discourses both permit and constrain, they can be complementary or contradictory. Sources of Internet discussion of these ideas are provided at the end of this chapter.

I was encouraged to read a review by Mary Thorton of the University of Hertfordshire, of the 4th Edition of *A Sociology of Educating*. It said, 'An old warhorse perhaps, but what a joy to read! It reminded me why the sociology of education became such a key part of my working life as an academic. Does it still inspire? Yes ...' (*The Lecturer*, December 2005).

Roland Meighan

Note to the reader:
All chapters are authored by Roland Meighan unless noted as being the work of other authors at the start of each chapter. Clive Harber has worked together with Roland Meighan to update material throughout for this Fifth Edition.

Preface to the 1st Edition

Many harsh things have been said about the writers of books. Samuel Johnson observed, 'Your manuscript is both good and original: but the part that is good is not original, and the part that is original is not good.' A gibe about bland writing comes from Charles Colton: 'Many books require no thought from those who read them, and for a very simple reason – they made no such demand upon those who wrote them.' But the most helpful advice I found came from Anthony Hope: 'Unless one is a genius, it is best to aim at being intelligible.'

This book is written with three audiences in mind. First, those who are beginning a career in education, such as students on initial teacher education courses. Second, experienced teachers on in-service courses with little or no sociological study in their previous courses. The third group that may find the material of interest is comprised of educationalists whose previous sociological study has been limited to the structural functionalist perspective.

The title of the book contains the verb 'educating' rather than the noun 'education', and this indicates that a particular perspective is employed for large sections of the book, namely the interactionist perspective. Since the perspectives are discussed at some length, it is sufficient to say that a key concept in the interactionist approach is that of the contradictions and ironies in social life. Key ideas in other approaches may be harmony in society and its organizations, or conflict in social structures.

This book is meant to be a progress report. Its intention is to stimulate sociologically informed thinking about educating rather than to provide any final conclusion or necessarily 'true' message. It is meant to be interpreted as constructive doubt and review, rather than the establishment of certainties.

The structure of the book is idiosyncratic and needs some explanation. Many sociology of education texts begin with an account of sociological concepts and theories and then use these to scrutinize education. Others develop a sociology of education which reflects on the theories and concepts of the parent discipline of sociology at the end. This book does neither. It begins with a light-hearted taste of sociology to give something of the flavour of this approach to thinking about society, and then gives three sociological accounts of topics unrelated except in their tendency to be provocative. These topics are assessment, the pupil's viewpoint and the teacher as a victim. I hope that this first part will establish some of the excitement and interest of sociology, as well as some of its relevance to an understanding of schooling.

The section on sociological theories and perspectives comes in the middle of the book, on the logic of a 'time out' in sports like basketball. It seems appropriate, after doing some sociological thinking, to reflect on the theoretical nature of the enterprise before undertaking some more investigation in the remainder of the book. (Len Barton and Stephen Walker have written this theoretical section at my invitation.) Users of the book are, of course, at liberty to ignore these ideas and use the material in any order they think fit.

Any selection of the concepts of a book is somewhat arbitrary. Those selected by the writer are: the hidden curriculum for Part Two, ideologies of education for Part Three, and educational life chances for Part Five. The final part, alternatives in education, uses the concepts of the previous parts to analyse various educational institutions. These are selected as the concepts that have emerged in the writer's teaching, reading and research as the most significant of those so far developed.

I have tried to write in an intelligible style and if I have been successful, there is the potential penalty of being interpreted as facile and simplistic, since, as research quoted in the book indicates, the same idea expressed in difficult and dense language gains higher applause as 'more academic' and 'superior in depth'. As Molière observed, 'That must be wonderful; I don't understand it at all.' However, I shall take the risk, and aim at communication rather than mystification.

ROLAND MEIGHAN

To Janet, James, Mark and Steve
In memory of Shirley
R.M.

To Mary
C.H.

Other books by the Authors

Roland Meighan

Sociological Interpretations of Schooling and Classrooms: A Reappraisal (with Len Barton, 1978)
Perspectives on Society (with Ian Shelton and Tony Marks, 1978)
School, Pupils and Deviance (with Len Barton, 1979)
Schooling, Ideology and the Curriculum (with Len Barton and Stephen Walker, 1980)
Alternative Educational Futures (with Clive Harber and Brian Roberts, 1984)
Flexischooling: Education for Tomorrow, Starting Yesterday (1988)
The Democratic School (with Clive Harber, 1989)
Learning from Home-based Education (1992)
Anatomy of Choice in Education (with Philip Toogood, 1992)
Theory and Practice of Regressive Education (1993)
The Freethinkers' Guide to the Educational Universe (1994)
The Freethinkers' Pocket Directory to the Educational Universe (1995)
John Holt: Personalised Education and the Reconstruction of Schooling (1995)
The Next Learning System (1997)
The Next Learning System: Pieces of the Jigsaw (2000)
25 Years of Home-Based Education: Research, Reviews and Case Material (2001)
Learning Unlimited: The Home-Based Education Case-Files (2001)
Natural Learning and the Natural Curriculum (2001)
Damage Limitation: trying to reduce the harm schools do to children (2004)
Comparing Learning Systems (2005)

Clive Harber

Authored Books
2005 *Global Citizenship Education: The Needs of Teachers and Learners* (Report on DfID Funded Research Project, Centre for International Education and Research, University of Birmingham) (with L. Davies and H. Yamashita)
2005 *Democratic Professional Development: a Guidebook for Supervisors and Inspectors of Teachers* (Reading: Centre for British Teachers)
2004 *Schooling As Violence: How Schools Harm Pupils and Societies* (London: RoutledgeFalmer)

2003 *Towards Ubuntu: Critical Teacher Education and Citizenship in South Africa and England* (Birmingham: Development Education Centre) (with J. Serf and C. Carter)

2002 *Democracy Through Teacher Education: a Guidebook for Use with Student Teachers* (Reading: Centre for British Teachers) (with L. Davies and M. Schweisfurth)

2001 *State of Transition: Post-Apartheid Educational Reform in South Africa* (Oxford: Symposium Books) pp 1–95

1997 *Education Democracy and Political Development in Africa* (Brighton: Sussex Academic Press) pp 1–168

1997 *School Management and School Effectiveness in Developing Countries* (London: Cassell) (with L. Davies) pp 1–189

1996 *Small Schools and Democratic Practice* (Nottingham: Educational Heretics Press) pp 1–73

1992 *Democratic Learning and Learning Democracy* (Ticknall: Education Now) pp 1–41

1989 *Politics in African Education* (London: Macmillan) pp 1–202

Edited Books

2002 Learning Democracy and Citizenship: International Experiences (Oxford: Symposium Books (Edited with M. Schweisfurth and L. Davies) pp 1–304

1998 *Voices for Democracy: a North–South Dialogue on Education for Sustainable Democracy* (Nottingham: Education Now in Association with the British Council) (Edited C. Harber) pp 1–138

1995 *Developing Democratic Education* (Ticknall: Education Now) (Edited C. Harber) pp 1–115

1989 *The Democratic School* (Ticknall: Education Now) (Edited with R. Meighan) pp 1–202

1987 *Political Education in Britain* (Lewes: The Falmer Press) (Edited C. Harber) pp 1–188

1986 *Social Education: Principles and Practice* (Lewes: The Falmer Press) (Edited with C. Brown and J. Strivens) pp 1–253

1984 *Alternative Educational Futures* (Eastbourne: Holt Rinehart) (Edited with R. Meighan and B. Roberts) pp 1–180

Part One
FAMILIARIZATION

The opening section is rather unconventional, since it is based on the ideas of browsing in libraries, familiarization through wandering around a new place, tasting or taking an aperitif. A rigorous, structured opening has been discarded for something more eclectic and appetite-whetting. Chapter 1 attempts to review observations made about sociology and the sociological enterprise rather than develop a conceptual map or a systematic account of the discipline. The remaining chapters of Part One are connected in two ways. First, they are rather provocative ideas: mass media, the pupils' viewpoint, the teacher as victim, and the parent as educator. Second, they can be seen as examples of the interactionist concept of layers of meaning mentioned in Chapter 1. The interpretation of the phenomenon of schooling varies according to the situation of the viewer: there is no objective entity called 'school'; only overlapping and varying accounts can be obtained. If, at the end of the section, the reader is not curious about the sociological contribution to the understanding of the processes of educating and is not intrigued by the possibilities of a sociological imagination, the writer has failed in his intentions.

A Taste of Sociology 1

Gossip: sociologists on a mean and petty scale.

Woodrow Wilson

INTRODUCTION

People usually ask for the recipe after tasting a dish rather than before tasting it. Following this kind of logic, this introduction will avoid definitions and lists of concepts in favour of observations about sociology. This approach is not original. Peter Berger used the same approach in his book *Invitation to Sociology* in 1966. The approach is also very much in keeping with Frank Smith's arguments regarding the means by which most of us first joined the *literacy club*. Smith (1985) argued that children begin reading because they wish to join others who seem to be getting something out of it. We have precisely the same aims regarding the sociology of schooling. We all started reading and writing because we found that we had interests in common with other readers and writers, and we committed ourselves to it because we developed an expectation that we would ultimately achieve all the fluency and capability of the experts. In just the same way, in terms of sociological literacy, we want you to become quickly involved in evaluating the arguments and researching and writing about the educational issues that concern you.

The *sociology club* has a long history; in fact there is a sense in which sociology may be seen as one of the oldest of the sciences. As Abraham (1966) noted, just as soon as people began to reflect on the way in which their society was or should be organized they were thinking in sociological terms. All those who have come to hold views on humanity and on its destiny, on the rise and fall of peoples and civilizations, are thinking in sociological terms even if they consider themselves philosophers, historians, law-givers or seers.

THE STUDY OF THE SOCIAL LIFE CREATED BY PEOPLE

Reflecting on society has not always been regarded as necessarily desirable:

> To quote from a matchbox – sociology is the study of those who don't need it by those who do.
>
> Weightman, 1977

This joke suggests a suspicion of those who study others. In addition, the common confusion between psychology and sociology is present, and the joke could more accurately be applied to psychology in its study of people as individuals, rather than to sociology, where the subject matter is more centrally, the institutions, cultures and social systems created by people, and, in turn, influencing people's behaviour.

Sociology is the source of fewer jokes than psychology, and this is an interesting feature for reflection. Psychologists seem to have been 'recognized' rather more than sociologists. One possible explanation lies in the success of psychology in establishing a claim to be special, and mysterious, rather like the impression many people have of physics:

> People do not expect to have a special knowledge of a subject like physics ... But because they are familiar with the objects the sociologist studies, they feel they already have a special knowledge of them and resent any sociological claim that they do not.
>
> McGee *et al.*, 1977

One sustained joke about sociology appeared in the form of an 'examination paper' in the satirical magazine *Punch* on 2 October 1974 (see Figure 1.1). Some of the questions in this spoof examination paper can be said to raise important issues about sociologists. Thus the statement 'Somebody introduced the Black Death. Somebody introduced Income Tax. Somebody introduced sociology' is stated in a sympathetic form as the point of a discussion by Cuzzort and King (1989):

> Even if the people who have the official title of 'sociologist' were to cease offering their interpretations of social conduct to the world, the world would still demand that somebody tell it what is going on.

The introduction of sociology or its equivalent is seen by Cuzzort and King as inevitable and desirable, though whether they would say the same about the Black Death and Income Tax is another matter.

Another source of humour in the 'examination questions' is the questioning approach assumed in the jokes to be revolutionary:

> As a 'mildly radical' sociologist, how would you set about undermining any *two* of the following:
>
> (a) The Bank of England;
> (b) Mr Hughie Green (a quiz show host);
> (c) Civilisation as we know it;
> (d) The international Freemasonry conspiracy.

GENERAL CERTIFICATE OF EDUCATION

ADVANCED LEVEL

SOCIOLOGY

Time: Two Hours

Only Six Questions To Be Attempted

1. *'Sociology is the study of people who do not need to be studied, by people who do.'*
   'Somebody introduced the Black Death. Somebody introduced Income Tax. Somebody introduced sociology.'
   'All the Golden Ages of man, all the Belles Epoques, were characterised by one thing: an absence of sociologists.'
   Which of these hostile assessments do you find most wounding? Which of them comes nearest to the truth? How would you attempt to improve the public image of sociology, while covertly furthering its subversive aims?

2. Johnny is a married man with ten children in institutions and a wife who resides in a battered wives' home. He has now found happiness with a 'Common Law Wife' just out of school who is about to bear him another child. They live in a retarded caravan which has broken down in North Ham, and Johnny draws Social Security. He is unable to work because, 'That's the way I've always been, innit?' He is claiming a council flat at North Ham, but the Council is reluctant to advance him over the heads of 15,000 people who have been on the housing list for an average of twelve years.
   Explain why we are all to blame for the dilemma in which Johnny finds himself. How would you set about fanning the country into a state of white-hot indignation on his behalf?

3. State which of the following you consider the ultimate in obscenity: (a) an unearned income of £50,000 a year; (b) *Oh Calcutta!*; (c) anyone over thirty enjoying sex; (d) the headmaster of a comprehensive school who dismisses his 'D' stream as 'a shower of dimmies'; (e) the Young Conservatives. Give reasons for your choice.

4. *'A democracy is that form of government which prevails in one form or another in the decay of a State.'* Though widely discredited at the time, this judgment by the Duke of Northumberland in 1909 is now recognised to be correct. Suggest ways in which the sociologist can contribute to the decay of the State and the enervation of the Constitution, while preserving lip-service to democracy.

5. Distinguish between:
   (a) a revolution and a revolutionary situation;
   (b) justice and social justice;
   (c) a committed person and a biased person.

Describe how a court of social justice would operate in a revolutionary situation.

6. As a 'mildly radical' sociologist, how would you set about undermining any *two* of the following:
   (a) The Bank of England;
   (b) Mr Hughie Green;
   (c) Civilisation as we know it;
   (d) The international Freemasonry conspiracy.

7. Len and Linda are living in London waiting and working for the Revolution. They pay a week's rent to a landlord and then sit tight, making no further payments, for seven months, which is the time it takes the landlord to get an eviction order. They then repeat the performance a few streets away.
   Given the exploitative world we live in, do you regard this as an acceptable design for living? Can you think of any reason why the rest of us should not do the same?

8. Compose a short Pop song embodying
   either
   The jubilant cry of an unmarried father who has broken his bourgeois shackles;
   or
   The lament of a Sixth Former who sees for the first time his classroom as the nursery of a counter-revolutionary ideology.

9. 'It seems to be a law of Nature,' writes Townend, 'that the poor should be to a certain degree improvident, that there may be always some to fulfil the most servile, the most sordid and the most ignoble offices. The stock of human happiness is thereby much increased.' Do you accept this law of Nature? If not, how would you work to overturn it? Is it better to leave the ignoble offices to immigrants, as at present? As a sociologist, what other ignoble offices would you be prepared to fulfil?

10. What are the epistemological problems involved in the tying of academic sociology, and in particular structural-functional theory, to a 'conservative' ideological standpoint, with its temptation to treat man as *homo sociologicus*? And do you think that people with white stone balls on their gateposts deserve everything that is coming to them?

Figure 1.1 A spoof examination paper in sociology by E. S. Turner. From *Punch*, 2 October 1974. Reproduced by permission of *Punch*.

The nature of this questioning approach is the subject of considerable comment by writers on sociology:

> Sociology is a subject with important practical implications. It can contribute to social criticism and practical social reform in several ways. First, the improved understanding of a given set of social circumstances often gives us all a better chance of controlling them. Second, sociology provides the means of increasing our cultural sensitivities, allowing policies to be based on an awareness of divergent cultural values. Third, we can investigate the consequences (intended and unintended) of the adoption of particular policy

programmes. Finally, and perhaps most important, sociology provides self-enlightenment, offering groups and individuals an increased opportunity to alter the conditions of their own lives.

Giddens, 1989

SOME SOCIOLOGICAL THEMES

The following poem combines a statement about the point of questioning institutions, cultures and social conduct, and a useful content list of themes covered in sociological writings. The exceptions are perhaps the themes of 'unconscious' and 'genes', which psychologists would claim as their particular province, 'climate', which is the concern of geographers, and 'deep linguistic structures', which are studied by psycholinguists. Additionally, a sociologist would study the phenomenon of 'belief in God' rather than a theological study based on the assumption of a God.

The Humanist's Sonnet
by Anthony Rudolf

I am determined by my sex
I am determined by my class
I am determined by my God
I am determined by my genes
I am determined by my unconscious
I am determined by my childhood
I am determined by my death
I am determined by my climate
I am determined by my homeland
I am determined by my work
I am determined by my newspaper
I am determined by my deep linguistic structures
I am determined by my etcetera
I am determined to be free

From the *New Humanist*. Reproduced with the permission of Anthony Rudolf.

This 'freedom' of the last line can easily be misinterpreted. The kind of freedom to which sociological inquiry contributes is a matter of continual debate among sociologists. Freedom is not seen as 'doing as one pleases'. Even choosing between alternatives is only a partial freedom.

Freedom is first of all the chance to formulate the available choices, to argue over them – and then the opportunity to choose. That is why freedom cannot exist without an enlarged role of human reason in human affairs.

Wright Mills, 1959

PERSONAL CONCERNS AND SOCIAL STRUCTURES

The issues raised in 'The Humanist's Sonnet' include a further theme, the link between personal concerns and social structures. A key feature of the sociological imagination, C. Wright Mills argued, was an awareness of this interplay. People in a mass society have personal problems which are intertwined with the social structure, but many do not recognize the connections. Knowledgeable people do. They understand that what they think of as personal troubles are very often also problems shared by others, and are incapable of solution by any one individual. Then only modifications of the structure of the groups in which they live, and sometimes the structure of the entire society, can be effective initiatives.

SOCIOLOGICAL QUESTIONS

Sociological questions are couched in terms of the social world that people create:

> The sociologist's questions always remain essentially the same: 'What are people doing with each other here?' 'What are their relationships to each other?' 'How are those relationships organized in institutions?' 'What are the collective ideas that move men and institutions?'
>
> Berger, 1966
>
> Copyright, © Peter Berger, 1966. Reprinted by permission of Penguin Books Ltd.

Another famous attempt to outline the kinds of questions of a sociological approach is that of C. Wright Mills. Classic social analysts, he suggests, have consistently asked three sorts of questions:

1. What is the structure of this particular society as a whole? What are its essential components, and how are they related to one another? How does it differ from other varieties of social order? Within it, what is the meaning of any particular feature for its continuance and for its change?

2. Where does this society stand in human history? What are the mechanics by which it is changing? What is its place within and its meaning for the development of humanity as a whole? How does any particular feature we are examining affect, and how is it affected by the historical period in which it moves? And this period – what are its essential features? How does it differ from other periods? What are its characteristic ways of history-making?

3. What varieties of men and women now prevail in this society and in this period? And what varieties are coming to prevail? In what ways are they selected and formed, liberated and repressed, made sensitive and blunted? What kinds of 'human nature' are revealed in the conduct and character we observe in this society in this period? And what is the meaning for 'human nature' of each and every feature of the society we are examining?

> Wright Mills, 1959
>
> From *The Sociological Imagination*. Reprinted by permission of Oxford University Press.

SOCIOLOGY – FOR WHAT PURPOSES?

Sociologists are not agreed on the purposes of their study. Although there is general agreement that understanding social life is a key feature, the uses of sociology are disputed. One point of view is as follows:

> Should sociologists themselves actively advocate, and agitate for, practical programmes of reform or social change? Some argue that sociology can preserve its objectivity only if practitioners of the subject are studiously neutral in moral and political controversies, but there is no reason to think that scholars who remain aloof from current debates are necessarily more impartial in their assessment of sociological issues than others. There is bound to be a connection between studying sociology and the promptings of a social conscience. No sociologically sophisticated person can be unaware of the inequalities that exist in the world today, the lack of social justice in many social situations or the deprivations suffered by millions of people. It would be strange if sociologists did not take sides on practical issues, and it would be illogical as well as impractical to try to ban them from drawing on their sociological expertise in doing so.
>
> Giddens, 1989

The products of an enquiry that is conducted in an effort to understand society may be used by different individuals or groups for differing purposes. Berger (1966) argued that there was nothing inherent in the sociological enterprise that leads to any particular practice or outcome. One's choice of an area of study is, however, bound to be significant.

An alternative view is held by those who see prescriptions for changing cultures and institutions as a major concern. The idea is contained in the statement of Marx: 'The philosophers have only interpreted the world in various ways; the point, however, is to change it.'

THE IRONY OF HUMAN ACTION

Those who would urge caution about this commitment to change society do so on various grounds, one of which refers to the difficulty of ensuring that change goes as planned. One finding derived from interactionist sociology is that of the irony of human action:

> the outcome of ideas is commonly very different from what those who had the ideas in the first place planned or hoped. Such a consciousness of the ironic aspect of history is sobering, a strong antidote to all kinds of revolutionary utopianism.
>
> Berger, 1966

Another reason for urging caution is that discovering 'error' does not automatically guarantee a superior alternative, since the alternative actions possible are multitudinous:

Some 'advanced thinkers' are of the opinion that anyone who differs from the conventional opinion must be in the right. This is a delusion; if it were not, truth would be easier to come by than it is. There are infinite possibilities of error.

Russell, 1950

Russell argued in his writings that the prior outcome of all critical and reflective thinking, not just sociological, was constructive doubt (see Russell, 1926). It follows that any social change should be subject to review and revision rather than implemented as the right answer.

SOCIOLOGY AS UNCOMMON SENSE

A view frequently encountered is that sociology is just common sense. Yet wherever sociology is studied, it tends to have a disturbing effect, a disturbing of that very common sense in question. Even though the sociologist investigates and reflects on the familiar society, and even though the categories employed in the analysis are only refinements of the categories which other people use – power, class, status, gender or race – the findings are often unexpected and can contradict common sense.

Therefore one claim made by some sociologists is that their intention is to 'improve' on common sense and 'expose' some of the folk interpretations of social behaviour as incomplete. Berger (1966) employed an interesting range of images to convey this point. He used phrases such as 'seeing through' and 'looking behind' very much as such phrases would be employed in common speech – 'seeing through his game', 'looking behind the scenes' – in other words, 'being up on all the tricks'. The sociologist is seen as trying to penetrate the smokescreen of the official versions of reality, those of the manager, the civil servant or the teacher, and to grasp the signals that come from the 'underworld', from the worker, the client or the pupil.

In setting about this kind of task, sociologists may find themselves in strange company, associating with the outsiders, the outcasts and the minorities, and on a broad range of missions. They may become involved in matters that others regard as sacred or distasteful. They will seek the company of judges or criminals, depending not on personal preferences but on the questions being asked. They will be interested in the human interaction that goes with warfare, with crime or with religion, and also in the relations between people in a classroom, or in a group of children playing in the street. The outcomes of these missions are not guaranteed. The investigation may yield something fresh and unexpected. This may be something totally unfamiliar or it may be the familiar taking on a new meaning. Sociology may make us see in a new light the very world in which we have lived all our lives.

Often, the uncommon sense of today becomes the common sense of tomorrow. As Giddens (1986) observes, a great deal of what we regard as common sense in this context, 'what everyone knows about society', has actually been based upon the routine work of social scientists for decades. We all know, for example, that divorce rates have risen since the Second

World War; we will also be aware of changes in the way teachers work in the classroom, in class sizes and in academic achievements. All this knowledge is based upon sociological research that has been publicized widely to inform social interest.

LAYERS OF MEANING

One reason why something fresh and unexpected is sometimes the outcome of sociological research is related to the complexity of human social behaviour, with its various layers of meaning. An individual may sample only a few of these layers of meaning in the routines of everyday life, e.g. teachers are unlikely to gain a view of school from the point of view of the pupils unless they make a special effort to gain this information. A sociologist is more likely to collect such data. A chapter that follows (Chapter 2) gives an account of the pupil's perspective and shows how the evidence demonstrates that holders of a transmission view of education have made unreasonable assumptions about pupils and that radical educationalists have sometimes embraced a delusion regarding pupils' aspirations. As we shall see in Chapter 23, this recognition has led some social theorists to adopt 'standpoint' theories of knowledge itself.

THE INVISIBLE SOCIAL WORLD

A large part of the introductory literature to sociology is taken up with questions of appropriate methods of study and the claim for the scientific nature of sociology. Sociology may be a network of propositions about the social life created by people, just as physical science is a network of propositions about physical reality, but the difficulties of procedure are increased when the invisibility of the subject matter is recognized:

> It comes as a mild shock to most people to be told that the entire web of human social interrelations is founded on many invisible and indirect meanings which we bestow on various individuals. Not only have we never seen a family. We have never seen a student or a teacher. Nor have we ever seen a scientist, a saint, or a sinner. So it is with socially defined statuses. We can observe the people who occupy such statuses: but, until we are informed that they occupy a certain status and are expected to behave accordingly, we cannot respond in any appropriate manner ... The social world is, then, largely an invisible world. This constitutes a major methodological problem for the sociologist. Sociology is supposed to be a science; and science, after all, is based on observation. What kind of science is it that devotes itself to an examination of events which are, by their very nature, not directly observable?
>
> Cuzzort and King, 1989

In fact, all this should not alarm us unduly if we recognize that the physicist's observations are often equally indirect, and the phenomenon studied, whether it be concerning forces, gravity, light, electricity or energy, is equally invisible and socially constructed.

The balance of power between the social structures that shape (or even determine) our lives and life chances (social class, gender, race) and individual agency (the ability of an individual to influence or control their life) is a significant debate in sociology. The relationship between the two has been extensively analysed by Giddens (1984).

CONCLUSION

Sociology, then, is many things, some of them seemingly paradoxical.

It is a relatively new discipline, yet its quests and questions are among the most ancient forms of reflective thought.

If sociologists were not available, some form of substitute reflection on social behaviour would probably emerge: yet sociological thought and inquiry are also resisted and resented.

Everyone tends to feel familiar with the world of the sociologist: as members of the social world we should be the experts on it. Yet common-sense views are frequently disturbed by the inquiries of sociologists.

Sociology, in attempting to free us from the determining effect of social frameworks, may only make the strength of the structures more apparent and the sought-after freedom more elusive.

Sociology attempts dispassionate inquiry, yet cannot eradicate values from its investigations, the investigator or the subject of the investigation. The sociologists, like good detectives, must suspect everything and everyone, including themselves.

Sociologists themselves are far from united on many issues related to their discipline, yet have some unity in their undertaking to meet argument with argument and to acknowledge the value of the constructive doubt, and in their willingness to live with the creative uncertainty of a constantly changing subject matter.

If this buffet, this smorgasbord, is to your taste, welcome to sociology!

Further Reading

Ball, S. (2004) *The Routledge Farmer Reading in Sociology of Educating*, London: RoutledgeFalmer.

Berger, P. (1966) *Invitation to Sociology*. Harmondsworth: Penguin. Well known as a lively, interesting and readable introduction to sociological thinking.

Berger, P. and Kellner, H. (1983) *Sociology Reinterpreted*. Harmondsworth: Penguin.

Brown, C. (1979) *Understanding Society*. London: John Murray Ltd. The opening chapter has a very intelligible introduction to sociological theory and the problems of social research.

Cuzzort, R.P. and King, E.W. (2002) *Social Thought into the Twenty-First Century*, 6th edn. Orlando, FL: Harcourt Brace. The first chapter of this book is a well written account of some of the basic problems of social thought, its premises, sources of error and degrees of objectivity. The rest of the book gives a very useful account of the work of well known sociologists, including Durkheim, Marx, Weber, Mead, Wright Mills, Becker, Goffman. Garfinkel and Berger.

Giddens, A. (1984) *The Constitution of Society: Outline of the Theory of Structuration*. Cambridge: Polity Press.

Lee, D. and Newby, H. (1983) *The Problem of Sociology*. London: Hutchinson. This book develops some of the themes of this chapter.

Wright Mills, C. (1959) *The Sociological Imagination*. Oxford: Oxford University Press. This is harder reading than the previous five. It is thorough and worth the effort of reading, but perhaps is best tackled after reading one or more of the above.

Discussion and Activities

1. Write down your definition of sociology. Compare it with the definitions written by fellow students, and check it against dictionary, particularly sociological dictionary, definitions. The working definition of this chapter is that sociology can be seen as the systematic study of the social life (institutions, cultures and behaviour patterns) created by people and in turn influencing their behaviour in a continuous interaction.

2. In C. Brown's *Understanding Society* there is an interesting activity: draw a picture or diagram which represents society to you. The first chapter of this book contains a discussion of common responses to this activity, including variations on circles, triangles, networks and stick figures.

3. Conduct an informal survey of opinions about sociology among your friends and relations. How many of these responses are misunderstandings of the kind mentioned in this chapter? Are there regular patterns in the responses? How can we cope with a diversity of interpretations?

4. Take some of the questions from the spoof examination paper (Figure 1.1) and discuss the ideas that are being parodied, misrepresented or accurately stated in each case.

5. Refer back to *The Humanist's Sonnet* by Anthony Rudolf. Prepare an account of how each influence has contributed to your own self-concept.

Signposts

1. The limitations of sociology

This chapter has suggested some of the positive features of sociology but an awareness of limitations is worth some enquiry. A start can be made with Shipman, M. (1972) *The Limitations of Social Research*, Harlow: Longman. Further sources are Burgess, R.G. (ed.) (1984) *The Research Process in Educational Settings: Ten Case Studies*, Lewes: Falmer Press; and Burgess, R.G. (ed.) (1984) *Field Methods in the Study of Education*, Lewes: Falmer Press.

2. The ethics of sociology

If you join a group to study it, what happens if you are required to follow the members into illegal or immoral acts? This was a dilemma presented in Patrick, J. (1973) *A Glasgow Gang Observed*, London: Eyre-Methuen. Further ethical issues are raised in Berger, P. (1977) *Facing up to Modernity*, Harmondsworth: Penguin.

3. The looking-glass self

The looking-glass self is an idea attributed to Charles Horton Cooley (1972). Our reflection in a mirror gives us information about appearance and Cooley proposed that our reflection in other people's attitudes to us, and our interpretations of how they see us, are used as key sources of information about our self-concept. George Herbert Mead (1934) took the idea further, in noting a process he called 'taking the role of the other', whereby a kind of internal debate can take place as an individual rehearses possible courses of action and possible consequences. Mead stresses that in play children develop this activity and develop their self-concept at the same time. An excellent summary of this aspect of interactionism, symbolic interactionism, appears in Chapter 1 of Hargreaves, D.H. (1972) *Interpersonal Relations and Education*, London: Routledge and Kegan Paul. As an activity derived from this concept, you should be able to interview yourself about your experience of schooling or pretend to be a stranger trying to interpret puzzling aspects of schools, such as bells, uniforms or compulsory religious assemblies.

2 Pupils as Clients?*

> I resented being told what to wear, what to think, what to believe, what to say and when to say it.
>
> C. Burke and I. Grosvenor, *The School I'd Like*

INTRODUCTION: SOCIOLOGICAL PERSPECTIVES

Some of the issues raised in this chapter require some awareness of the different perspectives within sociology. These are described in more detail in Part Four, and the account given here is only a brief introduction. One feature that complicates this issue is that there is no universally agreed categorization of the perspectives and the reader will encounter categorizations which are different from the one that follows.

Here, three broad groupings of the sociological perspectives – macro, micro and interactionist – will be proposed.

Macro Perspectives

There are several of these, but they all have a common feature: they start with a view of societies, cultures and institutions as having set patterns of rules and behaviours, with the result that individuals are seen as being forced, persuaded, manipulated or socialized into some degree of compliance with these patterns.

Two major sub-types of macro perspective are frequently described: structural functionalist and structural conflict.

Structural functionalist

This approach is based on an assumption that society is a structure or framework of parts which are closely linked together. Each of these parts (e.g. the economy, the family, education) performs a function in keeping society going. For the most part this structure is seen as

* An earlier version of this chapter appeared in *Educational Review*, Vol. 29, No. 2.

relatively harmonious, because there is seen to be general agreement or consensus about the usefulness of the whole pattern.

Structural conflict

This approach disputes that all groups are relatively well served by the structural arrangements and the idea of a conflict of interests is stressed. Some groups are seen as having advantageous positions over others and they will strive to keep this situation as it is, while other groups are seen as trying to obtain an alternative structure, with a redistribution of advantages and scarce items. One kind of conflict approach, known as Marxist, is derived from the ideas of Karl Marx.

Micro Perspectives

There is a variety of micro perspectives and a confusion of labels, including some lengthy ones like 'ethnomethodology' and 'phenomenology'. Other labels used are 'interpretivist', 'symbolic interactionism' and, confusingly, since it will be treated here as a separate category, 'interactionist'. At this stage these labels, and the variations they signify, need not detain us: they will be explained in Part Four.

What these micro perspectives have in common is a view that, instead of individuals being forced by the patterns of society or pulled by the strings of society like puppets, individuals create society every day by their social actions. Change occurs when individuals cease one set of social actions and start another. Social order is seen as an active production by members of society, and meaning is seen as being negotiated by social actors rather than being imposed upon them.

Interactionist Perspectives

There are several interactionist perspectives, some inclined towards a micro view, some towards a macro view. What they tend to have in common is a view of society as a loose network of related parts in a constant state of flux. This network can be sometimes harmonious, sometimes conflict-laden, sometimes rigidly structured, sometimes more open and flexible, and sometimes can contain some or all of these features in a contradictory state of affairs.

Interactionist perspectives tend to have a Janus view. Janus was a Roman god, the guardian of gates and doorways, who had two faces looking in different directions. Interactionist perspectives tend to look two ways, both at the patterns of society stressed by the macro sociologists and at the work and negotiations that individuals accomplish in keeping society going, as stressed in the micro perspectives.

THE STRUCTURAL FUNCTIONALIST VIEW OF PUPILS

A structural functionalist view of education tends to stress the activity of schools in training and selecting children so that they fit into some necessary slot in a relatively harmonious society. This view implies that children need to be manipulated in some way for that society's convenience or for some other reason. The images used by people who take this view stress this. The teacher is said to be like a potter moulding clay, or like a gardener cultivating plants, or a builder building a house on sound foundations. In each case pupils are seen as things being processed, and often as having no rights. Stone and Taylor (1976) researched legal cases involving pupils' rights. One example was that pupils who were pacifists could still be compelled to join the cadet force of the school: the right of conscientious objection allowable to adults could be overruled by the headteacher. In recent times some international legislation on the rights of children (the United Nations Convention on the Rights of the Child, 1989) could provide support for children to question impositions on their beliefs. Articles 14 and 15 of the Convention outline children's rights to freedom of thought, conscience and religion as well as freedom of association. Some European legislation has also strengthened individual rights, in particular the European Convention on Human Rights and the European Social Charter (see Signpost 4).

This is often the official view. In 1976, the Labour Prime Minister, James Callaghan, made a speech about education, and the Secretary of State for Education, Shirley Williams, followed this by starting a series of public debates about education. The people to be involved included teachers, employers and trade unions. Pupils were not mentioned at first. Later, a proposal to invite pupil representatives was negatively received by teacher representatives. This is consistent with a functionalist view: why should you consult the clay about what kind of pot it is to be made into?

It might seem that any attempts to establish the pupil's point of view and to take it into account are bound to be using perspectives other than the functionalist. Some headteachers consulted appeared to think like this (Meighan, 1977a). Here are some of their reactions to a research project on consulting pupils about teaching:

> It is dangerous to involve children in this kind of comment on their teachers.
> Discipline would be adversely affected by this kind of exercise.
> It is bad for classroom relationships.
> Children are not competent to judge these matters.

These reactions occurred despite the fact that the teachers had been provided with a written briefing that summarized several previous researches, both in the UK and in the USA, in which the findings contradicted all the above statements. (This is not particularly unusual. People operating with particular views of teaching might often behave like this when first given information that is contrary to their beliefs. We are all, from time to time, liable to prefer 'not to let the evidence confuse the issues involved'.)

However, it does not follow that consulting pupils automatically suggests a non-functionalist perspective, because there are several approaches to manipulating pupils. One is based on confrontation, where teachers order pupils to behave in certain ways and rely on fear and punishment to get their way. But other functionalist approaches are based on persuasion, coaxing and more subtle forms of control. Consulting pupils and using some of their responses can become a means of coaxing them into niches of society rather than ordering them into them. Nevertheless, many attempts to establish the pupil's point of view do use other perspectives, e.g. structural conflict and interactionist.

WHICH PERSPECTIVE IS IN USE?

This is often a difficult question to answer because the perspectives in sociology overlap a great deal and researchers often use more than one perspective in the course of their research. There are often clues to the perspective being used in studies of the pupil's point of view, in the concepts used, the methods of inquiry and the kind of questions asked. Studies using a conflict perspective may often use the concept of alienation in schooling. Studies using a functionalist perspective would be likely to ask a question such as, 'What are the best teachers you have had like?' rather than 'If you designed the ideal school, what would it be like?' The first question limits the pupils to the status quo, whereas the second question is more radical, in allowing the pupils to consider alternatives, whether or not they have experienced them. Micro-sociological studies would be likely to gain data from spontaneous discussion, conversation with pupils and 'uncensored' or anonymous written material that was not going to be used to grade pupils or be marked by teachers (see Woods, 1976).

AN INTERACTIONIST APPROACH

An interactionist approach would tend to explore the network of perceptions in play. This might result in studying several of the 'layers of meaning' referred to in Chapter 1, or concentration on one layer of meaning, in this case that of the pupils. The questions involved might include the following:

1. How do pupils interpret the experience of schooling? Are they critical? Is there a division of opinion? How do the 'successful' react? How do the 'unsuccessful' react? Do boys and girls react in the same way? How do 'deschooled' pupils educated at home react?
2. How reliable and valid are pupils as judges of their school experiences? Do they judge some aspects of schooling accurately and other aspects inaccurately? Is consultation welcomed by pupils?
3. What do pupils see as ideal in schooling? What is a 'good' teacher, as they see it? How do they define a 'bad' teacher?
4. How much are the pupils aware of any aspects of the 'hidden' curriculum?

5. Pupils' view of school includes their view of fellow pupils, and this raises even more questions. How do peer groups operate in schools? What is the influence of such groups? Is there a youth culture opposing a school culture?

STUDIES AVAILABLE

There is only a limited number of studies of the pupils' point of view of schooling in Britain available. Therefore a first conclusion is that this is a neglected issue in educational research.

In some studies the viewpoint of pupils has been one aspect of a larger study. In his analysis of a boys' secondary school, Hargreaves (1967) obtained information from the pupils about how they interpreted some of the features of school life, especially streaming by ability.

In contrast, the study by Blishen (1969) concentrates entirely on pupils' view of schooling by providing selections from essays, written mostly by secondary school children, on the theme of 'the school that I'd like'.

The educational weekly *The Times Educational Supplement* (1969) carried a two-part study entitled 'Child's eye view of teacher', which contained a summary of primary school children's comments on their teachers. In the following year there appeared a study of early school-leavers' views of teachers and schools by Maizels (1970), and three years later a pair of studies reporting the views of primary and secondary school children was produced by Blishen (1973a, b).

A comparative viewpoint was available in two educational paperbacks. One by Holt (1969) reported his observations of how pupils reacted to schooling in the USA, while the other was written by eight Italian boys protesting about their experience of schooling in Italy (School of Barbiana, 1970). Another writer in the USA, Jackson (1971), was writing about a 'hidden' curriculum of influences in school that affected pupils considerably but was hardly recognized by teachers.

However, since 1973, there has been a growing number of researchers interested in the pupils' view of schooling, and one collection of articles is entitled *The Learners' Viewpoint* (Meighan, 1978b).

The influence of growing youth unemployment is reflected in subsequent studies by Gow and McPherson (1980) and by White and Brockington (1983). Further collections are edited by Hughes (1984) and by Hammersley and Woods (1984).

Two perspectives presented in the *British Journal of Sociology of Education* (Vol. 12, No. 3, 1991) report on a US study into why pupils drop out of school (Stevenson and Ellsworth, 1991). Another perspective is presented by Furlong in the same issue of the journal: 'Disaffected pupils: reconstructing the sociological perspective'.

HOW DO PUPILS INTERPRET THE EXPERIENCE OF SCHOOLING?

The studies so far suggest some tentative conclusions. First, primary school pupils do appear to be more satisfied with their experiences than secondary school pupils, except of course the very large number of four-year-olds who are entering school in reception classes. Second, where dissatisfaction is expressed, it is just as likely to come from 'successful' as 'unsuccessful' pupils.

Primary School

In response to a request to seven- to eleven-year-old school children for written portraits of teachers came 1,200 replies, which were analysed by Makins (1969). She noted how children had watched their teachers with obsessive concern, noting mannerisms, subtle changes in mood and detailed variations in behaviour; they remark on teachers who talk to lonely, left-out children during playground duty and those who are angry with children because they are angry themselves. She concludes that, on the whole, these pupils love their primary schools: 'It is a sad fate to go home. I would like to stay for more education with the great 5'10" Mr Henshaw.'

The really popular teachers managed without many sanctions and did not shout at pupils very often. They let children talk, they explain clearly, they encourage, they are interested. Makins comments that the essays contained evidence that what children learn matters much less to them than how they are taught. Teachers who are good at something – music, art, photography, sport (it does not appear to matter what it is) – are appreciated, and so are student teachers who come prepared with new projects.

> On the evidence of our critics, hundreds of teachers are managing to make school so interesting that there is no time or reason for the old tricks and giggles and avoidance routines – and to establish a relationship with children makes the rituals of classroom warfare unthinkable.

Other studies (e.g. Blishen, 1972a, b) support these findings. A more recent study by Crocker (1988) is less positive and argues that capable young children are at risk of failing because of their infant school experience, suggesting that there is an overemphasis on conforming in schools and that by the age of six children 'closely mirror their teachers' opinions of their own and their peers' academic worth. By this age they have also learned to use the criteria that the teacher uses and can list them.'

Secondary School

The contrast with pupils' reports of their secondary schools is marked. For example, a study by Maizels (1970) concentrated on a sample of how 330 'unsuccessful' pupils who had recently left school at the earliest possible date, or were just about to leave, rated teachers in their secondary school. Schools and teachers were negatively rated for the most part. On the judgements given, Maizels concludes, few of the schools would get a 'pass' mark. Only a minority of pupils felt that their teachers had encouraged them, listened to what they had to say and praised them when they did well, had been pleasant, kind or sincere, or had kept their promises. Only 34 per cent of boys and girls had felt that their teachers had treated them like human beings.

The responses of some of the 'successful' pupils were obtained in an essay competition describing. 'The school that I'd like'. (Only children reasonably fluent in terms of literary skills and whose parents or teachers read the *Observer*, the newspaper which organized the competition, were likely to be included in such a sample.) Blishen (1969) comments that the essays amounted to an enormous, remarkably good-humoured, earnest, frequently passionate and, at best, highly intelligent plea for a new order in our schools, to replace what was currently seen as dreary and boring.

What the pupils mean by dreary and boring is diagnosed in some detail: 'Everything learnt is second-hand if it comes from the teachers and very often out-of-date and misleading if it comes from books. Far better to replace constipated ways of teaching with more active lessons.' The assessment of their experience of schooling was wide ranging and took in, among other things, the dullness of building design and dreary, unimaginative furniture, examinations and their distorting effect on learning, the role of the prefect as peer group policeman, the limiting effect of timetables, bells, the triviality of many school rules and the idea of compulsory worship and religious education as attempted indoctrination. Blishen comments that the image of the prison returned to him again and again as he read the essays. A further study of secondary school children was undertaken by Blishen in 1973.

HOW DOES IT AFFECT BEHAVIOUR?

In a survey of 15,000 British pupils carried out by the *Guardian* newspaper in 2001 some key findings were that pupils felt that schools were not happy places, that pupils' views were not listened to, that they were not treated and respected as individuals and that schools were rigid and inflexible institutions. (The survey was published later as *The School I'd Like* by Burke, C. and Grosvenor, I., London: Routledge Falmer 2003.

'Deschooled' Pupils

Some parents exercise their legal right to educate their children at home. (The organization that supports such cases is Education Otherwise, and it is studied in a later chapter.) The views of such children are of particular interest, since they often have an alternative experience with which to make comparison. Here are two examples:

> The school I'd like is what I have: my mother teaches my brother and me at home. We study maths, English, science, history, geography, French and scripture. This system has many advantages. The most important is that we can learn at our own speed: thus I have recently started A-level maths but am still struggling with O English, while my brother, who is three and a half years younger, is advanced in English but only average at arithmetic. Another advantage is that we have much more free time than other children: we don't waste time travelling to and fro and, as we have individual work, the education officer agreed to shorten lesson times for us. I spend a lot of my leisure time reading, bird watching, stamp and coin collecting, doing jigsaws, carpentry, painting, listening to radio, watching TV, swimming, playing chess, draughts, tennis and table tennis. Another advantage is that we are not hedged in by a lot of silly rules and regulations. We are also free from bullying big boys and from pressure to start bad habits like smoking and drug taking. We dress in comfortable, sensible clothes and do not have to wear some ridiculous uniform, nor do we have to play compulsory games. Again, we have home cooking all the time.
>
> When my mother started, a lot of people told her she was foolish because we would never learn to mix. I don't think this is true because, although I've always liked some time by myself, my brother likes and has lots of friends with whom he goes to play and who come and play with him ... It was also said that we would grow up selfish: I hope we're not. About once a fortnight we have a stall in our front garden to aid Oxfam and have collected £4 2s 3d so far this year. We also do a few odd jobs around the house. People also said Mother would find it too much. I know we get her down at times, but she survives and looks, so people say, much younger than she is ...
>
> The only disadvantage of the system to my mind is the difficulty of doing much advanced practical work in science because of the amount of apparatus required.
>
> I think it would solve a lot of problems if more people followed our system.
>
> Frank (aged 12)
>
> From Blishen, 1969.

Why I like to be taught at home

I like to be taught at home because I get more attention. For in a class there may be 40 or more children with only one person to teach them. Also if there are a lot of people in a class, each child can get only a fraction of the teacher's attention. Of course, not every pupil in a class behaves as he or she should and the teacher has to sort out fights and squabbles and make rules as to how to behave.

All this wastes time that you could be learning in. But when you are at home, there is no-one to fight with (except your Mum), no-one to queue with to get your books marked and find out what your next bit of work is. I have found, especially in maths, that some people are stuck with their sums and cannot get on without help from the teacher. It has taken me ten minutes standing waiting for my turn.

Another thing is that it is more peaceful and quiet at home because even when everyone is silent there is still a sound which you are only aware of if you have heard real silence.

Sophia Howard (aged 10)

From *Education Otherwise Newsletter*, No. 8, December 1978. Reprinted by permission of Sophia and Frances Howard.

HOW USEFUL ARE THE JUDGEMENTS OF PUPILS ABOUT SCHOOLING?

Beliefs about the usefulness of pupils' judgement of schooling are plentiful, whereas evidence is not. Investigations into the characteristics of pupil perceptions of schooling have taken place in the USA. The most systematic attempts appear to be those of Veldman and Peck (1963). The conclusion they reached was that pupil perception of teaching performance was reliable enough and valid enough in most aspects of classroom technique to be worth considering as useful feedback to teachers about their performance. The general conclusion from the limited research available is that this holds good for samples of British children (Meighan, 1974a, 1977a) although there appear to be a few technical aspects of performance, e.g. the effective use of questions and of teaching aids, where the perceptions of pupils are less reliable. 'Usefulness', however, can be interpreted in other ways. Are the perceptions useful as feedback so that performance is improved?

The impression of students who took part in research on pupils' perceptions was that it did make a difference and that they did modify or attempt to modify their classroom technique because of things that children had drawn to their attention.

Another aspect of usefulness is whether the act of consultation affects relationships. Some headteachers feared that it would lead to a deterioration, but the students reported otherwise. Several reported that they were less tense with the children concerned afterwards and, in one case, a 'difficult' group simply ceased to be difficult. Obstruction gave way to cooperation, to the surprise of both student and supervising teacher. The pupils appeared to regard someone who consulted them and took their opinions seriously as being on their side. Werthman (1963) reports some similar responses in his studies of delinquents in schools.

WHAT DO PUPILS SEE AS IDEAL?

There appears to be a high degree of consensus among pupils of all ages about the ideal teacher. The list of qualities children wish to see in their teachers is extensive:

They should be understanding, the children say, and patient; should encourage and praise wherever possible; should listen to their pupils and give their pupils a chance to speak; should be willing to have points made against them, be humble, kind, capable of informality and simply pleasant; should share more activities with their children than they commonly do, and should not expect all children to be always docile. They should have conscience about the captive nature of their audience; should attempt to establish links with parents; should be punctual for lessons, enthusiastic within reason; should not desert a school lightly; should recognise the importance to a child of being allowed to take the initiative in school work; and, above all, should be warm and personal.

Blishen, 1969

Blishen goes on to say how the children saw clearly that these 'new' teachers could not operate easily in the present context of secondary schooling, and that widespread changes in the organization of schools might be necessary.

The bad teacher, as defined by pupils, uses fear as a means of dominance, and is extremely moody, miserable, indifferent and lazy. The study by Maizels (1970) shows a similar picture. The unfavourable references to teachers in her study were overstrictness, having favourites, being sarcastic, being moody and overemphasis on time-keeping. Only a few teachers were remembered as kind, sincere, keeping their promises, reliable, pleasant, full of ideas, efficient and encouraging.

The bad teacher, in the essays written on the theme of 'The School that I'd like' (Blishen, 1969), is found guilty of remoteness, lack of sympathy and attachment to trivial rules, and fails to admit ignorance or uncertainty. Such teachers made schools unhappy places, and denied children the kind of relationship with teachers they were seeking and expressing in their view of the ideal teacher.

Teachers are a central focus in children's comments about schools, but the context in which teachers operate is also of concern. Blishen (1969) reports how children commented on various other aspects of secondary schooling. The overwhelming majority wanted mixed schools and comprehensive schools. The buildings came in for considerable negative comment: children were tired of square rooms, unimaginative decoration, desks and the lack of common rooms for pupils. Examinations were seen as a significant cause of 'constipated' teaching and distance in teachers, and alternative forms of assessment were desired. Prefects, homework, bells and religious education all received considerable scorn and alternatives for some of these were suggested. For example, religious assembly and instruction were interpreted as a form of indoctrination that represented a failure to look at a wide range of religions, philosophies and moralities. (It was six years later that a private member's bill was drafted to propose a remedy for precisely this failure: British Humanist Association, 1975.)

The comments of the children were surprisingly sober and considered, Blishen comments, and intelligent alternatives to the status quo were presented in most cases.

DO PUPILS RECOGNIZE THE 'HIDDEN' CURRICULUM?

'The hidden curriculum' is a term used to refer to those aspects of learning in schools that are unofficial, unintentional or undeclared consequences of the way teaching and learning are organized and performed in schools. A later chapter looks at this concept in detail.

Jackson (1971) uses the term to describe the unofficial three Rs – rules, routines and regulations – that pupils must learn in order to survive comfortably and effectively in schools. Other aspects include the messages learnt from school buildings, the influence of teachers' expectations, the kind of knowledge implied by teaching techniques, the effects of different usages of language and the sex roles projected by an institution. The idea of a hidden curriculum is closely linked with the notion of labelling processes and self-fulfilling prophecies, and one consequence may be the alienation of many pupils from learning.

The responses of the children in the various studies are often reminiscent of Goffman's theory of total institutions (see Goffman, 1961), in which he analyses in detail the coercive, non-negotiable and non-consultative nature of many contemporary institutions, including armies, asylums, monasteries, hospitals and prisons.

Goffman also talks about depersonalization, and this idea is also seen by a high school pupil in the USA:

> School is like roulette or something. You can't just ask: Well, what's the point of it? The point of it? The point of it is to do it, to get through and get into college. But you have to figure the system or you can't win, because the odds are all on the house's side. I guess it's a little like the real world in that way. The main thing is not to take it personal, to understand that it's just a system and it treats you like the same way it treats everybody else, like an engine or a machine or something mechanical. Our names get fed into it – we get fed into it – when we're five years old, and if we catch on and watch our step, it spits us out when we're 17 or 18, ready for college.
>
> Cited in Silberman, 1971

The effect of 'trading for grades' gradually replacing all other educational activity is described by Becker (1968), and also by the boys in the School of Barbiana:

> Day in and day out they study for marks, for reports and diplomas. Languages, sciences, history – everything becomes purely pass marks. Behind those sheets of paper there is only a desire for personal gain. The diploma means money . . . you have to be a social climber at the age of twelve.
>
> Letter to a teacher, 1970

The process of labelling and the consequence of alienation, for some pupils at least, are indicated in the above comments from pupils. Some pupils are able to recognize some aspects of the hidden curriculum. The material quoted earlier from pupils being educated at home shows an awareness of several other aspects, including 'denial, delay and interruption', key ideas in Jackson's analysis of the hidden curriculum, as outlined in Chapter 6.

CONCLUSION

Nice Strict and Nasty Strict

Your strictness is not strict (if you see what I mean). A nice strict.

Fourth year pupil

The research Roland Meighan conducted on pupils' views of teaching performance yielded these two categories of 'nice strict' and 'nasty strict', and they accord with the descriptions of good and bad teachers given earlier. These findings disappoint at least two audiences in education: the traditional transmission educationalists and the radical educationalists.

The traditional transmission educationalists tend to believe that pupils should not be consulted, are not competent to make judgements about schooling and will abuse any attempts by teachers to gain their views, leading to poorer discipline, and they generally accept the spirit of 'you do not consult the clay about what kind of pot it wants to be'. The findings that pupils make sound judgements, and that relationships do not deteriorate but often improve, do not match these beliefs.

The radical educationalists tend to believe that there is a pool of untapped radical desires in the consciousness of pupils, desires for democratic relationships and autonomous situations:

> Many of the pupils of the future will not accept, as many of us did and still do, the dictatorial
> methods of teachers who regard the classrooms as their own little despotic kingdoms.
>
> Kohl, 1970

The findings that most pupils ask for a more kindly authoritarian situation, the 'nice strict' regime, rather than for participation, autonomy and a democratic set of relationships, do not match these beliefs either.

In short, the research supports the proposition that the transmission view, as given above, is just plain wrong, and that the radical view, as given above, is a delusion. However, the study by Blishen (1969) holds a little hope for the latter view, since pupils in his sample, mostly the articulate and the highest achievers, did ask for a more participative and consultative relationship, and did ask for rather more than just 'nice strict'.

The View from the Girls

One serious limitation of the studies to date is the habit of putting boys and girls together and reporting the pupils' view of schooling. However, the evidence that school may, to some extent, present a different experience for girls has emerged. Schooling appears to be significantly sex-typed, a theme explored in Chapter 26. Other differences, like social class, ethnic origin and geographical region, are other important factors.

The Neglect of the Pupils' Viewpoint

The reasons for the neglect of the pupils' view may be related to the low power and status of both child and pupil roles, as Calvert (1975) suggests. The existing definitions of the situation appear to consider teaching as more important than learning, and the teacher's activity as more central than the pupils', despite the official rhetoric of educational writing and debate that makes claims for the pupils' welfare as the central focus. Calvert argues that this became clear after considering the politics of education. Every other group involved in education – teachers, administrators, planners, parents, employers – can obtain a better hearing for its point of view, through pressure groups or other channels, than can pupils. Moves to establish pupil pressure groups and children's rights are very recent, and often result in highly emotional, if not hysterical, responses from senior educationalists. In Europe, however, their rights are often recognized in legislation, and government resources are used to support pupil participation (see Davies, L. and Kirkpatrick, G. (2000), *The EURIDEM Project: A Review of Pupil Democracy in Europe*, London: Children's Rights Alliance).

Apart from the low status of both child and pupil roles, the writings about education are produced largely for an audience of teachers, who have the problems of teachers as their major preoccupation. The studies of the pupils' experiences themselves are mostly directed at the teachers and their problems. Few books are written about schooling for pupils, the *Little Red Schoolbook* being one exception.

This emphasis on teachers' views is reinforced by the apparent contradiction that the teacher needs the pupil more than the pupil needs the teacher. The teacher's position is an occupational one that requires some degree of commitment, since livelihoods are at stake. The pupil has no choice, and is not paid to pursue the role allotted, and many pupils remain uncommitted and indifferent, obtaining self-esteem in peer group and other activities. Successful performance of role can therefore be more important to a teacher than to a pupil.

For these reasons the role of pupil tends to be defined by the teacher, and the pupil's viewpoint neglected:

> Because the teacher thus defined the pupil role, he tends to see himself as the more decisive participant in the performance, and thinks of the pupil's role as more receptive than his own. Things are done by the teacher to or for the pupil, just as things are done by the doctor to or for his patient; and the pupil, like the patient, is expected to conform to the expectation thus set up for him.
>
> Calvert, 1975

In this situation, sociological studies of the pupils' view of schooling that are undertaken from perspectives other than the structural functionalist are likely to be disturbing and to yield the insights that radically question what was assumed about a familiar scene, thus producing the 'uncommon sense' referred to in the opening chapter.

Summary

Although research on the point of view of pupils is limited, there emerges a considerable degree of consensus in the general findings:

1. A larger number of primary school children tend to enjoy school, whereas secondary school children tend to be less happy with their school experiences. More recent studies are showing that some groups of primary children find their experiences are not enjoyable, e.g. four-year-olds in reception classes where there is a poor nursery education and formal classes are introduced too early.
2. Both 'successful' and 'unsuccessful' pupils in secondary schools record dissatisfaction. It is not just a reaction of the 'failures'.
3. The dissatisfaction appears to be marked, and not a minor feature. Only the minority of secondary schools appear to achieve even a pass mark in the eyes of the pupils.
4. The views of the pupils are not merely negative. They are sympathetic to the difficulties of teachers. They are able to offer a wide range of constructive, and mostly feasible, alternatives.
5. The perceptions of pupils show high degrees of reliability and validity.
6. Pupils' views about preferred teachers show a high degree of consensus, as do their views of 'bad' teachers.
7. Pupils are able to recognize some aspects of the hidden curriculum and some of the labelling processes, and record their feelings of alienation that result.
8. A structural functional view tends to dominate educational thinking, so investigations of the pupils' view are often seen as radical even when they are not.
9. The pupil's layer of meaning is rarely known to teachers in any systematic way, so findings are often disturbing and represent 'uncommon sense'.
10. The pupils' preference for 'nice strict' over 'nasty strict' disappoints the beliefs of both transmission educationalists and radical educationalists.
11. The experience of schooling of girls may well differ from that of boys, therefore making generalizations about the pupils' view open to question.

Further Reading

Blishen, E. (1969) *The School that I'd Like*. Harmondsworth: Penguin. One of the most readable accounts of the pupils' point of view.

Blishen, E. (1973) 'Pupils' Views of Primary Teachers', *Where?*, 84.

Blishen, E. (1973) 'Pupils' Views of Secondary Teachers', *Where?*, 86.

Burke, C. and Grosvenor, I. (2003) *The School I'd Like*. London: Routledge Falmer.

Cleave, S. and Brown, S. (1991) *Early to School: Four Year Olds in Infant Classes*. London: Routledge.

Crocker, A. (1988) 'Are some gifted children at risk because of their infant school experience?', *Education Today*, **38**, 3, 49–54.

Educational Review, **30**, 2. This special edition of *Educational Review* is entitled 'The Learners' Viewpoint', and was published in 1978.

Gow, L. and McPherson, A. (1980) *Tell Them from Me*. Aberdeen: Aberdeen University Press.

Hammersley, M. and Woods, P. (eds) (1984) *Life in School*. Milton Keynes: Open University Press.

Hughes, J. (ed.) (1984) *The Best Years: Reflections of School Leavers in the 1980s*. Aberdeen: Aberdeen University Press.

Newell, P. (1991) *The UN Convention and Children's Rights in the UK*. London: National Children's Bureau.

Sherman, A. (1996) *Rules, Routines and Regimentation: Young Children Reporting on Their Schooling*. Nottingham: Educational Heretics Press.

Stevenson, R. and Ellsworth, J. (1991) 'Dropping out in a working class high school: adolescent voices on the decision to leave', *British Journal of Sociology of Education*, **12**, 3, 277–91.

Stone, J. and Taylor, F. (1976) 'The Sad Tale of Pupils' Rights', *Where*?, 122.

Tucker, N. (1979) 'Pupils' Views of Teachers', *Where*?, 152; 155.

White, R. and Brockington, D. (1983) *Tales out of School*. London: Routledge and Kegan Paul.

Discussion and Activities

1. One straightforward activity is a replication of the study by Blishen. Either write your own account or ask some pupils to write their account of the school that they would like. The findings in *The School that I'd Like* could be used as cue material in any preliminary discussion if you think this is appropriate. Northamptonshire LEA organized a consultation with pupils over the curriculum. For an account, see Makins, V. (1984) 'Giving the Customers a Say', *Times Educational Supplement*, 23 November 1984.

2. An activity that might appeal to some readers is to research your own teaching style by getting a class to write answers to questions about classroom performance. Here are the questions used in previous research. (They could be extended or modified as thought fit.)

   (A) Preparation:

      (1) Do you think that my lessons are well prepared?

      (2) Do the lessons have enough interest for you?

      (3) Do you feel that I have organized everything well before the lessons start?

      (4) Do the lessons seem to have a pattern? (Or are they confusing?)

   (B) Presentation:

      (5) Do I speak clearly and use my voice well?

      (6) Are my explanations and instructions clear?

      (7) Do I use questions well?

      (8) Do I use teaching aids well?

   (C) Attitudes:

      (9) Do I treat you fairly?

      (10) Am I good humoured enough?

      (11) Am I too harsh or too soft with anyone?

      (12) Do I seem to be sympathetic with you?

(D) Class management:

      (13) Am I strict enough or too strict with the class?

      (14) Is my organization of activities during the lesson sound?

      (15) Are the start and end of lessons effective?

      (16) Do I manage the time available well?

An account of the research appears in the *British Journal of Teacher Education*, Vol. 3, No. 2. *Note*. Student teachers should make sure that their supervisors give clearance to this activity.

3. Client is an analogy. To what extent would other analogies help to describe the situation of pupils? Suggestions: prisoners, partners, apprentices, slaves, conscripts, parishioners. One interesting reference might be Easthope, G. (1980) 'Curricula are Social Processes', in L. Barton *et al.* (eds), *Schooling, Ideology and the Curriculum*, Lewes: Falmer Press.

Signposts

1. Gender

The experience of girls and their perspective may differ in some respects from those of boys. Some starting points are: Davies, L. (1984) *Pupil Power: Gender and Deviance in School*, Lewes: Falmer Press; Stanworth, M. (1983) *Gender and Schooling*, London: Hutchinson; Weiner, U. (ed.), (1985) *Just a Bunch of Girls*, Milton Keynes: Open University Press; and Herbert, C. (1989) *Talking of Silence: the Sexual Harassment of Schoolgirls*, London: The Falmer Press.

2. Pupil culture

The idea that peer interaction is a crucial feature of the pupils' perspective is developed in McPherson, J. (1983) *The Feral Classroom*, London: Routledge and Kegan Paul, and in Hammersley, M. and Woods, P. (1984) *Life in School: the Sociology of Pupil Culture*, Milton Keynes: Open University Press.

3. Employment and unemployment

How pupil viewpoints are influenced is the subject of Willis, P. (1977) *Learning to Labour*, Farnborough: Saxon House; and Hughes (1984) and Gow and McPherson (1980).

4. Children's rights

The world has over two billion children and young people and on 20 November 1989 the United Nations Assembly adopted the Convention on the Rights of the Child. How this international piece of legislation is of use to children (and those who work with them) is the subject of Newell, P. (1991) *The UN Convention and Children's Rights in the UK*. This has been published by the National Children's Bureau (8 Wakley Street, London EC1V 7QE), a body concerned with the welfare of children and young people.

5. The Children's Manifesto

In June 2001 the *Guardian* revisited the 'School That I'd Like' project first run in the Observer in 1967, when 1,000 children reported. This time 15,000 children responded. See *Guardian Education* 5th June 2001, stored on *www.Guardian-Education.co.uk*, and also stored on *http://bretton.ac.uk/schoolilike.html*

6. Pupil voice

Inclusionary and exclusionary processes in schools seem to involve the construction of pupil identities as either sociologically 'normal' or 'deviant'. Inclusivity as an educational goal or strategy attempts the normalization of the majority of pupils (Corbett, 1997). By contrast, pressures to exclude pupils from schools invite the identification of some as being fundamentally different 'others', marginal in status or sociologically deviant. Teachers in effect appear to be engaged in a societal process of patrolling the boundaries (Erikson, 1966) of the 'normal' social world and structuring the careers of children within schools and classrooms, or even manoeuvring them beyond their boundaries. See Waterhouse, S. (2002) 'Deviant and Non-deviant Identities in the Classroom: Patrolling the Boundaries of the Normal Social World', paper presented at the European Conference on Educational Research, University of Lisbon, 11–14 September 2002. The text is in the Education-line Internet document collection at: *http://www.leeds.ac.uk/educol/documents/00002140.htm*

Urquhart, I. (2001) '"Walking on air"? Pupil Voice and School Choice', *Forum* (for Promoting 3–19 Comprehensive Education), **43**, 2: Summer 2001. See also MacBeath, J., Myers, K. and Demetriou, H. (2001) 'Supporting Teachers in Consulting Pupils about Aspects of Teaching and Learning, and Evaluating Impact', *Forum* (for Promoting 3–19 Comprehensive Education), **43**, 2: Summer 2001.

7. ARCH

An organization that campaigns on behalf of children's rights is *Action On Rights For Children (ARCH)*. Check out their website at *www.arch-ed.org* for further information.

Teachers as Victims? 3

It is difficult to get people to understand something when their salaries depend on them not understanding it.

Based on an observation attributed to Upton Sinclair

We are just miserable rule-followers.

Verdict of a teacher in South Africa reported in C. Harber, *State of Transition*

INTRODUCTION

Description and analysis in human affairs often proceed by the use of analogies. Sociologists use a variety of these in their work. Each analogy presents possibilities of clarification as well as problems of distortion. The analogy of teacher as victim stresses the possibility of constraint, of limited choices, of imposed conditions of work. The distortions produced by the idea of victim include the possible conclusions that teachers are helpless victims, that constraints do not change and that limited choices are equivalent to no choices. An analysis taking the idea of teacher as victim takes up most of this chapter, and these distortions need to be borne in mind.

ANALOGIES OF THE TEACHER'S SITUATION

Role

A common analogy in sociological writings about teachers is that of role. In common with many sociological analogies, it is derived from drama. Some analyses of this kind proceed by listing alternative roles and describing the content of each. Two basic sets of roles are often proposed, one concerned with the activities of instruction and evaluation and the other concerned with maintaining control and generally creating the conditions for learning to take place (see Hoyle, 1969). These two main roles may be broken down into sub-roles, and Hoyle gives a list of examples that include:

1. Representative of society: inculcates moral precepts.
2. Judge: gives marks and ratings.
3. Resource: possesses knowledge and skills.
4. Helper: provides guidance on pupils' difficulties.
5. Referee: settles disputes among pupils.
6. Detective: discovers rule breakers.
7. Object of identification: possesses traits which pupils may imitate.
8. Ego-supporter: helps pupils to develop confidence in themselves.

Another use of role theory stresses the process of performing a role with the flexibility of conduct that is required, and the complexity of managing impressions in public (see Hargreaves, 1972). This approach is often referred to as dramaturgical, and the writings of Goffman provide many examples. In this analogy, social life is seen as an elaborate form of drama, requiring that people project a convincing image of themselves to their audiences. Therefore, a key idea here is that of the presentation of self, which is indeed the title of one of Goffman's books. But this analogy, too, has limitations. The teacher lacks a well developed script and has an unchanging audience, whereas actors in theatres commonly have both a full script and a succession of new audiences.

Cultural Worker

An analogy from the world of work is that of cultural worker. The worker is envisaged as someone who works to the designs of others: the bricklayer follows the architect's plan, the car assembler works to the specification of the designers and the navvy moves earth according to the maps produced by others. The cultural workers, whether they be teachers, journalists, artists or civil servants, are seen as people who reproduce culture in the form of language, values, attitudes, images, rules and information. They are seen as perpetuators rather than innovators, and their task is to reproduce the cultural apparatus to the design of others. C. Wright Mills argues that the cultural apparatus is composed of all the organizations in which artistic, intellectual or scientific work goes on, and therefore involves a complex set of institutions, including schools, theatres, newspapers, studios, laboratories, museums and magazines. He sees a strong likelihood that cultural workers will be in cooperation with the ruling group not least because of the prestige that this ensures. Association with authority lends increased importance to the work.

This analogy of cultural worker has limitations when applied to teachers. Not least of these is overgeneralization. Some teachers innovate, some marginally, some more radically: some change does occur from within schools. The autonomy of teachers may be overstated, but it can also be understated, and an analogy interpreting teaching as solely technical, as the activity of a cultural worker and nothing more, runs this risk. A further limitation is that the analogy of cultural worker may distract attention from the contradictions of the teaching task;

e.g. teachers are expected both to preserve the cultural status quo and to produce innovators who will develop new technologies, new industries, new sources of wealth and other fresh cultural ideas.

Other Analogies

The analogies of teacher as victim, the role of the teacher and teacher as cultural worker do not exhaust the possibilities. Other analogies that occur in sociological and educational writings from time to time include the teacher as a control agent, acting as a kind of police officer or prison officer. Other analogies may stress the manipulative task of teaching, seeing teachers as technicians of an educational production line, or potters moulding human material, or gardeners tending young human stock. An alternative occupational comparison is that of a profession. Teaching does not meet the criteria for a traditional profession, for example, having little or no autonomy, and has been seen as a semi-profession, and teachers as members of a qualifying association.

These analogies have several drawbacks, including the tendency to oversimplify by selecting one aspect of the complex task of teaching and thus being incapable of describing the diversity of actions and outcomes. They also share some of the limitations of the other analogies mentioned earlier, e.g. a strong tendency to overlook the contradictory nature of teaching actions.

A more complex analogy that has been used recently is that of scripts. Scripts appear both in music, as musical scores, and in drama, as play scripts, but a more modern version is the television script. The analogy of scripts may prove to be useful in the case of teaching if it extends the idea of role. Roles are seen as linked in a script which defines the setting, the action, varying audiences both in the studio and outside in their homes. The script also has a history behind it, exists alongside alternative scripts and is subject to various kinds of scrutiny as regards its suitability. The teacher may be seen as appearing in a variety of roles, including producer, actor-producer, producer-manager or director. At the end of this chapter you will be invited to use this analogy as a descriptive and analytical idea.

SOCIOLOGICAL QUESTIONS ABOUT TEACHERS

The questions asked in a sociological approach were discussed in a previous chapter. If we insert 'teachers' into one of the sets of questions given, it reads as follows. 'What varieties of teachers now prevail in this society and in this period? And what varieties of teachers are coming to prevail? In what ways are teachers selected and formed, liberated and repressed, made sensitive and blunted?'

One way of assembling some ideas and evidence about this set of questions is to adopt a biographical approach, to follow the experience of a teacher taking up an appointment at a school. The experiences of a student teacher starting a teaching practice would provide many similar features. Since few teachers are involved in designing and setting up a new school, the situation encountered is that of an assorted kit of items chosen and designed by others. The quality of the thinking behind this package is outside the control of the incoming teacher, and it may be resistant to change:

> each social situation in which we find ourselves is not only defined by our contemporaries but predefined by our predecessors. Since one cannot possibly talk back to one's ancestors, their ill-conceived constructions are commonly more difficult to get rid of than those built in our own lifetime.
>
> Berger, 1963

The situation facing the person in a new appointment can be described in various ways. It is a ready-made set of recipes; it is an existing perspective; it is a cultural world presented to the stranger; it is a kit of ideas issued to the new recruit. Whichever analogy is used, there is a complex of features involved. What follows is a catalogue of features, each briefly illustrated. A fuller treatment of each of these features will be given in later chapters. The analogy in use here is that of the teacher as victim.

THE TEACHER AS VICTIM

School Buildings

Kohl reports how teachers in his seminars drew or wrote about school. The drawings were dominated by boxes representing rooms, papers, books, tables and buildings. Memories of school were predominantly rectangular.

> It is no accident that spatial memories are strong. The placement of objects in space is not arbitrary and rooms represent in physical form the spirit and souls of places and institutions. A teacher's room tells us something about who he is and a great deal about what he is doing.
>
> Kohl, 1970

The spaces provided by architects tend to be permanent and may well outlast the beliefs about education that underpinned the design instruction. To an incoming teacher, the arrangement of rooms, corridors, furniture, display areas and specialized facilities, e.g. a library or a hall, is of interest in at least three ways:

1. It suggests possibilities and opportunities for teaching and learning.
2. It places constraints on what can happen for whatever spatial layout is met; some teaching and learning possibilities are eliminated or made very difficult.
3. It implies an ideology of education, i.e. a pattern of assumptions about knowledge,

teaching, learning, relationships, organization, assessment and resources. One such pattern might be that school knowledge is best regarded as different subjects, that teaching is essentially instructing, that learning is essentially absorbing the information and ideas of the teacher, that relationships are authoritarian, that organization is into groups of about 30 learners called a class, that assessment is the judging of written end-products and that appropriate resources are books, written by teacher-commentators, called textbooks. A building designed with these assumptions in mind presents problems to an incoming teacher who does not accept one of these propositions and severe difficulties to one who rejects the whole set. One interesting account of how a teacher dealt with his 'open' ideology of education in a 'closed' building and situation is Kohl's *The Open Classroom* but, for the most part, teachers can be seen as victims of the building design.

The Headteacher

Headteachers may be regarded as victims too: they receive a building, usually handed on from predecessors. They also receive, without much power of negotiation, many of the other features listed later, e.g. the external examination system. In C. Wright Mills's analogy, the headteachers are the foremen cultural workers, controlling those in their charge to some extent, but in turn controlled by others. However, in exercising their control over the particular schools in their charge, they have power to vary the regimes in various ways, e.g. by keeping power, by delegating or by democratizing.

Some strong clues may be present in the headteacher's room layout, although these are, of course, only clues, and not conclusive evidence. In a democratized regime the headteacher may not even have a room, if the decision of the school senate was that no room was necessary for this purpose. A decision of this kind was made by the Countesthorpe Community College in 1970, although later the decision was revised.

Research by Evans (1974a) suggests that varying patterns of headteachers' room arrangement may be found representing degrees of authoritarianism. In Figure 3.1(e) the most 'modern' headteachers, in the words of Evans, 'relegate their bureaucratic function to the wall'. The headteacher rotates towards the centre of the room in a swivel chair, and can arrange more democratic or consultative groupings around a coffee table if desired. But the layouts of most headteachers' rooms are of the other four kinds. The language of the arrangement and the objects in the room are authoritarian rather than consultative or democratic. Evans comments that these various layouts bear little relation to the practicalities of sources of light and heat, but are related to the way headteachers wish to present themselves and manage relationships. Teachers have little control over headteachers' choices of regime and therefore can be victims of a particular headteacher's ideology of education.

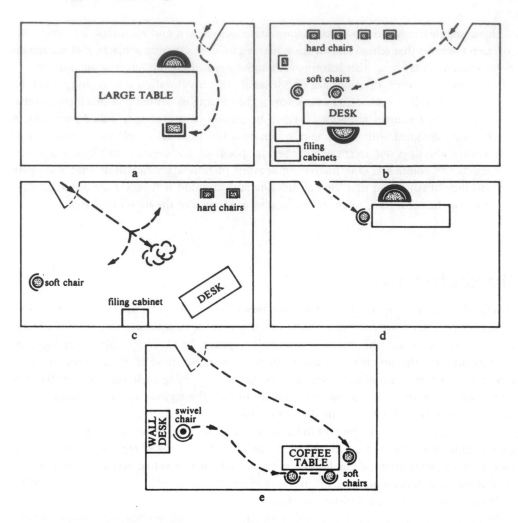

Figure 3.1 (a) The traditional layout of a public school headteacher's study. (b) Full frontal confrontation, the most common arrangement. (c) Ideal for the authoritarian; the visitor is left isolated in space. (d) The less authoritarian favour this arrangement; an open door is desirable. (e) A 'modern' headteacher may favour the informality of soft chairs around a coffee table. This first appeared in *New Society*, London, 24 October 1974, the weekly review of the social sciences.

The Timetable

Sooner or later the new teacher will be given a timetable. In a primary school this could be slightly more flexible. Certain fixed periods of time in a week might be labelled as assemblies, physical education, games or music, and the rest would be at the discretion of the teacher, provided that certain activities, such as reading, writing, mathematics and other areas of the National Curriculum, appeared regularly.

In a secondary school the 'cultural worker' interpretation is more clearly made, since decisions about which groups meet with a given teacher in which places, for how long and how often are usually presented to the staff and are open to only minimal negotiation.

The Organization

Underpinning the timetable there are many organization decisions also presented to a new teacher for largely unquestioning acceptance. The actual size of classes will depend upon decisions about how many senior staff need to be free for administrative tasks. The composition of classes will depend on whether the organization is a 'streaming by achievement' system, a mixed achievement grouping system, grouping for subjects by sex, or some mixture of these. Age grouping by years is a common feature of such plans.

Other organizational decisions to be accepted may include rules, punishments, dress, break times, house systems and midday meal arrangements.

The Curriculum

Since the 1988 Education Reform Act, all state schools in England and Wales are obliged to deliver a National Curriculum. The decisions about the content of the curriculum vary in scope, and several levels of decision can be described. The new teacher will be presented with a range of these decisions and those at the most general level are the least negotiable. Thus a teacher may feel that a compulsory National Curriculum or religious education is a dubious idea, but since it is required by law, no negotiation is possible.

At another level of decision-making, the curriculum may exclude some subjects. The incoming teacher might be a social science graduate or have a deep interest in cross curricular issues, e.g. multicultural education, but find that the social sciences are absent from the National Curriculum, and that the post offered is in English, history or some other National Curriculum subject only.

Within each area of the curriculum, decisions are likely to have been made about the programmes of study and about the appropriate external examination where this applies. This provides a useful example of the effect of the thinking of predecessors, since cohorts of children will already have experienced some years of the prescribed syllabus, making any changes difficult to implement and usually taking several years to phase in.

Therefore, in the area of the curriculum alone, the teacher may be presented with a wide range of ready-made practices within the external confines of the National Curriculum, with the expectation that they will be perpetuated. The analogy of the incoming teacher as a victim of circumstances therefore begins to gain plausibility.

Assessment

In Chapter 13, the wide range of possibilities in assessment is outlined and the frequent selection of certain kinds of assessment of a limited nature is indicated. The incoming teacher to a primary school may not believe in giving marks of a norm referencing kind, where pupils are compared with one another in performance, but may prefer to mark pupils against their own personal performance on a 1–3 system, where 1 means worse than the pupil's last work, 2 is as good as the last effort and 3 is an improvement on the previous performance. Yet the end-of-session report may insist on class positions because that is the assessment system operating throughout the school.

The system of assessing reading progress against a set reading scheme may be preferred to a teaching and assessment programme based on children's conversations and the writing of their own reading books and materials.

In a secondary school, an incoming teacher may not believe in the norm-referenced system of automatically failing a set percentage of pupils, but nevertheless may be required to prepare the classes for an external examination based on just such a 'rationing of success' assumption.

Teachers are now legally bound to undertake two kinds of assessments in both primary and secondary schools. One kind of assessment, known as teacher assessment, is based on the teacher's knowledge of the children and their work and is quite often described as formative assessment. This kind of assessment is usually based on long-term knowledge of what a child is capable of and is a continuous assessment which provides the teacher with information about the child's strengths and weaknesses. The second type of assessment can be described as summative, where the child undergoes a test or task which is given a score and which can be used to measure the child's progress against other children. In the UK, all schools are sent Standardized Assessment Tests (SATs) and all children are assessed in this way at ages 7, 11, 14 and 16 years. School test results are published in 'league tables' nationally and are available to the public.

Resources Available

The incoming teacher may find that the school has a fully operational resources centre with well developed retrieval, storage and indexing facilities for multimedia resources, a reprographic system and an equipment store with booking facilities. However, the teacher concerned may not believe in such a 'luxury' approach, preferring a 'no-nonsense, textbook-based system'. Alternatively, a teacher trained to use a resources centre may encounter a school with stockrooms filled only with textbooks.

In a less extreme situation, it may be that the range of resources is more limited than a particular teacher might wish: the carefully accumulated overhead projector transparencies may prove useless if the school has no suitable equipment. Or the reading scheme used by the school may be just the one the teacher has come to regard as a hindrance. Or, if the school has modern maths textbooks whereas the teacher trusts only traditional maths, the resources presented create problems. The possibilities of a mismatch between the kit of resources awaiting teachers and their personal preferences are considerable. In all cases the teacher has to accept, for some time at least, the resources based on decisions made by others and become, in some cases, an unwilling victim of circumstances.

Teaching Methods

The resources available imply a pedagogy: these teaching methods may also present problems of a mismatch between the school's existing recipes and the incoming teacher's beliefs and preferences. Thus a teacher who believes in having a class of children working from a standard textbook may be alarmed to find that the stock cupboard contains sets of five or six textbooks of varying kinds because the previous teacher believed in a groupwork system where pupils compared several textbooks in a research-based pedagogy. One of the writers had such an experience when this approach was so foreign to the views of the incoming teacher that he concluded that the pupils had stolen from the full sets available until only a small number of each remained.

Teachers who are used to an interpretation theory of teaching, which stresses dialogue with pupils, discussion and research-based written work, may encounter a school that has a transmission view, which stresses listening to the teacher and taking dictated notes. The pupils may quickly tell the teacher what they have learnt – that 'real' work is not discussion or research, but taking down notes from an 'expert' teacher. An increase in the content of what is to be taught through the National Curriculum is also likely to encourage more didactic methods of teaching.

Expectations of the Clients

The analogy of client presents problems in the case of teaching. Teachers appear to have multiple clients, including parents, employers and the pupils themselves. In addition, there are other sets of expectations to be considered: the headteacher's, those of colleagues, and those of inspectors from the local education authority and the Department for Education and Skills. (A student on teaching practice also has the tutor to consider.) The initial allocation of clients is not within a teacher's control. Like priests and prostitutes, they have little say in whom they serve.

As was indicated previously (Chapter 2), the expectations of pupils show a high degree of consensus: the 'nice strict' teacher is preferred to the 'nasty strict' teacher. In the cases of parents and of employers, there appears to be less consistency. For example, it is commonly asserted that the basic requirements of employers as regards maths and English are not being met, yet studies of employers' wishes show only limited agreement on these basic requirements (see Fitzgerald, 1976).

Whatever the particular features of these varying expectations of parents, pupils and employers, as well as the other people involved, they confront the incoming teacher, and the expectation is usually that they be accepted and accommodated.

Aims, Objectives and Outcomes

Since the objectives of education have been listed in impressive taxonomies, their quantity is known to be considerable: Bloom's *Taxonomy of Educational Objectives* fills three books. It is no surprise, therefore, to find that schools vary in the priority they place on their aims, objectives and outcomes. The aims may include:

1. Preparation for society as it is currently.
2. Preparation to perpetuate the way it is currently organized.
3. Preparation to change society through research and innovation.
4. Preparation to adapt to changes that occur in an uncertain future.
5. Preparation for personal development.
6. Preparation for the needs of the economy as a worker.
7. Preparation for life as a consumer.
8. Preparation for leisure.

Incoming teachers may find that the particular selection and the priorities already established in the school are not the same as their own preferences. The action required is likely to be the same as with the other parts of the 'kit' presented to the newcomer, i.e. accept and adjust.

Changes in Power Relations

According to Ball (1993) and Siraj-Blatchford (1993), the technical or craft element of a teacher's work has increased since the introduction of the National Curriculum and the imposition of national testing in schools. This has led to a reduction in the role of teachers as professionals who enjoyed a greater degree of autonomy prior to the Education Reform Act. With the introduction of national testing (related to a national curriculum) and published school performance league tables, the public is able to scrutinize and contrast school test results. This raises the possibility of comparisons with teacher performance and teacher appraisal. Ball (1993) provides a matrix of power relations between the curriculum, the marketization of education and the role of managers (Table 3.1). Note how the position of the teacher is influenced.

Table 3.1 A matrix of power relations

	Curriculum	The market	Management
Forms of control	Commonality Prescription Intervention	Variety Mechanism Responsivity	Consensus? Self-regulation Flexibility
System steering	*Ex post* processual and *ex ante*	Reputation *ex ante*	*Ex post/* feedback
Teacher as	Deliverer Tester Technician	Commodity-producer Performer Entrepreneur?	Resource Accountable Cost
Changes in	The balance between local and central curriculum	The values and the professional culture of institutions	The relationship of the managers and the managed

From Ball, 1993, p. 107.

CONCLUSION

This analysis based on the analogy of the teacher as victim may be used to stress an important sociological finding: that individual items in a network of influences may seem trivial if taken alone; it is the cumulative effect of such a network of influences that is significant.

The incoming teacher may have to accept a timetable: this seems to be trivial. And the headteacher's theory of education may have to be accommodated: still relatively trivial perhaps. But the newcomer also has to accept the particular organizational decisions, the building and furniture, the National Curriculum as adopted by the school, the assessment system adopted, the particular resources available, the approved pedagogy established in the school, the particular expectations of the clients and others, and the selection of aims, objectives and outcomes (with their established order of priorities). Thus the analogy of victim does not seem too far-fetched when the cumulative effect of all these features is totalled.

However, this chapter began with a caution about the use of analogies: the limitations of the idea of teacher as victim need to be considered in order to establish its usefulness. Furthermore, the contradictions that occur in such a complex network of influences may provide scope for either variation or change (see Grace, 1978).

Summary

1. Description and analysis in sociology often proceed by the use of analogies.
2. Analogies can clarify, but can also distort.
3. Many analogies in sociology are derived from drama: one example is that of the teacher as role player.
4. An analogy from the world of work is that of the teacher as a cultural worker who perpetuates the cultural apparatus to the designs of others, rather than innovating.
5. Teaching is seen as analogous to other occupations – police officer, technician and professional.
6. The analogy of teacher as victim gains plausibility if we list the kit of ideas given to a new teacher. This kit is made up of a given set of buildings, a headteacher who has a particular ideology of education, a timetable, an organizational style, a national curriculum, an assessment system, a set of resources, an expected teaching method, the expectations of various clients and a set of aims, objectives and outcomes.
7. The cumulative effect of a network of influences may be considerable, whereas individual items within a network may appear to be trivial when considered singly. This constitutes an important contribution of sociology to the understanding of social situations.

Further Reading

Ball, S. (1993) 'Education Policy, Power Relations and Teachers' Work', *British Journal of Educational Studies*, **41**, 2, 106–21.

Barton, L. and Walker, S. (eds) (1981) *Schools, Teachers and Teaching*. Lewes: Falmer Press.

Carter, C., Harber, C. and Serf, J. (2003) *Towards Ubuntu*, Birmingham: Birmingham Education Development Centre.

Gewirtz, S., Ball, S. and Bowe, R. (1995) *Markets, Choice and Equity in Education*. Buckingham: Open University Press.

Hammersley, M. (1977) *The Social Location of Teacher Perspectives*. Milton Keynes: Open University Press. An analysis of teaching as a profession. Section 4 is particularly relevant.

Hanson, D. and Herrington, M. (1976) *From College to Classroom*. London: Routledge and Kegan Paul. Contains an interesting account of a new teacher being the victim of the headteacher's ideology of education (pp. 44–52).

Hoyle, E. (1969) *The Role of the Teacher*. London: Routledge and Kegan Paul. The analogy of teacher as role player is the subject of this book.

Kohl, H. (1970) *The Open Classroom*. London: Methuen. An account of one teacher who refuses to be a helpless victim.

Siraj-Blatchford, I. (1993) 'Educational Research and Reform: Some Implications for the Professional Identity of Early Years Teachers', *British Journal of Educational Studies*, **41**, 4, 398–408.

Toogood, P. (1984) *The Head's Tale*. Telford: Dialogue Publications. A headteacher resigns rather than be a victim of LEA policy.

Discussion and Activities

1. The analogy of scripts was introduced in this chapter. Give an account of teacher behaviour using this idea. Are teachers both actors and scriptwriters?
2. Describe your teaching practice in terms of the teacher as victim, or interview someone who has just experienced a final teaching practice.
3. Is the analogy of victim more applicable to secondary school teachers than the primary school situation?

Signposts

1. Conflict theory

From a conflict theory point of view, professions can be seen as interest groups protecting their members' privileges rather than as groups operating a service-to-others ethic. A source on this approach is Johnson, T.J. (1972) *Professions and Power*, London: Macmillan. See also Lawn, M. (ed.) (1985) *The Politics of Teacher Unionism*, Beckenham: Croom Helm.

2. Bureaucratic settings

The traditional image of a professional is that of a person working alone to an ethical code of the occupation. What are the consequences of having professionals working in large bureaucratic organizations with rule systems and hierarchies with chains of command? A starting point is Ozga, I. and Lawn, M. (1981) *Teachers, Professionalism and Class: A Study of Organized Teachers*, Lewes: Falmer Press.

3. Influence systems

What influences teachers most? And what has least effect? One study is Taylor, P.H.T. *et al.* (1974) *Purpose, Power and Constraint in the Primary School Curriculum*, London: Macmillan.

4. Change

What changes in the activity of teachers can be expected? Several writers have addressed this issue, e.g. Wragg, T. (1984) 'Education for the Twenty-First Century', in C. Harber *et al.* (eds), *Alternative Educational Futures*, London: Holt, Rinehart and Winston.

5. Marketization

What impact has the Education Reform Act had on the professionalism and scope of teachers' work? The market-place in education puts the teacher in the role of 'producer' and the parent in the role of 'consumer'. See Ball, S. (1993) 'Education Policy, Power Relations and Teachers' Work', *British Journal of Educational Studies*, **41**, 2, 106–21.

6. Teachers and autonomy

According to Caroline St John-Brooks, editor of the *Times Educational Supplement*, professionalism in England and Wales has been linked to notions of autonomy, but important aspects of this have now been removed. Teachers with high levels of responsibility and low levels of autonomy are now one of 'the most dissatisfied group of workers in Britain'. Will they find the answer in a General Teaching Council? See St John-Brooks, C.

'The Meaning of Professionalism', paper available on the National Union of Teachers website: *http://www.data.teachers.org.uk/pdfs/atom1.pdf*

7. Teachers and Curriculum
The school curriculum is socially constructed. It is therefore interesting to compare the nature of the curriculum in different countries. A good example is to be found in Carter, C., Harber, C. and Serf, J. (2003) *Towards Ubuntu*, Birmingham: Birmingham Education Development Centre.

Parents as Educators?   4

> A partnership between teachers and parents: 'a working relationship that is
> characterised by a shared sense of purpose, mutual respect and the willingness to
> negotiate. This implies a sharing of information, responsibility, skills, decision-
> making and accountability.'
>
> Gillian Pugh and Erica De'Ath, 1989

> One head teacher told John's parents to make his home life less interesting so that
> he would not be so bored at school.
>
> Times Educational Supplement, 20 September 1996

INTRODUCTION

The concept of layers of meaning links the chapters of this first section. It draws to our
attention the notion that there is no one agreed or true picture of a complex institution like a
school. From the pupils' perspective, school looks different from either the teachers' or the
parents' viewpoints. Moreover, each layer of meaning is segmented, e.g. teachers vary in their
ideologies of education, parents vary in their social class identities and pupils vary in their
interpretations of the experience of schooling. Each layer of meaning turns out to be a rather
loose identity that accrues to the participants initially by force of circumstance – that of being
a five-year-old child in the UK rather than any other European country, or that of being
appointed to the staff of a particular school at a particular era, or that of a parent living in a
particular catchment area under a given political administration.

'SUCCESSFUL' PARENTS

The report of the Plowden Committee (1967), *Children and Their Primary Schools*, confirmed
the findings of research studies undertaken in the previous twenty years or so that there was a
statistically significant association between parental interest and encouragement of their
children at school and educational performance in academic tasks. Whether performance was

better where parents encourage or whether parents encourage where performance is notable was not clear. (Statistical associations are, after all, only clues: there is a high correlation between bed and death since so many people die there. From this it does not follow that bed is so dangerous that it should be avoided.) The committee gave the interpretation that it was very likely a matter of continuous interaction rather than a one-way causal effect.

The nature of such parental interest is not necessarily kindly. Musgrove (1966), summarizing research on the 'good' home as regards academic success, proposed that it was small and had ambitious parents, that the father was at least a skilled manual worker and, in the case of a working-class home, that the mother would have middle-class origins. (The problems associated with such a general social class dichotomy are taken up in a later chapter.) The father could be ineffectual or even feckless but one parent has to be demanding as regards school attainment. Musgrove concludes:

> Relationships in the home are emotionally bleak. The family is unstable and has moved often; the mother goes out to work. The children grow up to be rather withdrawn and solitary, conscientious and given to self-blame. They are 'good grammar school material'.

In the view of Musgrove this does not present too attractive a picture: ruthless, demanding relationships lacking in warmth, and a view that happiness is almost an irrelevance, lead him to observe that

> Neither humanity nor common sense seem to pay the highest dividends in the education system and social order which we have devised.

The American writer Eldridge Cleaver proposes that either you are part of the problem or you are part of the solution. Parents, homes and families are often presented to teachers in training as part of the problem, and this view tends to be confirmed by the behaviour and attitudes of experienced teachers. The process involved is identified in a study by Sharp and Green (1975). Much of the information about parents and homes is gained second-hand and then filtered through the concept of a 'good parent'.

Since the 1988 Education Act, we have been led to believe that the government is increasingly concerned to foster parental choice and participation in the process of children's education. Parents have, in line with market philosophy, more 'choice' in selecting the school that their child attends and a right to regular reports on academic achievement. In response to a perceived failure of schools to inform and involve parents, one government issued a parents' charter outlining the rights that parents have been given.

'GOOD' AND 'BAD' PARENTS

In the study of primary schooling by Sharp and Green, four key dimensions of the 'good' parent' role, as defined by the school, were identified.

1. The good parent needs to be knowledgeable about the way the school operates and its ideology of education.
2. There must be a strong interest in the education of their children and a motivation for them to succeed.
3. The parent has to be capable of cueing into the teachers' interpretation schemes, in particular the teachers' definition of the 'good parent'.
4. The parent has to be good at impression management and must be both willing and able to play up to the teachers' view of the 'good parent'.

The more any of these dimensions is missing, Sharp and Green proposed, the more likely it is that the relationship with the school will become negative and the label of 'bad parent' become affixed.

In the case of the first dimension of knowledgeability, the gathering of reliable information is not always an easy task. Visits to school-organized meetings, gleaning impressions from children, clues from the work brought home, talking with other parents – these were some of the methods available. Parents can occupy various stages of confusion about the school as a result; the more confused a parent, the less likely it was that dialogues with school staff would proceed smoothly and unambiguously. The variation among teachers regarding ideologies of education outlined in the previous chapter increases the difficulty of the task.

As regards the second dimension, there were differences among the parents as to their view of education. Almost all those in the Sharp and Green study registered interest but of different kinds. All appeared to regard reading, writing and numeracy as important, some supported a broader conception of education that valued an extended curriculum of creative and artistic activities, provided the three Rs were dealth with, and a minority had the personal happiness of their children as the top priority above instrumental concerns. Because of these variations, some parents would connect with the teachers' view in play in a particular school more than others. Parents' interest relates to their particular view of education and how well they think the school actually works for and achieves this. Interest is developed in interaction between homes and schools, not a fixed trait possessed or not possessed at the outset. The allegiances of various groups of parents are there to be won or lost.

Reading the teachers' view of a 'good parent' was the crucial part of the third dimension of the task before the parents. Sharp and Green concluded that this required a stance of deference to the teachers' claim of superior knowledge, expertise and competence, trust in the teachers' judgement and support for the teachers' definition of the situation. Parents vary in their effectiveness in this activity. Some are unsuccessful in the initial collecting of information about the school, and therefore misinterpretation results. Others may read the ideology of education of teachers and reject it, and so refuse to give the required deference. They fail in the fourth dimension of playing up to the teachers' definition of the 'good parent'. Through impression management the good parent convinces the teachers that he or she is in unison with them. 'Good parents' do not actually have to be knowledgeable about the school or really interested in the education provided, or genuinely defer to the teachers. They only have to convince the teachers by their role-playing skills that this is the case. Functional hypocrisy is sufficient and necessary, since if the parents actually did no more than really leave everything to the activity of the teachers, then their children would be at risk. Not that the impression management is one-sided, however, since teachers are involved in elaborate pretensions that all is well with the school in parents' evenings and school reports.

The successful parents, in terms of having their children successful at school, avoid the label of interferers while actually interfering persistently. They pretend to meet the definition of 'good parent' by not interfering, by not teaching their children at home, by not helping them to read, write and develop numeracy, while they actually do all these things and also teach their children to act discreetly at school by not letting on.

There are illustrations of the irony of human action here. If the parents did follow the teachers' definition of 'good parent', their children would be less likely to succeed. A further irony is that the school staff think they, by their teaching, make the difference in developing children well or otherwise, whereas Sharp and Green argue that the crucial factor is the activity or lack of it on the part of the parents – how good they are as behind-the-scenes educators. There is more irony yet:

> Additional irony – those parents who are most in favour at the school are usually those who, amongst other things, appear by their actions in consistently teaching their children to read etc., most critical of it.
>
> Sharp and Green, 1975

One of the features that connects here is that of social class. If we ignore for the moment the problems of oversimplification implicit in the division into middle class (white-collar occupations) and working class (blue-collar occupations), we can take up a point that Sharp and Green make that middle-class parents are more likely to have the impression-management skills since they are in the repertoire of so many white-collar occupations, ranging from lawyers, who have to pretend that they believe a client to be guiltless, to a bank clerk, who has to fake pleasantness to obnoxious customers.

Part of the explanation for this state of affairs is political. In the schooling system in the UK, parents have had relatively little power. Even those happy with a school did not set the terms of the bargain, but accepted them and manipulated them to their advantage. And if the parents are to some extent victims of the schools, pupils can be victims of both, being required to please teachers and please parents within a complex network of impression management which: 'may depend as much on mutual deception and misunderstanding as on a genuine communality of meaning' (Sharp and Green, 1975).

ALTERNATIVE VIEWS OF THE 'GOOD PARENT'

Alternative views of the role of good parent exist. One teacher in a reading workshop project that involved parents as educational helpers comments on the progress of a particular child:

He's come on in leaps and bounds. He's very confident. I'm surprised at how he's come on –
I couldn't have done it without his mum – it's a reading workshop success.

Weinburger, 1983

The definition of 'good parent' can vary with country. The Home School Movement, as a voluntary organization, occupies a modest place in the Swedish schooling system, but its goals are widely accepted: that the care of children is everyone's business; that homes, schools and society should work together to create a safe and enriching environment for growing up; that all people concerned strengthen their sense of community and find common interest in their local school and the immediate environment. Parents are encouraged, in the words of their brochure, to do the following:

- Care about the everyday work in the class; visit the class, take part in the child's work and the teaching materials, talk about school with them, read books and watch TV together.
- Contact the teachers and other personnel in the school when you feel it is necessary. Attend private conferences and class meetings.
- Get in on preparations for and the execution of activities such as field trips, project work and encampments, etc.
- Take care of the class if the teacher must be away temporarily during the school day.
- Volunteer to come to class, when it is appropriate, and tell about your job or something else that interests you.
- Get to know your own child's friends and their parents, meet them in your free time, at home or outdoors, children and adults together.
- Help out if your child's friends or their parents are having difficulties just now.
- Have the students present when class meetings are planned and held.
- Whenever you are in class think of things which can be improved upon or what ways we parents and students could help.
- Volunteer yourself as a leader for children's and teenagers' free time activities.
- Try to get your colleagues at work to be interested in the school.

That several of these ideas would usually get a defensive reaction from most school teachers in the UK is perhaps some measure of the differences in the dominant educational vision between the two countries.

PARENTS' CURRENT ACTIVITY AS TEACHERS

The title of this chapter implies that parents may increasingly come to be seen as having a teaching role, but this proposition disguises the characteristics of the current situation and obscures the range of existing parental activity. This existing activity is of several kinds.

Pre-school Activity

The education of children for the first five years of their lives is largely in the hands of parents. Pre-school educators have tended to develop a policy of working in partnership with parents rather than being *in loco parentis*. Pre-school education of this kind, including pre-school enrichment projects and playgroup schemes, does not assume that parents are automatically competent teachers, but that given support, advice and guidance, they frequently become so.

One project that indicates the possibilities has been developed in Sandwell in the West Midlands. The Child Psychology Service, directed by T.A. Kelly, established a parental involvement in a primary education project to help parents to increase their skills in helping the development of their young children. Sixteen schools were involved with a staff of four specially trained teachers whose task was to visit the homes of parents. These parents had older children in school who had been identified by a testing programme as failing to realize their potential and who also had younger siblings presumed to be equally at risk. The visits occurred weekly over a long period of time, up to five years in some cases, and attempted to establish relationships of mutual trust, to take equipment and toys and to provide advice, guidance and discussion about the pre-school education of the young children concerned. The results have proved encouraging, in that most of the children involved have produced higher test results than the 'contact' child when admitted to school. There have also been reported improvements in the learning attitudes and achievement of most of the 'contact' children as well (Stevens, 1984).

Families that had previously been overwhelmed with difficulties have discovered new resources within themselves to improve, to maintain their improvement and finally to cope independently. The relationship built up over time with the mothers, and also fathers (since unemployment is high in the area), through the weekly visit is seen as a crucial factor:

> These mothers, many of whom have given up in most areas of their lives, who constantly underachieve because they have no self-respect or motivation, now find themselves in a situation where:
>
> (a) Someone offers them a way to achieve.
> (b) Offers them motivation.
> (c) Offers them example – friendship, support, but never interference.
> (d) Offers them praise when they succeed and further encouragement when they fail.
> (e) Offers them consistency and an element of order and routine in which to operate (one weekly visit – same time – same day, etc.). Shows them that somebody cares very much what happens to them and their family.
> (f) Is often able to liaise on their behalf with other professional agencies with whom previous contact might have been inhibited or inadequate.
> (g) On a more material level, is in a situation to help with distribution of appropriate clothing and furniture – prams, cots, etc., between the network of families visited who all require certain material equipment at different stages of their child's development and then find it convenient to pass on or swap.
>
> Stevens, 1984

Similar findings are recorded in a larger project based in Coventry and based on the Community Education Development Centre (Widlake and Macleod, 1984). Encouraging parents, mostly from working-class backgrounds, to help with reading, language activities and other support raised standards, as the testing programme clearly demonstrated.

Projects Involving Parents as Teachers

It is an interesting question as to why only a few educators seem to regard parents as a resource. A common factor in conversations I have had with such educators is that they are both parents and teachers and have observed many limitations in what schools were achieving with their own children. They therefore devised strategies to remedy these limitations. It is then but a short step to advising other parents who are friends but not teachers and an even shorter step to seeing scope in the idea generally.

Sociological research findings related to social class play a part here. Studies of the superior formal school achievements of the middle classes have indicated that the home support given to children varies in *technique* rather than in motive (Jones, 1966). In both the middle classes as a whole and the working classes as a whole, the range of motives is rather similar. The majority desire that their children succeed at school, while another group is ambiguous in outlook and a small number rather opposed to school. The middle-class parents, some of whom are teachers anyway, are able to turn their desire into reality by appropriate techniques and by displaying the confidence to carry off the surreptitious teaching of reading, writing and arithmetic referred to earlier, as well as exploiting holidays, weekends and television viewing as sources of general knowledge and discussion. One of the achievements of the play group movement has been to pass on techniques to parents who previously lacked them.

In the USA the work of Dorothy Rich has been notable for using parents as teachers (Cookson, 1979). Her experience fits the profile outlined above. Her home learning methods evolved as she brought up her own daughters, and she introduced them into her teaching training activities at Trinity College, Washington. Out of this experience she developed the Home and School Institute. For some twenty-five years now she has run workshops and courses, producing written advice notes on specific techniques or 'recipes' that give parents clear straightforward instructions for using domestic items (e.g. refuse), and experiences, such as visits to the supermarket, to help children to acquire and develop skills in reading, writing and arithmetic, as well as other learning habits.

Many middle-class parents recognized these 'recipes' as things they were already doing but could improve. They were welcomed by many working-class parents as being the missing techniques they were in need of. To try to cope with the anticipated and actual hostility of many teachers, the 'recipes' concentrated on items and experiences more likely to be found associated with homes than with schools, so as to maintain a demarcation line. Parents were to be seen as complementing rather than rivalling the school.

Some schools in the USA have adopted the Rich 'recipes' in a variety of ways (Cookson,

1979). One use is in remedial teaching. Thus, at Damascus Elementary School in Maryland, parents with children having learning difficulties were persuaded to work with the recipes at home for four nights a week for a year. The wary parents found that the results paid off, since nine out of thirteen children avoided the repetition of the first-grade year that had been envisaged for them.

The remedial aspects have also been the subject of a project in Birmingham in Britain. Glynn (1980) introduced a remedial reading tutoring programme to the parents of four ten-year-old boys with reading problems. Marked improvements in the boys' reading skills as well as in the parents' skills of helping were recorded over as short a period as three months. Glynn had developed his ideas in New Zealand schools and the project results in the UK confirm the successes he had recorded in Auckland. Work by Hewison and Tizard (1980) in the UK has shown similar results.

The idea of involving parents in children's reading was welcomed in the case of UK primary schools. The Haringey Project based on an inner-city area in London was monitored by Tizard *et al.* (1982). Hewison concluded that the project: 'demonstrated that most parents are willing as well as able to help their children with reading', and that as a result the children concerned benefited compared with children lacking such help (see also Griffiths and Hamilton, 1985).

The Belfield Project, Rochdale, showed similar results (Wilby, 1981). The Fox Hill Reading Workshop, Sheffield, was the subject of another report (Weinburger, 1983), and apart from confirming the findings of the other projects, it demonstrated how both teachers and parents learnt from the experience. A parent commented that 'I understand better what a teacher has to cope with having to teach children', and a teacher approving of the work of the parents states, 'They could have done all this before, but we didn't know'. In all the projects the reading standards were shown to improve.

In the case of children defined as having special educational needs, the Portage Scheme, first set up in Wisconsin, USA, in 1969, set out to teach parents to teach their children at home with the aid of a home-visiting teacher. The Portage Scheme has been adopted at Winchester and South Glamorgan in Britain, and the conclusion is that this approach has helped parents to be effective in teaching their children with disabilities in using an agreed system and to record the progress made:

> The Portage model recognises that children gain most from education when parents are closely involved in the teaching. Until now professionals trying to help severely handicapped children have often looked for service improvements outside the home, e.g. smaller classes, purposebuilt centres, increasingly complicated teaching aids and teaching methods, etc. Perhaps the most valuable resource of all has been left at home preparing tea for a returning child!
>
> Cameron, 1984

Another project that ignored the demarcation line between home and school was the Parkway Programme, Philadelphia, where, among various radical aspects, only half the teaching was undertaken by teaching staff. The other teaching was performed by members of the community, many of them parents, who were recruited to match the declared interests of the students. Thus student requests to study psychology might lead to the recruitment of a local psychologist willing to take the class. This procedure of drawing course teachers from non-teacher trained members of the community is commonplace in further education and evening institutes but rare in schools.

One project with nearly a hundred years' experience of parents as educators is the World-Wide Education Service (WES) of the Parents' National Education Union, which was founded in the 1880s by Charlotte Mason. WES has concentrated on helping expatriate families in about a hundred countries to educate their children as an alternative to sending them to boarding school, but it also makes its service available to parents educating their children at home in the UK. The WES system provides guidance and training for the parents as an integral part of the course. One former WES pupil became chairperson of the Birmingham Education Committee and ultimately MP for Handsworth, Birmingham (see Boulter, 1984).

Education Otherwise

The role of parents as educators becomes total where they decide to take up their option in law to educate 'otherwise than at school'. The organization Education Otherwise was set up in 1977 as a mutual aid venture by the small minority of parents who had decided to undertake home-based education.

The equivalent organization in the USA, Growing Without Schooling, was set up at about the same time. The motives of *some* of these parents were based on genuinely held and articulated principles and their reaction to what they saw as some harmful effects of mass schooling as documented in the writings of the so-called 'deschoolers' and, more recently, in Hemming's (1980) work. However, the majority appear to be simply desperate because their children are so unhappy at school, or are achieving little, or are both unhappy and achieving little (Meighan, 1984). The members of the non-achieving group often express a desire for links with local schools in some cooperative partnership or flexischooling arrangement. Although this has happened in parts of the USA, few cases of British schools agreeing to this are known to the writer. Polarization is forced on such parents by LEAs that insist on either school or home education, but allow no cooperative partnerships. The nearest arrangement to a cooperative partnership that has been established so far appears to be that of supervision by the home tuition section of an LEA.

Parents who survive the various inquisitions of the school, the LEA inspectors and the School Psychological Service usually find the outcome is worth it. The success that can be achieved under a home-based scheme so startled one journalist that he wrote a book about one family's experiences (Deakin, 1973). My own research (Meighan, 1997) into Midland families has led me to the firm conclusion that the extreme suspicion, overzealous attention and often naked hostility of some LEA officials is unwarranted, disreputable and a misuse of public money. One Midland LEA used large sums of public money to pay a barrister in a magistrates' court hearing that resulted in an absolute discharge for the family.

PARENTS IN A CHANGING SOCIETY

There are a number of recent changes in the social context that have implications for education in general, and the potential development of parents as teachers in particular, not least because of the learning resources located in increasing numbers of homes. The credibility of parents as educators has increased as a variety of educational initiatives and projects have demonstrated positive outcomes to adopting various degrees of parental partnership.

Communication and Information Systems

It is no longer necessary to speculate about information systems since the television companies have already established CEEFAX, and other forms of teletext are already in use in many homes and are a familiar sight in the windows of TV rental shops. If the take-up of these services is as rapid as in the cases of radio, television and then colour television, over 90 per cent of homes will have them in the next five years or so. Personal computers with multimedia capabilities have been purchased for home use. The picture that emerges is of most homes gradually being equipped as sophisticated information retrieval centres, while schools have been doing the same.

Knowledge Explosion

It has been estimated that knowledge is expanding at the rate of a doubling in quantity every ten years. Some of this new knowledge renders existing knowledge inadequate, inaccurate or out of date, or all three. Schools depend on teachers who are now taking up to four years to train, and on books that take two or three years to produce and then need a sales run of several years to be commercially viable. Therefore, the basic sources of information used in schools easily become inadequate. Homes are less susceptible to such obsolescence since they have regular access to television and, increasingly, access to the information retrieval systems listed above.

Television

Pupils can quickly become aware of the gap between school knowledge and contemporary knowledge by viewing the latest TV documentary and news programmes. Schools are ill-equipped to cope, for few have more than limited TV and video facilities and some have none. In this situation, TV viewed at home becomes an alternative source of culture, information and education. In providing more up-to-date information, the home can become a competitive rather than a complementary source of culture.

Work, the Economy and Schooling

The relationship between work, the economy and schooling is problematic. Human capital theory, for example, assumes that formal education provides the skills that lead both to individual employment and economic growth for the society as a whole. Yet the level of investment in education varies considerably among industrialized countries and there are quite a number of 'less developed' countries with high levels of investment in education and high levels of unemployment (see, for example, the UNDP's annual *Human Development Index*). There doesn't seem to be any clear and consistent link between education and economic performance internationally. It might best be said that education can facilitate economic growth or not, but not cause it or stop it.

This, however, does not mean that the economic role of education is not a regular topic of both political and academic debate. If an economy is performing poorly and youth unemployment is high, there tends to be more public debate about the 'vocational' role of education than if the situation is the opposite. In Britain in the 1980s when youth unemployment was high, for example, there were a number of significant educational initiatives such as the Technical Vocational Educational Initiative and the Certificate of Pre-vocational Education which were aimed at making young people more 'prepared' for the job market. Since then this has been less of an issue as the economy has created more jobs and the proportion of young people leaving school and going to university (and thus not straight on to the job market) has increased from under 10 per cent in the 1970s to over 40 per cent in the early twenty-first century. In Britain we now hear much less about vocational education and much more about the relative performance of schools in terms of more traditional forms of academic assessment

In fact, the courses developed in the 1980s tended to be 'pre-vocational' rather than 'vocational' in the sense that they attempted to teach generic skills and dispositions thought useful for the world of work (communication, presentation, creativity, enterprise, flexibility) rather than training for a specific post. Vocational training in this sense has always been the role of colleges of further education. However, it is important to recognize that schooling has always been related to the world of work. Traditional academic education can be directly vocational if it successfully qualifies somebody to read medicine, law or dentistry at university and degrees in each of these high status and selective subjects have a strong academic input as well as a vocational one. Moreover, all formal education, sometimes well and sometimes poorly, equips learners with some generic pre-vocational skills such as literacy and numeracy. An interesting question for sociologists is whether all young people are equally equipped with such academic/pre-vocational skills and whether there is a difference in the type of knowledge, skills and attitudes that different groups acquire through schooling. This is further explored in Parts Four and Five of this book.

Learning Theories

Hemming (1980) claims that the theories of modern psychology about brain functioning and learning have been largely ignored. The work of Piaget, Bruner and others is set aside in favour of older but fallacious ideas:

> it is an extraordinary fact that the dominant influences operating in secondary education have no scientific basis whatever. They arise from dubitable philosophical ideas that had their origin in the distant past: the Greek view that the craftsman was inherently inferior to the thinker; Locke's presentation of the mind as a clean slate, as a *tabula rasa*; Descartes' over-evaluation of the intellect, and his division of the human being into mind (exalted) and body (debased); puritan ideas about the special value of making the young do what they don't like doing.
>
> Hemming, 1980

A similar point is made by Husen (1974) when he argues that the key assumptions about learning that underpin schooling are all dubious. These assumptions are (a) that people will only learn to avoid disagreeable consequences, (b) what pupils can achieve is rationed by the possession of 'ability' and (c) that formal textbook tasks indicate the best kinds of 'ability'. Until these false principles are abandoned, Husen and Hemming see schools as continuing to limit the development of young people.

A similar conclusion was central to the group of writers rather misleadingly known as the 'deschoolers', who, on the whole, were in favour of regenerating schooling rather than doing away with it altogether. The consequences of contemporary schooling based on fallacious principles were that:

> the students who endure it come out as passive, acquiescent, dogmatic, intolerant, authoritarian, inflexible, conservative personalities who desperately need to resist change in an effort to keep their illusion of certainty intact.
>
> Postman and Weingartner, 1971

The potential for homes to reverse this equation is clear in the responses of parents in Education Otherwise, where they report the liberating effects of developing home-based education (see Meighan, 1997).

Educational Developments

There have been educational developments that have involved homes in a systematic way as a learning resource and base. The first example is the Open University. Here learning at home is a key idea. The resources of the home, its television and radio, are taken into the network of learning experiences and the postal service is used as a major means of communication. The learning experiences are to some extent open to other members of the family to share, if so desired.

Deriving partly from the years of experience of the Open University is another idea, flexistudy. This approach has been adopted by many colleges of further education. As one prospectus states: 'Flexistudy enables students to study at home in their own time and at their own pace.' The students come to college from time to time to meet tutors and to use any college resources that they need.

Parents and Ideologies of Education

The existence of a series of competing ideologies of education, with competing definitions of learning, teaching resources, knowledge, assessment, language usage, location, aims and organization, has been the subject of research (see Part Three). The notion that there is one view of education, a politically neutral view, is shown to be mistaken. Therefore, the development of parents as teachers could follow several lines. It could be developed to serve any of the competing ideologies of education outlined in the research mentioned above. The example given earlier of parents used as remedial instructors at home shows how incorporation into the existing authoritarian system and its aims can take place. One example of parents operating with an alternative ideology of education is those parents in Education Otherwise who establish an autonomous education approach, with its stress on self-education, personal confidence, problem-solving, flexibility and adaptation (Meighan, 1984). Another is the democratic approach involving parents as equal partners, as found in the Danish Little Schools and proposed by the Campaign for State-assisted Alternative Schools (see Diamond, 1984).

CONSEQUENCES FOR TEACHERS

As parents become defined more and more as part of the solution rather than as part of the problem, one outcome is a changed role for teachers, who become more like their higher-status cousins – university teachers – in using a range of skills for tutorial, instructional, consultancy and research purposes. The model of teaching involved extends beyond the dominant idea of instruction, while the concept of 'good parent' becomes one of being an active rather than a passive supporter of teachers. The central concept of school becomes that of a learning centre (requiring similar kinds of adjustments already made in colleges of further education to the idea of flexistudy). The concept of flexischooling is the subject of a chapter in the final section of this book.

Part of the task of teaching can become 'training' parents by providing advice and guidance and monitoring their activities. The experience of pre-school educators and play group organizers argues that this cannot be left to chance. A study in Oxfordshire concluded that teachers seemed to believe that parents could just pick up the aims and techniques as they went along. Smith (1980) found that this was not true: the parents needed some guidance and knew that they needed it. The practice of Dorothy Rich in the USA has proved successful partly because it is so explicit and does provide training sessions. On the other hand, some families in Education Otherwise have had impressive results by avoiding the official wisdom and pioneering new approaches, e.g. some families have developed a non-sexist education – a problem that still baffles most schools in the UK (see Chapter 25).

Gilkes (1989) argues that schools have to get their ethos right: a supportive, even therapeutic, setting that creates confidence in those who come. She explains that an atmosphere or ethos that encourages a sense of belonging should aim to:

1. Make all feel that they are wanted and that they have a positive role to play in the setting.
2. Show parents that they can always make their feelings, views and opinions known to the staff, and that these will be dealt with respectfully and seriously.
3. Demonstrate that the parents' linguistic, cultural and religious backgrounds are valued and seen as positive assets to the setting.
4. Show that the early years setting is an organic part of the community it serves and so understands the concerns, aspirations and difficulties the members of that community might face.

The Children Act (Volume 2, 1989) states that parents of young children have certain parental rights which allow them to influence the quality of care and education their child receives. They should be able to acquire information about the setting, choose between settings and modify, express views about and contribute to their child's school. This has serious implications for parents who are not confident about their English. Early childhood educators need to ensure that they offer the whole community an equal chance to understand and use their service. If this means translating notices about the setting and putting them in areas where ethnic minority families will see them, e.g. doctors' surgeries, then this should be done as a first step to ensure initial interest.

Siraj-Blatchford (1994) argues that not all parents whose children attend school will have had a positive experience of education themselves, and because most of us draw on our past experiences to make judgements about matters of everyday life, parents might well hold negative views about teachers and the institutions they represent. They might even be sceptical or suspicious of professionals in general, particularly in areas where parents perceive 'professionals' as dominating and controlling their lives. Parents who are unemployed, who live in rented accommodation or suffer regular interventions in their family life by social workers and other support agencies may feel powerless over their lives or in making decisions.

This cumulative past experience and sense of outside control can make some parents feel disempowered and lacking in confidence in their dealings with schools. Their own academic failure may be attributed directly to schooling. Teachers have responsibility for building confidence and for getting to know parents as people with a life history which affects their everyday actions. Some parents will certainly be confident and will have had positive experiences of education, but it cannot be assumed.

Parents have culturally conceived ideas about the role of education and teachers and these are likely to be somewhat different. In some cultures the role of the educators is seen as distinct and separate from the role of parenting, and teachers may need to take some time explaining and illustrating how the child can benefit from partnership and continuity of educational experience across school and home. It is sensible for teachers not to make assumptions about parents' knowledge, beliefs or experiences but to create a friendly atmosphere where parents can talk openly about their feelings. Additionally, sufficient interest should be taken in each parent as an individual and his or her views and feelings should be sought on general matters pertaining to the school and particularly to his or her child. This sort of interest and care fosters trust and an open and secure ambience.

For parents to participate in the daily life of a school there must be real and obvious commitment from staff. It is not enough to use the rhetoric of parents as 'partners' in the education of their children. Some teachers do use such phrases, and through using these words feel committed to them. In reality this is not always the case, and it is all too easy to neglect the most vulnerable and needy parents. Regular scrutiny of the slogans and rhetoric we use is essential. For instance, what is actually meant by a 'partnership' with parents?

CONCLUSION

The educational role of a parent can be seen to be open to definition and redefinition as the identity is created and re-created in interactions among teachers, schools, politicians and social forces, such as a changing technology. Rival views exist in the UK, but the definition operating in the school studies by Sharp and Green (1975) is widespread, as surveys of teachers' and parents' attitudes have shown. According to this definition, parents are expected to avoid being either interfering by questioning school critically or admitting to direct teaching at home, or neglectful by not providing required clothing and skills of neatness and tidiness. The 'good' parent defers to the school and the professional claim of its teachers but becomes a victim if this is more than impression management.

The Taylor Report (1977) on the government of schools saw parents in a different light and sought to increase the power of parents to the point of power-sharing, for parents were seen as equal partners with teachers in terms of decision-making and responsibility.

The government Green Paper on parents (1984) took a different view: parents were to be given more power still by having an overall majority on school governing bodies. Three views of power are contained in these alternative views. Parents are, in turn, under orders, equal partners or in charge. There are other views too for those parents who educate their children at home rather than send them to school, undertaking the autonomous education already available to them in law. Another view is represented by the members of CSAS (Campaign for

State-assisted Alternative Schools), since they ask for a more active and embracing partnership than that of being on the governing body in their vision of democratically run schools (see Diamond, 1984).

The review of parents and their relationship to the process of educating and the system of formal education renders all the common views problematic. How much do the experts really know? Do parents need training in existing techniques or scope to develop new approaches? Is an effective relationship with teachers that of participants, partners or paymasters? A later section of this book concentrates on the concept of ideologies of education and you will be able to look again at the material on parents and reconsider it in the light of the authoritarian, autonomous and democratic groupings of educational visions.

Further Reading

Craft, M., Raynor, J. and Cohen, L. (1980) *Linking Home and School*. London: Harper and Row.

Cyster, R., Clift, P.S. and Battle, S. (1983) *Parental Involvement in Primary Schools*. Windsor: NFER-Nelson.

Gilkes, J. (1989) *Developing Nursery Education*. Milton Keynes: Open University Press.

Fortune-Wood, M. (2005) *The Face of Home-based Education: Who, Why and How*, Nottingham: Educational Heretics Press.

Harber, C., Meighan, R. and Roberts, B. (1984) *Alternative Educational Futures*. London: Holt, Rinehart and Winston.

Holt, J. (1981) *Teach Your Own*. Brightlingsea: Lighthouse Books.

Meighan, R. (2001) *Natural Learning and the Natural Curriculum*. Nottingham: Educational Heretics Press.

Meighan, R. (2004) *Damage Limitation: trying to reduce the harm schools do to children*. Nottingham: Educational Heretics Press.

Pugh, G. and De'Ath, E. (1989) *Working towards Partnership in the Early Years*. London: National Children's Bureau.

Sharp, R. and Green, A. (1973) *Education and Social Control*. London: Routledge and Kegan Paul.

Siraj-Blatchford, I. (1994) 'Some Practical Strategies for Collaboration between Parents and Early Years Educators', *Multicultural Teaching*, **12**, 2, 12–16.

Taylor Committee Report (1977) *A New Partnership for Our Schools*. London: HMSO.

Discussion and Activities

1. Compile a summary of the main points of the chapter and compare with the attempts of others if applicable.
2. Does the analogy of victim contribute to our understanding of a parent's situation in educational contexts?
3. In view of the quotation from Musgrove about the nature of homes that produce academic success, is the price too high?
4. Do projects that centre on mothers carry a hidden curriculum, in that pupils have a model of a female more firmly slotted into the traditional patriarchal system? Is this liberation or confirmation?

5. If the educational standards of parents have increased steadily over the past hundred years, does this mean that the success of the education system will ensure its own redundancy?
6. What should the role of the school be where parents are suspicious of professionals because of their own negative experience of schooling?

Signposts

1. Language development

The role of parents in language development raises a variety of issues. One is social class, for one study concludes that when their parents were encouraged to help, children from less privileged backgrounds were not 'doomed to fail' but did as well as and frequently better than their middle-class peers; see Widlake, P. and Macleod, F. (1984) *Raising Standards*, Coventry: Community Education Development Centre. Another issue is that of the efficacy of the parental activity of story-telling; see Wade, B. (1984) *Story at Home and School*, Birmingham: Educational Review Publications.

Other studies have concluded that parents, irrespective of social class, are usually very skilled at responding to children's interests, expanding their language facilities and feeding in relevant ideas and information, whereas teachers of young children are less skilled because of their anxiety to instruct; see Tizard, B. and Hughes, M. (1984) *Young Children Learning*, London: Fontana.

2. Social class and parents

See Gewirtz, S. (2001) 'Cloning the Blairs: New Labour's programme for the resocialization of working-class parents', *Journal of Education Policy*, **16**, 4. July–August; Solomon, Y., Warin, I and Lewis, C. (2002) 'Helping with homework? Homework as a site of tension for parents and teenagers', *British Educational Research Journal*, **28**, 4. August 2002; and Vincent, C. (2001) 'Social class and parental agency', *Journal of Education Policy*, **16**, 4: July–August.

Carol Vincent's *Including Parents*, Buckingham: Open University Press, 2000, and *Parents and Teachers Power and Participation*, London: Farmer, 1996, both examine the social factors that influence home-school relationships and teachers' perspectives on these.

3. Home-based education

In parts of the USA, 10 per cent of the school-aged population are educated at home rather than school. In the UK the number has grown from a handful in 1977 to about 1 per cent of the school-aged population and continues to increase. There are significant numbers in Canada and Australia. A recent research report is Fortune-Wood, M. (2005) *The Face of Home-based Education: Who, Why and How*, Nottingham: Educational Heretics Press. See www.homeeducationresearch.org and www.home-education.org.uk

5   Mass Media

IRAM SIRAJ-BLATCHFORD

Then it seems that our first business is to supervise the production of stories, and to choose only what we think is suitable, and reject the rest. We shall persuade mothers and nurses to tell our chosen stories to their children, and by means of them to mould their minds and characters which are more important than their bodies. The greater part of the stories current today we shall have to reject.

Plato, *Republic*

INTRODUCTION

The term mass media refers to the massive network of public communication which includes newspapers, television, radio and cinema. Nowadays, educational media would also include the huge growth in communication systems, including the Internet. Each medium has a powerful educating effect on children and adults. In this chapter we focus largely on the educational impact of television, but each aspect of the media has similar power to influence the masses. The mass media has been of interest to sociologists for many years. Educational sociologists look beyond the service and recreational functions of the mass media to examine how these media influence our attitudes and experiences in more hidden ways. The mass media provide much of the knowledge upon which decisions are made and attitudes formed. The most obvious example of this might be in national elections where voting is influenced by the response of the public to current political events and 'news items'. Television commercials and advertisements might have more subtle effects upon our tastes and preferences over a period of time.

All of this has major implications for schooling. We might well ask if the school can afford to ignore the effects of the mass media. Should we adopt more of the techniques of mass media to make schooling more popular? Should schools try to compensate for the negative effects of the mass media? It has been this latter question that has been given foremost attention. The anxiety has been widespread, but does the mass media have negative effects?

THE IMPACT OF TELEVISION

Statistics show that children in Western countries now spend more time watching television than they spend in school. As information technology advances, some form of interactive television may actually come to redefine the nature of school. Yet while the gurus (or anoraks) of information technology dream of a future world in which programmed learning dominates, it may well be that television has already taken the place of schooling as the primary institutional provider of education. Psychologists and sociologists have traditionally been concerned to find proof of the negative influences of the media and some of our discussions so far, on race and gender, may be considered to have uncritically accepted both the power of these effects and the special vulnerability of the young. Perspectives have changed over the years and research that used to be focused on what television does to children is now more commonly focused on what children do with television.

Ninety-two per cent of 10- to 14-year-olds watch some television every day. A study of over 5,000 11- to 15-year-olds in Dundee (Gibson and Francis, 1993) showed that boys spend slightly more time watching television than girls. It seems that the working classes also watch more than those in higher socio-economic groups. The boys watch more sport and the girls are more interested in soaps and light entertainment. The study confirmed previous research which showed that habitual viewers tend to avoid news and public affairs programmes. The findings were also consistent with the popular notion that the high-frequency viewers tend to be relatively more fantasy-oriented than average children. A major comparative study of viewing habits of nine- and ten-year-olds reported by Heal (1995) shows that:

> Cartoons, 'soaps' and series were the most popular programmes in most countries. News programmes were watched more by Italian children than by any others and least by British and Belgian children. More than half of the Portuguese, Spanish, Belgian and Swiss children spent the majority of their viewing time with their families. In contrast two thirds of the British and Italian children spent more than 50% of their time watching alone.
>
> Heal, 1995, p. 2

ADVERTISEMENTS

In Austria, terrestrial television is not permitted to broadcast any form of advertisement aimed at children or using children to convey the message. There are no advertisements at all during children's viewing hours. Yet Cullingford (1994) refers to evidence which suggests that there is little relationship between the presents bought for children and television advertising. While we may be unable to prove a direct correlation between advertisements and purchasing, the question does remain as to whether toy advertisements have an influence upon the types of toy chosen. Clearly children do watch and enjoy adverts. The question Cullingford asks is: do they see through them?

In this interesting survey of 320 seven- to eleven-year-olds we can see some of the difficulties involved in researching the opinions of young children. The children were asked if their favourite advertisements were true or not. Seventy-five per cent of the seven-year-olds said that they were true, yet by age eleven, 90 per cent of the children said that they were not. It seems that at seven the question was interpreted as a question related to the existence of the product: the children were aware that some element of fantasy was involved but were anxious to show that they knew that the product was real – and available in the shops. At eleven, the children's first reaction was to comment upon the fact that advertisements are not designed strictly to convey true information. It would seem that young children are aware that adverts are designed to be persuasive, as Heal (1995) found with the nine- and ten-year-olds:

> Children in four out of five countries (not the US) recognised the role of advertisements in providing information about products and about 'good' behaviour, such as caring for the environment. Children in the US were the only group to recognise that advertising could both persuade one to want something one had not previously wanted and associate a product with a certain image or lifestyle. British children by contrast especially emphasised aspects of presentation and production. There was particular concern in the UK, US and in Belgium that advertising can affect children's behaviour. With the exception of Germany, the children were concerned about advertisements which were misleading in some way – made exaggerated claims, involved deception or told lies.
>
> Heal, 1995, p. 2

It may be that children's responses to advertising change as they become more experienced and grow older. When Cullingford asked children if they were influenced by advertising, up to the age of eight half of them said that they were. Most of their references were to toys and especially those advertised at Christmas. Interestingly, by the age of nine only a third admitted to having been influenced.

TELEVISION VIOLENCE

Violence in research is defined as the threat or use of physical force, directed against the self or others, in which physical harm or death is involved. Extensive surveys have been carried out. Gerbner (1980) has been systematically analysing samples of prime time and weekend television from all the major American networks since 1967. The studies show that children's programmes tend to be the most violent, although killing is less often shown. Cartoons are particularly violent, although they often contain underlying messages regarding justice and retribution.

There is very little evidence to suggest that violence on television causes widespread 'imitative' behaviour. Children, even when they are very young, realize that media violence is not 'real'. Children might play at being Masters of the Universe but their blows don't usually connect and their weapons are 'pretend'. It is clear that we must consider the way in which children respond to television rather than take any simple relationship between their behaviour and the programmes for granted. As Hodge and Tripp (1986) have argued, what is important is not so much the level of violence in a programme but the underlying framework of attitudes and morality within which the violence takes place. This area is particularly relevant to young children's behaviour in school playgrounds. Children will often imitate the actions of people they see in their favourite programmes – even cartoons. For many teachers this creates behaviour management problems, particularly during playtimes and dinner break.

MEDIA BIAS

Very few of us escape the media's effects; they transmit a large volume of information quickly, frequently and to large audiences. We are subjected to a steady but intense bombardment of processed information that supplies the material on which we base our view of the world. Yet the mass media are not owned and operated by the masses, but tend to reflect the attitudes, opinions, tastes and preferences of dominant groups in society.

A central question here is how those with power within the media industry portray or represent those with less power. The representation of children provides a good example. In an influential review article Giroux (1996) argued that the 1990s have seen an 'ominous turn' in the representation and manipulation of youth by adult society. Giroux argued that while the filmmakers use images of youth to entertain their audiences and sell their products, support for young people in poverty and for youth programmes is systematically being cut. Young people are depicted without morals, without hope and without a future, and this gives viewers no reason to expect young people to take on their expected roles as responsible citizens; in fact it helps to justify their abandonment.

Giroux cites films such as *Natural Born Killers, Wayne's World, Boyz N the Hood* and *Kids* in support of his argument. In each case the horrific behaviour of young people is presented in a matter of fact way with no attempt made to show how their economic and social context shaped them. The young people are objectified. This may well be just one example of a wider and more pervasive problem with representations of youth that go back much further (Hatch, 1996) but that does not detract from Giroux's main argument or, for that matter, from the need to consider it further.

COMPUTER GAMES

The increased use of computer games has been a concern of educationalists, researchers and parents, and many consider that there are damaging effects on children. A number of studies have been concerned with the portrayal of violence and many have also observed a gender bias (Jessen and Holm-Sorensen, 1999). Some research does suggest that violent computer games will have effects on aggressive behaviour similar to – and possibly greater than – other media like television and movies (Anderson and Dill, 2000). But there is clearly a need for more research in this area. While most studies show an association between violent game use and aggression and delinquency, the evidence for any causality is weak. There is also evidence to suggest that any effects that may occur are most significant with individuals who are otherwise prone to (and/or victims of) violence (Linderoth *et al.*, 2002).

Akira Sakamoto (2000) has usefully summarized the reasons that many are concerned about the effects of computer games:

1. When engaged in aggressive games the players' own violence is often rewarded with high scores or access to higher levels.
2. While most people who feel anger are inhibited or control their violence because it is socially unacceptable, it may be that computer games teach children that violence is a legitimate option.
3. The virtual reality of video games are often similar to real life. If children learn there may be some advantage in using violence this may be acted out in the context of everyday life.

It may be that some dimensions of reality are lost in the simulations of video games. Sherry Turkle (1995) suggests that there may be two different effects that simulations have on children: the crocodile effect and the Disneyland effect. The crocodile effect is where the virtual drama might become more attractive then real life, while the Disneyland effect is where their real life becomes so artificial that the virtual simulations seem more real.

'EDUCATIONAL' MEDIA

The hidden bias in educational books is discussed in Chapters 6 and 9. Publishers have done a great deal to address the issue of sexist language, but bias is often subtle. A survey of geography texts published in 1991–2 (Connolly, 1993) showed that the illustrations of males were twice as numerous as those of females. Of the 31 authors of these texts, 24 were men and only seven were women. Of course, changes in society may eventually be reflected in our textbooks. In many cases it might, however, be more appropriate for educational media to take an active part in accelerating these changes. In most contexts, educational media continue to make this reflective response, and a major time lag is commonly noticeable.

BLACK PEOPLE AND THE MEDIA

Since the media have the potential to reach millions of people they have an enormous capacity to shape opinion and to change conceptions. As Cashmore and Troyna (1990) point out:

> The media is a hot-house for propagating notions that present black people as a problem or as inferior. This has important implications for the way communities with little black settlement view black people, as the media is their only source of information.

Television news reports have regularly presented groups of black people as a problem, as aggressors or as incompetent and unable to manage their affairs. News reports are frequently shown before 7.30 in the evening and political unrest involving black people is rarely analysed. In fact, it is more often sensationalized and the troubles are linked more closely to racial identity than to the root economic or social causes. The urban disturbances in Britain during the 1980s were often referred to as 'race riots' even when it was perfectly clear that white people were involved in all aspects of the alleged 'rioting'. Very little was made of the reasons why the people were angry. Little mention was made in any report of the unfair treatment of people from particular urban areas, of their poor conditions in housing and employment. The allegations of police brutality and victimization were rarely reported. Most significantly, this response of some inner-city people to economic and social crisis was only presented in terms of what was happening, and not why.

When news coverage includes reports on famine and war, black people are again presented as either mindless aggressors or passive and hopeless victims waiting for the benevolence of Western governments and charities to raise enough money to feed them. Children take particular note of these images because schools often help to raise the money, but the schools tend to fall into the same trap as the media by offering little explanation to children of how these situations arise. In fact, the teachers have often absorbed the media explanations of civil war as the cause for famine themselves. Issues of trade, Third World debt and the reasons for initial poverty and political instability are largely ignored. Documentaries sometimes deal with these issues, but they reach a far smaller audience outside of children's main viewing time.

Television programmes often promote racist views or stereotypes of South Asian and African-Caribbean people and at the same time acknowledge and give credence to the view that this is a 'normal', and therefore acceptable, part of our society. Programmes which try to deal with issues of racism more sympathetically often unintentionally present a caricatured picture of the way black people live and experience life, again tending to perpetuate views of them as passive victims or aggressors: in other words, as a problem, rather than ordinary people, families and community members.

Many old films continue to be televised despite the fact that they portray overt racist images. Old films such as *Tarzan* or *Gone With the Wind* portray black people as savages, slaves or servants who act as inferiors, objects of fun or 'problems' to white people. New movies that are popular with children, such as the Indiana Jones or Short Circuit series, continue the same trend in present-day society. The popular culture of television and the cinema therefore continues to promote racism, and children continue to absorb it. In their interviews with children, Troyna and Hatcher (1992) illustrate very powerfully the effects of television on primary children's perceptions of the Third World and the way that they view black and white people. The following responses from three of the children interviewed are typical. They were asked about their ideas about black people in the Third World:

J: ...the blacks in Africa and they think that white people are so great, they think they're brilliant because they've got all this water and food and these dead good clothes and that.

C: Yes like in *Indiana Jones and the Last Crusade*.

E: I think it was Princess Diana wasn't it sitting in the back once? Yes, that's it and they were all greeting them and everything and they took them to this dead nice...

J: They were just going like that to touch the elephant. They thought the elephant was good as well because of Princess Diana. They think Whites are brilliant but a white princess...

Troyna and Hatcher, 1992, pp. 139–40

In Troyna and Hatcher's book the children reproduced stereotyped images of white superiority and black inferiority, drawing out images of Africa as a primitive continent. When the children were asked how they knew these things, they said that they had seen it on television in Tarzan films and on the news. The authors assert that the powerful images portrayed by television of royal visits, famine relief and white intervention to 'save' black people offers a distorted and limited picture of Third World countries. We have all grown up with this distorted information.

The distortions perpetuated by television are equally present in the press and radio broadcasting. Newspaper reporting has less visual impact than television but sensationalist headlines sell newspapers. The press and radio reach a wide audience and are often equally guilty of focusing on black people only when reporting items of violence, famine, political unrest and sport. Some academics and researchers go further and have argued that issues of 'race' are not only reflected through populist understandings but also change and shape the attitudes and consciousness of the public towards black people. Siraj-Blatchford (1992) argues that people's attitudes towards black communities are negatively reinforced through this process. This has serious implications for white people who live in areas where few black people live, because they rely almost entirely on the media for their information about black communities. If this is largely negative, then it follows that people in white areas will have a misinformed view. This confounds the notion that anti-racist and multicultural education is only relevant in multiracial areas. On the contrary, it suggests that these approaches are even more needed in white areas.

MEDIA AND CULTURAL STUDIES

In recent years, early work on media audiences has been combined with the work on youth culture produced within the cultural studies tradition, to very interesting effect. As Buckingham (1993) argues, the approach that has developed within media and cultural studies appears to have a number of advantages:

> At least in principle, it offers an alternative to the psychological notion of young people as individual 'cognitive processors', while also avoiding the danger of regarding them merely as representatives of given demographic categories. On the contrary, this approach situates media use within the wider context of social relationships and activities, which are by definition diverse and particular. In this respect, 'being an audience' (or a member of an audience) is seen as a social practice, not as a fixed state of existence: it is something you do rather than something you are.
>
> Buckingham, 1993, p. 13

At its best such an approach will accept the possibility of ambiguity and contradiction, and of 'multiple readings' of media texts, while accepting that 'readers' are not free-floating individualists, that their readings will be influenced by established, and socially shared, orientations and expectations. There are dangers, however. In adopting such an approach we must be careful not to allow ourselves to become excessively romantic about childhood or youth culture. In attempting to identify ourselves with children and young people, to see things 'through their eyes', we may fall into the trap of celebrating forms of resistance that are far from progressive:

> In the case of younger children, it is often hard for researchers (and their readers) to avoid a Wordsworthian marvelling at children's innate wisdom and sophistication, or a vicarious identification with their anarchic – but nevertheless terribly cute – rejection of adult norms.
>
> Buckingham, 1993, p. 16

As Buckingham goes on to suggest, the difficulty that many adults have in listening to children without patronizing them is a direct consequence of their own power. In the celebration of childhood and youth culture, there is always the risk of understating the degree to which it is formed by its relationship to the dominant culture and of ignoring the 'hidden injuries' (Sennett and Cobb, 1972) of age, class, race and gender dominance. This is a theme to which we will return in Chapter 23, when we consider the influence of postmodernism on the sociology of schooling.

Activity

1. Summarize the main points from this chapter.
2. Read Paul Willis's *Common Culture*. To what extent do you feel that Buckingham is correct in arguing that Willis goes too far in romantically presenting the actions of young working-class people as entirely creative and worthwhile.

3. Conduct a small-scale study using qualitative methods to investigate the cultural significance of a group of children's reading of a popular television programme or comic.
4. Observe the play, during playtime, of a sample of boys and girls from a local primary school, and discuss it with them to determine where their ideas for play come from.

Discussion

American kids like watching violence on TV and in the movies because violence is being done to them, both at school and at home. It builds up a tremendous amount of anger ... The problem is not violence on TV. That's a symptom ... The real problem is the violence of anti-life, unaffectionate, and punitive homes, and disempowering, deadening compulsory schooling, all presented with an uncomprehending smile.

Jerry Mintz, quoted in Meighan, R. (1994) *The Freethinkers' Guide to the Educational Universe.* Nottingham: Educational Heretics Press

Further Reading

Buckingham, D. (1993) *Reading Audiences: Young People and the Media*. Manchester: Manchester University Press.

Cashmore, E. and Troyna, B. (1990) *Introduction to Race Relations*, 2nd edn. Lewes: Falmer Press.

Connolly, J. (1993) 'Gender Balanced Geography: Have We Got It Right Yet?', *Teaching Geography*, **18**, 2, 61–4.

Cullingford, C. (1994) 'Children's Response to Television Advertising: The Magic Age of 8', *Research in Education*, **51**, May.

Gerbner, G. (1980) 'The ''Mainstreaming'' of America: Violence Profile No. 11', *Journal of Communication*, **30**.

Gibson, H. and Francis, L. (1993) 'The Influence of Age, Sex, Social Class and Religion on Television Viewing Time and Programme Preferences among 11–15 Year Olds', *Journal of Educational Television*, **19**, 1, 25–35.

Giroux, H. (1996) 'Hollywood, Race, and the Demonization of Youth: The ''Kids'' Are not ''Alright''', *Educational Researcher*, **25**, 2, 31–5.

Hatch, T. (1996) 'If the ''Kids'' Are not ''Alright,'' I'm ''Clueless''', *Educational Researcher*, **25**, 7, 40–4.

Heal, C. (1995) 'Children and Television', *OMEP: Current Research in Early Childhood*, **72**, Spring.

Hodge, R. and Tripp, D. (1986) *Children and Television: A Semiotic Approach*. Cambridge: Polity Press.

Linderoth, J. and Lantz-Andersson, A. (2002) 'Electronic Exaggerations and Virtual Worries: Mapping Research of Computer Games Relevant to the Understanding of Children's Game Play', *Contemporary Issues in Early Childhood*, **3**, 2, available online at *http://www.triangle.co.uk/ciec/content/pdfs/3/issue3_2.asp*

Osler, A. (1995) 'Does the National Curriculum Bring Us Any Closer to a Gender Balanced History?', *Teaching History*, **79**, April, 21–4.

Sennett, R. and Cobb, R. (1972) *The Hidden Injuries of Class*. Cambridge: Cambridge University Press.

Siraj-Blatchford, I. (1992) *The Early Years: Laying the Foundations to Racial Equality*. London: Trentham Books.

Troyna, B. and Hatcher, R. (1992) *Racism in Children's Lives*. London: Routledge and National Children's Bureau.

Turkle, S. (1995) *Life on the Screen: Identity in the Age of the Internet*. New York: Simon and Schuster.

Signpost

1. The Internet

I wish to argue that where once we saw it our duty to impart as much knowledge as possible to our pupils and students, it is now our duty to impart as little knowledge as possible . . . The influence of the internet is mostly felt by the regime of explicit knowledge, the know-what. The internet, still in its infancy, is the wonder-child of education. It knows everything that is to be known. It forgets nothing. It is the intellectual equivalent of Aladdin's lamp. It will do anything within reason that you ask it to do and without question. It therefore absolves human beings from spending their lives accumulating knowledge as information. It therefore denies the hitherto accepted purpose of education.

Graham Hill, former Vice-Chancellor of the University of Strathcyde,
quoted in the *Independent*, 19 April 2005

Signpost

Part Two
THE HIDDEN CURRICULUM

This part attempts to show the range of the concept of hidden curriculum. The chapters that follow contain analyses that derive from the observation and interpretation of everyday events in classrooms, as well as propositions about the functions of the education system for a society and its economy. Therefore, the material ranges from the micro-sociological to the macro-sociological: the former shows how the participants create patterns in their social behaviour and achieve outcomes in their day-to-day activities, while the latter stresses the patterns of the social structure, the economy and other institutions, and shows how this framework has a powerful influence on the processes of educating.

6 The Hidden Curriculum: An Overview

Education is what remains when we have forgotten all that we have been taught.

George Halifax

INTRODUCTION

The notion of hidden curriculum was probably first identified by John Dewey, who referred to *the collateral learning of attitudes by children*. As a working definition, the hidden curriculum can be defined as all the things that are learnt during schooling in addition to the official curriculum. Both limitations and advantages of this broad definition should emerge during the discussion in this and subsequent chapters. As Reid (1986) puts it:

> Curriculum refers to *all* of the things that are learnt in school. In addition to the 'official curriculum' this includes the 'hidden curriculum', a concept that refers to all of those socialising practices that are not included in the official curriculum but that contribute towards the reproduction of our culture (e.g. boys being sent to do some photocopying, girls to wash the cups)

The hidden curriculum of most of our schools is such that students may also learn that:

- Passive acceptance is a more desirable response to ideas than active criticism.
- Knowledge creation is beyond the power of students and is, in any case, none of their business.
- Recall is the highest form of intellectual achievement, and the collection of unrelated 'facts' is the goal of education.
- The voice of authority is to be trusted and valued more than independent judgement.
- One's own ideas and those of one's classmates are inconsequential.
- Feelings are irrelevant in education.
- There is always a single, unambiguous Right Answer to a question.
- English is not mathematics and mathematics is not science and science is not art and art is not music. And art and music are minor subjects and English, history and science

major subjects. And a subject is something you take and, when you have taken it, you have 'had' it, and if you have 'had' it, you are immune and need not take it again (adapted from Postman and Weingartner, 1971).

One could add other possible 'learnings', including:

- Competition is more important than cooperation.
- Helping others is less important than getting on oneself.
- Reading, writing and arithmetic are more important than talking, thinking and creating.
- Adults are more important than children.
- Men are more important than women.
- White people are more important than Black people.
- The Western world is more 'advanced' and is superior to the rest of the world.

John Portelli (1993, p. 345), reviewing the literature on the subject of the hidden curriculum, refers to four 'major meanings of the hidden curriculum in curriculum discourse';

1. The curriculum as the unofficial expectations of implicit but expected messages.
2. The curriculum as unintended learning outcomes of messages.
3. The hidden curriculum as implicit messages arising from the structure of schooling.
4. The curriculum as created by the students.

AMBIGUOUS IDEAS AND THEIR VALUE

The notion of a hidden curriculum is highly ambiguous. Some of the competing meanings will be discussed in the following pages, but it is perhaps useful to outline the problems and possibilities of ambiguous ideas. de Bono (1972) categorizes such ideas as 'porridge words', which can be stirred around to stimulate further ideas and further connections because of the lack of precision. Precise words exclude a great deal more than porridge words. Since one aspect of sociology mentioned in Chapter 1 was the capacity to make connections between phenomena and events which people commonly regard as unconnected, these words are of particular use to sociologists. One danger lies in slipping and sliding the meaning without warning, so that attempted analysis is replaced by spurious association. An example was given earlier, in the assertion that sociology is the study of people who do not need studying by those who do. The ambiguous word here is people, because it can mean individuals or groups. Psychologists tend to study individual behaviour, whereas sociologists tend to study group behaviours, and this is why the writer got the joke wrong: it is more accurately a joke about psychologists.

DEFINITIONS OF CURRICULUM

The ambiguities spring from both words, 'curriculum' and 'hidden'. Many definitions of curriculum have been applied over the years, including:

> an ideological construction that is applied in the interests of reproducing culture, but is often resisted.
>
> M. Apple

> a rough and ready bargain between what some people are prepared to teach and others are prepared to learn.
>
> D. Riesman

> a mechanism for separating children into good learners and poor ones.
>
> J. Henry

> A social construction in which the selection and organisation of knowledge into the time-table of the school is the result of a choice from a number of possible alternatives.
>
> M. MacDonald

> The curriculum is all of the planned experiences provided by the school to assist the pupils in attaining the designated learning outcomes to the best of their abilities.
>
> Nagley and Evans

> A course of study.
>
> *Oxford English Dictionary*

These attempted definitions stress various features. Some stress the planned aspect, some hint at the possibility of spontaneity. Others stress the short-term immediacy of 'filling time', others still the long-term features of a course of study. One singles out the imposed nature of a curriculum, another the negotiation and bargaining aspects. One feature that the definitions appear to have in common is the idea of a sequence of events and experiences and the accumulation of ideas and information.

A number of academic approaches to curriculum studies have been taken over the years. These can be broadly divided into conceptual, cultural and critical approaches.

- *The conceptual approach.* Here curriculum has been seen simply as an interrelated set of plans and experiences (Marsh and Stafford, 1984). The conceptual approach includes the 'objectives model' of Hirst and Peters (1970, p. 110), where any 'social' influences were to be 'regretted' rather than acknowledged. These approaches to curriculum study have been widely criticized as technicist and ahistorical (e.g. by Giroux).
- *The cultural approach.* In these studies the curriculum is considered to be always culturally and temporally specific. The curriculum may also be seen as developmental; as a 'hypothesis testable in practice' (e.g. Stenhouse, 1976). For Stenhouse, curriculum development represented the 'applied branch' of curriculum study.

- *The critical approach.* Here the central concern has been with ideology, cultural reproduction and resistance.

The critical approaches included in Young's (1971) *Knowledge and Control*, a text widely considered to have launched the 'new sociology of education', included both *phenomenological* (Young/Keddy) and *structuralist* (Bernstein/Bourdieu) accounts. The critical approach has also included the neo-Marxist work of Sharp and Green (1975), and in recent years it has developed to focus more upon resistance and mediation studies focused on class, 'race' and gender. Work by Henry Giroux, Philip Wexler and Michael Apple has been particularly influential.

It is therefore possible to distinguish other definitions of curriculum.

- Ones which stress the official subject timetable: where the curriculum is seen as the planned instructional activities of the school.
- Others that stress intentions: the curriculum is everything organized by teachers, including lessons, clubs and out-of-school activities.
- Others which stress anything connected with school that results in learning, whether intended or not.

The notion of a hidden curriculum is given most scope in the last case, but there are also hidden curriculum aspects of the first two. The hidden aspects of the official curriculum are rather overlooked in the working definition given earlier, and this is also a limitation of some of the existing studies of the hidden curriculum. Since the advent of the National Curriculum in the UK the curriculum has increasingly been seen as the National Curriculum subjects alone, yet the National Curriculum Council's (NCC, 1990) guidance clearly emphasized the part to be played by a number of other essential cross-curriculum themes, skills and dimensions (see Chapter 13).

Quite a number of studies in recent years have referred to the hidden effects of 'institutional racism' and sexism. Hence German (1983), in defining the position of the Commission for Racial Equality in terms of the 1976 Race Relations Act, suggests that:

> The Act defines direct and indirect discrimination and, while the former is generally capable of recognition by reasonable people, the latter concerns a web of customary procedures and practices which militate against the interests of ethnic minority groups in particular, and about which there is generally little awareness of their ill effects . . . The latter has also been termed unwitting, unintentional or institutional discrimination.

THE NOTION OF 'HIDDEN'

The ambiguities in the idea of 'hidden' are considerable. The reason for a learning to be hidden presents one problem. Is it hidden intentionally to manipulate and persuade? Is it hidden because no one notices or recognizes it? Is it hidden because it has been forgotten or neglected? Is it hidden because the originator has left?

The outcomes of 'hidden' may be more significant than the reasons, and the analysis to follow will dwell on consequences. However, it is useful to bear in mind the variety of reasons lest the idea of a deliberate plot be assumed when none exists. The irony of human action was discussed in Chapter 1: the outcomes of ideas may turn out to be rather different from those originally intended. The case of play in the early years might be cited here. The schools that most of today's parents attended emphasized the need for pupils to work while they were in school – play was something to be restricted strictly for the playground. Most infant and pre-school educators believe that the child's play is highly educative. Yet attempts to introduce a play curriculum have often been opposed by parents who expect the teacher to provide their children with proper 'work' and to discourage play in school. An even more fundamental example relates to the fact that mass schooling was developed in an information impoverished society. Such arrangements may now be questionable given the informationally enriched circumstances that we now find ourselves in (Meighan, 1997).

A CLASSIC STUDY ILLUSTRATING THE HIDDEN CURRICULUM

A well known study in group behaviour is that of Lippitt and White (1958) on authoritarian and democratic regimes. Four small groups of ten-year-old boys were observed closely as they experienced three different regimes for craft-making activities such as mask-making. In the regime described as authoritarian, the adult leader determined all policies, techniques, activities and working companions, while using personal criticism of task performance and remaining aloof from the group. In the regime described as democratic, the adult leader encouraged discussion and used consultation about decisions while allowing a choice of both tasks and companions. (The use of the word 'democratic' to describe this kind of regime is perhaps misleading, and 'parental' or 'consultative' might have described more accurately what was an alternative kind of authoritarianism. This point is argued in Chapter 16.) In the third regime, *laissez-faire*, the boys were left more or less to their own devices, and this was effectively a non-leadership situation.

The same boys behaved quite differently under these different regimes, even though the task of craft work remained constant. For example, they were aggressive or passive in the authoritarian situation and friendly and cooperative in the democratic situation. Some of the contrasts in regime and consequential behaviour are given in Table 6.1.

The central ideas of a hidden curriculum are well illustrated in Lippitt and White's study. The official 'curriculum' consisted of the tasks of craft work. All the other learnings are unintended, incidental or otherwise 'hidden' in some sense or other. Yet these learnings are considerable in range and significance, and the list given above does not exhaust the features observed in this experiment.

Table 6.1 Lippit and White experiment on group regimes

	Authoritarian	Democratic
Policy	Leader determined	Group consultations
Task method	Leader decisions	Choice from alternatives
Companions	Leader chosen	Chosen by members
Leader	Aloof and withdrawn	Involved and approachable
Structure of groups	Atomized	Sub-grouped
	Resultant behaviour	
Attitudes to work	Agression or apathy	Interested
Attitudes to members	Competitive/scapegoating	Cooperative/friendly
Attitudes to leader	Submissive	Friendly
Leader leaves room	Work ceases	Work continues
Group morale	Unity low; tense	Unity high; relaxed
Task standards	High	Moderate
Response to problems	Disintegration into blame	Organized attack on problems

THE HIDDEN CURRICULUM OR 'HARDENED HISTORY' OF SCHOOLS

Each of the artefacts and environments that we encounter in our lives today were produced as an expression of the values of their creator/designers. In the sociology of technology this is referred to as hardened history. Many teachers have been heard to comment that when the classroom door closes, what happens next is within their control and direction: they claim complete autonomy. In considering this claim the notion of the classroom itself representating 'hardened history' has its uses.

Thus, Berliner (2001) quotes research that suggests that 46,000 secondary pupils are being bullied for their sexual orientation and that over half of young gay men and lesbian women have considered suicide because of homophobic bullying, while 40 per cent have actually attempted suicide more than once. In a survey of 1,177 sixth-formers, the overwhelming majority of whom were heterosexual, 43 per cent said their school was either not a safe place for gay pupils or only sometimes safe. Parallel interviews with 15 gay young people suggested that teachers were reluctant to deal with homophobia, with some teachers afraid of being called gay by pupils if they confronted the bullies. In America, New York City is set to open its first state school for gay, lesbian and bisexual students because of a severe rise in cases of harassment and assault.

Ghosts of the Architects

The classroom may be said to be haunted by the architects who designed it and their advisers. Attempts to reshape the classroom have to fight the ideas of the originators. The result is often a confusion of ideas rather than a reversal of the ideas embedded in the walls and fabric of the building.

Ghosts of the Book Writers

The classroom may also be said to be haunted by the book writers, resource designers and materials producers. Their inaccuracies, distortions and biases are embedded in their writing and designing, and may pass unrecognized and unchallenged. *They* become absorbed along with the accurate material present. Reading schemes for primary schools provide an interesting example. Here, analyses have shown that, along with the carefully graded reading books designed to build up learner reading skills gradually, there are often messages of nationalism, racism, sexism and social class bias. As early as 1975, a study by Lobban showed that the world portrayed in reading schemes was more sex biased than the real world. The world depicted was that of males who were active, dominant and involved in work and careers, whereas females were shown almost entirely in domestic roles. Since, even at that time, many children had working mothers, this was a distortion of the world as it was, let alone a limited vision of what the world could be, and, in the view of those seeking equal life chances for women, should be.

A second example may be taken from sex education books for secondary schools, which were surveyed by Hoffman in 1975. She concluded that most of these books passed on the prejudices of the writers, often based on erroneous information, rather than informing pupils dispassionately about sexual behaviour. One error concerned the notion of the low female sex drive:

> The message is clear: male sexuality is genital, easily stimulated and urgent; female sexuality, where present, is diffuse, easily sublimated and will probably go away of its own accord.

While many school texts have undoubtably improved greatly over the years, our critical analysis will have (inevitably) also changed. Many writers (for example, Epstein, 1995) now argue that anti-sexist education must, to be effective, also be anti-heterosexist. Even many of the most progressive sex education materials will undoubtably be found wanting from this perspective.

Ghosts of Our Ancestors' Language and Thinking

Other ghosts inevitably haunting the classroom are the ancestors who developed our language. Since language is a major, if not the major, means of communication employed by teachers and pupils, any unrecognized limitations, distortions and biases will be absorbed. Some of the constructions were established by groups long since dead and, as was suggested in Chapter 1, the fallacious thinking of our ancestors is often more difficult to get rid of than contemporary errors. Language is the subject of a later chapter, so one or two examples will suffice here. The English language has a marked tendency to use dichotomies, e.g. black/white, good/bad, strong/weak, and a consequence is the frequent oversimplification of complex phenomena (see de Bono, 1971). This limitation extends into sociology, and teaching is commonly analysed as if there were only two opposed types, e.g. open/closed, tradition/progressive, authoritarian/democratic. In the later section on ideologies it will be argued that there is a multiplicity of types of teaching.

Other commentators have noted the prevalence of rural imagery in an industrial society and, to a lesser extent, military imagery (Seabrook, 1971). John Holt wrote: 'School is the army for kids. Adults make them go there, and when they get there, adults tell them what to do, bribe and threaten them into doing it, and punish them when they don't.' Schooling here is compared to the military in terms of the element of compulsion and regimented authoritarianism. In many countries he could have added the existence of a standard school uniform. An article on school uniforms in the UK (*Times Educational Supplement*, 3 October 2003) quoted Halla Beloff, a social scientist at Edinburgh University as arguing that,

> We all know deep in our hearts that wearing uniform is a method of control. One of the aims of school is to get you used to the idea of obeying orders and to make you biddable. Sitting in rows, getting there on time, changing activity every 40 minutes, were useful if you were going to be cannon fodder or factory fodder or office fodder. But it isn't so useful these days, when there is more call for creativity.

Often these uniforms come with insignia of rank such as prefect, monitor or house captain, as well as regulated appearance such as length of hair. The requirements can change dramatically. In the UK, girls were, for many years, forbidden to wear trousers because the required school uniform was skirts. But a headline in the *Guardian* newspaper (22 June 2005) proclaims, 'School bans girls wearing skirts'. Furthermore, describing a conflict at the outset as a battle or a fight, rather than as a problem to be solved or a conflict of interests needing to be negotiated, may have consequences for the subsequent sequence of events. In the 1960s and 1970s, one of the comments often made by visitors from countries where industrial relations were rather less fraught than those in Britain was that if at the outset you define the situation as a battle it will always be seen by those concerned as a battle.

The analogy of ghosts could be pursued further or replaced by one from electronics, the idea of invisible force fields operating and invisible transmission through radio waves. Despite its disadvantages, one strength of this kind of analogy is that it helps to locate causes more accurately. Rather than assuming the malevolence or sinister nature of educators, these analogies suggest the possibilities of unwitting and unintended actions of those concerned and suggest a theory of a complex of causes. They are also optimistic analogies: ghosts can be laid, and force fields can be neutralized.

ATTEMPTS TO ANALYSE THE HIDDEN CURRICULUM

Jackson (1968) first used the term 'the hidden curriculum' to describe the unofficial three Rs of rules, routines and regulations that must be learnt by pupils in order to survive comfortably in most classrooms. Pupils must also learn to cope with the delay, denial and interruptions that accompany learning experiences in schools.

Delay occurs when pupils wait in assembly, wait in corridors, wait for their turn on the apparatus, wait for the lesson to start, wait for the teacher to become available or wait to be invited to answer a question. It is quite startling to add up this delay: some children spend the majority of their time coping with delay, and most spend almost half their time in this way.

Denial occurs when pupils are forbidden to talk among themselves, cannot ask questions, cannot pursue a chosen activity or cannot have a turn on apparatus because time has run out.

Interruption occurs when the bell rings in the middle of an activity, the equipment is needed elsewhere or the teacher is called away during a discussion. As Jackson (1971) concluded, 'for most students some of the time, and for some of the students most of the time, the classroom comes close to resembling a cage from which there is no escape.'

Faced with rules, routines and regulations and the consequent delay, denial and interruption, pupils have to devise strategies for survival. Some of these strategies, Jackson argues, avoid or reduce confrontation with teachers, but a price is paid, in that effective learning of the official curriculum is reduced. These strategies include 'resignation' or ceasing to hope that school makes sense, and 'masquerade' or faking involvement. A more positive strategy is 'patience', and some children are already well trained in this before they come to school, whereas others start handicapped in this respect.

Holt (1969) described another set of strategies children devise to reduce the fear and anxiety of classroom life: 'right answerism'. For Snyder (1971), the hidden curriculum was seen as associated most closely with the assessment system, and we will discuss this further in Chapter 13; for the time being 'right answerism' may be considered a collection of strategies to obtain the right answer or an approved response. These strategies have short-term survival value but, in replacing the activity of thinking out answers, in the long term reduce learning. The strategies include reading teachers' facial clues, noting the regularity of answer patterns and the prevalence of 'yes' answers, noting that freak questions are signalled by a change of voice, giving faint and mumbled answers that maximize chances of misinterpretation for the right answer and raising hands when many others are raised in the knowledge that the chances of being called on are small, and that this eventuality can be covered by a confused 'Oh, I forget'.

Holly (1973) developed an analysis of the curriculum of British schools as alienated and alienating for those subjected to it. He analyses four aspects of schooling: matters of organization, the content of learning, teaching methodology and general values which are promoted. Using these headings, a useful analysis of the hidden curriculum is developed, although the term itself is absent. He concludes that the curriculum is defined as a course to be run, an activity to be completed as smoothly and efficiently as possible without reference to what the race means:

> it is the finishing tape that matters, the mark, the examination pass, the entry to a career or further education. This is essentially instrumental thinking. It is also essentially alienated, separating the meaning of the activity from the activity itself.

As Connell and others have argued, the dominant liberal ideology of schooling in Britain has been significantly established upon 'meritocratic' assumptions regarding social mobility, where an individual's position in the class structure is assumed to be, at least in part, a result of his or her own qualities and endeavours (or the lack of them). While this notion has been widely contested by groups and individuals, and in particular by those involved in the various civil rights and women's movements, it remains a powerful assumption lying behind much of the popular discourse. In education, many early radical theorists argued that there was a direct relationship between labour and schooling. They identified the role of schools in the reproduction of capitalist economic relations. Bowles and Gintis (1976) thus developed a correspondence theory of the hidden curriculum. The proposition was that the attitudes engendered by most schools corresponded directly to those of the social relations of work in a capitalist economy and therefore constituted an attitudinal preparation for life in a class-divided society.

As McCarthy and Apple (1988, p. 18) have argued, 'racial' and gender divisions were also seen as the effects of economic divisions in society and as a by-product of more fundamental conflicts between the working class and their capitalist employers, who adopted 'divide and rule' policies to disorganize the working class. A major critique of this approach emphasized that it neglected and tended to characterize negatively the autonomous workings of racial and patriarchal structures of domination. The contribution made by earlier liberal researchers and 'policy intellectuals' to our understanding of school culture and politics were also ignored (McCarthy and Apple 1988). In more recent years, cultural reproduction theorists such as Apple (1982) and Giroux (1983) drew upon perspectives informed by the sociology of knowledge. Writing by Bourdieu and Passeron (1977), Bernstein (1977) and Wexler (1976) contributed to what increasingly became known as 'the new sociology of education'. Theories that emphasized the relative autonomy of schools to the social structure focused attention on 'hidden curriculum' and 'invisible pedagogies' which operated to the advantage of middle-class, male and ethnic majority pupils. A growing concern with the triad of knowledge, ideology and power offered a more hopeful way forward for 'race' and gender analysis, without at the same time ignoring the effects of economic and social class dynamics.

A useful framework for understanding schools as systems of control that help to maintain existing power relationships was provided by Michel Foucault (1977). Foucault questioned whether historical development was taking a linear path towards rationality, enlightenment and progress. He believed that, on the contrary, modern society had developed into a more limiting and inherently 'violent' form of rationality. He argued that the regulatory practices of contemporary institutions – including schools – are even more oppressive because they are more subtle and hidden. Schools, as other forms of modern institution, control through their bureaucratic, routinized authoritarianism – constantly measuring, categorizing, ordering and regulating so that control becomes accepted by the majority as normal and natural. The desired result is increased docility and obedience.

Feminist theorists such as Spender (1982) and Mahony (1985) have argued that schools reflect and reproduce patriarchal relations. While Barrett's (1984) analysis may be considered unduly deterministic and limited, her consideration of the four levels at which gender relations are reproduced in schooling is valuable. She argues that at the ideological level boys and girls are socialized into appropriate [sic] feminine and masculine behaviour. At the structural and organizational levels the gendered occupational structure of the school acts as part of the hidden curriculum. Mechanisms operate to channel pupils into gendered subjects reflecting gendered occupational structures outside of the school, and androcentric definitions of legitimate knowledge are taught as objective and neutral. School subjects are, in fact, themselves defined in these terms.

In the same way, ideologies of 'race' and ethnicism act to socialize Black and White pupils for their future roles. Research concerned with these ideological issues has tended to focus upon the alleged poor 'self-esteem' of Black pupils. Black teachers and assistants occupy inferior positions within the structure and organization of the school (Commission for Racial Equality (CRE), 1988), and researchers have been particularly concerned about the lack of positive role models. Black and White pupils are also channelled into subjects reflecting a racialized division of labour in society. Ethnocentric knowledge is equally legitimated and presented as objective and neutral.

Educational feminists have also drawn attention to the ways in which men and boys oppress and victimize women, and a number of studies have provided evidence of this in schools (Spender, 1982; Kelly, 1985; Mahony, 1985; Whyte, 1986). This process of oppression can be seen as completely overwhelming, as Thomas (1990) has put it:

> Many radical feminists see little point in attempting to change the education system because women are trapped in a vicious circle in which men keep changing the rules if women show any sign of becoming as successful as them. For feminists such as Spender, the only solution is a separatist one; for women to make their own education, their own rules.

Marxist feminists (Barrett, 1984; Wolpe, 1978) have argued that while women's oppression can be seen to be almost universal it has taken different forms at different times in different societies. Again, as Thomas (1990) effectively puts it:

> Thus under capitalism, women's oppression is not simply a question of individual men oppressing individual women nor of men in general oppressing women in general; it takes the form of exploitation in the labour market, which has become essential to maintaining capitalism – low wages, harsh working conditions, little job security – as well as exploitation in the home and family.

During the 1980s a growing interest in post-structuralism and postmodernism drew renewed attention to the essentialism of class analysis and led many women, Black and ethnic minority, homosexual and other marginalized groups to seek alternative theoretical models from a range of disciplines, including psychoanalytic theory, literary criticism and linguistics (Irigaray, 1982; Said, 1983). This has in turn given voice and legitimacy to the exploration and analysis of social phenomenon at the level of agency and experience as well as of structure. In education, 'critical educational theory' has been advanced by Wexler (1982), Apple and Weis (1983) and Giroux (1992) to look beyond class to analyse the inter-relationship and dynamics of 'race', gender and sexuality.

Siraj-Blatchford (1995) has argued that in research perspectives, as in school practices, 'multicultural' and 'equal opportunity' approaches have tended to focus upon the negative effects that education has had upon the educational performance of black and ethnic minority pupils in general and on girls in some subject areas. By contrast, anti-racist and anti-sexist approaches have more often emphasized the role that education has had in reproducing structural inequality through its preferential treatment of boys and ethnic majority pupils. While some anti-racist/anti-sexist writers have drawn attention to the importance of influencing the socialization of future adult males and ethnic majorities as potential discriminators, others have adopted more traditional structuralist approaches and emphasized the role of the state and of policy.

CONCLUSION

This chapter has attempted to show the range of the notion of a hidden curriculum. The various analyses outlined range from the observation and interpretation of everyday common-place events in classrooms to the function of the education system for society and its economy. In other words, some of the analyses have been micro-sociological, stressing how the participants create patterns and consequences in their day-to-day constructions and reconstructions within schools, and others have been macro-sociological, stressing the patterns of society and its economy that form a framework for educational activity and powerfully influence the system of schooling.

Others have adopted an interactionist perspective, looking for a network of influences and allowing for contradictions within the network. Interactionist approaches are summed up in the following passage:

In this perspective human action is not seen as fully determined by social, cultural, or psychological forces, and these forces are seen to be mediated in their impact by processes of social interaction. The outcome of any interpretive or interactional process is never entirely predictable, as it emerges from and is conditional upon the interplay of interpretations and actions.

Woods, 1977a

Most of the writings about the curriculum miss out the notion of a hidden curriculum and concentrate on the official curriculum. Many students find such writings alienating and unconvincing because they tend to represent an incomplete analysis as complete, and separate the activity of the curriculum from the pattern of schooling as a whole. The problems of definition remain. The hidden curriculum is probably best seen as a generalized concept or theme of hiddeness which turns out to be a linking feature in other concepts. Several limitations of the definition given at the outset may now be seen, in particular that defining the hidden curriculum as the form or framework of schooling as against the content of the official curriculum is too limiting, in that it obscures the hidden aspects of the official curriculum and ignores self-defeating processes, such as an assessment system encouraging selective neglect of parts of the official curriculum in the trading for grades.

Reactions to the idea of the hidden curriculum are worth noting. As noted above, many curriculum theorists ignore it or do not recognize it. Another reaction is to dismiss schooling and argue for a deschooled society.

An alternative reaction is pessimism and fatalism. Macro-sociological perspectives may contribute to this by stressing the enduring and powerful forces of a whole society socializing its members into compliance. Another reaction is management and administration. It is felt that, by careful administration, some of the most negative aspects of the hidden curriculum can be managed with less conflict.

A further response is reschooling. The view here is that different organizational patterns can be found in order to eliminate the hidden curriculum of contemporary mass schooling.

This differential response illustrates one of the points made in the opening chapter. The findings of sociological analysis may often lend themselves to widely differing, if not contradictory, policies. The good spy reports what is there. Others use the reports.

The remaining chapters of Part Two contain analyses of the hidden curriculum of selected aspects of schooling.

Summary

1. The hidden curriculum is an ambiguous idea, but one capable of making connections between phenomena and events which often go unrecognized.
2. The definition of 'curriculum' in use is often the broadest possible – anything that results in learning. However, the narrowest definition – planned instructional activities such as those defined by the National Curriculum – still yields a hidden curriculum.

3. The definition of 'hidden' often implies motives. These can range from deliberate manipulation, to non-recognition, to persistence beyond the original needs, to the irony of unintended consequences and institutional practices.
4. The Lippitt and White experiment illustrates the wide range of learnings beyond the instructional task of the official curriculum.
5. Teachers who claim that they control what happens when the classroom door closes may not have recognized the 'hardened history' or 'ghosts' of the architects' design, the influence of the book writers and the legacy of our ancestors' thinking enshrined in language.
6. The rules, routines and regulations of schooling, leading to various pupil responses and strategies like 'resignation' and 'masquerade', are one aspect of the hidden curriculum analysed by Jackson.
7. The strategy of 'right answerism' employed by pupils is described by Holt.
8. The assessment system has its own hidden messages and 'trading for grades as more significant than learning to think' is one of these.
9. One consequence of the hidden curriculum can be alienation and resistance.
10. The social control aspects of the hidden curriculum have been analysed in terms of 'correspondence theory', where the attitudes inculcated by school are seen as corresponding to those required to maintain a capitalist economy and a class-divided society. An important ingredient is seen as the learning of boredom and its toleration.
11. Reactions to the idea of a hidden curriculum can range from dismissal, to pessimism, to fatalism, to reschooling, to deschooling.

Further Reading

German, G. (1983) 'Some Thoughts on Institutional Racism', *Educational Journal*, November.

Giroux, H.A. (1981) *Ideology, Culture and the Process of Schooling*. Lewes: Falmer Press.

Harber, C. (2004) *Schooling as Violence*, London: Routledge Falmer.

Head. D. (ed.) (1974) *Free Way to Learning*. Harmondsworth: Penguin. The first chapter of this book has a clearly written account of the hidden curriculum.

Jackson. P. (1971) 'The Student's World', in M. Silberman (ed.), *The Experience of Schooling*. Eastbourne: Holt, Rinehart and Winston. One of the micro aspects of the hidden curriculum is the subject of Jackson's exposition of rules, routines and regulations and their consequences.

Meighan, R. (2004) *Damage Limitation: trying to reduce the harm schools do to children*, Nottingham: Educational Heretics Press.

Whyld, J. (ed.) (1983) *Sexism in the Secondary School*. London: Harper and Row. Explores the hidden curriculum in respect of sexist messages (see also Chapter 25).

Discussion and Activities

1. Is a hidden curriculum an inevitable part of any arrangement for educating?
2. The definition of hidden curriculum given at the start of the chapter was said to be faulty. Attempt a revised definition.
3. Try to distinguish between the hidden curricula of classroom practices, of schools and of education systems, giving suitable examples.
4. Are there 'ghosts' that haunt classrooms apart from the three mentioned? (Later chapters may contain ideas.)
5. What use can be made of the 'hidden curriculum' concept with a view to changing schools? The 'confidence-building curriculum' notion of Hemming (1980) is one starting point.

Signposts

1. Criticism of the 'hidden curriculum' concept
The concept of hidden curriculum has been the subject of critical comment. Two articles that attack the whole idea are Cornbleth, C. (1984) 'Beyond Hidden Curriculum?', *Journal of Curriculum Studies*, **16**, 1, 29–36; and Dreeben, R. (1976) 'The Unwritten Curriculum and Its Relation to Values', *Journal of Curriculum Studies*, **8**, 2, 111–24.

2. A hidden curriculum in further education
The hidden curriculum of further education has been a focus in the UK because of the establishment of youth training schemes as a substitute for employment and as a response to youth unemployment. Starting points: Gleeson, D. (ed.) (1983) *Youth Training and the Search for Work*, London: Routledge and Kegan Paul; Fiddy, R. (ed.) (1983) *In Place of Work: Policy and Provision for the Young Unemployed*, Lewes: Falmer Press; Barton, L. and Walker, S. (eds) (1986) *Youth Unemployment and Schooling*, Milton Keynes: Open University Press.

3. School as violence
There are three ways of looking at the relationship between formal education, individuals and society:
1. that education improves society;
2. that education reproduces society as it is;
3. that education makes society worse and harms individuals.
Clive Harber, in *Schooling as Violence*, argues that while school *can* play a positive role, violence towards children originating in the school system is common, systematic and widespread internationally, and that schools play a significant role in encouraging violence in wider society. Topics covered include physical punishment, learning to hate others, sexual abuse, stress and anxiety and the militarization of school.

4. The null curriculum
Those ideas and subjects that are excluded from the curriculum can be said to be a null curriculum. People from other cultures who settle in the UK can report the experience that their culture is overlooked altogether. Humanists with their philosophy of 'morals without religion' can feel the same. Logic and philosophy appear in the curriculum of other countries but usually not the UK. Vegetarianism, alternative health therapies and

medicine, green sustainability economics, the cooperative movement, contentment instead of competition as a life stance, Esperanto, are other ideas usually avoided (see *The School I'd Like* by Burke, C., and Grosvenor, I., London: Routledge Falmer, 2003, Chap. 4.)

Space Talks: The Hidden Curriculum of Educational Buildings

7

The thing which in the subway is called congestion is highly esteemed in the night spots as intimacy.

Simeon Strunsky

A safe haven, not a prison . . .
  Student reported in *The School I'd Like*, by Catherine Burke and Ian Grosvenor

INTRODUCTION: MESSAGES FROM SPACE?

Since many of the analyses used in sociology are derived from the theatre, it is perhaps surprising how little attention is given to analysing the setting in which the dramas of education take place. If we turn to those who do give attention to physical space (i.e. planners, architects, industrial designers), we find that their work is guided largely by tradition and accumulated experience: by common-sense recipes rather than systematic, reflective studies. A few educational writers have given attention to the spaces provided for schooling, and the ideas of one teacher trying to achieve changes in his classroom make a useful starting point:

> The placement of objects in space is not arbitrary and rooms represent in physical form the spirit and souls of places and institutions. A teacher's room tells us something about who he is and a great deal about what he is doing.

Kohl, 1970

In attempting to work out an alternative to the 'closed' teaching he saw around him, where classrooms were based on compulsion rather than participation, and imposing decisions rather than enabling choice making, Kohl found himself questioning the spatial arrangements provided for him:

> Why does a classroom have to have a front, a back and two sides? The notion that there is a 'front of the class' and the authoritarian mode of delivering knowledge received from above, to students who are below – both go together.
>
> Kohl, 1970

As we shall see, in recent years, such questions are increasingly coming to dominate the discussions of what constitutes good practice in British primary schools.

A RESEARCH ACTIVITY: THE SCHOOL BUILDING IN GENERAL

In the opening chapter, reference was made to the idea of layers of meaning and the view that an individual may sample only a few of these in the routines of everyday life. The school building provides an interesting example of layers of meaning.

The school building presents a different experience to each group of people involved. To an educational administrator it is a building of a certain size, for a defined set of pupils and having a detailed schedule of furnishings. To a pupil it is a place where a large part of one's life is spent, other children are encountered and teachers experienced. To teachers the school building is primarily a selection of rooms, perhaps inadequately equipped and serviced. To parents it may be predominantly the assembly hall where their child is performing or singing on a platform along with other children. To caretakers and cleaners it is often a place of problems in how to keep things clean, of pipes that burst, of floors to polish, windows to repair and fittings to maintain.

The research activity that follows will concentrate on the teachers' layer of meaning.

Background Propositions

The buildings available for schooling are of interest in at least three ways:

1. They suggest possibilities and opportunities for schooling.
2. They place constraints on what can be done.
3. They imply psychological, philosophical, sociological and pedagogical ideas about schooling that are often taken for granted, but are open to question.

Aim

The aim of this exercise is to analyse the various features of the building from the teacher's point of view, and to relate these to teaching possibilities, teaching constraints and the underlying theoretical assumptions about teaching and learning.

Procedure

1. Obtain a plan of a school or make a plan using paces as a measure or by sketching from memory.
2. Fill in the schedules below or design a preferred schedule suitable for the purpose.
    (a) General allocation of school spaces. Work out the percentage of school space given over to:
    (1) general purpose teaching spaces, e.g. classrooms;
    (2) specialized teaching spaces, e.g. science/technology rooms;
    (3) multi-purpose teaching spaces, e.g. halls;
    (4) circulation space, e.g. corridors;
    (5) administration space, e.g. offices;
    (6) other spaces, both teaching and non-teaching, e.g. playground, staff room, dining, caretaker.
    (b) What styles of furnishing are employed in each of the areas?
    (c) Write your comments, e.g. what assumptions are made here about how children learn, what they should learn, relationships between teachers and children, how the school is to be organized, sizes of groups appropriate for learning, structure of the staff, who has most space allocated, who has least, the key tasks of the institution.
    (d) How does the building differ from a factory?
    (e) What assumptions underlie the design of a factory?
    (f) How do these differ from assumptions underlying the design of the school you are analysing?
    (g) How are they similar to those of the factory?
    (h) Comment on the teaching possibilities of the building.
    (i) Comment on the limitations set by the building.
    (j) How does the building differ from the houses and flats of the pupils?
    (k) Any other observations.

Discussion

Clearly, findings will vary from building type to building type: a study of primary schools will not yield identical results to a study of secondary schools, nor open plan buildings to 'egg crate' plan buildings. However, some common propositions that emerge are:

1. A group size of 30 to 40 under the surveillance of one adult is often believed to be the most suitable for the learning process.
2. The process of education is seen as both orderly and apparently uncomfortable for the learners. The buildings tend to have the clinical austerity of places in which one is confined for purposes other than pleasure.

3. There is an asymmetrical relationship in the allocation of space and facilities: teachers have larger desks, padded chairs, lockable cupboards and access to more of the school territory, whereas pupils have inferior claims on the building's resources. It is a teachers' building rather than a pupils' building: it is 'their' building rather than 'our' building.

4. The design on which classrooms are based is not unlike a factory, in that the children pass through 'stages of production or process', according to certain criteria like age and sex, in regular sized compartments, in regular sized groups and at regular sized desks or tables.

5. A 'production manager' (headteacher) is allocated extra space and facilities to supervise the production activities of the teachers.

6. The buildings are not conducive to individual learning and small group learning.

7. The buildings tend to obstruct the development of cooperative and democratic relationships between teachers and pupils.

8. The buildings provide some facilities not available in homes, such as libraries, computer facilities and physical education equipment.

9. The buildings tend to introduce some ideas not present in houses and flats, like separate toilets for the sexes, learning regularly in large groups and large areas of space with access forbidden to children.

There are many other possible observations. One analysis (Hardy, 1977) stresses how the inadequacies of design may force teachers into an authoritarian role to compensate:

> One basic determinant of the relationship between teachers and pupils lies in the belief that where both see a system that is fair and sensible, there is less likely to be misunderstanding; but would a couple of 11 stone 16 year olds, rocking gently on a new upholstered bench seat, see this if persistently a teacher on social area supervision during the lunch hour tells them to sit still?
>
> Is the teacher being reasonable? What about the teacher who tells off a pupil for kicking the lavatory door open at the bottom with his foot? Unreasonable? Perhaps, but a metal kick plate has already been provided for just such a purpose.
>
> Surely the member of staff on outside break duty is being totally unreasonable in the eyes of the child when he insists that the two first year pupils playing tick and dodging from each other's clutches around a pillar with an attached drainpipe should go elsewhere. Is it fair on a group of pupils that they should be excluded from their social area by a deputy head, who is tired of asking them not to lean on an internal wall with their heels against the bottom of it, while chatting about the success of the local soccer team, or who is going out with whom?
>
> In these instances, most adults and children would feel the teachers are behaving unreasonably. It is just such petty attitudes of teachers that prevent many pupils from enjoying school.
>
> The teachers' actions cannot be excused on the grounds that any of these instances amount to vandalism. Yet the effect is to continuously and imperceptibly erode relationships between the staff and the pupils. And without cause?
>
> A closer investigation would show that the metal legs supporting the upholstered bench

seat were fixed on to chipboard by 1/2 inch screws. Above the kick plate on the lavatory door was a ventilation grill made of thin moulded plastic.

The problem with the pillar and its drainpipe was that they were attached by a thin plastic fastener. In dodging round the pillar from one side to the other with their hands on the pipe for support the fastener breaks, the pipe swings free, and water gushes everywhere when it rains.

The problem for the deputy head was that he knew that the interior wall was merely plaster board concealed by hessian, and that anyone leaning against the wall talking can place their heel on the base of the wall, and either through tapping or continual pressure, a hole would soon appear which would progressively grow in size.

The quality of these fixtures is poor, and certainly not able to stand for long the fair wear and tear of young adolescents behaving in a not unreasonable manner . . .

In all of the instances described above, the teachers have been forced into an authoritarian and custodial role to offset the inadequacies of design. Architects have a constructive part to play, therefore, in helping pupils and teachers to establish better relationships.

Hardy, 1977

Open plan schools provide interesting contrasts in a number of features of space and design, because the classrooms lose their 'front' and 'back', leaving teachers to move everywhere. Desks and tables are so arranged that pupils have eye contact with each other and are likely to share more experiences and communicate with each other more frequently. The learning environment is likely to be more relaxed. In some schools corridors were turned into work areas and book reference places. Washing and toilet facilities were planned in direct association with learning spaces (see Pearson, 1971).

Older schools provided their own particular problems of spatial layout for the users to solve. Gould (1976) comments that in an Edwardian school building where he once worked several classrooms were connected so that the entrance to the first was through a cloakroom, the second was entered from the first, and the third from the second. The middle classroom acted as a passageway and the teacher in this room had to accept that other staff and pupils would come through at various times, some scheduled, some unscheduled.

The spaces outside the school building may be indicative of assumptions about relationships. Evans (1974b) notes that it was Simmel who first drew attention to the significance that a border line has for a group. It defines who is included and who is excluded. In her study of infant schools, Evans notes that only one still displayed a notice saying that parents should not enter the school, but the same effect was achieved in other ways. Some headteachers wrote to parents asking them to say goodbye at the gate, and others did this verbally. In one school the parents toed a white line painted on the playground: beyond this they were not expected to pass.

Some of the territory within the school can be a source of dispute. Evans found that headteachers had mixed experiences with caretakers. One-third of the headteachers were full of praise for their caretakers, but another third reported constant difficulties. One headteacher commented that her biggest problems in running the school were with the caretaker, who neglected the floors and carpets, and let the toilets become smelly. For even the smallest jobs he insisted on sending for an expert.

A RESEARCH ACTIVITY ON CLASSROOMS

In the classrooms of Downers Grove school, Chicago, for children of junior school age, 'caves' once replaced desks. Each child had an octagonal plywood cave which was situated in a three-tiered honeycomb from floor to ceiling. The idea was analysed in a report by Bealing (1972):

> An article in this week's issue of *Educational Research* (Volume 14, No. 3). 'The organization of junior school classrooms', casts doubt on the revolution said to have taken place in the organization of the classrooms of Britain's primary schools in recent years. 'Despite the relatively informal classroom layout adopted by the vast majority of teachers, there was so much evidence of tight teacher control over such matters as where children sit and move that it seems highly doubtful that there is much opportunity for children to choose or organize their own activities in most classrooms.' Practical necessity, rather than pedagogical theory, probably accounts for this, says the author of the article, Deanne Bealing.
>
> Practical necessities do have a way of exerting their influence, so is it that to change the organization and behaviour in classrooms one needs to change the structure itself in a rather more adventurous manner than has yet been tried?
>
> All the children of Downers Grove school in Chicago would answer yes – for they inhabit classrooms unique in this respect. There are no desks – instead, each child has an octagonal plywood 'cave' which is piled with others in a three tiered honeycomb from floor to ceiling. The idea is to give every child his own area where he can stash his books, clothes, string and what-not and read or draw whenever he feels that he wants to.
>
> The project is the brainchild of the school head, Avery Coolney, who conceived the idea for the caves with educationist Larry Busch. The children climb into their hideouts by means of carpeted hand and footholds on the lower caves, and each space contains a seat, working surface, a light and storage space. The seat and storage space can be folded flush with the walls in order to give more room.
>
> The caves are – almost literally – the children's castles: they are assigned at the beginning of the year and from then on outsiders can enter by invitation only. The teaching day at Downers Grove is structured at present so that an hour and a half is set aside specifically to be spent in the caves, but children are allowed to spend as much time as they want there.
>
> Schoolwork, as a result of this project, says Coonley, has become more original even over the few short months it's been in operation. The children stick with their various academic activities longer now and because they can't look over each other's shoulders, there is more originality in their work. Often, just the opportunity to get away from the rest of the class is rewarding: fidgets often withdraw and only come back once they are more settled.
>
> The children themselves (up to age 11 or thereabouts) like the cave arrangement: being able to get away from others, and somewhere to leave things lying about, are the main attractions. In fact several want more privacy – the doorway closed up, for instance, and locks.
>
> But the biggest changes have occurred in the children who are from larger families and

who don't have rooms of their own at home. The caves are cheap to make, says Coonley, so they could be an effective help in inner city schools.

(This first appeared in *New Society*, 29 June 1972, London, the weekly review of the social sciences.)

The point of introducing these data on caves in classrooms is as an alerting device: classrooms can be quite different from those with which we are familiar.

Background Propositions

The spaces available specifically for teaching are of interest in at least three ways:

1. They suggest possibilities and opportunities for teaching.
2. They place constraints on what can be done.
3. They imply psychological, philosophical, sociological and pedagogical ideas that are often taken for granted, but are open to question.

Aim

The aim of this exercise is to analyse the various features of teaching spaces and to relate these to teaching possibilities, teaching constraints and the underlying theoretical assumptions.

Procedure

1. Make a sketch plan of a room or space known to you, including its furniture. This can be based on an actual visit or drawn from memory.
2. Make notes on the following features.
    - (a) The shape of the room/space.
    - (b) The arrangement of desks/tables.
    - (c) The arrangement of chairs.
    - (d) The position of the teacher's desk.
    - (e) The windows.
    - (f) The display boards (e.g. position, number).
    - (g) The storage units (e.g. position, access).
    - (h) Any other furniture and fittings.
    - (i) Has the room space a 'front' and 'back'?
    - (j) Access points (number, off a corridor?).
    - (k) Write your comments, e.g. what assumptions are made about how children learn

and what they should learn, the relationship between teacher and pupils, how the school is to be organized.

(l)   How does this room differ from a public house, a theatre, a crèche, a church or a youth club?

(m) What assumptions underlie the design of a public bar, a theatre, a crèche, a church or a youth club?

(n)   How do these differ from the assumptions underlying the design of the room you are analysing?

(o)   Comment on the teaching possibilities of the room/space.

(p)   Comment on the limitations set by the room/space.

Discussion

As in the case of the school building as a whole, there will be variations in the findings from classroom to classroom and space to space. Some propositions that emerge are:

1.   In most classrooms the placement of tables, desks and chairs gives the room a front and a back. The teacher's territory is usually well marked by a larger desk, the position of the backboard or white board, a space to the doorway, the position of a waste basket or some combination of these. This teacher territory may often occupy as much as a third of the space available.

2.   Many classrooms, particularly in secondary schools, are rather Spartan in appearance and in furnishings. The transitory nature of the pupils' stay is signalled by the relative lack of displays of work and other 'involvements' with the room, e.g. the occupants do not choose the decor or decorate the room themselves.

3.   The arrangement of seating indicates an expected channel of communication. In most cases this is seen as mostly teacher-centred or entirely teacher-centred. Teachers have the power to vary this and some do, particularly in infant schools.

4.   Classrooms tend to signal social distance and teaching styles which are authoritarian, i.e. the learners are dependent on the teacher throughout. The layout often suggests a confrontation. An analogy is that of battle: in battle, territories are clearly established, sorties into each other's territory are regarded with suspicion and there is victory, defeat or truce.

5.   Primary schools show some differences from secondary schools. Yet the teacher's territory remains well marked in most classrooms. In a study of infant schools in 1974: 'Of the 145 classrooms visited, there were only six which did not sport a teacher's desk or table. The most favoured position for this was still the traditional centre front, at right angles to the main access door. In 42 cases, the teacher was actually seated at her desk for the whole or part of the time the observer was in the room' (Evans, 1974b). While circumstances may have improved for some years it seems likely that recent educational initiatives may

encourage a return to such didacticism. Since the publication of *Classroom Organisation in the Primary School* (Alexander *et al.*, 1992) teachers have been increasingly under pressure to spend more time with whole-class teaching than with groupwork and in 'telling' children things rather than in setting questions. Evans concluded that, in her studies of infants' classrooms: 'elements of tradition and continuity are stronger in English infants schools than is sometimes assumed ... Many teachers were at pains to describe themselves as "old fashioned"' (Evans, 1974b). Such statements remain familiar today.

6. Comparisons with a modern public house are interesting. As in schools, large numbers of people are catered for over long periods of time. The standards of decor and comfort are usually higher in the public house and informal grouping and activity are encouraged by the layout.

7. A crèche is often equipped with comfortable furnishings, carpets and cushions. Distinct activity areas are defined and individual children are given a free choice in visiting them.

8. A theatre often has the territorial features of many classrooms, unless it is a theatre in the round. The performance is highly resourced, both professionally and technically, and the clients experience high levels of comfort and consideration.

9. The limitations set by classrooms can be overstated: theatre designers use a similar area to achieve remarkable variations. The Chicago experiment with 'caves' presents only one possible variation.

CONCLUSION

Environmental Competence

There are many practical implications of studies of space in schooling. One is contained in the idea of environmental competence. This is defined as:

> (a) a person's ability to be aware of the surrounding environment and its impact on him; and
> (b) his ability to use or change his settings to help him achieve his goals without inappropriately destroying the setting or reducing his sense of effectiveness or that of the people around him.
>
> Steele, 1973

On this definition, it can be argued that the behaviour of many teachers shows limited environmental competence. A common arrangement of furniture in a secondary school classroom is where the desks are set in rows facing the 'front' of the room, defined by the teacher's desk and other features like a blackboard. The teachers can usually see all or most of the pupils and from their point of view the classroom is ordered and tidy. The pupils can see only their neighbours and the teacher. The message of the arrangement is to look ahead. Unless the room is raked, what they actually see is a cluttered space of people's shoulders, heads and bits of the teacher.

The learning message is 'sit and listen': a lecture or instructional approach is implied. This style is appropriate some of the time, but if a teacher desires general discussion or group discussion, the furniture arrangements are opposed to it. The teacher may be attempting to exchange and explore ideas in a physical arrangement that inhibits this. In this situation many teachers accuse the pupils of being unresponsive, when in fact the teachers have not maximized the chances of getting responses. Discussion is also facilitated by comfortable furniture and pleasant wall and floor coverings, as evidenced in most modern public houses.

There are more mundane examples of environmental competence. Many student teachers have had to be warned about the territorial claims senior staff have on parts of the staff room and on particular chairs, and those who have not been given such warnings may find that their image with the staff quickly becomes an unfavourable one.

Walteenspuhl (1994) has suggested an architectural model developed from the curriculum and divided according to three distinct pedagogic categories, with the teaching being done in spaces which are themselves of three distinct architectural types (Figure 7.1):

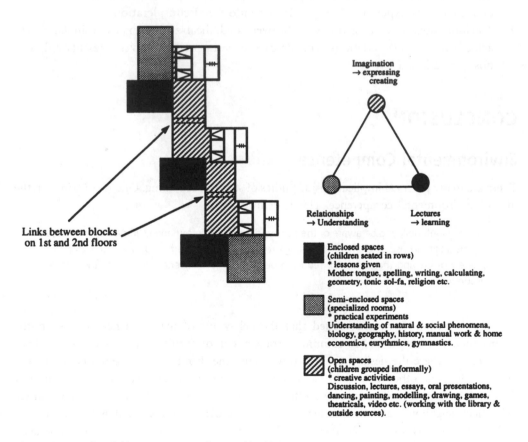

Figure 7.1 Use of available space. From Walteenspuhl, 1994.

This is so that the pupil can better distinguish the nature of the scholastic disciplines which are taught, each within a suitable ambience.

Walteenspuhl, 1994, p. 124

The Historical Dimension

One dimension of the descriptions and explanations for spatial layout largely overlooked in this chapter is the historical dimension. One of the continuities in educational activity lies in the relative permanence of buildings, which may well outlast the theories of education on which their design was based. Later users may find that their different teaching ideas are effectively reduced or outlawed by the inherited architecture. (See Seaborne and Lowe, 1977, for a useful treatment from the historical point of view.)

However, the furniture is less permanent and provides more scope for modification. School furniture before 1944 tended to consist of items like heavy cast iron frame desks, usually constructed in pairs. Light tubular furniture, stackable or mobile, increases the options open to teachers. Walls designed to have things pinned on them rather than painted brick designed purely to keep the roof up are another aspect of increased choice for teachers (Dale, 1972a).

The Pupils' Perspective

For the most part, the analysis so far has centred on the teachers' layer of meaning and the teachers' viewpoint, as have most of the limited researches available. To devote a little space to the pupils' viewpoint would seem to be appropriate.

> They cry out for colour, and are very conscious of the drab uniformity of many of the walls within which they sit. They would like to have some say in the ephemeral decoration of their schools. They long for attractive grounds and especially for trees ... the fabric of a school does speak to the children, and ... it says, 'I express the community's notion of what you are worth, of the environment you deserve.'
>
> Blishen, E. (1969) *The School That I'd Like*, Copyright Penguin Books.
> Reprinted by permission of Penguin Books

Theory and Practice

There is some light shed on the matters of theory and practice in the studies of educational spaces. The notion that 'theory' is opposed to practice is dubious in the light of evidence about space and behaviour. The theory underpinning the use of space may be implicit or explicit, recognized or unrecognized. A particular theory may be applied, misapplied or avoided. But one of the assumptions of this chapter is that all practices have an underpinning theory and that alternative practices and theories can be discovered. Teachers who do not recognize these competing theories are vulnerable to having decisions made for them, rather than exercising the choices that are open to them.

It would be misleading to see space as determining. In studies of classrooms (Evans, 1974b), headteachers' rooms (Evans, 1974a) and commercial offices (Joiner, 1971), the variety of uses of the same space and furniture is stressed. 'People, it seems, whatever the architect had in mind, can impose quite a lot of themselves on their surroundings' (Joiner, 1971). But as Mead (1934) points out, the changes individuals make in the social orders in which they are implicated usually involve changes in themselves and in their self-concepts.

Summary

1. Relatively little attention has been given to analysing the influence of the spaces provided in schools on educating.
2. Teachers' rooms may indicate a great deal about them and their views of education.
3. The experience of using a school building is one illustration of layers of meaning: it varies considerably with the groups of people involved.
4. A research exercise on the school building may yield a series of taken-for-granted assumptions about schooling.
5. Inadequacies of design may force teachers into a more authoritarian role to compensate. The promotion of authoritarian teaching styles may also result in the rearrangement of classroom furniture.
6. A research exercise on classrooms may yield further taken-for-granted assumptions.
7. Many teachers show limited environmental competence: room arrangements often fail to back up the teachers' intentions.
8. Buildings may outlast the theories of education on which their design was based, and create problems for later users who have different ideas.
9. Pupils have considerable awareness of the buildings, and many would like some say and involvement in improving them.
10. Spatial influences are important rather than determining, but their importance is often underestimated.

Further Reading

Alexander, R., Rose, J. and Woodhead, C. (1992) *Classroom Organization in the Primary School*. London: DES.

Bennett, S.N. *et al.* (1980) *Open Plan Schools: Teaching, Curriculum, Design*. Windsor: NFER-Nelson.

Burke, C. and Grosvenor I. (2003) *The School I'd Like*. London: Routledge Falmer.

Coopers, P. (2001) *Building Performance. An Emprical Assessment of the Relationship between Schools Capital Investment and Pupil Performance*. London: DfEE.

Cosin, B., Dale, R., Esland, G. and Swift, D. (eds) (1971) *School and Society*. London: Routledge and Kegan Paul.

Two articles in this reader are especially worth consulting: Chapter 11, by E. Goffman, and Chapter 13, by
D.J. Bennett and J.D. Bennett.

Dale, R. (1972) *The Context of the Classroom*. Milton Keynes: Open University Press. A very readable analysis of
spatial aspects of schooling.

Gordon, T. and Lahelma, E. (1996) ' '"School is like an Ant's Nest"': Spatiality and Embodiment in Schools',
Gender and Education, **8**, 3, 301–10.

Seaborne, M. and Lowe, R. (1977) *The English School: Its Architecture and Organization 1870–1970*. London:
Routledge and Kegan Paul. An investigation of the historical aspects of school buildings.

Foucault, M. (1977) *Discipline and Punish*. Harmondsworth: Penguin.

Walteenspuhl, P. (1994) 'Team Teaching and Didactically Defined Spaces in School Architecture: The Triadic
System Applied to Education', *Educational Media International*, **31**, 2.

Discussion and Activities

1. Using the two research activities in the chapter for ideas, devise your own list of questions for research into
   specialized spaces in a school, e.g. a secondary school science laboratory, a school library.

2. Teachers are sometimes thought to be akin to actors in having to give performances. Does this comparison
   break down in the case of environmental competence, with actors taking this much more seriously than
   teachers?

Signposts

1. Education without specialized buildings

The Open University, correspondence colleges and the radio schools of the Australian outback all operate
without the normal spatial features of special educational building. A state school in the USA operates in this
way too; see Farrington, P., Pritchard, G. and Raynor, J. (1973) 'The Parkway Programme', in J. Raynor and J.
Harden (eds), *Readings in Urban Education, Volume 2: Equality and City Schools*, Milton Keynes: Open University
Press.

2. Open plan classrooms in primary schools

About 10 per cent of primary schools in England and Wales are open plan. One study is Bennett, S.N. *et al.*
(1980) *Open Plan Schools: Teaching, Curriculum, Design*, Windsor: NFER-Nelson. Primary schools are the focus
of two articles: Cooper, I. (1982) 'The Maintenance of Order and Use of Space in Primary School Buildings',
British Journal of Sociology of Education, **3**, 3; and Cooper, I. (1981) 'The Politics of Education and Architectural
Design: The Instructive Example of British Primary Education', *British Educational Research Journal*, **7**, 2.

3. Grouping

Teachers often sit children in groups, and they argue that this supports small group teaching, collaborative
learning, 'ability grouping' and easy access to resources. But are these teaching practices actually pursued or
justified? Does group seating support or detract from children's engagement with learning in the classroom? See
Hastings, N. and Wood, K.C. (2002) 'Group Seating in Primary Schools: An Indefensible Strategy?', paper
presented at the Annual Conference of the British Educational Research Association, University of Exeter,

England, 12–14 September 2002. The text is available in the Education-line internet document collection at *http://www.leeds.ac.uk/educol/documents/00002181.htm*

4. International perspectives on school space
A five-nation study by Robin Alexander covering Britain, France, USA, Russia and India explored different uses of space in school in different cultures (see Alexander, R. (2000) *Culture and Pedagogy: International Comparisons in Primary Education*, Oxford: Blackwell).

8 Timetables

Suddenly a White Rabbit with pink eyes ran close by her. There was nothing so very remarkable in that; nor did Alice think it so very much out of the way to hear the rabbit say to itself, 'Oh dear! Oh dear! I shall be too late!' (when she thought it over afterwards, it occurred to her that she ought to have wondered at this, but at the time it all seemed quite natural).

Lewis Carrol, *Alice's Adventures in Wonderland*

Work expands so as to fill the time available for its completion.

Parkinson's Law

INTRODUCTION: THE ALLOCATION OF TIME

In situations where it is believed that there is not enough time to do everything, systems of allocating time to chosen activities have to be established. Schools face a time allocation problem. There are competing claims about what should be learnt in schools and the number of subjects to be included in the curriculum is seen as being greater than the time available, so time is defined as a scarce item that needs to be rationed in some way. At an early stage in the introduction of the National Curriculum, primary schools were required to audit the number of hours spent in teaching each subject. The apparently reasonable assumption being made was that the way in which time was allocated in the schools would contribute some insight into what goes on there and the hidden assumptions that were involved, as with the spaces and the architecture. In the case of the primary school curriculum, the reality proved more complex than the research instruments applied. It proved extremely difficult to allocate 'subject' hours to integrated topic work.

The timetable also becomes part of the consciousness of the pupils, and it is generally taken for granted. In fact, it is one of the features of the culture of the school that is often taken for granted by all those involved, as it may seem too obvious and unquestionable.

Within a very short time of entering a school, a pupil begins to take for granted that the school day is broken down into blocks of time called periods. Playtime is at a set time, and so is lunch time, the start of the afternoon and the end of the school day. This system was created by previous members of the school and has some theoretical base, but this is not explained to the pupil; and it becomes accepted as the 'natural', if not inevitable, way of doing things.

SOCIOLOGICAL QUESTIONS

A sociological approach tries to resist this 'taken-for-grantedness' and instead asks questions about the particular kinds of timetables in use, the assumptions underpinning these and the implications and consequences for the learning of all who are involved. A number of general questions may be asked:

1. Who timetables?
2. What is timetabled?
3. How is the timetabling undertaken?
4. Why timetabling and what are its consequences?

A RESEARCH ACTIVITY: THE SCHOOL TIMETABLE

Background Propositions

The allocation of time in school is deliberate and codified in a timetable. The principles that underlie this allocation are of interest, since they may:

1. have implications for what is learnt;
2. imply psychological, philosophical, sociological and pedagogical ideas that may be taken for granted, but are still open to question.

Aim

The aim of this exercise is to begin the process of questioning and analysing the underlying assumptions of school timetables.

Procedure

Obtain a copy of a school timetable or consider a timetable you have experienced, or obtain access to a timetable board. (A class timetable will yield some results if the school timetable is inaccessible.) It should be possible to deduce most answers from the timetable itself: any questions to school staff must obviously be handled with politeness and tact.

1. Who designed the timetable?
2. Who was consulted?
3. Who, in the school community, was not consulted?
4. When was it devised?

What assumptions are being made here?

5. How are groups formed: Allocated? Chosen? Age? Sex? Attainment?
6. Do all groups study the same subjects?
7. If not, when do differences begin?

What assumptions are being made here?

8. Which three subjects/activities are most frequently timetabled?
9. Which three subjects/activities are least frequently timetabled?
10. Which subjects/activities are absent from the timetable?
11. Does the frequency of subject/activity timetabling vary with different groups of children?

What assumptions are being made here?

12. How long are the periods allocated?
13. What subject/activities are given double periods?
14. Are activities planned to fit the timetable or are activities carried over to the next lesson?
15. Are the timetables of boys and girls the same?
16. If they differ, give details.

What assumptions are being made here?

17. How does the school timetable compare with:
    (a) A child's programme of choices in a crèche or nursery; or
    (b) A youth club programme (either one night a week or full time); or
    (c) A technical college timetable?
18. Why was the timetable devised in this particular way?

DISCUSSION

One general difference in timetables that can be seen is between those of infant, junior and secondary schools. The secondary school timetable tends to be made up of a wide variety of subjects and the task of fitting all these in with appropriate classes and teachers is complicated – so complicated that many schools use a computer for the purpose. Until recently, in infant school classrooms broadly defined activities were usual, like language work, number work and creative activities based on art and crafts. Junior and middle schools occupied an interim position, where the inclusion of subjects like history, science and music often meant that a finer division of time was required than in the infants' class. Some schools integrated these subjects to work on extended topics such as 'Ourselves', 'The seasons' or 'Transport'. Following the introduction of the National Curriculum, a good deal of this work is carried out in separate subject lessons and the influence of this statutory curriculum has been felt even in nurseries and play schools (Sylva and Iram Siraj-Blatchford, 1992).

Who Timetables and When?

The general question 'Who timetables?' raises some interesting issues. A hierarchy of some kind usually emerges. The pupils are rarely consulted. Usually only some of the teachers are involved, and these tend to be senior teachers. Caretakers and cleaners are usually expected to arrange their activities to fit in with the timetable. 'Outside' clients like parents are not usually consulted.

The answer to the question 'When was the timetable devised?' is usually that this takes place before the pupils arrive in school and, in the case of a new intake, before the children have been met. There is an assumption here that the needs, achievements and wishes of pupils can be predicated or are irrelevant. Some schools have challenged the assumption that a school timetable should be imposed in an authoritarian way upon learners, and have developed timetables based on negotiation:

> We talked . . . and about his timetable. On the basis of chats with his teachers at the other school, chats with me, and what he had heard from specialists here he chose the following subjects to study (in addition to what he would be studying in team time which would include maths, English, social studies and a variety of other things): art, visual communication, music, control technology, chemistry, PE and games. He had changed his mind about German after talking it over with his parents. He was especially excited by the idea of control technology because of the construction involved, music because of the possibility of using the organ and synthesizer, and visual communication because of a conversation with the person who was going to teach it who had talked about the possibilities of photography. Later he dropped PE and games and said he would play five-a-side 'during team time if he felt the urge'. He also added typing at my suggestion . . .
>
> At the start of term I'd suggested to Phil that he kept a journal. This is how he described his school life after two weeks.
>
> 'I have been at this school now for two weeks and now I have settled in and doing subjects I like to do and enjoy. Once you get to know the other students they are friendly towards you. When you get down to hard work, time seems to pass a lot quicker, but the

first week we were just working out timetables and going to different classes to see what the different subjects were like and so time seemed to drift slowly by! I like it at this school, you learn things at your own pace and not like at my last school where for example in maths you go through different subjects in that category like an express train so you don't gather much knowledge.'

Watts, 1977

What Is Timetabled?

Timetables indicate the dual nature of what is being processed in schools, knowledge and people.

People

Pupils are formed into groups and these groups tend to be allocated rather than chosen. Allocation takes place on the multiple criteria of age, sex and achievement. The first groupings experienced by pupils tend to be on the basis of age. Some infant schools developed a family grouping system where children of various ages worked with one teacher, but the most common system is to allocate children into groups defined by the National Curriculum; Reception, Year 1, Year 2, etc. Age grouping is less rigid in other educational institutions, e.g. in further and higher education.

The next experience of grouping may be by sex. Certain activities tend to be designated as boys' activities and others as girls' activities. Games provide an example: football for boys and netball for girls. Until relatively recently, domestic science for girls and metalwork for boys offered much more formally sex-typed aspects of the timetable. Most schools have adopted the alternative of non-sex-typed timetables, where all subjects are studied by both boys and girls. More commonly, children are given an 'equal opportunity' to select at least some of their examination subjects. In these circumstances many subjects remain highly gendered, and this tendency may be encouraged when option subjects that are especially gendered are set against each other (timetabled at the same time).

Grouping by achievement is encountered by most pupils. An early experience may be grouping within classes into 'top' tables and 'bottom' tables. Later experiences may involve streaming, when a whole class is grouped on the basis of similar achievement, and setting, where achievement in one subject or activity is the basis for grouping pupils together.

Teachers are allocated to the timetable on the basis of subject identification in most secondary schools, and on the basis of class teaching of a wide range of activities in primary schools. Middle schools and some secondary and primary schools have a mixed classification of subject and general teaching, and teachers do some of both. In recent years the Qualification and Curriculum Authority (QCA) has been encouraging primary schools to provide more subject teaching.

Table 8.1 Proportions of time on basic subjects and other subjects in a range of research studies and in National Curriculum policy guidance

	Percentage of curriculum time spent on	
	Basic subjects	Other subjects
(a) *Research*		
Bassey (1977) Junior	54	46
Bennett *et al.* (1980) Infant	53	25
Bennett *et al.* (1980) Junior	48	39
Galton *et al.* (1980) Junior	49	51
DES *Primary Staffing Survey* (1987) Junior	49	51
Tizard *et al.* (1988) Infant	52	40
Alexander (1992) Primary	52	48
Campbell and Neil (1992) KS1	51	39
Campbell and Neil (1993) KS2	49	45
Meyer *et al.* (1992) Primary/Elementary	50	50
(b) *Policy/Guidance*		
Guidance to National Curriculum Working Parties. KS1/KS2	40	60
NCC Planning the Curriculum at KS2 (1993)	37	63

Note: Other subjects are expressed either as in the research data, or if data were not given, by subtracting 'basic subject' percentages from 100. In the former cases, the proportions of time left for non-basis are consistently lower than in the latter cases.

From J. Campbell (1994) 'Managing the Primary Curriculum: The Issue of Time Allocation', *Education* 3–13, **22,** 1.

Knowledge

The knowledge to be processed is allocated to periods of time by being divided up into subjects. These subjects are more loosely organized in some schools than in others: in infant schools the organization is often broadly based in terms of number work, language activities, creative activities, etc., while in secondary schools the division of knowledge into a range of subjects is usually more rigid.

Some subjects and activities are allocated more time than others. Frequently English and maths, or their equivalent, head the list, and physical education, including games, is often third. Subjects that tend to be allocated least time are religious education and music. Despite calls for a 'back to basics' approach, classroom observation studies show that about half of the primary curriculum is devoted to the 'basics' of reading, writing and arithmetic. Campbell's (1994) study of 105 teachers showed that the calls for a 'back to basics' approach are actually a nonsense (see Table 8.1). As Campbell argues, primary teachers have always emphasized the basics and, in so far as there has been a real problem in managing the primary curriculum, the fundamental problem of manageability is not overload or over detailed prescription, important as these are, nor is it the teacher workload. The fundamental problem is ideological, in that the broad and balanced conception of the curriculum runs counter to the essentially traditional, elementary ideology and practice of most teachers on curriculum matters.

Campbell, 1994, p. 10

There are other ideological influences. Some subjects, such as ethics, philosophy, logic, sociology, anthropology, politics, psychology and even education, are missing from the timetables of most schools entirely. These omissions raise some interesting questions. For example, since logic, rather than mathematics, underpins most of the subjects on the timetable, there is a case for its being the basic tool subject. The courses in 'thinking' produced by Edward de Bono have been adopted on these grounds in some schools. Subjects are also placed at different times in the day: in primary schools English and mathematics are often taught in the morning, as it is assumed that children are at their best at that time. As Jones (1992) argues, research shows that this notion that children are more capable in the morning is actually a myth, yet children may well be quieter and more passive at that time. Jones argues that this might account for teachers organizing more active mental work in the mornings. The teachers are interpreting what is essentially a teaching problem as a learning problem: 'active minds and bodies are probably more difficult to manage' (p. 84).

The performance of tasks, with the exception of some limited short term memory tasks, actually improves as the day progresses. The evidence suggests that despite a short post-lunch dip in arousal and performance, performance continues to improve until the early evening.

The assumptions made about knowledge make an interesting list of propositions:

1. Knowledge is best compartmentalized into subjects.
2. Some knowledge deserves more timetable space than other knowledge, and knowledge is thus stratified.
3. Some knowledge is legally compulsory, e.g. the National Curriculum 'subjects'.
4. Some knowledge is examinable and some is not, e.g. physical education is not usually examined.
5. Different children should have different packages of knowledge, rather than there being a common curriculum.
6. Some knowledge is considered more suitable for boys and others for girls.
7. Some knowledge (e.g. economics, sociology, parenting) has been seen as worthy of timetable space by some schools and not by others.
8. The most suitable knowledge for schools is past-orientated and based on an ancient system of subject classification, rather than present-orientated and based on integrated themes like censorship, terrorism and environmental pollution, which cross the ancient subject boundaries.
9. Future-orientated knowledge systems stressing the skills of learning to create new

knowledge and cope with constant changes in information are given little space in most timetables.

10. Some knowledge within the subject traditions is best excluded from the timetable, e.g. logic, philosophy and psychology.

How Is Timetabling Undertaken?

The division of time into periods, days and weeks has consequences for the type of learning that can take place. All subjects or activities have to be taught and learnt in a similar way, in regularized blocks of time. Some concession to variations in learning may appear in the form of double periods, but this illustrates the point that, if double periods are needed, why not a half day, a whole day, several days or a week?

This division of time has implications for teaching methods. It tends to place a premium on third- and fourth-hand experiences. In history this may mean reading what a teacher other than your own has to say about manor houses rather than visiting the one a few kilometres away. It may mean seeing a short film about canals instead of travelling along one in a barge. It may mean copying pictures of locks and lock gates rather than sketching from the original. It may mean reading a play over a series of lessons instead of attending a performance at a local theatre. When outings of the above type are organized, they are special events rather than the basic mode of learning.

The timetable tends to be imposed: it is a set menu rather than a choice-based menu. A further or higher education college timetable is based on the same principle: students enrol for courses rather than have an allocation of subjects. A youth club timetable is negotiated even further, and is fashioned from the wishes and needs of the members.

Why Timetabling and with What Consequences?

At the beginning of the chapter we saw that breaking up time into small segments is a common activity. The timetable represents a school's attempt to cope with competing claims about what should be learnt in schools and by whom. Particular views of knowledge and a particular view of teaching and learning are implied in these arrangements. Therefore pupils involved in a timetable learn considerably more than where to go for a lesson at a certain time. They are being exposed to a series of hidden messages about what counts as knowledge, which knowledge is thought to be appropriate for them, and which knowledge is not made available to them. The questions surrounding what constitutes an appropriate 'canon' have caused a great deal more debate in the USA than in the UK, where the legitimacy of literary heroes and heroines is rarely questioned.

It may be that particular perspectives on time are related to social class. It has been suggested that the time perspective associated with white-collar workers tends to be future-orientated, impersonal, planned and built on the notion of deferred gratification, whereas the time perspective of blue-collar workers tends to be present-orientated, personal, spontaneous and implying immediate gratification. Schools and teachers tend to adopt the first view of time. Pupils used to the second view of time may quickly be seen as 'lazy, careless, impulsive, uninvolved'. A school's promise to pupils is that it will all be worth it in the long run:

> The pupils are promised that the value of subjects whose relevance is totally mysterious to them will some day be recognized, and with gratitude. Such encouragements and promises, it is argued, work very much better with the middle-class child, whose cultural background supports the deferment of gratification, than with the working-class child, whose time perspective leads him to want his cake now.
>
> Dale, 1972b

In the USA, Lois Weis also refers to the notion of CPT (Coloured People's Time). Weis argues that it is important to note that time, as expressed in street activity and adolescent ghetto culture, is not simply a deficient use of dominant time – it is oppositional in that it represents, as Horton (1979, p. 44) has put it, 'a positive adaptation to generations of living whenever and wherever possible outside of the sound and control of the white man's clock.' From the moment that they enter an educational institution students are bombarded with messages about the appropriate use of time. From this perspective, they are bombarded with dominant time – and they often resist.

THE SOCIOLOGY OF TIME, AND TIME IN SCHOOLS

So far the analysis has concentrated on school timetables, but there are other timetables in operation. The school timetable yields a class timetable, and a pupil's individual timetable may be derived from that. There are also year timetables and career timetables. The year timetable introduces other features. It is shorter than a calendar year and has within it paradoxes such as the compulsion to attend the school building for part of the calendar year, and exclusion, on the threat of trespass, at other times in the year.

A career timetable is built out of the year timetables. Although the years are of similar length, some are marked off as special. Years of transfer from one school to another, examination years and school-leaving years are examples. Some school career timetables are longer than others, for various reasons. Early starts are the experience of some because of accidents of birth dates or because of an 'optional' nursery school experience. The sixth form experience is for some but not for others. 'Schooldays' can mean anything from 11 to 16 years in school. Life chances are involved here, since length of school career is strongly correlated with job prospects and standards of living.

Time in school links with time outside school, and the social class links have already been mentioned. The school career timetable provides another example of this link in the concept of 'planners' and 'drifters': usually pupils who are 'pushed' by parents who tend to plan adopt the 'rational, future-orientated' time perspective of the school, whereas drifters do not. Planners know what goals exist in the school and how to reach them, when important turning points have arrived and what the consequences of the choices will be. Drifters are less certain of the goals and their order of importance, and where each of the possible choices will lead:

> Perhaps the differences between the two can best be summarized by a pair of similes. To the drifter the school career is like a pinball machine and he has little control over how he progresses from one end to the other. To the planner, on the other hand, the school career is like a road map with alternative but clearly marked routes to various valued destinations.
>
> Dale, 1972b

CONCLUSION

Many of the messages learnt from the spatial layout of schools and classrooms, as outlined in the previous chapter, are reinforced by the messages learnt from the timetables. To parody Kohl's comments about classrooms, a timetable is not an arbitrary arrangement of time: it represents in outline form the timetable designers' beliefs and assumptions about knowledge, about learning, about teaching and about the outcomes of schooling. This selection of beliefs, often made by ancestors long gone, is only one of several alternative sets of belief about these matters.

Summary

1. The activity of breaking time into small segments is common to many situations.
2. In school there are competing claims about what should be learnt and so time has to be rationed as a scarce item.
3. Timetables are some of the most taken-for-granted aspects of school culture and the hidden assumptions are rarely investigated.
4. A given timetable is only one of several possible ways of organizing, and the one chosen will reflect features of an ideology of education.
5. Some of the features of the implicit ideology of education are revealed by asking questions about who timetables, when timetabling takes place and what is timetabled.
6. From a timetable, pupils learn a great deal more than where to go at a certain time. They may also learn some messages of the hidden curriculum, e.g. which knowledge is seen as male knowledge and which is seen as female.
7. The hidden assumption of deferred gratification may be a more familiar message to one social class grouping than to another and consequent adjustment to it less of a problem.
8. The subjective interpretations of timetables by pupils and staff illustrate the ambiguity of many human experiences: the interpretations of like, dislike, useful and useless have to be learned.

9. Many of the hidden messages of the spatial arrangements of schools are reinforced by the timetable arrangements.

Further Reading

Ball S., Hull, R., Skelton, M. and Tudor, R. (1984) 'The Tyranny of Devil's Mill: Time and Task at School', in S. Delamont (ed.), *Readings in Interaction in the Classroom*. London: Methuen.

Bilton, H. (1994) 'Morning and Afternoon Sessions in the Nursery, Do They Have Equal Status? With Particular Reference to Stratum', *International Journal of Early Years Education*, **2**, 2.

Campbell, J. (1994) 'Managing the Primary Curriculum: The Issue of Time Allocation', *Education 3–13*, **22**, 1.

Dale, R. (1972) *The Use of Time in School*. Milton Keynes: Open University Press.

Jones, P. (1992) 'The Timing of the School Day', *Educational Psychology in Practice*, **8**, 2.

Horton (1979) 'Time and Cool People', in L. Rainwaer (ed.), *Black Experience Soul*. New Brunswick, NJ: Transaction Books.

Roth, J. (1971) 'The Study of Career Timetables', in B. Cosin *et al.* (eds), *School and Society*. London: Routledge and Kegan Paul. A useful summary of ideas.

Sylva, K. and Siraj-Blatchford, I. (1992) 'Top-down Effects of the National Curriculum on Pre-school Education', *International Journal of Early Childhood*.

Watts, J. (1977) *The Countesthorpe Experience*. London: George Allen and Unwin. This book contains some accounts of negotiated timetables.

Discussion and Activities

1. Obtain copies of some of the following: a further or higher education prospectus; an infant school timetable; an Open University student's personal timetable; any other educational timetable. Compare them using some of the analyses of this chapter.

2. Discuss how you would organize your time if you decided to educate yourself or your children at home. Analyse your timetable using any appropriate questions from the research exercise in this chapter

Signposts

1 Gender and the computer studies option in secondary schools
One study is Hoyles, C. (1988) *Girls and Computers*. Institute of Education Bedford Way Papers.

2. Transfer to secondary schooling
A new style of timetabling is encountered by those pupils who leave middle school for secondary school. See Measor, L. and Woods, P. (1984) *Changing Schools*, Milton Keynes: Open University Press. The same experience faces those who transfer from primary to secondary school, and a source here is Derricott, R. (ed.) (1984) *Curriculum Continuity: Primary to Secondary*, Windsor: NFER-Nelson.

3. Read the following account by Derry Hannam about Sudbury school and consider what it would be like without a timetable – can we trust students and teachers to manage their own time?

OK You're Certified!

'OK You're certified,' said the friendly twelve-year-old boy. Throughout 25 years of advocating the democratisation of schools I have often feared these words yet when they were finally delivered the context was delightful. I was visiting the Sudbury Valley School in Framingham, Massachusetts.

The introductory tour took us to the music room. As a one-time jazz musician I have a compulsion to try out musical instruments. On opening the grand piano our guide politely asked 'Are you certified to do that? I don't want to have to bring you up!' He explained that every specialist area of the school was managed by a 'corporation' of students and staff who had a particular expertise and interest in that area. I needed a member of the music corporation to certify me on the piano before I was free to play it. I asked who could do this.

'I can,' he said. 'Play me something you love.'

Eight bars of Satin Doll later – 'That's real pretty. OK You're certified'. He added my name to the list of the certified and in those few moments I learned a great deal about this truly and remarkably democratic school.

Had I not been certified I would have been brought up before the JC – Judicial Committee – for breaking one of the many school rules, all of which are agreed by the school meeting or the specialist corporation on a strictly one person one vote basis, and all of which can be changed democratically. The JC consists of students representing different age groups and a staff member, the business being conducted by two elected clerks who are always older students.

The first thing to strike a visitor to Sudbury Valley School is that there are a lot of people around. The school is currently full with 210 students aged from 4 to 19 and for the first time since its foundation in 1968 is oversubscribed with plans for extensions to the buildings. Yet although there is no overt adult supervision of anything, the facilities are well looked after, the extensive library is in good shape, computers work and normally rooms are reasonably tidy though everything is in constant use.

David Gribble of Sands School had told me that 'It will feel like break (recess) when you arrive'. He was right – and it went on feeling like break for the whole 4 days of our visit! There are no teacher organised lessons, the curriculum being totally generated by the students. The many rooms of varying sizes do not feel like classrooms. Individuals, small and not so small groups of students are everywhere. Occasionally they are with a staff member (not often referred to as teachers) working at anything from algebra to apple pie making. These tutorials/seminars are always at the request of students – either individual or group (often of mixed ages) – and will continue for as long as the students feel they need them. If after two sessions student interest fades no pressure at all will be exerted by staff for the 'course' or 'project' to be completed to the satisfaction of the adults.

The USA is mercifully free of national examinations. Each state accredited school can devise its own school leaving graduation. At Sudbury Valley this consists of a defended thesis, delivered to a full school assembly of students, staff, governors and parents, justifying that the student is ready to leave school and cope in the big wide world.

Of Ofsted's Assessment, Recording and Reporting there is no sign. There is no formal assessment of students' work. No records of achievement or progress are kept and no reports given to parents. There are currently ten staff but many are part-time. Their contracts are reviewed annually and by secret ballot students decide whose will be renewed and for how many days per week. Although fees are low by US or UK standards the school is in good financial shape. Co-operation with the local Framingham School Board is close and supportive. Roughly half the students are 'lifers' who have been at the school from early choice. The other half are 'refugees' from the region's public (state) schools.

The support for the school of all the students I spoke to was total but especially impressive were the comments of some of the refugees. Bullying was mentioned by several as their reason for transferring to Sudbury Valley. 'Does it happen here?' I asked.

'It's just not possible', was the reply. 'The bullies would be brought up at JC and it would stop. If it didn't the case would go to trial before the school meeting and if it still didn't stop they would be thrown out of school.'

'When was the last trial of a bully?' I asked. Nobody could remember. Several JC cases that we observed concerned what might be the first stage of bullying – they were all settled amicably but firmly after very fair exploration of both sides.

The first teacher that I met from the school was Mimsy Sadofsky. I asked the obvious literacy questions. 'They learn to read in their own time and when they feel the need,' she said. 'Nobody ever leaves the school unable to read though we have had quite a few who did not learn until they were nine or ten. Even though statistically we must have had our 10% of potential dyslexics there has never been a dyslexic student at Sudbury Valley.'

I pressed Danny Greenberg, a founder staff member and philosopher of the school, about what becomes of ex-SVS students after they leave. He directed me to Legacy of Trust – the most recent and extensive of two longitudinal studies of ex-students going back to the original intake in 1968. Virtually all have made a success of their lives in their own terms and look back to SVS as a time that truly belonged to them rather than some thing that was done to them by teachers or a national curriculum! It makes exciting reading.

From *Education Now News and Review*, **11**, Spring 1996, by Derry Hannam

9 The Official Curriculum

The wish to preserve the past rather than the hope of creating the future dominates the minds of those who control the teaching of the young.

Bertrand Russell

INTRODUCTION

This chapter concentrates on the hidden aspects of the official curriculum. Many of the writings on the hidden curriculum contrast it with the official curriculum, and the hidden aspects of the content of schooling, of school knowledge itself, can all too easily be missed in such an analysis. It is the 'ghosts of the school-book writers' referred to earlier and the ghosts of curriculum designers that are looked for in what follows.

The two examples looked at in Chapter 6 are worth considering again briefly to establish the approach. The world of the reading schemes in use in primary schools contains messages along with the carefully graded exercises to build up learner reading skills in gradual stages. These messages reflect the views of the writers about their world. One message is sexism: dominant males involved with careers and work are contrasted with passive females in domestic roles, and paralleled with similar roles for the children. Boys are involved in adventures, while girls help mothers with housework. Lobban (1975) concludes that this is even more sexist than the real world, and abdicates entirely any chance of helping boys and girls to think about possible future alternatives.

The other example given was sex education books, in which the writers pass on their views about chastity, marriage and sex rather than informing pupils dispassionately about human sexuality and the alternative views about it. Hoffman (1975) shows that in these accounts erroneous information is passed off as fact and Victorian beliefs about sex are dominant and expressed as the one right way of interpretation.

KNOWLEDGE IN SCHOOL IS NOT NEUTRAL

The proposition argued throughout this chapter is that the common-sense view that knowledge in school is neutral is mistaken. This is not a new idea. In 1916, Russell was writing about school subjects in this vein:

> It is in history and religion and other controversial subjects that the actual instruction is positively harmful. These subjects touch the interests by which schools are maintained; and the interests maintain the schools in order that certain views on these subjects may be instilled. History, in every country, is so taught as to magnify that country: children learn to believe that their own country has always been in the right and almost always victorious, that it has produced almost all the great men, and that it is in all respects superior to all other countries. Since these beliefs are flattering, they are easily absorbed, and hardly ever dislodged from instinct by later knowledge.

SOCIOLOGICAL QUESTIONS ABOUT SCHOOL SUBJECTS

The use of the word 'subject' here is not meant to exclude the content of infant and primary school curricula: 'reading', 'number' and 'creative activities' may be interpreted as broader, more loosely organized school subjects, and the subjects of secondary schools as narrower and more constrained versions of subjects.

Adopting a similar approach to that used earlier in an analysis of assessment, what follows will be an attempt to develop answers to the following questions:

1. Which subjects are selected, and which versions of subjects?
2. Whose subjects are these and who selects this knowledge?
3. Why subjects and what kind of knowledge is this?
4. How are subjects implemented and what kinds of presentation are adopted?

SCHOOL SUBJECTS

History

In the famous satire, *1066 and All That*, the outcome of much school history is portrayed as oversimplification:

> War with Zulus. Cause: the Zulus. Zulus exterminated. Peace with Zulus.

One aspect of this oversimplification is the charge that school history teaching promotes nationalism and ethnocentric attitudes:

> Every State wishes to promote national pride, and is conscious that this cannot be done by unbiased history. The defenceless children are taught by distortions and suppressions and suggestions. The false ideas as to the history of the world which are taught in the various countries are of a kind which encourages strife and serves to keep alive a bigoted nationalism. If good relations between States were desired, one of the first steps ought to be to submit all teaching of history to an international commission, which should produce neutral textbooks free from the patriotic bias which is now demanded everywhere.

Even though these comments were written by Russell in 1916, there appears to be only one case of their being taken seriously. The Scandinavian countries have a procedure for submitting their history books for scrutiny so that inaccurate or biased comments about each other can be identified. They can then be drawn to the attention of pupils, or the books can be rewritten or juxtaposed with alternative versions. In support of Russell's point, a recent survey of history books in use in junior schools in Britain came to the following conclusions about the teaching of the history of South Africa. Nash found that the bias of these books was evident in their selectivity. Only four of the books mentioned the existence of black slavery, and then only in passing:

> There were thousands upon thousands of slaves in South Africa during the seventeenth, eighteenth and nineteenth centuries, but children taught from these texts would never know. Even where proper mention is made, it is usually in emotionally neutral terms, as if making slaves of people were a quite acceptable and normal way of treating them. For example: 'To help them in their work they used slaves who were Negroes brought from other parts of Africa and poor people from Asia.'
>
> Nash, 1972

Nash comments that this is written in the same tone in which we might say that people use knives and forks to eat with, so that no reader would guess that the scars of over 200 years of slavery remain, and that they still have a powerful influence on South Africa. In Nash's view, the most significant evasion of the texts is that there is no mention of white supremacy. The total control by the white population of government, military, judiciary, police, industry and the mass media is not indicated by the books he studied. The books avoid the word apartheid: only one text contains it, even though all these books were published or revised after 1948, when the apartheid policy was implemented. When surveying the textbooks, Nash had before him the following five questions:

1. Is a history of South Africa given or only a history of European settlement?
2. Is the history of black slavery discussed?
3. Is white supremacy admitted?
4. Are derogatory terms used when discussing black or coloured South Africans?
5. Is apartheid or segregation admitted?

The results are shown in Table 9.1.

Table 9.1 Summary of bias in 14 primary-school textbooks in their accounts of South Africa

	No	Yes
History begins before European settlement	12	2
Gives account of slavery	10	4
Discusses apartheid	12	2
Admits white supremacy	13*	1
Uses derogatory terms when discussing native Africans	4	10

* In four of these cases a bright child might infer from the context that the whites are in control, but there is no clear statement.

It might be said that South Africa is a particularly sensitive example and that perhaps the treatment of other countries is less slanted. Nash disagrees. Here are his findings about the history of India in the same books:

> The history of India, for example, provides a parallel case. This is essentially the story of the East India Company (presented as a respectable body of merchants engaged in legitimate trade) and its wars with the French and the Indians. A great deal is made of native atrocities (always exemplified by the black hole of Calcutta) and of Robert Clive. In the following passage note how, in typical schoolmasterly language, Clive 'punishes' the 'cruel' native ruler:
>
> 'You will remember Suraj Dowlah, a cruel native ruler of Bengal. He attacked the East India company's fort near Calcutta, but he was punished by Bob Clive, who defeated his enemy at Plassey and then conquered Bengal.'
>
> And, of course British rule – just as it was in South Africa – is unreservedly maintained to have been beneficial to the development of India: 'During the first half of Queen Victoria's reign Britain had done much to help the millions of pesants who were ignorant and poor. Steamers now traded with all their ports, the first railroad was being laid between Calcutta and Bombay; and the telegraph enabled important messages to travel swiftly. Also, many cruel customs had been abolished and plans had been made to feed sufferers in time of famine and to educate native children.'
>
> One hardly has to be an expert on colonial history to appreciate that most of this is nonsense. The motives for expansion into India, even more than in Africa, were economic. The Indian subcontinent was virtually stripped of its wealth during the 200 years of British imperialism. Its thriving textile industry was ruined for the benefit of Lancashire and, by the end of the nineteenth century, returns from India provided more than two-fifths of Britain's balance of payments surplus. This surely benefited the Indians less than ourselves.
>
> Nash, 1972
>
> (This first appeared in *New Society*, London, the weekly review of the social sciences.)

Another hidden message of history teaching is sexism, according to various analyses of the content of textbooks and syllabuses. Millstein concludes from a survey of USA school books that history, as purveyed by such textbooks, was quite clearly *his*-story and not *her*-story (Millstein, 1972). An interesting example of how such a bias can influence a writer is given in the two illustrations in Figure 9.1.

Figure 9.1 The medieval illustration shows women rabbit hunting. *In A Portrait of Britain in the Middle Ages 1066– 1485*, men have taken over in R. S. Sherriff's otherwise similar illustration. From the *Times Educational Supplement*, 29 November 1974.

The conclusion of Davies (1974) about sex bias in history teaching is that:

> the hidden curriculum in history teaching is heavily biased towards sexual inequality. I am not complaining that most societies of the past were sexually unequal; that, fact or fiction, is beyond my desire or capacity to change. It is our present study of those societies that is sexist, and it bears a heavy responsibility for forming the belief that it is somehow abnormal to be female . . . the sexually prejudiced areas of our society are largely formed and reinforced by the way we teach and learn about the past.

Music

The content of school music has been subjected to analysis by Shepherd *et al.* (1977) and provides some very clear examples of selection in content. The consequence, they argue, is the alienation of pupils from music teaching: pupils in school are usually very interested in music, but they are usually not very interested in school music. The problem is rooted more in teachers' definitions of music than in the supposed lack of ability of pupils. The content of school music is usually defined so that:

> university students as much as kids in school music lessons get a hidden curriculum of themes like the following: that whilst popular music is socially significant and conditioned, 'serious' music is not, but reflects simply the creative purpose of the composer; that 'serious' music equals art, whilst popular music cannot be considered as 'proper' music at all; that 'serious' music is exempt from the commercial pressures which bedevil popular music; that

analysis of music presupposes analysis of musical notation and that musical analysis can objectively elucidate the meaning of music and act as a guide to relative musical value.

Vulliamy, 1978

All these assumptions, Vulliamy argues, can be shown to be dubious. First, the view that there is an objective yardstick by which you can measure classical music against jazz or rock music fails to recognize that the musical languages are quite different: the first uses a notated tradition, while the second two use improvisation in an aural tradition. It follows that there can be criteria for good and bad classical music and criteria for good and bad jazz, but not criteria to compare the two. The commercial pressures on popular music led to the pop musicians themselves identifying good 'pop' as against commercial 'pop', although the term 'popular' is a misleading oversimplification:

it must be emphasized that the term 'pop' music is a thoroughly misleading one, in that it covers many different types of music, some of which are popular and some of which are not, some of which are found on LP records (which since 1968 have outsold singles in absolute terms) and some on singles records. Various types of so-called 'pop' music (soul, Tamla Motown, teeny-bopper pop, rock, folk, reggae, 'progressive' music, to name but a few) not only have very different musical origins and qualities but also appeal to widely different social groups.

Vulliamy, 1978

Vulliamy states that the view that all 'pop' music is commercial is a vast oversimplification. Although the prime consideration of some musicians is money, others set out to create what they regard as serious artistic music. However, serious jazz or rock musicians who want to create music which, owing to its experimental nature, is unlikely to be commercial, rarely get help from the grant-aiding bodies. They also miss out on media exposure: the BBC policy appears to limit broadcasting serious jazz and rock. Radio 1, which is said to be the popular music provision, promotes commercial singles, and the two categories of music shown to be most popular with schoolchildren, namely progressive rock, and reggae and soul, are largely absent.

Vulliamy concludes that there has been an almost total neglect of jazz, rock and other forms of music in schools in both the USA and the UK. Academic music is totally dominated by so-called 'serious' music in the notated European tradition, and neither GCSE nor A level syllabuses consider the various forms of Afro-American music with their non-notational traditions. The conclusion is that pupils' musical knowledge and concerns are invalidly rejected: school music is 'their' music, not 'our' music, and the reasons for this tell us more about the misconceptions of the musical establishments in universities and elsewhere than about the nature of music.

Domestic Science

Domestic science was a regular feature of the school curriculum in the UK until the late 1970s when it was phased out by the National Curriculum legislation. As a subject, it illustrates several issues. First, it illustrates the idea of the stratification of knowledge, i.e. that some subjects are deemed to be more important than and superior to others. For the purposes of university entrance, an A level in domestic science is usually counted as GCSE only. In studies of the sixth form curriculum, it consistently comes at the bottom of the list of acceptable subjects, whether viewed by university tutors, employers, teachers or pupils. Yet as those who have experienced domestic science courses have consistently reported, the courses are demanding in both written and practical examinations.

Domestic science is a required study in some European countries, and required equally for boys and girls. In Britain, however, it is defined in practice as a girls' subject. The actual questions used in examinations signal this clearly:

> You and your husband are going to spend a weekend with your parents. Launder a selection of your own and your husband's clothes: these should include a variety of fabrics and finishes. Name these fabrics with labels, when displaying your finished work. Prepare a meatless evening meal for the two of you, using up leftover cooked vegetables and stale bread.
>
> Metropolitan CSE paper, 1974

Defined as a girls' subject, domestic science becomes a potential carrier for sexist assumptions about society. In a survey of textbooks available for teaching the subject, Wynn (1977) discerns these messages to girls and to the few boys who study domestic science. She concludes that any girl doubtful of the positive virtues of household tasks would be under attack. It would be suggested that her marriage would break down. She would be warned that her man would turn to drink if the home were not organized to his satisfaction. So any man who drinks to excess is in a position to blame his wife's failings.

> There have been some concessions made to the present interests of girls. One of these has been the development of courses in 'good grooming', which includes hygiene, appearance, make-up etc. These courses, whilst seen by some as an antidote to the 'future housewife' orientation of home economics, actually serve similar interests. Such courses help girls to think of themselves as ornamental creatures whose main aim in life should be to catch a suitable husband.
>
> Wynn, 1977

Wynn sees a theme which is missing from most domestic science courses: that of possible alternatives, especially those that would increase the chances of dual-career families. For Wynn, the characteristics of domestic science teaching in schools are sexist in that they mark out an almost exclusive domestic role for women. Employment is seen as a temporary activity that fills in awkward bits of time for women, rather than as a serious alternative to domesticity. Wynn concludes:

> Women's tasks in the home are envisaged as inevitable, as is the continuation of the family in its present form. Thus the stage is set for women to be used as cheap labour and to be exploited. The cultural pressures on women to conform to sex stereotypes start in infancy, and are reinforced in home economics.

Religious Education

Religious education had a unique place in the curriculum of schools in Britain before 1988 since here alone among the countries in Europe, it was compulsory by law. The only other compulsion of this kind was also religious – the daily act of worship in schools. RE is still compulsory but so are all the other subjects of the National Curriculum.

The hidden curriculum of RE teaching is perhaps indicated in the title of a document published in 1975 by the British Humanist Association arguing for the reform of the 1944 Education Act's provisions regarding the subject in schools. It was entitled 'Objective, Fair and Balanced', the assumption being that RE teaching was unbalanced and unfair and failed to be objective. One of the key objections of this document was that RE was often taught as if there were no alternative to Christianity, whether it be other religions or non-religious belief systems like humanism, existentialism or Marxism. Some advice to schoolteachers coping with young children's questions about religion will perhaps illustrate the point:

> Who made God? The simple answer to this is 'Nobody, God has always been there'. If He had been made by somebody else, we should then want to know who had made that person, and so we could go back until we got to someone who had started it all – and that Someone is God. If we reflect a little, we soon discover that all things begin with God. For instance, the table in the kitchen is made from wood, the wood came from a tree, but God put the tree there and made it grow. The child's woollen jersey came from a sheep – and who made the sheep and gave it life? – God.
> So we can go on, tracing all things back to God, who is the beginning of everything.
>
> Hunt, 1974

Objections to this advice as failing to be objective are made on two grounds:

1. The logical form of the question is not pursued: the next question, using such a logical sequence, must be 'and who started or created God?' It is just as logical to argue that the universe has always been there as it is to argue that God has always been there.
2. By omitting any qualification like 'the answer that believers or Christians give is . . .', the hidden message is that everyone agrees that this is the answer: alternative answers, by implication, simply do not exist, or are not recognized.

Figure 9.2 Different flat map projections of the globe. (a) Mercator projection. (b) Peters projection. (c) MacArthur's universal corrective map. (d) Peters/MacArthur projection.

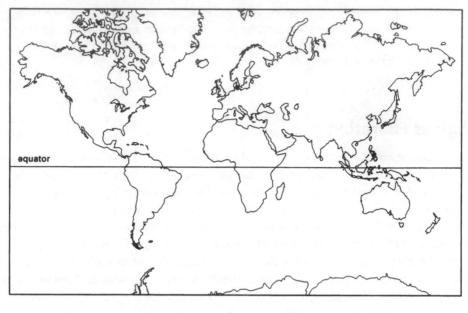

(a)

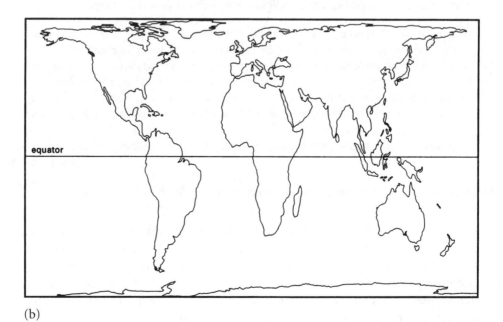

(b)

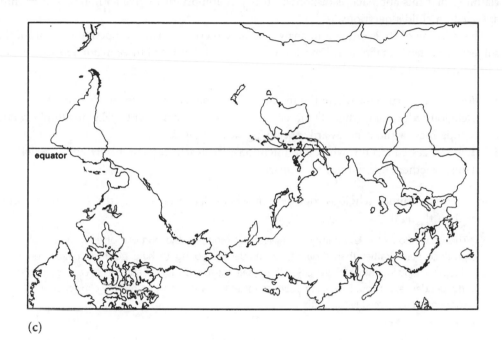

(c)

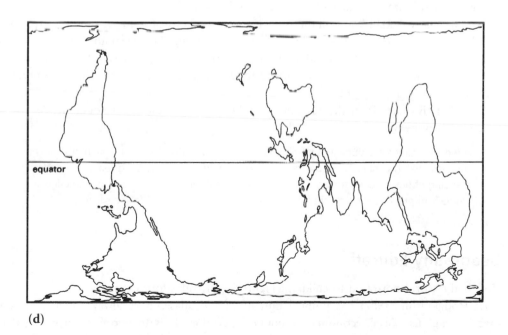

(d)

Interestingly, Hunt goes on to say, with unconscious irony in the light of the objection claiming that this approach is dishonest, 'It is very important to give an honest and truthful answer to a child's questions.'

The teaching of RE is difficult to analyse because there are many competing versions of the subject in existence at the same time. Stopes-Roe (1976) has listed three major versions, which can be described as:

1. Religious instruction, where the intention is to convert children to Christianity.
2. Religious education, where the intention is to convert children to religious thinking and sympathies, without necessarily specifying which religion.
3. Life stances education, where the intention is to teach dispassionately about belief systems, whether supernatural or secular.

The outcome of much religious education in schools has been seen as the advocacy of belief rather than thought:

> The prevention of free inquiry is unavoidable so long as the purpose of education is to produce belief rather than thought, to compel the young to hold positive opinions on doubtful matters rather than to let them see the doubtfulness and be encouraged to independence of mind. Education ought to foster the wish for truth, not the conviction that some particular creed is the truth.
>
> Russell, 1916

In contrast, the advice offered to teachers in 1974 by Hunt stressed belief rather than thought: 'We know that there is a heaven because Jesus told us so'.

The fact that we don't know all the answers can be one way of pointing out how great and wonderful God is – the only Being who does know everything. There is nothing wrong in thus instilling a sense of awe into a child, and little children will happily accept that there is One who is above (in the right sense) us all, and to whom we can safely leave these big puzzles, because He loves us all so much.

An alternative view from the advocates of religious education is less dogmatic. As Owen Cole (1978) writes:

> if we are helping the pupil in his search for meaning we must not predetermine the limits and say that his solution will be religious. He should, therefore, be given some understanding of how people can work out their place in existence without reference to religion. Humanism provides such a coherent alternative view of life.

Geography Education

How is the world portrayed to children? Figure 9.2 provides four examples.

As Hodgkinson (1987) has pointed out, maps and atlases have always been made for specific religious, social, economic or political purposes. It is therefore unsurprising that hidden biases may be found. Maps of the world seek to represent a three-dimensional reality on to a two-dimensional plane. The Mercator projection was developed in the sixteenth century primarily for navigation purposes. The map emphasizes those parts of the world considered most important at that time. Northern Europe provided the central axis to provide the traditional Eurocentric world view. Children take map design very literally, and the Peters projection was developed for UNICEF and Christian Aid in 1972. The Peters projection corrects the distortions introduced by Mercator; in particular it reduces the size of Europe and enlarges Africa to provide more realistic proportions. The map also restores the equator to the true centre of the map so that Africa can be seen to be a mainly northern, not southern, continent. It also shows India and Central America above the equator.

MacArthur produced his Universal Corrective Map by simply inverting the Mercator projection so that Europe is relegated to the bottom right-hand corner. As Hodgkinson says, the projection provides a fairly obvious piece of propaganda and is provided with an inset text: 'So spread the word. Spread the map! South is superior. South dominates! Long live AUSTRALIA – RULER OF THE UNIVERSE'.

Hodgkinson argues for an educational approach that makes the most of 'that most powerful pedagogic weapon, cognitive dissonance'. A course is outlined that provides a history of the development of our geographical framework:

1. Images of the world – Hindu, Amerindian, Eastern.
2. Early maps – ancient, medieval perspectives.
3. Carving up the world – Papal's line of 1494, Mercator and navigation.
4. World time – Harrison's chronometer, Greenwich, railway timetables, Universal Time.
5. Maps as world views, East/West and North/South conceptions. The politicization of maps.

Political Education

In the UK, political education has tended to be neglected as part of the official taught curriculum. This is not the case in other states, as Harber (1984) has noted. However, the hidden curriculum of the rest of school life is highly political, as was seen in the overview chapter of this section of the book. Harber (1984) quotes a cartoon that summarizes the findings well. A headteacher explains to an inspector, 'We concentrate on the 3Rs here: right wing views, reactionary ideas and respect for authority.' Harber's analysis concludes: 'The general thrust of schooling in terms of day to day messages and assumptions favours centre-right political values rather than centre-left ones.' It follows that the list of attitudes at the start of Chapter 6 and derived from Postman and Weingartner (1971) is, according to one point of view, the required outcome of education and is therefore good education.

The political education that does occur in the official curriculum has parallels with the case of religious education, in having various forms related to different ideologies of the subject.

1. The British constitution form – where the intention is to encourage children to adopt the British version of Westminister style representative democracy and therefore to perpetuate the status quo.
2. The democratic studies form – where the intention is to convert children to a generalized sympathy for democratic ideas without specifying a particular form of democracy.
3. The political enquiry form – where the intention is to explore critically all political belief systems and encourage political thinking and political skills rather than specific political beliefs.

The Curriculum Review Unit's Initial Training Panel has outlined five rather than three possible positions on political education. These are conservative, liberal, apolitical, reformist and radical (Porter *et al.*, 1983). However, Harber (1984) proposes that two positions occur more frequently in debates about the UK curriculum than any others. He describes these as the conservative and the liberal-reformist, the first limiting political education to the British constitution approach, the second favouring the democratic studies form, with the added idea of increasing the potential for democratic participation in economic, educational and political influence groups (such as pressure and interest groups). Harber (1984) argues that 'Conservative resistance to newer approaches in political education [is] not about a threat from the left but about a threat to their own hegemony'.

Russell, writing in 1916, saw the conservative approach as an infringement of the rights of children and tantamount to lying to pupils:

> Education is, as a rule, the strongest force on the side of what exists and against fundamental change: threatened institutions, while they are still powerful, possess themselves of the educational machine, and instil a respect for their own excellence into the malleable minds of the young. Reformers retort by trying to oust their opponents from their positions of vantage. The children themselves are not considered by either party; they're merely so much material, to be recruited into one army or the other. If the children themselves were considered, education would not aim at making them belong to this party or that but at enabling them to choose intelligently between the parties; it would aim at making them able to think, not at making them think what their teachers think. Education as a political weapon could not exist if we respected the rights of children. If we respected the rights of children, we should educate them so as to give them the knowledge and the mental habits required for forming independent opinions; but education as a political institution endeavours to form habits and to circumscribe knowledge in such a way as to make one set of opinions inevitable.

Russell's analysis is lost on those who respond to any attempt to reform political education with the comment that it is left-wing indoctrination.

In England, education for democratic citizenship has been compulsory in all schools. There are, however, large problems concerning the contradictory educational contexts into which this has been introduced, sometimes likened to 'reading holiday brochures whilst in prison' – Harber, C. (2002) 'Not quite the revolution: citizenship in England', in Davies, L., Harber, C.

and Schweisfurth, M. (eds), *Learning Democracy and Citizenship: International Experiences*, Oxford: Syposium Books.

Science

One view of science teaching in schools is that it serves as a sociological case study of the irony of human action. Science education was seen by its pioneers as radical, as leading to thought rather than belief, as undermining dogmatic forms of knowledge. Young (1976) argues that it has become almost the opposite, has developed as an alternative dogma, has become, in Russell's terms, 'a grave of intelligence'.

Young sees school science as carrying a series of hidden messages. The first, exemplified clearly in the specialized room of the laboratory, is that science is removed from everyday life:

> School science separates science from pupils' everyday lives, and in particular, their non-school knowledge of the natural world. It is learnt primarily as a *laboratory* activity, in a room full of special rules, many of which have no *real* necessity except in terms of the social organization of the school.

In contrast, the Open University foundation course in science operates without a laboratory, and undergraduate students do their experiments at home in the kitchen or garage, using a home experiment kit and improvised apparatus.

A second message, Young argues, is that if it is relevant science or applied science it is inferior. A rather startling example is the polarization of science and domestic science: the chemistry, physics and biology of kitchen, household, cooking, cleaning and house maintenance are so low in status that an A level in their study counts as a GCSE in one of the 'pure' sciences. Further examples are the separation of applied sciences like metalwork and woodwork, which then require a special project technology to try to upgrade these technological subjects in the knowledge hierarchy.

A third message stressed by Hine (1975) is that science, as presented in school, is dehumanized. He argues that there is no attempt to present Newton in the round, i.e. Newton as a person, his place in history, his non-scientific concerns. The work is extracted and presented out of human context as an explanation of so-called non-human events. This dehumanization makes the material completely different from that in other subjects.

> It is possible that a more complete study of Newton, including his preoccupation with magic, his relationship to his contemporaries, his particular use of the scientific method, to give only a few possibilities, could complement the study of Shakespeare, for instance. A study of Newton could show the fallibility of science, instead of emphasizing its dogmatic elements.
>
> Hine, 1975

The methods of teaching science in school are also held to carry hidden messages. In a study of how teachers use language in schools, Barnes *et al.* (1969) conclude about both arts teachers and later science teachers in their sample: 'teachers were teaching as though their tasks were more concerned with information than thought. If so, this is the version of the subjects that the children were learning.' This effect is reinforced by something like an obsession with technical terms: 'The act of giving a technical name seems for many teachers to have taken on a value of its own in separation from its utility.'

Barnes *et al.* find that, whether they intend it or not, by their use of language, science teachers were portraying their subjects as ready-reckoner systems of true answers, rather than principles of thinking through problems and constantly reviewing answers always held as probabilities, rather than certainties. In addition, they were signalling to pupils that their role as learners was passive: it was to reproduce information or reasoning, rather than to think for themselves.

None of these hidden messages is inevitable. An account by Hoskyns (1976) describes how he set about reducing both the message of laboratories as alien places and the message of the separation of pupils' everyday science and school science:

> I opened the labs in the lunch hour and after school and pursued a policy of reacting to whatever the students suggested with a 'yes' rather than a 'no'. I introduced a number of routines and activities which I dropped if students rejected them and kept if they were enthusiastic. The atmosphere in the lab was not right, so I fitted a hi-fi amplifier and speakers into the lab with a radio and turntable; some pupils actually found it easier to work with Radio 1 in the background, while others started to bring their own records. We started a record loan club. As I got to know the students (especially in the evenings when they came up to work in the Youth Centre) I decided to build on the success of the music and make available other facilities which could be loosely allied to physics. We introduced a loan service for equipment at the weekend. We designed and built radio-controlled cars and introduced photography with a permanent darkroom. We built a discotheque and used it in the school hall and local clubs. We encouraged those with an interest in electronics to build and test circuits out of *Practical Electronics* and similar magazines. We got some guitar amplifiers and cabinet speakers and let groups of two or three students use a room to practise with microphones and tape recorders in the Youth Centre in the evenings. I discovered that the computer terminal was free of charge after 6.30 p.m., so that students could run programmes up until 9.30 p.m. I got four people from Imperial College to help with the cars, the computing and the electronics in the evening. A number of third-year undergraduates came during the day and in the holidays to study the experiments in the Nuffield Course, to help students doing them and also to improve that section of the course for the following year. They responded particularly to the informality of the lab and the music and the confident way in which our pupils could talk about the difficulties they were having with the Physics.
>
> These sorts of facilities, which have developed over a number of years, are based upon an initial attempt to create the right atmosphere for mutual confidence between pupils and teachers. It is not particular innovations (music, model cars, etc.) that are important as any kind of magic formula. What is important is the continual effort to create a rich rather than a desiccated environment – one in which the activities and initiatives of the pupils and

teachers are stimulated rather than stunted, and one above all in which pupils have time to explore and familiarize themselves with equipment, ask questions and regain the confidence their earlier experience of schooling has so often removed.

In his account, Hoskyns notes how important it was to involve pupils in course planning to maintain pupil interest and concerns. Each holiday or the end of a term was a period of intense discussion about what was to be done in the next term or half term, and this ensured that pupils' needs were central to the work that followed. This approach also changed the use of resources. These became shelved until called on, rather than being fed in automatically to a preset plan. Such a course needed careful attention to structure, Hoskyns found, and, as a teacher, he could do too much or too little, for understanding came to be seen as a process that was full of contradictions. A student had to be free to pursue understanding in a way that was best for him, yet the information had to be available as he wanted it. Hoskyns found that the creative skills were given a chance to develop in the writing up of the work. To the question, 'What shall I write?', he learnt to reply 'Just anything you have done', instead of prescribing a rigid format. He found that his reply 'just anything you have done' stimulated a clear, often beautiful piece of work. Most science teaching in schools is not like this, Young (1976) suggests in his analysis of secondary school teaching. He argues that it tends to produce three broad groupings of people ready to fit into niches in society. These are the pure scientists, whose relations with the natural world are of a rather abstracted nature; the applied scientists, whose identity is essentially pragmatic – given something to be done, it is done, but ends are given, not selected; and third, there is the large group, the mass of people whose schooling teaches them that science is a specialized activity over which they neither have nor could have control.

Other Subjects

Most of the subjects in the school curriculum have been held to carry hidden messages, and a few are worth mentioning briefly.

Social science

Like science, social science was thought to be radical in its content and therefore to lead pupils to question and think rather than accept and believe. In practice, Reeves (1976) argues, the content:

> has passed through a complex filtration process, analogous to the processes of a sewage works. By the time it reaches the student, through the filter beds of various committees, examination board, schools council, publishing houses, headmaster, head of department and teacher, it is likely to have been cleansed of its most interesting radical pollutants.

The result, Reeves argues, is that pupils learn the hidden message that the parts of society fit together to form a relatively smooth-running machine of splendid complexity, with opportunities for small cogs to become larger cogs, provided they accept the modest starting positions awaiting the majority and believe in the virtue of the dominant group members.

Art

Art has been interpreted consistently as sculpture and painting, and the popular arts that many people practise, such as photography and gardening, have been either excluded or given supplementary status. The answer to the question 'Whose art?' often turns out to be 'their' art, high culture, upper-class art, and there are many similarities between art and music, examined earlier.

Languages

The case of languages raises an interesting issue. The attempts at future-looking, international cooperation- and communication-building languages like Esperanto are excluded from schools and universities. Examination boards refuse to recognize them. Latin, Greek and other ancient languages are 'suitable'; European languages are encouraged but in a form that stresses written rather than spoken skills; Russian and Chinese are reserved for a minority-interest group. These selections make plausible the charge that schools celebrate the past rather than prepare pupils for the future.

Mathematics

Maths dominates the curriculum as a 'true' subject of certain facts and reliable information, though many mathematicians would hold to a relativity view of their discipline and see school maths as 'imitation maths' of inferior quality (Sawyer, 1943). It dominates because it is held to be essential to so many other subjects. Yet logic, which is essential to an understanding of even more subjects, is excluded. School mathematics encourages belief and linear thinking, as Sawyer (1943) suggests, while logic encourages question, analysis and lateral thinking. One attempt to rectify this situation is that of de Bono and his CORT materials, designed to help pupils to learn to think logically.

THE SOCIOLOGY OF KNOWLEDGE

The sociology of knowledge is concerned with the existential conditions of knowledge and therefore with the study of the relationships between thought and society. Among the basic premises are that ideas are produced and received in a socio-historical setting and that knowledge is permitted or limited by social structures. Micro-perspectives in sociology stress that individuals are not entirely passive in this but are engaged in an active process of constructing their own knowledge and their own reality.

Putting this more simply, the proposition is that the knowledge needed at a particular time is produced in a society and restrictions are made on any knowledge produced that is not interpreted as desirable. For example, the technological knowledge to effect moon landings was produced in two societies when the political and military needs were established.

This kind of analysis can proceed only with a particular view of knowledge. It requires that the idea of 'best' knowledge or 'true objective' knowledge be suspended. Instead, knowledge is defined as what the participants believe or think is knowledge. It embraces the members' expectations, attitudes, myths, information and misinformation.

A SOCIOLOGY OF SCHOOL KNOWLEDGE

A number of questions are raised by a sociological approach to knowledge and schooling. They include:

1. What knowledge is available in classrooms?
2. If there are different stocks of knowledge, where do they come from?
3. What are the characteristics of school knowledge?
4. What happens if two stocks of knowledge are in competition?
5. Is some knowledge rejected or avoided?
6. Do the institutional features restrict knowledge?
7. How is knowledge assessed and with what consequences?
8. What alternative theories of knowledge are available?

Content

School knowledge may be interpreted as predominantly past-orientated, present-orientated or future-orientated. Past-orientated approaches will rely heavily on existing subject divisions on the grounds that the knowledge gathered in the past is comprehensive and reliable, and the allocation into subject areas soundly based.

Present-orientated knowledge approaches stress integration of some kind on the grounds that current 'problems' like terrorism, pollution, computer technology and mass media communication are both cross-disciplinary and in need of new kinds of knowledge to cope with them.

Future-orientated knowledge approaches stress that the rate of change in technology and society, and the rate of production of new knowledge, imply that learners need to acquire skills of learning, relearning and developing new knowledge. Generally, education needs to cope with the 'knowledge explosion', where, it is argued, the amount of knowledge is estimated to be doubling every ten years.

It follows that a past-orientated view would favour Latin as part of the curriculum, a present-orientated view contemporary French and German, and a future-orientated view

Esperanto as an international language with political implications for the 'problem' of nationalism.

Structure: Stratification of School Knowledge

Some knowledge in schools is granted high status and some low status. One division is between examined knowledge and non-examined knowledge. A case that illustrates this is that of the social sciences in the school curriculum. Cannon (1964) shows how social studies remained of low status until some of the individual social sciences became established as examination subjects at A and O level. Psychology, economics and sociology now attract large numbers of candidates, especially at A level examinations.

The examination subjects themselves are ranked though the perception of these rankings may vary. Among parents, perception varies with social class. Miles (1969) showed that the correlation between subjects at O level and social class of parents supported the interpretation that parents in higher social/economic groups favour non-practical subjects like Latin, whereas the reverse applies in the case of parents in lower social/economic groups. Using IQ as an indicator, Miles argues that an undue number of higher social/economic background candidates are missing from the practical subjects and vice versa.

The interpretations by university admission personnel are available from a study of the sixth form curriculum (Reid, 1972). This shows that science subjects have wide acceptability, although internally ranked in the order of maths, physics, chemistry and biology, whereas arts and social science subjects have less acceptability. Thus a stratification of subjects is found on attempting entrance to a university: some subjects have greater market value than others. The rankings are given in Table 9.2.

Table 9.2 Acceptability of 'A' level subject passes to a sample of university departments (n = 84)

Mathematics (Pure)	0.92	German	0.63
Mathematics (Pure w. Stat.)	0.83	Economics	0.62
Mathematics (Pure w. Mech.)	0.82	Greek	0.62
Physics	0.81	Geology	0.61
Mathematics (SMP)	0.78	Biology (Nuffield)	0.60
Mathematics (further)	0.78	Latin	0.60
Physical Science	0.71	British Government	0.49
Chemistry	0.70	General Studies	0.49
Further Mathematics (SMP)	0.69	Engineering Science	0.46
History	0.67	Scripture Knowledge	0.46
Biology	0.66	Music	0.44
Geography	0.66	Art	0.37
French	0.65	Elements of Eng. Design	0.27
English Literature	0.64	Geometry and Eng. Drawing	0.27
Chemistry (Nuffield)	0.64	Housecraft	0.15
Spanish	0.64		

Another aspect of stratification is that of subjects as opposed to integrated fields of study. Young (1971) argues that the modifications in the curriculum have been of two kinds. There are those that maintain the view of subjects as the most suitable way of organizing knowledge and therefore introduce new subjects or rewrite a syllabus for an existing subject. Second, there are those that propose an alternative view of knowledge, e.g. as integrated fields of study. Innovations are then restricted to low-status pupils, thus confirming their official 'failure':

> by creating new courses in 'low status' knowledge areas and restricting their availability to those who have already 'failed' in terms of academic definitions of knowledge, these failures are seen as individual failures, either of motivation, ability or circumstances, and not failures of the academic system itself. These courses, which explicitly deny pupils access to the kinds of knowledge which are associated with rewards, prestige and power in our society, are thus given a kind of legitimacy, which masks the fact that educational success in terms of them would still be defined as 'failure'.

Young has also suggested the main criteria for the established subjects with high status:

> These are literacy, or an emphasis on written as opposed to oral presentation; individualism (or avoidance of group work or co-operativeness) . . . which focuses on how academic work is assessed and is a characteristic of both the 'process' of knowing and the way the 'product' is presented; abstractness of the knowledge and its structuring and compartmentalizing independently of the knowledge of the learner . . . finally and linked to the former is what I have called the unrelatedness of academic curricula, which refers to the extent to which they are 'at odds' with daily life and common experience . . .

The consequences of this stratification of knowledge are that teachers became stratified, pupils became stratified, school organizational systems stratify and the school 'product' — pupils at the end of their school career — is stratified.

Subjects as Social Systems

The analogy of subjects as social systems includes the following propositions. Subjects tend to have:

1. *Intiation procedures.* Newcomers are required to prove their acceptability by undergoing examinations at various levels: GCSE, A level, university degree. This establishes their commitment to the 'tribe' of chemists, geographers, sociologists or whatever.
2. *Specialist languages.* Many of the terms used in subjects have everyday-speech equivalents, but a technical language is developed and subject members are required to use this to maintain credibility.
3. *Boundary maintenance procedures.* Considerable effort goes into marking off laymen from initiated members and also into defining how the subject differs from other subjects.

'Popularizers' are usually regarded with antagonism, because they appear to dispel some of the mystery of the subject.

4. *Research conventions*. The conventions of research paper production and subject conferences encourage researchers to stay within a discipline. Cross-disciplinary and inter-disciplinary efforts are less likely to be acceptable. Moreover, the finance of research is organized by subject committees.

The operation of subjects as social systems has at least three possible consequences:

1. Teachers' activities are constrained and the way they perceive school activities and possibilities is limited: 'Just as most secondary teachers take their pupils as they find them, so they take for granted what it is they are supposed to be teaching. What they are teaching, if vague ideals like "cultivation" and "liberal knowledge" are set aside, is a body of subject matter related to their college or university specialism. Sometimes this knowledge is seen as simply utilitarian and directly vocational, sometimes as a training of the mind or even as an opportunity for self-awareness' (Holly, 1973). Holly argues that subject specialists are recruited to teach predefined areas of knowledge in a way that is not really open to discussion. It is therefore a rationalization, not a rationale, for a true rationale is possible only where the decisions have not already been made. In most secondary schools all the real curricular decisions have been made, he suggests.

2. A rational debate about change is unlikely and the development of a present or future view of knowledge to replace the past orientation of subjects is made difficult: 'On the whole, the most well established secondary school subjects are those which were developed at universities during the nineteenth century, the time when the secondary curriculum was last basically reformed from the classical tradition of the Renaissance – hence English, history, geography, arithmetic of the stocks-and-shares variety, Euclidian geometry, algebra, Newtonian physics, inorganic chemistry, 'governess' French, muscular-Christian games, classificatory biology plus a residue of Latin' (Holly, 1973). This is still the curriculum of the majority of secondary schools. To say that this curriculum in the last quarter of the twentieth century is at all rationally derived would be to fly in the face of reason, Holly concludes. Demonstrably it is the result of a historical process.

3. The stocks of knowledge brought to school by pupils are rejected. The knowledge and its sources available in classrooms can be represented diagrammatically, as shown in Figure 9.3.

The result of such a situation is that one definition of knowledge, a subject definition, is usually imposed, or an attempt is made to impose it, on the pupils. The case of music illustrates this well. The pupils' knowledge of music is rejected in an attempt to replace it with a subject-defined and, as Vulliamy argues, fallacious version of music. The outcome is that large numbers of pupils are alienated from school music and are prevented from having a

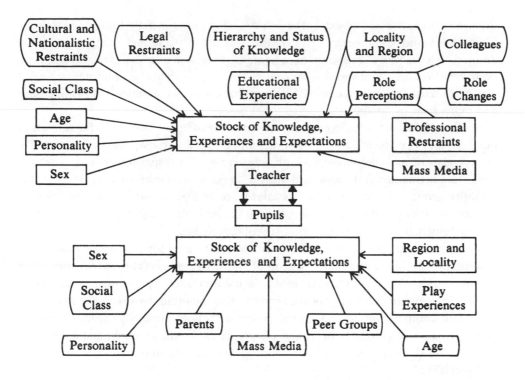

Figure 9.3 Teacher–pupil interaction as a confrontation of different stocks of knowledge.

sympathetic experience of classical among other musical forms, thus adopting an alternative fallacious view of music limited to African-American forms.

CONCLUSION

The case studies and the review of ideas from the sociology of knowledge should enable us to make some propositions in answer to the questions posed at the outset, which were:

1. Which subjects are selected, and which versions of subjects?
2. Whose subjects are these and who selects this knowledge?
3. Why subjects and what kind of knowledge is this?
4. How are subjects implemented and what kinds of presentation are adopted?

The following are some of the possibilities that were explored in this chapter:

1. The subjects selected tend to be those developed at universities during the nineteenth century. A few new subjects, e.g. sociology, have been partially adopted provided that

they were presented as 'subjects'. The versions of subjects include history with strong nationalistic and sexist perspectives, music and art with a 'high culture' selection, domestic science with a sexist outlook, a non-radical version of science and social science, both stressing acceptance and right-answer systems, a parochial and non-internationalist version of languages and a version of religion that excludes the outlook of many groups and individuals in Britain today.

2. Given the original date of many of these subjects, they often turn out to be the subjects of our ancestors: sex education has a Victorian morality and purpose; domestic science, the preservation of male dominance; RE, the prevention of a dispassionate look at alternatives to Christianity; and music and art, the subjects previously enjoyed by a wealthy minority group. The selection of this knowledge is maintained by the operation of subjects as social systems, thus tending to limit the outlook of teachers, to restrict change and to perpetuate a past orientation of school knowledge.

3. Subjects tend to persist for historical and social rather than for rational or educational reasons. Present- and future-based systems of knowledge are available outside more than they are inside schools, in the mass media, in industry and in government information services, in order to deal with modern problems like pollution, terrorism, the knowledge explosion, computerization and energy provision. School knowledge tends to remain past-orientated, to encourage belief and acceptance rather than thought and adaptation, to be a filtered and selected kind of knowledge. It is mostly non-integrated, fragmented and specialized.

4. Subjects are implemented by subject teachers' perception of their task as some kind of imposition requiring the rejection of much pupil knowledge. The social systems of subjects stratify teachers as well as pupils and schools, and limit perceptions of alternative ways of presenting knowledge.

Earlier in the book the limitation of analogies was mentioned; the hidden curriculum concept stresses selected features. The above summary is not meant to be a complete statement of what subjects achieve.

As a note of caution, the official curriculum teaches more than its hidden curriculum aspects, so pupils may be receiving complex and contradictory messages. A remaining question, therefore, is which set of messages is the most effective, or whether they cancel each other out. One answer is that of Postman and Weingartner, given in Chapter 6. However, it is not the only one.

Summary

1. The central proposition of this chapter is that the common-sense view that school knowledge is neutral is mistaken.
2. The case of history indicates how bias can enter a school subject through

oversimplification and selectivity. These biases may be systematic in promoting sexism, or an ethnocentric view of the world, or some other set of beliefs.

3. School music can be shown to teach a dubious view of musical styles based on the fallacy of objective standards across musical languages.

4. The characteristics of domestic science, as taught in most schools, can be shown to be sexist.

5. The only compulsory subject, religious education, is a potential and in many cases an actual source of indoctrination, and this is recognized by religious as well as non-religious critics. Political education raises similar issues.

6. The teaching of science frequently results in a view of the subject as more concerned with information than thought, as well as producing an alienated response from the majority of learners.

7. Other school subjects like art, languages and mathematics can be shown to lack the neutrality commonly seen as associated with them. Conversely, the supposed radicalism of social science in schools can be shown to be almost non-existent.

8. School knowledge can tend to be past-orientated, present-orientated or future-orientated. The first appears to be more common than the last.

9. School knowledge is stratified into high- and low-status subjects, and consequences of this include the eventual stratification of both teachers and pupils.

10. School subjects take on some of the characteristics of social systems and are therefore capable of perpetuating themselves beyond their time of usefulness, leaving us tied to the inadequate formulations of our ancestors.

11. The stock of knowledge brought to school by pupils is frequently rejected in favour of the teacher's stock of subject knowledge.

Further Reading

Goodson, I. (1983) *School Subjects and Curriculum Change*. Beckenham: Croom Helm.

Hammersley, M. and Hargreaves, A. (eds) (1983) *Curriculum Practice: Some Sociological Case Studies*. Lewes: Falmer Press.

Hodgkinson, K. (1987) 'Eurocentric Views – The Hidden Curriculum of Humanities Maps and Atlases', *Multicultural Teaching*, **5**, 2.

John, P. and Osborn, A. (1992) 'The Influence of School Ethos on Pupils' Citizenship Attitudes', *Education Review*, **44**, 2.

Whitty, G. (1977) *School Knowledge and Social Control*. Milton Keynes: Open University Press. Has three case studies of music, domestic science and physics in section 4 and a fourth – social studies – in section 7.

Whitty, G. and Young, M.F.D. (1976) *Explorations in the Politics of School Knowledge*. Driffield: Nafferton Books. A collection of sociological writings on the school curriculum.

Young, M.F.D. (1971) *Knowledge and Control*. West Drayton: Collier Macmillan. A well-known collection of papers on the sociology of school knowledge.

Discussion and Activities

1. Take a subject that is not discussed in the chapter, e.g. English, design and technology or physical education, and consider any hidden messages contained in their presentation in school.
2. Reading schemes are analysed by Lobban (1975) in terms of their sexist messages. Look at them in terms of their ethnic messages, their view of social class and their view of nationalism.
3. The compulsory act of worship has been seen as the source of varying degrees of attempted indoctrination. Discuss this aspect of the official curriculum. Useful sources are Hull, J. (1975) *School Worship: An Obituary*, London: SCM; and BHA (1979) *Objective, Fair and Balanced*, London: British Humanist Association. The first gives a Christian viewpoint, the second a humanist viewpoint.

Signposts

1. Microcomputers

The arrival of microcomputers in schools could make Russell's verdict quoted at the head of this chapter questionable. As Hart (2001) has argued, it is not too far-fetched to argue that Ivan Illich actually predicted the World Wide Web (www) 30 years ago (when he referred to 'opportunity webs'). Illich suggested a series of such networks which could replace schools, bringing together those who want to learn with those who want to teach voluntarily. He saw the process of education as a lifetime activity, the responsibility not of the state, but of individual learners. Illich (1971) proposed four interlocking 'educational networks', and Hart argues that the World Wide Web already provides each of them:

Network 1: Reference services

As Hart (2001) suggests, the Web provides a wealth of learning opportunities, 'from star charts to electronic circuits, from computer programs to pre-fabricated structures, from bookbinding to bombs'.

Network 2: Skill exchanges

Illich envisaged teachers advertising their services, and the Web already provides specialized lists of consultants that can be located with the use of sophisticated search engines.

Network 3: Peer matching

Illich described a communications network that allowed people to describe the learning activities in which they wanted to engage, in the hope of finding a partner for the enquiry. He was concerned to make the most of collaborative learning, and the sort of peer matching that he envisaged is now achieved through focused discussion groups which meet as Listservs and in online discussion forums.

As Hart points out, Illich even foresaw the emergence of Spam and other forms of system abuse:

> We must of course recognize the probability that such public matching devices would be used for exploitative and immoral purposes, just as the telephone and the mails have been so abused.

Network 4: Reference services to educators at large

Illich also described printed directories of those offering themselves as teachers, and it is clear that the entrepreneurial educator has already arrived in cyberspace, as evidenced by the following pages from a 'The Virtual University' website, where anyone can propose a course and teach it on the Web.

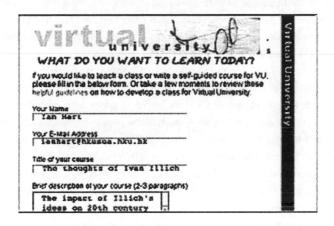

Figure 9.4 Invitation to teach.

It is perhaps surprising that despite so many of Illich's predictions of 30 years ago being realized, there is still no sign of a radical change in schooling. As Hart argues, the state continues to believe children need socializing, that they need to learn how to learn, and that this process needs to be accredited. But despite this, the Web will inevitably become more and more integrated in education. The real question may be whether it provides liberation, or is used to provide even more social control than we have already. To quote Hart (2001):

> There is a danger that in the multinational version of the Web (to paraphrase Illich) the cyberstudent will end up being schooled to accept entertainment in place of information, 'facts' in place of knowledge, affluence for the improvement of family life, the interests of shareholders with the wellbeing of society.

As educators we need to recognize that the anarchy of the Web is possibly the best hope for the survival of education, and so defend its independence. See Hart, I. (2001) 'Deschooling and the Web: Ivan Illich 30 years on', *Educational Media International*, **38**, 2–3; and Illich, I. (1971) *Deschooling Society*, New York: Harper and Row.

2. Political education
The issue of political education in schools has received attention in the UK recently. One collection of ideas is Harber, C. and Meighan, R. (1984) 'Political Education in 1981', special edition of *Educational Review*, **36**, 2. In Stradling, R. (ed.) (1983) *Political Education in West Germany and Britain*, London: Hansard Society, there is a checklist of twenty strategies for teachers to make sure pupils remain uncritically attached to the status quo. Sample strategies are:

- Do not allow the school council to develop to an extent where really important issues can be raised. The democratic decision-making in the school council is only a simulation. Safe agendas are best managed by the deputy head (pastoral), who understands the complexities of pupils' thinking. Free votes are usually safe however on subjects such as coffee-machines, fund raising, and prefect duties. N.B. If a school council does vote the wrong way on an important issue the following statement from the head is always a winner. 'In considering your proposal I have had to take account of the quality of the argument. Unfortunately other factors which you failed to consider have had to be borne in mind and I find myself having to overrule your proposition.'

- Label political education teachers who use a variety of learning strategies as 'progressive'. Any movement away from 'chalk-and-talk' is likely to cause you difficulties with your classes. Flexibility is anathema to the dedicated teacher who cannot afford to waste time preparing interesting or stimulating lesson material aimed at the ability levels of the pupils. Remember, uninterested pupils do not deserve time to be spent on them.

- Never feel guilty about showing favouritism to nice, clean, quiet, well turned-out pupils. This favouritism is good political education for the 'thickees' and 'louts' in a society where we know preference is always given to those who grease quietly against those who complain noisily, or try to change the rules of the system.

- Never allow pupils to participate in making decisions about planning after-school activities, trips abroad, or about the distribution of funds they have raised. Participation is time-consuming and never leads to the outcome you want anyway.

- Real-life experience of the pupils is to be ignored, since it confuses the formal learning they must acquire. In any case, textbook political theory is to be preferred because it remains non-active, and requires no real learning experience.

An interesting exercise would be to rewrite the twenty strategies to promote the opposite aim of encouraging political awareness.

3. International perspectives on the official curriculum

Again, it is useful to compare the official curriculum across different cultures. See Carter, C., Harber, C. and Serf, J. (2003) *Towards UBUNTU: Critical Teacher Education for Democratic Citizenship in South Africa and England.* Birmingham, Development Education Centre.

4. Green education

The various environmental crises, and specifically climate change, make it urgent that these issues are made available and presented as part of any curriculum. By the time they reach 18, it now seems almost certain that the current cohort of primary school children will be living in a different climate to that of today.

See Woodin, M. and Lucas, C. (2004) *Green Alternatives to Globalisation: A Manifesto*, London: Pluto.

A free booklet entitled *Issues in Green Education* is available – while stocks last – from Educational Heretics Press, 113 Arundel Drive, Bramcote, Nottingham, NG9 3FQ.

Organization

Institutions are to be judged by the good or harm they do to individuals.

Bertrand Russell

A school is an organization consisting of classrooms (environment) in which pupils (subjects) are brought together for the purpose of learning (object) through the direction of teachers (agents).

Whittaker, 1993

INTRODUCTION

Three terms that are found in sociological writings to describe the patterned activity of a place like a school are 'social system', 'organization' and 'institution'. These terms have various meanings and can be used to mean very similar things, or, with other definitions, to stress different aspects of patterning.

The concern of this chapter is not to discuss these concepts but rather to focus on organizational or institutional style to see whether there are hidden messages in the form of organization adopted for mass schooling.

One approach to organizational theory has been to look for the aims of the organization. Using this approach the question becomes one of whether or not schools are 'successful' in achieving their aims. One successful institution is an army. It sets out to turn men and women into killers, given certain stimuli like the 'enemy', 'patriotism' or 'survival', and has a long record of success in achieving this. Among unsuccessful institutions are perhaps large prisons like Pentonville, which set out to reform inmates, make the public safer, and deter criminals. From the sociological studies available, such institutions tend to have a reverse effect, in that they confirm criminality, 'educate' inmates into more sophisticated criminal methods (thus making them more dangerous to the public) and provide marks of status, since inmates are considered 'experienced' criminals in criminal circles (see Morris and Morris, 1963). A partially successful institution is a hospital, which has high rates of success with some ailments and low rates with others.

The analysis of schools, then, becomes a question of locating them alongside armies, prisons or hospitals in terms of success in achieving aims. Different writers have come to contrary conclusions here, because the aims of schools are not agreed; an agenda of aims is given a different order of priority by different people (see Chapter 3 for a list of aims). To the parents of a sixth former who achieves university entrance a school is successful, while to other parents the success of this small minority is seen as being achieved at the expense of the rejection of the majority. We saw in Chapter 4 how parents had various agendas of aims and in Chapter 3 how teachers varied in their priorities. Aims and goal are a practical problem for judging school effectiveness. This is especially a problem in different ideological contexts (see Harber, C. and Davies, L. (1997) *School Management and Effectiveness in Developing Countries*, London: Cassell).

ORGANIZATIONAL STYLES

The question investigated here is not related to a particular set of aims but rather what alternative organizational styles can be identified and what consequences these have for the behaviour of the people involved.

Etzioni's Classification

Etzioni suggests a ninefold typology summarizing different kinds of compliance, based on three kinds of power and three kinds of involvement of members. The three kinds of power are:

1. Coercive, based on punishment.
2. Remunerative, based on positive incentives.
3. Normative, based on agreed rules.

People go along with these kinds of power in three ways:

1. Alienative: grudging compliance.
2. Calculative: calculating involvement.
3. Moral: morally identified with the regime.

The most common patterns from the nine possible combinations are where the type of compliance is apparently matched by the type of power, i.e. alienative – coercive; calculating – remunerative; and morally involved – normative.

Etzioni's classification provides some interesting ideas, but has been criticized for a number of hidden assumptions as well as for the failure of this typology to take into account some examples of educational organization, such as the Hitler Youth or Spartan education:

this very neat set of types harbours a whole series of psychological assumptions which are an integral part of the democratic ideology but which may be empirically incorrect. There seems, for example, to be as much valid educational evidence in support of a relationship between coercive power and moral involvement ... as there is evidence supporting an association between coercive power and alienative involvement.

Swift, 1969

Weber's Classification

Weber distinguishes between charismatic, traditional and bureaucratic forms of authority. Charismatic authority rests on the personal magnetism and public performance skills of an individual to persuade followers to become disciples. The organizational style that results can often be arbitrary and loose:

Because charismatic power rests, ultimately, on the unique impressions of the individual, it has an arbitrary and eccentric quality about it which makes it a potential source of disruption to more rational forms of power utilizations. The charismatic leader, as Weber nicely put it, is not congenial to the idea of routine. To the contrary, because that person's power is lodged within personal qualities, he or she exists as a threat to routine and to the established order.

Cuzzort and King, 1976

Charismatic organizational styles usually give way to a more routinized form, which may be traditional or bureaucratic, to introduce stability and perpetuation. Traditional forms may find new leaders by searching for a new charismatic power in appointed persons, e.g. priests, by hereditary systems, as in monarchies, or by selection or election.

Bureaucratic forms establish leadership by promotion. Bureaucracy, as Weber analysed it, in its ideal type was a detailed rule system for organizing large-scale administrative tasks rationally, to minimize personal idiosyncrasies of individuals, including charismatics. A useful summary of the key features is contained in Swift (1969):

Fundamentally, a bureaucracy is a rational arrangement of offices providing certain means for administration and control of the office-holders' actions. Officials enter the bureaucracy expecting security, specialization, salary and seniority based upon achievement and examinations. The rights, duties and qualifications of the official will be carefully defined so that he is replaceable with a minimum of upheaval to the smooth running of the organization. Offices will be hierarchically arranged so as to facilitate demarcation of responsibility and promotion according to ability.

Swift sees that among the intended consequences of all these arrangements are two that social commentators tend to fear – impersonality and uniformity. For goals to be achieved, the actions of each office-holder have to be predictable according to the rights and duties of the positions, and personal idiosyncrasies minimized.

There have been several attempts to elaborate and develop Weber's concept of bureaucracy. In the case of schools, one view is that an alternative mode of organization, the professional, exists alongside some of the features of bureaucracy. The professional is believed to have appropriate skills, qualifications and attitudes related to a particular occupation which has its own professional code, ethic and organization, licensing practitioners to serve in or out of various kinds of organization. Bidwell's (1965) attempt to incorporate these two forms in relation to American schools leads to the listing of four major organizational features on which schools may be composed. These were the grouping of pupils into age cohorts, the contractual hiring of teaching staff as licensed professionals, the mixed organizational system of bureaucracy and professionalism, and the dual responsibility of educationalists to a clientele and to a public.

Another contribution has been the distinction between 'tall' and 'flat' organizational styles. Tall organizations have many levels of authority, and these are arranged in a tight hierarchy so that the shape of the authority structure is that of a pyramid. Flat organizations have few levels of authority and operate on the basis of teams making collective decisions, allowing for more professional and democratic forms of activity (see Cooper, 1965).

Goffman's Classification

Goffman's work on organizational style has produced the concept of a total institution. This describes the characteristics of a place of residence and work where the inmates are cut off from outside society for considerable periods of time. Prisons, mental hospitals, armies, monasteries and residential schools are examples. Although Goffman's work is related to such 'closed' organizations, the characteristics he describes provide one means of describing and comparing the organizational styles of other organizations, in this case schools. These characteristics include the following:

1. All aspects of life are conducted in the same place and under the same single authority.
2. Each phase of activity is carried on in the immediate company of a batch of others, all treated alike and required to do the same things together.
3. The day's activities are tightly scheduled, with one activity leading to another at a pre-arranged time.
4. The sequence of activities is imposed by a system of explicit formal rulings and a body of officials whose task is surveillance.
5. The various activities are brought together in a single rational plan designed to fulfil the official aims of the institution.
6. There is a basic split between a large managed group, the inmates and a small supervisory group.
7. Each group tends to conceive of the other in terms of narrow, hostile stereotypes. Staff tend to feel superior and righteous: inmates to feel inferior, blameworthy and guilty.

8. Social mobility between the two groups is severely restricted: social distance is great and formally prescribed.
9. The passage of information about staff plans for inmates is restricted and inmates are excluded from decisions about their fate.
10. Incentives for work have little significance outside the institution. Groups have only official points of contact.
11. There is a barrier between inmates and the outside world. Inmates are dispossessed of basic rights.
12. High-ranking inmates have more authority than low-ranking supervisors. Inmates are expected to internalize the norms of the staff.

This list raises a key sociological issue: that the effect of a pattern like this is cumulative. Taken individually, each of these features could be interpreted as trivial, but the cumulative effect of a set of features operating together can be powerful. Goffman says that institutions like this are the forcing houses for changing people and each is a natural experiment on what can be attempted on the self. Thus armies convert people into killers by using a total-institution pattern for their organizational style.

There is also a qualitative aspect to be taken into account. How coercive is each of the above features? Is negotiation possible? Can some kind of truce be called? The existence of a particular feature may vary in its effect according to who decided that that feature was desirable. An example is the existence of a school uniform. The effect is qualitatively different if a headteacher imposes a uniform, or if pupils and staff are consulted and a majority agree that it is a good idea.

The application of this list of characteristics to schools can indicate an index of how far a particular school is taking on the features of a total institution and how it compares with other schools in that respect. Some of the variations to be found may be as follows:

1. 'The same place' – the school building – is a constant, but the freedom and frequency of visits, expeditions, field work and other uses of the 'outside' is a variable. 'The same single authority' varies according to the decision-making procedures, for in some schools the headteacher delegates and involves staff, sometimes parents and occasionally pupils, while in others the headteacher retains all powers of decision-making.
2. Grouping systems vary from set 'batches', e.g. class or stream groupings, to other systems like setting, family grouping or individualized systems.
3. The timetable, as looked at in a previous chapter, shows variations in rigidity and flexibility. In secondary schools tight scheduling is very common.
4. There are variations in the amount of explicit ruling and surveillance needed.
5. The timetable embodies the 'single rational plan', but there are qualitative differences in when it was produced and how widely consultation was conducted.
6. The split between teachers and pupils varies with schools: in many, relationships are rather distant, in some they are closer and in a few they are almost equal.

7. The hostility between the two groups is well documented in some cases. One teachers' union leader believed that 'the swish of the cane may be one of the essential sounds in education' (Casey, 1974). In other schools, cooperation, sympathy and mutual concern are in evidence.

8. The variations in feelings of superiority and inferiority tend to parallel the incidence of hostility between the groups.

9. Pupils are rarely called on to help in teaching and mobility is restricted to some pupils becoming teachers through teacher-training establishments.

10. The secrecy of records about pupils and staff is still an emotive issue in education. Pupils usually learn about decisions on their fate after the event has taken place.

11. Ticks, stars, house points and grades have no value outside schools, although the minority who achieve certificates have a marketable commodity in terms of job applications, etc.

12. Most interaction takes place in classrooms; the amount taking place elsewhere varies from none to a substantial minority of time.

13. The 'symbolic barrier' is the white line on the playground or the printed notice commanding visitors to report to a particular place to state their business. An interesting contrast is with another public building, the public library, which has open access, and a few schools operate rather like this.

14. The basic rights Goffman discusses include rights of dressing in clothes of one's own choice, of being able to use the toilet facilities whenever desired, of eating with some choices about times and foods, of being addressed by chosen names and of being protected from body searches or physical assault, including physical punishments. Schools clearly vary in how much they infringe these 'rights'.

15. It is harder to find examples of high-ranking inmates, like tobacco barons in prisons; the nearest equivalent would appear to be prefect systems, where old-established prefects may appear to be more powerful than new young teachers on the staff.

16. Few schools appear to operate on the assumption that teachers can learn from the pupils even when the pupils have considerable knowledge, e.g. about forms of music other than the classical.

One analysis of secondary schooling that contains many of the features of Goffman's total institution is that of James (1968):

> If for a moment we forget our preconceptions about secondary schooling and imagine ourselves able to start fresh, can we really be content with the way in which our young people's days are spent? Would we allow them, if we had the choice, to spend this time in squads (group is too rich a word) being addressed or grilled by adults, one adult after another and in a totally incoherent order? ... Would we not like them to learn to work cooperatively rather than in a moral climate so competitive that sharing is denigrated as 'cheating' and actually punished? Would we really wish them to find much of their satisfaction in having some others to be better than? ... Who rescues the children at the bottom

of the heap, the bottom children in the bottom stream? Sometimes a kindly, occasionally a superbly imaginative remedial teacher; certainly, never their peers in higher streams.

Again, how do we explain a youth-time arbitrarily divided into spasms of 30, 40 or 45 minutes, punctuated by the clanging of bells, and often followed by a massive flocking in and out of corridors? How do we reconcile this planned incoherence with our knowledge of the different rhythms of learning different individuals have, of their different ways of thinking and learning? Are we allowing millions of people in schools, children and adults, to spend their time disagreeably when it is quite unnecessary that they should do so?

In this passage, James also indicates some of the hidden curriculum of an organizational style with a high index on 'total' features. She includes:

1. Competition rather than sharing.
2. Superiority rather than equality of consideration.
3. Incoherent learning rather than coherent.
4. Learning being unpleasant rather than joyful.
5. Learning consisting mostly of listening in groups.
6. Fragmented knowledge.

Reynolds and Delinquent Schools

A study of school organizational styles in South Wales by Reynolds (1976) serves to emphasize the consequences of variations in some of the features Goffman described. Differences between nine schools in a Welsh valley were located in terms of rates of attendance, academic attainment and delinquency. Influences outside the school were found to be comparable for all the schools, suggesting that it was school differences that would yield possible explanations. The more 'successful' schools, with higher rates of attendance, higher academic attainment and lower levels of delinquency, tended to:

1. Be smaller in size.
2. Be lower in staff turnover.
3. Have smaller classes.
4. Have older buildings.

Reynolds investigated organizational features, and gives these particular stress in his analysis. Differences in organizational style were that the more 'successful' schools:

1. Were more likely to have prefect systems.
2. Enforced school uniform rules with less rigour, especially for fourth- and fifth-year pupils.
3. Enforced rules against three key behaviours, i.e. smoking, chewing gum and outside

school behaviour, in a less obsessive and relentless manner; in Reynolds's terms, they opted for 'low rather than high control', over senior pupils in particular.

4. Used lower levels of physical punishment; the 'unsuccessful' schools use higher rates of coercion and produce lower commitment to the school on the part of the pupils as a result.

Reynolds describes the 'successful' schools in the sample:

> The successful school, on the other hand, does not fight battles over chewing gum, smoking and out-of-school behaviour that it knows it cannot win, and does not even attempt to enforce the wearing of school uniform when that enforcement becomes problematic. It does not use high rates of physical punishment and is not harshly authoritarian in its mode of control.

Reynolds summarizes the 'unsuccessful' schools as follows:

> The conflict between pupils and teachers is continually fuelled by the attempt of the staff to exercise control in areas of the pupils' lives where they expect autonomy, such as in their behaviour outside the school, and in some aspects of their behaviour inside it. In the schools like this one that have no truce, there are many pupils who wish for one.

Reynolds observes that where there is this sort of conflict in a school, there will invariably be vandalism within it, truanting from it and delinquency outside it. The attempt of the teachers to exercise control over the pupils in areas of their life where they feel they should have some autonomy is likely to set in motion a circular process of deviancy amplification. The pupils will see the teachers as using illegitimate authority, and they are then less likely to be responsive in other areas of school life. Teachers will tend to respond by increased coercion, leading to a reaction in an increasingly alienated pupil body of defiance to the 'oppressors'.

This research raises important issues for educational policies, Reynolds concludes, for his research supports the proposition that the organizational style of a school is an important influence upon its pupils' levels of vandalism, truancy, delinquency and educational failure. The common response has been to appoint more educational psychologists, advisers and social workers, and more recently to create 'disruptive pupil' units. These 'helping' professions 'help', or, Reynolds argues, 'force' the child to adjust to the school, whether the reality of the school is worth adjusting to or not.

> Instead of continually merely treating the deviant and delinquent children, we should perhaps begin to look and see if the reason for their rebellion lies squarely in the nature, process and operation of some of the schools that we offer them. If the reason does lie there then perhaps we should seek changes in some of our delinquents' schools.
>
> Reynolds, 1976

CONCLUSION

One theme that emerges from these various approaches to the study of the organizational styles of schools is that some are capable of transmitting a marked authoritarian message. The message is that you are to do as you are told without question. Woods (1977b) sees this as contrasting with messages transmitted in families and other institutions in society, for with the reduction of the working week, greater affluence, mass production, the mass media and increased mobility, patterns of leisure and behaviour have changed:

> Today, children have more freedom and independence, more discussion and contact with their parents, more money and material things, more outings and holidays, more lenient discipline, and fewer rules to obey and duties to perform, all of which increase the social distance between total institutions and the rest of society . . . Schools have been developing totalizing tendencies in a society which has not stood still, which, indeed, has been moving in the opposite direction.

Woods also sees this organizational style as opposed to some educationalists' views:

> Modern educationist thought, of course, explicitly rejects many of the features of total institutions which have long taken hold in schools. The split between inmates and staff, for example, regarded as inevitable by Waller in terms of 'social distance' . . . is deplored in the Plowden Report, which denounces the division into 'them and us' in many schools, and recommends more 'kindness, humanity and personal contact, and less authoritarianism' . . . One of the main changes, sought also by the Newsom Committee, was a 'change of heart in teachers'.

Finally, some psychological studies link in here: a study by Biber and Minuchin (1971) in the USA demonstrated how self-concepts of children varied with school regimes. The work of Milgram (1971) on the tendency of people brought up in authoritarian regimes to go along with orders even when those orders are malevolent indicated that behaviour similar to that of officials in Nazi Germany could be replicated in citizens of New York and other cities of the USA. In an authoritarian situation, people could be induced to hurt each other with electric-shock machines because the authority said it was necessary. The estimates of experts and others were that about 1 per cent of the population would do this, whereas incidences ranging from 33 to over 50 per cent were actually recorded.

Summary

1. One approach to organizational theory is to locate the aims of an organization and then judge whether it is successful in achieving them.
2. This approach yields different conclusions in the case of schools, since the aims of schools are in dispute: the agenda of aims is given different orders of priority by different people.
3. Etzioni's classification yields three common kinds of institution with contrasting patterns of control and response from the membership.

4. Weber's three types of authority – charismatic, traditional and bureaucratic – have stimulated further work on organizational style. These include analyses identifying the tensions and contradictions between the concepts of bureaucracy and of professional.
5. Goffman's theory of total institutions has been used to describe some of the characteristics of schools. An index of how far a particular school is exhibiting the characteristics of a total institution can be the outcome of this kind of analysis.
6. The hidden curriculum of organizational style can include messages like: competition is preferred to sharing; incoherent learning, rather than coherent, is experienced; and learning is unpleasant.
7. The research of Reynolds supports the proposition that the organizational style of a school can influence levels of vandalism, truancy, delinquency and educational failure.
8. The marked authoritarian message of many schools can be seen as contrasting with the less authoritarian messages of other institutions in UK society.

Further Reading

Ball, S. (1987) *The Micro-Politics of the School*, London: Methuen.

Barton, L. and Meighan, R. (eds) (1979) *Schools, Pupils and Deviance*. Driffield: Nafferton Books. This collection of papers addresses the question of how far the organizational style of schools can create deviance in pupils.

Goffman, E. (1961) *Asylums*. Harmondsworth: Penguin. The idea of total institutions is analysed in this book, especially in section 1, pp. 15–115.

Handy C. (1990) *Inside Organizations*. London: BBC Books.

King, R. (1983) *The Sociology of School Organisation*. London: Methuen.

Milgram, S. (1974) *Obedience to Authority*. London: Tavistock. Obedience to authority in general, and obedience to malevolent authority in particular, is the subject of this book.

Reynolds, D. (1976) 'The Delinquent School', in M. Hammersley *et al.* (eds), *The Process of Schooling*. London: Routledge and Kegan Paul. A study of the influence of organizational style on schooling.

Rutter, M., Maughan, B., Mortimer, P. and Ouston, J. (1979) *Fifteen Thousand Hours*. London: Open Books. Another study of the influence of organizational style on schooling.

Whittaker, P. (1993) *Managing Change in Schools*. Buckingham: Open University Press.

Discussion and Activities

1. A Marxist view that schools correspond to the values of the other institutions of a capitalist society was given in Chapter 6. Contrast this with the interactionist view, given in this chapter, that schools are out of step with the other institutions in society.
2. Take the list of Goffman's characteristics of a total institution and analyse an educational institution known to you. Compare your results with the discussion at the end of the section on Goffman's classification.
3. Do the messages of organizational style tend to reinforce the hidden curriculum messages of spatial layout and timetabling? Specify any messages they have in common.

Signposts

1. Open schooling

Some schools and writers have tried to establish the organizational patterns of non-authoritarian schooling. Some examples are: Watts, J. (1980) *Towards an Open School*, Harlow: Longman; Toogood, P. (1984) *The Head's Tale*, Telford: Dialogue Publications; Neill, A.S. (1968) *Summerhill*, Harmondsworth: Pelican; Moon, B. (ed.) (1983) *Comprehensive Schools: Challenge and Change*, Windsor: NFER-Nelson; Fletcher, C., Caron, M. and Williams, W. (1985) *Schools on Trial*, Milton Keynes: Open University Press; Davies, L. and Kirkpatrick, G. (2000) *The EURIDEM Project: A Review of Pupil Democracy in Europe*, London: Children's Rights Alliance.

2. You can't get an education from school books

One good way to see the difference between school books and real books is to examine the different customs that separate librarians from school teachers ... somewhere in the differences we're going to find a key to unlock the secret of the war between *education* and *schooling*.

To begin with, the libraries I've visited have always been comfortable and quiet, places where you can read instead of just pretending to read. People of all ages work side by side in a library; not just a pack of age-segregated kids. For some reason libraries are not age-segregated; nor do they presume to segregate readers by questionable tests of ability ...

The librarian doesn't tell me what to read, doesn't tell me what sequence of reading I have to follow, and doesn't grade my reading. The librarian appears to trust me. The librarian lets me ask my own questions and helps me when I want help, not when it's decided that I need help. If I feel like reading all day long that's OK with the librarian. I'm not told to stop reading at regular intervals by ringing a bell in my ear. The library keeps its nose out of my home too. It doesn't send letters to my mother reporting on my library behaviour ... or issue orders about how I should use my time at home.

There are no records at all detailing a reader's past victories or defeats. If the books I want are available, I get them – even if that deprives a reader more gifted and talented than I am of the book ... the library doesn't play favourites for any reason. It's very class blind. It's very talent blind. And that seems proper in a country that calls itself a democracy. The library never humiliates me by posting ranked lists of good readers for all to see. It presumes good reading is its own reward ...

One of the strangest differences between library and school is that you almost never see a kid behaving badly in a real library, although bad kids have exactly the same access to libraries as good kids do. I've taken literally thousands of bad kids into real libraries ... not once in 29 years did I have a complaint. The library never makes predictions about my future based on my past reading habits; nor does it imply that my days will be carefree if I read Shakespeare and troubled if I read Barbara Cartland. It tolerates eccentric reading because it realises that free men and women are always eccentric.

Finally the library has real books, not school books. Its books are not written by collective pens, nor selected by screening committees. Its real books conform only to the private curriculum of each author, and not to the invisible curriculum of a government bureaucracy. Real books are a vehicle to transport us into an inner realm of absolute solitude where nobody else can come. Real books generate unmonitored ... mental growth. School books are tools made of paper. They are vehicles of training; they reinforce the school routines of close order drill, public thinking, endless surveillance, endless ranking, and endless intimidation. Real books educate. School books school. When you take the free will out of education, that turns it into schooling. You cannot have it both ways.

From John Taylor Gatto's keynote speech at the US Options in Learning conference, 1992.

3. Schools as authoritarian organisations
'... despite most countries having signed the UN Convention on the Rights of the Child, for the majority of pupils schooling is essentially an authoritarian experience ...'

In this observation from *Schooling as Violence*, Harber argues that the dominant form of school organization globally is authoritarian.

In Chapter 8 of *Comparing Learning Systems*, Meighan proposes that school as a concept has its roots in totalitarian thinking: 'you will do it our way – or else!'.

4. Small schools
The organization of small schools is often different from that of their larger counterparts (see Harber, C. (1996) *Small Schools and Democratic Practice*, Nottingham: Educational Heretics Press; Carnie, F. (2003) *Alternative Approaches to Education,* London: Routledge Falmer; Ayers, W., Klonsky, M. and Lyon, G. (2000) *A Simple Justice: The Challenge of Small Schools*, New York: Teachers College Press).

1 Teacher Expectations

I am not an underachiever. My teacher is an over-expecter.

Child's response to a school report

INTRODUCTION

If the hidden curriculum is broadly defined as everything else that is learnt in addition to the official curriculum, the research on the expectations pupils either read or absorb from their teachers' behaviour is worth careful scrutiny. The central proposition in studies of teacher expectations is that pupils tend to perform as well or as badly as their teachers expect. The teacher's prediction of a pupil's or group of pupils' behaviour is held to be communicated to them, frequently in unintended ways, thus influencing the actual behaviour that follows. A brief account of four of the studies follows and is intended to be an alerting device, to signal the thinking of this type of research

FOUR STUDIES IN TEACHER EXPECTATION

Garwood and McDavid (1975)

This study established that teachers had stereotypes related to first names. Boys named David were viewed as good, strong, wise, active, serious, complex, sociable, excitable and masculine. The same teachers viewed the name Harold as signifying weak, bad, foolish, passive, humorous, simple, unsociable and calm. Names rated as desirable included Craig, Gregory, James, Jeffrey, John, Jonathan, Patrick, Richard and Thomas. Names rated by teachers as undesirable included Bernard, Curtis, Darrell, Donald, Gerald, Horace, Jerome, Maurice, Roderick and Samuel.

The evidence of a further study by Garwood (1976), seeking to relate teachers' ratings of first names to pupil self-concept and school achievement, supported the hypothesis that male pupils with first names that teachers considered desirable score higher on measures of self-concept and achievement than do those with first names that teachers rate as undesirable. The same effect had been shown in experiments where teachers graded work which was linked in authorship to desirable and undesirable names (Harari and McDavid, 1973). The authors saw this as evidence of teacher expectancy at work. A study in England noted similar results (Erwin and Caley, 1984).

Palardy (1969)

The subject of a second study was expectation and sex typing. Palardy (1969) compared five teachers of infants in the USA who believed that boys were almost as good as girls at learning to read, with five teachers who thought that boys were only about half as good as girls. At the outset the boys and girls had similar scores on pre-reading tests, and were from similar home backgrounds. After a period of time spent with their teachers, the performance of the children varied according to the teacher they had. The boys taught by the teacher who believed that they were almost as good as the girls had progressed as well as the girls in their reading. The boys taught by the teacher who believed that girls were superior had not progressed as well as the girls in their class, and their performance was clearly below that of the boys working with the first teacher. The author concluded that a self-fulfilling prophecy was in evidence, so that the beliefs of the teachers were influencing the actual outcome in terms of reading performance.

Harvey and Slatin (1976)

A study by Harvey and Slatin (1976) used photographs of pupils to investigate expectations. The teachers, 96 in the sample, were shown 18 photographs of children from different social class groups, evenly divided between the sexes, and evenly divided between white and black. The teachers were invited to rate the children in the photographs on estimated school adjustment, aspirations, homework attitudes, parental involvement and general school performance.

The lower-class children were rated in markedly less favourable terms, especially when they were black. The more experienced teachers were firmer in their categorizations than the less experienced, expecting the black children, whom they saw in general as lower class, to be failures. When asked how they arrived at their conclusions, teachers said that they based their ratings on similarities of the children in the photographs to those they had taught in the past, and on facial expressions.

Charkin *et al.* (1975)

If the studies are correct in concluding that pupils read teacher expectations and may be influenced by them, the problem of how these messages are passed on remains. A study by Charkin *et al.* (1975) investigated the possibility of non-verbal communication being one medium. A group of undergraduates comprising 24 men and 24 women taught a short lesson on house safety to a ten-year-old boy. A third of the sample were told that the boy had a high motivation to work and an IQ of 130. Another third were given no information and the remaining third were told that the boy did badly at school and had an IQ of 84. An analysis of the videotaped lessons that followed showed that the non-verbal behaviour of the teachers varied. Those in the 'high expectancy' group leaned forward more than those in the other two groups, looked pupils in the eye longer, nodded their heads up and down more and smiled more. The researchers concluded that these gestures provided easily recognizable indicators of approval which could be read by pupils, though not necessarily consciously.

FALSE EXPECTATIONS

Forming impressions of others serves an important function in everyday life, and categorizing others is necessary, or remembering all the vast amounts of detailed information about all the people we meet would prove an impossible task. However, if these impressions are inaccurate or false they may end up hindering rather than helping. In the four studies quoted, teachers were prepared to make inferences about pupils (whom they had not even met in some cases) on the basis of their first names, their sex, their appearance and information about their supposed ability. The effect of teacher expectation can start with false diagnosis:

> It is because most people are prepared to make inferences on the basis of the most slender evidence that so many of our initial inferences about other people are misleading and sometimes completely false . . . An elderly teacher once boxed the ears of a student teacher on his first day of teaching practice for running along a corridor. He had inferred from the student's age that he must be a sixth form pupil.
>
> Hargreaves, 1972

THE SEQUENCING OF TEACHER EXPECTATION

The build-up of expectations and the consequent actions and reactions make for a complicated story. It is possible to discern a number of stages:

1. Predictions based on a teacher's interpretive schemes or ideologies of education before meeting pupils for the first time.

2. The initial meetings.
3. Subsequent pattern of interaction.
4. Retrospective assessment and reflection, leading to reinforcement or modification of interpretive schemes.

The various studies of teacher expectation tend to try to illuminate one or other of these stages: studies following through all the stages are difficult to mount and therefore are rather rare.

This sequence, seen here for convenience as having four stages, will be followed in the analysis that follows, in an attempt to locate a number of the studies on teacher expectation. However, it is as well to remember that these stages are not always present in teacher–learner situations: sometimes learners are not actually met by their teachers and, in the absence of such meetings, inferences are made on even more limited evidence. A study of the behaviour of tutors in the Open University illustrates the point.

A study of the effects of penmanship and physical attractiveness on essay marking by Open University tutors was undertaken by Bull and Stevens (1976). The essay always had the same content but it was given to markers in variable handwritings or typed, and with different photographs, ranging from unattractive to attractive, attached. The judgements about good and bad handwriting and physical attractiveness were made by observers. The researchers found considerable variation in the marking that resulted. For 'style', the essay in typed form believed to have been written by an unattractive female received highest marks. The same essay in poor handwriting from an unattractive female received lowest marks. For 'talent', the essay in good handwriting from an attractive female was highly rated, but in the same handwriting from an unattractive female it was rated lowest of all. When markers believed the writer to be male, fewer differences related to handwriting and physical attractiveness were found. Half the markers were male. The results were complex, but evidence of the effect of expectation upon marking and grading was present in the data, the researchers concluded.

Predictions Based on Teachers' Interpretive Schemes

A later chapter looks more analytically at the interpretive schemes of teachers, under the heading of ideologies of education. Here the purpose is to review some studies that show some of the features related to teacher expectations and consequent pupil behaviour.

A study by Nash (1973), using a repertory grid technique, revealed a number of constructs employed by primary and secondary school teachers in Scotland. The repertory grid method is derived from Kelly (1955). Nash presented each teacher with three cards, each bearing the name of a child in the class, and asked how one differed in some significant way from the others. If the teacher comments on one being quiet and another noisy, the assumption is that this is part of that teacher's perceptual scheme. When no further differences emerge from this technique, the teacher's repertoire of personal constructs is assumed to be exhausted. A particular teacher's constructs may turn out to be:

bright – dull
quiet – noisy
mature – immature
well behaved – badly behaved
independent – gang member
able to work alone – unable to work alone
vivacious – subdued
good humoured – ill tempered
likeable – not likeable

Nash then compared the performance and behaviour of the pupils with the teachers' evaluations of them and concluded that the way the pupils were perceived by their teachers had a great influence upon their attainment. This was a greater influence than that of the pupils' social class, as indicated by parental occupation.

Nash also followed the progress of some of the pupils into secondary schools, and concluded that their behaviour varied with different teachers according to the teachers' perceptions. Where pupils were perceived favourably they did well and said they liked being with that teacher. Where they did not do well, they were in the situation of not being favourably perceived by the teacher, and reported that they did not like being with that teacher. The profile of a particular child's performance thus varied according to teachers' perceptions of him or her more than according to other features, like social class.

The work of Nash is in many respects a replication of the work of Becker (1952) in Chicago schools, where he demonstrated similar results. Both pointed out that their researches did not remove social class as a source of influences on pupils, and concluded that the teachers' perceptions of working-class children as less able meant that these children could have no favourable evaluations from any teachers during their school experience. Nash quotes the work of Goodacre (1968) in support of his conclusions, since she showed that the perceptions of teachers about home background were least accurate in areas of low social class.

Part of a teacher's interpretive scheme may be expectations about gender. The study by Palardy (1969) quoted earlier gives one indication of the possibilities in primary schools: the outcome was that the teacher's expectation was met in that if boys were expected to do worse than girls at learning to read they did, and if they were expected to do as well as girls, they did. In a study by Davies and Meighan (1975) of sex typing in secondary schools, teachers of both sexes, in a forced-choice question, showed a marked preference to teach boys rather than girls. Davies estimates that, on the basis of expectations theory, this preference is likely to be communicated to girls, and may help to explain the deterioration of academic performance of girls in general during the secondary phase of schooling.

A study of how teachers plan their teaching (Taylor, 1970) throws some light on the interpretive schemes of teachers. The strongest influences reported by teachers were within schools, so the views of colleagues, particularly the headteacher, counted for much more in decision-making than outside influences like advisers, inspectors, teaching associations, parents, books or educational journals. The expectations of teachers, this study would suggest, are most heavily influenced by parochial features: studies of attempts to change curriculum practices by 'outsider'-based projects have frequently found this to their cost (e.g. Shipman, 1977). Thus, if the local influence system stresses orderly classrooms and low noise levels, outside influences advocating alternative practices creating more noise and reordered classrooms have little chance of becoming established in the teachers' interpretive schemes.

Initial Meetings

Teachers take their expectations, based on their interpretive schemes, into the initial meetings with a new group of pupils. There are only a few studies that have followed what happens next. Experiments by Lippitt and White (1958) indicated that the behaviour of pupils soon took up a distinct pattern according to whether the regime of the teacher was 'authoritarian' or 'democratic'. The expectations of the teacher were read within a few minutes and the pattern became habitual within a few meetings.

Older pupils may be more deliberating in their evaluation of their teachers. Werthman (1963), in a study of secondary-age pupils defined as delinquent gang members, showed how the pupils make decisions about whether to accept or reject the authority of a teacher on various criteria related to how the teacher treats them, and how fairly marking of work is done. The initial meetings are key occasions, when the interpretive scheme of the teacher is 'researched' extensively by these pupils. Werthman reports how the marking characteristics of the teachers were established:

> As soon as the grade is handed down, gang members behave like good social scientists. They draw a sample, ask it questions, and compare the results with those predicted under alternative hypotheses. The unit of analysis is a set of relevant grades. The one received by a particular student is only a single member. No interpretation of a grade can be made before the others are looked at.

When their 'research' is complete, the delinquent gang members have their evidence about whether the teacher is fair, and is for them or against them. If the verdict is 'for them', they give cooperation; if 'against them', they obstruct.

In a study by Lacey (1970), he isolated two mechanisms at work in initial meetings with pupils in the grammar school he studied. These were differentiation and polarization. *Differentiation* referred mainly to the activity of the teachers in ranking and categorizing pupils in their meetings with new classes, whereas *polarization* referred mainly to the activity within the pupil body as a reaction to differentiation, resulting in the emergence of pro-school and anti-school sub-cultures. The first few days established the bases for the later hardened and habitual patterns:

> As soon as the highly selected first-year population meets at the Grammar School and is allocated to the four first-year classes, a complex process of interaction begins. It takes place through a variety of encounters. Boys talk and listen to each other; talk and listen to teachers; listen to conversations; notice details of accent, gestures, clothing; watch others at work and at play in various situations and in innumerable different permutations.

The effect of differentiation and polarization was to reverse the self-concepts of a proportion of the pupils on intake, since the new arrivals at the grammar school consisted of 11-year-olds accustomed to playing what might be termed the 'best pupil' role, and having a correspondingly positive self-image. Lacey reports that after six months in the second year the 'bottom' stream was already becoming polarized. This reversal of the performance and self-image of these pupils had taken only 18 months, and Lacey concluded that the interpretive schemes of the teachers, represented in particular in streaming practices, were a significant factor, and these operated swiftly: the die was cast in the initial meetings.

Subsequent Patterns of Interaction

There are many studies that concentrate on subsequent events when an expectation is in operation. Most of these have been in intellectual activities, so one that concentrates on the motor skills of swimming is interesting, if only for its novelty. Burnham and Hartsough (1968) administered a fake test supposed to predict psychological readiness to swim. The instructors, armed with this false information, gave their courses of instruction. Children designated as 'ready' tended to pass more of the tests than the average for their group.

Perhaps the most famous, as well as the most scrutinized and criticized, study is that of Rosenthal and Jacobson (1968) in the USA. Rosenthal noted that rats became brighter when expected to by their researcher, and wondered whether it was possible that children also become brighter when their teacher expects them to. He and Jacobson, of the south San Francisco unified school district, set out to see if this was so. Every child in an elementary school was given an intelligence test, a test described as one that would predict 'intellectual blooming'.

The school was in a lower socio-economic area on the West Coast. There were three classrooms for each grade – one for children of above-average ability, one for children of average ability, and one for children of below-average ability. About 20 per cent of the children in each class were chosen at random to form the experimental group. The teachers were given the names of this group and told that these children had high scores on the test for intellectual blooming, and would show remarkable gains in intellectual development during the next eight months. In reality, the only difference between these children and the rest was in the minds of their teachers.

At the end of the school year, all the children were again given the same IQ test. In the school as a whole, the children who had been designated as 'bloomers' showed only a slightly greater gain in verbal IQ (two points) than their classmates. However, in total IQ, the experimental group gained four points more on average than their counterparts did, and in reasoning IQ the average gain was seven points more.

Various reviews of the work of Rosenthal and Jacobson have cast doubt upon the statistics (Snow, 1969), the technical design (Thorndike, 1968) and the failure of replication attempts (Claiborn, 1969). As a pioneer study, it stimulated considerable research, and by 1973 Rosenthal was able to report that 242 studies had been completed, and that 84 had demonstrated that teachers' expectations do affect learners' performances. The other studies gave some clues that learners could resist expectation effects or be stimulated into 'confounding' behaviour to prove the teacher wrong, so that the expectation chain of events had several possible outcomes: self-fulfilling prophecy effects were not inevitable.

The expectations of lecturers and students regarding assessment and the effect on subsequent interaction were a central theme of a study by Becker (1968). Lecturers operated on a rhetoric of educational activity, e.g. learn the information and ideas of the course, or learn to see the world differently through a discipline, whereas students learned that what really counted for them, as well as in the final analysis the lecturers, was the grading of work. 'The realities of the situation lead him to define his classes as places in which he can get the grades he wants by performing as the teacher wants him to' (Becker, 1968). The students therefore indulged in a complicated activity of 'trading for grades', of reading the lecturer for grading clues, preferences and idiosyncrasies, and this activity gradually squeezed out or eventually dominated all other kinds of learning. 'Trading for grades' largely extinguished education.

This is not unlike the conclusion of Holt (1969) regarding children in schools; he sees his pupils concentrating on obtaining the right answer by the use of a complex series of strategies of reading the teacher's face, voice, gestures and responses, which may gradually exclude thinking through the logic of problems, especially since wrong answers obtained in this way are usually heavily penalized. Strategies for deducing the right answer largely extinguish thinking, he concludes.

The work of Good and Brophy (1972) has concentrated on the differential expectations of teachers of different members of the same class. Teachers of primary school children named pupils in their classes who fell into each of four groups – attachment, concern, indifference and rejection. The attachment group members initiated contact with teachers about work more often than the others and conformed to classroom rules, therefore receiving few chastisements. In return they received praise and more reading turns, and were asked more questions requiring conceptual thought. The concern group, though initiating contact with teachers, were prone to guessing and were less accurate in their work, thereby having more opportunities to ask questions, and teachers initiated more private conversations with members of this group. Teachers tended to praise them more often for success and criticize them less often for failure.

The indifference group members were passive and initiated few contacts with teachers. Although teachers asked them as many questions as other children, they made less individual contact with them and did not call on them to run errands or do special tasks. The rejection group sought out the teacher frequently and, particularly through calling out, received most disciplinary responses. They were active in class, but were given fewer reading turns and received less response from teachers for their work efforts.

These patterns were dependent on the teacher's expectations, and Good and Brophy (1970) indicated in another study how teachers behaved differently with a sample of high achievers and with a sample of low achievers. The former were consistently favoured, in demands for good performance, lower rates of criticism for wrong answers, help in rephrasing or repeating questions asked and the giving of praise for correct answers. When the teachers were informed about these patterns they changed their behaviour so that pupils were treated more equally, and the behaviour of the low-achieving group changed in respect of an improvement in behaviour and achievement.

Retrospective Assessment and Reflection

The initial meetings and subsequent interaction yield experiences which appear to reinforce or modify interpretive schemes of teachers, as well as those of pupils. However, only a few studies have monitored this feature. One such study is that of Fuchs (1968), of 14 newly qualified teachers in New York. She describes the process of the modification of their interpretive schemes by the influence of the 'parochial' features outlined in Taylor's study (previously mentioned).

First, the new teacher of class 1–5 in a slum school begins her career with a warm, friendly attitude towards her students. Early in the new teacher's career, however, a more experienced teacher exposes this new teacher to the widely held belief that the inferior backgrounds and the deficits in homes, e.g. lack of newspapers and parental care, prevent educational achievement. That the teachers and the school as an institution could contribute to the failure of the children is not considered.

Early in her career this new teacher is aware of her deficiencies. As yet, she has not unconsciously accepted the belief that the failure of children stems from gaps in their backgrounds.

By the end of the term, the eventual failure of most of class 1–5 has been virtually assured, for the teacher has come to rationalize this failure in terms of pupil inadequacy. Fuchs sees the good intention of the teacher defeated as her interpretive scheme is modified by in-school theories of pupil failure. The teacher has internalized the attitude that deficits of the children themselves explain their failure in school:

> The teacher of class 1–5 has been socialized by the school to accept its structure and values. Despite her sincerity and warmth and obvious concern for the children, this teacher is not

> likely to change the forecast of failure for most of these children – because she has come to accept the very structural and attitudinal factors that make failure nearly certain.

Fuchs notes that this teacher came to her job with very positive attitudes, but that her good impulses were not enough. This young teacher was socialized by the attitudes of those around her, and by the availability of a suitable rationale to explain her and the school's failure to fulfil their ideal roles:

> she came to accept traditional slum-school attitudes towards the children – and traditional attitudes towards school organization as the way things have to be. This teacher is a pleasant, flexible, cooperative young woman to have on one's staff. But she has learned to behave and think in a way that perpetuates a process by which disadvantaged children continue to be disadvantaged.

The study by Harvey and Slatin outlined at the beginning of this chapter showed that the judgements of teachers based on photographs of children were more firmly stereotyped in the case of experienced teachers. The interpretive schemes of inexperienced teachers were less stereotyped and judgements less dogmatic.

The account by Hoskyns (1976) of his experiments in physics teaching was outlined in Chapter 9 and provides an interesting case study of a reverse process. Here the interpretive scheme of the teacher was revised on the basis of a series of experiments in teaching methods.

CONCLUSION

A great deal of observational material reported in over a hundred different published articles lent support to the proposition that teacher expectations can have a self-fulfilling prophecy effect. There are, however, many remaining areas of doubt. First, it is not clear how frequently this effect occurs. Second, it is not clear whether it affects some aspects of interaction, e.g. grading, more than others, e.g. praising and blaming. Third, it is not clear how significant teacher expectations are: they may be a minor rather than a major feature.

The studies have often proved to be difficult to replicate. The wide publicity given to the Rosenthal and Jacobson experiments may have made it more difficult to convince teachers about false information. In addition, the long chain of circumstances of a self-fulfilling prophecy means that breakdown can occur at various points, making replication problematic. This chain has been clearly spelt out by Barber and Silver (1968):

1. The student experimenter attended to the expectancy communication from the principal investigator.
2. The experimenter comprehended the expectancy communication.
3. The experimenter retained the communication.
4. The experimenter (intentionally or unintentionally) attempted to transmit the expectancy to the subject.

5. The subject (consciously or unconsciously) attended to the expectancy communication from the experimenter.
6. The subject (consciously or unconsciously) comprehended the experimenter's expectancy.
7. The subject (consciously or unconsciously) retained the experimenter's expectancy.
8. The subject (wittingly or unwittingly) acted upon (gave responses in harmony with) the experimenter's expectancy.

As Nash (1976) comments:

> When one researcher, repeating another's work, fails to get the same result, it may be that the chain has failed at some point. And, since any replication involves a different set of people, this is hardly to be wondered at. This built-in problem of replication must be held in mind throughout.

However, as regards the hidden curriculum of schooling, the area of teacher expectations is potentially a considerable source of hidden messages, though precisely what weight is to be attached to it awaits the findings of more research.

Self-fulfilling Prophesy

As Merton (1948) argued, the self-fulfilling prophesy begins with the false statement of a situation, and this, in turn, leads people to act in such a way that creates the situation.

> Public predictions of future developments are frequently not sustained precisely because the prediction has become a new element in the concrete situation, thus tending to change the initial course of developments.

Desegregation of schools in the USA was achieved in large part because of the evidence of 'self-fulfilment' contributed by Clarke (1955). The evidence presented in *Brown* v. *Board of Education* (1954) suggested that black children brought up in a society that held them to be inferior learned to feel and act inferior. As Wineburg and Shulman have suggested, as the perceived benefits of desegregation were seen not to be realized, another form of the self-fulfilling prophesy was introduced. This time it was the teachers who were fulfilling their own prophesy. They didn't expect black children to succeed so they saved their resources and time for those who would most benefit. Subsequent test scores reinforced the teachers' mis-conceptions regarding the children's ability.

In Rosenthal and Jacobson's *Pygmalion in the Classroom* (1968), statistically significant results were found in the first two grades but the findings were exaggerated, the tests were inappropriate and the book was heavily criticized by reviewers. *Pygmalion* did, however, pave the way for a number of other more adequate studies that have provided more adequate evidence. As Wineburg and Shulman put it, a large number of studies have now 'supported the hypothesis that expectations can lead to marked variations in teachers' responses to pupils. Those responses, in turn, are associated with important variations in a variety of pupil performance measures.' It does, however, remain the case that 'the claim that teachers' expectations could influence measured intelligence has yet to be supported empirically'.

One of the major problems in all of this is that the teachers are often seen to be responding quite rationally to the evidence they have before them:

> Although there are relationships between teacher expectations, teacher–student interaction, and student achievement, most of these are more accurately construed as student effects on teachers rather than as teacher expectation effects on students. Most differential teacher expectations are accurate and reality based, and most differential teacher interaction with students represents either appropriate, proactive response to differential student need, or at least understandable reactive response to differential student behaviour ... although the potential for teachers' expectations to function as self-fulfilling prophesies always exists, the extent to which they actually do so in typical classrooms is probably limited.
>
> Brophy, 1983, p. 634

But, of course, this is problematic in itself. Why do teachers prioritize the very children who would appear to be the least in need of assistance? The TESA (Kerman, 1979) programme provided some clues. Kerman found that teachers asserted that:

- Asking the less able questions might embarrass them.
- Asking the more able meant that all of the class could benefit from their answers.
- It was important to cover the curriculum content, and this meant there was little time to give to the unprepared, slow or confused.

The TESA project involved teacher training and peer observation of teacher–pupil observation. The results have been fairly positive, with increased academic gains, and decreased absenteeism and disciplinary referrals (Wineburg and Shulman).

> Whereas the self-fulfilling prophesy involves a false definition of a problem the 'self-sustaining prophesy' (Cooper and Good) begins with the status quo, and assumes that because something is, it must be.

For Merton, a 'belief system' represented just as much a 'prophesy' as any individual belief. The self-fulfilling prophesy may therefore be seen to be a restatement of the principle that scientific paradigms determine what may be observed rather than reality, or, to put it another way, 'we see what we want to see'. As Harry Nielsen put it, 'Have you ever been to Paris? Have you ever been to New Delhi? There you are then.'

Summary

1. The central proposition in studies of teacher expectations is that pupils tend to perform as well or as badly as their teachers expect.
2. Some support for this proposition is given by studies of teacher ratings of pupils by first names, a study of variable reading performance according to teacher beliefs about boys' and girls' reading achievements, a study of teacher ratings of pupils by photographs and a study of the non-verbal behaviour of student teachers in micro-teaching.
3. It is when the first impressions that a teacher forms are false or inaccurate that problems arise.
4. It is possible to discern four stages in the build-up of expectations: (a) predictions based on interpretive schemes; (b) first meetings; (c) subsequent patterns of interaction; (d) retrospective assessment leading to reinforcement of interpretive schemes or their modification.
5. Teachers' interpretive schemes can be investigated using a repertory grid technique.
6. Studies by Nash and Becker suggest that teacher expectations can be a more powerful influence than social class features.
7. Part of a teacher's interpretive scheme may be expectations related to beliefs about gender.
8. The strongest influences on teachers' interpretive schemes appear to be parochial rather than outside-school influences.
9. In initial meetings, the interpretive scheme of the teacher may be researched intently by the pupils, who may modify their behaviour accordingly.
10. Initial meetings may show two mechanisms at work – differentiation and polarization. In some circumstances, pupils' self-concepts can be reversed in the process.
11. The studies of Rosenthal and Jacobson were an attempt to demonstrate how a self-fulfilling prophecy derived from teacher expectations can develop.
12. Becker's notion of 'trading for grades' and Holt's notion of 'right answerism' are other illustrations of the consequences of teacher expectancy.
13. A study by Fuchs indicates how the interpretive schemes of a new teacher can become modified by the theories of experienced teachers, to the disadvantage of the children she teaches.
14. There are considerable areas of doubt regarding teacher expectancy: its frequency and its significance are open to varying interpretations. Replication of studies has proved to be difficult owing to the long chain of circumstances involved.

Further Reading

Connell, R.W. (1985) *Teacher's Work*. London: George Allen and Unwin.

Good, T.L. and Brophy, J.E. (1984) *Looking in Classrooms*, 3rd edn. London: Harper and Row. An account of techniques to increase teacher awareness.

Holt, J. (1969) *How Children Fail*. Harmondsworth: Penguin. An account of a teacher observing some of the mechanisms of expectancy at work in his own classroom.

Merton, R.K. (1990) *Consensus and Controversy*. Lewes: Falmer Press.

Nash, R. (1976) *Teacher Expectations and Pupil Learning*. London: Routledge and Kegan Paul. A review of the material on teacher expectations.

Pidgeon, D. (1970) *Expectation and Pupil Performance*. Windsor: NFER. A review of the material on teacher expectations.

Rosenthal, R. and Jacobson, L. (1968) *Pygmalion in the Classroom*. Eastbourne: Holt, Rinehart and Winston. An interesting case study despite the various criticisms levelled at it.

Woods, P. (1983) *Sociology and the School*. London: Routledge and Kegan Paul.

Discussion and Activities

1. Some of the studies reported in the chapter could be replicated in the form of an exercise, e.g. Harvey and Slatin's study based on photographs or Taylor's study of how teachers plan their courses. Start by reading the original study in full.

2. Do delinquent gang members or other 'troublesome' groups in the UK research their teachers as the USA teenagers reported in Werthman's study do? Wills, P. (1977) *Learning to Labour*, London: Saxon House, is one source of material if you have no direct friendly access to such a group.

3. Read the study by Fuchs, E. (1973) 'How Teachers Learn to Help Children Fail', in N. Keddie (ed.), *Tinker, Tailor … The Myth of Cultural Deprivation*, Harmondsworth: Penguin, and then interview some student teachers after a teaching practice, or teachers during their first year, to test for any evidence of the same resocializing effects.

4. Discuss the proposition that the road to becoming an oppressive, bullying teacher is paved with good intentions. (See Chapter 3 for material.)

Signposts

1. Improving teacher awareness

This is the subject of Good and Brophy (1984), who set out both to survey research on expectations and to demonstrate how teachers can implement the findings to develop their teaching techniques. See also books by John Holt (1969, 1971, 1973).

2. Teacher happiness

A survey on happiness at work by City and Guilds was reported in February 2005. It asked 1,500 people from 15 jobs to rate their satisfaction at work on a series of criteria. Well down the list were teachers. Only 8 per cent said they were happy in their work – which means that a massive 92 per cent were not.

'… the general context of tests, inspections and league tables is also very stressful for teachers who themselves become ill …' Clive Harber in *Schooling as Violence*, p. 115. There have been a few cases of teachers committing suicide under the pressure of it all.

12 The Hidden Curriculum of Language

ROLAND MEIGHAN AND STEPHEN WALKER

It ain't what you say but the way that you say it.

From a song by 'Trummy' Young and Oliver

INTRODUCTION

The previous chapters of this book have been concerned with the exploration of a simple, though not unimportant, observation. This is that our understanding of life in schools will be incomplete unless we include in our analysis consideration of the hidden as well as the overt messages embedded both in the settings in which teachers and pupils operate and in the practices in which they engage. Of all the factors which contribute to the working of the process of educating, it is arguable that the way in which language is used in schools and classrooms can be regarded as the element of most obvious, and perhaps most crucial, significance.

First, it is significant because of the close relationship that exists, in our culture, between educational activities and language. The strength of this relationship is nicely pointed by Stubbs (1976), in his observation that:

> For us teaching and learning typically comprise linguistic activities such as: lecturing, explaining, discussing, telling, questioning, answering, listening, repeating, paraphrasing and summarizing.

It should, therefore, come as no surprise to us when observers of classroom interaction like Flanders (1970) report that two-thirds of the time spent in most lessons in 'traditional' classrooms is made up of talk and, furthermore, that, typically, two thirds of this talk is done by the teacher. If one adds to this the time spent in the classroom on two other linguistic activities, reading and writing, it becomes clear that classrooms are language-saturated environments. Interestingly, however, the language used in school environments is often highly stylized, in terms of both its content and its structure. Consider, for example, the following three fragments of talk. One is taken from a cross-examination in a court, one from an exchange between a teacher and a pupil and one from a conversation which formed part of a radio 'phone-in' programme.

(1)

    A: I like tuh ask you something.

    B: Shoot.

    A: Y'know I'ad my licen' suspendid fuh six mumts.

    B: Uh huh.

    A: Y'know for a reaz'n which, I rathuh not mensh'n tuh you, in othuh words – a serious reaz'n, en I like tuh know if I w'd talk to my senator, or – somebuddy, could they help me get it back.

(2)

    A: You had had bronchitis, had you not?

    B: Yes.

    A: You have mentioned ... about wearing a coat?

    B: Yes.

    A: It was not really a coat at all, was it?

    B: Well, it is sort of a coat-dress, and I bought it with trousers, as a trouser suit.

(3)

    A: No. No, it is not a pickpocket on the move. Mister Atkins?

    B: Is it about a bird – that flies around?

    A: About a –?

    B: A bird that flies a–

    A: A bird that flies around. No. John?

Now, even though these fragments have been separated from their context and contain no obvious references which would reveal the sources from which they have been taken, we can easily distinguish between the speech of the casual conversationalist, that of the lawyer and that of the teacher, and thus identify which fragment belongs to which setting. We recognize, in the way the teacher uses a certain style, a familiar pattern of communication which we associate with the speech modes and language patterns of teachers in general. What is the precise nature of these 'styles' of communication? What purposes do they serve and what consequences might they have? Who determines the acceptability or non-acceptability of certain patterns of usage and on what criteria are these decisions made? Most importantly, what messages might be hidden in the manner in which communications are organized in social settings like classrooms, as well as in the content of what is said, written or read? These kinds of concerns provide a focus for what follows.

Before examining these questions, however, let us consider briefly a second reason for proposing that language usage has significance for the educational experiences of both pupils and their teachers. Language serves different, although not unrelated, functions; it allows communication, thought, social interaction and control. Thus, on the one hand, language is a device for the transmission of ideas, perceptions and concepts between individuals and, on the other, it is a means by which individuals order and direct both their personal social experiences and conceptualizations and their relations with other people. But these functions do not operate independently. Individuals come to recognize the ways in which others communicate – the linguistic rules they seem to obey, the styles to which they appear to conform, and the particular symbols they employ to describe the world and to order their knowledge of it. In learning how to use these practices for their own purposes, they internalize certain representations created by other people which can be used in the formulation of their own understandings and interpretations of the world. To this extent, the language environment in which school pupils are immersed will influence not only how they communicate with other people in school but also how they conceptualize and think about the messages to which they are exposed. In short, it will have an effect on their learning. As Douglas Barnes (1976) argues:

> we cannot consider language in the classroom only in terms of communication, but must consider how children themselves use language in learning. The major means by which children in our schools formulate knowledge and relate it to their own purposes and view of the world are speech and writing.
>
> Not only is talking and writing a major means by which people learn, but what they learn can often hardly be distinguished from the ability to communicate it. Learning to communicate is at the heart of education.

But what kind of talking and writing is done in school? We need to have some idea of how this question has been answered and of suggestions about the specific messages transmitted through such communication practices before we can consider how these might be related to how learning itself is defined and accomplished.

SCHOOL LANGUAGE

Pre-school Experience

In some senses communication in schools and classrooms is not different from that regularly used in settings outside this environment – not surprisingly, as individuals communicating in any walk of life work with the same language base. Teachers and pupils bring with them into school a stock of meanings of words, understandings of linguistic rule systems and knowledge of language etiquette which they share because it is drawn from a linguistic heritage common to the culture in which they are located and which exerts a pressure upon them to conform to certain conventions affecting everyone. Such conformity is necessary, because without it, although language could serve as a means by which individuals made subjective representations of the world to themselves, it could not act as a basis for the transmission of such ideas and perceptions from one individual to another. Indeed, as Berger and Luckmann (1967) argue:

> As a sign system, language has the quality of objectivity. I encounter language as a facticity external to myself and it is coercive in its effects on me. Language forces me into its patterns, I cannot use the rules of German syntax when I speak English; I cannot use words invented by my three-year-old son if I want to communicate outside the family; I must take into account prevailing standards of proper speech for various occasions, even if I would prefer my private 'improper' ones. Language provides me with a ready-made possibility for the ongoing objectification of my unfolding experience.

What is significant about this observation is that, in acquiring a language under these constraints, an individual is not simply learning a neutral sign and symbol system for personal and idiosyncratic use, but is also taking on ideas, meanings, conceptualizations, theories, attitudes and judgements which were deposited in the language system when they were first produced. In a very real sense language represents a huge repository of interpretations and knowledge by which the ideas and recognitions of our ancestors are preserved and handed on to succeeding generations. Thus, in learning a language we are exposed not only to pre-determined definitions of the world, but also to predetermined explanations of it. Again, as Berger and Luckmann observe:

> With language, and by means of it, various motivational and interpretative schemes are internalized as institutionally defined – wanting to act like a brave little boy, for instance, and assuming little boys to be naturally divided into the brave and the cowardly. These schemes provide the child with institutionalized programmes for everyday life, some immediately applicable to him, others anticipating conduct socially defined for later biographical stages ... Finally, there is internalization of at least the rudiments of the legitimating apparatus; the child learns 'why' the programmes are what they are.

Thus, before the child even reaches school, he or she will have been exposed to predetermined language patterns and the descriptive, prescriptive and evaluative messages hidden within them. This exposure has relevance for the process of educating in different ways.

First, it might be argued that the early language experience of school pupils encourages the employment of explanations and views that are taken for granted and seemingly self-evident, as opposed to encouraging them to use language boldly to create understandings, to question their experience. In Seabrook's discussion of the obsolescence and essential conservatism of much of the imagery which is used in modern English, especially in what he calls 'the language of suburbia', we can find illustrations of how this happens.

Seabrook (1971) claims that the English language abounds with words, phrases and maxims which not only are relics of another age but which seem peculiarly inappropriate to contemporary life. He notes the pervasiveness of imagery based on rural and military analogies which refer to experience no longer central to social life and which have little relevance in modern circumstances:

They have become figurative and allusive designations of something quite different. Not many people set hand to plough, separate the wheat from the chaff, make a killing, make a last-ditch stand, sail near the wind, pay the piper or find a hard nut to crack. These expressions have been extended to cover a wide range of human situations, which they indicate only obliquely. Their homely reverberations often conceal, rather than illuminate, the context in which they are used.

The images mask, distort or hide what life is really like, giving it an appearance of homeliness, familiarity and simplicity. Of even greater concern to Seabrook is the possibility that popular usages of either redundant imagery or even more up-to-date set phrases and clichés serve not only to narrow our chance of engaging with conflicting ideas and sceptical interpretations by making attempts to explore more unfamiliar forms of expression more difficult and more threatening, but also to weaken our sense of responsibility for the reliability and the validity of the descriptions and judgements contained in our application of these formulations. He argues that:

> the familiar phrases do not only give us the consoling illusion that we understand, and can cope with, the world we live in and all its contingencies. Often there is also an implicit moral judgement. People shouldn't play fast and loose, blow hot and cold, be unable to see beyond noses, make mountains out of molehills, have bees in their bonnet, fish in troubled waters, build castles in the air, kick over the traces. These phrases, which present themselves so readily, diminish the ability to assess situations objectively, because of their ready-made judgement.

The child's pre-school language experience has relevance for later educational contact in another way. In learning a language the individual is also exposed to the often hidden message of what constitutes 'proper' usage. Whether the environment in which language acquisition takes place is one in which a dialect variation of a language is the norm, or one in which a standard version of a language is the accepted mode, in their initial encounters children are presented with a situation which, albeit for the time being, represents the particular mode used as the form of expression. However, in accepting allegiance to a particular form of speech and expression, children are made vulnerable to fairly persistent social attitudes to different modes of language usage as they come into contact with other speech communities. These arise from the fact that, in learning language, we also learn ideas about what constitutes appropriate usage in different contexts and, on the basis of this, we also come to recognize that judgements of other users are made according to beliefs about what constitutes appropriateness; we learn how to use our understanding of language and appropriateness as a basis for ordering our impressions of others, as demonstrated in the way *they* organize communications. As Stubbs (1976) has noted:

> British people are very sensitive to the *social* implications of dialect and accent, and the characteristic speech of our large cities, especially Birmingham, East London, Liverpool, Newcastle and Glasgow, is often regarded as 'slovenly' and 'ugly'. Giles (1971) carried out experiments in which people listened to standard and regional dialects. In fact, they heard

the same speaker using different language varieties, but they did not know this! Speakers of standard English were *perceived* as more ambitious, more intelligent, more self-confident and more reliable.

Stubbs comments that, unreasonable as such linguistic stereotyping might appear to be, we need to be aware of the extent to which it is used in social interaction as a basis for evaluating individuals' intelligence and personal worth.

The importance of such stereotyping becomes critical if we consider how it might work in school. When we look at patterns of communication in classrooms later in this chapter, the proposition emerges that, at the very least, teachers sometimes show more concern with the form of their pupils' communications than with the content.

Perhaps the most significant message about schooling transmitted in the process of language acquisition concerns the assumptions to which children are exposed which refer to an education world they have yet to experience. In learning a language a child internalizes not only words and concepts which refer to objects, but also some which describe social categories and social roles. Thus the pupil entering school already has ideas about what terms like 'school', 'learning' and 'classroom' mean and about expectations which surround the general role categories 'boy' and 'girl', 'teacher' and 'pupil'. This should not be taken as a claim that the activities and understandings of the child in school are massively predefined or culturally determined. The specifics of classroom life will be created, negotiated and developed *in the course of interaction* in school, but this interaction takes place against a background of previously acquired expectations and understandings. We have only to observe groups of four-year-olds 'playing school' to notice that such children already have ideas about what activities in this setting are like and mean. What is important is that such ideas have been transmitted through a filter of values contained in other people's subjective interpretations of that setting; in taking on the perceptions of others the child is almost inevitably involved in taking on some of the judgements and evaluations carried in these perceptions.

Much of the discussion in this section has been to do with the way in which language might be seen as the vehicle by which general social messages relevant to the processes of educating are transmitted. But, in the distinctive way language is used in schools we can identify other types of subtle communication, and it is with these that the next sections will be concerned.

School Experience: General Patterns of Language Usage

As was noted earlier, language practices in schools have characteristics which distinguish them from those used in other social settings. While we might not agree that communication in schools conforms to a type which Waller (1932) termed 'the didactic voice', i.e. dry, un-emotional, impersonal and repetitive, there do seem to be certain regular patterns concerning writing and talking, the persistence of which is curious. What patterns can we distinguish?

In the work of Basil Bernstein we find some suggestion of how we might attempt a description of some key elements of these patterns. Bernstein's writing (1973, 1977), concerned with his sociolinguistic theory and the relationship between language and education, is complex and often highly abstract. However, because it represents one of the few sustained attempts to explore language in education and because Bernstein's theory, in its development, has influenced the thinking of many educational practitioners and policy-makers, it is worth making a brief detour from the main discussion of this chapter to consider certain features of this work. Bernstein began his work in the late 1950s with the aim of devising a conceptual framework upon which the relatively poor educational attainment of working-class pupils (early leaving, poor test performances and low rates of 'academic' success), as against that of their middle-class peers, could be explored. In attempting this he concentrated upon 'how the class system acts upon the deep structure of communication in the process of socialization' (Bernstein, 1973).

This framework is based upon the postulate that the social relations of particular social groups (i.e. their work relationships or place in the scheme of how the social division of labour is managed, the nature of the belief system which holds their particular group together, the way in which family life is organized) will generate a *system* of communication specific to that group and their conditions of life. This system, once established, sensitizes or orientates both those using and those acquiring language to distinct 'orders' of meanings, relationships and relevances. Bernstein argues that these systems are distinguishable and can be placed on a continuum, moving from what he calls the restricted code, at one end, to the elaborated code at the other (RC/EC). Different orders of meaning, or the 'dominant principles' humans use to organize their thought about the definition of and the relations between objects and people, are distinguishable according to the criteria of *universalistic* characteristics (EC) – in which meaning is independent of the context in which it is being made, does not depend upon shared and taken for granted assumptions, is generally available and is therefore *explicit* and *particularistic* characteristics (RC), in which the circumstances or context in which meaning is being made are essential for understanding; this renders such meaning useful only at a local level, it being *implicit*. The extent to which the major socializing agency, the family, favours one meaning system or another depends, in the main, upon the class position of the family and upon the role system dominant in the life of that family. By role system Bernstein means 'how families determine the allocation of decision-making on the extent and kind of interaction between members of the family'.

These role systems are themselves, in part, a reflection of the family's place in the wider social system. Bernstein distinguishes between *positional* families (in which decisions about interaction are made by reference to the formal position or the commonly held notions about roles in the family – father, mother, daughter, son – and hence involve role ascription) and *person-orientated* families (in which decisions rest upon individuals' unique attributes, and hence involve role achievement). The link between the family role system and communication codes is that, for Bernstein, the principles of management and control used to sustain one role system or another focus upon different orders of meaning. Or, in his own words:

inasmuch as a role system is personal rather than positional, then it is a relatively more unstable system. It is continuously in the process of assimilating and accommodating the verbally realized but different intentions, qualification and motives of its members. Tensions will arise which are a function of the characteristic of the role system. Special forms of arbitration, reconciliation and explanation will develop. These tensions only in the last resort will be managed in terms of the relative power which inheres in the respective statuses. Social control will be based upon linguistically elaborated meanings rather than upon power.

Bernstein, 1973

Now, the crucial element of Bernstein's theory is that the particular orientation of specific meaning systems (communication codes) and the particular forms of social control inherent in a specific role system (family types) are *realized* or actualized in distinctive speech forms (linguistic codes or speech variants) which are either elaborated or restricted. Because working-class families are, as a consequence of the social relations of their cultural position, more likely to develop a positional role system, members of these families are more likely to make significant use of a speech variant which requires little linguistic elaboration, i.e. is based upon the restricted code. The individual child acquires language in four crucial contexts – the regulative, the instructional, the interpersonal and the imaginative – and the words, structures and discourse possibilities to which the child is made sensitive are both transmitted and regulated by the communication code used by the family of socialization to order their understanding of the world. For most working-class children this code will be the restricted code.

The link between language usage and educational process, as framed by Bernstein, can now be considered. Because he believes that schools, almost by definition, 'are predicated upon an elaborated code and its system of social relationships', those children who, through primary socialization, have not been orientated or sensitized to such a code, and thus have not learned when meaning needs to be made explicit, will experience feelings of cultural discontinuity between life at school and life at home. This, Bernstein argues, is because:

the school is necessarily concerned with the transmission and development of universalistic orders of meaning. The school is concerned with making explicit and elaborating through language, principles and operations, as these apply to objects (science subjects) and persons (art subjects).

Thus, most middle-class children can always be expected to perform more successfully in the present school system because the code around which the system is organized is that which is typical for middle-class family life, or, again in Bernstein's own words:

The sequencing rules of educational transmissions, the pacing of this transmission (the rate of expected acquisition), its future relevance and its immediate irrelevance are, to say the least, based upon performance rules which the middle-class child embryonically possesses. Class regulates the elaborated codes of education and the family.

Bernstein, 1977

As the above exposition of Bernstein's sociolinguistic theory has been, necessarily, over-compressed, two further points must be emphasized. First, it is important to recognize that *codes* are defined as underlying or generative principles. As Stubbs (1976) observes, 'people do not speak codes, just as they do not speak grammar: both grammar and codes are abstract, underlying systems'.

Second, and related to the last point, Bernstein insists that in suggesting that some children 'do less well' in school because they are made sensitive to a particular linguistic variant he is saying nothing about the child's linguistic or intellectual potential. Rather, the theory focuses upon the kind of rules that the child or adult user will determine as appropriate to certain speech and cognitive contexts.

If Bernstein's account has validity, what implications might it have in terms of the hidden messages carried in school language? Perhaps the following:

1. That certain ways of thinking demand certain ways of communicating and talking – complex, explicit, elaborate and abstract. The message for some children is that the modes of communication most prevalent in their out-of-school experience are inappropriate in this domain. They must, therefore, decide whether to accept or reject a context which effectively devalues elements of the world from which they originate.

2. That learning and educational concerns are significantly to do with abstract principles and operations. The message for some children is that the affairs of everyday life, as expressed in the language of their culture, are distinctly separate from the world of learning.

3. That the apparently superior/inferior educational performances of their peers that pupils observe are explicable by reference to characteristics they bring to school rather than to aspects of how schools and classrooms are defined and managed. The message for some pupils is that their lack of achievement in school is not because the school is making an inadequate adjustment to their needs but because they are different from what is celebrated in school as the 'normal' pupil.

4. That the world is describable in concepts which are organized in a hierarchical structure. The message for all pupils is that modes of communication, like most other social phenomena, can be perceived and evaluated in a ranked order. Ways of speaking are subtly represented to them in a framework based upon notions of better/worse, richer/poorer, high-status/low-status, most-acceptable/least-acceptable, rather than as being simply different.

However, it is important to emphasize that Bernstein's work received a great deal of criticism. Lawton (1968) criticized the constraining nature of the conditions of experimentation upon which Bernstein formulated some of his assertions; Rosen (1972a) called into question Bernstein's definition of class and his characterizations of the life experiences of the various social groups he identifies; Trudgill (1974) and Labov (1969) regarded Bernstein's work as involving serious misunderstandings of the relationship between language and thought, explicitness and logic, and have suggested that we should regard elaborated and restricted speech variants as differences of style rather than of substance. For our purposes, however, the central critical concern must be with the explanatory power of Bernstein's theory with relation to the links between language usage and educational processes. Are patterns of communication in school based on an elaborated code? In his critique of Bernstein's 'idealized' portrayal of school language, Edwards (1976) suggested that this is not necessarily so, and came to some rather different conclusions about the message the pupil receives when he or she experiences this communication form. He suggested that if we consider the typical characteristics of 'traditional' or 'hierarchically organized' schools, where, it can be argued, it is often the case that:

> meanings are too often 'given as part of a natural order which cannot be questioned . . .
> [and] that the boundary between teacher and learner is often too clear, the latter having too
> little discretion; and that the individual child is so submerged in the pupil role that meanings
> relate not to him but to the category in which he is fitted . . .'

then we are left with an impression of a context which, according to Bernstein's own theoretical analysis, would be more likely to be predicated upon a restricted code than on the elaborated version.

Perhaps, then, we are not at present in a position from which we can talk about the 'underlying principles' which shape school language in general, but we can certainly scrutinize some of the actual communication practices found in schools, even if a comprehensive theory which explains why they are as they are is elusive.

The Written Language of Schooling

One distinctive feature of communication in schools and classrooms is that it involves fairly extensive deployment of the written word. Apart from talking, textbooks, worksheets and printed resource packages are by far the most popular and common devices used by teachers to stimulate pupils and introduce material for learning; and requiring pupils to write something about the things to which they have been introduced – short descriptions, essays, test answers or notes – is the main strategy by which children in schools are encouraged to record and demonstrate their knowledge and understanding. An almost unavoidable impression created in the classroom is that the literary mode is the best mode of communication for organizing learning and thinking about new ideas and experiences. But there is more to it than this. Other impressions are also created in the forms these writings take and the purposes for which they are used.

Consider first the language of textbooks. As was suggested in Chapters 6 and 9, a good deal of the *content* of the books used in schools carries covert judgements about what is often presented as 'objective' information. But in the *form* of the language regularly employed in some textbooks for school pupils there are also implied evaluations. Compare the following extracts quoted by Wilkinson (1975). The first is taken from a 14-year-old girl's notes on a text, the second from the text upon which she was working:

> There are two forms of energy. One is Kinetic energy when something is moving. When a man pedals a bicycle down a hill it is Kinetic energy. A body possesses potential energy if we force it to change shape. When we wind up a clock we force the spring to change shape.

> There are two forms of mechanical energy. A body has Kinetic Energy when it is moving; the more massive the body and the faster it moves, the more energy it has. A body possesses Potential Energy if a force has been applied to it to change its position or shape. A bicycle at the top of a hill and the wound-up spring of a clock have potential energy. Potential energy is stored energy.

How does the second extract differ from the first? It contains more technical terms; it is more impersonal; it is highly condensed and compressed; it is formal and somewhat colourless in tone; it is assertive in tenor; it is highly abstract, the information given being decontextualized, separated from an everyday world which would give it purpose and relevance. Indeed, in some ways it seems to have different points of reference from those to which the girl's own formulation is addressed. For example, the terms 'energy' and 'force' appear to refer to general common-sense understandings in the pupil's version, and are associated with the activities of people, while in the textbook they have special reference, associated with objects and abstract ideas. (And, we might observe, this difference of reference seems to have interfered with the process by which the girl comes to terms with the information being presented.)

The point here is that, in the course of giving information which is considered necessary to the development of a child's scientific understanding, the world from which such information is being drawn and to which it is applicable is presented, by virtue of the language used, as foreign and strange, set apart from the one which the learner inhabits. Might there not be two messages here, the one contingent upon the other? Not only is the language used to describe the concept dry, unfamiliar and out of touch with a living world, but so also, by implication, are the ideas which the language is expressing. Might an unintended consequence of using language which is different from that which we use to understand and organize our personal experiences and everyday lives be that it signals to the pupil that such is the character of the very knowledge and concepts we are trying to impart, that the concerns of schooling are similarly dry and alien? Furthermore, might such usage not also convey the impression that what counts as learning, being able to move around in this curious educational domain with some familiarity, depends more upon an ability to articulate ideas and thoughts in abstract, remote and impersonal formulations than on being able to apply the ideas acquired to practical situations and everyday encounters? Harold Rosen (1972b), in his discussion of this formal and conventionalized language found in many of the texts used in classrooms, describes vividly some of the possible impressions its usage has for the reader:

Language like this looks at children across a chasm. The worst way to bridge this chasm is to encourage children to take over whole chunks of it as a kind of jargon (examinations have been the great excuse). For fluent children, such as moderately successful grammar school pupils, this process is fatally easy. Probably few of us who have grown up in the system are free from some taint of this schooling. Instead of the new formulations representing hard-won victories of intellectual struggle or even partial victories, there are not even half-hearted skirmishes. Instead there is empty verbalism, sanctioned utterance and approved dogma; behind them is a void or a chaos. The personal view is made to seem irrelevant; it is outlawed.

For other pupils, however, the gap between their own language and the textbook is so great that the textbook is mere noise. Their own language has not organized their thinking in such a way that they can be cognitively responsive in even a minimal sense. The textbook is alien both in its conventions and its strategies. The subject never comes through: it is another way of life. Though this is not a matter of language alone, language plays a big part. The willing bright pupil has sufficient language achievement behind him to enable him to mime the textbook though his hold may be precarious and over-dependent on verbatim memory. At least the morale will be high when he is confronted with new verbal experience. He has done it before; he will do it again. At the other extreme is the pupil who receives nothing but scrambled messages. He has failed to decode them in the past; he will fail again.

All this is not to claim that pupils should never be introduced to technical language, high-level conceptualization and the specialist linguistic conventions used to manage complex thought and interpretation. Rather, it is to suggest that unless we are sure that, first, we make such introduction in a way which permits the pupils to handle initial encounters with these forms by using their own existing language competences and skills and, second, that we are not using these conventions to give the material status rather than to clarify meaning, then the message for many pupils is likely to be that the concerns of schooling have little to do with the concerns of life.

One dimension of this 'unreality' and the impact it has is caught by Jennifer, aged 15, when she writes:

People who write in textbooks do not make mistakes – and the best way to learn is by your own mistakes.

In Claxton, 1978

However, the language of textbooks is not the only area relating to pupils' experience of the written word in which they might be exposed to some complex messages. In the writing that they themselves do we can identify the impact of other hidden communications. To help make such an identification we can ask three, not unrelated, questions. What do pupils write about? What form does their writing take? Why do they write?

Pupils' Writing

It is difficult to generalize about 'what' pupils in school write about, as this will vary from school to school and according to the demands of different teachers. Certainly pupils seem to do a lot of writing. For example, Nancy Martin (1971), in her study of the total writing done in one week by three classes of seven-year-olds, nine-year-olds and eleven-year-olds, reports that, for the seven-year-olds:

> The average amount written by each member of the class was 20 full pages, excluding pictures, and this covered about 15 different items . . . Within the average of different pieces of written work each child had made four or five diary entries and had written one or two generally long stories; he had also done two or more pieces of work headed 'Mathematics' and two or three brief reports of scientific experiments.

It is worth noting that quite often what children are asked to write about represents a subject division between areas of knowledge carried in the minds of the teacher. The observation made in Chapter 9, that school knowledge is 'mostly non-integrated, fragmented and specialized', is thus reinforced through this exercise. Equally significant is that, in many classrooms, writing represents the area in which a pupil makes his or her most major *individual* and *active* contribution to the communication process. Although much time is devoted to talk in schools, the individual's contribution to any period of talk is usually small, in that he or she is only one of many who share this period and so writing about what they have been taught has become one of the principal methods by which pupils are given the opportunity to produce some kind of individualized response. The nature of this response can vary in type. James Britton (1971) suggested that we can differentiate between different types of language usage (spoken and written) according to the nature of the 'typical functions' their production is designed to serve, and he proposed that these differences can be conceptualized according to the following continuum: *transactional–expressive poetic*. What distinguishes these categories is the relationship between what is being expressed and the purpose of making that expression. Language can be used to 'get things done', in which case we are directly concerned with the consequences our usages have, the end in view, and we work with transactional language. Alternatively, language can be used to reflect on and evaluate reality, in which case we are concerned with the validity of our reflections rather than with any instrumental purpose, and we work with poetic language. In the former instance we assume the role of participant, and in the latter the role of spectator. The way in which Britton contrasts the extremes of his systems is shown in Table 12.1.

It is tempting to speculate that, although we can make few generalizations to describe what children write about in schools, as they progress through them they are increasingly required to produce writing from the point of view of the participant; that is, transactional writing, writing to report on the matters to which they have been introduced in lessons, to recount them or to record them. Necessarily, this means that the practice of using language to stand apart from actuality and to contemplate it, the spectator role, is neglected – meanings and

Table 12.1 Contrast of the extremes of Britton's system

Transactional (participant role)	Poetic (spectator role)
The utterance is an immediate means to an end outside itself.	The utterance is an immediate end in itself, and not a means, i.e. it is a verbal artifact, a construct.
The form it takes, the way it is organized, is dictated primarily by the desire to achieve that end efficiently.	The arrangement *is* the construct, i.e. the way items are formally disposed is an inseparable part of the meaning of utterance.
Attention to the forms of the language is incidental to understanding, and will often be minimal.	Attention to the forms of the language is an essential part of a listener's (reader's) response.
The speaker (writer) is concerned in his utterance to enmesh with his listener's relevant knowledge, experience, interests; and the listener is at liberty to contextualize selectively what he finds relevant.	The speaker (writer) is concerned to create relations internal to the utterance, and achieve a unity, a construct that is discrete from actuality.

interpretations are taken up and used rather than explored and evaluated. Hence, implicit in much of the writing that pupils do, which is aimed at 'enmeshing' with the teacher's knowledge and interests, is, perhaps, a message that the affairs of school are to do with acceptance and conformity rather than with questioning and creating. We cannot, of course, be sure of this. Yet if we examine differences between how pupils write and how they talk about the same thing in school we can find some clues to what they appear to think is required of them in 'school writing'. Compare, for example, the differences between one nine-year-old girl's written and spoken accounts of a holiday episode:

The leaning tower pisa
We went to piza. We all had an ice-cream. It was a very hot day I had a chocolate one. then we went to the tower I was the first one to the top. Piza is a very small town.

It was a few months ag ago/ about half a year/ I think it was/ we went we went I think/ it was in italy/ and we/ we went to a big tower and it/ one of the seven wonders of the world and it was crooked it went like that/ and there were 200 steps and we had to go all the way up and/ I was the first one up and we/ I I almost got blown off the side when the bells went/ we had it was about you had to put earplugs in mm but we didn't have any/ cause we didn't know they were going to go/ then then we had to go down again/ and then/ just across/ across the road there was another place when mm/ i think it was a/ it was round with a/ long round roof on/ and and/ somebody came in it made such an echo/ it was very very loud/ he was talking softly and when/ when he went in it made a very loud echo/ and then after that we went out again and we went down to the graveyard/ I dont know if we were allowed in but we did go in/ and mm/ there was a few graves and/ I wish Id seen some bones but I didnt/ I looked in every single grave that hadnt a grave top on/ but I didnt find any

In Wilkinson, 1975

It could be that some of the differences we can observe in the two pieces above can be explained by saying that the girl found writing more difficult and demanding. But does this entirely explain the formality of the written version, the lack of interconnection, the absence of the spontaneity and attempted development of ideas demonstrated in the spoken version, that impersonality? Could it be that she has learned and is acting upon a message about writing in school – that accuracy and correctness of form are higher goals to strive for than is struggling to express personal feeling and emotions. Harold Rosen (1972b) reports that a 16-year-old boy wrote in his geography book:

> An erratic is quite an exciting result of glaciation as a large rock not geologically the same as it surroundings may be found perched incredibly precariously on smaller stones. This is an erratic.

His teacher ringed the word 'exciting' and wrote by it 'No need to get excited. "Spectacular" a better word to use here'. Rosen comments: 'Every need to get excited, one would have thought; excitement about erratics cannot be so abundant that teachers can afford to dampen it.'

More seriously, it can be argued that when teachers make this kind of insistence, which places conventions above subjective responses, they are not merely 'correcting' the pupils' writing but communicating to them expectations about what counts as acceptable education, knowledge and expression and about the status of these forms compared with more personal responses to the world. From instances of this kind we can also develop a more general realization about communication practices in schools, a realization which gets to the core of the idea of the hidden curriculum of language. When teachers set up and either insist upon or encourage their pupils' conformity to certain *styles* of communication in school, they are not just making use of a form of language to allow the mutual exchange of ideas and information. They are also making statements about their tacit understanding of *what* is being dealt with in this exchange, of *how* such exchanges are most appropriately managed, of *why* such exchanges are being promoted in that particular setting and of the position particular individuals occupy in relation to one another in the exchange process and to the material that is being moved around. They are making a covert but influential statement of how they define the situation in the classroom – of what they regard as educational knowledge, as learning, as the purpose of education and as the roles of the teacher and the pupil.

An analysis made by Barnes and Shemilt (1974) of the responses of teachers in 11 secondary schools to questions about their reasons for setting written work and about how they evaluate it provides an illustration of what possible statements about how they define the situation teachers might make in this particular area of classroom communication. They found that, in their replies to questions, teachers described attitudes to written work in ways which could be categorized into two groups. The groups were distinguishable in terms of their justifications of why they set written work, what they were looking for in the work and how they used this work as part of their general teaching schemes.

The first group indicated a feeling that written work was designed to enable the pupil to record and acquire knowledge presented, that work could be judged against some fair objective of correctness and thus production of something which conformed to the strictures of a predefined exercise, and that such products could be used to assess the pupil's response in terms of how close this came to what the teacher expected or understood the exercise to be about, and could thus be marked or handed back for correction.

The second group indicated that written work was mainly aimed at providing a means by which pupils could extend their understanding and develop their personal feeling about and awareness of the material under consideration, that it could be judged in terms of what the pupil saw as the purpose of the work and of how it related to each particular pupil's individual circumstances, and that the responses the pupils made could be used as the basis of a dialogue between teacher and pupil, in which the teacher would reply to the pupils' writing, could be used by the teacher to formulate how future work should be organized or could be displayed publicly and given a wider audience.

Barnes and Shemilt regard the first group of teachers as conforming to a stereotype they call the *transmission* teacher, and the second as conforming to a type they label *interpretation* teachers. They suggest these differ in their attitudes to written work as follows:

1. 'The Transmission teacher ... is primarily aware of writing as a means of measuring the pupil's performance against his own expectations and criteria. When he sets written work his attention is focused upon the kind of writing he wants ... He assumes that it is his business to define the task for the pupils, and to provide them with information about their success in measuring up to his standards. He values writing as a record to which his pupils can later look back, but assumes that they will address it to a general disembodied reader rather than to themselves or to him.'

2. 'The Interpretation teacher sees writing as a means by which the writer can take an active part in his own learning; as pupils write they can – under certain circumstances – reshape their view of the world, and extend their ability to think rationally about it ... He tries to ensure that his pupils see the written work as relevant to their own purposes and sees writing as contributing to a dialogue in which he plays a crucial part.'

We can get some general impression of how writing might differ according to the type of teacher for whom it is being done, by comparing Stubbs's (1976) constructed examples of alternative ways pupils might write about a chemistry lesson, one personal, the other 'stylistically conventional'.

> Few things can be more beautiful than to watch crystals grow before your eyes in various shapes and hues. Yesterday, my friend and I dropped some warm, strong copper sulphate solution onto a microscope slide, and watched with delight as the liquid cooled and the tiny crystals took shape.

> Two or three drops of warm, concentrated copper sulphate solution were placed on a microscope slide. As the solution cooled, crystals were deposited. Solutions were selected so that varieties of crystal form and colours were investigated.

However, the important suggestion that Barnes and Shemilt (1974) make is that the communication system set up by teachers in classrooms is a reflection of their beliefs and assumptions about the business of educating – underlying ideologies of what constitutes learning and teaching. They hypothesize that these ideological differences can be summarized as in Table 12.2.

Table 12.2 Ideological differences between the 'transmission' teacher and the 'interpretation' teacher

The transmission teacher	The interpretation teacher
Believes knowledge to exist in the form of public disciplines which include content and criteria of performance.	Believes knowledge to exist in the knower's ability to organize thought and action.
Values the learner's performance in so far as they conform to the criteria of the discipline.	Values the learner's commitment to interpreting reality, so that criteria arise as much from the learner as from the teacher.
Perceives the teacher's task to be the evaluation and correction of the learner's performance, according to criteria of which he is the guardian.	Perceives the teacher's task to be the setting up of a dialogue in which the learner can reshape his knowledge through interaction with others.
Perceives the learner as an uninformed acolyte for whom access to knowledge will be difficult, since he must qualify himself through tests of appropriate performance	Perceives the learner as already possessing systematic and relevant knowledge and the means of reshaping that knowledge.

What is important for the present discussion is that, although few teachers make open and explicit statements about their views of knowledge, learning or the roles of individuals in the classroom, in the kind of writing they ask their pupils to do, in their communications about how it should be done, in the situations they create to promote writing and in the way they react to it, they cannot avoid making implicit indications of their views on all these things. Pupils faced with writing tasks which require them to conform to a particular linguistic mode and to demonstrate their knowledge of the details of predefined material, and which are being done to be presented for assessment, are likely to build up very different ideas about what they are doing in school from those of pupils who are asked to write as part of a collaborative enterprise in which they are exploring reality with the teacher and other pupils.

Classroom Talk

Barnes (1976; Barnes and Todd, 1977) suggested that similar messages are conveyed in the way in which talking is organized in classrooms, an aspect of communication in school we have so far neglected in this chapter. As research in this area is fairly prolific, it is not possible to include all the details of such work. However, some of the more general observations that have emerged are as follows.

The teacher talks most

It has been found that most of the talk in classrooms is done by the teacher. Even in those classrooms where we find pupils talking to each other, be this officially sanctioned or privately established conversations, control of the main discourse system is maintained by, or quickly reverts back to, the teacher. As Edwards and Furlong (1978) observe:

> Verbal encounters are still the main means of transmitting knowledge, and they are encounters of a very distinctive kind. For older children especially, the main characteristics of classroom talk are not only that there is much of it, but that so much of what is said is both public and highly centralized.
>
> In traditional classrooms, the communicative rights of teachers and pupils are very unequal indeed. To adapt Flander's comment ... teachers usually tell pupils when to talk, what to talk about, when to stop talking and how well they talked.

Restricted communication

When pupils do talk their communications are remarkably restricted. Bellack *et al.* (1966), for example, suggested that the language interaction in classrooms can be broken down into four basic moves or categories which relate to the recognizable functions of language being used and to how instances of talk are structurally related. These are *structuring* moves (utterances working to create and direct the setting for talk and activity in a lesson), *soliciting* moves (designed to elicit some kind of response), *responding* moves (which are directly tied to structuring moves) and *reacting* moves (talk designed to clarify, expand or evaluate a prior move without being directly elicited by the prior move). In classrooms, teachers seem to use the soliciting moves most, while the pupils' contribution to the 'language game' is restricted mainly to making responding moves.

Using a more sophisticated analytical system, which is based upon describing how each item of talk in a stretch of discourse or speech interaction is related, Sinclair and Couthard (1974) confirmed this picture of the organization of talk in classrooms. They suggest that the structure of discourse in classrooms (i.e. those times when the pupil is asked to take a role in the talk, as opposed to when the teacher is conducting a monologue) quite regularly follows a three-move exchange pattern of:

Initiation → Response → Feedback

Or, to illustrate this sequence more concretely:

Question → Answer → Evaluation

More significantly, they observe that when this pattern is operating, it is the teacher who initiates and gives feedback, and the pupils who respond. Deviations from this course are noticeably rare. A great deal of teacher–pupil talk in classrooms, they suggest, follows the kind of pattern illustrated below:

> *Teacher:* Those letters have special names. Do you know what it is? What is one name that we give to these letters? (Initiation)
> *Pupil:* Vowels. (Response)
> *Teacher:* They're vowels, aren't they? (Feedback)
> *Teacher:* Do you think you could say that sentence without having the vowels in it? (Initiation)
>
> Coulthard, 1977

Even when exchanges are enlarged, through one participant or other extending their turns at talking, the basic pattern of initiation–response–feedback remains the underlying principle of the exchange. Two points are worth noting. First, the pupil's part in the dialogue is structurally contingent upon the teacher's; hence control of the content or direction of talk is difficult for him or her to achieve. (The pupil also has less opportunity to speak, the teacher having the option of taking two turns to every one of the pupil's turns.) Second, even though the pupils are being constrained or invited to take part in a dialogue, it is a subordinate role they are being given; in the structure their chances of initiating talk or introducing topics, of making statements, of asking questions and, crucially, of making evaluations and judgements are significantly low.

An important consequence of teachers regularly taking control of who talks to whom about what in the classroom dialogue is that it can influence the development of pupil identities. In distributing speakership rights, the teacher might be tempted to give preference to those pupils who display a perspective of the classroom situation which conforms to that of the teacher. Or, as feminist writers have observed, the communication system in the classroom can operate in a way which reinforces stereotypical gender roles and relations. Michelle Stanworth (1983), for example, in her study of the patterns of talk in a coeducational humanities lesson in a college of further education, notes not only that it is common for boys to be selected to talk much more frequently than girls, but also that boys are invited to give views and build arguments whereas girls are invited to make passive responses.

'Recitation' and questioning

It has been found that a high proportion of teachers' talk consists of either 'recitation' or, particularly when they wish to bring the pupils into a dialogue, asking questions. To explore these two practices, Barnes (1976) analysed recordings he had collected in the course of following some first-year secondary school pupils through their lessons for a day. He noted two important regularities in 'recitation':

1. As with the language of textbooks, teachers in their talk make extensive use of terminology which is special to the subject they are teaching. Very often they are well aware of this and 'present' the specific meanings to the class. However, even when they do

this, Barnes suggests, 'the act of giving a technical name seems for many teachers to have taken on a value of its own in separation from its utility', and he argues that, although the use of subject terminology is seen by many teachers as an efficient way of expressing difficult concepts, it also serves a cultural function of preserving and signalling aspects of the teacher's role as being 'superior' to that of the pupil.

2.   Teachers also make use of a language which, though not special to a subject, is strictly peculiar to school, the language of 'secondary education'. It is less likely to be explained to pupils, as it is part of the teacher's taken-for-granted perception of what is appropriate in school; indeed, it is sometimes used to explain subject-specialist terminology. For example, consider the abstract formulations this teacher uses to explain the concept 'city states':

> Teacher: They were called 'city states' because they were *complete in themselves* ... They were governed by themselves ... *ruled by themselves* ... they *supported themselves*.
>
>   These states were complete in themselves because the terrain *between cities* was so difficult that it was hard for them to *communicate* ... Now because these people lived like this in their own cities *they tended to be* intensely patriotic towards their own city ... Now, what's 'patriotic' mean?
>
> Barnes, 1976 (our emphasis)

Barnes makes other important observations about the practice of questioning, albeit on a rather 'impressionistic' basis. He argues that we can distinguish at least four broad types of questions: factual ('what' questions), reasoning ('how' questions), open (questions which permit a wide range of answers) and social (questions used to direct the course of a lesson rather than to work on the content). The teachers whose lessons he analysed asked mostly factual questions, some reasoning and few open ones, perhaps thus indicating to pupils, as Edwards (1976) suggests, the extent to which what is being considered in the lesson 'is to be received ready-made, whether it can be challenged and whether their own experience has anything relevant to contribute'.

Although a great deal of work on how talk is managed in classrooms is yet to be done, from the above we can suggest some of the messages to which pupils might be exposed which are hidden in the *way* talk is organized:

1.   That school knowledge is something fairly fixed and closed and that it is quite different from, and of a higher order than, the knowledge they already possess.

2.   That their role in the classroom is very subordinate to that of the teacher; they are required to be passive and to listen to those who are in authority over them by virtue of their possession of this 'superior' form of knowledge.

3.   That learning involves 'answering' and not 'questioning', and that they will be judged to have successfully mastered something when their understanding approximates that of the teacher.

CONCLUSION

In this chapter the concern has been to explore how the *form* of language might carry hidden messages to the pupil as he or she prepares for or experiences schooling. There is one further point to be made. We may not like the contents of some of these messages. Yet, although teachers may have limited power over space, organization, subject and school knowledge, timetables and other carriers of the hidden curriculum, in the way they use language there is considerable power under their direct control. Perhaps they need be much less of a helpless victim in this aspect of schooling than in many others.

Summary

1. Classrooms can be seen as language-saturated places and educating can be seen as revolving around activities like lecturing, explaining, discussing, telling, questioning, answering, reading, writing and listening.
2. Messages may be contained in both the manner in which language is used in classrooms and the content of the communications.
3. Language serves at least three functions simultaneously in school: communication, thought, and social interaction and control.
4. For communication between people to take place there must be some agreed set of ideas, and this linguistic repository of interpretations and symbols was largely the work of our ancestors.
5. The world of our ancestors was rural and military, many of the images embedded within our language refer to experiences no longer central to life in a complex, industrial society and our thinking is constrained and distorted as a consequence.
6. In learning language we also learn ideas about forms of expression and the social evaluations of dialect and accent.
7. Bernstein proposes that the social relations and lifestyles of particular social groups generate variable systems of communication, and that these can be placed on a continuum ranging from a restricted code through to an elaborated code.
8. The extent to which a particular family will favour one meaning and communication system over another is related to its social class position and its family role system.
9. Most pupils from the middle class are likely to perform more successfully in the present school system because the code around which it is organized is the same one that is more frequently found in extensive use in middle-class family life, namely the elaborated code.
10. Most pupils from the working classes are likely to find that the modes of communication most prevalent outside school are often inappropriate in school, with the result that their school experience is one of conflict and potential alienation.
11. The theory of Bernstein has been subjected to a range of criticisms since it was first developed in the 1960s and 1970s. Much of this criticism has questioned the reliability of the description he offers of how language is actually used.

12. The written word is extensively used in schools in textbooks and other teacher-initiated material, as well as in pupils' work.
13. This written language tends to be formal and conventionalized, and a potential source of alienation from learning, for this transactional form of language contrasts with expressive and poetic forms, which encourage exploration and meaning-making.
14. The use of spoken language in classrooms shows some similar characteristics.
15. The use of language in classrooms varies according to ideologies of education: transmission and intepretation teachers have different theories of communication, and these are related to their theories of knowledge, learning, teaching, assessing, etc.

Further Reading

Barnes, D. (1976) *From Communication to Curriculum*. Harmondsworth: Penguin. An important book which looks at how patterns of communication in classrooms reflect different ideologies of learning and educating.

Barnes, D., Britton, J. and Rosen, H. (1969) *Language, the Learner and the School*. Harmondsworth: Penguin. This book, too, considers in greater depth some of the propositions in this chapter.

Edwards, A.D. (1976) *Language in Culture and Class*. London: Heinemann. Contains more detailed and critical reviews of issues concerning the relationship between patterns of communication and the processes of educating.

Postman, N. and Weingartner, C. (1969) *Teaching as a Subversive Activity*. Harmondsworth: Penguin. Chapters 2, 6 and 7 are lively and provocative sections on language and educating.

Stubbs, M. (1976) *Language, Schools and Classrooms*. London: Methuen. Another book containing critical reviews of issues concerning the relationship between patterns of communication and the processes of educating.

Discussion and Activities

1. Flanders found that two-thirds of the time spent in traditional classrooms is made up of talk, and two-thirds of this talk is done by the teacher. Observe any classrooms available to you to see if this conclusion still holds. Attempt to identify some of the main ways in which ideologies of educating are displayed in the organization of talk in this setting.

2. Bernstein proposes a relationship between social relations, lifestyles and language patterns. Does an examination of newspapers such as the *Guardian*, *The Times*, the *Daily Express*, the *Sun* and the *Mirror* provide support for this view?

3. Analyse any piece of writing produced by a pupil in school and attempt to determine the audience and purpose the writer seemed to have in mind and the distinctive characteristics of the style used.

4. Since television is beamed across social classes, does it operate as an ameliorating influence on language variations?

Signposts

Pre-school and early childhood education

It is interesting to explore how the patterns of verbal interaction a child experiences in the home, before he or she ever attends a school, prepare the child for life in classrooms. Several writers have suggested that a hidden curriculum operates in these situations just as much as in the classroom, and that in pre-school conversations the child is already learning important things about learning, the role of the learner and the role of the teacher. For a general overview of patterns of discourse development through interaction, readers should consult Wells, G. and Nicholls, J. (eds) (1985) *Language and Learning: An Interactional Perspective*, Lewes: Falmer Press. Two very good studies of the influence of early language experience upon how the child responds to interaction in the classroom are: Tizard, B. and Hughes M. (1984) *Young Children Learning: Talking and Thinking at Home and at School*, London: Fontana; and Wilies, M.J. (1983) *Children into Pupils*, London: Routledge and Kegan Paul.

13 Assessment

Assessment, far more than religion, has become the opiate of the people.
Patricia Broadfoot

INTRODUCTION

This chapter demonstrates how a sociologist may use a series of apparently simple questions to analyse behaviour. The behaviour chosen is that of assessment in schools. This is an activity commonly regarded as a very important aspect of schooling, and a 'good' school is often defined as one where pupils achieve higher than average grades in Standard Assessment Tasks (SATs) or many examination passes in the General Certificate of Secondary Education (GCSE).

Many concepts in the human sciences turn out to be ambiguous. It often helps to select from the competing ideas a working definition. Such a definition may be refined and clarified during subsequent analysis, but it establishes a starting point. The working definition adopted here will be a broad and general one, in the hope of opening up a wide range of issues. At the outset, assessment will be taken to mean collecting information, on which to base judgements about learning experiences, in schools. Outside school, assessment is a regular feature of social life. We continually collect information about people, places and products, on the dress, behaviour and values of other people, on television, news, consumer goods and sport, and pass judgement on them.

In Chapter 1, it was stated that a key question asked by sociologists was: 'What are people doing with each other here?' To pursue this question in the case of assessment, we will ask four related questions:

1. Who assesses?
2. What is assessed?
3. How is assessment undertaken?
4. Why is assessment taking place?

WHO ASSESSES?

The participants in the assessment activity in schools appear to be teachers, pupils and inspectors. Several combinations of the participants are possible:

1. Pupils could assess pupils.
2. Pupils could assess teachers.
3. Pupils could assess inspectors.
4. Teachers could assess pupils.
5. Teachers could assess teachers.
6. Teachers could assess inspectors.
7. Inspectors could assess pupils.
8. Inspectors could assess teachers.
9. Inspectors could assess inspectors.

These interactions do all take place in schools within the definition of assessment which has been stated, but, based on observations and experiences of schools, the incidence and the significance accorded to them appear to vary considerably.

Pupils Assess Pupils

The highest incidence appears to be that of pupils assessing pupils. They are together for much longer periods of time both in and out of classrooms. Dreeben (1968) discussed the complexity of this activity, since the classroom is a public place where a pupil has to please at least two audiences that are present, teachers and fellow pupils, and possibly also 'absent' audiences of parents and examiners. This public assessment, Dreeben suggests, relates to at least three things:

1. Learning.
2. Institutional adjustment.
3. Character.

Dreeben argued that, in the way schools are organized and operate at present, peers are more involved in the last two processes, and 'being smart', 'cissy', 'teacher pleaser' or 'cool' are examples of these assessments. Even 'private' consultations between one teacher and one pupil usually take place in the presence of an attentive set of pupil eavesdroppers.

Despite the high incidence of this form of assessment, it is not accorded the highest significance (at least not formal significance), since at the end of the schooling experience the certificates and reports record other kinds of assessment, not pupils' assessments of each other. These assessments of each other do have some effects, however, that are now well documented. We now know that peer group assessment of what is appropriate for girls counts as one of a number of powerful influences that shape a girl's self-concept and that these influences, in the vast majority of cases, steer her gently but inevitably away from some careers (e.g. computers, engineering) and into others. The influence of peer group assessment has also been considered significant in explaining the underachievement of Black and ethnic minority pupils.

Pupils Assess Teachers

Little formal notice is taken of this activity, high in incidence though it may be. Indeed, attempts to research this activity and to establish the validity and reliability of these assessments and possible uses of such feedback have been treated with hostility by some teachers, as was shown in Chapter 3. So, although pupils are often the most experienced assessors of teachers, little formal significance has been attached to this.

Teachers Assess Pupils

The incidence of this activity is high and assessment covers at least the three areas mentioned, i.e. learning, institutional adjustment and character. When a teacher makes the judgement of 'good pupil', it tends to cover all three. This activity is accorded more formal significance, since written reports, record cards and marking of work stem from it. Much of their assessment is school based and undertaken entirely by a teacher who is in frequent contact with the pupil, but pupils may also be assessed by teachers from other schools who act as 'external examiners'. Here an assumption is made that those unaware of the pupils' 'adjustment' and 'character' may be able to achieve greater objectivity in assessing their 'learning'.

External examiners assess pupils only at certain prescribed times, and only at certain stages in a pupil's school career. Yet this is accorded especially high significance. Examination and 'standard assessment' results, grades and certificates are heavily stressed and considerable expenditure of money and resources is involved.

Inspectors Assess Pupils

As the National Curriculum first appeared on the political agenda in 1987–8 two major concerns were widely voiced. The first was regarding the proposal for a ten subject structure. As Lawton (1994) argued, this was defended by the 'empty promise' that 'cross-curriculum elements' would be applied to fill the gaps. The second was the concern that any national curriculum should provide an entitlement rather than a back-to-basics, assessment-led core curriculum that might encourage teachers to 'teach to the tests'. The Task Group for Assessment and Testing (TGAT) provided a model 'entitlement' criteria-led approach that provided integrated 'standard assessment tasks', providing a formative model of good teaching and learning that augured well for the future. The revision of the National Curriculum masterminded by Dearing has now resulted in a distinction being made between formative 'teacher assessments' and the summative national standard 'tests' that are applied to facilitate the construction of school league tables.

The simple question 'Who assesses?' therefore yields a puzzle for sociologists. Why are the assessments of most incidence given least significance and those of least incidence given highest significance? The mystery is deepened when you gain information that the external examiner activity is absent from equivalent schools in other countries like Sweden, where assessment is always school-based and undertaken by the teachers. Indeed, this system replaced an external examiner-based system many years ago.

There are, of course, comments to be made on other possible assessment combinations, e.g. teachers assessing teachers (a more frequent activity where team teaching and appraisal systems have been introduced). It is also significant that the Office for Standards in Education (OFSTED) inspectors also assess teachers, but this is an exercise readers will be invited to undertake for themselves at the end of the chapter.

WHAT IS ASSESSED?

A lot of things happen in classrooms. People talk, people listen, people make decisions, people produce written material, people work in groups, people work on their own, people laugh (sometimes), people learn. Activity includes reading, writing, answering questions, drawing and reasoning. Among the learning outcomes are blocks of information, attitudes, thinking skills and manual skills. Mammoth taxonomies exist to indicate the vast quantity and diversity of classroom activity. Bloom's *Taxonomy of Educational Objectives*, which has three separate volumes, is one example.

From this wealth of happenings, some are habitually selected for assessment by the participants. The selection differs according to the point of view. For examiners and inspectors, the written end product of an examination is selected. For pupils, the characters of their teachers, in terms of good humour and patience and their instructional skills of explaining clearly and organizing effectively, are given emphasis (see Chapter 3). Teachers appear to select scholastic behaviour, institutional adjustment and personal character when assessing pupils, though their final judgements emphasize written end-products, as in the case of the examiners and inspectors.

The assessments of teachers, examiners and inspectors tend to stress end-products rather than processes. Diagnosis, adjustment, reappraisal and adaptation appear to be accorded little respect in terms of assessment. One outcome Holt (1969) demonstrates is 'right answerism'. Pupils absorb the idea that learning means finding the right answer, whereas the way of obtaining it is seen as of much less significance and, moreover, doubt and reservation are not welcome. Holt's remarkable journal records some of the strategies developed by his pupils for gleaning the right answer from him in order to please teacher.

Miller and Parlett's (1983) research suggested that pupils tend to fall into one of three groups: the cue-conscious, the cue-seekers and the cue-deaf. The cue-conscious recognized that they needed to work out certain things in order to do well under assessment. These included working out which pieces of work really counted and which were exercises, which method of presentation would get highest marks, what hints were available about examination topics and what would please the staff marking particular work. None of this was declared – it was all part of the hidden curriculum. The cue-conscious group were alert and took up any information that came their way. The cue-seekers were much more active. They quizzed members of staff, sought out information about external examiners, checked the research interests of staff and deliberately set out to create a good impression. The cue-deaf remained largely oblivious that this was an important feature of assessment: they had failed to become aware of this aspect of the hidden curriculum.

Another related phenomenon was first identified by Becker (1968). Becker found that two activities were rivals for a group of medical students' attention. One was 'learning to think independently and critically' and the other was 'trading for grades'. The experience of the students led them to abandon the former in favour of the latter. Over time they gave more and more time to searching for cues to get the best grades from the lecturers and less attention to developing independent thought.

Yet another feature common in the experience of teachers in secondary schools and further education settings is that students claim that debate and discussion is not 'real learning' – they consider that dictation of the right answer is real learning. Then by written recall of these right answers students can demonstrate that they are worthy of a certificate saying that they are good learners.

There is one other possible subject of assessment; that is, the courses or learning experiences themselves. Although it is people and their performance that are usually assessed, there have been some attempts to assess courses rather than learners. One was the programmed learning movement of the 1960s, which resulted in carefully structured courses that were tested for their effectiveness in teaching. Courses that did not teach over 90 per cent of the target learners were rejected as unsuitable. This was perhaps the most radical idea of the whole movement, because it shifted blame for failure to learn from the learner to the learning experience provided, in these cases a learning programme. The Open University has adopted a similar approach to its tuition services through its educational technology staff.

Such an approach could be applied to the National Curriculum. The 1988 Education Reform Act (ERA) placed a statutory responsibility upon schools to provide 'a broad and balanced curriculum'. Yet the ten subjects (English, maths, science, design and technology, geography, history, art, music, physical education and foreign languages) and their assessment have entirely dominated the curriculum at the expense of all of the cross-curriculum elements.

The first National Curriculum Council (NCC) curriculum guidance originally referred to three major dimensions that should 'permeate every aspect of the curriculum': 'Gender equality', 'Cultural diversity' and 'Special needs of all kinds' (Curriculum Guidance Three, p. 2). These dimensions relate to children's current experiences at school, to equality of opportunity and their access to the curriculum, and also to their preparation for their present and future lives as citizens in a free and fair, democratic and diverse society. People who are prejudiced usually believe that the inequality in attainment or capability that they see is sufficient evidence to infer inferiority. Yet in this rapidly changing world we cannot predict what capabilities will be most relevant for the future. It often seems difficult for schools to give pupils the kind of education that seems relevant for today rather than yesterday. The NCC curriculum guidance also referred to six cross-curricular skills:

- communication;
- numeracy;
- study;
- problem-solving;
- personal and social;
- information technology.

However, despite the NCC's suggestion that 'what is beyond dispute is that in the next century these skills, together with flexibility and adaptability, will be at a premium' (Curriculum Guidance Three, p. 3), the National Curriculum has not been structured around these – a subject approach has been adopted instead. Even the 'desirable outcomes' (SCAA, 1996) for pre-school and nursery settings have been structured according to the National Curriculum subject structure rather than from these essential skills.

The simple question 'What is assessed?' thus yields another puzzle. Why is this particular selection of what will be assessed made? Who decides, and for what reasons? Some light may be thrown on these questions by considering how assessment is undertaken.

HOW IS ASSESSMENT UNDERTAKEN?

The definition of assessment given earlier implies five processes. These are:

1. Deciding what information to collect.
2. Deciding on a format or means of collecting it.
3. Collecting the information.

4. Recording it.
5. Using the information.

The second, third and fourth processes appear to be essentially technical problems in deciding which method is appropriate to achieve the ends specified in the first and last of the processes listed. Therefore, the use of the information seems to be one of the critical questions in finding out how assessment takes place.

There are several possibilities. First, there is a *diagnostic* possibility. The information is gathered to tell the teacher what the next stage of learning should be. An assessment of this kind might show that the learner has gained sufficient understanding of one stage to proceed to the next. Alternatively, it might show that further work on the first stage is necessary. An example is that of reading schemes, where performance on one book is used to decide whether the pupil transfers from, for example, level two, book 2A, to level three, book 3A, or has further practice at level two by going on to book 2B or 2C.

A variation of this is diagnostic self-assessment. Here the information tells the learners themselves what the next activity might be, e.g. a new activity or further work on the current learning. One firm produces a reading scheme, consisting of boxes of reading cards, in which pupils can assess their own performance. Another possibility is formative assessment.

Formal tests and examinations may also be used to provide summative statements of achievement. The pupils' scores or grades on these tests may determine their place at the secondary school or university of their choice, and they will often be referred to by prospective employers as well. The main function of summative assessments is therefore to allocate the best courses and jobs to those pupils who achieve the highest grades. The principle in play here appears to be that of rationing. There are only a limited number of places, so the summative assessments are to be gained competitively. Tests and examinations are usually norm-referenced, where the performance of one individual is compared with the performance of others to arrive at a rank order of candidates. Test results may also be used to construct crude school performance tables, although it is widely recognized that the performance of a school depends upon the *progress* made by its pupils rather than simply their final examination grades. No matter how many GCSE grades are awarded to its pupils, a school that uses entrance examinations to ensure that only those pupils most likely to gain high grades are admitted may actually achieve less than a school that achieves fewer grades with less 'promising' pupils. Various schemes for measuring the 'value added' have been tested and some versions have been applied. Curiously, while the term 'value added' is currently being widely used in this context, there seems to be little recognition that the actual values involved are extremely narrowly and uncritically defined.

One alternative to all of this could be provided by criterion-referencing. Here criteria of performance are available to show whether a minimum standard has been reached and, if more than the minimum, what standard has been reached. Individuals are tested, either by themselves or by others, against the criteria rather than against other people. The National Curriculum was first presented as a criteria-referenced system, yet the level descriptions often provide only a crude indication of 'levelness', and teachers fall back upon norm-referencing for want of adequate moderation practices and procedures. The average pupil is thus assumed to have achieved the average grade and the most capable and least capable pupils are graded above and below this benchmark.

As Murphy (1994) has said, Dearing's decision to give teachers more responsibility for assessing their own students is: 'conceptually very different from having end results criterion-referenced, and places the emphasis for development work much more firmly upon In-service training ... the problem with a national system of criterion-referencing is that it is irreconcilable with the breadth and diversity of National Curriculum subjects and the diverse achievements of the nation's children' (p. 11). Later, Murphy adds a rider: 'particularly where there is a requirement to produce simple summary grades'. And here is 'the rub' – the aims of producing both summary grades and criterion-referencing are actually incompatible.

The publication of examination results each year is met with a storm of critical publicity. If the average grades are higher than the year before the examiners are told they have made the tests too easy; if the average grades have fallen then we are told that the schools are under-achieving. For many, given the critical climate and the assumption of hopeless subjectivity, norm referencing provides the only 'objective' criterion for evaluating standards. As long as it is the same limited proportion of pupils who achieve the highest grades then all is considered well. An acceptance of criteria-referencing, by contrast, might bring the unsettling prospect of more pupils achieving the highest grades each year, even the possibility that all but those with special educational needs might one day achieve these highest grades before leaving school.

In criteria-referenced assessment many (sometimes an unlimited number of) attempts may be allowed. Practical examples of this process are the driving test, first-aid proficiency tests, physical and athletic tests and reading schemes. If the driving test, which tests a very complicated and sophisticated set of psychomotor skills, quick decision-making and information usage, were to be based on norm-referencing, the assumption would have been made that there was only a limited 'pool of ability' to drive, so that only a minority of the population could pass the test. However, the driving test is criteria-referenced and most of the population therefore can, and do, become qualified drivers. The National Curriculum could be applied in the same way if the will was there to do so.

WHY ASSESSMENT?

Earlier we noted that what is assessed with most significance in schools tends to be end-products rather than processes of learning, learners rather than courses, teachers or examiners, and written material rather than other activities. Moreover, this assessment is norm-referenced rather than criterion-referenced, or diagnostic and performed by others rather than self-assessed. This suggested the idea of rationing, so what might be being rationed?

First, since the certificates accorded so much significance are used to get jobs, occupations are rationed by this kind of assessment. Why schools are used in this way is not immediately clear, as more than one writer has noted. Holly (1973) has described the schools as being used to do the employers' sorting task for them instead of educating pupils. It does not always happen like this in other countries, and the case of Sweden, where the whole norm-referenced external examination system is simply absent from schools, has already been mentioned.

Second, occupations are given different social ranks, some being seen as 'superior', 'upper class', 'white-collar' or 'professional'. So perhaps along with occupational placement goes social placement into a social class and a linked set of life chances. In Swedish society social placement appears to be more muted and the distinctions between social classes less marked, with life chances less differentiated. The theme of social class difference is developed in a later chapter.

Third, not all the reasons are likely to lie outside the school, and listening to talk in staffrooms suggests another possibility: examination classes are said to be easier both to control and to teach, for the pupils can constantly be reminded of the consequences of failing the examination and thereby are 'motivated' and brought under control. Husen (1974) describes this view of education in the following way: 'Pupils undertake to learn mainly to avoid the disagreeable consequences if they do not: low marks, non-promotion, censure, punishment, etc.' Husen argues for an alternative criterion-reference approach which he sees as preferable to this.

However, the case can be overstated and contradictions overlooked, because there are other ideas talked about in schools, e.g. diagnostic reasons for assessment, personal development based on personal profiles and the autonomy that derives from self-assessment, but if we stay close to Berger's question, 'What are these people doing with each other here?', the picture is closer to Husen's description. To go further into the question of 'Why assessment?' will require the more systematic use of concepts. The one we have chosen to use here is the concept of ideologies of education.

WHAT IS THE IMPACT OF ASSESSMENT ON PUPILS?

Schooling is a competitive assessment and selection mechanism with 'winners' and 'losers' at all levels. This overemphasis on testing and examinations is causing unacceptable levels of physical harm to pupils (and to teachers).

> One survey of more than 8000 secondary school pupils in England and Wales in 2000 led to a report entitled *Testing to Destruction*. The report claimed that stress is damaging teenagers' physical and emotional well-being. It claimed that children suffer severe stress from the endless tests. Physical symptoms included difficulty with sleeping, and eating disorders such as bulimia and anorexia. A cartoon attached to an article describing the survey has a child returning home from school and saying to her mother, 'We had a lesson in the break between tests today'. More than a third of 7-year-olds suffer stress over national tests and one in ten lose sleep because they are worried about them according to a poll of 200 parents. The pressure starts in infancy and increases as children move through the school. By

the age of eleven, two thirds of children show signs of stress as they revise for national tests. Around 34% suffer from general stress, a quarter have lost confidence and 20% are so busy revising they have no time to play with their friends. More than one in ten children have been reduced to tears in the run up to the tests, 12% have refused to go to school to sit the tests, and 9% have suffered anxiety attacks. (See Ward 2003 'Infants in Test Distress', *Times Educational Supplement*, 25 April)

from Clive Harber, *Schooling as Violence*, p. 113

IDEOLOGIES OF EDUCATION AND ASSESSMENT

'Ideology' may be defined in various ways. The meaning intended here is that of a broad but interlinked set of ideas and beliefs about the world which are held by a group of people and which those people demostrate in both behaviour and conversation to various audiences. These systems of belief are seen by the groups holding them to be descriptions of the way 'things really are', and they are the means by which sense is made of the world. 'Ideologies of education' refer to the broad set of ideas and beliefs held by a group of people about the formal arrangements for education, specifically schooling, and often, by implication and extension, also about the informal aspects of education.

An analysis of competing ideologies can be attempted by comparing them on a series of key component features which will be called 'theories', bearing in mind that this is an ambiguous word that has both common and technical uses. In general, any ideology of education will contain various theories, including:

1. A theory of knowledge.
2. A theory of learning and the learner's role.
3. A theory of teaching and the teacher's role.
4. A theory of resources appropriate for learning.
5. A theory of organization of learning situations.
6. A theory of aims, objectives and outcomes.
7. A theory of assessment to discover whether learning has been successful.

The use of the concept of ideology here is to enable the puzzle about assessment outlined earlier to be explored further by showing how the selections of who assesses, what is assessed and how assessment takes place form part of one of several competing patterns of ideas and beliefs about education.

A wide variety of ideologies of education has been described in educational literature. They include: transmission and interpretation (Barnes and Shemilt, 1974); authoritarian and democratic (Lippitt and White, 1958); open and closed (Kohl, 1970); meaning-making and meaning-receiving (Postman and Weingartner, 1971); autonomous study (Husen, 1974); competitive academic (Connell, 1985); bully (Meighan, 1997); and the ubiquitous 'traditional' and 'progressive'.

Table 13.1 Comparison of ideologies and education

Transmission ideology	Interpretation ideology	Autonomous ideology
Knowledge is believed to exist in the form of public disciplines known as subjects, developed in the past and currently being extended.	Knowledge is believed to exist in the knower's consciousness and in the ability to organize thought and action. Subjects are one of several available resources.	Knowledge is believed to exist in the present and future, since existing subject knowledge is seen as limited in coping with modern complex problems.
The learner's performance is valued so far as it measures up to the standards and criteria of the subjects.	The learner's activity to interpret his or her reality is valued, so that criteria arise from both learner and teacher.	The learner's performance in learning techniques of learning and developing new knowledge and understanding is valued.
The teacher's task is perceived as correcting the learner's performance according to the subject criteria known by the teacher.	The teacher's task is perceived as the setting up of a dialogue in which the learner can reshape his or her knowledge through interaction both with others and with subjects seen as resources.	The teacher's task is perceived as organizing learning experiences so that the learner gradually learns how to make all the decisions about learning.
Assessment will be of the end product in some examination probably written, supervised by teachers or examiners, and where entry to the subject is rationed for some reason, norm-referencing will be the system adopted.	Assessment will take place throughout the course as a means of monitoring the reshaping of knowledge, phase by phase. It will tend to be criterion-referenced wherever possible to achieve this result.	Assessment will gradually pass from the control of the teachers to the learners as they learn how to access effectively their own learning. It will tend to be criterion-referenced throughout.

A comparison of three of these ideologies on four of the features given above (i.e. theory of knowledge, theory of learning, theory of teaching and theory of assessment) will show how the ideas about assessment vary with the ideology of education concerned. Table 13.1 makes such a comparison.

The central point that emerges from Table 13.1 is that there appears to be no neutral view of assessment: all the alternatives can be said to be political because they make assumptions about what counts as good education and bad education, and each has consequences for what happens to the learners after assessment is over. Under one system they may go into a lower-paid occupation, believing that they had their chance and were not 'up to standard', and that is that. Or they may go to such a job believing that second and third chances are available and that they may well achieve more later. Or, under another system, they may go to such a job believing that they are capable of learning and relearning whenever an opportunity arrives.

CONCLUSION

All sociological analyses tend to be incomplete, and this attempt is no exception. The approach adopted has been an interactionist one and the four questions chosen ask about the interactions of the participants with each other, with their school institution and their society, and with the network of alternative ideas about education and assessment. An important question is: what is missing from this kind of analysis?

One missing idea is that of a historical discussion. Norm-referenced assessment was seen as a better way of allocating scarce occupations and life chances than patronage, and merit was seen as a fairer rationing idea than favouritism. Out of this view grew ideas such as equality of opportunity and the wastage of talent. A structural conflict approach such as the Marxist sociological perspective would usually give a prominent place to a historical discussion in the analysis. The differences between the various sociological perspectives are the subject of later chapters.

Summary

1. Some kinds of assessment occur very frequently in British schools. Examples are pupils assessing each other and pupils assessing teachers.
2. Some kinds of assessment happen less often in British schools. Examples are inspectors and examiners assessing pupils and inspectors assessing teachers.
3. The rarest assessments, those with low incidence, are given the highest formal significance or valuation, whereas the most frequent assessments, those with high incidence, are usually given least formal significance.
4. Of the wealth of happenings in classrooms, certain things are selected for formal assessment. These tend to be written work taken as the end product of the learning process.
5. For pupils the characters of their teachers are given most emphasis.
6. The consequences of stressing written end products for formal assessment may be right answerism, the development of strategies to find approved answers without necessarily developing thinking strategies and other outcomes, such as the belief that recall is the highest form of intellectual activity.
7. The assessment of courses and learning experiences tends to be overlooked in favour of assessing the learners' performance. Blame for poor performance tends to be attached to the learners rather than to the learning experiences.
8. Formal assessment in British schools is usually norm-referenced, specifying that only a fixed proportion of candidates can be successful, and the alternatives of diagnostic assessment and criterion-referenced assessment, where most candidates are expected to succeed eventually, are largely overlooked.
9. Assessment of a norm-referencing kind may have more to do with allocating occupations, social class positions and life chances than with anything else.

10. Within schools, norm-referenced assessment systems may be seen as one means of motivation and one method of control.

11. The choice of an assessment system may relate to other ideas and beliefs about education that form a coherent pattern described as an ideology of education.

12. Competing ideologies of education exist, each making assumptions about what counts as good or bad education and each having consequences for the learners' fates: this suggests that there can be no neutral view of assessment or education. Each competing ideology of education is political because of its assumptions and its consequences.

13. The interactionist approach adopted in this chapter has strengths and weaknesses. One weakness is the tendency to overlook the historical dimension.

Further Reading

Blishen E. (1969) *The School That I'd Like*. Harmondsworth: Penguin. The pupils' viewpoint is the subject of Chapter 7, 'This Almighty God'.

Broadfoot, P. (1979) *Assessment, Schools and Society*. London: Methuen. Few books appear to approach assessment from a sociological perspective, but this is one exception. Another follows below.

Broadfoot, P. (ed.) (1984) *Selection, Certification and Control*. Lewes: Falmer Press.

DES (1988) Education Reform Act. London: HMSO.

Dore, R.P. (1976) *The Diploma Disease*. London: Allen and Unwin. This book develops the proposition that schooling is increasingly dominated by the business of qualification at the expense of the business of education.

Hartog, P.J. and Rhodes, E.C. (1935) *An Examination of Examinations*. London: Macmillan. A classic study of examinations.

Hextall, I. (1976) 'Marking Work', in G. Whitty and M.F.D. Young (eds), *Explorations in the Politics of School Knowledge*. Driffield: Nafferton. This is a paper analysing the implications of the daily task of marking.

Murphy, (1994) 'A Farewell to Criterion Referencing?', *British Journal of Curriculum and Assessment*, **4**, 3.

Schools Curriculum and Assessment Authority (1996) *Desirable Outcomes*. London: DfEE.

Discussion and Activities

1. Write comments on the combinations of participants in assessment not developed in the chapter, e.g. teachers assessing teachers, teachers assessing inspectors, inspectors assessing teachers.

2. Discuss whether the quotation given at the head of this chapter is justifiable.

3. Discuss the questions about technical aspects of assessment given at the end of the section 'How is assessment undertaken?'

4. Conduct an informal survey of beliefs about assessment among your friends and relations.

   (a) Do they believe that examination (e.g. GCSE) grading systems are consistent? Compare with the findings of A. Wilmott and D. Nuttall in a Schools Council investigation in 1975: they found that the life chances of large numbers of candidates are based on a statistically unreliable examination system. Their findings indicate that:

when it comes to an individual candidate every grade on a five-point scale should be read plus or minus one. That is, a real distinction can be drawn between two candidates with grades separated by two points, but if you are comparing a grade one with a grade two, or a two with a three, the difference quite likely depends on the luck of the draw.

A quarter of GCSE candidates are given the wrong grades as indicated above, and the chances of substantially improving exam consistency are remote.

(b) Do they believe that script markers are reasonably consistent? Compare with:

All the experimental data has shown that for a particular performance expressed in terms of an exam script, assessment by different examiners produces marks with considerable variability such that in the determination of these marks, the part played by the examiner can be greater than that of the performance of the examinee.

Pieron, 1969

the standards set by examinations whether those of a basic pass or an ABC ... grading system are in the last analysis wholly subjective. They are based on what candidates, in the opinion of the examiners (or chief examiner) should attain; no internal consistency or other form of reliability is published. The exam boards do not consider it part of their duties to inform teachers and pupils of the reliability and validity of their products.

Lewis, 1978

(c) Do they believe that the standards in one subject at 'A' level are similar to those in another subject? Compare with:

Recent research by Alison Kelly of Edinburgh University has produced evidence that there were wide variations in the standards expected by different disciplines at the Higher Grade Exams of the Scottish Certificate of Education. Research in Britain suggests that such variability is not affected by national boundaries.

'Tough Exams', *New Society*, 13 April 1976

(d) Do they believe that the standards of different examination boards are similar? Compare with the findings that candidates can improve results by changing boards, in Scott, J.F. (1975) *Comparability of Grade Standards in Mathematics at GCE A Level*. London: Schools Council/Evans/Methuen.

5. Conduct a survey on the impact of assessment on pupils.

Signposts

1. Assessment in primary schools
Much of the writing concentrates on secondary schooling and beyond. Work on primary school assessment can be found in Black, H. and Broadfoot, P. (1982) *Keeping Track of Teaching*, London: Routledge and Kegan Paul; Richards C. (ed.) (1982) *New Directions in Primary Education*, Lewes: Falmer Press; and Galton, M. and Simon, B. (eds) (1980) *Progress and Performance in the Primary School*, London: Routledge and Kegan Paul.

2. The assessment of teachers
There is a link here with the chapter on teachers as victims and a starting point is Grace, G. (1985) 'Judging Teachers: the Social and Political Contexts of Teacher Evaluation', *British Journal of Sociology of Education*, **6**, 1.

3. Should children assess teachers?
Go back to Chapter 8, read the account by Derry Hannam of the way he was assessed by a 12-year-old boy and consider the implications of systematic assessment of teachers by pupils.

4. Punished by rewards
Start investigating this topic with the book Kohn, A. (1993) *Punished by Rewards*, Boston: Houghton Mifflin. Then see Chapter 8 of *Schooling as Violence* by Clive Harber.

5. Personalized learning and assessment: the celebration of learning rather than stultifying testing
Assessment (an idea derived from taxation – deciding what somebody is *worth*) and *Inspection* (an idea found in military circles) are terms favoured by the authoritarian approach. Advocates of personalized learning, reject the government's pure domination approach of *'you will do it our way – or else'* as both counter-productive and anti-democratic.

There appears to be no neutral view of assessment. All the alternatives can be said to be political because they make assumptions about what counts as good education and bad education, good people and bad people, and who should have the power to decide.

Each system has consequences for what happens to the learners after 'assessment' is over. Under one system they may go into a lower-paid occupation, believing that they had their chance and were not 'up to standard' and that is that. Or they may go to such an occupation believing that second and third chances are available and that they may well achieve more later. Or, under another system, they may go to such employment believing that they are capable of learning and relearning whenever an opportunity arrives.

Review (taken from 'walking' – the action of looking back at the pathway just walked, and looking ahead to the route to follow) is the preferable term in the personalised education approach, as part of the cycle 'plan, do, review'. *Celebration* is preferred to imposed testing. *Self-evaluation* and *agreed peer group review* are acceptable ideas.

There is a tension between autonomous approaches – *'leave me alone to do it my way',* and democratic – *'we must have monitoring to protect everyone's human rights'*. This tension has to be recognized and dealt with in some way. An everyday example, the driving test, shows that this can be done. The 'right of everyone to be safe on the roads' means a test that is seen to be as fair as possible is agreed, but individuals can have many attempts at it, whenever they feel ready, and can drive under supervision and with L-plates in the meantime.

The *tools* of celebration are worth investigating and they include:
- profiles of achievement,
- portfolios of work,
- exhibitions of projects completed,
- performance,
- publication,
- presentations via exposition, videos, tape-slide or CD compilations.
- tests and accreditation are fine if the learner chooses them or agrees to them.

(see www.c.person.ed.gn.apc.org)

Part Three
IDEOLOGIES OF EDUCATING

The word 'ideology' has had a chequered career, as Chapter 14 will show. Currently it can be used for the purposes of preaching and prescribing a one right way, as an insult in locating opposing or different beliefs as lunatic or misguided, or as a means of comparing sets of ideas. The last use is the one that is advocated here.

For some, the very word 'ideology' is negative or tainted, and replacing the word with a synonym like 'philosophies of education' or 'alternative visions of education' may be advisable.

14 The Concept of Ideology

Every dogma must have its day.

Carolyn Wells

INTRODUCTION

Ideology is a highly ambiguous concept, and it is necessary to have some discussion of the competing uses at the outset.

The Science of Ideas

An early usage of ideology was as a philosophical concept to distinguish a science of ideas from an ancient metaphysics. The use of ideology in this sense is now rare.

Revolutionary Thinking

Another usage of ideology as a concept, traced to Napoleon Bonaparte (R. Williams, 1977), was that of revolutionary thinking, this revolutionary thinking being interpreted as an undesirable set of ideas. Ideology thus threatened 'sound and sensible' thinking about a vision for a society. From this developed the notion of ideology as fanatical or impractical theories about society, and it was largely a term of abuse.

False Consciousness

One use of ideology by Marx and Engels in *The German Ideology* (1845–7) is related to the earlier view of undesirable sets of ideas. Ideology is interpreted as abstract thought about human society which was false:

> Ideology is a process accomplished by the so-called thinker consciously indeed, but with a false consciousness. The real motives impelling him remain unknown to him, otherwise it would not be an ideological process at all. Hence he imagines false or apparent motives.
>
> Engels, Letter to Mehring, 1893

The true consciousness is sometimes referred to as 'science', setting up a distinction between Marxism, as science, and other social thought, as ideology. This notion of ideology as illusion has become a common view:

> Meanwhile, in popular argument, ideology is still mainly used in the sense given by Napoleon. Sensible people rely on experience, or have a philosophy; silly people rely on ideology. In this sense, ideology, now as in Napoleon, is mainly a term of abuse.
>
> J. Williams, 1977

Elsewhere Marx uses ideology in a more neutral sense, where he refers to the legal, political, religious, aesthetic or philosophic as ideological forms in which men become conscious of conflict arising from conditions and changes in economic production. Ideology is not seen as false consciousness here (see Marx, *Contribution to the Critique of Political Philosophy*, 1859).

Competing Belief Systems

This second use of ideology by Marx is close to a more sociological use of the concept, where it refers to a group philosophy. Ideology is defined as a broad interlocked set of ideas and beliefs about the world held by a group of people that they demonstrate in both behaviour and conversation to various audiences. These systems of belief are usually seen as 'the way things really are' by the groups holding them, and they become the taken-for-granted way of making sense of the world. It is this last use, of ideologies as competing belief systems, that is used in the analyses of ideologies of education that follow, since this makes the concept capable of being used as an analytical tool to demonstrate alternative patterns of ideas that coexist and compete for acceptance.

INDIVIDUALS AND IDEOLOGY

A psychological view of ideology begins with the attitudes and opinions of individuals, and sees these as structured in a hierarchical manner. One attempt is that of Eysenck (1957) (Figure 14.1). Specific opinions uttered on one occasion, such as 'what a naughty child that was in the supermarket', may give rise to habitual opinions uttered on several occasions, e.g. 'children should be seen and not heard'. A large number of habitual opinions about one central issue, e.g. the place and behaviour of children in society, is defined as an attitude. When groups of attitudes are related, this is referred to as an ideology. This raises a difficult issue, that of the relationship between an individual's consciousness and the social world. The

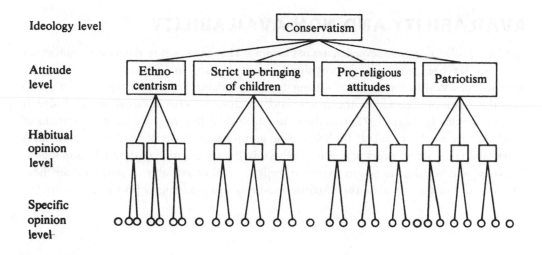

Figure 14.1 Eysenck's hierarchy of attitudes and opinions

psychological analysis above tends to a psychological reductionist approach: the ideology is constructed out of the opinions of individuals. An alternative possibility is that individuals' attitudes and opinions are fashioned out of the ideologies available in an inherited language, inherited institutions and the situations that present themselves over which individuals have limited control – a cultural formation approach. It is not necessary to decide for or against either of these positions if they are both seen as partial explanations: both can be seen as having some credibility, as well as there being an interaction between the two sets of influ ences. For the purpose of some sociological analysis it is useful to operate on the distinction that individuals have beliefs and opinions, whereas organized groups of people have ideologies. These ideologies are not just the sum total of the relevant opinions and beliefs of those concerned, unless they shared identical opinions, and we assumed that you could add up opinions like coins.

> But if you 'add' one opinion to another, you get not only two opinions, but an argument, a debate, a belief and one of its presuppositions, a qualified agreement, an exemplification of a general idea in a particular situation, and so on. Since relations between ideas can assume different forms, and since ideas must be understood in terms of their relations to other ideas, we must be prepared to find an ideology containing more than all the relevant opinions and beliefs of those who adhere to it.
>
> Cosin, 1972

AVAILABILITY AND NON-AVAILABILITY

Systems of belief may have several states of existence. They may exist in theory only, since they have not yet been adopted or recognized, except perhaps in science fiction writing or futuristic novels. Ideologies may exist but be non-available because the sponsoring group lacks the means of transmitting the beliefs widely or chooses to remain small and exclusive. It has been argued by Allen (1975) that the term 'ideology' is best reserved for those systems of belief that are available, in that the sponsoring group has a means of transmitting the ideas widely and takes the necessary action to achieve this. For the purpose of the analysis to follow, 'ideology' will be taken to be any system of beliefs, whether available or not, whether theoretical or in practice, to allow the discussion to be as wide-ranging as possible.

TRUTH AND FALSITY

The question of true and false ideologies would be important in a philosophical approach to ideology. For the purpose of sociological analysis, however, this question is often suspended, and the definition of knowledge is taken to be what the participants define as true information, beliefs, ideas and attitudes. This allows any ideology to be investigated in terms of how far it functions to advance or defend the interests of a particular group, and the consequences of actions derived from that ideology. Nothing about the truth or falsity of an ideology is indicated by this kind of analysis.

IDEOLOGIES IN COMPETITION

The idea of competition introduces an analogy with possible distorting effects; e.g. ideologies can coexist in a state of mutual tolerance with no competition. However, where the ideologies conflict and compete, several outcomes are possible.

Domination

One ideology may achieve a position of dominance over the others. One way in which this may be done is through cultural domination. Gramsci calls this cultural hegemony, where a dominant culture represents itself as the natural, obvious or mainstream culture and attempts to contain all others within it. Such a dominant culture becomes the basis of a dominant ideology.

Incorporation

One ideology may absorb, take over or combine with another in a variety of ways and, if this is successful, it is referred to as incorporation. One example is the proposition of the incorporation of radical educational ideas about equality in educational provision into the traditional educational ideology, by the offer of equality of opportunity in the form of an apparently equal start in the race to become unequal. This preserves the traditional idea of an elite but appears to shift the means of recruitment from aristocratic inheritance and patronage to merit. The incorporation is completed by ensuring that the competition is of such a nature that those who enter the elite under the merit system are similar to those who would have entered under the inheritance/patronage system.

Legitimation

To become dominant, one ideology has to achieve acceptance of its beliefs. One form of this is direct repression through armies, police, secret police and prisons. Esland (1977) makes the point that:

> Of course, in many societies where the dominant group is insecure legitimation occurs through the methods of overt repression. Armies, secret police, machineries of summary imprisonment, torture and execution have been, and continue to be, used by rulers and their socially-powerful supporters to enforce their view of social order. Whether we talk about the Inquisition during the sixteenth century, or Stalinist Russia in the 1930s, or the student uprisings of 1968, we have to take account of the 'legalized' use of force which is always available to the controlling groups in a society.

Esland comments that, in contemporary Britain, it is important to remember that, just by being there, they are secondary reinforcement if the first line of legitimation gives way. There are also numerous techniques of counter-intelligence and monitoring dissent, so that an attack on the social order is likely to be anticipated. A softer form of legitimation is in the use of major institutions, such as education, mass media, religion, law and the economy, to put over a 'consensus', 'common-sense' or 'sensible person's' point of view as against the 'lunatic fringe' view, which turns out to be almost any view inconvenient to the group with the dominant ideology. Control of the mass media and education may be one way of preventing an alternative ideology from becoming available; for example, the British television companies and the schools combine to give special privileges to one form of the Christian viewpoint and to deny similar access by either other religions or non-religious life stances.

CONCLUSION: THE MULTIPLICITY OF IDEOLOGIES

The concept of ideology is ambiguous not only because of competing definitions but also because it is used to describe sets of ideas operating at various levels in society and in various contexts. A ruling class, a middle class or a working class: all may be said to have an ideology. Banks, retail organizations and trade unions may also be said to have ideologies. So may the professions, education, the mass media and the nation. Pressure groups of various kinds, whether for car owners, for pedestrians, for motorways or against motorways, may be said to have ideologies. It helps to try to specify the level or context of the ideologies in question, and when this shifts. This is not always easy. In the analysis that follows, ideologies of education operate at various levels, having several layers of meaning: nationally in the Education Acts, regionally in local education authority policies, locally in a particular school and internally between rival groups in a school. Furthermore, ideologies of education are linked with other ideologies: ideologies of politics, of the economy, of social classes. Failure to grapple with this has created considerable confusion in educational writing in the past.

Summary

1. Ideology is an ambiguous concept: its meanings range from fanatical visions of society, to the false visions of others, to sets of belief that can be compared and analysed.
2. The approach employed in this book is the last – ideologies as competing belief systems.
3. For the purposes of sociological analysis, it is useful to see individuals as having beliefs and opinions, and organized groups of people as having ideologies.
4. Ideologies may be: theoretical, in not yet having been adopted; non-available, because a sponsoring group lacks the means or the desire to transmit its belief system widely; or available, if it has both the means and policy of promulgation.
5. Issues of truth or falsity are seen here as philosophical rather than sociological concerns.
6. Where ideologies exist in a state of competition there are several possible outcomes, including domination by one, incorporation and legitimation.
7. Another aspect of ambiguity is that ideology can be used to describe sets of beliefs operating at various levels and in various contexts with several layers of meaning.

Further Reading

Althusser, L. (1971) 'Ideology and the State', in L. Althusser, *Lenin and Philosophy and Other Essays*. London: New Left Books. A Marxist approach is given in this book, where a distinction is drawn between the role of ideology in repressive state apparatuses like the police and its role in ideological state apparatuses like the education system.

Cosin, B. (1972) *Ideology*. Milton Keynes: Open University Press. A discussion of the concept of ideology.

Siraj-Blatchford, I. (1994) *Praxis Makes Perfect: Critical Educational Research for Social Justice*. London:

Education Now Books. Incorporates a critique of dominant educational research reflecting Eurocentric and patriarchal ideologies.

Williams, R. (1961) *The Long Revolution*. Harmondsworth: Penguin. A general analysis of ideologies and society.

Discussion and Activities

1. An informal survey of friends, relations and colleagues might establish which of the definitions of ideology given in this chapter is the one most commonly in use.
2. What distortions might arise by adopting a psychological reductionist version of ideology that sees it as being constructed out of the opinions and beliefs of individuals?

Signposts

To what extent is the compulsory act of worship in schools an attempt at 'cultural domination' and 'legitimation of a dominant group ideology'? A useful starter is Hull, J. (1975) *School Worship: An Obituary*, London: SCM.

15 Ideologies of Education

Do not do unto others as you would they should do unto you; their tastes may not be the same.

George Bernard Shaw

INTRODUCTION

An ideology of education may be defined as the set of ideas and beliefs held by a group of people about the formal arrangements for education, specifically schooling, and often, by extension or by implication, also about informal aspects of education, e.g. learning at home.

DICHOTOMOUS APPROACHES

There have been attempts to describe alternative ideologies of education. Some of these have been theoretical, while others have been based on empirical studies. A common approach has been to contrast two polarized types, a dichotomous approach:

teacher-centred *v.* child-centred (Plowden Report, 1967)
open teaching *v.* closed teaching (Kohl, 1970)
meaning-receiving *v.* meaning-making (Postman and Weingartner, 1971)
authoritarian *v.* democratic (Lippitt and White, 1958)
traditional *v.* progressive (Bennett, 1976)
transmission *v.* interpretation (Barnes and Shemilt, 1974)
open schools *v.* closed schools (Bernstein, 1967)
dependent study *v.* autonomous study (Husen, 1974)

As an example of this approach, look back at the conclusions of the empirically based study of Barnes and Shemilt (1974), referred to in Chapter 12. Their study concerned the way in which teachers use language in classrooms. Two contrasting patterns of language usage emerge: these were described as transmission and interpretation. These patterns were associated with two different ideologies of education, each having four elements (see Table 12.2).

The limitations of approaches based on dichotomies emerge if an attempt is made to link the ones listed above. There is some similarity in the ideas of teacher-centred, closed, meaning-receiving, authoritarian, traditional, transmission, closed schools and dependent study, although there is considerable variety of emphasis. But the other partners of the pairs have little in common other than being contrasted with a similar alternative. Child-centred, open teaching, meaning-making, democratic, progressive, interpretation, open schools and autonomous study vary considerably, and can be seen as alternatives to each other.

This becomes clear if we consider just one aspect, the activity of the learner. In one child-centred approach, the learners choose from a range of activities provided by the teacher, whereas in open teaching the learners make decisions about how learning is best undertaken. In meaning-making, the activity of learners is similar. In the misleadingly named democratic system, learners respond to a pleasant authoritarian teacher who allows learners some privileges in a contrived, pleasant working atmosphere. Progressive teaching is seen as something similar. In interpretation teaching, a negotiation takes place and a dialogue emerges at the initiative of the teacher. The learners in open schools are also involved in negotiations and dialogues. In autonomous study, the learners gradually take on all the decision-making about what to learn and how to learn until they are able to control all aspects of learning themselves.

The activity of teachers also varies. In some cases they make all the decisions but implement them in a pleasant, 'nice strict' fashion; in others they negotiate; in others they facilitate the decisions of the learners; in others they initiate a dialogue; in others they gradually hand over decision-making to the learners in a systematic way.

The conclusions are that these pairs of ideologies are operating at different conceptual levels and that there is a selection of contrasting pairs from a wider range of alternatives. The latter point is clear from the analysis above. The former point is clear if we note that some of these pairs are describing classroom teaching ideologies, others ideologies of the whole education system and others ideologies of whole schools.

ATTEMPTS TO IDENTIFY MORE THAN TWO IDEOLOGIES OF EDUCATION

A number of attempts go beyond dichotomies. One well known attempt is that of Raynor (1972). He outlines four ideologies of education: aristocratic, bourgeois, democratic and proletarian. He defines as aristocratic the view which sees education as a means of preparing a young person for his social role as a gentleman and as a leader, so education is seen as a means of confirming a person in the social status into which he was born.

The bourgeois is that view of education which sees the examination system as the principal means of selecting the individuals who are to fill the elite roles in society, so success in education is seen as the means by which a person achieves the right to hold prestige positions in work and public life.

The democratic view of education is concerned with the problem of distributing education to everyone as a fundamental right, regardless of his social background and without concern for the social position he will eventually fill. The child's full development is the centre of the educational process.

Finally, proletarian is that view of education (initially held by the aristocratic sections in society, but later having a wider acceptance) which sees its purpose as fitting the mass of young people for the kind of work and lifestyle of the subordinate groups in society. It holds that the education offered should be utilitarian, practical and relevant. Here, too, education is seen as a means of confirming a person in his social status.

Another attempt is that of Cosin (1972). He distinguishes between elitist/conservative, rationalizing/technocratic, romantic/individualist and egalitarian/democratic, and sums up the key differences between them as follows. Elitism is concerned with the maintenance of the established standards of cultural excellence through traditional methods of selection. Technocratic/rationalizing has as its central concern the vocational relevance of education. Romanticism is concerned with the development of all an individual's innate abilities. Egalitarianism concentrates on the principle that all have an equal right to be educated.

Davies (1969) also distinguishes between four ideologies of education: conservative, revisionist, romantic and democratic. They are defined as follows:

> Educational ideologies fall into four categories: conservative, revisionist, romantic and democratic. The first, obviously, is concerned to maintain something like the status quo though conservative positions range from crude dogmatism (which characterises many of the essays in the Black Paper) to carefully formulated versions of Elite culture (T. S. Eliot, F. R. Leavis and G. H. Bantock). The revisionist arguments are couched in economic language or in a pseudo-sociological concern with the 'wastage' created by the educational system. Its emphasis is on improving the system's efficiency in terms of the job requirements of the market. Not surprisingly, successive governments – Labour and Tory – have found this the most attractive stance to adopt, and most of the official reports have incorporated its logic. The romantic attitude (which might also be called the psychological) owes much to a concern with individual development and derives from the work of Froebel, Montessori, Freud, Pestalozzi and Piaget. It was central to the establishment of the private 'progressive' schools and has had considerable influence on some forms of curriculum revision and on the primary schools. Its official monument is the Plowden Report. Finally, the democratic socialist tradition, stemming from socialist and liberal thinkers of the nineteenth century, seeks equal opportunity for all (recognising the difficulties presented by class and patterns of socialisation), and the progressive elimination of the Elitist values inherent in established education. In its most recent articulate form (Raymond Williams' *The Long Revolution*), the democratic socialist approach called for a 'public education designed to express the values of an educated democracy and a common culture'.
>
> This first appeared in *New Society*, London, the weekly review of the social sciences.

Bennett and Jordan (1975) attempted to go beyond the traditional/progressive dichotomy in an empirical study based on primary school teacher self-reported teaching strategies. They established 12 types of teaching style among these teachers, based on six areas: classroom management and organization, teacher control and sanctions, curriculum content and planning, instructional strategies, and motivational techniques and assessment procedure. Most teachers could not be firmly identified as traditional or progressive (taken as equivalent to informal/discovery based teaching style) but had a mixed strategy. The 12 types identified were as follows.

1. These teachers favour integration of subject matter and, unlike most other groups, allow pupil choice of work whether undertaken individually or in groups. Most teachers in this cluster allow pupil choice of seating; fewer than half curb movement and talk. Assessment in all its forms, tests, grading and homework appear to be discouraged, while intrinsic motivation is favoured.

2. These teachers also prefer integration of subject matter. Teacher control appears to be low, but there is less pupil choice of work. However, most of these teachers allow pupils choice of seating, and only one-third curb movement and talk. Few test or grade work.

3. This group favours class teaching and groupwork. Integration of subject matter is preferred and pupils are taken out of school. These teachers appear to be strict; most of them curb movement and talk and smack children who step out of line. The amount of testing is average, but grading and homework are below average.

4. These teachers prefer separate subject teaching, but a high proportion allow pupil choice of work in both groups and individual work. None seats pupils by ability. They test and grade more than average.

5. A mixture of separate subject and integrated subject teaching is characteristic of this group. The main teaching mode is pupils working in groups of their own choice on tasks set by the teacher. Teacher talk is lower than average. Control is high with regard to movement, but not to talk. Most give tests every week and many give homework regularly. Stars are rarely used as rewards. Pupils are taken out of school regularly.

6. These teachers prefer to teach subjects separately, with emphasis on groups working on teacher-specified tasks. The amount of individual work is small. These teachers appear to be fairly low on control, and are below average on assessment and the use of extrinsic motivation.

7. This group teaches separate subjects, using class teaching together with individual work. Teacher control appears to be tight; few allow movement or choice of seating, and offenders are smacked. Assessment is, however, not used much.

8. This group of teachers has very similar characteristics to those in type 3, but they prefer to organize the work on an individual rather than on a group basis. Freedom of movement is restricted and most of the teachers expect pupils to be quiet.

9. These teachers favour separate subject teaching, with pupils mainly working on tasks set by the teacher. Teacher control appears to be high; most curb movement and talk, and

seat by ability. Pupil choice is minimal. Regular spelling tests are given, but few mark work or use stars.

10. The teaching mode favoured by this group is teacher talk to the whole class within separate subjects. Pupils work in groups, determined by the teacher on tasks set by him or her. Most teachers in this cluster curb movement and talk, and over two-thirds of them smack for disruptive behaviour. There is regular testing and most of them give stars for good work.

11. All members of this group stress separate subject teaching by way of class teaching and individual work. Pupil choice of work is minimal, although most teachers allow choice of seating. Movement and talk are curbed, with smacking used as punishment.

12. This is an extreme group in a number of respects. None favours an integrated approach, subjects are taught separately by class teaching and individual work. None of the teachers allows pupils choice of seating and every teacher curbs movement and talk. These teachers are above average on the use of all assessment procedures and extrinsic motivation predominates.

The types have been placed, for the sake of clarity, in increasing order of 'formality'. This procedure may suggest that the cluster can be represented by points along a continuum of 'progressive–traditional', but this would be an oversimplification. The extreme types could be adequately described in these terms, but the remaining types all contain elements of both 'progressive' and 'traditional' practices.

These approaches have several features in common. They all attempt to go beyond dichotomous models to more complex versions, but the problems associated with the former remain:

1. They appear to be selecting from a wider range of alternatives, since the attempts do not match up well.
2. They are operating at different conceptual levels: some at the level of classrooms, some at the level of comparing educational systems across states and nations.

A Network of Ideologies

It is tempting to try to solve the second problem, i.e. operation at different conceptual levels, by categorizing into levels of operation. This would allow a comparison of ideologies of whole education systems, competing ideologies within a national system, ideologies within schools and ideologies of classroom practice. However, level is an analogy with the built-in assumption of a hierarchy of power or influence of significance, and it therefore prejudges the relationships between these levels. One attempt to avoid this has been the distinction between ideologies of legitimation and ideologies of implementation. The first addresses the question of why, the second the problem of how. Legitimation refers to the goals, values and ends an education system should foster, whereas implementation refers to organizational alternatives, methods of attempting to achieve the legitimated goals and, in general, the means. A limitation of this approach is that most ideologies of education contain ideas about both ends and means.

A further possibility is to regard the ideologies as networked. The ideologies of education systems and of classrooms have some links, though they are not seen as tightly and completely linked. The ideologies of education in the classroom may have some links with other parts of the network, but also have logics of their own at the same time, according some autonomy of action. An example from RE teaching shows the possibilities of this pattern. RE teaching is compulsory by law, so secondary schools have appointed staff for the subject and allocated time on the timetable for an agreed syllabus to be taught. Many teachers, however, find this unteachable, either for their own personal reasons or because of the reaction of pupils, or both, and so they spend the time teaching and learning about issues like morals and decision-making in personal relationships, often without a specifically religious interpretation. The national ideology here has consequences for the school ideology but does not determine it.

Thus the notion of a network of ideologies allows contradictions to emerge which might be hidden in a view of levels, or a view of legitimation distinct from implementation.

ANALYTICAL MODELS BASED ON CRITERIA

An alternative approach to describing ideologies of education is to establish criteria of the major features of such ideologies and then to plot all the combinations that are possible. Some will exist in practice and others may not.

One attempt to identify national ideologies of education in this way is that of Smith (1973), and another is that of Hopper (1971). Smith's attempt is as follows:

Some Major Elements in a Provisional Model of Education Systems

I Assumptions

(i) An education system in an industrial society participates centrally in a complex series of distribution processes which include: the distribution of each generation among positions within the social structure, in particular to positions within the occupation structure; and the distribution among future role occupants within the occupational and other structures of 'knowledge', skills and perceptions.

(ii) Processes of selection (the distribution of students among educational routes leading to 'qualifications') and transmission (the distribution to students, within educational routes, of educational 'knowledge', training in technical and social skills, and ways of perceiving and thinking about the world) occur within an education system and represent its mode of participating in the wider societal processes of distribution.

(iii) The way in which the education system participates in these wider societal distribution processes varies according to: the character of the 'external linkages' of the education system with hierarchically ordered social strata and the occupational structure; the character of the structure of power relations through which constraints are imposed upon processes of educational selection and the transmission of educational knowledge; the character of the ideological forms which express valued objectives and procedures with respect to the education system.

II Structural aspects

The above assumptions direct attention to four structural aspects of an education system:

(i)   The structural relationship between the education system and social stratification; that is, the relationship between distribution processes occurring within the education system and distribution processes occurring between the education system, social strata and the occupational structure.

(ii) The structure of administrative control; that is, the power relationships among agencies exercising continuing and direct control over the organization of selection and transmission.

(iii) Ideologies of implementation, which specify the appropriate criteria of student selection, character of educational knowledge and mode of transmission, and ideologies of legitimization, which justify the possession of power by controlling agencies and the objectives that should be furthered by the use of this power.

(iv) The organization of selection and transmission; that is, the administrative practices actually put into effect with respect to student selection, the character of educational knowledge and the mode of transmission.

This model can be used to compare features of different education systems in different countries and rival ideologies at the national level within one nation.

A model that concentrates on the ideologies within and among schools is that of Hammersley (1977a, b). He develops five criteria – teacher's role, pupil action, view of knowledge, view of learning and teaching techniques – and breaks each of these down into sub-divisions:

1. Definition of the teacher's role:
    (a) authoritative role ↔ no distinct role
    (b) curriculum ↔ method
    (c) narrow ↔ wide
    (d) high degree of teacher control ↔ low control
    (e) universalistic ↔ particularistic
    (f) product ↔ process
2. Conceptualization of pupil action:
    (a) licensed child ↔ apprentice adult ↔ adult
    (b) individualistic ↔ deterministic vocabulary of motives
    (c) pessimistic ↔ optimistic theory of human nature
3. Conceptualization of knowledge:
    (a) distinct curriculum ↔ no distinct curriculum

(b) knowledge objective and universally valid ↔ knowledge personal and/or tied

(c) hierarchical structure ↔ no hierarchy

(d) discipline-bound ↔ general

4. Conceptualization of learning:

(a) collective ↔ individual

(b) reproduction ↔ production

(c) extrinsic ↔ intrinsic motivation

(d) biological ↔ cultural learning path

(e) diagnosis ↔ pupil intuition

(f) learning by hearing about ↔ learning by doing

5. Preferred or predominant techniques:

(a) formal ↔ informal organization

(b) supervision and intervention ↔ participation and non-intervention

(c) imperative mode plus positional appeals ↔ personal appeals

(d) class tests ↔ assessment compared to past performance ↔ no formal

(e) assessment

(f) grouping ↔ no grouping

(g) grouping by age and ability ↔ random, friendship or pupil-choice grouping

An attempt which includes features from the approaches of both Smith and Hammersley, to give a model that might serve to analyse particular classrooms, schools or systems, is that of Meighan (1978a), mentioned briefly in Chapter 2. Here an ideology of education is taken to have various component 'theories'. 'Theory' here is used in its colloquial sense of a view about something rather than in its scientific sense. These components are as follows (the order is not significant):

1. A theory of discipline and order.
2. A theory of knowledge, its content and structure.
3. A theory of learning and the learner's role.
4. A theory of teaching and the teacher's role.
5. A theory of resources appropriate for learning.
6. A theory of organization of learning situations.
7. A theory of assessment that learning has taken place.
8. A theory of aims, objectives and outcomes.
9. A theory of parents and the parent's role.
10. A theory of locations appropriate for learning.
11. A theory of power and its distribution.

There may be other candidates for inclusion in this list, e.g. a theory of language and its usage, and the components given above should not be regarded as exhausting the possibilities.

Each of these component theories can be analysed in detail by being broken down into sub-divisions. The following discussion gives some examples of such sub-divisions.

A Theory of Discipline and Order

People sometimes think that discipline is the simple problem of adults making children behave to instructions. This is only one kind of discipline – the authoritarian. Three kinds can be identified. They are:

1. *Authoritarian* – where order is based on rules imposed by adults. Power resides in an individual or group of leaders.
2. *Autonomous* – where order is based on self-discipline and self-imposed rational rules. Power resides with the individual.
3. *Democratic* – where order is based on rules agreed after rational discussion, i.e. based on evidence, human rights values and the logic of consequences. Power is shared amongst the people in the situation.

There has been a centuries-old debate about which of these three is the best system of discipline. It is increasingly a sterile debate. The complexities of modern life are such that *all three types of discipline* have a place to play in the scheme of things. Sometimes we need to follow instructions or take on leadership roles, thus following the authoritarian approach. In an aeroplane, debating who should fly the aircraft and the rules of flying is not the appropriate form of discipline that matches the situation. In a car, drivers needs autonomous discipline and to make the decisions about driving the car without the confusions of being overruled by an authoritarian or advised by a committee of back-seat drivers.

In many other situations, 'several heads are likely to be better than one' in deciding the rules to be adopted based on the evidence and the rights of all involved: power-sharing, although time-consuming, is then likely to lead to better, fairer and accepted decisions with a cooperative system of order.

It follows that there are three types of error as regards discipline. One, the current error of most UK schooling, is to select the authoritarian as the exclusive or predominant approach. The second, the error of some radical thinkers, is to make the autonomous the One Right Way. The third error, from another radical tradition, is to make the democratic the exclusive approach. All these One Right Way approaches fail to match the need for young people to learn how to be competent in the logistics and practice of all three types of discipline and to select them appropriately.

A fourth error is to regard all three as of equal status and allocate equal time to them. In the modern world, the democratic form of discipline is, in the end, the most significant, on the grounds that Winston Churchill proposed: that democracy is the worst form of organization – except for all the alternatives. Clive Harber, in his book *Democratic Learning and Learning*

Democracy, develops the idea that this implies the dual task of both learning about democracy through effective political education and learning how to do democracy by acquiring the necessary behaviour patterns and skills.

The democratic form of discipline has another feature: it can incorporate the others. To illustrate this point, when Roland Meighan and Clive Harber trained teachers using the democratic approach, where the group planned, administered and evaluated their own programme of learning, and with the services and support of paid tutors acting as learning coaches, the group would delegate considerable amounts of the preparatory work to be done autonomously by individuals. In deciding the best way to learn a particular theme or skill, the group would often choose to submit to an authoritarian form of learning as appropriate for that particular task.

Teachers have proved that the democratic approach is effective with all ages of children. Headteacher Bernard Trafford, in his book *Sharing Power in Schools: Raising Standards*, shows how this is working in a Wolverhampton Grammar School (Trafford, 1993, 1997, 2003). John Ingram and Norman Worrall, in their *Teacher–Child Partnership: The Negotiated Classroom*, show how this works with infant and junior classes. The sad conclusion is that most schools in the UK, by ignoring the democratic form of discipline, are doing their pupils a grave disservice. The result, Chris Shute argues in his *Compulsory Schooling Disease*, is that the obsessive use of authoritarian imposed discipline is the *cause* of many of the social problems it sets out to 'cure'. Such schools are involved, as they have been since the start of compulsory schooling, in compulsory mis-education.

A Theory of Knowledge: Its Content and Structure

Knowledge may be interpreted as predominantly past-orientated, present-orientated or future-orientated. Past-orientated approaches will rely heavily on existing subject divisions, on the grounds that the knowledge gathered in the past is comprehensive and reliable. Present-orientated knowledge approaches will stress integration, on the grounds that current problems like terrorism, pollution, computer technology and mass media are both cross-disciplinary and in need of new knowledge to cope with them. Future-orientated knowledge approaches will stress the rate of change and the rate of production of new knowledge, and the consequent need for learners to acquire skills of learning, relearning and developing and adjusting to this 'knowledge explosion'. It follows that a past-orientated view would favour Latin, and a future orientated view Esperanto as an attempted international language.

School knowledge may be interpreted as distinct from pupils' everyday knowledge. The teaching task, consequently, will vary, from replacing the false or inadequate knowledge, to establishing a dialogue, to grounding learning in the existing knowledge of the learners.

School knowledge may be seen as hierarchically structured, in terms of perceived difficulty and status of subjects, or of equal availability and similar status, or may not be seen as subjects at all. In the first case, high-status subjects, e.g. mathematics, may be contrasted with low-status ones, e.g. domestic science, so GCE A level in the latter will be interpreted as equivalent to only a GCSE for the purposes of university entrance. This also illustrates a contrast between the view that knowledge is sex-typed, with some more appropriate to females and others to males, and the view that all knowledge is equally suitable for both sexes.

The view of knowledge which holds that only a limited number of subjects or studies are appropriate for schools may be contrasted with the view that a wide range should be included, with few exceptions, and with the view that there should be no exceptions. In the case of foreign languages, the first view might imply that one stipulated foreign language should be offered, the second view that a range of Western European languages should be available and the third that any language, including attempts at international languages like Esperanto, should be available. (Currently, few schools teach Esperanto, and they cannot get it established as an examination subject. In 1984, however, London University began its first course in the language as part of a degree course in linguistics.)

A Theory of Learning and the Learner's Role

One view of learning is that it is predominantly a collective activity best organized in groups, another that it is predominantly an individual activity. The contrast between a conventional university, with students attending lectures and seminars, and the Open University, with students at home studying from units and broadcasts, shows how the difference in emphasis leads to different organizational solutions.

A view of learning as competitive against others may be contrasted with a view that it is competitive against criteria of achievement. A further view is that it is a cooperative venture.

In one view learners learn to avoid disagreeable consequences, like low marks, censure, non-promotion and punishment; in another view they learn to increase desired personal competence; and in another, intellectual curiosity is a feature of human consciousness unless it is discouraged.

In one view learning is related to ability manifested in the successful performance of the increasingly complex tasks provided in schools. In an alternative view, learning is related to the skill with which the learning situation has been devised: you do not kick the piano for playing the wrong notes, the argument runs.

Learning is best undertaken by listening; alternatively by seeing; alternatively by doing.

The learners' role is to receive without question decisions made by the teachers, or to engage in consultations and negotiations of the teachers' initiatives, or to make decisions for themselves.

The learners' role is to reproduce what the teacher knows, or to produce a personal synthesis from the resources available, or to produce new insights and knowledge. Learners are trainees, or scholars, or explorers.

A Theory of Teaching and the Teacher's Role

The expertise claimed for the teacher's role can be of various kinds. It can be based on the knowledge to be acquired where teachers are single subject teachers or multiple subject class teachers. Alternatively, the claim can be based on methods of achieving learning in learners, an educational technology or learning systems expertise. A third possibility is that of facilitator and consultant, where the teacher responds to the initiatives of the learners for instruction, advice on learning systems, or whatever counselling is appropriate. In this case the teacher is acting almost *in loco parentis*.

The teaching role is closely linked to the claim for expertise. Teachers may be predominantly instructors, learning-systems designers and administrators or learning counsellors.

Teaching may stress product or process. If the stress is on product, the task is to get learners to give correct answers. Where the stress is on process, the task is to achieve thinking, e.g. thinking historically, thinking scientifically or thinking critically. The latter is not entirely specifiable or simple to assess, and requires some notion of 'constructive doubt' rather than the comfort of certainty.

Teaching may imply coercion, negotiation or control by democratic principles, with pupils' responses tending to compliance, bargaining and participant decision-making. The various forms of authoritarian teaching, where learners remain dependent on teachers, and non-authoritarian teaching, where learners either have or eventually gain independence, are discussed in detail in the next chapter.

A Theory of Resources Appropriate for Learning

Resources may be first-hand, second-hand or third-hand experiences. First-hand experiences are research studies, simulations or making one's own text or reading books. Second-hand experiences are accounts of first-hand experiences given in books, in films or by visiting speakers. Third-hand experiences are contained in items like textbooks, which give summaries of what people other than the writer experienced. Schools differ in the emphasis they place on these kinds of resources.

Resources may be books, multimedia materials or first-hand experiences. In the first case the prime resources for learning will be a school library, a class library and subject book storerooms. In the second, the outcome may often be a multimedia school resources centre. In the third case the whole environment of the learners, both in and out of school, is defined as the prime resource.

Resources may be available to learners with varying degrees of access. Access may be very limited, with resources available only through a teacher, or resources, such as domestic science facilities, may be limited to one sex, or a resources centre may be open to teachers and sixth formers only. Alternatively, access may be licensed to insiders only: community schools operate on a different assumption – that both insiders and outsiders may have access to some resources. Open access to resources is another possibility.

A Theory of Organization of Learning Situations

The general organization of a school may be seen as one individual's responsibility – the headteacher's – as a senior staff concern, as a whole staff concern, as the concern of the whole staff and senior pupils or as the concern of the whole learning community, including service personnel such as caretakers and cleaners.

Grouping of learners may be organized on the basis of age, sex, achievement, some combination of these or none of these.

Timetables may be decided long before the arrival of the learners, thus predicting their activities, or as a result of learners' options, or negotiated with learners as a first activity of a new school year.

Teachers may be organized as subject teachers, as class teachers teaching a range of topics or as a team of teachers working with a large group.

Other details of school organization may be expressed in various ways.

Resources

There may or may not be a resources centre, with various kinds of access.

Records

There may be open record systems or secret record systems, with reporting systems of various kinds.

Rewards and punishments

These may range from individual incentives to team incentives, from physical punishment to loss of privileges to restitutionary activities, decided in authoritarian or non-authoritarian ways.

School uniforms

These may be present, absent or voluntary, with styles imposed or negotiated, and decisions imposed or arrived at democratically.

House systems

These, or other sub-groupings of a school, may exist for various purposes, pastoral, sporting, or social.

Extra-curricular activities

These may range from school choirs, orchestras, plays, clubs and societies to none at all, as in many European countries, where schooling is limited to classroom learning.

A Theory of Assessment that Learning Has Taken Place

Views as to who is best able to assess learning range from the external examiners of an examination board, to the teachers of the learners, to the learners themselves.

Notions of what should be assessed vary: the courses, for their efficiency in achieving learning; the teachers, for their results; and the pupils, for their achievement in learning.

The purposes of assessment may be diagnostic, to direct further learning, or for selection of some kind.

The method employed may vary from criterion-referencing, performance against known criteria, to norm-referencing, to produce an agreed proportion of successes and failures.

The assessment may focus on the processes of learning, adapting, revising and thinking, or on an end-product of written right answers.

Assessment may refer to written performances, non-written performances, institutional adjustment or personal character.

The form of assessment may vary, from references to reports, to profiles, to certificates, to self-report profiles.

A Theory of Aims, Objectives and Outcomes

There is an agenda of aims from which different approaches to education select their priorities.

The society for which education is thought to be preparing pupils can be characterized in various ways. It may be seen as a society of rigid inequality where pupils are eventually allocated to occupational roles according to birth or patronage. It may be seen as a state of fluidity, with mobility for a minority based on some means of competition and selection. Other visions of society stress some form of equality. Another alternative proposes a pluralistic society with conflicts of interest resolved by democratic means. These do not exhaust the possibilities. The aims given most priority vary according to which vision of society is being promoted and they will be selected from an agenda that includes the following. Education should aim at:

- preparation for living out the prescriptions of a particular religion;
- preparation for personal autonomy and personal development;
- producing people who will serve the needs of the economy;
- preparation for constructive leisure;

- producing people who will be participating citizens in a democracy;
- preparation for economic activity as a consumer;
- developing people who will conform to the society as it is;
- producing people who will change society through research and innovation;
- preparing citizens who are capable of adapting to changes that occur in an uncertain future;
- producing people who will serve their nation without question;
- preparing people for an increasingly international identity.

According to which order of priority these are given in a nation, and which are excluded, we can begin to classify that country as being predominately fascist, religious fundamentalist, nationalist, democratic, pluralistic, totalitarian, communist, capitalist or some combination of these, such as welfare capitalist. There are other possibilities still, such as internationalist. In the UK, the nationalist-economic and conformist aims appear to be held as paramount and this rather limited vision can be seen as contributing to the rigidity of the present system.

A Theory of Location

An expensive decision in terms of money to be spent concerns the theory of location adopted. Learning may be seen as best undertaken in a special building, which may be a school, a college or a university. Alternatively, it may be undertaken in a community operating from an organizational base, as in the case of the 'anywhere' or 'everywhere' or 'street' schools that have been experimented with in the USA (e.g. the Parkway Project in Philadelphia). Or learning may be organized using home as a base, as in the case of the Open University or Education Otherwise families. In another view, the City as School in New York has defined workplaces as the central focus for high school pupils and a succession of work experiences makes up the core of the curriculum.

Under a flexible system of education, a wide variety of locations can be used for learning and this theme is pursued in the final section of this book.

A Theory of Parents

The role of the parent can be seen in different ways and one of these will be selected as the predominant outlook. In one view, parents are spectators, preferably admiring, for if they are not admirers they may become problems to be dealt with by professionally trained teachers. Alternatively, they are the customers or clients who should control the activity of potentially wayward teachers through governing bodies. In another view, they are para-professional aides who can be useful to teachers providing they do what the teachers say. Next they may be seen as partners with teachers, working to agreed schedules that involve negotiation and inputs from both parties. In the last view, parents are the primary educators, who may, or may not, decide to involve teachers in their educational programme in various ways.

The first role defintion of parents as spectators, whether admirers, interferers, neglecters or something else, has been predominant since the 1870s, when mass schooling was established. Since most parents were then assumed to be illiterate with no experience of schooling, it was thought that education was best left to the professionals. As schooling has been partially successful the other definitions of the parent's role have been emerging with growing but irregular frequency, often with strong opposition from schools.

A Theory of Power and Its Distribution

Power and order appear in rival forms. In authoritarian systems, power is concentrated in the hands of one or a small group of people (e.g. a headteacher or a senior management team) who believe they have the right or have been appointed to impose the decisions they make upon others.

In non-authoritarian systems, power is dispersed. This has two major forms, autonomous, where power is devolved to individuals, and democratic, where power is dispersed to groups. In democratic systems power is shared in some form or other and to some degree or other, so that decisions are made collectively or have some collective base or approval.

As regards order or discipline systems, authoritarian order is a matter of imposition, coercion or manipulation via 'leadership' or some other device, such as inheritance, as in the case of a monarchy. Democratic order and discipline is a matter of negotiation, agreement and contracts involving dialogue and discussion. Autonomous order stresses self-regulation and self-discipline.

CONCLUSION

These are examples of how the theories can be analysed further by proposing sub-divisions, and do not exhaust the possibilities. Future work no doubt will extend the list. But enough has been achieved here, it is claimed, to demonstrate that, although the concept of ideologies of education is highly ambiguous, it is capable of being used as an analytical tool.

The attempts confined to dichotomies, it has been suggested, have severe limitations: first, because they select two from a range of possible alternatives (frequently a different pairing each time); second, because these attempts operate at various conceptual levels, ranging from national systems to individual schools, without always specifying the level in question.

Attempts to establish more complex typologies of four or more ideologies of education have pointed the way to a more systematic attempt based on criteria of comparison.

The attempt to establish an analytical model based on criteria has centred on the establishment of various component theories that make up an ideology of education. These theories can be looked at in detail by outlining sub-divisions within these theories.

A previous attempt along these lines (Hammersley, 1977a, b) suggested that these sub-divisions were dichotomous, but the attempt discussed here has demonstrated that frequently three or more alternatives can be discerned.

Summary

1. An ideology of education may be defined as the set of ideas and beliefs held by a group of people about the formal arrangements for education, particularly schooling.
2. A common approach to describing alternative ideologies has been the dichotomy, which contrasts two patterns of assumptions.
3. Dichotomous approaches tend to understate the complexity of the activities of teachers and learners.
4. Attempts to locate more than two ideologies get nearer to the complexities of schooling, but still appear to be selecting from a much wider range of alternatives.
5. Analytical attempts based on criteria allow a wide range of actual and potential patterns to be identified.
6. The version used here proposes that any given ideology of education can be compared with others on the basis of a series of component theories about knowledge, learning, teaching resources, organization, assessment and aims.
7. Although the concept of ideology is ambiguous, it is capable of being used as an analytical tool to compare various patterns of educational beliefs and practices.

Further Reading

Bennett, N. (1976) *Teaching Styles and Pupil Progress*. London: Open Books. A complex attempt to describe ideologies of education.

Freire, P. (1972) *Pedagogy of the Oppressed*. Harmondsworth: Penguin. Uses a dichotomous approach.

Kohl, H. (1970) *The Open Classroom*. London: Methuen. Another interesting book which uses a dichotomous approach.

Postman, N. and Weingartner, C. (1971) *Teaching as a Subversive Activity*. Harmondsworth: Penguin. Also uses a dichotomous approach.

Raynor, J. (1972) *The Curriculum in England*. Milton Keynes: Open University Press. A more complex attempt.

Taylor, L.C. (1971) *Resources for Learning*. Harmondsworth: Penguin. A particular component of an ideology is the focus of the whole book.

Toogood, P. (1984) *The Head's Tale*. Telford: Dialogue Publications. One headteacher's attempt to establish a variant ideology of education.

Watts, J. (1980) *Towards an Open School*. Harlow: Longman. Another headteacher's experiences and reflections.

Discussion and Activities

1. Take the list of dichotomous approaches given at the start of the chapter and compare as many as you can, using the component theories approach.
2. Using the material in Chapter 12, produce an account of a further component – a theory of language and its usage.
3. Is the components approach, which aims to identify a variety of ideologies of education, itself ideological?

Signposts

1. Parents

A further component theory of an ideology of education may be that of a theory of parents and the parents' role. The materials and reading suggestions of Chapter 4 should provide a starting point.

2. How to democratize a school

In two short and lively books, head teacher Bernard Trafford describes and analyses the process of trying to move a school into more democratic behaviour patterns over a five-year period: Trafford, B. (1993) *Sharing Power in School: Raising Standards*, Derby: Education Now; Trafford, B. (1997) *Participation, Power-sharing and School Improvement*, Nottingham: Educational Heretics Press; Trafford, B. (2003) *School Councils, School Democracy, School Improvement*, Leicester: Secondary Heads Association; Welgemoed, A. 'Democratising a School in South Africa', in Harber, C. (ed.) (1998), *Voices for Democracy*, Nottingham: Education Now Books; Apple, M. and Beane, J. (1999) *Democratic Schools: Lessons from the Chalkface*, Buckingham: Open University Press.

3. Political ideology

Is New Labour's education policy centrist, liberal (in the late nineteenth-century British sense), centre-left, updated social democratic, centre-right, Thatcherite, post-Thatcherite, neo conservative or neo-liberal? Or is Labour's education ideology inchoate and contradictory – a mixture of ideologies? Is there a 'Third Way' in education and elsewhere? Or does New Labour's much-vaunted policy priority of 'Education, education, education' represent, in fact, the triumph of Thatcherism, subservient to the interests of 'Business, business, business'?

See Hill, D. (1999) '"Education, Education, Education", or "Business, Business, Business"? The Third Way Ideology of New Labour's Educational Policy in England and Wales', paper presented at the European Conference on Educational Research, Lahti, Finland, 22–25 September. The text is in the Education-line Internet document collection at *http://www.leeds.ac.uk/educol/documents/00002208.htm*

16 Authoritarian and Non-authoritarian Ideologies of Education

The golden rule is that there are no golden rules.

George Bernard Shaw

INTRODUCTION

The model proposed in Chapter 15 has component 'theories' which make up an ideology of education. A specific ideology is seen as containing a view, stated or implicit, on most, if not all, of these theories. However, previous attempts to identify ideologies have given priority to one or other of these component theories and usually are given a label that indicates this.

The first example we will look at is that of Raymond Williams (1961). In devising his fourfold typology of Liberal/Conservative, bourgeois, democratic and populist/proletarian, Williams has implicit theories of knowledge, learning, teaching and the other component theories given earlier, but locates his classification, both by name and content, in the component of aims, objectives and outcomes.

By contrast, the attempt by Kohl (1970) to juxtapose open and closed classrooms gives priority to the components of teaching and the teacher's role and learning and the learner's role. The classification of Bernstein (1967) also uses the terms 'open' and 'closed', but gives stress to the components of organization of learning situations and of aims and objectives.

The classification of Barnes and Shemilt (1974) concentrates on the components of teaching language usage in particular, and the teacher's role, and develops from this an explicit account of the components of knowledge, its content and structure.

It follows that one advantage of the proposed model is that it enables the existing attempts to be located and compared, and goes some way towards reducing the confusion created by these rival attempts. Table 16.1 shows the picture that emerges as a first attempt at such a comparison.

Table 16.1 Comparison of component theories

	TK	TL	TT	TR	TA	TO	TAO	TLL
Williams (Liberal/Conservative, bourgeois, democratic, populist/proletarian)						X		
Kohl (open and closed classroom)		X	X					
Bernstein (open and closed schools)					X	X		
Barnes and Schemilt (transmission and interpretation)	X		X					
Postman and Weingartner (meaning-making, meaning-receiving)		X						
Lipitt and White (authoritarian, democratic)		X	X				X	
Raynor (aristocratic, bourgeois, democratic, proletarian)							X	

X = priority or stress given to this component or components
TK = theory of knowledge, its content and structure
TL = theory of learning and the learner's role
TT = theory of teaching and the teacher's role
TR = theory of resources appropriate for learning
TA = theory of assessment of learning situation
TO = theory of organization of learning situation
TAO = theory of aims, objectives and outcomes
TLL = theory of the location of learning

There are attempts that stress a theory of resources. Taylor (1971) juxtaposes learning based on resources with learning based on formal teaching, and proposes a changed role for learners in the process. An attempt that gives priority to a theory of assessment is the proposal for an integrated social sciences advanced level GCE which links a school-based assessment system, similar to the Swedish system, to a theory of learning through student decision-making, first-hand experiences and a network theory of knowledge. Both the Open University and Education Otherwise are examples where priority is given to the home as a learning location.

Another advantage of the approach based on component theories is that it enables ideologies of education that appear to be similar to be shown to vary in key details: they may share several component theories in common but vary crucially in one or two others. Sometimes it is possible to show that ideologies that are said to be contrasting in type are actually very close, because they have more in common in a range of component theories than is recognized. An example of this is the Lippitt and White pair of ideologies of education, authoritarian and democratic. It will be argued that the term democratic is highly inappropriate, because it turns out to be a variant form of authoritarian.

AUTHORITARIAN AND DEMOCRATIC IDEOLOGIES OF EDUCATION

Alternative Authoritarian Forms

If 'authoritarian' is taken to mean a discipline system with a dependence relationship in which one person is dominant and another or others dependent, it is possible to suggest several forms. One is the autocratic form. Here order is imposed through fear, which may be either physical or psychological. The images related to this form are those of a dictator, commanding officer or ringmaster. It is this form that is most frequently meant by the term 'authoritarian' and it is the form predominantly investigated in the Lippitt and White (1958) experiments.

Next there is a parental form. Here order is obtained through deference. The related images are those of a father, a mother, a priest or a village policeman. The paternal variant may be seen in many secondary schools, while the maternal variant occurs in many primary schools.

Third, there is the charismatic form. Here order is obtained through personal magnetism, public performance skills or emotional persuasion. The related images are those of a leader with his disciples, entertainer or pied piper.

Fourth, there is the organizational form. Here order is obtained through detailed organization, indicating a clear structure, giving full instructions and deciding ends and means in a systematic way. The related images are those of an architect, production planner or quantity surveyor.

Fifth, there is the expertise form. Here order is obtained through the possession of information demonstrated to be useful or believed to be necessary by the non-expert. Related images are a doctor or a scientist.

Sixth, there is the consultative form. Here order is obtained through the use of feedback from the learners so that they feel that the teacher has taken account of their ideas and responses. The related images are those of a market researcher or a diagnostician.

In all these cases the dependence relationship tends to persist unless the dominant person decides otherwise, though reactions from the submissive persons can occur. However, the degree of dependence appears to vary with each type. With the autocratic it may be 100 per cent, whereas with the other forms it may often be less than this.

The concept of authoritarian order thus breaks down into the types shown in Figure 16.1. (There are echoes here of the classical analysis by Max Weber of three types of authority – traditional, charismatic and bureaucratic.)

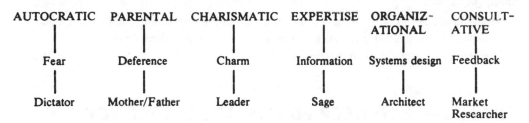

Figure 16.1 Authoritarian order

The various forms of authoritarian order shown in Figure 16.1 can be seen in classrooms in a single manifestation, where a teacher relies almost exclusively on one type to establish and maintain order. They are also seen in combination, where teachers use a variety of forms according to the situation, their moods or the stage of their relationship with the class (the 'start autocratic and ease up later to become consultative, parental or charismatic' principle frequently advocated in the phrase 'start tough and ease up later').

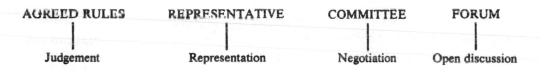

Figure 16.2 Democratic order

Alternative Democratic Forms

The concept of democratic order suffers from a similar lack of clarification, and again there is often a failure to distinguish between several types. If 'democratic' is taken to mean that a discipline system has an independence element in the relationship, with the possibility of all the persons in it having some agreed level of participation in decision-making, there are various possible forms.

One is the *agreed rules* form. Here order is obtained by appealing to rules agreed at some previous date. The teacher administers the rules, but these are open to appeals or changes. The related images are those of referee or judge.

Second, there is the *representative* form. Here the class elects spokesmen, either formally or by an identification process, and these spokesmen can influence the decisions made.

Third, there is the *committee* form. Here several representatives are elected or nominated to meet to make decisions. This is often in connection with a particular project, but it has a potential wider application.

Fourth, there is the *forum* type. Here all members of a class are involved in open discussion about decisions.

(In all these cases the amount of real independence in the relationship can be manipulated by the teacher, and sometimes eradicated, so that it becomes pseudo-democratic.)

The concept of democratic order thus breaks down into the forms shown in Figure 16.2.

SHALLOW AND DEEP FORMS OF DEMOCRACY

In shallow forms of democracy only a small amount of power is shared, often under limited licence which those in power can withdraw at will, and often confined to marginal activities. As an example, many schools organize schools councils. They are usually allowed limited time and limited scope, and if they try to extend their range of tasks, they are reprimanded or shut down. Teachers retain a veto and use it whenever it suits them.

Such shallow democracy can degenerate to such a sham as to be counter-productive in leading to cynicism, fatalism and a belief that 'democracy does not work'. Sham democracy certainly does not work. On the other hand, shallow democracy can lead on to a gradual development into more participation and influence for the learners, as Trafford (1993) demonstrates.

Deep democracy is not simply about the number and range of items where power is shared. It is also about the levels of decision-making. It is not just being involved in more items on a longer agenda, but also having the opportunity to decide the agenda itself. In shallow democracy, children may decide how to redesign and landscape the playground. In deeper democracy, they may be involved in appointing new teachers, as they are in some Scandinavian countries, and in redesigning the curriculum.

The terms 'deep' and 'shallow' only indicate a general dimension. Hart (1992) has developed a 'ladder' of eight levels of children's participation. By leaning his ladder against a school it is possible to see how many rungs children have the opportunity to climb in a particular case. At the lowest rung is 'manipulation', where children are making choices in an activity designed by adults which is not subject to any feedback or modification. At the top rung is 'child-designed activity with shared decisions with adults'. Among other rungs below are 'adult designed with shared decisions with children', 'child designed and directed' and 'consulted and informed'.

Another approach that indicates levels of democracy in operation in a school is that of Davies (1994), where she develops a series of performance indicators of democracy covering such areas as the structure of school management, decision-making arenas, practice opportunities in democracy and preparation for active citizenship. Most secondary schools in the UK score nil or little more on these performance indicators, supporting Carl Rogers (1993) where he points out that schools, for the most part, despise and scorn democracy:

> Students do not participate in choosing the goals, the curriculum, or the manner of working. These things are chosen for the students. Students have no part in the choice of teaching personnel, nor any voice in educational policy. Likewise the teachers often have no choice in choosing their administrative officers ... All this is in striking contrast to all the teaching about the virtues of democracy, the importance of the 'free world,' and the like. The political practices of the school stand in the most striking contrast to what is taught. While being taught that freedom and responsibility are the glorious features of our democracy, students are experiencing powerlessness, and as having almost no opportunity to exercise choice or carry responsibility.

MISUSE OF THE TERM 'DEMOCRATIC'

A summary of the Lippitt and White analysis of authoritarian and democratic regimes is given in Chapter 6. From this analysis it is clear that Lippitt and White's 'democratic' is a misnomer. The independence relationship basic to the classification 'democratic' is missing, and the characteristics match none of the democratic forms briefly outlined. It is, however, close to the notion of parental authoritarian previously described. The conclusion is that, far from the Lippitt and White regimes being a contrasting pair, they are similar and represent two variants of the authoritarian group of regimes: autocracy and parentalism.

INADEQUACIES IN THE AUTHORITARIAN– DEMOCRATIC CONTINUUM VIEW

The above attempt to develop the concepts of authoritarian and democratic ideologies of education seems inadequate on at least four counts:

1. The placing of each type on a continuum obscures the possibility that each may have its own continuum that can bridge into democratic forms. Thus the organizational regime can remain extremely authoritarian, or can operate to transfer learners gradually into more independent systems of learning. This may be presented diagrammatically as shown in Figure 16.3.
2. The use of the term 'democratic' rather than 'non-authoritarian' effectively prevents the discussion of ideologies of education involving an independence element for individuals

rather than groups of learners. Such individually based independence systems of learning have been called by various names, including individualized study and independent learning. The term used here will be autonomous study, the term adopted by the Council of Europe Committee for General and Technical Education in 1975.

3. The analysis is based predominantly on one component feature of ideologies of education, the theory of teaching and the teacher's role. The other features are not clearly indicated.

4. The possibility of there being ideologies lying between the authoritarian and democratic regimes which could operate as bridges in either direction, i.e. towards more or less independence for learners, is overlooked. One such possibility is a consultative ideology of education, where negotiations take place at the initiative of the teacher at first, but later may become more democratic.

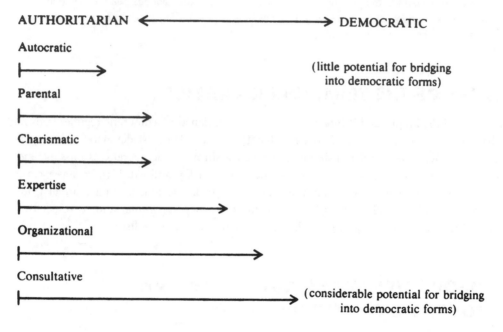

Figure 16.3 The potential of the various forms of authoritarian regime for bridging into democratic forms

AUTHORITARIAN AND NON-AUTHORITARIAN

One limitation of the term 'democratic' has already been suggested: it obscures the possibility of other alternatives to authoritarian ideologies of education. One candidate for consideration is autonomous study, with its stress on individual learning rather than group learning, and this is the subject of the next chapter.

This suggests that there are at least three groups of ideologies of education: authoritarian, democratic and autonomous study. There can be overlaps, interactions and combinations among these, but they can also be identified as having distinct characteristics. 'Non-authoritarian' allows for alternatives other than democratic to be considered.

A second advantage of these terms is that they have reference to several of the component theories of ideologies of education, whereas some terms apply to only one, as was demonstrated earlier; it is possible to talk of authoritarian teaching, learning, knowledge, aims, objectives and outcomes, organization, resources and assessment. The term 'non-authoritarian' also applies to these various components. This is not, of course, returning to simple dichotomies, since these terms categorize groups of ideologies of education, and not simple alternatives.

BRIDGING

A consideration of autonomous study raises another issue regarding ideologies of education which leads to confusion. Autonomous study can be interpreted as:

1. a method of teaching and learning within an ideology of education, e.g. transmission; or
2. an ideology of education in its own right; or
3. an option available to learners operating in a democratic ideology of education.

In the first case we have a teacher-based system which uses, as one of a repertoire of techniques, autonomous study methods, whereas in the second case the notion of autonomous study dominates the theories of aims, learning, resources, etc. This dual interpretation raises some practical possibilities of moving gradually from the situation where autonomous study is one item in the repertoire of one ideology of education to the situation where it is dominant, in other words the possibility of bridging from one ideology of education to another, if a teacher so desires. The necessity for developing such bridging techniques is signalled in a discussion by Goodson (1975) of the failure of one attempt, at Countesthorpe College, to move from a 'teachers' curriculum' approach to an 'integration and individualization' approach. Here, it would appear, bridging strategies had not been clearly thought out, so the enterprise failed. Where bridging is taking place, a hybrid ideology of education may emerge which has some features of, say, the authoritarian group and some features of one of the other groups. Bridging and hybrid ideologies of education appear to be significant for the understanding of the processes of curriculum change.

CONCLUSION

This chapter has tried to show how the approach using component theories that make up an ideology of education can be used to clarify some of the confusions that exist in this field:

1. Existing attempts to describe ideologies of education can be compared to show how they tend to give priority to one or other of the component theories. The labels used indicate this: compare 'bourgeois', stressing aims, 'transmission', stressing teaching and knowledge, and 'open', stressing teaching and/or organization.
2. Attempts at typologies claiming to be contrasting can sometimes be shown to be similar, e.g. Lippitt and White's authoritarian and democratic turn out to be autocratic authoritarian and parental authoritarian.
3. Another alternative can be identified, e.g. the autonomous study group of ideologies.
4. The possibility of developing bridging techniques to allow movement from one ideology to another emerges.

Summary

1. Previous attempts to identify ideologies of education have tended to focus explicitly on one of the components and contain implicit theories of the other components.
2. One advantage of the component-theories approach is that previous attempts can be compared to reduce some of the confusion created by their different emphases.
3. Another advantage is that two apparently similar ideologies of education can be shown to vary in one or two component theories.
4. Authoritarian ideologies of education have a common view of the learner's relationship to the teacher: it is one of dependence.
5. Various forms of dependence give rise to different types of authoritarian approaches, including autocratic, parental, charismatic, organizational, expert and consultative.
6. Democratic ideologies of education have a common view of independence in the teacher–learner relationship.
7. Various forms and degrees of independence give rise to different types of democratic approaches, including agreed rules, representative, committee and forum.
8. The component-theories approach allows confusions, like that of the Lippitt and White misuse of the term 'democratic', to be located.
9. The view that authoritarian–democratic is a simple continuum is open to a series of doubts.
10. The adoption of the term 'non-authoritarian' allows for other types of ideology of education to be discerned, e.g. the individual learning approaches of the autonomous education group.
11. The notion of bridging from one ideology to another emerges as a possible practical consequence of the component-theories approach to ideologies of education.

12. The identification of hybrid forms of ideologies of education may further the understanding of the processes of curriculum change.

Further Reading

Fletcher, C., Caron, M. and Williams, W. (1985) *Schools on Trial*. Milton Keynes: Open University Press. An account of four schools that developed non-authoritarian approaches.

Hammersley, M. (1977) *Teacher Perspectives*. Milton Keynes: Open University Press. Contains an account of four ideologies of education located using a checklist of features of educational practice that can be compared with the component-theories approach.

Husen, T. (1974) *The Learning Society*. London: Methuen. There are few attempts to describe the practice of non-authoritarian ideologies of education, but this and the following reference are two.

Freire, P. (1972) *Pedagogy of the Oppressed*. Harmondsworth: Penguin.

Moon, B. (1983) *Comprehensive Schools: Challenge and Change*. Windsor: NFER-Nelson. Accounts of six schools that developed non-authoritarian ideas.

White, P. (1983) *Beyond Domination*. London: Routledge and Kegan Paul. A philosophical approach to the issues of this chapter.

Discussion and Activities

1. Using the component-theories approach, analyse the ideology of education of a school known to you.
2. Analyse the ideology of education of *The Countesthorpe Experience*, by J. Watts (1977), or *Pedagogy of the Oppressed*, by P. Freire (1972).
3. Take Table 16.1, which compares various attempts to locate ideologies of education, and develop it, e.g. by filling in the implicit theories of each component of the attempts listed.
4. Is the Open University an example of a hybrid ideology of education?

Signposts

1. Deschooling

The deschooling writers, writing in 1971, concluded that most children left school after ten years of schooling with little to show for it. Using a range of metaphors, e.g. prisons, hospitals, museums, the proposition was that schools made most young people hostile to the idea of education. An analysis of the ideas of these writers using the component theories approach is an interesting research activity. References: Freire, P. (1972) *Pedagogy of the Oppressed*, Harmondsworth: Penguin; Goodman, P. (1971) *Compulsory Miseducation*, Harmondsworth: Penguin; Holt, J. (1969) *How Children Fail*, Harmondsworth: Penguin (the ideas of John Holt about how children learn to fail in schools, based on observations of his own teaching); Illich, I. (1971) *Deschooling Society*, Harmondsworth: Penguin; Kozel, J. (1968) *Death at an Early Age*, Harmondsworth: Penguin; Lister, I. (ed.) (1974) *Deschooling*, Cambridge: Cambridge University Press (an attempt to assemble the ideas about deschooling in one volume); Reimer, E. (1971) *School Is Dead*, Harmondsworth: Penguin.

2. Management of schools

The notion of organization and management of schools has developed in recent years, particularly on in-service courses for aspiring headteachers. What ideologies of education underpin such courses? See Handy, C. (1984) *Taken for Granted? Understanding Schools as Organizations*, York: Longman; and Meighan, R. (2005) *Comparing Learning Systems*, Nottingham: Educational Heretics Press.

3. Multicultural education

The term multicultural is highly ambiguous and covers a variety of contradictory ideologies of education. Some sources are Willey, R. (1984) *Race, Equality and Schools*, London: Methuen; Barton, L. and Walker, S. (eds) (1983) *Race, Class and Education*, Beckenham: Croom Helm; and Cherrington, D. (ed.) (1985) 'Ethnic Minorities in Education', special edition of *Educational Review*.

17 A Case Study in an Ideology of Education: Autonomous Study*

ROLAND MEIGHAN AND MICHAEL ROBERTS

The object of teaching a child is to enable him to get along without a teacher.
Elbert Hubbard

INTRODUCTION

It was personal experience of the limitations of the formal class lesson as a device for teaching adolescents of varying attainments that led both writers to experiment with pedagogical alternatives and to consider the notions of individualized learning, learning from resources, and autonomous pupil learning.

In one case this took the form of an indexed work-card system in geography teaching and, later, individual study folders in social studies. The individual study folders were of various kinds – stimulus, linear structured, multiple-staged, networked, learning choices and research folders – allowing pupils to move from highly structured work to more open-ended, autonomous work. (For a fuller account see Meighan, 1975.) In the other, Michael Roberts devised a complete business studies course, the basis of which was a collection of linear and multistage folders with access to further multimedia resources. The course was designed to allow students choice of topic sequence. It contained built-in student self-assessment, which took the form of multiple-choice and sentence-completion tests and comprehension exercises, and more formal means of teacher assessment, such as essays, were also employed.

These initiatives were based on a hypothesis similar to the following:

> Individualised instruction, properly implemented and executed, holds its own in traditional measures of academic achievement and promises more in the development of personal characteristics; such as self-direction, self-respect and responsibility.
>
> Talbert and Frase, 1969

---

* This chapter first appeared, in a different form, in the *Journal of Curriculum Studies*, **11**, 1, 1979.

The success of these two experiments led the writers to consider further possibilities. The incidental gain of self-direction, self-respect and responsibility might, after all, be a major outcome, and there emerged the possibility of seeing individualized work as more than just an extension of the repertoire of techniques available for the traditional task of knowledge transmission. The new hypothesis seemed to be:

> What we have is a teaching-based system which provides some opportunities for independent learning: an alternative would be an independent learning system which provides opportunities for teaching.
>
> Taylor, 1971

The experience of the writers also illuminated a crucial practical problem. Given the status quo of transmission teaching, how could a teacher move to a situation of autonomous study? The individualized approaches held out promise as both the means and the end. They could act as bridging techniques by starting with highly structured, individualized work to lead to more and more pupil-directed opportunities over time, and ultimately to autonomous study. Or, to put it another way, the approaches developed by the writers appeared to have potential for shifting from one educational ideology, transmission, to an alternative, autonomous study.

PROBLEMS OF TERMINOLOGY

Even in the brief discussion so far a number of related terms have been used. They include 'individualized learning', 'learning from resources', 'autonomous pupil learning', 'individualized instruction', 'independent learning' and 'autonomous study'. Other terms used elsewhere include 'personalized instruction', 'programmed self-instruction', 'programmed learning' and 'self-instruction'.

The term 'autonomous study' is adopted here, since it is the term adopted by the Council of Europe Committee for General and Technical Education in 1975. Until then, the expression 'independent study', a term used in the USA, had been used, but the view was taken that this had connotations of non-direction and unstructured exploration which could be seen as threatening the assumptions of existing school organization. 'Autonomous study' was thought to avoid this problem, since it did not define in advance whether the study was closed or open-ended, structured or unstructured (see Marbeau, 1976).

What the term 'autonomous study' did signify was that pupils were afforded a greater degree of responsibility in their learning. The emergence of this as an essential objective of European education systems is traced by Marbeau (1976). He notes that the Berne conference of European Ministers of Education in 1973 acknowledged the need for a diversity of learning and teaching methods to achieve a more individualized education and promote independent study by pupils. The same conclusion emerges from a study of the objectives implicit and explicit in reports submitted by member states of the Council of Europe in preparation for the Klemskerke symposium in Belgium in 1976.

THE EMERGENCE OF THE AUTONOMOUS STUDY CONCEPT

In the view of Marbeau (1976) there were three main reasons why European school systems were paying attention to the idea of autonomous study:

1. Changes in the social and economic environment of pupils.
2. Changes in information techniques.
3. Changes in theories of learning.

The first reason refers to the rapidity of social and technological change, requiring that members of modern societies face the necessity for constant adaptation. Husen (1974) argues that:

> people will have to learn new job skills many times in a lifetime . . . urban life will make even more strenuous demands on the intelligence and adaptability of city inhabitants: when, in fact, only the man who has never stopped learning will be able to cope.

All this implies emphasis on self-education and self-teaching, and the ability to do this will depend to a large extent on learning approaches gained during school years.

The second refers to changes in information techniques. The information provided by cinema, radio, television, newspapers, magazines and computer storage and retrieval systems has developed into an information source so rivalling the traditional school as to be described as the parallel school and to be seen by some deschoolers as the basis of a preferable educational experience. Marbeau argued that the school finds itself in a situation where young people need the technical knowledge, critical attitudes and learning techniques to help them to sift this welter of information throughout their lives.

The third reason, Marbeau suggests, is the development of theories of learning, especially those of Bruner (1966), which lay stress on the idea of pupils making meanings rather than passively receiving them, and of learning methods of learning and thinking rather than how to recall set bodies of information. Piaget (1964) is also concerned with the means by which learners actively construct and arrange their knowledge as their interpretational schemes develop. Particularly significant from the point of view of autonomous study is Bruner's stress on individual differences, and the consequences of this recognition for schooling:

> If a curriculum is to be effective in the classroom it must contain different ways of activating children, different ways of presenting sequences, different opportunities for some children

to 'skip' parts while others work their way through different ways of putting things. A curriculum in short, must contain many tracks leading to the same general goal.

Bruner, 1966

A fourth reason that emerged since 1976 is the growth of youth unemployment throughout Europe, which has been particularly severe in the UK.

AUTONOMOUS STUDY AS AN IDEOLOGY OF EDUCATION

It was noted earlier that autonomous study can be regarded as a method that can serve various educational ideologies. First, it can be seen as serving a transmission ideology, as part of the repertoire of techniques available to a teacher for instructing pupils and helping them to pass their subject-based examinations. Second, it can serve an interpretation ideology by helping pupils in preparing projects, studying particular themes and mounting investigations to further the dialogue between teacher and taught about the interpretation and reinterpretation of their world. Third, autonomous study can also serve an open, democratic ideology by being available as a technique when a learner or learning group chooses to call on it. Viewed thus, autonomous study is seen as a means to some other end. It is because of this flexibility as a means that it has potential as a bridging technique for changing from one ideology to another.

However, autonomous study can also be seen as an end in itself, and it therefore becomes, in this case, an alternative educational ideology. This ideology has theories of knowledge, learning, teaching and assessment that can be identified.

A Theory of Knowledge: Its Content and Structure

In an autonomous study ideology, knowledge is seen as having a flexible structure, an expanding network, since it is believed to be fluctuating and growing quite rapidly. Traditional subjects are viewed with less reverence than in a transmission ideology, since they are seen as bodies of information with severe limitations for solving those contemporary 'problems' that cut across several disciplines, e.g. the problems of mass communication, pollution, terrorism and alienation. The view of knowledge is future-orientated, predicting that the methods of learning with a lighter loading of information will be more useful to pupils as they grow up than a heavy loading of existing information with a minor loading of methods of learning.

Existing subject bodies of knowledge are dethroned. They become useful, though limited, resources alongside other available knowledge resources, rather than the key resource.

A Theory of Learning and the Learner's Role

To learn in a transmission ideology is to be passive and receive a content decided by someone else; it is 'meaning-receiving'. In the interpretation ideology, the learner is more active, in entering a dialogue with the teacher to interpret and reinterpret the world, using resources especially in traditional subjects, but the end is still tending to come to terms with a content selected by someone else. In the autonomous study ideology, the learner 'makes meanings' by mastering methods of learning to explore past, present and future problems of existence. The learners eventually arrive at a point where they are capable of making all the decisions about study, appropriate content, appropriate methods and appropriate assessments. The motivation for learning is intrinsic, rather than the extrinsic assumptions of pupils undertaking to learn in order to avoid disagreeable consequences if they do not, e.g. low marks, non-promotion, punishment, censure. The learners are encouraged instead to strive to create new knowledge and fresh understandings. Their role is dynamic, not static.

A Theory of Teaching and the Teacher's Role

The teacher's task in an autonomous study ideology is arranging learning activities so that pupils gradually learn to make more and more decisions about learning for themselves. In the study-folder system used by one of the writers, the first folders were highly structured, allowing a few decisions by the learner, the later ones allowing for more and more decisions by the learner, to the final step of a 'how to make your own folder' folder, where pupils learned to execute the whole process from topic selection, through information assembly, to assessment of the end-product. The teacher moves from being an organizer of learning experiences to being a learning consultant during this process. This can be seen as a much more creative and dynamic role than that of the instructor in the transmission ideology and, arguably, a more professional role if it requires more skills and more complex techniques. But, as both writers found, it requires a change in self-concept, since identity and security no longer rest in being a subject expert. One result is a release from instruction and formal class teaching to give much more individual consultation and to have sustained personal contact with many of the pupils on a one-to-one basis during lesson time. Hunt (1976) summarizes the position as follows:

> When instruction is designed on an individual-needs basis, the teacher emphasis is likely to change from that of the 'fountain of knowledge' to one of an on-going learning counsellor. That is, professional responsibilities are likely to lie in his abilities for:
>
> (i) Identifying relevant student characteristics for a given task.
> (ii) Marshalling the instructional resources to facilitate maximum individual learning.
> (iii) In concert with the individual, selecting goals and determining performance standards.

To date, we are a long way short of the realisation of this utopia. It may take time to come; but the knowledge is already here. What is needed is a more careful examination of the individual qualities which affect learning, and the nature of the goals which society and the individual wish to acquire.

A Theory of Resources Appropriate for Learning

An ideology of education wedded to subjects will concentrate on those resources that encapsulate the material, i.e. books, and teachers, seen as initiated subject 'experts'. The autonomous study ideology, being future- and present-orientated, implies that any resource that enables learning to learn to take place is potentially acceptable, whether it be books, discussions, television, photoplays, investigation, sociodrama, computers or trails. A particular situation may restrict this choice, for a school with no access to closed-circuit television cannot use this resource for pupils to make programmes. But in theory there is no restriction.

The relationship of learner to resources is direct, whereas access to resources is usually seen as monitored by a teacher in a transmission ideology, where the appropriate resources are selected and defined by someone other than the learner.

A Theory of Assessment

In the autonomous study ideology the teacher's role as assessor is a temporary one, since the learners are seen as engaged in a process of learning to assess their own learning appropriately. Ideas like self-assessment and groups assessing their members' learning, as well as external types of assessment (e.g. objective tests, standardized tests, teachers' judgements), are given credence. This is in contrast to the transmission ideology, where assessment is seen as initiation or verification of a candidate's suitability or performance by an initiated teacher or examiner. Assessment, in this view, is done by someone to someone else, and self-assessment is not seen as appropriate.

A Theory of the Organization of Learning Situations

In the transmission and interpretation ideologies the teachers organize the learning situation, in the former without consultation with pupils, in the latter often with some consultation. In the early stages of an autonomous study ideology, this teacher-based organization is similar, but the eventual outcome is that of adults directing their own learning for a whole lifetime, so the process of organizing the learning context itself is implicit in the theory. Since thousands of Open University students do this already by organizing their learning context (though not, in this case, the content) at home, this is not a novel idea. The theories of *education permanente* (where members of a society continue learning throughout their lifetime, in an organized way) are implied here (see Husen, 1974).

The organization of resources for learning by learners, rather than teacher organization of pupils in classes to receive the same instruction, raises other issues. Mixed ability 'teaching' now becomes feasible, since in a classroom the learners increasingly diversify and pursue different contents and different methods, while the teacher has time to conduct individual consultations to help and advise.

A Theory of Aims and Outcomes

Aims of education have been expressed in hundreds of statements. The general aim of an autonomous ideology can be expressed as follows:

> At the end of it all, the educator will insensibly stop being an educator, and find that he is talking to an equal, to an educated man like himself.
>
> Hare, 1964

This is in contrast with the outcomes of the transmission ideology, as shown in the research of Wankowski (1973), which included an analysis of sixth-form tuition experienced by undergraduates at Birmingham University. The author comments: 'it became apparent, during interviews, that many students were not adequately prepared for the more independent study techniques essential to University education' (Wankowski, 1973).

He suggests that sixth-form pedagogy, far from producing independent learners, trains students to depend on others, especially teachers. In the teaching of science subjects, Wankowski found predominant the 'one-way' method of communication, in which the teacher, having organized his or her body of scientific knowledge, systematically presents it to the students with the directive, 'this is what you need to learn'. In the teaching of humanities there was less direction, communication between teachers and students being more reciprocal, with the attitude 'let's see what we can learn from this' being adopted by the teacher. In the former, student participation in discussion and question framing was minimal. The extent of teacher direction of student note-taking was considerable; indeed, Wankowski estimates that at least one teacher in five regularly dictated notes to students. Such evidence suggests that traditional sixth-formers are often in the hands of transmission teachers who direct and control the content, style and pace of student learning without regard to the possibilities of their students becoming independent learners.

Wankowski's research, which suggests a lack of emphasis upon the development of independent learning in sixth forms, points to the existence of a serious pedagogical gap in the transition from school to university which may contribute to learning difficulties and even failure for some undergraduates. Clearly a university education demands the ability to learn independently: students must, for example, be able to organize a large amount of material into some sort of priority for exploration and learning, and prepare exercises, papers and essays with little or no direction or supervision.

Wankowski argues that sixth-form pedagogy, by 'spoonfeeding' the student, creates a protective structure around him or her which may create a false illusion of himself or herself as a competent and autonomous learner, and masks or accommodates anxiety and learning weakness. The illusion is created largely by the sixth-form environment, in which objectives in terms of A level performance are precise, there is copious and instant reinforcement of the 'body of knowledge' by feedback from a pedagogy in which the teacher systematically plans, directs and tests the students' acquisition of the 'body of knowledge', and the teacher is omnipresent for support, guidance and advice. Instead of being able to learn independently, the student learns to depend on his or her teachers. It is not surprising, therefore, that some students experience problems when exposed to the different learning requirements of university education. Wankowski prescribes a greater emphasis in the sixth form upon learning how to learn as a preparation for university pedagogy: 'the preparation should be active and exercised over a long period of time if it is to be effectively integrated by the pupil' (Wankowski, 1973).

It is reasonable to suggest that such preparation, to be effective, should commence long before students reach the sixth form. It might arise naturally from a lower-school curriculum based more on learning from resources than from teachers. To confront students in the sixth form with an entirely different set of pedagogical expectations which entail a large degree of independent learning is perhaps to make unacceptable demands upon them.

THE GENERAL STUDIES PROJECT (GSP) AND AUTONOMOUS STUDY: AN INVESTIGATION

The case for an empirical investigation of independent student learning as an example of autonomous study at sixth-form level in general studies is considered fully by Roberts (1977), the object of inquiry being the utilization of the resource packages produced by the Schools Council General Studies Project, which offered the means by which autonomous study might occur.

'Individualization of study' in the sense of giving students choice of topic for study and method of learning was a fundamental GSP precept. The Trials Officer perceived the resources as:

> making individual work a practical possibility by freeing both teacher and pupil from reliance on textbook and blackboard and class size units of instruction.
>
> Smale, 1974

GSP resource materials were structured in such a way that 'guided individual learning' by students could occur. Student instructions to work through source documents and other resource materials were contained in the study guide booklets, which, the project claimed, could be used by the teacher as an 'alternative voice in the classroom' (Smale, 1974). 'Reference units' with additional details of source material were supplied to be used for further depth research by students on their own. It was hoped that teachers would emulate the GSP idea by producing their own materials and study guides, and by modifying those provided. The project suggested that 40 per cent of timetabled time for general studies be used for independent student work on GSP materials.

The expectation by the project that its resources would be used for student-centred activities, within which autonomous study was emphasized, was thus quite explicit in GSP dissemination literature.

METHOD OF INVESTIGATION

A pilot study of local GSP users indicated that the resources were not being employed for autonomous study and the objective of the main study, which was conducted in six institutions in the Birmingham area, was to investigate reasons for non-adoption. The principal research instrument was the semi-structured interview of the head of general studies. This was employed to allow depth probing of teacher perceptions and the pursuit of leads not envisaged in the interview schedule. A questionnaire to all general studies teachers in the six institutions surveyed was used as a supplementary instrument to yield quantifiable confirmation of the trends suggested in the interviews.

THE INTERVIEWS

Obstacles Perceived by Teachers

The interviews revealed the predominant use of GSP materials for 'class teaching', teacher-directed discussion being the norm. Restricted use of the materials for autonomous study is partly explicable by teachers' responses to the question, 'Why not let students work on their own from the study guides, or produce your own guides?'

Teachers challenged the technical feasibility of GSP materials for autonomous study, claiming that content was 'loaded academically' and therefore was unsuitable for non-selective sixth-formers, and that its style and approach would not maintain sufficient student interest or involvement for independent learning. One teacher, who had never actually used the materials in their existing form for autonomous study, believed them to be inadequately structured for that purpose, since guide instructions lacked detail and material required simplification.

Of various institutional barriers, shortage of time was a frequently perceived obstacle. This

Table 17.1 Obstacles perceived by teachers to the implementation of autonomous study using GSP resource materials

Implicit source of obstacle	Nature of obstacle as perceived by teacher	Example of teacher response
Materials	Content of study guides	Concepts, language too difficult
	Structure of study guides	Instructions lack sufficient detail
School	Limited time for student research	No sixth-form private study periods allowed
	Insufficient time for teacher to organize GSP materials for independent learning	Head of general studies has other duties
	Lack of resources in schools	Library facilities inadequate
Students	Students could not work independently	Students have never been trained to work independently
	Students would not work independently	Students are motivated only by an exam in general studies
Teachers	Autonomous study precludes pursuit of other objectives	Discussion with groups ruled out
	Autonomous study incompatible with teacher's style	Teacher likes to take active role
	Autonomous study implies loss of control over student learning	Students would reach too narrow conclusions

may be partly attributable to the low status of general studies in some of the schools. Thus one teacher was reluctant to encourage independent student research in general studies because he feared it would be conducted at the expense of more important A level work. Where general studies received low priority in timetabling and staffing, teachers felt they lacked incentive, preparation time, and length of experience, which they deemed essential for experimentation with autonomous study.

Several teachers believed that only their 'most able' students were capable of conducting their own research or beneficially choosing their own topics for study: the majority required close teacher direction and control. Students' inability to learn independently was attributed variously to literacy problems and previous lack of heuristic training, with assertions like: 'they prefer to be told what to do rather than choose for themselves. It's less demanding for them.' Teachers also doubted their students' motivation to work independently. Intrinsic interest in general studies was often deficient, they claimed, and students would not work independently without instrumental motivation such as an external examination.

An underlying message was transmitted in the interviews that autonomous study was not valued significantly by the teachers. While some gave explicit justifications for this in personal terms (see Table 17.1), interview probes elicited a degree of teacher anxiety about autonomous study, associated with an implied loss of teacher control over the learning situation. This anxiety was expressed in the following way by one teacher:

> Perhaps it stems from a sense of insecurity – you feel you would like to know exactly what the kids are taking in – a feeling that they are becoming conversant with information that you are already aware of. Whereas – perhaps branching out too much one could be in a situation where you are not in control of the learning situation. I want a clear idea of what the actual material is that they are going to be involved with and how they are going to tackle it.

Pressed to reveal what he perceived might happen in the absence of his control of the learning situation, he replied:

> Students can take too finite an approach to answering the problem set – their conclusions are too limited. Whereas – if you are going over a complex topic with them, various sides of the argument can be brought out.

One way of interpreting this comment is that this teacher's anxiety appears to stem both from a fear that his students may come to possess knowledge with which he is unfamiliar and from alarm at the prospect that they might not reach the kind of conclusions he wants them to reach.

From the evidence collected it seems that teachers deny both the suitability of GSP materials for independent learning and the feasibility of autonomous study *per se*, with the latter receiving the greatest weight of objection. Hoyle and Bell (1972) suggest that when an innovation is rejected teachers may attribute this to external factors, when the more fundamental reason lies in the teachers' own attitudes. In the present context it is possible that, where teachers express reservations about autonomous study and ascribe as obstacles the unsuitability of GSP materials and their students' inability or unwillingness to work independently, it is in fact their own anxieties and perceptions which are the obstacles. Thus, as in the example described above, it may be that the teachers' own fear of losing control over their students' learning is the real barrier to their adoption of autonomous study. This view gains some support from the fact that few of the teachers interviewed had actually attempted to put the materials to the latter use, and some of their objections may therefore be considered as being largely hypothetical.

Teacher Understanding of Autonomous Study

Teacher ignorance or misunderstanding of autonomous study was suggested by responses to those interview questions in which teachers evinced failure to appreciate certain implications and possibilities of student learning from resources: indeed, two teachers commented that interview probes were making them aware of it for the first time.

In their views on the use of autonomous study as a technique for mixed-achievement groups, teachers' responses ranged from astonishment at the novelty of the idea to puzzled scepticism: 'it is theory rather than practice'. One teacher's insistence that all her students must cover the same knowledge content appeared to blind her to the possibility of pupils working on different aspects of a study guide, each suited to the achievement level according to the teacher's judgement.

Three of the teachers interviewed accepted that individual tuition was hypothetically desirable and even necessary for autonomous study, yet rejected it as impractical because of lack of time, and one commented: 'it's disruptive since when you are dealing with one person you cannot deal with the rest of the class'. They had missed the implication that, with students occupied in independent work during lesson time, the teacher would be released to give tuition to individuals.

All department heads interviewed expressed reluctance to persuading colleagues to adopt the GSP approach:

> that doesn't leave any freedom for individual teachers to do their own course, and one approach, however good, is not suitable for everybody all the time.

The implicit inconsistency in such assertions about teacher individuality and choice is significant: only one teacher interviewed permitted his students any choice of topic for study, and none allowed choice of learning technique. Direction was the common, and apparently unquestioned, method. The transmission ideology of education was suggested by these teacher responses.

The interviews raised doubts about the effectiveness with which GSP philosophy had been disseminated, and this may partly account for teachers' misunderstandings. With one exception, all those interviewed claimed to have read the GSP unit 'Teaching and Learning', which expounds GSP philosophy and contains various references to independent learning. Only one teacher had further contact with the project, through attendance at a dissemination day conference in Birmingham. There had been no GSP information or guidance from any LEA representative; indeed, an inspector had visited one teacher seeking information himself.

One explanation of teacher attitudes may be found in the fact that only two of the teachers had attempted even limited experimentation with GSP resources for autonomous study. If it is only through experience born from experiment that teachers become aware of the implications and possibilities, then the responses reported here are not altogether surprising.

THE QUESTIONNAIRE

Of 50 general studies teachers responding to the questionnaire, only six reported frequent use of GSP materials. Among different GSP resources available, study guides and source documents were used with twice the frequency of teaching notes or reference units, and three institutions reported little or no use of the latter. No teacher reported using secondary source material from the GSP resource bank.

Table 17.2 suggests that most respondents directed students to a varying extent – responses (b) to (d) – the most frequent use of GSP materials being as 'class teaching aids'. Only one teacher appears to have used the materials significantly for autonomous study or even

Table 17.2 Teaching approach using GSP materials

	Teacher responses	
	n	%
(a) Allow students to work on their own, following study guides	5	14
(b) Work through materials with students, largely following the approach suggested in teaching notes and study guides	6	17
(c) Work through materials with students, largely following my own approach	10	29
(d) Use source documents as teaching aids to illustrate points, etc.	14	40
	35	100

discerned a connection between them. He alone perceived GSP materials as advantageous, in the following terms: 'it gives opportunity for students to pursue independent studies and to follow up their own interests'. The main value of the GSP perceived by other respondents confirms the pattern of use reported earlier, e.g. 'good starting point for discussion' and 'useful as back-up material after teaching'.

Questionnaire responses also suggest that the GSP philosophy had not effectively permeated to the teachers. Eight respondents reported having read 'Teaching and Learning', but only one knew of the GSP 'Trials Report'. Apart from the interviewed teacher who had attended a GSP conference, and one other who had participated in a workshop, no further contact with the GSP was reported. Accordingly, it seems that few teachers knew that the GSP was advocating independent student work.

RESULTS OF THE INVESTIGATION

Limited Use of GSP Resources for Autonomous Study

Despite the provision of resources and explicit GSP recommendations, autonomous study was not significantly employed, there being only limited experimentation with topic choice and structuring, and little or no independent student research from GSP secondary resources. Teachers absorbed the resources into their existing pedagogical styles, which permitted close supervision and direction of student learning. The transmission ideology of education is in evidence here.

Suitability of GSP Resources for Autonomous Study

Doubts were expressed about the suitability of GSP resources for autonomous study, especially by teachers of non-selective groups who believed material content to be beyond the intellectual capabilities of their students. Resources were also criticized for being inadequately structured for independent learning. Since, however, these objections were largely conjectural, little weight can be attributed to them.

Teacher Rejection of the Feasibility of Autonomous Study

Teachers perceived a number of obstacles to autonomous study which emanated from their particular school or college situation, their students' capabilities and motivation, and their own attitudes and beliefs. These rationalizations appear to reflect their own anxieties about their capabilities.

Teacher Misunderstanding of Autonomous Study from Resources

There was some misunderstanding and ignorance of the implications and possibilities of independent learning with respect to the roles of both teacher and student. Imperfect understanding might be attributed to inexperience of the situation and unfamiliarity with the GSP philosophy pertaining to autonomous study.

GSP Dissemination Failure

GSP pedagogical suggestions advocating autonomous study were not effectively transmitted to the study teachers through literature, conferences, workshops or any other way. It may be that autonomous study was not employed because the possibility of using the resources in this way had simply not occurred to the teachers. The efficacy of the GSP diffusion programme might offer a fruitful area for further research.

CONCLUSION

In the schools studied the transmission ideology of education, with its particular theories of knowledge, learning, relationships, assessment, etc., appears to be dominant. The GSP, which has been described as the Schools Council project with the most potential for radical alternatives within it (Holly, 1973), was possibly ahead of its time, since neither the possibility of autonomous study as a strategy within transmission ideology nor the possibility of it as an end in itself appears to have been exploited. The criticisms of Wankowski (1973) about the consequences of this for the study techniques of sixth-formers entering university will, it would seem, hold for some time yet.

From the point of view of those who consider the transmission ideology of education to be inadequate as the dominant ideology for a modern industrial society, these results are disturbing. It appears that schools are not coping with the three aspects of such societies discussed earlier, i.e. rapidity of social and technological change, changes in information techniques and changes in the theories of learning. Marbeau (1976) claims that educational trends in the UK are less favourable than those in other European countries in this respect, but considerably more evidence would be needed to establish this.

The use of autonomous study as a strategy within a transmission ideology has been developed by the Open University, albeit with a different clientele, but the practicalities of such an approach have been coped with in this case. From the research described above, it can be concluded that lack of understanding of, and sympathy for, autonomous study approaches appears to be a significant factor, for even when the General Studies Project provided the practical means, the opportunity was still disregarded.

Summary

1. Individualized learning can be seen as one extension of the repertoire of techniques available for the traditional task of knowledge transmission.
2. Alternatively, it can be seen as autonomous education: an independent learning system aiming at self-direction and self-responsibility that provides opportunities for other forms of learning, e.g. by submitting to teaching when it is recognized as useful.
3. Individualized approaches can be seen as both a means and an end, by being used as a bridging technique to lead to autonomous learning.
4. Autonomous study emerged as a concern in European school systems because of changes in the social and economic environment of pupils, changes in information techniques and changes in theory of learning.
5. Autonomous study, as a distinct ideology of education, has specific theories of knowledge, learning, teaching, resources, assessment, organization of learning situations and aims.
6. The study of one attempt to facilitate the development of autonomous learning, namely the General Studies Project, suggests that the concept of autonomy is foreign to teachers schooled in a transmission ideology of education.
7. If the transmission ideology of education is seen as inadequate for the needs of a modern industrial society, schools are not coping with the aspects of social and economic change, changes in information techniques or changes in theories of learning.

Further Reading

Bruner, J. (1965) *The Process of Education*. Harmondsworth: Penguin. Discusses changes in learning theory.

Flude, R. and Parrott, A. (1979) *Education and the Challenge of Change*. Milton Keynes: Open University Press. The idea of recurrent education is taken up in this book.

Husen, T. (1985) *The Learning Society Revised*. Oxford: Pergamon Press. A useful book to follow up some of the ideas in this chapter.

Jenkins, C. and Sherman, B. (1979) *The Collapse of Work*. Discusses changes in economic circumstances leading to a need for autonomous education.

Marbeau, V. (1976) 'Autonomous Study by Pupils', *Education and Culture*, **21**. A debate on autonomous study in a European setting.

Meighan, R. (2005) *Comparing Learning Systems*. Nottingham: Educational Heretics Press.

Roberts, M. (1994) *Skills for Self-managed Learning*. Nottingham: Education Now Books.

Skager, R. (1984) *Organizing Schools to Encourage Self-direction in Learners*. Oxford: Pergamon Press. Four case studies of schools are given in this book.

Discussion and Activities

1. What is the relationship between autonomous study and democratic education?
2. Discuss the significance of developments like CEEFAX and PRESTEL and the Internet for autonomous education.
3. Interview any Open University students you know, to establish how far autonomy has been developed as a strategy for achieving transmission within the Open University system of learning. Questions may be devised from the case study material in this chapter.

Signposts

Study skills

The idea that study skills are automatically absorbed by learners has been questioned recently as evidence emerged that achievement could be related as much to strategies of learners as to anything else. Study skills are of particular importance in autonomous forms of education, since the learners learn independently. See Tabberer, R. and Allman, J. (1983) *Introducing Study Skills*, Windsor: NFER-Nelson; Skager, R. (1984) *Organizing Schools to Encourage Self Direction in Learners*, Oxford: Pergamon; Marshall, L.A. and Rowland, F. (1983) *A Guide to Learning Independently*, Milton Keynes: Open University Press; Gibbs, G. (1981) *Teaching Students to Learn*, Milton Keynes: Open University Press; Miller, C.M.L. and Parlett, M. (1983) *Up to the Mark*, London: Society for Research into Higher Education; Marton, F. *et al.* (1984) *The Experience of Learning*, Edinburgh: Scottish Academic Press; Roberts, M. (1994) *Skills for Self-managed Learning*, Nottingham: Education Now Books.

18 Case Studies: Democratic Education

Democracy is the worst system devised by the wit of man, except for all the others.

Winston Churchill

INTRODUCTION

Most organized education operates under one of the versions of the authoritarian ideology of education described earlier. This can lead to considerable ironies, ignorance and false information. Bartholomew (1976) outlines one as he shows how teachers in training can be urged to operate non-authoritarian approaches in schools by lecturers using authoritarian methods for this advocacy. In addition, teacher trainers may believe that they are advocating radical approaches when they are merely describing one variation (e.g. consultative) rather than another (e.g. autocratic). In schools, young teachers may then be advised to 'forget all that radical nonsense they taught you in college', when it was not the least bit radical in terms of moving out of the authoritarian grouping of ideologies of education. Holt (1969) saw this as the myth of the progressive teacher. Progressive education, Holt argued, really meant a benign variation of authoritarianism:

> They thought, or at least talked and wrote as if they thought, that there were good and bad ways to coerce children (the bad ones mean, harsh, cruel, the good ones gentle, persuasive, subtle, kindly), and that if they avoided the bad and stuck to the good they would do no harm.

CASE STUDIES OF DEMOCRATIC LEARNING

The following four reports are from people who have experienced democratic practices in education. For Sonia Bonner, her A level sociology course left a lasting impression. James Baldaro, a student on one of these A level courses, is now training to be a teacher. Lesley

Browne encountered democratic learning methods on her initial teacher training course for her post-graduate certificate of education. She subsequently offered her students the chance to experience the same process. Her course had been tutored by Clive Harber and Roland Meighan.

THE DEMOCRATIC LEARNING COOPERATIVE – REFLECTIONS OF A SECONDARY SCHOOL STUDENT

Sonia Bonner reports: 'Although my memories of sixth form are fading fast, the one thing still highlighted for me is the sociology democratic learning cooperative (DLC). After twelve years of "traditional" learning and soaking up the information I was fed, it was a most refreshing change to be given a choice.

'On starting A level sociology I was pleasantly surprised by the democratic attitude taken towards our course. At first many of us were unsure about taking on so much responsibility for our education, what with the extra pressure of just beginning A levels. Also the thought of putting our learning in the hands of our classmates, no matter how much we liked them, was a bit daunting. However, it soon came to light that the idea appealed to our academic curiosity and after much debate we all agreed to give it our best shot.

'It took a great deal of deliberation before the contract was signed by everyone, as we all thought it too important to rush. Some obvious clauses were introduced into the contract at the beginning. For example, *we must share work for mutual benefit*, which was the whole backbone of the DLC. Also *every lesson should be attended and deadlines should be met and essays completed*. Later, we added into the contract that someone should chair each lesson.

'Furthermore, the fact that we were taking responsibility as a group was of paramount importance. This gave us a collective concern for our learning and a strong group bonding. We agreed to evaluate our progress at the end of every term, so we were all able to express our thoughts and air any problems. We also understood throughout the contract that our teachers were to be used as a resource for the group and were requested to stand in if anyone was off ill. With this in the contract everyone felt as if they had some support and were not totally alone.

'The reasons we had clauses, like *We must be kind, respectful and competent, not right,* was to remind everyone of the principles of the cooperative. So the contract helped us to form an understanding of our rules and contributed significantly to the DLC's success.

'It soon became apparent that everyone was very dedicated, perhaps because it was a different way of learning or because it was what we had wanted all along. The bonding of the group was very strong straight away and the first lessons were full of enthusiasm. I remember being entertained by quizzes, cartoon drawings, new and topical material, including current affairs. All of these new stimulants made the whole learning experience very enjoyable and, more importantly, effective.

'The success of the cooperative was also shown through its failures! For example, when lessons didn't go according to plan or if the group member who was taking the lesson didn't turn up, then the group reacted very differently than before. We became outraged that a fellow student would let us down like this. However, before experiencing the DLC we would have all been very happy to have gone home for the afternoon if the teacher had failed to turn up. However, for a while when our teacher was ill we continued with the lessons, sticking to the timetable and motivating ourselves.

'I remember when I prepared my own lesson. I took considerable time planning it and was very proud of the work I had done. It was a wonderful feeling teaching your peers, and providing them with quality information. I took as much time over their lesson as I would have expected them to do for me.

'Although we didn't follow the DLC through to our final exam, the time we spent doing it was invaluable. It made me take an active part in my education, helped me understand what a group effort could produce, and how important it is to experiment with teaching methods and not always to be the receiver.'

EMBARKING ON TEACHER TRAINING – THE VIEWS OF A FORMER PARTICIPANT IN DEMOCRATIC LEARNING

James Baldero reports on his experiences of democratic learning:

> I have never let my schooling interfere with my education.

'Mark Twain's quote perhaps best sums up my experiences of education up until the age of sixteen. There I left secondary schooling relatively successful but ultimately disillusioned with the institution of the school and its teacher-dominated learning.

'Upon returning to education a year later I found such fears and prejudices challenged by my involvement in a democratic learning cooperative during an A level politics course. The formal creation of the cooperative, its structure and implementation, are discussed elsewhere. What I hope to offer here are my recollections. Importantly, I aim to look at how these experiences have helped shape my perceptions and influence my actions throughout university and beyond, as today I myself move towards a career in education.

'In 1981 HMI in *Teacher Training and the Secondary School* (DES) commented that: "There is scope for more small group work which genuinely involves student participation and far less reliance upon the set lecture and tutor dominated seminar." This key notion of "student participation" was an essential and recurrent theme of our democratic learning cooperative. As students, we were involved in every aspect of the decision-making process. I can remember the surprise of all the group members at being given the power to choose the particular syllabus we were to follow, the actual subjects within the syllabus we were to cover and, most surprisingly of all, the specific teaching methods the course would involve. Any understandable apprehension quickly vanished as we were reassured by the language of the cooperative: negotiation, tolerance, choice, mutual support and, of course, democracy. Not just as politics students but as a representative group of sixth-formers these key words appealed to us and to our sense that we deserved a certain level of responsibility.

'Within the group each of us took an active role in the creation of a positive classroom atmosphere, something my experience had only ever previously defined in negative terms. As a cooperative we felt that our role in the initial decision-making process was crucial. Obviously, individuals had little working knowledge of the syllabuses so we recognized at an early stage the benefit of using the teacher as a resource. More importantly though, the group highlighted the fact that individual group members, being equal to the teacher, could also suggest topics and ideas not previously considered.

'Essentially the group was able to construct its own study programme using the resources available. Significantly my one outstanding memory of this time is the overwhelming sense that this was our course. Indeed, after listening back over the interview tapes from 1991, this proved to be the most commonly used phrase. Tina's comments on the initial course choices underlines this:

> I think it's really good, but I think more courses should be like this. It's more our course. We
> are teaching each other ... I'm proud of myself and it's given me more confidence.

This last point, that of increased confidence amongst group members, leads me to what I believe was the key success of the democratic learning cooperative: *the development of transferable skills*. Another comment from a group member relates specifically to this: "Democratic responsibility, as opposed to sitting back and always receiving, means that we have a chance to use existing skills as well as learning new ones."

'It was not until my time in higher education that I began to acknowledge such skills and trace them back to my democratic learning experience. Perhaps the most obvious of these transferable skills was seminar work. Seminars were not so overwhelming for me, as I felt, to some extent, that I had experienced the possibilities and problems of communication and confidence through the DLC. Moreover, in negotiating course choices and in advising and supporting other group members we had developed key political skills. These, too, were useful at university and appear essential to any career in education!

'Obviously such a radical change in approach to our studies did present some early problems. These were rarely of a truly negative nature and the established group structure was successful in offering reassurance and encouragement. To me at the time and still today, I believe that the creation of this group culture is essential for any school wishing to offer a positive learning experience away from the long-established care and support structures of the school and sixth form. The cooperative represented a kind of inner circle that quickly began to tackle the kind of minor problems of confidence and motivation within the group that are so often the principle worries of sixth-form students. As Nicole commented: "Everyone did a little bit, we all helped each other. If I hadn't done my part, other people would have suffered. I felt responsible for them."

'I feel that this point was particularly significant with relevance to the age of the group members. Being 16–18, we were seeking to redefine our pupil–school relationship. A common complaint throughout sixth forms is "stop treating us like kids!" The DLC offered us not only a different pupil–teacher relationship, but perhaps more importantly, it rewarded us with a quintessential responsibility for our own learning, development and destiny.

'The relative success of the group in external examination results, despite seeming to mean "everything" at the time, is actually secondary. The real success of the democratic learning cooperative lies in how it instilled key notions of cooperation, mutual support and tolerance in a group of 16–18 year olds. These are skills which reach far beyond the short-term goals of A level examinations and university graduation. Coupled with the confidence developed through the DLC's reliance on continued public speech, teaching and discussion with others, I believe our experiences equipped us with essential transferable skills. In my own case it was an experience which has ironically helped to change and shape my own perceptions and expectations of teaching as I embark on a career in education.'

DEMOCRATIC PRACTICE IN A SECONDARY SCHOOL

Lesley Browne reports on her experiences of democratic learning:

'Democratic approaches to learning are a rarity in the British education system. However, in 1985 I was given the opportunity to participate in a democratic learning environment on a teacher training course run by Roland Meighan and Clive Harber. This experience provided the most positive and satisfying educational experience I have ever encountered. I found the process so worthwhile that for the last five years advanced level sociology and politics students at the school where I teach have similarly been given the opportunity to choose how they learn.

'The courses begin with an initial discussion and presentation which looks at different methods of learning. The choices include the conventional teacher-directed course, a teacher-based consultative model, a democratic learning cooperative and an individualized course of the Open University type. The teacher also suggests that a mixture of these options is possible to allow for some individual preferences.

'The aim of setting up a democratic learning environment is to enable young people to take responsibility for their own learning. This means that they decide their own agenda, then they work individually or in small groups preparing lessons, making visits, planning and leading presentations, organizing visiting speakers and so on. Other aims are to increase students' self-reliance, to increase confidence, to develop skills of articulation and investigation, and to remove the myth that the teacher is expert in all things.

'The initial discussion is an exercise in the important skill of group decision-making. After much debate the 1989/91 A level group – and more recently the 1992/4 group – decided on the democratic model of learning. Whenever this choice is made, it is important to create a classroom atmosphere that promotes the values of tolerance, fairness and openness to change. These encourage student contributions and participation.

'At the pre-democratic stage the students are given a specimen democratic learning contract. This consists of a written contract which lays down the ground rules for the cooperative. The original contract presented to the students was one devised by Harber and Meighan for the PGCE course in social and political education at the University of Birmingham.

'The process of devising a contract can be a long and at times painful one. The students then go on to choose a syllabus that they wish to follow and the areas they wish to be responsible for. All students take part in a number of presentations which use the full range of teaching and learning styles. In fact the range is far greater than the teacher would normally use. The final session of each term includes a review of the course.

'Possibly one of the most important practices in democratic learning environments is that of dialogue between students and teachers, questioning and discussing together how they might improve their practice. If democracy in the classroom is about anything, it is the free exchange of ideas. Without this open continuous debate, power-sharing is pointless.'

Some of the comments of students on Lesley Browne's courses were as follows:

> Because people know that they have the responsibility of taking lessons they are likely to put a lot of effort into their presentations.

> The democratic way of learning has been very interesting and enjoyable. It has proved that learning can be fun and interesting.

> I think having to do the research for the lessons ourselves is a good way to learn the topic; it improves our research skills and you have to understand it better so you can explain it to others.

> Pupils contribute more in discussions so grow in confidence when talking in groups. Skills such as these may not be used so much if another form of learning was used.

> I used to see you as the 'expert', because of your knowledge of the subject, but now I see you as more of a resource directing us to places.

> It makes you think more, doesn't it, it makes you feel a bit more responsible.

> It was refreshing to be able to choose the syllabus and topics that interested you.

> I have not only learnt a lot but experienced much. I feel motivated to work and get involved because it is our course.

> By setting up a democratic learning environment, power was shared by all members of the group.

TEACHER EDUCATION AND BREAKING THE CYCLE

A key feature of democracy is the principle that those who are affected by a decision have the right to take part in the decision-making. This is expressed in slogans such as 'No taxation without representation!' If we apply this to schools, we get, 'No learning and therefore no curriculum without the learners having a say in the decision-making.'

In the usual approach to schooling, however, there is a chronic fear of trusting students and sharing power with them. In the everyday life of schools, we find a fear of opting for the discipline of democracy. Instead, teachers resort to an exclusive diet of hierarchical order and authoritarian discipline. Indeed, Carl Rogers in *Freedom to Learn for the Eighties* noted that democracy and its values are actually *scorned and despised*:

> Students do not participate in choosing the goals, the curriculum, or the manner of working. These things are chosen for the students. Students have no part in the choice of teaching personnel, nor any voice in educational policy. Likewise the teachers often have no choice in choosing their administrative officers ... All this is in striking contrast to all the teaching about the virtues of democracy, the importance of the 'free world,' and the like. The political practices of the school stand in the most striking contrast to what is taught. While being taught that freedom and responsibility are the glorious features of our democracy, students are experiencing powerlessness, and as having almost no opportunity to exercise choice or carry responsibility.

THREE KINDS OF DISCIPLINE

As noted earlier, people sometimes think that discipline is the simple problem of adults making children follow instructions. This is only one kind of discipline – the authoritarian. But, as we saw, there are three kinds:

1. *Authoritarian* – where order is based on rules imposed by adults. Power resides in an individual or group of leaders.
2. *Autonomous* – where order is based on self-discipline and self-imposed rules. Power resides with the individual.
3. *Democratic* – where order is based on rules agreed after discussion based on evidence, human rights values and the logic of consequences. Power is shared among the people in the situation.

There has been a centuries-old debate about which of these three is the best system of discipline. It is now a sterile debate. The complexities of modern life are such that *all three types of discipline have a place to play in the scheme of things.* This point is developed in the final section of this book, on educational alternatives, with reference to the concepts of flexischooling and flexi-education and their capacity to incorporate all three types of discipline.

Any 'One Right Way' approach fails to match the need for young people to learn how to be competent in the logistics and practice of all three types of discipline, and to select them appropriately. This is one argument for the inclusion of democratic practice in mainstream education.

Teacher education has been part of a cycle whereby authoritarian classrooms pass students on to authoritarian teacher courses, which produce authoritarian teachers who go back into schools, to sustain and perpetuate authoritarian classrooms, round and round in a closed circle. Breaking out of this cycle is not easy, even when it is seen as desirable. But if it is not broken at the learner–teacher point, teachers go into their careers with no vision of alternatives and no experience of democratic learning. It is usually more difficult to change later.

So, what happened when we tried a democratic approach on a teacher education course? After a short settling-in period, when the students had introduced each other to the group, the news was broken by the tutors, Clive Harber and Roland Meighan, that although there was a planned course ready in the familiar authoritarian expert style, there were other options open to the group. They could consider operating as a democratic learning cooperative which would devise and plan its own programme of studies using the tutor as resource if and when deemed appropriate. A specimen contract was available for discussion purposes if this option required any elaboration.

Specimen Group Learning Contract

We agree to accept responsibility for our course as a group.

We agree to take an active part in the learning of the group.

We agree to be critical, constructively, of our own and other people's ideas.

We agree to plan our own programme of studies, implement it using the group members and appointed teachers as resources, and review the outcomes in order that we may learn from any limitations we identify.

We agree to the keeping of a group logbook of work completed, planning decisions, session papers and any other appropriate documents.

We agree to share the duties of being in the chair, being meeting secretary, session organizers and contributors.

We agree to review this contract from time to time.

The course thus began as a consultation about the approach to be adopted for the course itself. There was, in fact, another option made available to the group and that was of a mixture of approaches, e.g. adopting one approach for one term and another for another term, or some members choosing an individualized course if the majority wanted either a lecturer-taught course or a learning cooperative.

There is a need to clarify what 'a course' actually meant. In one case it referred to the 'methods of teaching' module of the post-graduate certificate of education year, taking up about one third of the total time. During the period 1976 to 1990, considerable experience of this approach was accumulated as thirteen courses approached their learning in the democratic mode. One course decided to begin with the authoritarian mode and change to the democratic when they felt appropriate. This took about four weeks. This particular course was evaluated by an independent observer and an account published (Fielding *et al.*, 1979).

In two cases, part of the course was run democratically, in one case one day a week, in another, the summer term. The majority of members of these two groups expressed regret in the end of course evaluations that they had not chosen to do the whole of their course as a learning cooperative.

The tutors had to adjust to a different theory of teaching and so did most of the students. All were agreed, however, that the effort was well worth while. The new habits were a great improvement on the old ones.

RATIONALE FOR A DEMOCRATIC APPROACH

If teaching in secondary schools in the UK is seen primarily as a decision-making activity, one appropriate way of learning to teach may be simulating the process on the training course itself by selecting the aims, content, methods and evaluation methods for their own group. In effect, teachers in training can experiment on themselves, practising many of the skills they will need for the rest of their careers, in contrast to the authoritarian approach of listening to someone else tell them how to make appropriate decisions. Since currently a central activity in secondary schools is formal instruction, students will practise this activity by taking the role of instructor to their fellow students.

In most teacher training there is a marked contrast between the essentially passive role assigned to students at the training institution and the active role on teaching practice. The adoption of a democratic approach weakens this dichotomy since the students become active in both situations.

THE OUTCOMES – FROM THE LEARNERS' VIEWPOINT

No student involved in the thirteen courses wrote an evaluation regretting the debate over the methods they should adopt for the learning, and none of those who opted for a democratic mode has evaluated the experience negatively. No course chose the individualized option, and one student explains the rejection of this approach:

We decided upon the democratic working cooperative for the following reasons. To begin with we felt that individual work was too isolated. We all felt that the work we had been engaged upon for our first degree courses had been too competitive and too isolated. Therefore, we all agreed that something else had to be attempted for our year within the faculty. At the beginning the course tutor was to be absent from our meetings and later allowed into the group as our confidence grew.

One course resulted in the consultative mode being adopted as a compromise:

Members of the group decided to choose Option 2 as the most useful method of learning, i.e. a course which begins with tutor direction and then gradually handed over decision-making to the group. This was essentially a compromise between individuals who wished for a conventional tutor-directed course and those who wanted to try a Democratic Learning Cooperative.

The written evaluations produced by the various group members contained a number of regular themes. One was that of confidence:

Democratic responsibility, as opposed to sitting back and always receiving, meant that students had to use the skills they already had, as well as learning new ones. Such a situation was a good one in which to develop confidence in one's own thinking.

Most students had something to say about motivation, and always in favourable terms:

I felt great responsibility for the course and this involvement meant always taking a mentally active part. I felt no resentment against somebody trying to impose work or a situation on me. Thus motivation was high.

Personally for me the course was very stimulating theoretically and practically. I not only learnt a lot but experienced much. I felt motivated to work and get involved because I felt it was our course.

There was intellectual enjoyment. Intellectual exploration became an exciting and satisfying end in its own right, rather than a means to a boring and worthless end (e.g. exams, assessment, achieving the teacher's aims, etc.). Ultimately the only end was personal satisfaction, thus the only pressure was personal. Personal pressure stimulated, and made exciting, my learning. Outside pressure always deadened and styled it.

Several students noted that the discussion techniques of the group members were utilized to the full and developed in the process:

The discussions were conducted on a relaxed and friendly basis and were therefore enjoyed by most students. Most students felt able to contribute their ideas and opinions to some or all of the topics discussed. Personally I have found this aspect of the course very beneficial because it has facilitated the exchange of ideas and information between group members and the exploration of many different aspects of key issues.

One of the conventional objections to democratic learning is that the content may be deficient if the 'experts' let go of the selection of the 'best' content for the task in hand. The students did not support this interpretation:

> With all students choosing the range of subjects the content, inevitably (in my mind), was of a greater range and more relevance than if the 'teacher' had done all the choosing. A group of students, especially from different specialist backgrounds, were able to provide more resources than one teacher could.

> The standard of papers given was generally very high – probably much higher than if the work had been set by the tutor.

> A wide variety of topics relating both to the practical and philosophical aspects of social science teaching have been covered by the course. In addition the content of the course has reflected the interests of the students because of their role in choosing the topics to be discussed.

The democratic nature of the course meant that decision-making was practised and that responsibility was shared. The students found this a favourable feature of the course.

> Responsibility and authority were dispersed among all members of the group, meaning that the assumption of these was voluntary, rather than them being concentrated into one person's (teacher) job. The taking of responsibility on a voluntary basis did not present any problems as all members of the group were happy to take it.

> A system whereby 'rules' were made, but made by ourselves as we went along, meant that the group had security and direction, but also adaptability and flexibility

> One was encouraged to recognize the value of other students as a resource.

> The content of the course would be decided by the group. Essentially this meant that the group decided its priorities – what the particular members of the group felt would be most useful to them as future teachers. It allowed members of the group to follow up personal interests and also allowed the group to draw upon the expertise that did exist within the group.

A regular theme that occurred in the student evaluation was that of the bridging of theory and practice. Since a dichotomy is frequently reported between those two, it is interesting to see what the learners in a democratic situation had to say about this matter:

> With regard to the 'methods' course, any gaps between theory and practice were, I think, well bridged. The peculiar nature of the course, with its options (including the more radical democratic learning cooperative), offered and put into practice, meant that we did not just talk about alternative ways of teaching and learning but to a certain, albeit perhaps limited, extent, experienced and experimented with alternative methods.

There was also comment on a related tension between the problems of preparing for survival in schools as they were, while considering any vision as to improvements on the status quo or alternatives to the current orthodoxy:

> The course, in practice, therefore, seemed to me to cope nicely with the idealism of educational change and the practicalities and constraints involved in operationalizing such changes. In this way the course provided a realistic 'vision' for changed procedures in teaching while not ignoring the problems of practice, or survival, which face all teachers.

> The experience of a democratic learning cooperative is valuable in itself for intending teachers since it presents them with an alternative method of learning and teaching for future use with their own pupils. Unless this is actually experienced by students, it is unlikely that this important innovation will reach schools in any significant degree.

> One of the roles of teacher training should be to investigate and experiment with alternative methods of teaching and learning, in a practical way, and to provide working models of the alternative methods.

The cooperative outlook to learning basic to the democratic approach extended in influence beyond the methods course in the university to the teaching-practice situation:

> During the major teaching practice and in other instances the cooperative tended to be very supportive and relationships proved to be advantageous, especially during the ten long weeks of teaching practice in the spring term.

The enthusiasm of the students for their democratic learning cooperative did not prevent them from identifying problems, and one student commented on a difficulty, not exclusive to democratic approaches of course, regarding lateness:

> one obvious 'problem' in the group was never really brought out into the open and tackled: the 'problem' being that of lateness. Presumably no one member was willing to take the authoritarian role of instigating a discussion on the subject. Lateness did not impair the content of our sessions – we simply finished later. But such a casual approach can cause personal organization problems for some. The point of lateness is really insignificant, but the principle is important. No one, within the group situation, had a role which legitimated instigation of questioning group behaviour. I don't think this ever caused us any important problems, but with different personalities and circumstances a dilemma could be produced.

Most of the evaluations concluded with an overall verdict on the course:

> The group enjoyed the methods course very much. It was extremely beneficial both academically and practically. Highlights and reservations along with possible improvements and alterations were suggested, and a general report on the course was made which had the consent of the whole group.

> I hope other groups will learn from our experiences and enjoy their year as much as I believe our course has.

Our course certainly could not be taken as a blueprint for democratic learning. It was unique, like every learning situation should be, based on the idea that every group of students is different. However, within our own terms and circumstances, I consider the system to have been a success and one which could be adapted, with great benefits to many situations.

The cooperative spent many hours in discussion and formulated opinions and views (often varying) in relation to our timetable of work. All the group members felt without any reservation whatsoever that the co-op was a new working experience which was stimulating, enjoyable and very worthwhile. We all gained an enormous amount from it, academically and in relation to the new relationships we formed. Everyone in the working cooperative agreed that it was an invaluable, exciting experience and one which we would advise any PGCE students to take part in regardless of discipline.

THE OUTCOMES – FROM THE TUTORS' VIEWPOINT

The tutor involved in the first attempts and the second tutor involved later kept personal notes week by week on the democratic learning cooperatives. Some of the themes that are selected from these notes as significant are as follows.

A potential conflict was seen in the transfer from the democratic course to the authoritarian schools in which teaching practice took place. The tutors were surprised at the pay-off from the course, which seemed to more than offset any expected responses of alienation and rejection. The students approached the teaching practice with considerable confidence, and this was remarked upon by the teachers in the school. Since the students were used to making decisions about what to learn and how, assembling appropriate materials and using them, they appeared to transfer these behaviours to school scheme and lesson preparation without any nervousness. They were also used to working cooperatively and so fitted into team situations with teachers with relative ease. Tutors' visits held little fear for them, since they were already used to the tutor's presence at their 'performances' at the university. None attempted to implement learning cooperatives, with the exception of one attempt at sixth-form level, which was reportedly successful, but all approached pupils in either the 'nice strict' mode or the consultative mode, and relationships with classes were remarkably smooth from the outset in most cases.

The tutors had to adjust to a different theory of teaching since they had been educated in authoritarian styles. They had to learn to listen much more, learn to resist the previous habit of dominating the decision-making and discussions, and to cope with anxiety when their expertise was seen to be less significant than they had previously supposed. There was irony in feeling anxious at having helped students to manage competently on their own when this is exactly what they will need to do for the rest of their professional careers. The facilitative role was demanding, since making contacts, identifying resources and solving operational problems on the spot or at short notice were different experiences from the authoritarian approach (where, having made the decisions as to content in advance, a tutor was in a position to produce hand-outs and identify resources some time beforehand). The tutors also had to cope with their ideas and suggestions being either rejected or scrutinized closely, with justification requested.

There were tensions with the other courses that the students were required to attend as part of their PGCE year. The confidence of members of the learning cooperative in challenging other tutors in formal lectures was not always welcome, and other students did not always find their enthusiasm and commitment appealing. On one occasion there was a joint session with another methods group to work with a visiting speaker. When she phoned to say she was unable to come due to a school crisis, the learning cooperative immediately set about organizing a substitute programme for the morning for themselves. The other student teacher group declined to take part or devise something similar for themselves, and went away to take the morning off with some parting remarks about the others being far too keen.

Any anxieties the tutors had about the quality of student input or the 'covering of key topics' proved groundless. The students exceeded what the tutors had planned and added ideas that had not been included, so that the tutors were learning new material in some of the sessions.

The tutors were curious as to how the students would cope with applications for posts and interviews. Potential teachers of social and political studies sometimes have to cope with hysteria about their subject – not unlike that biology teachers used to face in Bible-belt communities because of their identification with evolution theory – but, in addition, this group had a democratic experience that had appeared to increase confidence, commitment and awareness of alternatives in approaches to education. It seemed a potentially explosive combination. However, the pay-off from the course appeared to be positive rather than negative. The approach of the students seemed to appeal to many interviewers. Some headteachers responded to the effect that 'this is a whole new generation of teachers, articulate, enthusiastic, industrious and challenging'. Perhaps the tutors should have known better because when they had organized teach-ins with in-service courses using the members of the democratic learning cooperative as a resource, the response of the experienced teachers had frequently been similarly enthusiastic.

CONCLUSION

If democratic ideologies of education have in common a view of independence in the teacher–learner relationship, the outcome is a type of power sharing and an exercise in freedom in the sense that Wright Mills (1959) expounded:

> Freedom is, first of all, the chance to formulate the available choices, to argue over them and then the opportunity to choose. That is why freedom cannot exist without an enlarged role of human reason in human affairs.

The democratic learning cooperatives appear to exemplify this principle and also allow a bridging back into the authoritarian situations of schools with positive effects, so that the student teachers appeared to be well prepared to cope well with schools as they are, but having experiences and visions of possible alternatives and possible modifications to the status quo should the situation allow or require them.

Further Reading

Bartholomew, J. (1976) 'Schooling Teachers: The Myth of the Liberal College', in G. Whitty, and M.F.D. Young (eds), *Explorations in the Politics of Knowledge*. Driffield: Nafferton Books.

Chamberlin, R. (1989) *Free Children and Democratic Schools*. London: Falmer.

Davies, L. (1994) *Beyond Authoritarian School Management*. Ticknall: Education Now Books.

Engle, S. and Ochoa, A. (1989) *Education for Democratic Citizenship*. Columbia, NY: Teachers College Press.

Friere, P. (1972) *Pedagogy of the Oppressed*. Harmondsworth: Penguin.

Gordon, T. (1986) *Democracy in One School?* London: Falmer.

Harber, C. and Meighan, R. (1989) *The Democratic School: Educational Management and the Practice of Democracy*. Ticknall: Education Now Books.

Harber, C. (1995) *Developing Democratic Education*. Ticknall: Education Now Books.

Hart, R. (1992) *Children's Participation: From Tokenism to Citizenship*. Innocenti Essays, No. 4. London: UNICEF.

Kelly, A.V. (1995) *Education and Democracy*. London: Paul Chapman.

Kohl, H. (1970) *The Open Classroom*. London: Methuen.

Meighan, R. (1994) *The Freethinkers' Guide to the Educational Universe*. Nottingham: Educational Heretics Press.

Rogers, C. (1983) *Freedom to Learn for the Eighties*. Colombus, OH: Merrill.

Nicholls, J.G. (1989) *The Competitive Ethos and Democratic Education*. Cambridge, MA: Harvard University Press.

Watts, J. (1980) *Towards an Open School*. Harlow: Longman.

White, P. (1983) *Beyond Domination*. London: Routledge and Kegan Paul.

Discussion and Activities

1. How do leadership styles vary with each ideology of education? Consider how appropriate this quotation is for democratic education: 'Of a good leader, when his task is finished, his goal achieved, they say, "We did this ourselves".' Lao-tse c.600 BC (with apologies for the sexist language!).

2. In Russell's 'control in the spirit of freedom' concept, authoritarian forms of education can be seen as possibly necessary and certainly temporary expedients. When and how can moves to non-authoritarian forms take place?

3. Without assertiveness training, will females be disadvantaged by democratic forms of education?

Signposts
---

1. Relationship between interactionist sociology and non-authoritarian ideologies of education
Central concepts of interactionist sociology include bargaining, negotiation, reality construction, mandates, self-concepts and reconstruction of self, and layers of meaning. This raises the question of whether there is a necessary link between this kind of sociology and non-authoritarian ideas. The references listed under Further Reading above may provide some starting points. See also Chapter 20.

2. Forms of democratic education
The degree and kind of power sharing may mark off different forms of democratic education. In teacher education, syndicate approaches may be another form where the learners make a wide range of decisions within the confines of a set syllabus. See Collier, G. (1983) *The Management of Peer Group Learning*, London: Society for Research into Higher Education.

3. Children's rights
The most radical analysis of children's rights appears in Holt, J. (1975) *Escape from Childhood*, Harmondsworth: Penguin. A recent account appears in Franklin, B. (1995) *The Handbook of Children's Rights*, London: Routledge. Davies, L. and Kirkpatrick, G. (2000) *The EURIDEM Project: A Review of Pupil Democracy in Europe*, London: Children's Rights Alliance. See Chapter 2.

4. Early childhood education and democratic practice
The idea that young children do not have the skills and experience to be democratic is refuted by studies such as: Paley, V.G. (1992) *You Can't Say You Can't Play*, Cambridge, MA: Harvard University Press.

5. Investigate the following themes

(a) Schools councils. Children can only learn about democracy if they take part in it. Read the chapter 'Little citizens' by John Siraj-Blatchford (1995) from the book *Educating the Whole Child*, Iram and John Siraj-Blatchford (eds), Buckingham: Open University Press.

(b) Cooperative learning. There is an assumption by some educationalists that working together is a natural way of learning. However, cooperative learning is a skill which has to be practised before it is perfected. Read Galton and Williamson's (1992) *Groupwork in the Primary Classroom*, London: Routledge.

(c) Circle time. Peter Lang has written about the importance of personal and social education (PSE) for children as part of a holistic programme. It is also a key cross-curricular area as defined by the Schools Curriculum and Assessment Authority. Look at the curriculum guidance on the various cross-curricular themes, e.g. PSE, environmental education, economic and enterprise education, health education and education for citizenship. How do these relate to the Core and Foundation subjects of the National Curriculum and how relevant is it to have these themes in schools? Even the youngest children can work on each of these areas: see Iram and John Siraj-Blatchford (eds) (1995) *Educating the Whole Child*, Buckingham: Open University Press; in particular the chapter by Peter Lang on circle time.

6. International Perspectives

Some countries have consciously designed their formal education systems to foster democracy for some time (see Chapter 10 of Harber, C. (2004) *Schooling as Violence*, London: Routledge Falmer).

Ideologies of Education: Section Summary

The Authoritarian View of Education

Authoritarian education, in its various forms, has one person, or a small group of people, making and implementing the decisions about what to learn, when to learn, how to learn, how to assess learning, and the learning environment often before the learners are recruited as individuals or meet as a group.

Discipline is ... learning to obey the rules and instructions decided by the management.

Knowledge is ... essentially, information contained in the traditional subjects.

Learning is ... mostly, listening to subject experts and reading their books.

Teaching is ... usually, formal instruction by trained or approved adults.

Parents are ... expected, for the most part, to be spectators to the experts.

Resources are ... predominately, subject textbooks.

Location is ... a central place (school) where the experts (teachers) can easily be assembled together cheaply, with large groups of pupils.

Organization is ... usually in classes formally arranged.

Assessment is ... mostly, by tests of how well pupils can repeat the subjects.

Aims are ... essentially, to produce mini-academic subject experts, with those who fail in this enterprise, required to be useful in industry/commerce.

Power is ... in the hands of the appointed individual or a senior management team or governors who believe that they have the right to impose their decisions on others.

The Autonomous View of Education

In *autonomous education*, the decisions about learning are made by the individual learners. They manage and take responsibility for their own learning programmes. They may seek advice or look for ideas about what to learn and how to learn it by research and consultation.

Discipline is ... that form known as self-discipline.

Knowledge is ... essentially, the repertoire of learning and research skills needed to cope with new ideas.

Learning is ... mostly, self-directed activity and personal research to gain experience, information or skills.

Teaching is ... usually, self-teaching; the purpose of other teachers is to teach you how to teach yourself better.

Parents are ... expected to be part of the team supporting the learner's growth in learning skills and confidence.

Resources are ... predominately, first-hand experiences as the basis of personal research backed up by any other resources seen to be appropriate.

Location is ... anywhere that useful or interesting learning can take place.

Organization is ... often in individual learning stations in institutional settings, but remains flexible to match the variety of learner-managed tasks.

Assessment is ... commonly, by self-assessment using any tests, devised by the learner or by others, that are seen to be appropriate to the situation.

Aims are ... essentially, to produce people with the confidence and skills to manage their own learning throughout their entire lives.

Power ... is seen as devolved to individuals who are seen as morally responsible for the exercise of their autonomy.

The Democratic View of Education

In *democratic education*, the learners as a group have the power to make some, most or even all of the key decisions, since power is shared and not appropriated in advance by a minority of one or more. In many 'democratic' countries, such educational practices are rare and often meet with sustained, hostile and irrational opposition.

Discipline is ... democratic discipline by working cooperatively to agreed rules and principles.

Knowledge is ... essentially, the skills and information needed by the group to maintain and develop its cooperative culture.

Learning is ... activity agreed by the group to gain experience, information or particular skills working either together or delegated to individuals.

Teaching is ... any activity, including instruction, that the group judges will lead to effective learning.

Parents are ... seen as part of the resources available.

Resources are ... anything appropriate to the group's research and learning including people, places, experiences.

Location is ... anywhere that the learning group can meet to pursue effective learning.

Organization is ... commonly in groups where democratic dialogue and cooperative learning can take place.

Assessment is ... by any form of assessment using any tests, devised by the learners or by others, that are seen to be appropriate to the situation.

Aims are ... essentially, to produce people with the confidence and skills to manage their own life-long learning within a democratic culture.

Power is ... shared in the group who are seen as responsible both individually and collectively for its exercise.

Part Four
SOCIOLOGICAL PERSPECTIVES AND THE STUDY OF EDUCATION

LEN BARTON AND STEPHEN WALKER

WHAT IS A PERSPECTIVE?

In Chapter 1 the sociologist was likened to a spy, an 'agent' involved in the business of collecting key information on the mechanisms and processes of social life. Much of the material presented so far has been concerned with the reports made by those sociological spies who have investigated the world of education. However, the validity of any spy's report has to be scrutinized. The spy who infiltrates the organization is likely to depict the scene under investigation in a very different way from one who looks through the keyhole, and so the vaildity of what he or she reports is closely related to the position from which the observations were made. Similarly, no sociologist can approach the study of social life without making some selection from the various perspectives available, and, if the information offered by such sociologists is to be of use to people in their daily lives, it is necessary to know both the perspective from which the sociologist is working and the ways in which this perspective is distinct from other sociological stances.

In this section the intention is to introduce the reader to some of the various perspectives used by sociologists in their endeavour to analyse human conduct. Initially, therefore, it is important to understand what we mean by the term 'perspective'. A perspective is a frame of reference, a series of working rules by which a person is able to make sense of complex and puzzling phenomena. For the sociologist the phenomenon is social life and, in adopting a particular stance towards this, he or she makes use of a set of assumptions upon which analysis can be based and which, typically, includes ideas about the following:

1. A view of humankind, i.e. an idea about what distinguishes human beings from other species.
2. A view of society, i.e. a picture of the structural features which emerge, develop, persist and change as a consequence of people acting in association with others.
3. A view of the interrelation between the individual and society.
4. A view of what should be taken as the crucial properties, the fundamental factors, which condition human conduct and experience in a social order.
5. A view of what it is to 'know' or 'understand' the properties of those aspects of social life under investigation.
6. A view of the relationship between 'academic' explanations of social life and the formulation of policies which can be used to direct the everyday affairs of members of society.

All these issues can, of course, be interpreted in different ways. However, what is important for our purposes is that the specific interpretation adopted by a working sociologist will influence both what is seen to be problematic about a topic for investigation and the kind of explanation which will emerge from such investigations.

PERSPECTIVES IN SOCIOLOGY AND EDUCATIONAL ISSUES

It may appear that the preoccupations listed above are unnecessarily complicated and are divorced from the down-to-earth study of either social life in general or education in particular. However, consider the controversy concerning so-called 'compensatory education'. How can we best explain and react to the relative failure of large numbers of working-class pupils in our schools today? Some sociologists, accepting prevailing definitions of school success and failure, have attempted to explain the causes of this occurrence. In doing this they have explored questions like:

1. The extent to which the problem resides in the individual pupils, in that they lack certain skills, abilities and aptitudes.
2. The extent to which the problem is caused by the inadequacy of some pupils' home background.
3. The extent to which the problem is concerned with the way in which inequalities in society are reproduced in the educational and social experiences of such pupils.
4. The extent to which the problem is the result of attempts to impose a uniform school experience in a multicultural society.

More recently, other sociologists, maintaining that the essence of the problem is concerned with how educational success and failure is defined, and how individual pupils come to be given success and failure identities by teachers and educational administrators, have attempted to explain the processes by which categories of success and failure are constructed, organized and applied in the course of everyday life in schools. In so doing they have focused on questions about:

1. What teachers take to be valid educational performance.
2. How pupils perceive and react to such definitions.
3. What pupils actually fail at.

It seems likely that the extent to which one of the above sets of questions is seen as more appealing than the other as a basis for making an examination of the issue of educational 'failure' is fundamentally concerned with the perspective one has of the person, of society and of the interaction between the two. The position one adopts from which to view something will determine what one sees and hence what one takes to be important aspects of the object under scrutiny.

DETERMINISM VERSUS VOLUNTARISM

Underneath a great deal of the conflict of opinion contained in the perspective debate in sociology is a tension which is well illustrated in 'The Humanist's Sonnet' quoted in Chapter 1. The poem raises the issue of the extent to which individuals are determined by their class, culture or circumstances, or are free agents, controlling their own destiny. It is interesting to note that teachers themselves often experience a similar kind of tension when they explore questions about the working of the education system or about their own place within it. When challenged to express their feelings on educational issues or to explain their reasons for adopting particular classroom practices, many teachers regularly fall back on the argument that, although they would like to follow all kinds of innovative and imaginative educational principles, they cannot do so because they are constrained by the curriculum, their senior colleagues, the pupils' parents, the inspectorate – in short, the system (see Chapter 3). In a very real sense, this kind of explanation involves a sort of intuitive 'sociological' reasoning. It is an expression of an awareness of a difference between the reality of the constraints of the structured system in which they find themselves, on the one hand, and their ability to decide upon their own course of action and implement the dictates of their own wills and volitions, on the other. However, it would be wrong to imagine that one could study the conduct of teachers in particular or of people in general solely in terms of this very basic dichotomy. We need to question not only what might constrain our lives and actions but also how these 'external' constraints find their way into individuals' lives and activities. Clearly this is a complex question. Just as complex are the methods used to explore the issues raised, and in this part of the book we hope to introduce some of the ways in which these kinds of questions are both conceptualized and handled by sociologists. Much of the following discussion will be concerned with sociological insights and interests of an abstract nature, and we would suggest that if the reader keeps in mind that much of the debate is tempered by a consideration of the 'free or determined' problem outlined above, then the relevance of the discussion might be seen more easily.

Exercise

To clarify the issues introduced so far it might help if the reader spends a short time on the following project. Ideally the project should be undertaken in groups (see item 1 below).

1. Select a topic which you consider an important educational problem. For example, you might focus upon truancy, discipline in classrooms, the role of the teacher or any area suggested in the material of the previous chapters. (This project might be usefully extended if you work in groups and if two groups decide to work on the same topic. Each group should discuss independently the issues raised in items 2, 3 and 4 below and then compare their accounts in a joint session.)
2. Devise a study programme which allows you to explore the crucial properties of the problem you have isolated with a view to providing an explanatory account.
3. Justify the basis upon which you intend to collect evidence in your search for an explanation and explain the criteria you would apply to distinguish between valid and invalid evidence.
4. Determine what views of the person, of society and of the interrelation between people and society are embedded within your chosen study programme.

Further Reading

Barton, L. and Walker, S. (1978) 'Sociology of Education at the Crossroads', *Educational Review*, **30**, 3. A discussion of the factors which influenced the emergence of various perspectives within the sociology of education.

Bernstein, B. (1977) 'Sociology and the Sociology of Education: A Brief Account', in B. Bernstein, *Class, Codes and Control, Vol. III*. London: Routledge and Kegan Paul. A detailed review of the ways in which perspective shifts have influenced attitudes to theorizing and research in the sociology of education.

Cohen, P. (1968) *Modern Social Theory*. London: Heinemann. A comprehensive account of the emergence and development of major schools of thought in general sociology.

Eggleston, J. (1974) *Contemporary Research in the Sociology of Education*. London: Routledge and Kegan Paul. The introductions to both this and the following reference contain reviews of the ways in which perspective shifts have influenced attitudes to theorizing and research in the sociology of education.

Karabel, J. and Halsey, A.H. (1977) *Power and Ideology in Education*. Oxford: Oxford University Press.

19 Social Systems, Structures and Functions

LEN BARTON AND STEPHEN WALKER

INTRODUCTION

Sociologists study a wide variety of questions about human conduct. However, a basic theme which underlies many of these questions is a puzzle very similar to what has become known as the Hobbesian 'problem of order'. Why is it, asks Hobbes (1651), that when individuals come together in societies there is not a constant 'war of everyone against everyone', with each individual person fighting for his or her own survival or self-interest using whatever means are available? Why, he wonders, is social order necessary and how is it achieved? If the processes by which social life proceeds in an orderly and coherent fashion are to be identified and explained, we must first explore the basis upon which these processes rest, the mechanism which enables or restricts collective human behaviour.

Berger (1966) likened social life to the workings of a puppet theatre. Is it accurate, he asked, to see people as puppets, manipulated by some force from above so that some order is imposed upon the social drama? Accepting for the moment the basic idea of this analogy, i.e. that it might be useful to identify those factors which work upon individuals to render their behaviour orderly, we still need to ask questions about the nature of the social puppeteer. What is this power or force? It is no accident that early attempts to handle this question were, in the main, concerned with identifying those features of social life which provide for stability, cohesion and integration, i.e. the social system. Although in the period when sociology first emerged as a distinctive form of study many of the individual's actions seemed to be a consequence of personal or local interests being pursued, for 'society' itself to exist as a framework in which the conditions for the individual's existence are made possible, it was thought that the crucial feature of social organization was the system by which individual social members were related to the social whole.

Nevertheless, it is important to appreciate that the emergence of sociology as a discipline in the nineteenth century took place during an era of considerable historical and cultural upheaval. First, the Industrial Revolution, the increase in urbanization, the political revolutions in Europe and the relative decline in the power of the church meant that previously held notions of society and social order ceased to provide a meaningful explanation of the situation in which individuals found themselves; the right of certain groups to rule and the basis upon which one individual was related to another could no longer be justified in terms of traditionally held concepts like divine ordinance or 'natural' social justice. Second, the publication in 1859 of Darwin's *The Origin of Species* and the subsequent impact that evolutionary theory had upon thought created a kind of reverence for 'scientific' methods of study and, more importantly, put the whole question of social order back into the melting-pot. In effect, Darwin's work provided an academically and philosophically respectable base upon which misgivings about previously cherished notions of social organization could be consolidated. The 'social order' of any given society became nothing more than a particular organizational form created by people for the governing of their affairs as part of their collective struggle to survive the natural environment. Given these upheavals, it should come as no surprise that the major concerns of sociologists present at the birth of the discipline were with:

1. explaining the socially devised structures which allow individuals to act as relatively independent beings, yet also provide a system which prevents complete anarchy and confusion;
2. adopting a 'scientific' approach to the formulation of such explanations;
3. providing knowledge which would allow people to understand and direct the social forces which seemed to be something more than the power of any single individual.

DURKHEIM AND THE SOCIAL ORDER

In the work of one of the 'founding fathers' of sociology, Emile Durkheim (1858–1917), we find a very clear statement of what this social force, this power behind the 'social puppeteer', was taken to be. Central to Durkheim's sociology is the notion of the primacy of society over the individual. If there were no agency to regulate and direct the activities of people then human association would be impossible, social life would become chaotic and society would disintegrate. Durkheim is, therefore, in absolute opposition to the ideas of utilitarian theory, which stress that social order is achieved through unrestricted competition, through each person pursuing his or her own best interest, which will often conflict with the interests of others. For Durkheim this agency is the moral order, the central value system which, though created by people, has an independent and external existence and acts as a constraining and conditioning force upon individual people. His view is perhaps best illustrated in his famous statement that:

> Society commands us because it is exterior and superior to us, the moral distance between it and us makes it an authority before which our wills defer.

People act as they do in compliance with the demands of the society in which they live, and these demands are enshrined within the moral code. But what is this moral code and how is it to be recognized? It is, Durkheim (1968) explains:

> the totality of beliefs and sentiments common to average citizens of the same society [and this totality] forms a determinate system which has its own life; one may call it the collective or common conscience . . . it is, by definition, diffuse in every reach of society. Nevertheless, it has specific characteristics which make it a distinct reality. It is, in effect, independent of the particular conditions in which individuals are placed; they pass on and it remains.

It follows that any other social agency or institution, such as the political system, the economic system or the education system:

1. is shaped by the basic principles of the common moral order;
2. functions so as to ensure that these principles are put into practice and obeyed;
3. allows for behaviour which does not conform to these principles to be defined, explained and controlled.

Durkheim did not ignore the fact that in a complex society such ideals would not be achieved easily. An important element in such societies is that individuals increasingly take on specialized roles and activities to enable and help the society to develop; although these individuals are, therefore, mutually interdependent, a common value system is necessary, both to relate different individuals and their work to each other and to provide continuity between successive generations. From Durkheim's model for sociological analysis, then, three key words emerge: system, structure and function. The social system is the totality of organizations which emerge to satisfy the needs carried in the central value system of a society. The structure of this system is similarly defined by these values. Any particular institution in the structure functions to provide a link with other elements and, more importantly, to ensure that the principles of the value system are realized in everyday life. So, institutions like the political, economic and education systems provide a basis for determining what is and what is not acceptable social conduct, and the means by which individuals are introduced to and taught the common values of the society. The relevance of this Durkheimian perspective is, perhaps, more clearly seen if one applies it to a particular instance. What, for example, would an analysis of the education system based on this perspective look like? Very basically, it would always begin by examining the relationship between the structure of society and the function of education as a sub-system of the society. Like any other social organization, the system of education can be analysed primarily in terms of the functions it serves, notably its function in providing for the maintenance, legitimation, transmission and internalization of the 'collective conscience' (the moral order). In Durkheim's own words:

> Society can survive only if there exists among its members a sufficient degree of homo-
> geneity; education perpetuates and reinforces this homogeneity by fixing in the child, from
> the beginning, the essential similarities that collective life demands.
>
> Durkheim, 1956

The consequence of viewing education in this way is that any question about the organization and process of education is always to be framed in terms of the system's function, i.e.
in terms of education's role in providing for the adequate socialization of the individual. This
view has massive implications. First, in broad terms, education must be seen as a conservative
or an integrating force. As Gouldner (1971) notes:

> Durkheim ... regarded moral values as pattern-maintaining forces ... their significance was
> primarily social; they contribute to the solidarity of society and to the integration of indi-
> viduals into society.

If the education system functions to transmit these values, it too must work towards solidarity
and integration rather than towards differentiation and managed pluralism. Second, and
more specifically, let us consider briefly how the view influences interpretations of three key
areas of schooling. For example, we can ask how the perspective conditions questions like:

1. What should be taught in schools? (The curriculum.)
2. What are the responsibilities of teachers? (The role of the teacher.)
3. What is the pupil's 'purpose' in school? (The role of the pupil.)
4. How should teachers and pupils relate? (Interpersonal relations.)

Of course, these are only a selection from a wider range of issues concerning education which
might be explored in terms of the Durkheimian perspective.

A DURKHEIMIAN VIEW OF SCHOOLING

The Curriculum

If education is to be successful in fulfilling its transmission and socialization functions then
choice of curriculum content in schools is strictly limited. Specific ideas, concepts, topics or
segments of knowledge included in the curriculum will, of course, vary from society to society
and from era to era. What is important is that an item can only justifiably find its way into the
school curriculum if it is part of the common collective culture. The specific nature of the
contents of the curriculum is largely irrelevant, as long as the curriculum is designed to
conform to the ideals of the following statement:

> The man who education should realize in us is not the man such as nature has made him,
> but as society wishes him to be ... It is society that draws for us the portrait of the kind of

man we should be, and in this portrait all the peculiarities of its organization come to be reflected.

Durkheim, 1956

The Role of the Teacher

Here again the dominance of social needs over those of the individual is paramount. Teachers must ensure that their activities in school:

1. Encourage in their pupils group involvement, allegiance and responsibility.
2. Enable pupils, where necessary, to recognize that their allegiance to societal goals and values comes before personal or familial concerns; to this extent the teacher may have to work to resocialize those children whose previous formative experience has taken place in an environment which celebrates sectional rather than collective interests.
3. Develop and extend in their pupils those skills which society needs in order to function and which the children need in order to survive in society.

Teachers must never lose sight of the fact that, although they are agents of transmission, they themselves are under obligation to the same societal requirements. Teachers, then, are simultaneously moral models and moral beings, constraining and constrained:

> The teacher must therefore be committed to presenting (the rule), not as his own personal doing, but as a moral power superior to him, and of which he is an instrument, not the author. He must make the student understand that it imposes itself on him as it does on them; that he cannot remove or modify it; that he is constrained to apply it; that it dominates him and obliges him as it obliges them.

Durkheim, 1961

The Role of the Pupil

The child was always seen by Durkheim as an empty vessel, a blank sheet, waiting to be filled by the agents of society; 'the child', writes Durkheim (1956),

> on entering life, brings to it only his nature as an individual. Society finds itself, with each new generation, faced with a *tabula rasa*, very nearly, on which it must build anew. To the egoistic and asocial being that has just been born it must, as rapidly as possible, add another, capable of leading a moral and social life. Such is the work of education.

The image of the pupil, then, derived from this view of the child, is of a passive being, in need of restraint and having to be led away from selfish intentions towards a self-disciplined and cooperative identification with the common social good. Pupils must be passive because they lack experience and knowledge; they must be restrained because, initially at least, they are motivated by selfish desires which are vague and indistinct. However, Durkheim insists that the process by which this is achieved is not one of indoctrination or forced compliance. To be properly socialized the pupil's acceptance of common social values must be based upon understanding, which is to be derived from reasoned explanation, i.e. the child must come to want what society needs him or her to want; socialization in schools which is not based upon this principle will produce an educated person who might know the common culture, morals and mores but who will be unable to identify with them personally, and such a being is likely to become a danger to both self and society.

Interpersonal Relations

Given the roles of teachers and pupils outlined above, it follows that interpersonal relations in schools are to be characterized in Durkheimian analysis by three elements. First, teachers are, by definition, dominant partners: as agents of the state, and, therefore, of the common value system, they are superior.

> The ascendancy that the teacher naturally has over his pupil, because of the superiority of his experience and of his culture, will naturally give to his influence the efficacious force that he needs.
>
> Durkheim, 1956

Second, teachers are constrained from treating their pupils as individuals. A classroom, for Durkheim, is a society in miniature, and as such, 'must not be conducted as if it were only a simple agglomeration of subjects independent of one another' (Durkheim, 1956). Rather, interpersonal relations in schools must be carefully structured to reflect and realize homo-geneity, cooperative interaction and mutual interdependence. Third, and slightly paradoxically, there is, overarching interpersonal relations in schools, an impersonal force. Teachers' authority and pupils' passivity are not defined by personal needs and interests. Indeed, the behaviour of either is not governed or justified in personal terms at all, but through reference to the system of education which defines both roles according to the tenets of the collective culture. Personal whims, wishes and volitions are always subordinate to larger, more general 'societal' evaluations.

PARSONS AND SOCIALIZATION

Before some evaluation of this particular perspective is made, it is worthwhile to explore how both it and its application to the study of education have been extended in more recent sociological writings. Although a great deal of Durkheim's work was published at the turn of the century, it should not be imagined that either his approach to generating explanations of social life or his analysis of the education system fell out of use when he died. In the work of the American sociologist, Talcott Parsons, we can find a considerable refinement of some of the basic ideas postulated by Durkheim, an extension of the structuralist perspective.

Parsons was concerned with providing a schema which enabled an analyst to map not only the structural and systematic properties of a given social order, but also the way individual social actors come to know and behave in accordance with the constraints of that system. In this sense the Parsonian perspective has two important strands. First, Parsons, like Durkheim, saw social order achieved through the operation of an integrating system common to all members of society. Second, however, Parsons, borrowing from Freudian psychoanalytical theory, attempted to establish a link between the reproduction of society and the production of individual personalities, and the way in which he believed this could be achieved was through scrutinizing the process of socialization. Socialization involves the way in which:

> the main structure of personality is built up through the process of social interaction. It (personality) develops through the internalization of social objects and of the normative patterns governing the child's interaction in social situations.
>
> Parsons, 1964

Parsons argues that, in order for social integration to be achieved, society has, through a process of gradual evolution, thrown up a number of institutions which function as agencies of socialization – the church, the family and, importantly, the education system. As part of their everyday lives in society, social actors, like actors in the theatre, take on specific roles, depending upon the part of the social system, the institution, in which they are interacting – roles such as priests, fathers, mothers, teachers and pupils. The behaviour appropriate to these roles is defined by society. Society has what Parsons calls 'patterned expectations of the behaviour of individuals who occupy particular statuses in the social system'. In other words, for any given social role, society has, on the basis of past experience, evolved a system of 'rules and regulations' governing what is generally considered to constitute proper behaviour for those playing the roles, and these 'rules' gradually become crystallized into a set of 'expectations'. These expectations are shaped by the need society has to preserve itself; that is, its 'functional requirements'. For Parsons, all societies had four main functional requirements. These are:

1. Pattern maintenance, i.e. the preservation and passing on of social norms, values, rights and prohibitions.
2. Internal integration, i.e. the provision of the means by which one part of social life is linked to another or by which one sector of the social system (e.g. family life) is related to another (e.g. the economic system).
3. Goal attainment, i.e. the provision of the means whereby both individual and collective aims and needs can be realized.
4. Adaptation, i.e. a capacity for people to make a controlled reaction to changes in the physical, technological and cultural environment in order to maximize any productive

benefit to be derived from these changes and to minimize any threat of disruption to the overall integration of society.

Clearly, different functions will be emphasized and satisifed through activity in different social sub-systems, but two important processes, which are interrelated, were singled out by Parsons as being vital sociological concerns. The first of these was the process of institutionalization, or the way in which human behaviour becomes systematically regularized and standardized. The second was the process of internalization, or the way in which social expectations surrounding different social roles (as shaped by the functional requirements of society) are encountered, understood and learned by individuals. It was through a consideration of this latter process that Parsons attempted to handle differences between instinctive and learned behaviour, to bridge the gap between actions which arose in response to the individual's will and desires (personality) and those which were determined by the social structure and culture. He wrote:

> while the main content of the structure of the personality is derived from the social system and culture through socialization, the personality becomes an independent system through its relations to its own organism and through the uniqueness of its own life experiences: it is not a mere epiphenomenon of the structure of society. There is, however, not merely interdependence between the two but what I call interpenetration.
>
> Parsons, 1964

Parsons went on to propose that, in learning to play predetermined social roles (in becoming socialized), men and women preserve the common culture, find a place in a network of interrelated roles, discover an organized way of satisfying and developing personal needs and establish a base from which they can react to new situations confronting themselves in particular or the species in general. The part played by schooling and the system of education in allocating men and women to specific roles and in teaching them their 'parts' is obviously tremendous. 'The school class', Parsons (1959) maintained, 'is an agency through which individuals are trained to be motivationally and technically adequate to the performance of adult roles'.

However, in a complex society schools satisfy two broad functions for society. They provide a basis for socialization and they work as the mechanism by which individuals are allocated their adult roles – both work roles and wider social ones. In a sense there is a contradiction here between a celebration of similarity and a celebration of differences. Parsons exploited this contradiction by working on the assumption that the child in school had to be socialized to accept the legitimacy of a highly differentiated society in which individuals are selected for different roles which carry unequal status and reward, and also the acceptability of the criteria by which such selection is made. This last point is worth re-examination. In Part Two of this book some subtle aspects of schooling were discussed in terms of a hidden process, often the implication being that the differential treatment, the hidden ranking and the covert processes by which pupils are identified and labelled educational successes and failures are an undesirable consequence of the school system. For Parsons this process was not a latent function of the system at all: it was a necessary activity which one part of the social system, education, performed for the social whole.

Parsons (1959) maintained that schools foster two types of commitment: on the one hand commitment to broad social values, and on the other commitment to specific types of roles played in adult life. Elementary or primary education emphasized the first and secondary education the second, although both sectors of education worked to develop in the child both the capacity to perform roles and the capacity to be aware of and to live up to the obligations of different roles, both general and specific. Thus schools socialize pupils. But they socialize in ways which are specific and special to the particular social system, education, of which they are a part. Because the system also functions as an agency of 'manpower allocation', an organization which selects and trains the young for different, specialized roles in adult life, it must also provide a basis for establishing differences between individuals. The individual must be brought to an awareness that:

> it is fair to give differential rewards for different levels of achievement, so long as there has been fair access to opportunity, and fair that these rewards lead on to higher-order opportunities for the successful. There is thus a basic sense in which the elementary school class is an embodiment of the fundamental American value of equality of opportunity, in that it places value both on initial equality and on differential achievement.
>
> Parsons, 1958

This last function, Parsons suggested, is fulfilled by pupils identifying with the teacher, with what he or she represents and with the beneficial nature of education. Achievement itself has two facets. The first is cognitive, i.e. to do with activities and performances 'appropriate to the school situation'; the second is moral, i.e. to do with acquiring the necessary attitudes and behaviour for life in society. Both facets are, necessarily, always defined by adults and, like Durkheim, Parsons presents teachers and parents as superior to and in authority over their pupils and children. One final point. Schooling in advanced societies was viewed by Parsons as an indispensable section of the whole social structure:

> Relatively speaking, the school is a specialized agency. That it should increasingly have become the principal channel of selection as well as agency of socialization is in line with what one would expect in an increasingly differentiated and progressively more upgraded society.
>
> Parsons, 1959

THE STRUCTURALIST PERSPECTIVE AND THE SOCIOLOGY OF EDUCATION

The peculiar characteristics of a structuralist sociological perspective applied to the study of education and schooling – and, it is important to add, some of the weaknesses associated with such usage – are most clearly illustrated by an examination of the activities, attitudes and concerns of British and American sociologists of education working in the 1950s and the early 1960s. Although various writers developed some distinctive approaches to their work, the following comment made by Olive Banks (1978) remains substantially correct: 'It is fair to say that the main thrust in the sociology of education in the 1950s and 1960s was structure functionalism and this was true of both this country and the United States.'

Central to the work produced during this period was a concern with exploring and explicating the relationship between education and the structure of society. Indeed, it is hard to see how anyone working in the structuralist tradition could proceed otherwise, in view of the fact that in this sociological stance institutions in society were seen as functionally interrelated. It was thought, therefore, that an analysis of the functions of the education system and the extent to which these were being efficiently met would reveal:

1. The nature of the relationship between education and other social organizations.
2. Important insights into the way in which people can be expected to behave within educational settings.
3. The contribution education makes to the maintenance and the development of the social fabric.
4. A method by which dysfunctions in education, and the social malaise which would attend such dysfunctions, could be identified and redressed.

The question was, however, 'Functions for what purpose?' Durkheim had suggested that different functions could be reduced to the main need for social organizations to transmit the collective conscience. In the rapidly developing and changing post-war society, however, it was difficult to reconcile such a model with the realities of emergent values, new technological achievements and changing patterns of social groupings; traditional values seemed to be inadequate tools to cope with shifting situations. The major focus, therefore, was upon economic needs and the close relationship between education and the economy, which arose from what Parsons described as education's dual function of socializing and selecting people for adult roles. Thus, in the introduction to their influential reader concerning the sociology of education, Floud and Halsey (1961) asserted that:

> In modern society, the major link of education to the social structure is through the economy and this is a linkage of both stimulus and response. Contemporary educational organizations stimulate economic change through research and, in turn, they respond to economic change in carrying out the functions of selection and training of manpower. The implications for schools and universities, as organizations, are unending.

But what kind of activity did this kind of attitude generate at the empirical level? Essentially, the major interest was with identifying and mapping inefficiencies in the education system to sort, train and allocate individuals. This interest influenced what was taken to be the main problem area for sociologists of education, the main properties to be studied in pursuit of a solution to this problem area and the main methods judged as appropriate for such investigation.

The Problem

The problem was to investigate why the education system was failing to draw upon and use 'pools of ability' conceptualized along social class lines. For the economy to reach optimum development and growth, it needed a steady supply of skilled and flexible personnel, yet it appeared to observers in the 1950s and 1960s that large numbers of able pupils, mostly from working-class backgrounds, were failing to achieve satisfactory standards in the primary schools, were being excluded from entry to the academic sectors of secondary education because of their inability to satisfy the 11+ entry examination requirements, were not being entered for or were failing in public examinations and certificate assessments, were leaving school early, were failing to gain places in higher education and were entering semi-skilled or unskilled employment after completing their formal education.

Explanations

Explanations of this problem were conceived, as the perspective demanded, in terms of dysfunctions either in the internal structural organization of the education system or in the structural relationships between education and other social subsystems. In the former, research concentrated on areas like regional variation in the quality of schools available (Banks, 1955), the selection procedures used in schools (Floud and Halsey, 1956; Jackson, 1964), teachers' role performances (Musgrove and Taylor, 1969; Cohen, 1965) and the internal organization of the school, streaming and the generation of anti-school attitudes (Hargreaves, 1967; Lacey, 1970). In the latter, there was an extensive amount of research which investigated such issues as the relationship between aspects of home life and school achievement (Jackson and Marsden, 1962; Douglas, 1964), the relationship between attitudes to education of pupils' parents and success in school (Newsom Report, 1963; Plowden Report, 1967), the impact of local environment and neighbourhood upon educational performances (Mays, 1962; Wiseman, 1964) and the interrelation of pre-school language socialization, social class and classroom life (see Bernstein, 1975).

Methods

Because the topics selected for investigation were fundamentally concerned with large questions about relationships between substantial aspects of social life, the methods used to conduct such investigations were designed to provide data and explanations which would be valid across the wide area selected for research. Thus, for example, in order to make a longitudinal study of the educational experiences and performances of children from different social backgrounds (in terms of such properties as class of origin, family size, family income, birth order, type of housing, parental attitudes, etc.), Douglas (1964) found it necessary to work on a sample of some 4,700 children, and the techniques he used to collect information included administering standardized tests to all members of the sample population, extensive interviewing and consultation of records, reports and school assessments of the pupils who made up the sample. Looking back over this period of research it is tempting to view the issues mainly in terms of a political and ideological concern with a search for equality of educational opportunity, a quest for the achievement of greater social justice through education and a movement towards a meritocratic society. While there is no doubt that these concerns represented the values of many sociologists of education working in this period, we should not lose sight of the fact that there was also a concern that education was dysfunctional. As Karabel and Halsey (1977) comment on this period, 'The attack by British sociologists on inequality of educational opportunity was not only that it was unfair, but also that it was inefficient.'

This last point is important, because it illustrates, in a way which concentration upon ideological concerns obscures, the powerful tendency within the structure-functionalist perspective to conceptualize social life in terms of the 'fit' between the parts of the social system and their functional contribution to the smooth running of the whole – a tendency which has come to be regarded as one of the major weaknesses of the perspective.

CONCLUSION: EVALUATION OF THE STRUCTURALIST PERSPECTIVE

A perspective contains important assumptions about the individual and society, and for functionalism the question of order is paramount. The importance of these factors is underlined by Dawe (1970), when he says that:

> In this sense, the problem of order is a label for a doctrine which defines a universe of meaning for sociological concepts and theories ... The progression begins from a view of human nature from which follows a view of the relationship between the individual and society.

Many criticisms have been made about the structural functionalist perspective, and here we will refer briefly to three main weaknesses, which we hope will provide a basis for discussion.

Society: An All-pervasive Entity

Society is presented as an all-pervasive entity which has a life apart from the individual. It is depicted as overarching individuals, constraining, moulding and regulating them, and as such it is invested with human motivations and characteristics, so that society is described as having 'needs', 'purposes' and 'functional requirements'. An idea is thus treated as a being, and an analytical category reified, yet where this externalized life form is to be found, except in the consciousness of individuals, is somewhat obscure. If it is to be found only in the consciousness of the individual, how is it external? If not, where is it? One of the consequences of this reification is that in the educational sphere the effectiveness of any school structure can be measured only in terms of the needs of the system. Problems of disorganization or conflict are thus largely attributed to poor organizational factors, the lack of 'fit' between role and personality, inadequate adaptation to emerging social systems or deviance. What is inadequate about this approach is its lack of consideration of how pressures for change arise within social systems as a result of conflicts of interests over the balance of power. As Worsley (1973) argues in his criticism of Durkheim:

> What Durkheim did not show was how men use ideologies as well as being used – not by 'reified' society – but by men who have power to make others accept their ideologies, and hence make ideologies work.

In short, social order might well be achieved not by all coming to want what society requires them to have, but by a few having the power to define social necessity and imposing their definitions on the less powerful. It would seem more acceptable to depict the 'social puppeteer' as a group of real people acting for their own interests, rather than as a mystifying entity called 'society'.

'The Oversocialized Conception of the Individual'

A further, not unrelated, criticism concerns the view of the individual that such a perspective presents. It has been described as: 'the oversocialized conception' of individuals (Wrong, 1961), 'oversocialized' in that individuals are depicted as being at the receiving end of dominant influences rather than being creators of them; an 'absolutistic view' of humanity (Douglas *et al.*, 1971), in the sense that people are seen as confronted by forces beyond their control; and as an example of 'repressive sociology' (Gouldner, 1971), in that the perspective led sociologists to place more emphasis on exploring the conditions that determined the individual's life than on the ways in which an individual or group of people could become controllers of their own destiny.

The Problem of Meaning

Lastly, a problem that arises with this perspective is that of meaning. If society makes the rules, the values and the cultural norms of social life, it must also greatly influence how social objects, concepts and relations are defined and understood. Thus, as Blum (1974) points out:

> To describe society is to chart the concrete influence of the social . . . sociology is in the grip of that which it is discussing; consequently sociology can make its case not on the basis of differentiating itself from that which it describes, but only in terms of its efficiency in affirming the authority of that which it describes as authorizing its very description.

In other words, if meanings are defined by social conventions, then sociologists, who are, after all, fundamentally products of the system in which these conventions operate, are constrained to use analytical categories, descriptions of the world which are far from objective; sociology, therefore, is itself constrained by the very forces it seeks to describe.

Further Reading

Archer, M. (1979) *The Social Origins of Educational Systems*. London: Sage. Although highly sophisticated, provides one of the best illustrations of the insights that can be generated by a macro-sociological analysis.

Giddens, A. (1978) *Durkheim*. Glasgow: Fontana. A very clear introduction to some of the basic ideas of this writer.

Gouldner, A. (1971) *The Coming Crisis of Western Sociology*. London: Heinneman. Offers a critical appraisal of the assumptions and implications of the structuralist perspective in sociology; a review which pays special attention to the ideas of Durkheim.

Signposts

Read the paper by Earl Hopper himself in his collection of readings, Hopper, E. (ed.) (1971) *Readings in the Theory of Educational Systems*, London: Hutchinson. Although the typology of the basic mechanics of educational systems is a bit dated, it still provides a stimulating basis for asking questions about contemporary educational policy to do with the educational system. Identify policies which you think might be changing the degree of centralization and standardization in the UK education system and, using Hopper's model, try to articulate some of the less obvious consequences of these changes.

20 The Action Perspective

LEN BARTON AND STEPHEN WALKER

INTRODUCTION

In his analysis of the development of the different 'doctrines' which shape sociological perspectives, Alan Dawe (1970) wrote:

> There are, then, two sociologies, a sociology of social system and a sociology of social action. They are grounded in the diametrically opposed concerns with two central problems, those of order and control. And, at every level, they are in conflict. They posit antithetical views of human nature, of society and the relationship between the social and the individual. The first asserts the paramount necessity, for societal and individual well-being, of external constraint; hence the notion of a social system ontologically and methodologically prior to its participants. The key notion of the second is that of autonomous man, able to realize his full potential and to create a truly human social order only when freed from external constraint. Society is thus the creation of its members; the product of their construction of meaning, and of the action and relationships through which they attempt to impose that meaning on their historical situation.

It is with the second of these two doctrines, what Dawe calls 'a sociology of social action', that this chapter is concerned.

First, while it is true to say that the question of how order is achieved in social life, of how the relationships between individuals are regulated and their individual affairs constrained, has formed a basic framework for a great deal of sociological thought, it should not be imagined that this concern has been developed in isolation or without challenge. An alternative vision has also been much in evidence in a great deal of sociological writing. This alternative has a more optimistic view of humanity: while the possibility that some human acts are motivated by self-interest is not discounted, the ability of the species to create meanings, to constitute social situations, in short, to control the social and natural world, is emphasized.

What is seen to be remarkable about human beings as a species, then, is not so much the instances of their obedience and compliance to larger forces and powers which work upon them but, first, their genuinely creative ability to build out of nothing, as it were, that intricately arranged and delicately balanced mechanism which is the social structure and, second, their capacity to endow the various elements of this mechanism with meaning and significance. There is, in this vision, a kind of reverence for that uniquely human characteristic, the capacity of members of the species to react imaginatively to their environment and to construct creatively the means by which humankind can be liberated from various kinds of subordination.

It follows that sociological inquiry which celebrates the kind of recognition outlined above will have a very different shape and bias from that which Dawe calls 'a sociology of social system'. If humanity is seen as creative rather than constrained, then the kinds of social phenomena which are of interest to, and in need of explanation by, the sociological observer are likely to be:

1. The ways in which members of society, through their individual and collective actions, create and maintain the social fabric within which they live.
2. The ways in which members of society come to recognize, understand and assess the social arrangements and structures by which they manage both to act socially and to impose a form of control on the conditions of their existence.

WEBER AND SOCIAL ACTION

The extent to which this distinctive sociological concern differs from those discussed in the previous chapter is shown clearly if we examine Max Weber's definition of the sociological endeavour. Although Weber (1864–1920) was writing in exactly the same period as Durkheim, albeit in a different intellectual tradition, his sociology is dramatically different from that of his contemporary. He asserts:

> Sociology . . . is a science which attempts the interpretive understanding of *social action* in order thereby to arrive at a causal explanation of its course and effect. In 'action' is included all human behaviour when and in so far as the acting individual *attaches a subjective meaning to it* . . . Action is social in so far as, by virtue of the subjective meaning attached to it by the acting individual (or individuals), it takes account of the behaviour of others.
>
> Weber, 1964 (our emphasis)

There are, of course, all kinds of issues raised here. To what extent can sociology be a science? What is meant by 'interpretive understanding'? However, before we can consider these methodological problems we need to examine two core concepts used by Weber in his definition: 'social action' and 'subjective meaning'.

Weber is fairly insistent on grounding his sociology in the development of an understanding of the totality of social life which begins by building up a description of the workings of the basic components of this totality, the 'atom' of the societal structure. For him, says MacRae (1974):

this atomic unit of the social is the single deliberate action of an individual directed to affecting the behaviour of one or more persons.

While Weber would not deny that individual human actions might be susceptible to the influence of larger collective elements in society, like the state, the form of family life or the education system, we should recognize that these are:

solely the resultants and modes of organization of the specific acts of individual men, since these alone are for us the agents who carry out subjectively understandable action.

MacRae, 1974

The danger, therefore, of starting sociological investigation with an analysis of these larger features, with a view to working down to an explanation of individual behaviour, is the temptation to treat such representations (which, after all, are only concepts that individuals use to describe circumstances which arise from their collective action) as if they have a mind, a consciousness, an intentionality of their own – that is, to reify them. Similarly, Weber is sceptical of analysis which starts at the other extreme, i.e. with a consideration of the internal mental states, the psychological make-up of human beings. To view individuals' acts solely in terms of the consequences of inner drives is to see them acting in a social vacuum. Thus, according to Weber, sociology can only move *towards* an understanding of both social institutions and individual psychological conditions *from* an understanding of the practical form which gives these two sets of properties their realization, the specific acts of individuals.

But how are these acts to be analysed, or described? We could adopt either or both of two approaches. First, we could note directly the characteristics and consequences of an act as they appear to an observer and, by relating such observation to our existing knowledge of human behaviour derived from past observations, we could arrive at an explanation, comparing the act observed to already accepted theories and interpretations of action and its context. So, for example, if we observe a pupil in school writing out the same sentence 200 times and we weigh this observation against our more global intelligence of what constitutes appropriate conduct in the context in which this writing is being done, we can work out some 'causal explanation' of the act. However, Weber would argue that, at best, in doing this we would succeed only in making a 'peculiarly plausible hypothesis'.

This problem is acute when placed in the context of what Weber regards as the basic intentions people have in carrying out acts. He suggests that, on an abstract level, we can distil these intentions into four pure or 'ideal' types, which he groups under the divisions 'rational' and 'non-rational' (the second not to be confused with 'irrational' or 'unreasonable'). Rational intentions might take either of two forms: 'purposefully rational' (by which there is an instrumental intention behind an act, in the sense that the person performing it has weighed up the cost, the means of achieving a certain end and the desirability of such an achievement, and has designed his conduct accordingly) and 'value rational' (by which the intention behind an act is the pursuit of some virtue or ideal, the attainment of which is not questioned, only the means being debatable). Similarly, non-rational intentions are separable into two sub-types: 'affectual' orientations (by which the act performed is done in response to an emotion) and 'traditional' orientations (by which an act is done according to the dictates of habit, custom, ritual or tradition).

Accepting, at least in part, the usefulness of this typology, it becomes apparent that sociological explanation based solely on direct observation of the overt features of action will be problematic in at least two of the types of acts thus identified – value rational action and affectual action – the motivations or intentions of such conduct not being obviously available for public scrutiny. This is why Weber introduces into his definition of sociology the second concept isolated above – the concern with the identification of 'subjective meaning'. As Giddens (1971) explains, adequate sociological understanding of social action, for Weber, necessarily involves 'the elucidation of an intervening motivational link between the observed activity and its meaning to the actor'.

This, of course, is extremely difficult. How can we know the ways in which other humans understand the consequences of their actions and have intentions for them? Weber was not unaware of these problems, but suggests that a way of cutting through them is for the sociologist to make formal use of the same devices that members of society use to understand the conduct of others in everyday life: observation; the making of inferences about the motives behind the acts observed, which is achieved by empathizing with the subject performing the act; the testing of the validity of such inferences against existing knowledge of what is 'normal' in the context in which the behaviour is located; the construction of generalized interpretations of the conduct against which to measure particular instances of it and thus identify acts which conform to or deviate from these normal patterns; and finally, the comparison of this understanding of specific cases of action with similar instances in other circumstances. Nevertheless, Weber (1964) is insistent that:

> A correct causal interpretation of a concrete course of action is arrived at when the overt action and the motives have both been correctly apprehended and at the same time their relation has become meaningfully comprehensible.

While 'one need not have been Caesar in order to understand Caesar', one does need to be able to move around in his world with some surety to understand both the world and his conduct within it.

We pointed out earlier how Berger, using the simile of social life being like the workings of a puppet theatre, suggests that one question we explore in sociology is concerned with the forces in society which govern the movement of the human puppet. However, Berger is not so naive as to imagine that human beings are merely puppets. Indeed, he points out that an important difference between puppets and humans is that, while the actions of the former are wholly dependent upon some power above them which is pulling the strings, humans, through their power to think, are not only capable of looking around, and thus of being aware of external forces, but are also able to resist and react to various attempts to manipulate their lives on the social stage. Berger (1966) writes:

> We see the puppets dancing on their miniature stage, moving up and down as the strings pull them around, following the prescribed course of their various little parts. We learn to

understand the logic of this theatre and we find ourselves in its motions. We locate our-selves in society and thus recognize our own positions as we hang from its subtle strings. For a moment we see ourselves as puppets indeed. But then we grasp a decisive difference between the puppet theatre and our own drama. Unlike the puppets, we have the pos-sibility of stopping in our movements, looking up and perceiving the machinery by which we have been moved. In this act lies the first step towards freedom.

This emphasis upon human beings' ability to recognize and influence the world about them and the part they play within it provides the cornerstone for the sociological perspective under consideration in this chapter. Those influenced by this emphasis work on the notion that there is both an objective and a subjective social reality. The situations in which an individual lives out his or her life have an objective reality in the sense that various social organizations and institutions, like the political structure, the economic order and the edu-cation system 'are *there*, external to him; persistent in their reality, whether he likes it or not' (Berger and Luckmann, 1967).

However, although such things may be there, outside of people, they are, first, built and constantly in the process of being reconstructed and modified as a direct result of the decisions and actions of individuals as they seek to control the conditions of their everyday affairs. Second, they are real and of consequence only through a person's subjective or individualized awareness of them. Thus, for example, to imagine that there might be such an institution as schooling that did not first evolve as a consequence of intervention in their social arrangements or that would continue to exist as a systematic social organization if contemporaries did not recognize it as such and have awareness and definitions of what it means and does, would be absurd. This, then, is the subjective dimension – the human being's capacity both to produce and to maintain his or her social universe.

SUBJECTIVE REALITY

For a number of reasons sociologists working with such ideas insist that sociological analysis begin with and concentrate on the subjective dimension of reality. First, it is argued that a serious limitation of the perspective outlined in the previous chapter, which emphasizes the objective reality, is that the observer of society is seduced into caricaturing individuals as being determined, assigned to their role by some force more powerful than themselves or, in Garfinkel's poignant image, as being 'cultural dopes'. The problem here is not just that it is difficult to capture and describe a reality which, though 'social', excludes real people from its analysis, but, more seriously, that the tradition tends either to overlook or to treat as constant the unique actions of the individual. If we view humans as being predominantly 'determined' in their conduct, it is difficult to account for idiosyncratic and situationally specific features of human behaviour. Yet in our daily lives we notice that these very features, these mundane and everyday occurrences in which individual social actors display and act upon private and subjective understandings, choices and intentions, are both routine and regular, and appear to be at the foundations of social life. To assume, therefore, that we could explain an event like an act of truancy from school without reference to the way in which the 'truant' perceives his or her world and judges the kind of response appropriate to that perception would be unacceptable to those taking this perspective, because such an explanation would represent a distortion. The extent to which those developing this alternative approach are critical of simple determinist explanations and insist on the importance of taking into analysis the subjective vision is succinctly summarized by Blumer (1962) in the following way:

> These various uses of sociological perspectives and interests, which are so strongly entrenched to-day, leap over the acting units of a society and by-pass the interpretative process by which such acting units build up their actions.

He continues his exhortation for sociologists to make the actions and the subjective interpretations carried out by real mean their focal concern, by remarking that, for these individuals:

> Structural features, such as 'culture', 'social systems', 'social stratification' or 'social roles', set conditions for their action but do not determine their action. People – that is, acting units – do not act towards culture, social structure or the like; they act towards situations. Social organization enters into action only to the extent to which it shapes situations in which people act, and to the extent that it supplies fixed sets of symbols which people use in interpreting their situations.

A second reason why those who favour a concentration upon the subjective dimension of social action insist upon making this the base for sociological analysis is concerned with their attitude to what constitutes acceptable sociological knowledge. Certainly, they would argue, in our investigations of the social world we can make use of concepts which refer to collective behaviour, to general patterns of conduct applicable to large sections of the population, to notions of whole groups of people and the objectified relationships between them. But we should never lose sight of the fact that these concepts are concepts: they are not descriptions of actual behaviour or concrete phenomena, but images, possible interpretations of the complexity of human life. True, some of these concepts might be used by real people in their real lives, but the extent to which this is so and the manner in which it takes place is an empirical question and cannot be left to mere assumption. Thus, to explain pupils' 'failure' in school in terms of their being victims of the social class from which they originate might be a useful tool for pointing out possibilities, but it does not give a full explanation of the particular activities of an individual pupil or of how that pupil came to be categorized 'educational failure'. Through following this kind of argument, sociologists working within the action perspective develop a concern to redirect investigation towards an understanding of everyday life, rather than one based on grand theoretical debate, survey data, the scrutiny of social rates or statistical measures of behaviour patterns and/or comparative historical analysis. Jack Douglas (Douglas *et al.*, 1971) is particularly strong in his condemnation of investigation which is not orientated towards the systematic observation and analysis of everyday life, and concludes that:

> Any scientific understanding of human action, at whatever level of ordering or generality, must begin with and be built upon an understanding of the everyday life of the members performing those actions. (To fail to see this and to act in accord with it is to commit what we might call the *fallacy of abstractionism*, that is, the fallacy of believing that you can know in a more abstract form what you do not know in the particular form.)

A significant consequence of this overall concern with exploring the subjective dimensions of human action in everyday situations is that the knowledge people have of their world and the meanings they themselves give to the objects which constitute it become crucial substantive areas for the sociologist to explore. If we wish, as writers like Douglas have suggested, that sociologists should 'retain the integrity of the phenomena' under observation or, in other words, avoid distorting reality in the name of analysis, then we will need to ensure that the gap between a social actor's own interpretation of his or her actions and an observer's interpretation of them is minimal. Two important questions concerning the methods sociologists use are pushed to the fore if one accepts the need to adhere to this structure.

The first is that observers cannot assume that the interpretation and understanding of a situation under study that they bring with them at the start of an investigation have much more than a tenuous validity, because the 'meaning' of all the properties which make up the situation is problematic in the sense that these properties will have already been interpreted by those participating in the events, and it is their understanding of these and their assumptions that will influence the course of events in the situation and in which the observer is interested. As Gorbutt (1972) notes:

> The observer must be careful to recognize that different parties in any interaction may have different interpretations of it and that these interpretations cannot be assumed in advance of empirical investigation. We cannot merely describe a school assembly, for example, as a consensual ritual which binds staff and pupils together. This indeed may be the stated intention of the headmaster but the interpretation put upon the event by others, even though they may outwardly conform, cannot be assumed.

However, to analyse behaviour yet at the same time to suspend assumptions about it is very difficult. Sociologists, as well as being observers or spies, are also members of the community which they are investigating, and to move suddenly from a position where objects, activities and relationships in the world are familiar, recognizable and significant to one in which these same items are treated as problems, as hardly knowns, or as objects of inquiry, requires constant effort. Becker (1974) illustrates the full force of this difficulty by pointing out the problems for the observer of everyday life in the classroom:

> We may have understated a little the difficulty of observing contemporary classrooms ... I think ... that it is first and foremost a matter of it all being so familiar that it becomes almost impossible to single out events that occur in the classroom as things that have occurred,

> even when they happen right in front of you ... it takes a tremendous effort of will and imagination to stop seeing only things that are conventionally 'there' to be seen.

Nevertheless, it was a vision of the tremendous insights into the process of education that would be gained through adoption of this technique of treating the categories and meanings used by members of the educational world as problematic which both excited those involved and gave impetus to the so-called 'New Direction' movement in the sociology of education which emerged in Britain in the 1970s. Examining not only how teachers and pupils act and interact in schools but also how they construct and understand the definitional categories on which they base activity – the assumptions they have of what counts as knowledge, learning, intelligence and even schooling and education itself – was seen as a way of revealing the bedrock upon which the schooling system rests and thereby providing an opportunity for bringing the system into the more direct control of its creators and users. As Gorbutt, in his discussion of the 'New Direction' approach, asserted in 1972:

> It should be clear that the kind of research I have in mind would not be based on a social science which merely elaborates and reifies existing educational categories like intelligence and the disadvantaged child. It would be based on the interpretive approach ... and would question the very assumptions which underlie conventional sociology of education, educational psychology and philosophy of education and the prevailing educational practices which they support.

The second methodological implication of the stress on the relativity of knowledge and the subjectivity of meaning made within the action perspective is that sociologists themselves can claim no privileged status for their own interpretations and understandings. Sociological research, like any other attempt to order perceptions of the world, is a social act itself, and as such is open to the same kinds of scrutiny and analysis used in the exploration of the social. This has meant that a great deal of work based upon this perspective has involved a considerable amount of self-criticism by those carrying out the work, particularly with reference to the methods employed, so that the 'integrity of the phenomena' is retained (notably participant observation and ethnographic study), and it has also proved a popular point for criticism by those dubious of the main concerns of the perspective. It is argued by some that, even if one accepts that it is important to suspend one's own presuppositions in the relentless pursuit of meaning, one must still accept that there comes a point when one grounds one's definitions on a base which, for all practical purposes, is accepted as valid. Otherwise it would be impossible to know anything. While it is possible to suggest that sociologists in the past have been guilty of employing too little rigour in their examination of their assumptions, this is not the same as saying that they must never make assumptions. Indeed, Douglas himself admits that:

> there inevitably comes a point at which one either accepts total solipsism and the impossibility of 'knowing' anything or grounds one's thought in some presupposed (commonsensical) experience.

INTERPRETATIVE PERSPECTIVES

So far in this chapter we have treated the action perspective as if it represented a uni-dimensional doctrine among sociologists. It is important to note that several different schools of thought are often grouped together under the one generic umbrella of interpretive or appreciative sociology – for example, symbolic interactionism, phenomenology or ethno-methodology – and, while it is true to say that these all share a common concern to develop an appreciative understanding of social action in everyday life, they differ in their meth-odological persuasions. The main emphasis in the rest of this chapter will be upon the first of these specific approaches, because it is arguable that interactionism has had the greatest impact upon educational research, but first let us consider the main differences between these three branches of interpretive sociology. Hammersley and Woods (1976) offer a useful articulation of such differences which can be summarized as follows.

Interactionism

Interactionism stresses the 'partial independence from social structural, cultural and psychological forces of the sense people make of the world and of action based on such perspectives'. For the most part individuals absorb given interpretations of the physical and symbolic universe from others and act accordingly, yet the task of the interactionist sociologist is, claims Blumer, 'to reveal the process' through which individuals 'construct' their actions. The emphasis, then, is upon *process*.

Phenomenology

Phenomenologists place the emphasis differently. Hammersley and Woods argue that this movement 'is concerned with the knowledge and assumptions which must be possessed and acted upon by people in order for the social world to exist'. Their task, then, is to reveal this knowledge, which is not always available at a conscious level; indeed, is more often taken for granted by individuals in the course of their everyday lives. So the objective of the phenomenological sociologist is to provide a description of what people think they know, of 'how individuals define their world and typify both it and their position within it'. Or, as Sharp and Green (1975) assert, 'the basic preoccupation of the sociological phenomenologist is with the subtle texture of meaning which constitutes reality'. The emphasis, then, is upon *meaning*.

Ethnomethodology

Ethnomethodologists, like the sociologists described above, are concerned with the ways in which actors construct their social worlds, but they stress the capturing of the methods, the devices, the practical activities which, it is argued, must underlie this construction for it to take place at all. Perhaps it is useful to examine briefly the research strategies of ethno-methodologists, as this reveals something of their distinctive stance. Garfinkel has used the technique of 'making trouble', or disrupting real, everyday situations 'to expose the back-ground assumption underlying them'. Placing subjects in bewildering, confusing or even senseless environments and observing how they then 'make sense' of these, i.e. negotiate a new social order, should, claims Garfinkel (1967), 'tell us something about how structures of everyday activities are ordinarily and routinely produced and maintained'. Ethnomethodo-logists, then, attempt to answer the question 'What are the rules of social interaction?', and in answer to the criticism that this begs the question 'Where do these rules come from?' they would reply that their form of analysis can answer this too, because rules are 'only established as such by their ability to organize the settings of practical common-sense actions – an ability which is proven in so organizing these actions' (Garfinkel, 1967). The stress here, then, is upon the nature, construction and expression of the regulative techniques, the conventional routine, the *practical accomplishments* by which members of society make their actions rational and comprehensible for others.

There is, of course, considerable overlap between these separate sociological programmes. It is difficult to imagine, for example, how one could describe the processes of classroom life without taking into account both the meanings that participants in that world take from it and the details of the practical activities in which they engage to signal and order their understandings and to render their behaviour accountable to others. To a certain extent the interrelation between these concerns is illustrated in the work of interactionists, and so it is to a more detailed consideration of this single approach that we will now turn.

INTERACTIONISM

A great deal of the work which is identifiably 'interactionist' draws upon the theoretical perspective to be found in the writings of G.H. Mead (1863–1931). Mead begins his analysis by making a distinction between non-symbolic communication (or the use of gestures) and symbolic communication (or the use of ideas and concepts), the difference between these being nicely illustrated by Mennell (1974) thus:

> The difference between a gesture and a symbol for Mead is the difference between punching someone and shaking a fist at him. Shaking a fist normally communicates not the possibility of attack, but the *idea* of anger in the shaker's mind. The person at whom the fist

is shaken is able to interpret it as meaning hostility; it is the idea of anger which has been communicated from one mind to another.

Human beings are unique in being able to make massive use of this second form of communication, symbolic communication. This ability derives from the development in the species of those anatomical and neurological features which enable members to carry and make use of a complicated symbol system, language. This faculty opens up a number of possibilities of organization of behaviour.

Language allows people to reflect upon their situation and their place within it. The importance of this seemingly simple observation is vast. Mead argues that, because language is available to humans, they are able:

1. To organize and store up impressions and understandings of the social and physical world.
2. To transmit these understandings to others who share the language form.
3. To apply already acquired understandings held in the mind to new situations, perceptions or symbolic communications received from others and, therefore, to deliberate upon these and create newly fashioned understandings of such signals.

Thus, from birth onwards, humans are exposed to a host of signals and symbols carried in the language form which are put out by others and, as they learn to understand and interpret these signals, they develop not only an accumulated collection of other people's perceptions, impressions and beliefs but also the capacity to consider this body of knowledge. In learning a language the individual acquires the ability to use it for his or her own purpose and to turn it back upon the direct stimulus of experience. Mead describes this as the development of a conception of 'self' – the process by which, through the acquisition of a form of symbolic representation, individuals achieve the means by which they are empowered to share and understand the accepted and conventional symbolic interpretations of the world, are given a tool with which they can reflect upon these representations and the significance these have for their own particular being, and, in so doing, are able to recognize and realize their own individuality. Mead depicts this development in terms of the emergence of distinctive 'I' and 'me' sections of the individual mind. Possessing language, humans are able to see themselves as both objects in the world and subjects acting upon that world. But language allows more than this: it enables the object side of humans, the 'me' to which things happen, to be held up for inspection by the subject side, which is reacting to these happenings, the 'I'. The full force of the Meadian concept of self is articulated by David Hargreaves (1972) thus:

> In Mead's analysis of the self, the individual becomes a kind of society in miniature, for he can engage in a form of internal social interaction. When, through the process of taking the role of the other, the self acquires its reflexive quality and attains self-consciousness, the individual is no longer at the mercy of the forces of nature. He does not merely respond to those forces which play upon him from inside or outside, as is the case with objects or

organisms that lack a self. In short, his behaviour is no longer determined. With a self, the individual ceases to be subject to the direct impact of other stimuli, for he can withhold his response to such stimuli and estimate their significance and consequences for particular lines of action towards them. His ability to anticipate makes several possible future lines of action available in the present; and from such future possibilities he can make a choice. The person thus constructs and chooses what he does; his acts are not predetermined responses.

Language allows people to respond to and direct the experience and actions of other persons. Indeed, an important dimension of the formation of 'self' involves just that. Implicit in the process of 'self' development is the idea, introduced in the quotation above, of 'taking the role of the other'. Mead argues that language is one of the main mechanisms by which new members of society, rather than engaging in the cumbersome process of noting, classifying and interpreting every new object, person, idea or experience encountered, instead take on the ready-made understandings of others. This involves coming to see the world as they see it, and also means that individuals learn to see themselves as others see them and are thus able to anticipate the responses of others to their own actions.

Consider, for example, some of the points raised in Chapters 2 and 3. How do individuals become either pupils or teachers? Can we assume that this is a relatively simple process by which the social actors involved internalize a 'ready-made set of recipes' (see Chapter 3) which have been compiled by society and are easily available for the newcomer to note, comprehend and follow? Does moving from being a non-teacher to being a teacher involve simply the finding out of what teachers do and replicating such practices? Clearly, even from a common-sense point of view, this is unacceptable. While novices in any social situation will receive from others who are involved in the situation a whole variety of directives about what constitutes 'proper' behaviour in that setting, they will also carry with them to the situation personal views of the world, acquired in the past, which they will bring to bear upon these directives and thereby accept, adjust to, modify or even reject them. Furthermore, there is no guarantee that attitudes and understandings adopted one day by a pupil or a teacher will be constant for ever: ongoing interactional experience creates the demand for further reflection by the individual, the construction of new responses and the making of gradual shifts in the definition he has of his role, the roles of others and the whole meaning of the situation. Taking on a role, then, is filtered through the recipient's self-concept and is a continuous process, not a unique, easily completed event. As Mead (1934) himself observed:

> This taking-the-role-of-the-other is not simply of passing importance. It is not something that just happens as an incidental result of the gesture, but it is of importance in the development of co-operative activity. The immediate effect of such role-taking lies in the control which the individual is able to exercise over his own response.

In attempting to explore how social actors present, understand, take on and act on their interpretations of the roles of others and how the resultant patterns of conduct emerge from this intersubjective organizing of perceptions, meanings and behaviour to form what we might call the 'interactional situation', sociologists working within the interactionist perspective employ a variety of additional concepts which enable analysis to move from simple descriptions of the unique experiences of isolated individuals towards a full description of the locations of these experiences.

As we have already noted, from this perspective humans are viewed as active participants in the social world. Through the complex and flexible processes of interaction, social identities, meanings and roles are created, maintained, modified or changed. Combined with this is an awareness of and interest in the interplay of personal, social and structural features and how these influence social situations. Thus, as Rock (1979) points out:

> The Symbolic Interactionist rejects subjective idealism because they acknowledge the stubborn facticity of the world, yet they also resist the gross empiricism which depicts objects and relations as laden with innative meaning.

Individuals act *within and towards situations*; their actions are related to their processes of interpretation, and thus a person's definition of the situation is a vital ingredient in all social interactions. It relates to what a person hopes to get out of the situation, which features within the situation are taken to be more important than others and, as Stebbins (1975) maintains:

> to put it concisely, a definition of the situation is the meaning an individual attaches to the ongoing events in which he finds himself. Perception or recognition of specific aspects of the environment is invariably the first step in this process, and some sort of action (or inaction) is the necessary consequence.

This process of defining the situation is very much a part of the task of 'taking the role of the other', in which individuals act in relation to their interpretation of what they think others expect of them. What is important is that this experience entails conscious reflection on the part of the people concerned. Imagine a person entering a new social situation, i.e. one of which he does not have a clear definition; for example, a student teacher entering a school staffroom for the first time. What factors would we need to consider to make sense of such an encounter? From the student teacher's point of view, his conduct is determined largely by his reasons for being involved in that situation and his theories about what he believes it will be like (built up through communication with other students, other teachers, and, perhaps, his tutors), the things he perceives on entering the staffroom (the physical surroundings and the clues his new acquaintances give him through their dress, gestures and manners), his understanding of what the other teachers he meets communicate to him, through their talk and their behaviour, about what they think will constitute appropriate conduct by him in the situation in which they are all engaging and, most importantly, the assessment he makes of all these inputs through reflecting upon them. In short, he constructs a definition of the situation as a basis for his action. But so do the other participants. So, to arrive at an adequate description of this little drama, the sociologist would have to comprehend both the various definitions of the situations by participants in the interaction and the ways in which these different definitions rub against each other, involving a series of negotiations of the acceptable role definitions for the different individuals involved so as to produce that totality which is the interactional setting.

It is important at this point to caution against the idea that individuals are always aware of the nature of the processes which make up their social interactions. The extent of such awareness is open to question and the social observer is, therefore, constrained to be alert not only to the overt intentions and understandings of his or her subjects but also to the results of unexpected events within the interaction and the unintended consequences of action. Thus, as Martin (1976) points out:

> Neither the idea that everything is negotiable nor the idea that interlocking roles are set by status within a social organization is adequate to describe the dynamics of interactions that take place in ordinary daily living.

It is through careful exploration of these dynamics, which are, perhaps, revealed through coming to appreciate the differences between one partner's intentions in interaction and co-participants' interpretations and reactions to them, that the 'hidden' elements of interaction are revealed. An influential writer on this type of approach is Erving Goffman (1971), who, using metaphors drawn from the theatre, seeks to show the intricate strategies by which people endeavour to present or manage various images of themselves in social interaction. He argues: 'When an individual appears before others he will have many motives for trying to control the impression they receive of the situation.' And he attempts to show how, in a wide variety of social contexts involving several different 'audiences', people seek to exercise and maintain some degree of control over their situation so that they do not suffer the embarrassment and personal distress that results when an asserted identity is seen as a facade or sham. This 'presentation of self' is an important influence on the dynamics of social interaction, and Goffman (1971) maintains that:

> The self then, as a performed character, is not an organic thing that has a specific location, whose fundamental fate is to be born, to mature and to die. It is an effect arising diffusely from a self ... the crucial concern, is whether it will be discredited.

Thus people are seen as being involved in attempts to manage the impression they 'give off' to others; social interaction is, therefore, about deceit and counter-deceit, about people adapting and accommodating in their endeavour to impress a definition of the situation and themselves upon others. The definition of the situation which is used as a basis of action by participants in that situation is a 'working consensus' arrived at by those involved in the specific social encounter. The level of this consensus is variable. Where people involved in a social situation share common understandings and accept the validity of each other's definitions it will be strong; however, if there is disagreement or lack of awareness by participants of their associates' interpretations, consensus will be weak. Nevertheless, some 'workable' basis for interaction must be reached if the association which gives rise to the situation is not to be terminated abruptly.

Recognition of these variations in the nature of the 'working consensus' has led interactionists to a consideration of certain techniques used by social actors to resolve those problems which arise when definitions of the situation are in conflict. Resolution can be through either negotiation or the imposition by dominant partners in the interaction of their own particular desires and designs. A great deal of the material presented earlier in this book was selected to demonstrate the extent to which the different individuals involved in schooling see this life differently, have different interests and reasons for participating in it, and gain different satisfactions from their contributions to this social experience. We have here, then, a situation which looks as if definitions of the situation are in serious competition. How is it, therefore, that life within school is able to proceed at all?

An interactionist would have to look for an answer to this question in the methods by which the people involved come to terms with this conflict of interests. One explanation of how some agreement is reached is made in terms of the enormous difficulty most individuals have in sustaining a relationship in which a lack of harmony means that continued involvement in it is more costly than profitable. An easy solution in these circumstances is for the individual to withdraw completely from the relationship. Within the school situation this remedy, although not impossible, is problematic in itself. Few teachers or pupils can take themselves out of the encounter because to do so would perhaps upset the equilibrium of other situations in which they are involved and which they would wish to preserve because of the high dividends to be secured from this involvement. Although deliberately absenting oneself from school resolves one set of conflicts, it may create new and more costly problems in other environments, e.g. in the person's interaction with parents, peers or the police. Thus the meaning of action has to be viewed in terms of the interlock between various definitions of situations which are contingent upon an individual's understanding of his or her place in any single situation.

Given that withdrawal has a high cost (as shown by the remarkable fact that, despite schooling being a fairly unpleasant experience for some pupils and for some teachers, most of them battle on gamely within the boundaries of the school situation), what alternative methods for the resolution of competing definitions of the situation are routinely adopted?

First, through a series of negotiations and bargainings, a number of compromises take place. Strategies are developed by which some concessions are agreed by the various social factors involved; certain interests are renounced in return for reciprocated accommodation. An uneasy truce is reached. This may seem pessimistic, but some interactionists would argue that it is through identification and exploration of such practices that a point of intervention is revealed: in coming to know the real basis for action, we make available those areas upon which people could act in order to regain control of essential elements which influence social conduct.

Second, where compromise is unattainable, a 'workable' consensus is achieved by the most powerful partners in the interaction imposing their definitions. Hargreaves (1975), for example, lists a number of techniques teachers can and do use to make manifest their dominant position within an asymmetrical interpersonal relationship and to impose their definition upon the interaction. These include threats, appeals to reason or tradition, with-holding of privileges, rewards, opportunities and mystification, and we would add to these straightforward physical coercion. However, this kind of interpretation introduces into the discussion a concept and a form of explanation which certain critics of interactionism see as a difficult notion for the perspective to manage – the concept of power. It is argued that if, as is the case with this perspective, individuals are seen as having the freedom to define reality and to act upon their definitions, where does the ability come from which allows some individuals to make their definitions count more than those of others? As Sharp and Green (1975) have argued:

> the ability of the headmaster to influence the actions of his teachers, the ability they have to process pupils, the ability of teachers collectively to protect themselves against the felt threats of parents, lie not merely in their linguistic and conceptual superiority but in their position in the power structure. If they are linguistically and conceptually superior it is only because those who have power in the macro structure define it to be so and have given them available sanctions to reinforce their definition of reality against others.

CONCLUSION

As Hargreaves (1978) has sought to demonstrate, the interaction perspective has the power to allow us to:

1. Appreciate crucial dimensions of everyday activities.
2. Formulate a conceptual framework, a vocabulary, with which we can talk about these various dimensions with greater confidence.
3. Reflect upon the consequences of particular elements which make up everyday life.
4. Find a way into the reality of social experience with a view to changing that reality.
5. Embark upon correctionist programmes with greater awareness of how the social body upon which we are operating will react to such attempted surgery.

Nevertheless, equally important is the question of the ways in which the everyday affairs of individuals are related to the particular material, social and political circumstances in which they are located, specifically to the distribution of power in society. It is this kind of issue which will be considered in the next chapter.

Further Reading

Delamont, S. (1976) *Interaction in the Classroom*. London: Methuen. Describes the ways in which the perspectives outlined in this chapter have been applied to analysis and research in education.

Giddens, A. (1976) *New Rules of Sociological Method*. London: Hutchinson. This is not a book which will be easily understood by newcomers to sociology, but its importance justifies perseverance. An important book in terms of the philosophical and methodological issues raised in this chapter.

Hargreaves, D.H. (1972) *Interpersonal Relations and Education*. London: Routledge and Kegan Paul. Discusses the application to analysis and research in education of the perspectives considered in this chapter.

King, R. (1980) 'Weberian Perspectives and the Study of Education', *British Journal of Sociology of Education*, **1**, 1. The distinctive contribution the ideas of Weber can make to the study of education is concisely reviewed in this article.

Meltzer, B., Petral, J. and Reynolds, L. (1975) *Symbolic Interactionism; Genesis, Varieties and Criticisms*. London: Routledge and Kegan Paul. A discussion of both the advantages and the problems of symbolic interactionism developed by writers who work within this tradition.

Woods, P. (ed.) (1980) *Teacher Strategies*. Beckenham: Croom Helm. The ways in which the perspectives outlined in this chapter have been applied to analysis and research in education are to be found in both this and the following reference.

Woods, P. (ed.) (1980) *Pupil Strategies*. Beckenham: Croom Helm.

Signposts

The 1980s and 1990s have produced a number of detailed accounts of teachers' and pupils' experiences of schools. Read Woods, P. (1979) *The Divided School*, London: Routledge and Kegan Paul, and try to assess:

(a)   how his research methodology influences the explanations about school processes; and,

(b)   the usefulness of his observations about life in classrooms, schools and staffrooms for student teachers.

21 The Conflict Perspective: A Marxian Approach

LEN BARTON AND STEPHEN WALKER

INTRODUCTION: CONFLICT AND POWER

In the preceding two chapters a problem has arisen which we have left unattended. Whether one is considering social behaviour at the macro level, in terms of the interrelation between individuals' actions and the structure of society, or at a situational level, in terms of the understandings, intentions and methods people use in the organization of their daily lives, the question remains of why there are some systematic social arrangements and some interactional social situations which seem to work against the interests of certain of the individuals involved and in favour of others. The central issue is concerned with explaining differences experienced by both individuals and groups in terms of their access to and ability to use resources in society and also in terms of the nature of the resources these different people have at their disposal or under their direction. These resources include material benefits and wealth, privilege, status and knowledge, and an adequate explanation of social conduct must surely be able to offer some explanation of how it is that some people, who receive only a trivial allocation of such resources, continue with their societal membership. Or, to turn the question around, how it is that some individuals can use their social association to accumulate benefits vastly superior to those enjoyed by others. The centrality of this issue to sociological debate arises from the fact that when people enter into forms of social relationships with other people, they do not only enter into an association which involves making decisions about either the moral basis for their collective lives or the ways in which this life form is definable and has significance, they also enter into economic relationships.

We can attempt to come to terms with making an investigation of the economic dimensions of human behaviour by establishing how the economic order is related to, and, perhaps, directed by the central value system of society or, alternatively, we can try to cut into this aspect of social life by building up a perception of how people understand their economic relationships with others and their intentions in economic action. However, to an extent, to follow either course is to treat economic order as unproblematic, to assume that we know the main parameters of economic action and have only to investigate their empirical realizations. The sociological perspective which refuses to make such assumptions is that which is based upon the writings of Marx (1818–1883), and in this chapter we shall be concerned with introducing two essential elements of a Marxian approach: the analysis Marx made of the economic development of social organization and the use made of this analysis in attempts to identify the main properties of the economic order prevalent in modern society (i.e. the capitalist mode of production). We shall also be concerned with outlining the impact this approach has had upon those seeking insights into the working of educational systems in modern societies and the experiences of all those involved with these systems.

However, before we turn directly to these concerns it might be helpful to explore some aspects of the broader sociological perspective in which the Marxian endeavour is sometimes located. This perspective is popularly referred to as 'the conflict perspective'. Conflict theorists have, as their point of departure for sociological analysis, the concern introduced at the beginning of Chapter 19, the Hobbesian question of how societies hold together. Unlike the Durkheimian view, which presents the individual as being restrained from unfettered pursuit of his own self-interest by his association with, and by the restrictions which arise from, the collective value system of society, conflict theorists view social order as being achieved through a continual process of disputed interaction between individuals and groups, of sectional struggles and of the imposition of order by those who win power. Dahrendorf (1959) distinguished between these two explanations thus:

> There is one large and distinguished school of thought according to which social order results from a general agreement of values, a *consensus omnium* or *volonté générale* which outweighs all possible or actual differences of opinion and interest. There is another equally distinguished school of thought which holds that coherence and order in society are founded on force and constraint, on the domination of some and the subjection of others.

If we accept the essential premise of the first of these schools (or consensus theory), in which individual wills and volitions are seen as being subordinated in the interest of the general good, then even fairly routine deviations from the 'normal' – strikes, petty thefts, racial disharmony, truancy from school, anti-establishment protests and opposition – become problematic. Can we, for example, explain away all such behaviours with notions of the individuals involved being victims of poor socialization, of their being ignorant of the 'common good', or of their not understanding that their welfare depends upon the successful development of the collective interest? Even more difficult to explain is the phenomenon of social change, which tends to be seen by consensus theorists as a process of gradual adaptation.

Equally, the second school of thought (conflict theory) throws up some areas requiring deeper consideration. Although the kind of routine deviations listed above are explicable in terms of individuals seeking to further their own particular causes and interests, the idea that social life is made up of a series of unruly episodes in which unrestrained individuals seek fulfilment of purely selfish motives is difficult to sustain. To manage these problems, while retaining the basic notion that human beings are driven by personal interest, conflict theorists introduce into their sociological analysis the notion of power. This notion is usually used to refer to the concerns, interests and relationships people experience in group life. Conflict theorists note that, although individuals form certain associations with like-minded others from which they derive the benefit of collective effort, the groups which emerge from such affiliations do not always coexist harmoniously because separate groups will, necessarily, pursue interests defined according to their unique perceptions of the world and according to those needs articulated through the very act of affiliating with others. Every group, if it is going to satisfy the reasons individuals have for joining it and therefore preserve itself, will be under pressure to put the interests of its members above the interests of other groups. Where these do not compete, a peaceful pluralism can be accomplished; however, where there is competition, some management of the conflict becomes necessary, and it is in these circumstances that the notion of power becomes crucial, on two levels. First, it is crucial in terms of the ability of individuals within a group to shape, direct and define the objectives and practices of the others who constitute the group, i.e. the management of intra-group conflict. Second, it is crucial in terms of the ability of informal and formalized associations of individuals to overcome successfully opposition from other groups, or even from other individuals, i.e. the management of inter-group conflict. John Rex (1961), in discussing the second of these levels, both identified possible causes of inter-group conflict and points to the reasons why such tensions require some management:

> As between groups, we should first make clear the points of conflict in their separate aims. We might find that the conflict was a total one or we might find that there were areas of agreement including agreement as to how conflict might be carried on. But, given that there was a conflict of aims, we should expect each group to seek to enforce upon the other behaviour which at worst did not interfere with and at best actually promoted the achievement of its own aims. If each group did this there would be some sort of power contest using various forms of power and some sort of conflict would ensue until each side recognized that compliance to a certain degree was more profitable than a continuance of the conflict.

The attraction of conflict theory, then, is that it allows us to generate explanations of social behaviour at both the micro- and the macro-analytical levels. For example, by noting differences in interests between, say, some teachers and their headteachers, or between whole groups of pupils from common social backgrounds and the manifest aims of a system of schooling, and by proceeding to work out how these differences are either resolved or controlled, one can begin to understand how order is achieved in situations which are differently interpreted or reacted to by those participating in them. However, to accomplish this it is necessary to have some idea of the main parameters and essential techniques used in this kind of social stage-management. In other words, the assumption that these conflicts are worked through by the exercise of power constrains the social analyst to devise some conceptualization of the nature of power, the source from which it is derived and the mechanisms by which it is realized.

Precise formulations of exactly what power *is* are difficult to devise. For example, when we say teachers have *power* over their pupils, what do we mean? Are we referring to their observable practices and the extent to which they can promote their own interests and inhibit those of their pupils by actually directing behaviour, or are we referring to a more nebulous property, a force or means which provides the basis for action but the existence of which does not depend upon its exercise? Anthony Giddens (1979) provides a definition which allows us to conceive of power in a way which enables the term to be applied to both the 'actual' and the 'potential' dimensions of the notion, when he writes:

> a person or party who wields power *could* 'have acted otherwise', and the person or party over whom power is wielded, the concept implies, *would* have acted otherwise if power had not been exercised.

He goes on to assert that:

> power ... concerns the capability of actors to secure outcomes where the realization of these outcomes depends upon the agency of others. The use of power in interaction thus can be understood in terms of the facilities that participants bring to and mobilize as elements of the production of that interaction, thereby influencing its course.

But if power is a 'capability to secure outcomes' from where is this capability derived, and by what methods is it realized? Does the power of the teacher, say, spring from personal charisma, experience, position in the social system, superiority of knowledge, cognitive capacity and command of language, or simple physical dominance? All these possibilities are problematic in the sense that what counts as charisma, experience, the rights and obligations of social roles and the statuses of knowledge forms is relative, contingent upon the capability of some groups to make their definitions of these elements legitimate and accepted by those members of society involved with their usage. We can, then, either resort to explaining teachers' power in terms of their physical strength (which is hardly persuasive, given the fact that in most classrooms the pupils heavily outnumber the teacher) or look for the basis upon which certain definitions are projected as the definitions par excellence. One explanation of how certain social groups, i.e. dominant groups, come into the possession of a capacity to define and enforce their definitions, ideas and practices as superior and proper and to impose these upon other groups, i.e. subordinate groups, is through their winning control of the basic resources essential to human beings in the creation and maintenance of their biological and social existences. To develop such an explanation it would be possible to investigate the social institutions that such dominant groups devise and manage in order to protect and further their interests (for example, the political system, the media or the education system) or their manipulation of values, knowledge and beliefs (for example, their control of accepted moralities, forms of reasoning or cultures), or the governance such groups have over the creation, distribution and usage of the concrete resources upon which individuals depend for survival (for example, the production and allocation of food, goods and objects of utility); in short, we could examine the capabilities groups have at a structural, ideological or material level. Marxists would argue that distribution of the first two of these resources is contingent upon the arrangements which arise from attempts individuals make to manage their material environment, and in the next section we shall examine the reasons for this insistence and how a consideration of the material conditions of social organization is developed in Marxian analysis into a comprehensive sociological perspective.

THE MATERIALIST CONCEPTION OF HISTORY

At the heart of Marx's analytical endeavour lies a vision of the evolution through history of forms of social organization which is based upon a belief that the essential property which characterizes human beings is their need and ability to work upon nature as they find it and thereby to transform it – or to engage in production. Social history begins at the point when human beings first engaged in this work, and indeed, the original human attempt to produce marks the exact moment at which humankind as a specific, identifiable species is distinguishable from the rest of the animal world, when the 'human animal' transforms himself into the 'social human'. Thus the materialist view is, first and foremost, based upon the notion that human beings, lacking the physical equipment to survive nature as animals do (by having a simple, mechanical, instinctive reaction to their material environment), have to work on nature, to change, adapt to and modify the physical world, to produce a means of subsistence. In doing this, people produce and reproduce the conditions of their existence and create new situations which throw up new needs and capabilities. Through work, humans find solutions to the problem of survival, but they also create new problems in that, as they produce, they create a material world which is different from that which existed before they began to work on it. As Giddens (1971) observed, for Marx, human history is:

> a process of the continuous creation, satisfaction and re-creation of human needs. This is what distinguishes men from the animals, whose needs are fixed and unchanging. This is why labour, the creative interchange between men and their environment, is the foundation of human society.

The essential logic of relating the origin of social development and the continued impetus given to this development to humankind's attempt to control its material world is encapsulated in Engels's (1969) declaration of the distinctive feature of the materialist conception of history:

> History was for the first time placed on its real basis; the palpable but previously overlooked fact that men must first of all eat, drink, have shelter and clothing, therefore must work, before they can fight for domination, pursue politics, religion, philosophy, etc. – this palpable fact at last came into its historical rights.

The process of social evolution which necessarily arises from the activity 'work' is conceptualized by Marx in terms of a *dialectic*, a moving interpenetration of separate forces or forms; it is a dialectic between the individual in society (subject) and the natural and human-created material world (object) in which humans gradually come to gain control of the elements in the material world so as to satisfy their own needs, and by so doing they change both that world and their own needs: a person both makes his or her world and is made or shaped by it.

However, through work, through production, people produce not only objects but also the conditions under which they relate and are related to others. This interrelation is founded on two elements. First, through engaging in production, humans create the need for the regulation of how they can cooperate, or not, in their productive activities. Even if people determine to produce in isolation, independently, this determination itself is a social act (it represents a decision to organize production according to a distinct rule or set of rules), the act being the basis for the formulation of a set of social relations. Second, they create the need for the regulation of the exchange of the products, for the circulation of the objects they make in their work. Whatever decision they may have reached about how they will organize production itself, in engaging in labour they create the dilemma of what to do with their products, a dilemma which becomes acute with respect to how they see others being related to these products. In developing these two sets of regulations human beings evolve a set of *relations of production* because, Marx (1958) argues:

> In production men not only act on nature but also on one another. They produce only by cooperating in a certain way and mutually exchanging their activities. In order to produce, they enter into definite connections and relations with one another and only within these social connections and relations does their action on nature, does production, take place.

Two key concepts, then, emerge: the *forces of production* (i.e. the material conditions of nature and technology, the things used for production) and the *social relations of production* (i.e. the division of labour and the market relations created by people to facilitate production and exchange), and these also stand in dialectical relationship. To enable a realistic exploration of social history to take place, Marx calls for the development of an empirical science to explore how this dialectic has differently influenced the form and structure of society through various eras and epochs of history – a science of historical materialism. His own typology of societal evolution explores how the division of labour has gradually become more differentiated and specialized:

> One thing is clear – nature does not produce on the one side owners of money or commodities, and on the other, men possessing nothing but their own labour power. This relation has no natural basis, neither is it common to all historical periods. It is clearly the result of past historical development, the product of many economical revolutions, of the extinction of a whole series of older forms of social production.

In his own portrayal of this historical development, Marx sees a gradual evolution from primitive, classless societies to modern, class-based social organization, the dynamic for which arises from the essential condition which results from individuals cooperating in production. The divisions of labour which pertain to this cooperation enable working groups to realize a surplus of goods over their own needs. The existence of this surplus thus creates a new condition, the potential for the development of trade, which itself creates the problems of ownership and of the establishment of the social relations necessary for the exchange of goods. The dialectical relationships, then, between human beings' productive life and their other social activities can be represented thus:

1. That from each kind of production system evolves a unique set of social relationships according to the circumstances of ownership and the social division of labour. (For example, freeman/slave, patrician/plebeian, lord/serf, guildmaster/journeyman, bourgeois/proletarian.)
2. That the form of social relationship established around production (i.e. base structure) conditions the other forms of social organization – political forms, cultural life, religion, family form, legal structure – which emerge (i.e. superstructure).
3. That classes emerge only when one group of people who stand in a common relation to production unite in a conflict with other groups of people.
4. That, most importantly, social change or the transformation from one social order to another is a result of a contradiction between existing productive forces and existing relations of production, i.e. the social relations of production become, as a result of technological or cultural change, inadequate for the regulation of production itself. Marx (1970) observes that: 'No social order ever disappears before all the productive forces for which there is room in it have been developed and new, higher relations of production never appear before the material conditions of their existence have matured in the womb of the old society.'

What might sometimes be an unintended consequence of productive activity is that it promotes the development of new technologies, inventions, ideas or instruments of production. The very appearance of these renders existing ideas and practices of production, and the forms of social relations which have emerged to support such practices, obsolete, and thus forces a change within the system. For some time societies may successfully resist the impact of these pressures; however, the momentum for the development of increasingly efficient techniques of production which will lead to the extension of humankind's mastery over nature compels these societies to react to the existence of these new creations, to make use of them in production and hence to change the social relations in the society to accommodate the new forms of production that emerge.

The materialist conception of history is sometimes depicted as supremely deterministic, as encapsulating a view of humanity and social life largely directed by economic and productive forces. Certainly Marx would have us accept that the individual is not free from the constraints of the material reality which he, she or his or her ancestors have created. Yet the emphasis is upon creation, and, as Garaundy (1970) observes, the concept

> starts not from a negation, but from an affirmation; it affirms the autonomy of man and it involves as a consequence the rejection of every attempt to rob man of his creative and self-creative power.

We should recognize that

> Men make their own history, but they do not make it just as they please; they do not make it under circumstances chosen by themselves, but under circumstances directly encountered, given and transmitted from the past
>
> Marx, 1969

and thus realize that this knowledge gives us a basis for real intervention in the process of history, the principle being that an understanding of the world as it is provides the basis from which we can work for change.

PRODUCTION AND CONFLICT IN MODERN SOCIETY

Using the principles established in the materialist conception of history, Marx attempted to delineate the peculiar dynamics of that form of production which supports social organization at its most recent stage of development – the capitalist mode of production. What Marx is concerned with is the mode of production at a given point in time, not production in general, because, while human beings will always produce things which have utility for them, can be exchanged or can be used to support production, how this is managed is the important variable. Thus the capitalist mode of production has to be seen as a form of production which has developed out of the forms or modes which preceded it but which, nevertheless, is based upon characteristics that are unique to a specific stage of social development.

As Giddens (1971) notes, 'in Marx's view, the search for profit is intrinsic to capitalism'. In one sense the capitalist mode of production is no different from any other mode of production, in that, unless a portion of the products created through production is reserved, to be converted back into the means of production (so that the 'materials' consumed in the initial phase of a production process might be replaced), the reproduction of life through production is quickly played out. In other words, any form of production needs to create a surplus of goods over those produced for consumption, in order for the cycle of production to continue. However, the capitalist mode of production *is* different from others in terms of the form this surplus takes, how it is created and, importantly, who 'owns' it.

To work towards some answers to these questions we have to recognize two basic features of the capitalist mode of production which are a direct consequence of the place the mode occupies in the overall socio-economic development of human history. The first is that it is a process concerned with the production of commodities; the second is that the process is carried out by people with different economic interests.

Commodity production concerns people working upon nature to create objects which are not intended to satisfy their own private needs, but which can be traded or exchanged for other objects or services. What makes this kind of production the focal concern of capitalism arises from the birth and adoption of the money form as the main basis for regulating exchange between social groups or between individuals, an adoption which took place during a stage of development long before capitalism emerged as the mode of production. Marx argues that, initially, money was used as a simple and convenient device to enable people to represent the value of the different things they had produced; it was a convenient measure, but it had no intrinsic value, no 'use value' of its own. However, as the money form gradually became the universal base for calculating rates of exchange for things which do have the capability to satisfy needs, or use values, by virtue of this social function money acquired a use value of its own: it became a commodity in itself. This simple development metamorphosed the whole process of trade and exchange, because as soon as money became 'the universal material representation of wealth' (Marx, 1973) – i.e. used to calculate and to express the value of all commodities – it also became the most desirable commodity of all, and hence the circulation of commodities took on a new form. This was because the possession of the commodity 'money' became the starting and finishing point of each cycle of production. The simple exchange process of 'commodity → money → commodity' was transformed, inverted into 'money → commodity → money', and it is this cycle of transactions which forms the basis of the capitalist economic order – a buying-to-sell cycle.

Clearly, the circulation of money for money would be absurd if nothing extra or of surplus value was to be gained in the process. Why should the owner of money or capital risk his resources if there were no benefit to be derived from so doing? This surplus value, argues Marx, is created in the production of the commodities in circulation in the society, but is extracted in the process of exchange, and it derives from the difference between the 'cost' of production and the exchange value or 'worth' of the produce. To put it another way, money is laid out to buy those things necessary to produce a commodity – this represents the cost of production. Money is clawed back when these commodities are sold. For a profit to be realized the articles must be sold for more than they cost to produce. One way of achieving this would be simply to 'fix' the sale price above the cost price, but Burns (1952) draws our attention to Marx's observation that the source of profit:

> could not possibly come from capitalists selling the products above their value – this would mean that all capitalists were all the time cheating each other, and where one made a 'profit' of this kind the other necessarily made a loss, and the profits and losses would cancel each other, leaving no general profit. It therefore follows that the value of an article on the market must already contain the profit: the profit must arise in the course of production, and not in the sale of the product.

Yet it is in the sale of the product that any surplus is made real, is extracted in the form of money. However, for this money to have value it has to be converted back into commodities, and if this conversion is to be done profitably then the whole exchange cycle of 'money → commodities → money' must begin again. Thus, as Marx (1970) observes:

> The circulation of money as capital is an end in itself, for the expansion of value takes place only within this constantly renewed movement. The circulation of capital has therefore no limits.

The vital compulsion for capital to be accumulated in order for the capitalist mode of production to be maintained, then, is determined not by some subjective factor, such as greed or a passion for accumulation, but by an objective and necessary condition of the mode of production itself, commodity production.

What is it about actual production, however, that allows it to be organized so as to enable some surplus to be created? To answer this question we need to look at the way in which, through the development of history, there have emerged two groups of people whose involvement in production is sharply different. A whole host of gradual changes in social affairs – urbanization, expansion of trade, increased industrialization and commercial innovation, the development of progressively more specialized methods of manufacture – have led to increased polarization in the division of labour in society, out of which have emerged two classes who stand in opposition to each other. These are the owners of the means of production (capitalists) and the men and women who exist as a means of production (wage-labourers). Each class supports itself differently: capitalists by using their accumulated resources to initiate and control production by buying essential materials and hiring labour, and then selling their products; and wage-labourers by selling their labour power to the capitalists, an arrangement to which they are compelled to agree, since they have no other means of subsistence.

Thus there is a separation between workers and their means of production; indeed, human labour becomes just another commodity necessary for production to take place. The cost of labour, like that of any commodity, is determined by the 'labour-time socially necessary' for its own production in other words, the cost incurred by workers in producing and maintaining themselves. However, human labour-power as a commodity is unique in the sense that, although the capitalist buys it 'at its daily value', the worker is able to produce more in an average working day than is needed to meet the cost of his own subsistence. For example, suppose the daily subsistence cost of the worker is £20, and it takes an average of four hours to realize that value in production, and the average working day is eight hours; the value of commodities produced during one half of the working day is greater than that necessary for the subsistence of the worker, and is, therefore, surplus value, and is appropriated by the capitalist.

Thus the capitalist doesn't 'cheat' the worker: rather he exploits the capacity of human labour to produce more than is necessary for its own production. The worker must acquiesce in this exploitation of his labour power so that commodities necessary for his own subsistence are produced, and also to gain a wage, and the capitalist is compelled to exploit labour in order to realize surplus value so that the circulation and accumulation of capital continue.

However, to appreciate fully the impact of the kind of analysis presented above, it is important to recognize, as Bowles and Gintis (1976) argue, that:

> Capitalist production . . . is not simply a technical process; it is also a social process. Workers are neither machines nor commodities but, rather, active human beings who participate in production with the aim of satisfying their personal and social needs. The central problem of the employer is to erect a set of social relationships and organizational forms, both within the enterprise and, if possible, in society at large, that will channel these aims into the production and expropriation of surplus value.

Surplus value is increased only to the extent to which the difference between 'necessary labour' and 'surplus labour' is maximized, i.e. the degree to which the capitalist wins a prolongation of the time in which the worker is producing value or its equivalent beyond that necessary for his own reproduction. Clearly, the worker will resist attempts to extend the length of the working day and, in any case, unlimited extension of the working day, by reducing the time for activities necessary to the proper physical and social development of workers, would quickly exhaust the labour force and decrease its productivity. So, surplus labour-time has to be increased inside the normal working day. For this to happen, control and manipulation of the labour process, the activities in which workers engage to produce things, are vital to the capitalist, because a reduction of the 'necessary labour-time' which will give an extension of 'surplus labour-time' is possible only through an increase in the productivity of labour.

There are several ways in which the labour process can be brought more directly under the control of capital. Marx identifies at least two. First is the way in which increased differentiation between labour skills on the part of the employer not only provides an increase in the cost benefit derived from greater cooperation in production, but also leads to increased alienation of individual workers from the fruits of their labour; in contributing to only a limited part of the total production of a commodity and thus being dependent on other workers, and ultimately the employer, for the finished production of a complete product, the worker effectively loses control of what he creates by work. Second, increased mechanization and use of technological advances in the production process also provide a means by which the employer can dominate the labour process and subjugate the worker; machines can replace workers, facilitate the employment of weaker and less skilful workers and, by replicating the activities involved in a productive task in a fixed, mechanical pattern, subordinate the worker to the machine, in the sense that his movements and pace, and the degree of mental activity involved in work, are all determined by the machine.

To these two elements Harry Braverman (1974) adds a third: the application of a management structure and the principles of scientific management, which he represents as an additional weapon for the employer in his quest for increased control of the labour process in order to yield increased productivity and hence increased profit. Any form of management has the consequence of separating planning and design activities from actual production, and Braverman (1974) argues that, through scientific management, through relating the activities and organizations of production to scientific principles, capital seeks to eliminate the 'capriciousness of human labour' and the incursion of change elements from the production process. By the same token its application serves 'to strip the workers of craft knowledge and autonomous control and confront them with a fully thought-out labour process in which they function as cogs and levers'. Thus, as we indicated at the start of this discussion, the capitalist mode of production has as its motivating force an endless quest for the maximization of profit, but to this point we can now add that this can be achieved only if the inequitable social relations of production described above are sustained and developed, so that the dominant class is able to exercise ever-increasing control over the use of labour-time, the organization of the labour process and the deployment of the labour force.

To appreciate how this rather economic analysis is developed within Marxian sociological perspectives to allow for the exploration of social conduct in all its manifestations, we need to return to a point made by Bowles and Gintis in an extract quoted earlier – that capitalism is not just a technical process but a social one. From this perspective it is argued that social systems, the structure of social institutions, the creation and dissemination of organizing ideas and interpretations of the world, and even the consciousness of individuals in society, which form the basis for the everyday actions and interactions, emerge from (and work back upon) those relations essential to the production process.

Forms of political administration, legal systems, family life, communication systems, religious practices, educational processes and, importantly, the ways in which those involved in these social institutions relate to one another are all inextricably linked with the form of the social relations of production, and in capitalist society these relations are necessarily hierarchical, exploitative and antagonistic. It follows, then, that the structure and institutional arrangements of such a society will:

1. Reflect such hierarchical relations.
2. Serve to produce and reproduce conditions necessary to sustain it.
3. Provide the opportunity for dominant groups to legitimize both their position and their interpretations of social order and, where necessary, to control groups which develop interests and activities contrary to their own.

Thus sociologists working within a Marxian framework would attempt to explore the following:

1. The management by capitalists and workers of the social relations of production, which will involve investigation of the nature, extent and consequences of the struggle between these groups, the historical location in which such struggles take place and the development of the mode of manufacture which is promoted and impeded through such conflict.

2. The nature and workings of the dialectical relationship between the capital form of economic life and other social institutions and arrangements.
3. The way in which social institutions not directly concerned with production are internally organized so as to reflect, reproduce and reinforce socio-economic relationships.
4. The overarching structure (and the principles upon which this is constructed) which allows various institutional arrangements to be interrelated.
5. The identification of correspondence and/or contradictions within institutions and both between various institutional forms of life and between these forms and the overall social structure.
6. The everyday experience individuals have of social life, and the extent to which these experiences are conditioned by or are a reaction to those hierarchic relations which have their roots in the material base.

One of the major institutions in capitalist society is the education system, and, not surprisingly, its nature and working are of great interest to sociologists working with a Marxian perspective. Interestingly, Marx himself wrote very little about education, although in *The Communist Manifesto* we find some indication of what he and Engels saw as an important concern for materialist analysis in this area. They assert:

> And your education! Is not that also social and determined by the social conditions under which you educate, by the intervention, direct or indirect, of society, by means of schools. The communists ... do but seek to alter the character of that intervention and to rescue education from the influence of the ruling class.

In many ways a search for the main dimensions of this 'intervention' has formed the basis of a great deal of recent sociological work on education. It is to an exploration of some of the main features of this endeavour that we will now turn in order that the impact of the six characteristics identified above upon sociological perspectives of education might be demonstrated.

MARXIAN ANALYSIS AND THE STUDY OF EDUCATION

Although we intend that some overview of Marxist writings and ideas on education will be presented here, the reader should be aware that, as with those perspectives identified in Chapters 19 and 20, there is a considerable difference of opinion among sociologists of this persuasion about what constitutes the most appropriate analytical path. An important point of difference is between those whose main interest is exploring the structural 'fit' between the education system and the economic order (see, for example, Bowles and Gintis, 1976) and those who seek to explore the ways in which certain cultural beliefs and practices that support capitalist society are created, transmitted and reproduced within educational worlds (see, for example, Bourdieu and Passeron, 1977; Willis, 1977; Apple, 1979, 1980).

However, most Marxian analysis can be seen as an attempt to identify what Apple has called 'the deep structure' of education, the ways in which the systematic arrangements of schooling and the day-to-day organization and routine activities of life in classrooms (and also the ways in which both of these impinge upon the social experience of teachers and pupils) are explicable through reference to the distribution of power in society. What distinguishes Marxian analysis of education, then, is that schooling is seen not as a process which serves to socialize new members of society into the collectively established, consensual moral order, simply as the outcome of the rule-governed creative interaction of local groups of social actors, but rather as a phenomenon which is related most profoundly to the distribution of resources and opportunities in a society. As Corrigan and Frith (1977) maintain:

> The importance of education for capitalism is clearly revealed by the state's action in taking control of educational institutions and expanding them; the question for Marxists is why.
> We can take as given that education does fulfil a basic function for capitalism, the task is to understand this function. But there is a further task for Marxists; to relate this theoretical understanding to day-to-day education practice.

Of course, in an effort to answer these questions Marxian analysis of education has attempted to explore a wide variety of areas in which it might be shown that educational affairs are influenced by the ideologies or direct intervention of socially and politically dominant groups – for example, at the level of educational provision, the social relations established in contemporary schools, the organization of knowledge and the curriculum, the links between educational and industrial sectors in the creation and application of new knowledge and technology or the cultural ethos on which education is predicated – and although it is not possible to examine in detail all such work, to capture the flavour of this kind of analysis we include below a brief description of some of it.

Without doubt, many sociologists of education in Britain have been greatly influenced by the thoughts of Bowles and Gintis, particularly as developed in their book *Schooling in Capitalist America* (1976). In what they described as an attempt to construct a political economy of education, Bowles and Gintis isolated many features of schooling in modern capitalist societies which, they claimed, corresponded to the 'social relations of work roles' and thus, they argued, education could be seen as a crucial element in the preparation of individuals for their roles in the world of work. In general terms, they saw education functioning both as a transmission and as a control mechanism in the reproduction of the social relations which underpin the capitalist mode of production. First, education plays an important part in forming the skills and attitudes that workers need in order to be fully productive in work; second, education

> helps defuse and depoliticize the potentially explosive class relations of the productive process and thus serves to perpetuate the social, political and economic conditions through which a part of the product of labour is expropriated in the form of profits.

The bureaucratic and hierarchically structured order which characterizes school was seen by Bowles and Gintis as the main dimension by which pupils' personal development and learned behavioural characteristics were nurtured in a specific way, i.e. their socialization was in a climate which celebrated and was based upon relationships of dominance and subordination, and was thus compatible with the social order of the workplace. That such an order is perpetuated in British schools is supported by studies of schooling in this country. With regard to teacher–pupil relations, for example, Sharp and Green (1975), in their study of a progressive primary school, found that even in a setting based upon a child-centred ideology, the power of the teacher to shape pupils' identities and create a stratification system within the classroom is enormous:

> The teacher is crucial to this process not simply because she is the reality definer but because . . . she can be regarded as a scarce resource in that she possesses and can transmit the means whereby the careers of pupils can be facilitated or held back.

Paul Willis (1977), on the basis of his study of life in an urban comprehensive school, argues that the authority of teachers is not merely a consequence of their being given control over pupils by the state, but must be seen as part of a collection of assumptions about what education entails, an educational paradigm. Teachers, he notes, control use of space, property and time, dictate the rules of interpersonal relationships, and, most importantly, see and represent themselves as controllers of 'what is implied to be the scarce and valuable commodity of knowledge'.

Bernstein (1975) argues that even the ritual order of schools, which serves as a symbolic representation of the prevailing value system of the institutions, similarly works 'to deepen respect for and impersonalize authority relations'. The school assembly, house rituals, the prefect system, setting and streaming practices all remind pupils and teachers of their place within the hierarchy and, more importantly, that a hierarchical structure is in legitimate operation.

At a different structural level, the differential ranking of types of educational routes (public school/state; grammar/comprehensive/modern; top stream/bottom stream; university/polytechnic/further education college/apprenticeship), the differential patterns of socialization which operate in differentiated routes (individual responsibility being emphasized at the 'higher' levels, close supervision of students being the norm at the 'lower') and the differentiated allocation of resources between ranked sectors of education are also seen by Bowles and Gintis as emphasizing a hierarchical rule and the individual's place within the hierarchy.

Perhaps the most crucial aspect of education which can be seen as defining hierarchy as normal is the way in which educational knowledge, the central concern of schooling, is selected, classified and evaluated. Bernstein (1971) has argued that 'educational knowledge is the major regulator of the structure of experience', and that it can be categorized according to the strength of its classification (i.e. how units of knowledge are related to other units) and its frame (i.e. how the transmitters and receivers of knowledge are related and interrelated). He suggests that in English education knowledge is strongly classified or bounded, although the system allows some weakening of frame. The idea of strong insulation of content areas of educational knowledge means that it is distributed and evaluated 'through a series of well-insulated subject hierarchies'. This hierarchy permeates the structure of the curriculum (which represents a movement towards 'higher' forms of knowledge), the educational careers of students (which involves a movement towards increased specialization) and even the relationships of teachers and pupils (who are ranked according to subject and mastery of subject). Bernstein (1971) argues, however, that it is necessary to relate 'patterns internal to educational institutions to the external and social antecedents of such patterns'.

It may well be, therefore, that, taking into consideration the way knowledge is organized in British education, there is a case to be made for viewing the dialectical relationship between education and the capitalist mode of production in terms of how the mode shapes social patterns. Whatever the nature of the relationship might be, Bowles and Gintis would still maintain that school work – the acquisition of knowledge – is very like productive work: fragmented, differentiated and not in control of the worker.

The most developed part of Bowles and Gintis's argument about the role of education in the transmission of behavioural characteristics important for capital to maintain and extend control of the labour process concerns the way in which schools foster and reward certain personality traits. Using data from research by Meyer (1972), they attempt to discover the relationship between certain personality traits and school success, as measured by ability to achieve high marks or grades, which schools use as a major motivational device. They note that, even when IQ is held constant, there is a high correlation between pupils' ability to achieve a high 'grade point average' and their possession of personality characteristics of submission to authority, passivity, conformity and perseverance, and a negative correlation between such success and traits of creativity, aggression and independence. Comparing these data with those presented by Edwards (1976) in a study of the characteristics valued by managers in industry, Bowles and Gintis observe that managers rate negatively the last three traits in the school research. Thus, they conclude (with some qualification in terms of the influence of other personality attributes), 'the personality traits rewarded in schools seem to be rather similar to those indicative of good job performance in the capitalist economy'.

As was noted earlier, Bowles and Gintis also argue that schools act as control agencies by defusing potential conflict which might arise if workers were to question the legitimacy of their occupational placing or status. It is clear that occupation placement and the levels of qualifications obtained through schooling are increasingly related (see, for example, A. H. Halsey's study of education and socio-mobility in Great Britain in Karabel and Halsey, 1977). This is traditionally explained and justified by reference to the notion that educational attainment represents an objective measure of cognitive merit. However, this justification is contradicted by evidence that suggests little correlation between educational achievement and productivity (Berg, 1973) or between occupational status and cognitive skills (Bowles and Gintis, 1976). Bowles and Gintis explain this contradiction by asserting that the idea of educational success being determined by merit or superior cognitive ability is an illusion fostered in the schools: educational success is much more likely to be determined by the possession of the personality traits listed above and by conformity to the school norms, characteristics acquired, they argue, in family and home backgrounds. The systems of education, streaming structures and grading devices, while claiming to advance those possessing some objective characteristics of merit, in fact can be shown as rewarding behavioural characteristics already possessed, and in one sense exclusively, by individuals from a specific social background, i.e. the middle class. (See Chapter 24 of this book for details of research into the relationship between social class and educational success and failure.) Thus, Bowles and Gintis contend, 'the legitimation process in education assumes a largely symbolic form'. That it is symbolic is important, in that it preserves class-based inequality without the foundation of this inequality being brought into serious debate: it both preserves and legitimates this inequality. In a review of their book, Gintis and Bowles (1980) rephrase one of the more important features of their analysis thus:

> the current relationship between education and economy is ensured not through the *content* of education but its *form*; the social relations of the educational encounter Education prepares students to be workers through a *correspondence* between the social relations of production and the social relations of education.
>
> Like the division of labour in the capitalist enterprise, the educational system is a finely graded hierarchy of authority and control in which competition rather than co-operation governs the relations among participants, and an external reward system – wages in the case of the economy, and grades in the case of schools – holds sway.

In the same paper, they also recognize a certain weakness in the 'correspondence principle'. As Sarup (1978) has noted, Bowles and Gintis tended to assume that social institutions like schools have a massive capacity for achieving comprehensive realization of their 'functions', overemphasizing the constraining influence of social structure to the neglect of an examination of the micro-sociological issues like the individual's response to these pressures or consideration of the ways in which 'consciousness' in social actors is created, realized and maintained in everyday life. Such a response is important to Marxian analysis because an essential feature of the perspective is that capitalist social relations of production inevitably allow for the development of contradictions. The existence of distinguishable and irreconcilable social groups upon which the mode of production depends also means that each group can and will create cultural forms and life-worlds which are based upon their different definitions of reality and relationships with the material world. What is needed, therefore, is an extension of the correspondence theory that enables the student of educational life to account for not only the correspondence between education and the economy but also the struggles in which individual people engage in their daily experiences when they encounter contradictory expectations, pressures or definitions. We need to be able to decide, for example, whether those pupils who passively accept the label 'educational failure' and their placement low down in the educational and occupational hierarchy do so as a response to the message of schooling or, alternatively, as a response to a communication which has little to do with education and its directives and signals, and may well contradict them.

In *Learning to Labour*, Willis (1977) goes some way towards filling this gap in the work of Bowles and Gintis. His basic concern is with questioning why the illusion of people being ranked according to objective criteria of merit (or meritocratic stratification) works. It is absurd, he argues, to assume blind acceptance of the illusion, since educational and occupational 'failures' would thus be involved in judging their own position by reference to their own relative stupidity, and hence individuals in the lowest stratum 'would scarcely rate a score for being alive'. Rather, Willis suggests that the boys in his study, 'the lads', 'the educational failures' and members of the school counter-culture, far from being forced into positions of subordination, make a voluntary 'choice' to reject school and to accept manual work as their occupational destiny, and that the origins of this decision-making are to be found outside the education system, in the cultural conditions of their working-class origin. The working class, far from being members of a culture which is shaped, directed and supremely controlled by dominant group interests and machinations, develop and create their own cultural activities, their own interests and understandings and their own 'lived-out experiences'. Contradictions inherent in capitalism make this unavoidable.

In doing this they achieve two things. First, they provide a basis for action, a logic for individuals within the culture. Thus, for example, attitudes and conduct at work and school have their roots not simply in life in the institutions but in the ideologies and practices groups create as their class culture. Willis (1977) argues:

> this class culture is not a neutral pattern ... It comprises experiences, relationships, and ensembles of systematic types of relationship which not only set particular 'choices' and 'decisions' at particular times, but also structure, really and experientially, how these choices come about and are defined in the first place.

Second, they provide for the possibility of what Willis calls 'a partial penetration' – the creation of a perception which enables the reality of the conditions of social life, be they inequitable, exploitative or whatever, to be exposed. As Apple (1980) explains, with reference to the educational context:

> By penetration, he [Willis] means those instances where students have developed responses to schools and work that see the unequal reality they will face. Their rejection of so much of the content and form of day-to-day educational life bears on the almost unconscious realization that, as a class, schooling will not enable them to go much further than they already are. The culture the lads create inside and outside the school actually constitutes a rather realistic assessment of the rewards of the obedience and conformism which the school seeks to extract from working class youths.

Now, while the analysis of both working-class cultural forms and penetration that Willis provides is complex and subtle in nuance, the important theoretical point he establishes is that explorations of pupils' school experience cannot be made simply in mechanistic terms of their being conditioned and constrained by the system. Rather it has to take into account a realization that attitudes and conduct in social life (including that of the school) are not mechanically reproduced but are the product of an interplay between:

1. The dominant ideologies and interests of institutions.
2. Those contradictory features and expectations associated with such institutions.
3. That degree of autonomy of individuals which has been created by their active engagement within or upon institutions and which arises from the consciousness that the individual carries from his or her own cultural setting into institutional life.

While the mode of production remains the most profound influence upon both the structural organization of society and its institutional arrangement, and upon the settings in which cultural forms and penetrations are created, human behaviour is not to be regarded as a simple response or reaction to either of these but as arising from the dynamic association between them. In these terms, then, an analysis of education that attempts to investigate how the system and practices of schooling serve to produce and reproduce the social relations necessary for the maintenance and development of the capitalist mode of production cannot assume any simple 'correspondence'. Certainly, the choice Willis's 'lads' make does work to support this reproduction. But if choices are available, so are alternative outcomes. Recognition of the importance of this last point has led Reynolds and Sullivan (1980) to call for a socialist sociology of education which brings together Marxian analysis at the cultural and structural levels, and in making this exhortation they remind us of one of the most important features of Marxian endeavour: its optimistic vision. Thus, they assert:

> The adoption of a Marxist sociologist perspective, then, would suggest an urgent need for rapprochement between uncontextualized micro level analyses that neglect to focus on societal constraints and rather abstract ... macro level accounts that grant human consciousness and action little independence from the societal material base. Man can, and classical Marxists are quite clear on this point, affect his development and his surroundings as well as being affected by them.

CONCLUSION

The perspective with which this chapter has been concerned is distinguishable from other sociological stances by the central place it affords to and the specific explanations it offers of the nature, source, exercise and distribution of power in society. While the writers who work within this perspective are interested in understanding and articulating the contradictions and conflicts that are endemic to a class-divided society, they also share an attitude to sociological investigation that is premised upon a desire for change. What is important for our purposes, however, is that such an attitude arises from the basic vision of human beings and society upon which this perspective is based. Humans are seen, at one and the same time, as both the creators of their social world and a product of the systematic social arrangements which have emerged during the history of collective behaviour. A major task of this type of sociological analysis, therefore, is to facilitate humankind's creative potential by increasing people's understanding of the real workings of the social system: in short, to demystify the world at the level of both action and structure.

Further Reading

Corrigan, P. (1979) *Schooling and the Smash Street Kids*. London: Macmillan.

Sarup, M. (1978) *Marxism and Education*. London: Routledge and Kegan Paul. A most helpful overview of how Marxist ideas have been developed within the field of education.

Young, M. and Whitty, G. (1977) *Society, State and Schooling*. Lewes: Falmer Press. An illustration of how Marxist ideas are applied in the field of education.

Signposts

1. Materialist analysis

It is important that one recognizes that different Marxist critiques of schooling and educating emphasize different aspects of what we have generally described as 'materialist' analysis. Bowles, S. and Gintis, H. (1976) *Schooling in Capitalist America*, London: Routledge and Kegan Paul, stress the importance of the hidden curriculum of schooling in the reproduction of the social relations of production. Willis, P. (1977) *Learning to Labour*, Farnborough: Saxon House, explores how 'the lads', a group of working-class boys in a secondary school, respond to the ideologies of schooling. And in the book produced by the Centre for Contemporary Cultural Studies (1979), *Unpopular Education*, London: Hutchinson, you can find a superb discussion of how the state is implicated in the manipulation of educational enterprises. Pierre Bourdieu's work has emphasized the importance that education plays in the reproduction of 'cultural capital' as well as economic capital, and the role of social class actors themselves in reproducing their own circumstances. Bourdieu's emphasis is on the 'habitas' or status qualities and their associated ways of behaving that are derived from education rather than the economic and technical skills that have been acquired. These habits then influence the way people understand and interact with social structures, particularly in relation to social contacts and perceived opportunities. Bourdieu, P. (1983) 'The forms of capital' in Halsey, A.H., Lauder, H., Brown, P., and Wells, A.S. (eds), *Education, Culture, Economy and Society*, London: Sage 1990.

2. Schooling can seriously damage your health?

It has been argued that schooling not only reproduces social inequality, but also actively perpetuates violence in society (see Harber, C. (2004) *Schooling as Violence*, London: Routledge Falmer).

22 Doing Research in Schools and Classrooms

LEN BARTON AND STEPHEN WALKER

TAKING A STANCE

So what do you think of this book so far? You might have dipped into earlier chapters and come across stories about how everyday events in schools and classrooms are mysteriously created through the interactions of teachers and pupils. You might have read whole sections, perhaps as part of a course assignment or in preparation for seminars and discussions about different perspectives of educating or about different accounts of the effects of day-to-day activities in schools. But ask yourself this. What are *your feelings* about the stories, the analyses, the accounts of life in classrooms you have been given in other parts of this narrative?

Why are you reading this now? What are you hoping for? How do you think we feel in writing these accounts, these stories? What hopes and fears do you think we have about educating? Crucially, when you are testing your visions and views of schooling against the ones we offer in this book, can you detect any shared understandings, any meeting points?

If you find these questions difficult to answer, or if they disturb or puzzle you, you are already into the kind of experiences which challenge anyone concerned with analysing social life, with producing accounts of social behaviour, with doing research. The point of the questions is this. Even something as commonplace as reading a book like this, or writing a text like we are doing, is a complex act in which we invest our unique personal ambitions and interests and to which we bring our own singular interpretations, backgrounds and under-standings. You might be reading this text to prepare for an exam or to structure an essay or to help you think about your actions and experience in the classroom – or simply because it's a prescribed book. Some of the accounts you read might amuse you or make you angry; they may cause you to rethink some of your beliefs about educating or to act differently in the classroom; or they may leave you cold. And what about us? What draws us into this attempt to put certain ideas about educating before you, and how do these interests influence our selection and interpretation of the stories about schooling we introduce? All difficult questions. Nevertheless, whatever it is that motivates any of us involved in the present dialogue, it is certain that how we see the activity and what we want from it will shape how we respond and what we make with it. Or, to put it another way, our behaviour, our actions, our strategies for dealing with even quite routine experiences like reading a book or writing a text are not independent of the stance we adopt towards such an experience – how we make sense of it, how we interpret the conduct of others involved, how we evaluate the experience. In fact, quite the contrary. Each and every one of our daily actions and interactions is fundamentally dependent on our subjective understanding and interpretations, our world-view. Indeed, as we suggested in a previous chapter, 'The Action Perspective', it is difficult to imagine how we could engage in social interaction at all without constant recourse to the various views, definitions and motives we hold, to the personal beliefs and assumptions, hopes and fears we cling to and which we use to make sense of our experiences and to direct our behaviour.

In interaction, then, we constantly theorize about social life, about our own place in daily affairs and about how we can best cope in each of the fresh and familiar situations we encounter. And as we theorize, we develop a stance – a personal perspective of what social life is about, of possible lines of action in specific circumstances, of what counts as a problem for us in a situation and what counts as a solution.

It is, of course, one thing to recognize that everyday life in seminars, in classrooms, in colleges and in schools, or anywhere, is produced by those involved in it negotiating how they will conduct their affairs according to their personal ideas of what it is all about and what they want from the situation. It is quite another thing to find a way of producing narratives about such affairs, of creating stories that illuminate the darker and more mysterious features of these encounters, of doing research which keeps faith with the basic recognition that social events are built upon people's common-sense knowledge and motives. If we are to hold true to an appreciation of the crucial importance *subjective* understanding and interest has for human behaviour and experience, then researching social actions and social situations is made difficult in at least two significant ways.

First, we have to discover research strategies which allow us to get close enough to those we are studying or working with to be able to establish an appreciative understanding of their view of the activities and circumstances in which they are involved, close enough to be able to glimpse both the idiosyncratic and the shared preoccupations, values and interpretations of the 'insider'. And we can work towards this by always being alert to the danger of substituting our (observer) versions and interpretations of what we see happening for those accounts and evaluations held and acted upon by those (insiders) who are making it happen.

Second, we have to face up to the fact that doing research is itself a social act. Real, live people are both the subjects and the doers of investigations of human behaviour, and the doers, the researchers, bring to their investigations their own views, hopes and fears. They carry out their studies at particular moments in history, in particular material circumstances, and they cannot suddenly switch off their personal predilections and purposes and stop being human in the name of 'objective' research. To imagine, therefore, that a first priority in starting out on a piece of social research is for the researcher to confront the problem of whether she or he has an 'objective' approach and technique or one based on values on commitment and personal motives, is a rather pointless concern. For such a dilemma to exist, observes Becker (1970):

> one would have to assume, as some apparently do, that it is indeed possible to do research that is uncontaminated by personal and political sympathies.

And he continues by arguing that:

> the question is not whether we should take sides, since we inevitably will, but rather whose side are we on?

For educational research, this question from Becker seems particularly pertinent. Educating is never a neutral nor a mechanical activity, in which all that matters is that we establish the right inputs, press the right buttons and check the end-product. If it were, doing educational research would be no more difficult than driving a car. Rather, as has been clearly demonstrated in the earlier chapters of this book, what makes educating both exciting and frustrating is the infinite number of choices and decisions we keep on having to make about matters like the needs of pupils, our motives in assessing work, on the use of time and space and words in schools, about teaching materials, methods and so on. And each of our decisions, each of the strategies we choose to implement our plans, reflects our interests-in-hand, our different beliefs about what we hope to achieve, our different ideas about ways of getting there and our different fears of possible, unintended outcomes of our actions. And there is certainly no universal consensus about the goals, methods or pitfalls of educating. In teaching and in learning, we take a stance. But neither do we come 'uncontaminated' to the study, the analysis, of educational processes. Wanting to find out what's going on in schools and classrooms might be inspired by a desire to make life with 2A manageable or by a worry about the effects on education of certain government policies or by a dream of academic or professional fame and fortune – but it is never without purpose. Further, whatever obvious or hidden motives a researcher might have, she or he brings to the research a biography, a history, a set of sympathies which provides her or him with the means of making some sense of the affairs under scrutiny, with ideas about lines of investigation and with the basis for interpreting what's going on.

Educational research, then, involves two kinds of subjectivity: the subjectivity of the 'insiders', the people producing educational events, and the subjectivity of the observer, the researcher. With this in mind, let us return to Becker's question of whose side we are on. This is made doubly difficult. How can we get to know which 'side' those we are studying are on and and, at the same time, reveal to ourselves the ways in which our 'personal and political sympathies' permeate our studies? We would like to suggest that one way forward is to reduce Becker's large question into three smaller ones, and to use these to interrogate each episode of our research activities. The three, interrelated, questions we suggest are these:

- By whom is the research being done?
- For whom is the research being done?
- For what purpose is the research being done?

Obviously, this list is not exhaustive. Probably, you will want to propose alternative versions. In what follows, however, we will use these questions to discuss ways of dealing with subjectivity in different stages of the educational research process. One note of caution. Most investigations of schools and classrooms do not follow the 'tidy' plan we use to explore the difficulties of doing educational research. As Pollard (1985) admits, the process involves difficulties, uncertainties and setbacks and is, itself, a learning experience, not easily contained in neat, preplanned stages and sequences.

STARTING OUT

The typical image of the educational researcher is very like the 'spy' character with which we began the discussion in this part on sociological perspectives – an outsider looking in, motivated by concerns which are different from those on whom she or he is spying, and often remote or coldly detached from the everyday struggles, ambitions and troubles of those in the schools and classrooms being investigated. To a large extent this image, often quite a reasonable portrayal, has gained sway because of the patterns employed by educational researchers in 'getting started' on research, or, to put it more formally, because of the traditions established in the formulation and selection of research problems. The history of sociological research in education is littered with projects in which the 'issue' which gave energy and purpose to the research has been determined and defined by individuals one step or more removed from the world of those who were making schooling happen and with scant attention to how the researcher's version of educational 'problems' might relate to the practical concerns of teachers and pupils. It has been frequently taken for granted that teachers must share a concern that researchers had with constructing theories about the impact of culture, family life, mobility norms, childrearing practices and the like on educational performance and achievement. Or it has been frequently assumed that teachers will recognize the value of empirical investigations and explanations of how knowledge is defined in the education system, or of the organization of schools and learning situations. As a result, the levels of problems given priority in research projects have:

1. Often been derived from the major concerns facing policy-makers and planners rather than teachers.
2. Often been associated with a view of educational 'troubles' which emphasized a supposed failure in the schooling system, or an inefficiency or inadequacy on the part of individuals and groups working within schools.
3. Often been selected because they seemed to provide an opportunity to further a general

interest about education, widespread in sociological circles, which rested on the desire to promote greater justice through piecemeal social engineering and school reform.

Now, any one of the above motivations might be defended as wholly laudable, with general appeal to teachers. The point is that to exclude educational practitioners – teachers, students, pupils, administrators – from the process in which research problems are selected and formulated almost inevitably produces a chain of consequences which either distort the research or make researching futile. First, this kind of exclusion is either based on or lends support to the view that analysis and practice (or researching and teaching) are distinct, separate activities, requiring different skills and techniques and involving different perceptions of the schools and classrooms in which they take place. Analysis is concerned with theory; practice is to do with action. Since teachers do not have the time, the opportunity or (presumably) the skills to pursue research, it follows that 'theory' is something created by educationalists and researchers. Once this absurd division of educational labour is given currency, the path which leads initially to mutual disregard between teachers and researchers and eventually to mutual distrust becomes dangerously seductive. Using Lampert's (1984) observations, we can trace the kind of outcomes likely when the separation between research and teaching is established at the very beginning of an analytical project. The following set of assumptions would seem to pertain:

1. Theory is that which is created by professional academics and researchers.
2. Teachers, therefore, need to use the language of theorists both to define problems and to understand solutions.
3. Teachers think, but they do not think critically.
4. Teachers think, but it is low-level thinking.
5. Teachers undertake personal inquiries within their classrooms but these do not constitute proper research.

What makes this particular set of assumptions objectionable is not just that they are wrong, but also the damage caused by those who, in writing educational reports and critiques, operate as if they were true. What makes them wrong and what makes them dangerous?

To start out on research with a belief that teachers can't, don't or won't theorize about their work, their experiences and their achievements is to adopt a very strange view indeed of what teaching entails – suggestive of teaching being a series of robotic acts involving the application of unproblematic rules and procedures and the simple implementation of clearly defined and agreed strategies and principles. Ah, were it so easy! In fact, teaching is just the opposite – problematic, full of uncertainty and challenging teachers to draw on their own resources to cope as best they can with the steady flow of decisions and interpretations they are required to make and to act upon. Andy Hargreaves (1978) gives some idea of the significance of teachers' interpretative work, of their decision-making involvement, in his description of just one of their interactive roles, as 'processors of the curriculum':

> Teachers are the immediate processors of the curriculum for the child. They are the evaluators of pupils' academic work and the assessors of their overall ability. Teachers are the immediate adjudicators of children's moral worth and the direct arbiters of the appropriateness of their everyday behaviour. It is teachers most immediately and perhaps most significantly who therefore create, transmit and attempt to impose definitions of children as successes or failures, ideal pupils or deviants.

Daily, teachers operate in a variety of situations in which there exist no preprogrammed 'answers' to their concerns, but rather, where they have to decide upon their own individual aims and purposes, where they have to check out the situation and select an approach from the many available, and where they have to put that 'approach' to work and evaluate the results in terms of their original aims. They also have to live with the consequences of their deliberations and their decisions. In effect, teaching demands that teachers routinely engage in effective research; isolating problems, following up hunches on ways of coping with these problems and sifting the evidence to assess the validity of their particular hunches or theories. True, these research moments are fleeting and often expressed in terms like 'Does it work or solve the immediate pragmatic interests?', but that doesn't mean that they are either lacking a critical edge or are necessarily low-level.

But the dangers of the separation between researchers and teachers which arises where, to use the distinction suggested by Young (1971), researchers 'take' educators' problems and 're-make' them to suit their own research purposes, is that students and teachers gradually become more and more suspicious and uneasy about the alleged connection between what researchers say and do and the realities of school life. Educational theory comes to be regarded as being too remote from schools and classrooms. Researchers come to be seen as exploiting schools, with little, if any, return for the teacher. And, as Burgess (1980) warns, the language in which theory and research literature is couched comes to be seen, at best, as threatening and, at worst, as incomprehensible. Bolster (1985) offers the following possible explanation of why it is that research on education and teaching has had so little influence on practice or is viewed with suspicion by teachers:

> The major reason, in my opinion, is that most such research, especially that emanating from top-ranked schools of education, construes teaching from a theoretical perspective that is incompatible with the perspective teachers must employ in thinking about their work. In other words, researchers and school teachers adopt radically different sets of assumptions about how to conceptualize the teaching process. As a result, the conclusions of much formal research on teaching appear irrelevant to classroom teachers – not necessarily wrong, just not very sensible or useful. If researchers are to generate knowledge that is likely to affect classroom practice, they must contrive their inquiries in ways that are much more compatible with teachers' perspectives.

So, is there an approach to educational research which would enable us to make a constructive response to the problems we have sketched so far in this chapter and, maybe, overcome some of the more vexatious issues? Reviewing the discussion so far, we would suggest that such an approach would have to satisfy the following requirements:

1. It would have to recognize the impact of subjectivity on the process of educating and on the study of those processes; ideally, it would be sensitive to the belief succinctly stated by Shotter (1982) that 'there is a sense of knowing something from the "inside" which is quite different from that knowledge we may have of things from the outside'.
2. It would have to provide an opportunity for 'outsiders' and insiders to get into purposeful dialogue and shared enterprises to do with the design of research concerns, analytical processes and the building of explanations and theories.
3. It would have to allow for the identification and articulation of the kinds of personal commitment, the 'sides', which those doing research are acting upon.
4. It would have to be used as a basis for implementing new practices or for starting fresh inquiries.

We believe that such an approach does exist. Indeed, it is an approach which developed as a direct attempt to confront the kinds of issues we have been discussing. It is variously called 'classroom-based research', 'the teacher-researcher movement', 'teacher-based research' or, more frequently, *action research*, and draws inspiration from the pioneering work of the late Lawrence Stenhouse. Starting with the assumption that teachers are already 'problem-solvers', 'inquirers' and 'self-evaluating professionals', the approach of action research is to extend and activate the idea that teachers' theorizing about their practices can be enhanced by research methodology and can contribute to the creation of theory that focuses on school and classroom interaction and can be used to interrogate larger theories and ideas about the workings of educational systems or public policy. Research techniques merge, but the essential emphasis in action research is based on a relationship between classroom teachers, students, teacher-educators and social science research which is best described as a collaboration. Look at the definitions of action research below and try to determine your own answers to the questions of by whom research is being done, for whom and to what purpose, questions which are implicit in the statements, quoted in Hopkins (1985):

> Action Research ... is about the systematic study of attempts to improve educational practice by groups of participants by means of their own practical actions and by means of their own reflection upon the effects of those actions.
>
> Ebbutt (1983)

> Action Research is a form of self-reflective enquiry undertaken by participants in social (including educational) situations in order to improve the rationality and justice of:
>   (a) their own social or educational practices,
>   (b) their understanding of these practices and
>   (c) the situations in which the practices are carried out.

It is most rationally empowering when undertaken by participants collaboratively, though it is often undertaken by individuals, and sometimes in cooperation with outsiders.

Kemmis (1983)

RESEARCH IN ACTION: ACTION IN RESEARCH

If you have sorted out the basic aims of action research, you are now probably asking what it looks like in practice and how it is done. Participants in action research generally start with (often loosely defined) worries, irritations or puzzles about their classroom experience which they want to understand and change, or with ideas about new teaching methods or materials that they or the group to which they affiliate want to try out. Sometimes hypotheses are formed about the nature of the 'problem' or about strategies suitable to solve whatever dilemma is being acted upon.

Then the action-and-research twin initiative begins. The participants begin to implement their action programmes, and as they do so they begin to reflect on and explore the 'theories' they hold about themselves, the material, the pupils, the situation, the school, learning, pupil responses – whatever elements seem pertinent to the action 'problem' being worked through. 'Theories' to explain the progress of a project are generated, checked-out, worked into the project, and so on – the end in view being the generation of practical, usable theories rather than the testing or application of existing theories.

But how, you might ask, are data collected from which working theories are generated and in what ways are theories checked, tested or scrutinized? How is the 'research' bit done? Action research, while systematic and thoughtful, tends to be essentially pragmatic in the selection of research recipes or data collection and evaluation techniques adopted. A rule of thumb would be, if it helps you to understand your situation and further your action components, then use it, albeit critically and reflectively. For example, Rob Walker (1985) lists the following as techniques used in the Ford Teaching Project, a programme mounted by teachers and researchers wanting to explore their experience and problems of what the teachers described as 'inquiry' and 'discovery' approaches to teaching and learning. It is worth reading the full discussion Walker provides of the advantages and disadvantages of the various research techniques used, which he lists as:

Summary of Classroom Research techniques

Method	*Administration and equipment*
1. Questionnaire	Outsider–teacher/question sheet
2. Questionnaire	Teacher–child/question sheet
3. Questionnaire	Outsider–child/question sheet
4. Observation	Teacher–self
5. Observation	Outsider–teacher/tape-recorder, notebook, camera, documents or whatever the observer requires

6. Observation	Outsider–child/tape-recorder, activity list, inventory
7. Tape-recorder	Teacher/cassette-recorder
8. Tape-recorder	Outsider/cassette-recorder
9. Slides	Teacher/camera and accessories
10. Video TV	Cameraman? Expensive equipment
11. Question analysis	Teacher–child? Question analysis sheet
12. Field notes	Teacher/notebook
13. Standard assessment tests	Teacher–child/tests
14. Interview	Teacher–child
15. Interview	Outsider–teacher
16. Interview	Outsider–child
17. Case study	Teacher/any methods available to the teacher

Clearly, each technique, like any research tool, needs to be sharpened, assessed and evaluated – in action research a key element is the purchase the method gives to the action element in the enterprise – and the use of a multiplicity of techniques will yield vast quantities of data. But teachers and researchers who participate in this kind of educational enterprise are encouraged to generate their own categories for handling data and to attempt the techniques of TRIANGULATION, of contrasting the 'messages' found in data collected through different methods or from different participants or as seen by different analysts. Perhaps the best way in which we can introduce the distinctive features of action research is to ask you to consider how it compares with other ways of involving teachers in research and of developing methods of inquiry about life in schools and classrooms. To do this, we ask you to contrast the lines of action suggested in the model (Figure 22.1), designed by Ebbutt (1982) and reproduced in Walker (1985).

It seems to us that action research offers attractive and promising opportunities for both teachers and researchers. But what do you think? And why?

Further Reading

As we have only sketched the bare characteristics of action research, you might like to consult the following two excellent texts in which both techniques and commitments are discussed, and which offer many illustrations.

Hopkins, D. (1985) *A Teacher's Guide to Classroom Research*. Milton Keynes: Open University Press.
Walker, R. (1985) *Doing Research: A Handbook for Teachers*. London: Methuen.

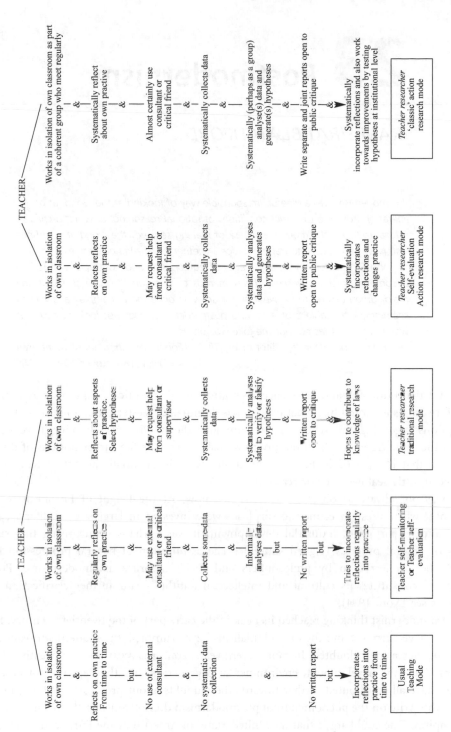

Figure 22.1 Classification of a range of insider activity currently occurring in UK schools

23 Postmodernism

IRAM SIRAJ-BLATCHFORD

Postmodernism was a gleeful, irresponsible way of looking at the world, at best a liberation from the too-strict conditions of rational reasoning, at worst a childish refusal to tackle the momentous task of making sense of the world. It could not last. Now we are used to fragmentation; whether it is the various bodies that used to form British Rail, the many pieces of equipment (and contracts) needed to become a 'portfolio worker', the numerous cultures on the high street of any major urban centre. Now, we look for answers once more: complex answers to seemingly intractable problems; and postmodernism does not look so clever. It was fun while it lasted, but the joke was on us.

Peter Aspen (Deputy Editor of the *Times Higher Education Supplement* until 1994), *THES*, 18 October 1996, p. VIII

The idea that humanity and its science, its culture and its political economy moves inexorably forward as a natural historical process has dominated Western thinking for centuries. Assumptions regarding the school curriculum and the quality of schooling have often followed the same trend. Yet 'natural' progress, just as much as the earlier notions of divine providence that it replaced in Europe, constitutes what is essentially an act of faith. It is grounded in little real evidence or reason.

This was not always as obvious as it may be now. At the height of European world dominance, when Western economic surpluses were invested in large-scale military, agricultural and in particular, industrial development, it was perhaps unsurprising that such notions of natural progress reigned supreme. The assumption of natural progression has generally been referred to by philosophers and social theorists as 'modernism'. 'Postmodernism' constitutes its cultural and intellectual antithesis (for further clarification on definitions see Lyon, 1994).

Western modernist thinking reached its peak in the early part of the twentieth century. But as empires have been lost and the old colonialisms have crumbled, the modernist dream has come to be increasingly doubted. In more recent years, concerns regarding the negative side-effects of economic development, environmental degradation and the depletion of natural resources have all contributed further towards these doubts about progress. However, many authors who write on the phenomenon of postmodernism do not consider the realities of the 'new' empires. One could argue that the United States of America or the European Union, in their domination of world markets, have simply instituted new (more subtle) forms of economic imperialism.

The social sciences, just as much as any of the so-called 'hard' sciences (e.g. physics, chemistry), were grounded on the modernist assumption of an ever developing tree of knowledge, securely rooted in the ancient world and upon a set of 'objective' empirical observations. These roots of knowledge thus provided foundations for a great tree that was seen as branching out ever further to provide in future centuries insights and discoveries beyond our wildest dreams. Yet increasingly, the very possibility of making objective observations has been questioned. Philosophers of science have increasingly become aware that it is extremely difficult to make judgements between alternative scientific explanations and different paradigms or world-views. At the same time, we have seen an ever more confident critique of empiricism and the introduction of more relativist approaches and uncertainty in the arts, humanities and cultural studies.

All this has had little effect upon the day-to-day work or procedures of many professional scientists and researchers in industry or in university laboratories. But an increasing number of social scientists are now aware that empirical quantification has served to hide the sexist, racist and social elitist assumptions that provided the foundations of many research problematics. While feminist, African-American and 'Third World' (Majority World) critiques of established science may have sometimes come close to adopting the very orthodoxies they have opposed, the postmodern turn in the social sciences (if that is not a contradiction in itself) is now becoming increasingly popular.

WHAT DOES IT MEAN TO REJECT FOUNDATIONALISM AND EMBRACE RELATIVITY?

When we question the legitimacy of those empirical observations that provide the foundations of a form of knowledge then we are also bringing into question all of the reasoning that has been drawn from them. Yet in doubting the power of reason we must accept that all claims to truth may ultimately be discredited. More seriously perhaps, if reason itself is to be questioned then our ethics and morality may have no grounding. Although this is accepted by many postmodern social/cultural commentators, they reject the notion of progressive knowledge production entirely. In its place they posit discursive engagement, critique and interpretation. Unfortunately, while we might well be willing to reject the role of contributing to some questionable notion of natural progress, a sociologist who accepts the role of postmodernist is, in effect, denying the sociological enterprise itself. And, as we noted in Chapter 1, C. Wright Mills (1959) identified the implications of this very clearly when he wrote:

> Freedom is first of all the chance to formulate the available choices. To argue over them – and then the opportunity to choose. That is why freedom cannot exist without an enlarged role of human reason in human affairs.

While we may wish to reject the idea of natural progress, as sociologists we would find it difficult to reject the need for 'progress' away from poverty, ignorance and suffering. If there is no basis for knowledge construction then there is no basis for social action at all. We will be left with a cult or a culture of individualism. If the traditional notion of shared knowledge is rejected and we are left with nothing more than 'networks of language games', as some commentators suggest, then there can be no social science.

For many postmodernists the changes that we have been seeing in society in recent years are related closely to the growth of consumerism and *post-industrialism*. Bauman (1991), for example, argues that what Western countries are experiencing is actually the development of new forms of society where the place of work in the capitalist system is now being replaced by consumption as an organizing principle. The market is still central but the emphasis is now upon consumer freedom and not the 'labour market'. Seduction, as Bourdieu has put it, has taken over from coercion as the dominant means of social control.

According to Bauman we can no longer attempt to 'correct' the views of others, we can only represent their views in a critical commentary. Before we return to this question of whether or not a postmodern social science is possible let us see what a postmodern education system might look like.

POSTMODERN SCHOOLING?

Taken to its extreme, in a postmodern school all the current bases for defining ability could be considered arbitrary: there would be no examinations, tests or league tables. No particular choice of curriculum could be demonstrated to be superior to any other, so the pupils, acting as educational consumers, would select whatever lessons they chose.

Mass communications and information technology would provide a means by which the 'child as consumer' might be prioritized over the 'child as worker'. Just as shopping is now being transformed from a domestic chore to a leisure pursuit, we could expect education to involve children in the free selection of 'hands on' exhibitions, interactive museums and multimedia products from around the world. Knowledge would be reduced to 'sound bytes', and only the 'big ideas' would be prioritized.

Given the effects of modularization, this process may already be advanced in some higher education institutions, although it has contradictory tendencies, as Pat Ainley (1994) puts it in his book *Degrees of Difference*:

> Crude reductionism, which imports language and explanations from one level and subject of study, to apply across all levels of explanation, is but the obverse of simple relativism, which abandons any attempt at causal connection or even integration between levels and subjects of study. Examples of reductive thinking that have recently originated in higher education are monetarism in economics and geneticism, which has migrated from biology to socio-biology and psychology. Relativistic nihilism has also reasserted itself in the 'anti-essentialist' fashion for facile intellectual deconstruction, which categorises any attempt at totalising

reconstruction as 'totalitarian'. This approach is now so ubiquitous as almost to present itself as the new orthodoxy in the social sciences. Both reductionism and nihilistic approaches are likely to be accentuated by the dismantling of discrete disciplines into under-resourced, unsupported and isolated modules of study.

Ainley, 1994, p. 184

What Ainley is suggesting here is that the postmodern intellectual euphoria of 'anything goes' is bringing us to a point where marginal (or even antisocial) ideas may be promoted (and taught) without challenge as long as students/readers have chosen them. Postmodernism and information technology may ultimately make schools and other forms of institutionalized education redundant. Yet postmodernism is actually anti-educational, it threatens the very basis of education, it threatens its founding assumption that there is actually worthwhile knowledge to be transmitted and reproduced. Postmodernism provides perhaps the ultimate in deschooling rationales. Many organizations in the UK and USA are already hard at work developing new learning systems. One such organization in the USA, TRANET International, wrote in its 1996 annual report:

> Thinkers in every walk of life are recognizing that our current form of governance threatens ecological, political, social, and economic failure . . . Management guru Peter Drucker says in his *Post Capitalist Society* 'there is a need to restore community.' He sees a new community-centred society . . . in which schools are replaced by an open life-long learning system which any person can enter, at any level, any time . . .
>
> The 'Learning Community' theme is echoed by holistic educators who now recognize that 'child-centred education', much as it is needed for the flexibility inherent in the age ahead, is inconsistent with 'schooling'. 'Teaching' or 'schooling' implies that society or someone is acting on, inductrinating some amorphous blobs. 'Learning', on the other hand, implies a self-actualized process of creating skills, taking in knowledge, and satisfying one's natural curiosity . . . Learning, like politics, must be reinvented.
>
> The vision of a 'World Without Schools' is being developed by organizations such as the Educational Futures Project. Schools fade into the background as the community as a whole becomes a network of learning centres; and the people themselves take control of their own and their family's whole-life learning. Museums, libraries, churches, businesses, YMCSs and a growing set of other learning centres (mental fitness centres not unlike today's physical fitness centres) provide all citizens with the knowledge they need for their own right livelihood . . . 'mentors' (whom we now call 'teachers') provide a personal consulting and advisory service to people of all ages. They keep detailed databases on learning opportunities throughout the region and by counselling and guidance help each family and individual reach self-set goals for gaining knowledge.

As Bob Carter (1993) has suggested, schools have already proven to be no more immune from the development of postmodernism than any other institution. In England and Wales examination results are now published in league tables to allow parents (as the consumers) the 'freedom' to play the market in pursuit of educational advantages. Schools are also being encouraged to provide centres of excellence in different curriculum areas and thereby increase choice and variety. In Part Six we will look more closely at some of the alternatives that will be open to us in the new millennium.

THE TYRANNY OF THE 'HISTORICAL META-NARRATIVES'?

In many ways postmodernism may be seen as a reaction against the assumed certainties of the past. For many, the collapse of the Berlin Wall provided a graphic illustration of the collapse of communism as a 'grand narrative' in the former USSR. Marxism attempted to make some kind of overall sense of history. For many sociologists, Marxism and the history of class struggle provided analytical foundations for their thinking and action. But in recent years the feminist critique of patriarchy in particular has been applied to this and every other 'grand narrative' to administer it a crushing blow. Even among non-Marxists, Marxism was of central importance to critical social thought, and this may no longer be the case. As Giddens *et al.* (1994) suggest:

> Ideals of socialism still persist and there are many who would wish to claim that socialist thought should continue to be defended today. Others, however, have abandoned Marx's idea of a 'union of theory and practice' altogether, or have come to recast critical theory in quite a different light from previous generations. We cannot say at the moment what is likely to emerge from a situation of some intellectual turmoil; but if new forms of critical practice emerge, they will certainly have to incorporate the issues raised by feminism, ecological movements and other groups that have stamped their mark on current debates.

For Giddens (1990) and for Habermas (1987), modernity remains an unfinished project. For both of these theorists all the above phenomena that have associated with postmodernity simply constitute the features of an advanced form of capitalism. A similar position is taken by Reeves (1995), who also refers to the resultant terminological problems:

> A variety of terms for the changes occurring to contemporary society is available: modern, post-modern, advanced, post-industrial, post-Fordist, service, leisure, information or knowledge societies. Their appropriateness depends on the features emphasised, the systems or institutions affected, and the perceived severity of the break with the past.

Postmodernism has been particularly attractive to many feminists because it has rejected the truth claims and scientific authority of an intellectual world that has been dominated by men. To embrace postmodernism has been to embrace pluralism, to declare a tolerance for different voices and to provide a platform for those previously silenced. Yet postmodernism is a two-edged sword that can just as easily deny the foundational grounding of feminist social theory. The organization of resistance and opposition to social dominance has previously been based upon common assumptions, principles, knowledge. So what is the alternative?

THE APPLICATION OF POSTMODERNISM IN EDUCATIONAL RESEARCH

To be truly objective is, according to Bauman (1991), to place reason in a transcendental, out-worldly region that towers above the daily human bustle at a height at which it cannot be reached, or glimpsed or tarnished, from the lowly world of common daily experience:

> Only the few, capable of the formidable effort of transcendental reduction (an experience not unlike the shaman's trances, or forty days of desert meditation), can travel to those esoteric places where truth comes into view.

It is now widely recognized that this kind of intellectual gymnastic is impossible, that metaphysics have no place in social theorizing. Bauman (1991) argues that this does not mean that we must abandon systematic social reflection and moral standards. An alternative argument based on a reading of Habermas and Gramsci, considering the notion of the 'organic intellectual', may be found in Siraj-Blatchford (1995). It is suggested that the postmodern critique has been helpful in questioning many of the dominant assumptions of our time. Our claims must from now on be more modest but they should still demonstrate rigour. More importantly, postmodernity itself should be questioned, along with its claims to freedom of choice and democracy. In particular, postmodernity should be questioned from the perspective of those who remain without choices or democratic freedoms – from the perspective of the unemployed, of single parent families, of the disenfranchised minorities and majorities both within Western societies and outside in the wider (so-called) Third World.

POSTMODERNISM AND THE KALEIDOSCOPE OF IDENTITY

One of the most valuable products of the recent debates on postmodernity has been a growing recognition of the importance of ethnic, gender, class and sexuality identity in social theory. The notion is not, on its own, a new one, of course: identity was recognized as an important concept for bilingual and ethnic minority children in the Swann Report (DES, 1985), a report on the achievement of ethnic minority children in the British education system:

> membership of a particular ethnic group is one of the most important aspects of an indi-vidual's identity – in how he or she perceives him or herself and in how he or she is perceived by others.

But this statement is not elaborated further, or analysed, in the whole body of that report. Most significantly, there is no recognition of the fact that the child may be classed, gendered or racialized in more than one way. Yet Stuart Hall (1992), for example, discusses not only the discourses of identity but also those of 'difference' within ethnic groups. As Hall argues, in the very act of identifying ourselves as one thing, we are simultaneously distancing ourselves from something else. In terms of 'race' and ethnicity, Hall argues that there are contradictions within these categories as well as between these and other categories, such as sexuality, class and disability.

The way we perceive identities is very much shaped by how they are produced and taken up through the practices of representation (Grossberg, 1994). In Chapter 5 we discussed the means by which the media represent inequality and difference. Many other forms of representation are referred to throughout the book. Groups of students are often differentially represented in educational resources and guidance materials, in school publications and displays and in conversations between teachers, parents and governors.

Individuals are often 'essentialized' as members of particular groups; their identity is 'reduced' to some limited category or 'essence'. Making use of the metaphor of a kaleidoscope in understanding identity based on a range of inequalities, Bailey and Hall (1992) argue that there will be differences within any identity-forming category, such as 'race'. As they put it, 'black signifies a range of experiences, the act of representation becomes not just about decentering the subject but actually exploring the kaleidoscopic conditions of blackness'. Grossberg (1994) argues that this notion of the 'kaleidoscopic conditions of blackness' (and presumably gender and class) is related to a 'distributive map of the social terrain' where difference is (re)created depending on how and where one is situated.

It is important to highlight the complexity of identity formation in children. To ignore it is to ignore the child's individuality. The notion of the 'kaleidoscope' explains why each ethnic minority child and every girl or disabled child does not perceive himself or herself in the same way. In fact it explains why children from different structurally disadvantaged groups often hold contradictory positions, which is why we might find in our classrooms black and other ethnic minority children who are very confident and academically successful despite the structural, cultural and interpersonal racism that we find in society. Similarly, we will find working-class boys who are caring and unaggressive and African Caribbean boys who are academically capable and well behaved. We should not be surprised at any of this. The sexism, racism and other inequalities in society explain why at a structural level certain 'groups' of people have less power while others have more. But at the level of interpersonal agency we should beware of the stereotypes and focus on individual people. This is not to suggest that we should ignore structure; far from it, we need to engage in developing the awareness of children and staff in schools through policies and practices which explain and counter group inequalities. Educators need to work from a number of standpoints to empower fully the children in their care, and children need to be educated to deal confidently and fairly with each other and with others in an unjust society (Siraj-Blatchford, 1994).

REFLEXIVITY

In Chapter 20, references were made to the relativity of knowledge and the subjectivity of meaning inherent to the action perspective, and also to the implication that sociologists could claim no privileged status for their interpretations and understandings. As Barton and Walker suggest, even if one accepts that it is important to suspend one's own presuppositions, one must still accept that one needs to ground one's definitions on some kind of base or foundations: otherwise it would be impossible to know anything. 'Reflexivity' refers to the process by which the observations that we make are dependent upon these foundational ideas – the process by which the observations we make 'refer back' to them. It is a concept of central importance to philosophical, social-scientific and psychological constructivism.

Arguably the two most extreme responses to reflexivity in the social sciences have been deconstruction, a post-structuralist technique associated with Jacques Derrida, and cultural studies on the one hand and ethnomethodology (see Chapter 20) on the other. Post-structuralism may be considered the linguistic variant of postmodernism, and deconstructionists try to overcome reflexivity by writing texts that ultimately deny meaning entirely. Ethnomethodologists, by contrast, aim to achieve the opposite, trying to reduce the effects of reflexivity by interrogating their respondents and by including literally everything in their accounts. As a methodological response to reflexivity, symbolic interactionalism might be considered to occupy the mid-point between these two extremes. While ethnomethodological accounts restrict their concern to the actors' 'point of view', symbolic interactionism has tended to relate this view to the wider contexts of society, social research and explanation. It has confronted the challenge of reflexivity directly; it has also built around the conception of an essential reciprocity between the socially determined and social determining 'self'. Symbolic interactionists have rejected the idea that the actions of individuals and groups are in any way passively determined by psychological attributes such as drives, attitudes and personalities or simply by external structures such as class, race or gender.

For symbolic interactionists it has been the interactions between individuals that have provided the best explanation for their actions. Individuals have been seen as active in accepting, modifying and resisting the influence of others. As Cohen and Manion (1994) suggest, these models seem to 'fit' quite naturally with the kind of concentrated action found in classrooms and schools, environments where 'pupils and teachers ... [are] continually adjusting, reckoning, evaluating, bargaining, acting and changing' (Woods, 1979). And as Barton and Walker suggest, the difficulty of this research approach is that the structural effects of adult, class, 'race' and gender dominance could still be understated. Powerful social actors are able to impose their 'meanings' upon others. The realities of social structure and the inequalities of power that are a consequence of these structures must always be recognized. In this Willis's (1977) contribution has been especially important in its identification of resistance.

The challenge of reflexivity is undoubtably great, yet both Giddens and Habermas see possibilities for taking social science forward. In the meantime, as Reeves (1995) suggests:

Education is affected in a number of ways, for example, in the tendencious relationship between the formal school or college curriculum and popular culture, in the growing uncertainty over the legitimacy of official definitions of what constitutes knowledge, culture, and taste, and the means by which their acquisition might be assessed, and in the apparent failure of education as a whole to grasp the impact of the information revolution and its possibilities for empowering individual learners.

CONCLUSIONS

The rise in 'postmodernism' has drawn with it a wide recognition that the search for absolute foundations of truth in research is no longer tenable. The term 'postmodernity' or 'post-modern condition' refers to what is considered to be our new social order, perhaps most graphically illustrated by the collapse of the Berlin Wall and Eastern European and Soviet communism, but applicable to all forms of social action where the 'meta-narratives' of yesterday, such as Marxism, are being rejected wholesale in favour of consumption and a reliance on the consumer market. As Giddens (1991) asserts, postmodernists consider that they now live in societies where the nation state is in decline and the cohesive totality has been replaced by a multiplicity of sites of social reproduction, where 'Cultural pluralism is matched by structural pluralism: the post-modern order is split into a multitude of contexts of actions and forms of authority.'

Postmodernism has provided a critique of naive positivism and the recognition of a trend towards 'Big Brother' manipulation by the media. Giddens suggests that there are two possibilities. If we accept that such trends exist, we can adopt one of two courses. The first is to emphasize 'the end'; the death of the author; the disappearance of art; the end of history. The alternative is to start to talk about beginnings. He argues that it is no longer purely utopian to anticipate

> the possible emergence of a truly global order, a global cosmopolitanism in which recognition of pluralism goes along with, and is supported by, the endeavours of collective humanity.

As Lyon (1994, p. 62) suggests, heresy may also serve to encourage a reassertion of pre-modern faith. Martin Scorcese's *Last Temptation of Christ* and Salman Rushdie's *The Satanic Verses* have certainly demonstrated the continued vitality of religion, and not just the fundamentalist forms of it. And even if the postmodern condition continues to develop, do we have to embrace postmodernism? Can we still pursue social science or must we accept the more relativistic approaches of cultural studies? Some clues as to the author's answers to these questions may be found above, but it is too early to predict where these arguments will lead the sociology of schooling. We can only hope that the reader will take up the challenge to become actively involved in the debate.

Further Reading

Ainley, P. (1994) *Degrees of Difference: Higher Education in the 1990s*. London: Lawrence & Wishart.

Bailey, D. and Hall, S. (1992) 'Critical Decade: Black British Photography in the 80s', *Ten-8*, **2**, 3.

Bauman, Z. (1991) *Modernity and Ambivalence*. Cambridge: Polity Press.

Beck, U. (1989) *Risk Society; Towards a New Modernity*, London: Sage.

Carter, B. (1993) 'Losing the Common Touch: A Post-modern Politics of the Curriculum?', *Curriculum Studies*, **1**, 1.

Department of Education and Science (1985) *Education for All*, The Swann Report. London: HMSO.

Giddens, A. (1990) *The Consequences of Modernity*. Cambridge: Polity Press.

Giddens, A. (1991) *Modernity and Self-Identity: Self and Society in Late Modern Age*. Cambridge: Polity Press.

Giddens, A. et al. (1994) *The Polity Reader in Social Theory*. Cambridge: Polity Press.

Giroux, H. and McLaren, P. (eds) (1994) *Between Borders: Pedagogy and the Politics of Cultural Studies*. New York: Routledge.

Grossberg, L. (1994) 'Introduction: Bringin' It All Back Home – Pedagogy and Cultural Studies', in H. Giroux and P. McLaren (eds), *Between Borders: Pedagogy and the Politics of Cultural Studies*. New York: Routledge, pp. 1–28.

Habermas, J. (1987) *The Philosophical Discourses of Modernity*. Cambridge, MA: MIT Press.

Hall, S. (1992) 'Race, Culture and Communications: Looking Backward and Forward in Cultural Studies', *Rethinking Marxism*, **5**, 10–18.

Lyon, D. (1994) *Postmodernity*. Buckingham: Open University Press.

Reeves, F. (1995) *The Modernity of Further Education*. London: Bilton College Publications and Education Now.

Sarup, M. (1996) *Identity, Culture and the Postmodern World*. Edinburgh: Edinburgh University Press.

Siraj-Blatchford, I. (1994) *The Early Years: Laying the Foundations for Racial Equality*. Stoke-on-Trent: Trentham Books.

Siraj-Blatchford, I. (1995) 'Critical Social Research and the Academy: The Role of Organic Intellectuals in Educational Research', *British Journal of Sociology of Education*.

Wright Mills, C. (1959) *The Sociological Imagination*. Oxford: Oxford University Press.

Signposts

1. Read Reeves, F. (1995) *The Modernity of Further Education*, London: Bilton College Publications and Education Now. Do the many changes in further education follow a discernible pattern of development? If so is this a positive process? Could we or should we do something to intervene?

2. Marxist critique of postmodernism

See: Kelly, J., Cole, M. and Hill, D. (1999) 'Resistance Postmodernism and the Ordeal of the Undecidable: a Marxist Critique', paper presented at the British Educational Research Association Annual Conference, University of Sussex at Brighton, 2–5 September. The text is in the Education-line Internet document collection at *http://www.leeds.ac.uk/educol/documents/00002211.htm*

24 The Discourses of Education

STEPHEN WALKER

> Every educational system is a political means of maintaining or of modifying the appropriation of discourse, with the knowledge and the powers it carries with it.
>
> Michel Foucault

INTRODUCTION

A widespread perspective in postmodernist social analysis is that of discursive texts. Giddens's notion of structuration is useful in discussing how language is used in the social interactions of schools and classrooms.

Putting it simply, Giddens proposes that the macro-sociological (social systems and structures) and the micro-sociological (the actions and interactions of social actors or agents) exist together in a complementary and contradictory relationship. So, social structures such as social norms or customs only come into existence when someone enacts them, and that act or set of actions is only possible because the person has a sense, a knowledge and an idea of what the norms and the culture expect. Structure and agency are different but you can't have one without the other. Of course, it is through language or discourse that the structuration process is carried out. It is through language and signs and the use of symbols that a person manages to interact with another; and it is through these discursive means that the person can think and recapture some consciousness of what the norms and the culture allow and disallow; and it is also through such discourse that a person learns and internalizes the prevailing norms and culture as he or she acquires knowledge, identity and a sense of how to behave, to communicate and to interact.

Discourses, then, are central to the formation of the individual in society and they provide the rules for the conduct and interactions of any individual in all social situations and encounters. Discourse enables social action and carries social structures.

WHAT EXACTLY DO WE MEAN BY 'DISCOURSE'?

Discourse analysis and the deconstruction of 'texts' (conversations, documents, signs, images, sounds – whatever serves as a medium of communication) is a fairly recent approach in post-modernist thinking and draws on the theoretical writings of linguistic philosophers such as Derrida (2003), Habermas (1996) and in educational investigations, Michel Foucault. It should not be confused with the kinds of discourse analysis we explore in Chapter 12 of this book, 'The Hidden Curriculum of Language', which concerns itself with charting the patterns of talk in any social context. Modern discourse analysis is concerned with trying to discover the 'deep' meanings carried in a text. The best explanation of this approach, as applied to processes of educating, comes from McDougall (2005). He explains it this way:

> Schooling and assessment are contingent cultural practices, producing forms of self, knowledge and legitimation. The classroom is a site of production, at once factory in this sense and also laboratory, as educational practice is always experimental, arising out of specific historical conjuncture. Teaching is informed by an eclectic range of influences, training, academic histories and institutional trends as well as externally contingent discourses.
>
> McDougall, 2005

Educating, then, in any form, happens in places where people come together and, through the discourses they use to make the meetings happen, produce and reproduce who they are, what they know and what are the accepted 'rules' for the social encounters. In doing so, they consciously or unconsciously refer to what they have learned before from 'others' or 'outsiders' about what is appropriate or inappropriate behaviour, relationships and purpose.

EDUCATIONAL DISCOURSE: THE READING OF A TEXT

Discourse simultaneously enables and constrains.

> We know very well that, in its distribution, in what it **permits** and what it **prevents**, it [education] follows the lines laid down by social differences, conflicts and struggles.
>
> M. Foucault, 1971 (bold added)

In this section, to illustrate the whole approach and how powerful it is, there is an exploration of the discourse and the educational edifice constructed through the Programme for International Student Assessment (PISA) (OECD); 'investigations' is presented as an example. Obviously, this text, this political artefact, is no different from other educational policy objects, being neither unique nor free-standing (Ball, 1990). The prevailing discourses it brings with it all use and abuse other discourses prevalent in wider policy contexts and across a broad spectrum of discursive practice in education.

Significantly, PISA is a regulatory device, an instrument to discipline and to order struggles around what is taken for granted as 'effective schooling' in relation to 'pupil performance', how all pupils should progress and what teachers should expect them to achieve. The authority, the legal standing and the moral certainty appropriated and revealed in this carefully crafted statute are all easily available. Below is a small fragment of the text which is about the measures used to evaluate and to co-relate national educational performances.

Box 24.1   PISA variables used in the analysis of the relative impact of policy-amenable school characteristics

1. Student characteristics (6)

Socio-economic status; gender; age; immigration status; grade level; type of study programme

2. School context (3)

School type; school location; school average socio-economic status

Policy-amenable school characteristics

School resources (8)

School size; index of the quality of a school's physical infrastructure; index of the quality of a school's educational resources; proportion of computers available to 15-year-olds; proportion of teachers with an ISCED 5A qualification in the language of assessment; index of teacher shortage; student:teaching staff ratio; professional development

School climate (8)

Index of disciplinary climate; index of teacher support; index of achievement press; index of teacher–student relations; index of students' sense of belonging in school; index of principals' perceptions of teacher-related factors affecting the school climate; index of principals' perceptions of teachers' morale and commitment

School policies (13)

Instructional time; index of monitoring of student progress; index of school self-evaluation; student's performance is considered for school admission; study programme for 15-year-olds is based on students' academic record; study programme for 15-year-olds is based on students' placement exams; transfer of low achievers to another school is likely; transfer of low achievers to another school is very likely; performance information is communicated to parents; performance information is communicated to school principal; performance information is communicated to local education authority; index of school autonomy; index of teacher autonomy

---

Notice two recurrent concepts which provide the foundations of the discourse as revealed in what is 'permitted' reference with respect to 'policy-amenable school characteristics' –

index and *performance*. In different ways, both concepts are simultaneously reductionist and normative. They 'reduce' the ways in which it is imagined we can evaluate how schools operate to numbers, to a score, to an index. They also make the (incorrect) assumption that there are some single, unambigous 'normal' standards or benchmarks. In fact, as Meighan argues passionately elsewhere is this book, the goals and the methods of educating and of schools are hotly contested. In this discourse, indices reduce human characteristics and endeavour to create simple, calculable benchmarks; and in statements of performance the value of social actions is reduced to comparison against a standard. Maybe this need not be a sociological problem – if the instrument outlined above is a simple tool to stimulate more divergent and creative analysis and research. Unfortunately, it is not. As the quotation from a speech by Prime Minister Blair illustrates, both the instrument itself (PISA) and the ideological devices carried in the discourse shape the ways in which public educational policies are rationalized, defended and evaluated:

> Science is just knowledge. And knowledge can be used by evil people for evil ends. Science doesn't replace moral judgement. It just extends the context of knowledge within which moral judgements are made. It allows us to do more, but it doesn't tell us whether doing more is right or wrong. We should not ignore our strengths in science education. The recent, highly respected OECD PISA study ranked British 15-year-olds fourth internationally for science literacy, well ahead of most of our competitors.
>
> Tony Blair's speech on scientific research to the Royal Society, 23 May 2002

It has been the case that performativity, competition and standardization have been inserted as the keystones of discourse across the whole field of educational planning and management by the state modernizers in their project to manipulate how we think, talk and act in educational zones. They provide grounding for publicly sponsored research; they provide a base for the governance of pedagogy; and they provide the foundation on which students' and teachers' roles and relationships are regulated.

The emphasis is upon performance, and the performance of education systems, schools, teachers and students is frequently expressed in terminology more usually associated with industrial production – output, quality control, accountability and human resource management. As the OECD suggests,

> The resources devoted to education are among the most important investments that countries and their people make. The OECD's work on education takes a lifelong learning perspective in its attempt to identify policies that will build human and social capital. Both are needed; physical capital alone cannot ensure either wealth or happiness.
>
> Modern knowledge economies require a highly skilled workforce, not just an elite, since economic growth is driven by a powerful interaction between increased human competence and the adoption of new technology. Individuals need high level skills as well since, without them, they are at great risk of exclusion.[1]

---

[1] OECD (2001), *The Well-Being of Nations*, Paris: OECD.

The discourse of performativity can be found in every aspect of current educational policy and evaluation. How children perform on tests of their academic potential is assessed as they enter schooling – benchmark assessment. How students perform in the mastery of the 'basic skills' is calculated through frequent progress checks, end-of-school examinations and international comparisons and competitions. How teachers perform is measured though appraisal as a contractual obligation, though external, standardized inspection regimes and through performance management operations which link teacher performance to pay and promotion. How schools perform is demonstrated in the publication of inspection reports in the UK, in different types of external evaluation elsewhere, and in performance league tables. How systems perform is revealed through the performativity research conducted by agencies like the OECD and international comparisons.

Performance discourse is about measurement. Performance discourse is about regulation. Performance discourse is also about shaping and disciplining subjective identities.

> Performativity is a technology, a culture and a mode of regulation, or a system of 'terror' in Lyotard's words that employs judgments, comparisons and displays as means of control, attrition and change. The performances (of individual subjects or organizations) serve as measures of productivity or output, or displays of 'quality', or 'moments' of promotion . . . or inspection. They stand for, encapsulate and represent the worth, quality or value of an individual within a field of judgment.
>
> Ball, 1999

The central place of 'performance' in discourses which define educational purpose, curricular framing and educational achievements can, in some ways, be explained by the capacity it has for conflating, in a single agenda, the two ideological platforms of state modernization projects – neo-liberalism and neo-conservatism. The first of these is a concern to release the efficacy of free-market operations and relationships to stimulate economic growth, work flexibility, consumption and competition and to 'roll back' the bureaucratic state. The second, neo-conservatism, focuses on a rolling-forward stronger state control and governance, especially in areas where the behaviour of citizens has to be held to account to protect the operations of market-regulated economies. In managing the contradiction between liberating enterprise and private investment, on the one hand, and in securing both a mandate for free-market reforms and in winning acceptance for the promotion of individualism over collective interests, on the other, 'performance' serves as a mechanism through which success of the economic project is demonstrated in incontestable, 'neutral' valuations and as a device which regulates in a similarly incontestable 'neutral' manner the competitions between individuals.

The significance of performativity discourse in education is the power it carries to govern both the subjective identities of teachers and students and the value of their actions. In the PISA index (see Box 24.1), we are given a code system that defines such complex, contested practices of schools as 'climate', 'sense of belonging' and 'autonomy' in norms provided by a mysterious agency outside the influence of students and teachers and which represents a measure, a standard, against which teachers and students are encouraged to police the relative success or failure of their own behaviours. Lawson and Harrison (1999) use Bentham's notion of the panopticon to reveal the regulatory power of a set of educational discourses, which brings together standards, performance, accountability and surveillance. The panopticon is a prison in which prisoners are separated from each other and believe that those in authority can observe them at any time. The pressure is, therefore, upon self-regulation. Teachers, under the potential gaze of politicians, managers, inspectors and parents (through control of their timetables, their assessment arrangements, their professional codes of practice and their performances against international standards in the classroom, the examination hall and in the whole school climate), are encouraged to align their professional values and evaluations with those of government. Furthermore, these are not usually those values of elected governments but of the shadowy figure of bodies like the OECD or of QUANGOs. 'Disciplinary power', argue Lawson and Harrison (1999), 'is thus concerned with the individual as both the object and the instrument of its exercise; the individual is the object because disciplinary power is aimed at the production of a certain subjectivity, and it is the instrument because disciplinary power operates as a system of self-surveillance, in which the individual "polices" his/her own actions.'

The discourse operating in education can be depicted as a set of interrelated 'disciplines'. How can we best understand the dynamics of the discourses represented above as semi-permeable codes or cells of social disciplines? How can we justify the central significance of the discourses about *standards* as the central locking structure? And how can we explain the social transformations through which these discourses gained such significance in political thought, in social policy and in social praxis? Both the neo-liberal and the neo-conservative transformative projects for the modernization of advanced capitalist economies and states depend upon the energies released through the application of market forces and market principles. In the 1970s, governments in the UK, the USA and in Europe put into place a series of 'reforms' to manage the ecomony and to manange how citizens in a society related to the state and to each other. Essentially, they introduced 'free-market capitalism' as the way of manging these affairs. There were two main strands to these policies. One was a reduction in the involvement of state governments in industry, social services and investment. The main thrust here, in concrete terms, was 'privatization', the selling of publicly provided operation to private groups or individuals, and this is oftern referred to as 'neo-conservatism'. The second was to put into place policies which encouraged people to take care of their own finances and arrangements for things like pensions, education, health care and security, and this is frequentually referred to as neo-liberalism. The dynamic of free-market capitalism is *competition*. In a globalized economy, both entrepreneurs and transnational corporations are in a permanent state of competition. The competitions are over the creation and appropriation of profit or, in Marxist terms, surplus value. They are, therefore, in competition over levels of investment, over energy, materials and labour costs, and in competition over sale prices in the distribution of commodities and services. The discourse of competition is both enabling and regulatory. The texts, which realize the discourse, abound with references to the key signifiers of value, cost efficiency, deregulation and privatization. In educational policy, the application

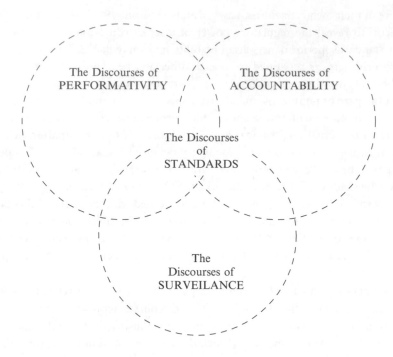

Figure 24.1

of market principles redefines schools, colleges and universities as quasi-markets, and institutions compete for funds, for lower costs of provision and for consumers (students).

Free markets, because of the vagaries of competition, require at least two kinds of regulation: the regulation of the production processes (to guarantee that goods and services are of the highest quality); and the protection of the rights and welfare of citizens and consumers in a deregulated market-economy. This requirement, in effect, generates the discourse of *performance or performativity*. The performativity discourse is saturated with textual references to thresholds, targets and normative, measurable criteria or indices. To ensure the acceptance and validity of the performance operations, this discourse cell itself generates a corresponding discourse of *accountability* – a discourse through which performance is audited and displayed, and in which the language and approach of financial accounting are applied to social processes. In turn, accountability requires a further discursive development, the discourse of surveillance, through which audits are both managed and legitimated – through such technologies as inspections, the public display of performance audits, and the central control of work methods and purposes.

The discourse of *standards* holds these three interconnected discourse cells together. Each cell is semi-permeable. So, in education for example, the discourse of accountability (school inspection and evaluation) is sometimes permeated by the discourse of performance (student examination scores). The three discourses rely upon 'standards' and construct them in the language of each cell. In reality, the discourse on standards is both empty and full. It is empty in the sense that we know that standards are not universal and can only be seen as defined through other discourses – performance standards, audit standards and surveillance standards. So 'standards' only exist in relation to the judgement call made about what counts as 'quality'. But the discourse around standards is full in that it provides the significance and validity of the other three cells.

Further Reading

Ball, S.J. (1999) 'Performativities and fabrications in the education economy; towards the performative society?', keynote address to the Australian Association of Research in Education, Annual Conference, Melbourne.

Blair, T. (2002) 23 May 2002, speech on scientific research to the Royal Society, London.

Derrida, J. (2003) *Structure, Sign, and Play in the Discourse of the Human Sciences*, trans. Alan Bass. London: Routledge.

Foucault, M. (1986) 'Kant on Enlightenment and Revolution', *Economy and Society*, 15, 88–96.

Habermas, J. (1996) *Between Facts and Norms. Contributions to a Discourse Theory of Law and Democracy*. London: Polity Press.

Jensen, K. (2004) 'Agency and structure in the systematic production and reproduction of alienation in industrialized service societies: The social conditions of public service'. Paper IIS 36th World Congress and RC36 Midterm Conference, Beijing, 7–11 July 2004, published in RC36 newsletter.

Jensen, K. and Walker, S. (2000) 'A contribution to the mapping of alienation: Alienation and how to get rid of it'. Paper RC36's Midterm Conference, Washington, July 2000, published in RC36 newsletter.

Jensen, K. and Walker, S. (2000) 'The Modernisation of Western European States And Its Implications For Public Sector Professionals. "Getting further out of Chaos".' Conference of ISA Research Committee, Sociology of Professional Groups, RC52, Lisbon, September 2000.

Lawson, T. and Harrison, J.K. (1999) 'Individual Action Planning in Initial Teacher Training: Empowerment or Discipline?,' *British Journal of Sociology and Education* 20, 1, 89–105.

McDougall, J. (2005) 'Subject Media: A Study in the Sociocultural Framing of Discourse', unpublished PhD thesis, University of Birmingham.

OECD (2001) *The Well-Being of Nations*. Paris. OECD.

Saussure, L. and Schulz, P. (2003) *Manipulation and Ideologies in the Twentieth Century: Discourse, Language, Mind*. University of Neuchâtel/University of Lugano.

Signposts

1. This chapter has introduced the reader to the ideas of discourse analysis and provided a glimpse of how it can be used to explore how educational texts work. It has demonstrated how discourse analysis can be used to reveal all kinds of ideas and ideologies which operate in and around educating. As a follow-up, why not try some of the following activities:

- Record a conversation between teachers and learners and try to describe what 'rules' they appear to be following to make their encounter happen.
- Take an educational text and by digging deep into how it is presented, the words and images and fonts used, the recurrent 'themes' included, try to uncover the underlying assumptions in the text.
- Hold a seminar on the positive and the negative features of 'standards in education'.

Stephen Gorard's *Education and Social Justice*, Cardiff: University of Wales Press, 2000, provides a useful statistical discussion of education and social diversity at the end of last century, arguing that social justice and equality in educational provision has improved in some ways, while remaining problematic in others.

2. The most up-to-date discussions on educational discourse are mostly on the internet. You can check: Discourse Analysis Online: *www.extra.shu.ac.uk/daol/resources/* or you can browse through the back and current editions of the journal *'Discourse', Studies in the Cultural Politics of Education*, published by Routledge.

Part Five
EDUCATIONAL LIFE CHANCES OR WHO GETS WHAT?

The concern of this part is to explore some of the regular patterns of the educational experience of people in the UK. These educational life chances are seen to be persistent, and there are competing explanations of them. The aspects selected are gender (since girls tend to receive different educational outcomes from boys), social class (since educational life chances tend to be persistently superior the higher the social class), ethnicity (since black and ethnic monority pupils tend to experience different patterns of education from white pupils) and finally the categorization known as special education. These are not the only regular patterns. One that is less well documented is that of region. The educational life chances of rural children tend to differ from those of urban children, and those of the pupils in the south-east tend to differ from those of pupils in the north-east. A contribution to an understanding of these patterns from the interactionist sociology is derived from labelling theory, and therefore this is the subject of the first chapter in this part.

25 Labelling Theory and Life Chances

STEPHEN WALKER

One of the commonest ailments of the present day is premature formation of opinion.

Frank McKinney Hubbard

INTRODUCTION

In Chapter 11, the expectations of teachers as a factor in the hidden curriculum of schooling were examined. The central proposition was stated as:

> pupils tend to perform as well, or as badly, as their teachers expect. The teacher's prediction of a pupil's or group of pupils' behaviour is held to be communicated to them, frequently in unintended ways, thus influencing the actual behaviour that follows.

It was argued that this was a matter of particular concern to educationalists where inferences about pupils were based on false diagnosis. There are several potential sources of false prediction, including expectations based on age, sex, ethnic identity, religion, name, physical appearance and social class 'indicators' such as speech and dress, which become established in the interpretive schemes of the participants. The outcome can be the establishment of a self-fulfilling prophecy, when the false diagnosis influences the self-concept of the learner, who then learns to behave as expected, thus 'verifying' the initial false diagnosis (see Chapter 11).

These concepts of expectations and self-fulfilling prophesies are derived from a larger theoretical perspective called labelling theory, which is a set of ideas related to the interactionist perspective (see Chapter 19). The purpose of this part of the book is to use labelling theory to explore the question of 'who gets what in education'. The assumption made here is that the life chances of individuals and groups vary according to certain regular features, and that the educational life chances vary in a similar way: e.g. the chance of a girl having a university education is much less than that of a boy; the chance of a working-class boy is less than that of a middle-class boy; the chance of a black, working-class girl is very low indeed; and so on. The concepts of life chances and educational life chances and the related patterns and evidence will be examined later in the chapter. At this point we shall attempt to establish the key features of labelling theory.

LABELLING THEORY

Labelling theory features in the work of Lemert (1951), Becker (1963) and Matza (1964), as well as other writers. It is mostly in the fields of criminology and the sociology of deviance that the theory has been developed. A basic proposition is that deviant behaviour has the characteristics of a transaction between the deviant person and another or others. (Another term for this theory is transactional theory.) Particular behaviour is deviant because it is defined as such by groups in society, particularly by those groups who have some power to establish that their definitions carry weight.

As an example, a headteacher suspended a 15-year-old schoolboy in a secondary school in England, in November 1978, for asking his friends if they wanted a copy of the National Union of School Students magazine, *Blot*. The boy was labelled as deviant by someone with the power to enforce his definition by using sanctions against the person defined as undesirable (Giddens, 1993, p. 755). The suspension might well have been reversed in Sweden, where headteachers are required to facilitate pupil organization in their schools. Failure to do so may result in the headteacher being defined as deviant and sanctioned accordingly!

Labelling theory raises some questions about the conclusions regarding deviance that are reached in structural functional approaches in sociology, where social control is seen as a reaction to deviant behaviour. An alternative proposition is mooted: that social control may create deviance.

> Older sociology . . . tended to rest heavily on the idea that deviance leads to social control. I have come to believe that the reverse idea, i.e. social control leads to deviance, is equally tenable.
>
> Lemert, 1972

Both sociological approaches – the interactionist, stressing labelling, and the structural functionalist, stressing the social control of rule breakers – run counter to those psychological approaches that propose individual causation because of biological factors. However, labelling theory, unlike the other approaches, calls for an examination of the labellers and their assumptions as much as an examination of the persons or groups being labelled.

Deviance Involves a Social Process

Deviance is seen as a social process with a series of stages, and the participants in this process are rule makers, rule enforcers and rule breakers. This approach entails a resistance to the idea of a single act of categorization that has permanent consequences encompassed in the idea of 'once a criminal, always a criminal'. Instead, there emerges the possibility that labelling may have varying effects at different stages in an individual's life, so that an individual may drift in and out of activities defined as deviant.

A Deviant Is One Who Has Been Successfully Labelled

Since deviance is not seen as something into which an individual has been inevitably pushed by biological or psychological factors, labelling theorists stress the consequences of the application of rules by others to the deviant. In the case of the schoolboy quoted above, he is only deviant because the headteacher in a particular culture successfully labels him so, by defining the distribution of NUSS magazines as deviance and then having the power to enforce that definition. A now famous quotation makes the point:

> Deviance is not a quality of the act the person commits, but rather a consequence of the application by others of rules and sanctions to an 'offender'. The deviant is one to whom the label has successfully been applied: deviant behaviour is behaviour that people so label.
>
> Becker, 1963

Labelling Activity Affects Those Labelled in Various Ways

An individual does not become labelled as a deviant simply by breaking a rule, or even several rules. Many people break rules, but only some are subsequently labelled. The social process that follows the breaking of a rule may involve individuals in negotiating, rejecting, accepting, reinterpreting or modifying. A key issue for Lemert (1972) is whether primary deviation becomes secondary deviation.

A primary deviant has committed a rule violation but claims that this is uncharacteristic and maintains a self-concept of being non-deviant and upholding socially accepted roles. A secondary deviant has undergone a reorganization of self-concept and has accepted the label of deviant. Lemert (1951) described the transition from primary to secondary deviation as a sequence of interactions:

> 1) primary deviation; 2) societal penalties; 3) further primary deviation; 4) stronger penalties and rejections; 5) further deviations, perhaps with hostilities and resentments beginning to focus upon those doing the penalizing; 6) crisis reached in the tolerance quotient, expressed in formal action by the community stigmatizing the deviant; 7) strengthening of the deviant conduct as a reaction to the stigmatizing and penalties; and 8) ultimate acceptance of deviant social status and efforts at adjustment on the basis of the associated role.

In the case of the self-fulfilling prophecy, secondary deviation can occur even when no primary deviation exists. Chapter 11 indicated how the initial diagnosis by a teacher may be false; i.e. no primary deviation exists except in the imagination of the teacher or as an expectation built into an interpretive scheme.

Deviance May Be Amplified

One of the puzzling features of institutions for deviants that are based on traditional theories of social control is that outcomes are frequently the opposite to those intended. Studies of prisons, mental hospitals and schools for offenders show that criminals tend to become hardened criminals and first offenders often become recidivists. Labelling theory offers some explanation of this. In such institutions opportunities to withdraw from deviance are reduced, a new identity as a 'social outsider' is established and a change of self-concept may result whereby individuals see themselves as irrevocably deviant. The social reaction to deviance establishes a deviant career: deviance is amplified. An aggressive social policy of 'tightening up' and 'establishing firmer law and order' may have a similar effect. A vicious circle that creates more deviance may be set in motion: more 'tightening up' leads to more acts defined as deviant, which lead to more action against deviants, which leads to more alienation of deviants and more changed self-concepts, which lead to more deviance by those so affected, which leads to more attempts to 'tighten up', and so on.

In the case of schools, the work of Reynolds and Sullivan (1979) has illustrated effects of this kind. The schools that produced most deviants had a zealous social control policy; for example, cigarette smokers, when caught, had their smoking materials confiscated and were then punished, at that time often physically. In some cases 'patrols' of teachers looked out for smokers around the schools, and smokers found in other places, like cinemas or parks, were dealt with at school. The same zealous attitudes were shown in other areas of control, e.g. policy regarding school uniform and chewing-gum consumption.

The schools that produced fewest deviants had a 'softer' approach. Rules regarding the same matters existed and were enforced, but with less aggression; for example, the confiscation of cigarettes was considered enough punishment, and the school was considered to be sufficient territorial range, so incidents in parks and cinemas were not dealt with.

Persons Labelled 'Outsiders' May Offer 'Accounts' and Seek Support Groups

Just as new identities as 'social outsiders' are established within institutions, changes of self-concept often result when individuals are considered irrevocably deviant by the wider society. The process by which individuals come to recognize themselves as having been labelled as outsiders can often be traumatic. Black and ethnic minority people often talk of a particular individual or a particular incident that finally brought about this change of self-concept. In describing the events they often refer to being 'given their blackness'.

Labelling can have a crushing effect on an individual's or a group's identity and social behaviour: people are involved in various degrees of suffering. If life becomes difficult, labelled persons often offer 'accounts' to justify their conduct and identity. Scott and Lyman (1968) indicate that these may take the form of a variety of excuses. Attempts to reduce the effects may take the form of avoiding situations in which labelling occurs or covering-up tactics. Often it is found useful to seek the support of similar people or groups who may have solved some of the difficulties, or who at least understand the problems. Such groups often come to resist and even to confront and try to transform their situation. Such groups may attempt to change laws and values by campaigning: feminist, anti-racist and homosexual equality campaigns offer classic examples.

'Successful' Labelling Depends on a Variety of Factors

Writers developing labelling theory are not suggesting that labelling is always successful: they are not claiming that if someone is labelled stupid that person will necessarily become mentally handicapped. However, they draw attention to the questions of why people are categorized as deviant and who it is that labels, based on what has been defined as a deviant or 'outsider' in that society at that particular time. The factors involved in the successful application of a label include the frequency of the labelling, the status of the labeller, the degree of damage done to others, the nature of the 'account' rendered and the power of the person to resist or reduce labelling effects. Scheff (1966), investigating the power of the person concerned, demonstrated that, in diagnosing an identical behaviour pattern in high social status and low social status clients, there was less willingness to diagnose the pattern as indicative of serious mental illness in the highest status clients. As Rist (1977) puts it, 'The crux of the labelling perspective lies not in whether one's norm violating behaviour is known, but whether others decided to do something about it.'

EDUCATIONAL LIFE CHANCES

The concept of life chances is one of the more straightforward concepts in sociology. It has been defined as the probability of a person of specified status achieving a specified goal or suffering a special disadvantage (Reading, 1977). When the concept of life chances is used to describe general patterns in a society rather than to account for the fate of a particular individual, it provides one kind of answer to the question 'who gets what?' The assumption that there are regular patterns to the biographies of individuals and groups underpins the concept of life chances.

The notion of educational life chance is derived from the main concept to focus attention on the regular features found in educational biographies and group experiences. From empirical studies, a number of propositions can be made about educational life chances. One study of pupil careers came to a range of conclusions, including the following:

> The social class differences in educational opportunity which were considerable at the primary school stage have increased at the secondary and extend now even to pupils of high ability. Thus nearly half the lower manual working-class pupils of high ability have left school before they are 16 1/2 years.
>
> Early leaving and low job aspirations make it probable that as many as 5 per cent of the next generation of manual workers will be recruited from pupils who, in other circumstances, might have qualified for administrative or professional occupations.
>
> The manual working-class pupils, compared with those of the middle class, are least handicapped when they are in the best staffed and best equipped schools.
>
> An analysis of the length of school life among the lower manual working-class pupils of borderline ability and above shows that both parental interest and school staffing and equipment are associated with age of leaving. These two factors are of course highly correlated, but neither adequately compensates for the deficiency of the other – the interest of the parents alone is insufficient to counter the deficiencies of the schools.
>
> The interest and encouragement that parents give their children is closely linked to their own educational history. Any attempt that the parents made to secure for themselves education beyond the elementary school level, even if this was not successfully completed, is associated with higher aspirations for their own children's educational success.
>
> Children from large families make low scores in all attainment tests at all ages. There is, however, no evidence of an increasing educational handicap at secondary school; indeed, in the manual working class there is rather less difference in the attainment of children from large and small families at 15 than there was when they were first tested at eight.
>
> The more young children there are in the family when a child is learning to talk, the lower his score in the eight year old vocabulary test. This early deficiency in the understanding of words is not made up later.
>
> Pupils from large families leave school earlier than expected at each level of measured ability. Financial reasons alone are insufficient to explain this, for the youngest in large families also leave early, even though there are likely to be fewer calls on the family income than when their elder brothers and sisters were the same age.
>
> First-born boys in families of two or three achieve higher scores in the attainment tests and are academically more successful and more aspiring than their younger brothers and sisters. They are also superior in attainment to only children. For the girls, this difference is not found.
>
> Pupils from two-child families with birth intervals of two to four years make higher scores in all tests than those with either shorter or longer intervals; they get superior 'O' level results and leave school later. This holds for both older and younger boys and girls: the advantage of those with two to four year intervals being as great at eight as later.
>
> The short-sighted pupils have, at each age tested, superior attainment scores to those with normal vision; their non-verbal intelligence scores are, however, similar. They have higher job aspirations at each level of ability than those with normal vision, and more academic hobbies.
>
> From Douglas *et al.*, 1971

CONCLUSION

According to the particular study mentioned above, educational life chances are related to a variety of factors, including social class, size of family, school staffing and equipment, parents' educational experiences, spacing of children in families and myopia. This kind of investigation is largely descriptive; that is, it identifies the patterns. Explanations of the pattern are a different matter, and in the next four chapters we shall examine the kinds of explanation generated by interactionist approaches, particularly labelling theory, for four aspects of life chance and identity: gender, social class, ethnicity and 'special', designating various kinds of disability.

Summary

1. Labelling theory explores the proposition that social control may create deviance, while the structural approach proposes that social control is a reaction to deviance.
2. Labelling theory calls for an examination of the labellers, their assumptions and their power to establish their definitions, as much as an examination of the person or group being labelled.
3. Deviance is seen as a learned activity with a series of stages rather than as a personal attribute or a single act defined as folly.
4. Many perform deviant acts, but only those successfully labelled are deviants.
5. Secondary deviation, where an individual reorganizes his or her self-concept to accept the label of deviant or 'outsider', follows a sequence of interactions.
6. Social reactions to deviance may amplify it rather than reduce it.
7. Labelled persons may seek the support and comfort of others similarly labelled.
8. The assumption that there are regular patterns to the biographies of individuals and groups gives rise to the concept of life chances.
9. Educational life chances are related to a variety of factors, including gender, social class, ethnicity, size of family, parents' education and membership of any minority seen as 'special'.

Further Reading

Dahrendorf, R. (1980) *Life Chances*. London: Weidenfeld and Nicolson. A more complex theory of life chances than that given in this chapter.

Douglas, J.W.B., Ross, J.M. and Simpson, H.R. (1971) *All Our Future*. London: Peter Davies. A longitudinal study of educational life chances.

Giddens, A. (1993) *Sociology*. Cambridge: Polity Press.

Halsey, A.H., Heath, A.F. and Ridge, J.M. (1980) *Origins and Destinations*. Oxford: Oxford University Press.

Rist, R. (1977) 'On Understanding the Processes of Schooling: The Contributions of Labelling Theory', in J.

Karabel and A. Halsey (eds), *Power and Ideology in Education*. Oxford: Oxford University Press. A review of labelling theory and schooling.

Discussion and Activities

1. View the film *Eye of the Storm* (on hire from Concord Films, Nacton, Ipswich) and discuss the examples of labelling shown, based on colour of eyes.
2. 'Labelled people may seek the support of others similarly labelled.' Obtain literature from groups often seen by the mass media as deviant. Why are they seen as deviant? How do they counter this label? What social rules are they seen to be infringing? Examples of such groups are Alcoholics Anonymous, Campaign for Homosexual Equality, Education Otherwise, Voluntary Euthanasia Society.

Signposts

1. Regions

Reference to *Educational Statistics for the UK* and *Social Trends* (both published regularly by HMSO) shows that educational life chances vary with region. See Byrne, D., Williamson, B. and Fletcher, B. (1974) *The Poverty of Education*, Oxford: Martin Robertson, and the 'New Society' Social Studies Reader on Regions.

2. Pupil labelling

Read Elliott, J. (2001) 'Motivation in the Junior Years: International Perspectives on Children's Attitudes, Expectations and Behaviour and their Relationship to Educational Achievement', *Oxford Review of Education*, **27**, 1, 37–68. This article discusses the results of a survey of nearly 3,000 children aged 9–10 from England, Russia and the USA.

26 Gender Identity

The trouble with some women is they get all excited about nothing – and then marry him.

Cher

Genius has no Sex.

Madame de Staël

INTRODUCTION

From the 1944 Education Act until the late 1970s, the main focus of sociological analyses of equality of opportunity was on social class rather than on gender or race. As a result, many books on the sociology of education rated at best a page or two on women or on sex differences and, at worst, not even a reference in the index. 'Compensatory' education for girls did not emerge as an issue and any disparities that did emerge were part of larger studies (Douglas, 1964).

The reasons for this comparative neglect were complex. First, educational research followed contemporary definitions of what constituted an educational problem, and so looked at wastage of talent, inequality of opportunity, school leaving ages and school organizational features. Inequality of opportunity between the females and males was rarely recognized as a problem, or at most was seen as an anachronism that would disappear with coeducation. Second, sex stereotyping appears to be a deeply embedded and taken-for-granted aspect of the social structure, so the 'common-sense' explanations about the assumed innate intellectual differences between man and woman were all too readily acceptable as a complete explanation. The lack of a well developed comparative perspective of education may have been contributory here, since a systematic comparison with other countries (e.g. Russia, Sweden) would have presented some disturbing information about women, education and occupations elsewhere.

Recognition of sex differences in education as an 'official' problem came with an announcement in September 1973 that the government planned to ask Her Majesty's Inspectorate to undertake an inquiry into the extent to which differences in school curricula and customs contribute to unequal opportunities for boys and girls (DES, 1975). The influence of various feminist and women's liberation groups at that time was especially significant (Knight, 1973; Smoker, 1973). Official opinion was influenced strongly by the evidence to the House of Lords Select Committee on the Anti-Discrimination Bill in 1971–72 and 1972–73. The evidence collected by a group within the Labour Party was particularly influential (Rendel, 1968; Labour Party, 1972).

In the period after 1973, a number of articles and books thus focused on the life chances of girls in particular. As a result the issues became more clearly identified. As Byrne wrote in 1978:

> One message is clear. The education service has also a good deal of homework to do, the first task of which is to raise the debate about sex roles in education to a serious intellectual level, and to vote research funds to relevant and more substantial field-work. We should moreover begin to make socially unacceptable the common attitude of triviality and, occasionally, mockery, which has so far characterized public reaction to the intelligent questioning by a few in the leadership of education, as to why the education of girls should be any different from that of boys; and how solid is the ground for alleged norms of sex differences used to justify different curricula and methods for girls and boys respectively.

It should be borne in mind that a distortion is produced by looking at gender in isolation. Other variables, such as social class, ethnicity and geographic location, are intertwined with gender.

THE EDUCATIONAL LIFE CHANCES OF GIRLS AND BOYS

The concept of educational life chances was outlined in Chapter 25 and was taken to refer to the probabilities of a person of a specified status, in this case a boy or a girl, achieving a particular goal or experiencing a particular disadvantage. The educational biographies of girls and boys in Britain followed a fairly regular pattern up until the late 1980s, with a smaller proportion of females than males achieving success at all levels. However, since the beginning of the 1990s the situation has changed significantly and we can now see that:

1. In Britain for pupils aged 7 and 14 teacher assessments and tests indicate that girls outperform boys in both English and mathematics. There appears to be very little difference in attainments even in National Curriculum science at either age (Social Trends, 1996).

2. Girls are more likely than boys to gain five or more GCSE qualifications at grades A to C and, even more notably, there is now a higher proportion of girls than boys achieving these grades in all the core National Curriculum subjects (English, mathematics, science and a foreign language). However, many of the traditional gender differences in subject

Table 26.1 Pupils achieving GCSE grades A–C or equivalent: by selected subject and gender, Great Britain, percentages

	Males			Females		
	1988/89[a]	*1991/92*	*1993/94*	*1988/89[a]*	*1991/92*	*1993/94*
English	38	41	45	53	57	62
Any science	35	39	43	33	39	43
of which: Biology	13	7	7	19	9	8
Chemistry	17	10	9	13	8	7
Physics	21	11	10	10	6	5
Double award science[a]	7	23	32	7	24	34
	36	38	42	32	37	42
Mathematics	19	20	25	30	33	40
Any modern language	17	18	20	27	29	33
of which: French	16	15	18	18	20	24
History	21	22	23	18	19	21
	19	18	19	5	8	10

[a] Data are for England only.
From Department for Education and Employment; Welsh Office; The Scottish Office Education and Industry Department.

choices do still remain, as girls are still underrepresented in GCSE physics, chemistry and craft, design and technology. But this may not always be the case; an increasing number of girls are now taking up these options and when entered for these examinations they are showing themselves to be particularly capable. The one exception to this trend appears to be the case of computer studies, which has remained unpopular for girls. Boys are particularly underrepresented in English, history and foreign language classes.

3. Girls have also overtaken boys in terms of GCE A level success. In 1978 the subjects taken showed marked variation according to gender. The ratios of boys to girls in different subjects were physics 6:1, mathematics 4:1, chemistry 3:1, biology 9:8, technical drawing 200:1, languages 1:2. By 1996 the ratio of boys to girls entering GCE A level in most subjects had narrowed markedly. In physics the ratio was down to 3:1 and the girls who were entering were showing a significantly higher performance and lower failure rate than the boys. The same applies to mathematics, where the ratio of entries was nearer 3:2. Perhaps most significantly, technology (CDT) was showing the same pattern and the ratio was down to 4:1. It was only in computer studies, where the ratio of boys to girls was 4:1, that the boys were outperforming the girls.

4. Roughly the same number of boys and girls now gain places in higher education. Yet the greater the prestige commonly accorded an institution, the fewer girls are present. In 1992/93 girls made up 46 per cent of all university students and 53 per cent of polytechnic and other college students. (Approximate figures are: Oxbridge, 10–20 per cent; large civic, 20–35 per cent; small civic, 35–50 per cent, depending on year taken.) The

Table 26.2 Qualifications attained: by gender, England, percentages

	Males			Females		
	1980/81	*1990/91*	*1993/94*	*1980/81*	*1990/91*	*1993/94*
3 or more GCE A levels[a]	10	13	14	8	14	15
1 or more GCE A levels[a]	16	21	21	15	23	23
5 or more GCSE grades A–C[b]	24	36	39	26	44	48
1 or more GCSE grades A–C[b]	50	63	64	55	73	75
1 or more GCSE grades A–G[b]	87	95	91	90	95	93

[a] Students at school aged 16 to 18 at start of academic year as a percentage of 17-year-old population.
[b] Pupils aged 15 at start of academic year as a percentage of the 15-year-old school population.
From Department for Education and Employment.

differences in some of the subject choices remain substantial at this level, with the ratio of boys to girls in engineering and technology being 5:1. Girls are overrepresented in arts courses, whereas they make up only one in three of enrolments in science courses.
5.   The number of women pursuing teacher training courses exceeds the number of men, particularly for primary school teaching. The ratio is currently close to three girls to every one boy on teacher education courses.

(In all cases the current situation may be checked from several sources, including the most recent versions of: *Statistics of Education, Vol. 2, School Leavers; Social Trends; Educational Statistics for the UK*, all published by HMSO; and The Universities Central Council on Admissions Annual Report.)

The significance of boys and girls choosing, or being directed into, different subjects may be illustrated by the international comparison presented in Table 26.3. The table shows the perceptions held by the general public regarding the relative importance of different secondary school subjects. There can be little doubt that the main criteria being applied here are economic. In the job market there can be little doubt that science and technology qualifications have greater currency and provide the best career opportunities.

Women's Employment

One of the implications of the different subjects taken by girls and boys is that girls are therefore denied the financial rewards of employment in some of the best-paid sectors of the economy. In the professions as a whole the ratio of men to women is approximately 5:1. If we consider those people currently in employment or working in the past eight years (Table 26.4)

Table 26.3 Public opinion on subjects regarded as essential or very important in secondary schools[a]: international comparison, 1993/94, percentages

	Arts	Sciences	Technology/ technical studies	Foreign languages	Education for citizenship[b]
Austria	43	67	60	91	64
Belgium[c]	29	57	53	88	66
Denmark	36	46	–	79	46
Finland	31	53	39	87	67
France	31	63	47	87	67
Netherlands	31	64	42	85	41
Portugal	55	76	66	85	73
Spain	44	65	63	72	66
Sweden	31	65	38	87	70
Switzerland	58	63	52	77	65
United Kingdom	26	66	57	56	36
United States	47	85	36	53	77

[a] Respondents were asked 'The following are examples of things that young people study in secondary school. In your view how important are each of them?'
[b] For example civic or social education.
[c] Flemish community.
From OECD.

we can see that the occupational structure of women is much more concentrated in the intermediate and skilled, non-manual groups.

These statistics also demonstrate the importance of considering 'ethnic identity' alongside gender. South Asian women are notably overrepresented in the 'partly skilled' group. It is also significant that while women outnumber men in both the health and education sectors, they tend to be found in the less senior posts. Women make up 81 per cent of all teachers in nursery and primary schools, yet they represent only 57 per cent of headteachers and deputy headteachers. In secondary schools, women make up 49 per cent of staff yet only 30 per cent are deputies or headteachers.

Women are also channelled into specific areas of the labour market and, even in those areas that they dominate, such as education, they are to be found in the lowest positions. In higher education, women have gained a foothold in areas such as sociology and women's studies. But the opportunities for black and ethnic minority women remain relatively limited (Beechey, 1986).

In summary:

1. Girls have demonstrated their academic ability in all subject areas.
2. Fewer girls than boys enter the most prestigious universities.
3. Fewer girls than boys take GCSEs in physics, chemistry and technology.
4. Fewer girls than boys take A levels in science and technology subjects.
5. Fewer boys than girls prepare for teacher education.

Table 26.4 *Social class[a]: by gender, spring 1995, Great Britain, percentages*

	Profes-sional	Inter-mediate	Skilled non-manual	Skilled manual	Partly skilled	Unskilled manual	All[b] (=100%) (thou-sands)
Males							
Black	6	23	13	31	19	8	212
Indian	13	27	15	24	17	–	261
Pakistani/Bangladeshi	–	18	13	35	22	–	149
Other ethnic minorities	14	33	14	26	10	–	174
White	8	29	12	32	14	5	15,484
Females							
Black	–	29	33	11	16	9	243
Indian	6	20	34	7	31	–	194
Pakistani/Bangladeshi	–	20	39	–	31	–	62
Other ethnic minorities	–	31	32	9	18	–	157
White	2	28	37	9	18	7	13,165

[a] Based on occupation of males aged 16 to 64 and females aged 16 to 59.
[b] Excludes those who were serving in the armed forces, those who did not state their previous occupation and those who had not worked in the last eight years.
From Labour Force Survey, Office for National Statistics.

Things have definitely improved for girls in the past twenty years yet we can still see that after leaving primary school, girls experience an ever-decreasing set of possibilities in educational achievement, with the exceptions of preparation for primary school teaching and preparation for nursing.

EXPLANATIONS

There have been several attempts to provide explanations for the different sets of educational life chances outlined above. Some are derived from psychology: one proposition based on the idea of inherited abilities is that girls inherit a different set of abilities and aptitudes from those of boys, so schools follow a natural pattern and presumably could not alter this even if they wished to do so. History appears to be proving this proposition incorrect.

An alternative explanation offered by psychologists is related to inherited personalities and different motivations influencing achievement. It is that girls inherit a different set of personality traits from boys, so schools follow a natural pattern in providing different motivations, with consequent different subject choices and achievements in boys and girls.

From sociology there are derived a range of explanations that stress the learning of a culture, with its in-built gender definitions. The role of schools is seen variously: in one proposition it is seen as repeating the labels of a culture, since a society has a traditional allocation of roles of men and women, and the agencies of socialization of the society socialize boys and girls to fit in with that pattern. Schools as an agency of socialization follow suit, and in this they neither increase nor decrease nor decrease the options open to pupils.

Alternatively, schools can be seen as continuing the process started outside school by closing off further options. A society has a traditional allocation of the roles of men and women and schools actively contribute to the further differentiation of roles by effectively closing off more options.

A further proposition stresses the possibility of schools changing the traditional allocations of roles. Schools are active in resisting the allocation of roles for men and women and increase the range of choices. Therefore, they are instrumental in starting to change the social structure by altering the expectations of pupils and increasing their educational life chances.

Marxist interpretations are derived from the concepts of 'capitalism' and 'patriarchy'. The family is seen to be crucial to legitimizing unequal profit sharing, with the control of work, marriage and property being in the hands of men. The second-class roles of childrearing and care of the elderly are allocated to women, with any involvement in work regulated by males.

EXPLAINING GIRLS' EDUCATIONAL ACHIEVEMENT: THE CONTRIBUTION OF LABELLING THEORY

Mathematics

As a case study, in earlier editions we examined the experience of girls in mathematics in schools. Until the early 1990s, when girls started to outperform boys in mathematics at all levels, 11-year-old girls were seen to perform as well as boys, yet by the age of 16, when GCE O levels and CSEs were, at that time, encountered, girls were performing less well, and at A level four boys were achieving mathematics passes for every one girl. Studies of this phenomenon were often undertaken by psychologists who looked for an ability peculiar to boys and absent in girls. The 'missing ability' was identified as spatial 'ability', since girls consistently did poorly on certain types of question requiring geometric/spatial understandings. The fault was therefore located in the girls themselves, as a biological difference that the school could do little to alter. This belief entered the consciousness of both teachers and taught, so that both were frequently convinced that most girls were 'unmathematical'.

The contribution of labelling theory here is in the identification of a powerful self-fulfilling prophecy. The process began with a false diagnosis, in this case that girls lacked an ability called 'spatial ability'. This false diagnosis set in motion a typical sequence: the girls were labelled as unmathematical, their performance was noted and the outcome of poorer performance was used as 'conclusive evidence' that the label was accurate and the explanation of a biologically situated difference was sound. The educational 'labellers' were powerful, while the girls who were labelled were not.

Discussion Activity in Classrooms

Contrary to popular belief, it has been found repeatedly that males talk more than females. Here is one experiment that illustrates the discrepancy between the belief and the evidence:

> The greater amount of man-talk and the greater frequency of interruptions is probably something that few of us are conscious of; we believe so strongly in the stereotype which insists that it is the other way around. However, it is not difficult to check this. It can be an interesting classroom exercise.
>
> It was an exercise I set myself at a recent conference of teachers in London. From the beginning the men talked more because, although there were eight official male speakers, there were no female ones. This was seen as a problem, so the organizing committee decided to exercise positive discrimination in favour of female speakers from the floor.
>
> At the first session – with positive discrimination – there were 14 male speakers and nine female; at the second session there were 10 male speakers and four female. There was almost twice as much man-talk as woman-talk. However, what was interesting was the impression people were left with about talk. The stereotypes were still holding firm. Of the 30 people consulted after the sessions, 27 were of the opinion that there had been more female than male speakers. This helps to explain some of the contradictions behind sex differences in language. On the one hand we believe that females talk too much; on the other hand we have ample evidence that they do not talk as much as males.
>
> Spender, 1978

Spender suggests that there are some regular patterns of interpretation here: a 'talkative' female is actually one who talks about as often as a male; a 'dominating' female talks about half as much as a male. Therefore, at the conference reported above, although the number of female speakers was fewer than half the total number of speakers, most people thought they had dominated the talk. Males would have to have talked almost all the time before they would have been seen as dominating the talk. This pattern, Spender argues, is related to differences of power:

> When it comes to power, some very interesting sex differences have been found. Although we may have been able to predict some of them, there are others which completely contradict our beliefs about masculine and feminine talk.
>
> The first one, which was to be expected, is that females are more polite. Most people who are without power and find themselves in a vulnerable position are more polite. The shop assistant is more polite than the customer; the student is more polite than the teacher; the female is more polite than the male. But this has little to do with their sex, and a great deal to do with their position in society.

Females are required to be polite, and this puts onus on them to accommodate male talk...

It is not polite to to be the centre of conversation and to talk a lot – if one is female. It is not polite to interrupt – if one is female. It is not polite to talk about things which interest you – if one is female. It *is* polite to accommodate, to listen, to be supportive and encouraging to male speakers – if one is female.

So females are kept in their places. They enjoy less rights to talk. Because they have less power and because politeness is part of the repertoire of successful feminine behaviour, it is not even necessary to force females to be quiet. The penalties are so great if they break the rule, they will obligingly monitor themselves.

Spender, 1978

In the classroom, boys conform to expectations and live up to their label when they dominate classroom discussion or question and answer sessions, whereas girls meet the expectations for their sex when they are quiet or accommodate male-directed talk. Single-sex situations give girls more opportunity, because in single-sex schools with female teachers, girls are not obliged to defer to male authority, to support male topics, to agree to interruptions or to practise silence. There is relatively 'free' speech, as Spender puts it, and this could explain the frequently claimed superior achievement of females in single-sex schools. Where females are free to use their language to learn, they learn more. This provides another example of labelling theory. Girls who deviate from the expectations risk acquiring a deviant label of 'dominating', 'talkative' or 'intellectual', and an accompanying set of penalties. Those who conform have to develop a self-concept that allows for their silence and their submissive role.

Spender (1978) asked a group of girls at an inner London secondary school whether they thought it was unfeminine to speak up in class, and they agreed.

The girls thought it natural that male students should ask questions, make protests, challenge the teacher and demand explanations. Females on the other hand should 'just get on with it' – even when they, too, thought the work was silly, or plain boring.

Spender concludes that, although it is unlikely that teachers consciously practise discrimination against their students on the grounds of sex, by enforcing the social rules for talk they are unwittingly penalizing females. Since there is no physical reason, no sex difference, that is responsible for the relative silence of females, this situation is not inevitable, and teachers have the power to do something about it.

Gender Identity in Pre-school and Primary School

At birth children are given a clearly identifiable sex label – their first name. Boys and girls are dressed differently, given different types of toys, reinforced for different types of behaviour. Mothers typically treat their male and female infants in different ways (Moss, 1967). Parents tend to shape the behaviour of their children: fathers especially discourage any 'feminine' behaviour in sons (Pitzner, 1963). Boys tend to be encouraged to show tenacity, aggressiveness and curiosity, girls to show kindness, obedience and cheerfulness (Brim, 1960). Any biological differences are thereby accentuated.

Children thus learn what Danziger terms a gender identity: 'Once they have grasped that they are characterized by their membership in a gender category, this colours their evaluation of persons and activities' (Danziger, 1971). An experiment that illustrates this is that of Montemayor (1974), who played a game with six- to eight-year-olds with an asexual toy clown. With some children he described the clown as a toy for boys, with others a toy for girls and with others in sex-neutral terms. Boys performed better in the game when the boy label was given; girls when the girl label was given. Montemayor's conclusion was that sex labels were influencing behaviour even in the absence of any outright reward and punishment.

Since the 1970s, research has focused on how very young children, even those under seven, learn about gender identity. Young children learn about and experience class bias, sexism and racism. We know that children absorb biased knowledge and understanding from their environment. This can be from parental views, media images and the children's own perceptions of the way people in their 'image' are seen and treated. In the absence of strong and positive role models, children may be left with a rather negative perception of people like themselves. This bias can start from birth.

Barbara Lloyd (1987) conducted a number of studies in the late 1970s and the 1980s which illustrated how sex-biased behaviour by mothers towards babies and infants contributed to the gender stereotyping of boys and girls. One of her most interesting studies was conducted with Caroline Smith. Both researchers observed mothers of firstborn six-month-olds while they played with babies who were systematically presented to the mothers as either a boy or a girl. The mothers responded, using their preconceived ideas of how boys and girls should behave. The same baby when presented as a boy was encouraged to play with a hammer and engage in vigorous activity. Conversely, when the baby was presented as a girl it was offered a soft doll and praised for being pretty and clever. Mothers appeared to favour gross motor movements for boys.

By the age of thirteen months, boy infants engaged in more large motor movements while girls made more fine motor responses. As Lloyd (1987, p. 148) puts it:

> The gender differences at thirteen months may reflect babies' experiences at six months which are shaped by mothers' social representations of gender. I interpret the thirteen-month-olds' gender differentiated toy choice and play styles as evidence that these children are beginning to construct a concept of gender, albeit in practical activity and with some help from their mothers.

Many parents and educators conclude from children's behaviour that they are 'naturally' different, without considering their own contribution to the children's socialization. Difference, therefore, can be a matter of social learning as well as physiology. This has implications for practice and the kinds of activities which all children should have access to regardless of gender preference.

Early childhood teachers are often inexperienced and lack knowledge and understanding about how children become biased, and in dealing with these matters they often display a profound sense of inadequacy when faced with sexism and racism from children. Yet it is natural for children to learn the behaviours that they have been exposed to by parents and other significant adults.

Some Aspects of the Hidden Curriculum

Practices like lining up boys and girls separately, physically punishing boys but verbally chastising girls and commenting on girls' appearance but boys' achievement were shown in a study by Ricks and Pyke (1973) to be common in secondary schools. While the most extreme practices may now be outlawed in our schools, we continue to tolerate different standards of behaviour, e.g. discouraging girls from fighting but not boys, expecting boys to be chivalrous by standing if there are not enough places or to carry desks. Teachers, therefore, may cumulatively pass on expectations of different behaviour or, at the very least, grossly exaggerate any differences which do exist, based on selective generalizations. (Examples of selective generalizations in reverse might be: men cannot be hired for this job because they may have a heart attack and die, men having a higher incidence of heart disease than women; or, men cannot be considered for executive positions because they become violent too easily, since men have the male hormone testosterone, often considered to be a major source of aggression.)

Part Two of this book, on the hidden curriculum, provides further examples of sexism in the education system.

CONCLUSION

The proposition that our society has institutions and cultural features which are intentionally or unintentionally harmful to both the self-concepts and the life chances of women includes schools. On the evidence of this chapter, despite major advances, this would seem to remain the case. A complex network of influences is involved, and the effect of a wide range of apparently minor behaviours is powerful because it is cumulative. Labelling theory provides one way of explaining some of the characteristics of this network of influences and how they operate in institutions like schools. If the causes are complex, so are the practical implications, as Murphy and Gipps (1996) recently wrote:

> While there is evidence that strategies to make the curriculum and teaching more 'girl-friendly' have worked with girls from majority, middle class backgrounds . . . they have not worked with other girls; furthermore, they have often generated a 'male backlash'.

As Murphy and Gipps have argued, there is now evidence to suggest that the recent pattern of boys' lower achievement may be explained by their tendency to favour approaches to learning that are at odds with current practice. What is now required is a clearer recognition that pupils do not all learn in the same way and that a class of pupils require a variety of different strategies:

> Changing teachers' approaches so that they consider a range of pedagogic strategies appropriately for various pupils, subjects and tasks, places a tremendous demand on teachers and on how they are educated. But the task is not about gender equity or working with feminist teachers; it is a much broader agenda of engaging with the learner, while being conscious of the 'white, male, middle-class' nature of knowledge as it is defined, so as to offer appropriate and effective teaching for all pupils. In western countries ethnic minority and disadvantaged boys and girls are underachieving.
>
> Murphy and Gipps, 1996

Summary

1. Gender intertwines with social class ethnicity to make a complex pattern of influences on life chances.
2. After leaving primary school girls tend to experience an ever-decreasing set of possibilities for their educational and other life chances.
3. Among psychological explanations are those that stress inheritance, either of abilities or of personality traits.
4. Sociological explanations are derived from the concept of culture: definitions of gender are seen as learned.
5. Labelling theory gives rise to the idea of a self-fulfilling prophency: in the case of mathematics, girls were falsely diagnosed as lacking in 'spatial ability', when it was different curricular experiences that gave rise to the differences in spatial thinking.
6. Discussion activity in schools discriminates against girls because of the conventional rules about talk in mixed company.
7. Where girls are free from the unwritten obligations to defer to male-dominated talk, as in single-sex schools, they may perform better at educational tasks.
8. Gender identity is established and reinforced through a complex web of influences that take effect from birth onwards.
9. Both the official and the hidden curriculum contribute a variety of influences to this web.
10. The wide range of apparently minor behaviours inside and outside school is powerful because of its cumulative effect.

Further Reading

Byrne, E. (1978) *Women and Education*. London: Tavistock.

Davies, L. (1984) *Pupil Power: Deviance and Gender in School*. Lewes: Falmer Press.

Deem, R. (1978) *Women and Schooling*. London: Routledge and Kegan Paul.

Lloyd, B. (1987) 'Social Representations of Gender', in J. Bruner and H. Haste (eds), *Making Sense: The Child's Construction of the World*. London: Routledge, pp. 147–62.

Lloyd, B. and Duveen, G. (1992) *Gender Identities and Education*. Hemel Hempstead: Harvester Wheatsheaf.

Murphy, P. and Gipps, C. (1996) *Equity in the Classroom: Towards Effective Pedagogy for Girls and Boys*. Lewes: Falmer Press and UNESCO Publishing.

Reid, I. and Wormald, E. (1982) *Sex Differences in Britain*. London: Great McIntyre. A comprehensive review of the evidence available.

Reynolds, H. and Davies, L. (1977) 'Sex Roles and Society', special edition of *Social Science Teacher*, **6**, 4. Contains analyses and teaching suggestions.

Sharpe, S. (1976) *Just Like A Girl*. Harmondsworth: Penguin.

Siraj-Blatchford, I. (ed.) (1992) *'Race', Gender and the Education of Teachers*. Buckingham: Open University Press. Read the chapter by Ann Flintoff on sexism on PE courses.

Spender, D. and Sarah, E. (1980) *Learning to Lose*. London: The Women's Press.

Whyld, J. (ed.) (1983) *Sexism in the Secondary Curriculum*. London: Harper and Row.

Discussion and Activities

1. Examine school textbooks for evidence of sex typing. A useful source book is *Sexism in Children's Books*, published by the Children's Rights Workshop (1977).
2. Repeat the exercise on talk patterns described in this chapter, in the section 'Discussion activity in classrooms', and see if your results agree with those of Spender.
3. Prepare a checklist of sex-discriminating features of schooling and use it to study a school or schools known to you. A useful checklist appeared in *Where?*, **130**, July 1977.

Signposts

1. Sexism in higher education

Consider how sexism operates in higher education. One source is Acker, S. and Piper, D.W. (eds) (1984) *Is Higher Education Fair to Women*, Guildford: SRHE and NFER-Nelson. Another is by Siraj-Blatchford, I. (ed.) (1992) *'Race', Gender and the Education of Teachers*, Buckingham: Open University Press. Read the chapter by Ann Flintoff on sexism on PE courses.

2. Single-sex schooling

Evidence about the way in which mixed schooling can help to disadvantage girls has led to a reconsideration of single-sex schooling. See Deem, R. (1984) *Coeducation Reconsidered*, Milton Keynes: Open University Press; and Mahony, P. (1985) *Schools for the Boys? Coeducation Reassessed*, London: Hutchinson.

3. Teachers as gendered role models

Should there be more male primary teachers? Are we failing boys and encouraging male working-class disaffection? These accusations are implicated in present publicity campaigns. The following paper sets out to explore how established stereotypes have contributed to maintaining a highly gendered work force. Voices from female and male primary teachers illustrate the discussion. Read Burn, E. (2001) 'Do Boys Need Male Primary Teachers as Positive Role Models?', paper presented at the British Educational Research Association Annual Conference, Leeds University, 13–15 September. The text is in the Education-line Internet document collection at *http://www.leeds.ac.uk/educol/documents/00001884.htm*

4. Masculinity

There is an increasing concern about the ways in which school promotes different forms of masculinity:

> Among the characteristics of this hegemonic form of masculinity are misogyny, homophobia, racism, compulsory heterosexuality, the importance of sport, a denial of emotions, competition, success, individualism, strength, toughness, and the threat or use of violence to get what is wanted or, often, what it is assumed the male is entitled to and has a right to. Boys or men who deviate from this model can be seen, labelled and treated as 'unmanly'.
> Harber, C. (2004) *Schooling as Violence*, London: Routledge Falmer, p. 106

5. Statistical Review

The press regularly carries articles about achievement by gender, as well as race and class. Collect these and compare with the statistics in this chapter and note any changing patterns.

27 Social Class

INTRODUCTION

The links between social class and education in the UK have been researched frequently and persistently. The reasons for this concentration are both historical and political:

> The development of the British education system, from the point where education was wholly the preserve of the rich, through forms of voluntary education for the poor, to compulsory education for all, has been characterized by concern about social class and about equality.
>
> Silver, 1973

The relics of the earliest structures can still be seen today, in the continuance of independent and 'public' schools alongside those provided by local authorities. The work of psychologists of education in the 1930s and 1940s in trying to relate intelligence, as measured by IQ tests, to social class set the scene for later work by sociologists on the theme of the 'wastage of talent'. The view held by psychologists and sociologists alike was that equality of educational opportunity was not in evidence, since many working-class children with high intelligence were either not reaching grammar school or underachieving if they did get there. IQ tests are no longer used to select pupils for entry to grammar schools. In fact, the number of grammar schools has radically declined. In 1971, 19 per cent of all secondary schools in the UK were grammar schools and by 1995 this was reduced to just 5 per cent. Five out of six pupils are now educated in comprehensive schools, although the proportion of pupils in the private sector has hardly changed at all. About 1 in 16 of all pupils go to independent and 'public' schools. While the proportion of pupils successfully completing GCSEs and GCE A levels, and the number of students going on to university, have increased in recent years, there has been little change in the overall pattern of social class advantage. The children of working-class parents continue to be underrepresented at every level.

Table 27.1 Average real annual income of higher education students, United Kingdom, pounds at 1992/3 prices

	1986/87	1988/89	1992/93
Grants/awards	1,604	1,592	1,715
Parents	1,757	1,573	1,277
Earnings	138	240	230
Loans/overdrafts	141	139	147
Other income	372	527	293
All sources	4,010	4,071	3,662

From Department for Education.

DEFINING SOCIAL CLASS

Social class is a highly ambiguous concept. The complications only begin with distinguishing among its uses as (a) a common, everyday expression, (b) an administrative, demographic concept, (c) a concept within sociology and the social sciences in general. Further complications stem from the fact that it is ambiguously used within each of these three areas as well as across them. Many researchers have found it necessary to adopt an operational definition that is either the administrative categories of the Registrar General's Classification of occupations, or a modified version of it. Although this means that there is some basis for comparison between various studies, the links with sociological theories of social class outlined by Weber or Marx are somewhat tenuous; for example, in the case of the latter, class is defined in relation to the ownership of the means of production.

Subjectively social class raises other problems of definition. Various national opinion polls have shown that people accept the existence of different social classes, will assign themselves to upper, middle or working classes, and think that the major factor in judging position is accent, ahead of occupation, money or education.

However, the findings regarding educational life chances are consistent no matter which definition of social class is employed: in general, the children from higher socio-economic classes have much better educational life chances than the children from lower classes, and this relationship has held throughout the grammar school/selective school phase, through comprehensive reorganization and the designation of educational priority areas, with their various compensatory schemes for schooling. ('Better' here signals the introduction of a value interpretation: to obtain a degree, experience extra full-time education or gain GCE/GCSEs are all assumed to be superior.)

EDUCATIONAL LIFE CHANCES AND SOCIAL CLASS

In the previous chapter it was pointed out that looking at gender in isolation involved distortion, since class, ethnicity and region are intertwined with it. The same thing must be said of social class. Since the early 1980s governmental priorities changed and many of the official annual sources of statistical information related to social class and to poverty have now been lost. Both the Royal Commission on Income and Wealth and the Supplementary Benefits Commission, which both regularly published information, have now been abolished. The priority in recent years has been to reintroduce all the selectivity of the 1940s, and to increase the 'opportunities to be unequal', as the former Conservative Prime Minister Mrs Thatcher put it. In 1990 the Child Poverty Action Group concluded that the long-term trend towards improving the lot of the poorer sections of UK society had reversed (Oppenheim, 1990). Department of Social Security (DSS) statistics showed that, between 1979 and 1988, income inequality increased. In fact Department of Employment statistics (1990) showed that the gap between the highest and lowest paid employees was wider than at any time since the records began in 1886.

Skellington (1992) summarized the major research reports of 1991:

- In March 1991, research by Peter Townsend, Professor of Social Policy at Bristol University, showed that the incomes of the poorest 20 per cent of the population fell by just under 5 per cent between 1979 and 1989, while the income of the richest percentile increased by 40 per cent (Townsend, 1991).
- In April 1991 the EC (European Community) found that between 1980 and 1985 the increase in the number of people living in poverty – from 8.2 million to 10.3 million – was greater in the UK than in any other EC country. One in five of all EC residents defined as poor lives in the UK (*Guardian*, 8 April 1991; *Independent*, 17 May 1991).
- In May 1991, a House of Commons committee estimated that between 1979 and 1988 the number of people with incomes below half the national average grew by 3.7 million to 9.1 million (Social Security Committee, 1991).
- In October 1991, the Child Poverty Action Group reported that 11.8 million people lived in poverty, more than double the figure in 1978 (*Guardian*, 23 October 1991; CPAG, 1991).

Given the increased inequality, few readers will be surprised to note the following observations regarding educational life chances.

Table 27.2 Highest qualification held[a]: by socio-economic group, 1992–3, Great Britain, percentages

	Professional	Employers and managers	Intermediate non-manual	Junior non-manual	Skilled manual and own account non-professional	Semi-skilled manual and personal service	Unskilled manual	All persons
Degree	61	19	21	3	2	1	–	12
Higher education	16	19	29	6	9	4	2	13
GCE A level[b]	7	16	12	13	14	7	3	12
GCSE, grades A–C[b]	7	21	20	35	23	21	12	22
GCSE, grades D–G[b,c]	1	7	5	16	15	12	10	10
Foreign	4	3	3	3	2	4	3	3
No qualifications	3	15	10	24	36	51	70	28

[a] Persons aged 25–69 not in full-time education.
[b] Or equivalent.
[c] Includes commercial qualifications and apprenticeships.
From Office of Population Censuses and Survey

Table 27.3 Highest educational qualification attained by persons[a] aged 25–49, by sex and social class of father, Great Britain 1981/2[b], percentages

	Father's social class						
	1	2	3	4	5	6	ALL
Males							
Degree or equivalent	40	20	22	6	5	4	10
Higher education below degree	17	15	13	10	7	8	11
GCE A level or equivalent	13	12	12	9	8	6	10
GCE O level/CSE, higher grades or equivalent	16	20	17	15	11	8	15
GCE/CSE other grades/commercial/ apprenticeship	2	6	8	13	12	12	11
Foreign/other	5	6	5	4	3	2	4
None	7	22	22	44	55	60	40
Females							
Degree or equivalent	23	8	9	2	1	1	4
Higher education below degree	27	15	15	7	5	4	9
GCE A level or equivalent	9	8	6	3	3	1	4
GCE O level/CSE, higher grades or equivalent	22	25	22	17	13	8	17
GCE/CSE other grades/commercial/ apprenticeship	6	11	14	12	11	9	12
Foreign/other	6	6	4	3	3	3	4
None	7	27	30	57	64	75	50
Social class of sample	3	17	10	44	19	7	100

[a] Not in full-time education.
[b] Data for 1981 and 1982 combined.
Taken from Reid, 1986.

Entry to Grant Maintained and Grammar Schools

The children of parents in social class I (professional and managerial occupations) still have a substantially better chance of gaining entry to grant maintained and grammar schools than children of social class VI (unskilled manual occupations).

Length of Full-time Education

The length of full-time education is still strongly related to parental occupations. Children with parents who have gained further and higher education are thus more likely to enjoy the same advantages themselves.

Educational Qualifications

The higher the social class, the greater the chance of achieving educational qualifications. This is summarized in Table 27.3. The contrasts between the figures for no qualifications and for obtaining a degree illustrate the issue of educational life chances. Male children of professional and managerial parents (social class I) are the most likely to obtain degrees (40 per cent of them) and the least likely to achieve no qualifications (7 per cent of them). The corresponding figures for children of unskilled manual parents (social class VI) are 4 per cent obtaining degrees and 60 per cent achieving no qualifications. At that time female children brought up in unskilled manual households fared even worse, with 75 per cent gaining no qualifications.

The social class profile of university and advanced further education students shows a similar pattern (see Table 27.4). A clear overrepresentation of the upper and middle classes is apparent. While they only represented 35 per cent of the population their children took 80 per cent of the places in universities. The working classes, by contrast, made up 65 per cent of the population but gained only 19 per cent of places.

Table 27.4 Percentage distribution of full-time university entrants, UK 1984, and advanced FE students, GB 1977, by social class

	I	II	III(nm)	III(m)	IV	V	Middle	Working
University	22	48	10	12	6	1	80	19
Advanced further education	13	37	19	20	9	2	69	31
18-year-olds[a]	5	20	10	40	18	7	35	65

[a] Based on 10–14 year-olds in 1971 Census.
The UCCA social class classification is based on occupational information provided by candidates and does not always include employment status.
Taken from Reid, 1986, p. 183.

Adult Education

More than one-third of higher education students and half of all those in further education are aged 25 and over and most of these students study part-time. The Open University in particular provides students with a second chance for higher education and its recruitment profile is less strongly related to either gender or the social class of parents than are other educational opportunities. Table 27.5 provides some interesting evidence of regional differences in enrolments in adult education in Britain.

Table 27.5 Enrolment on adult education courses[a]: by region and gender 1991 and 1994, percentages

	1991		1994	
	Males	*Females*	*Males*	*Females*
North	1.7	4.3	1.3	3.5
Yorkshire and Humberside	1.0	2.7	0.9	2.4
East Midlands	2.0	4.8	1.8	4.6
East Anglia	2.2	5.7	1.6	4.4
South East	2.5	6.0	2.0	5.2
Greater London	2.8	6.6	2.3	5.5
Rest of South East	2.4	5.7	1.9	4.9
South West	1.5	4.1	1.3	3.6
West Midlands	1.7	4.0	1.3	2.8
North West	1.1	2.8	1.1	2.8
England	1.9	4.6	1.6	4.0
Wales	1.7	4.1	1.2	3.1

[a] Percentage of the population aged 16 and over.
From Department for Education and Employment; Welsh Office.

EXPLANATIONS

A variety of explanations exists to account for the relationships listed above. Some psychological attempts have proposed that middle-class children are genetically superior, because middle-class parents pass on through inheritance superior qualities that result in better school performance. This approach raises a whole host of problems:

> This would involve you in a series of assumptions about the relationship between physiology and behaviour, and mind and behaviour, and about the efficiency of the selection processes in society. What is the point, you might ask, of positively discriminating in favour of socially disadvantaged children if their intelligence potential is fixed at a low point at birth? Why try to compensate for social inequality if individual inherited inequalities determine ability to

take life-chances? Such questions could then become the motifs for research, such as that undertaken by Jensen. We could investigate how (or even whether) mental behaviour as displayed by performance in an intelligence test can be correlated with genetic character-istics; or we might attempt to measure the efficiency with which the tasks of particular occupations sort and select people according to these genetic characteristics. But we would then have to explain knotty paradoxes like the following: if clever people have fewer chil-dren than less clever ones, why is the average national intelligence creeping upwards?

Swift, 1978

Despite the contradictions these theories have continued to be applied to explain the underachievement of working-class children in the same way as they were routinely used to explain the underachievement of girls a decade ago. As we shall see, they have also been applied to provide reasons for the underachievement of black and ethnic minority children, and it may be that it will be in the context of this latter application of genetics that they will finally become universally discredited. This is a subject to which we will return in Chapter 28.

Other theorists have proposed a psychology of motivation: either the children or their parents, or both, are inadequately motivated towards success in school. Attempts at explana-tion derived from sociology include the notion that the institutional regimes of educational institutions tend to favour middle-class pupils; alternatively, education, as currently practised, tends to alienate working-class pupils. Therefore the range of explanations runs from those that locate causes in inadequate pupils to those that stress inadequate institutions – a very similar range as that seen in the attempts to explain the educational life chances of girls.

The problem is complicated by the existence of relationships between educational life chances and other factors. As Mackinnon (1978) argues, the tendency for middle-class children to do better in education than working-class children is only a beginning. We want to know how this happens, and why. Interpretation of the research is notoriously difficult and controversial. We can demonstrate that educational success is correlated with social class, but that it is caused by social class is a proposition that raises difficulties. Without qualification, such a claim is unjustified, because the correlation is not exact, and therefore social class can be only a partial explanation of attainment. Educational success and other factors – for example, the children's intelligence as measured by IQ tests, and parental attitudes – may also be correlated.

> Often these correlations are as high as, or even higher than, that between class and attainment, so that on the face of it we have as strong grounds for saying that intelligence or parental attitude causes educational success as for saying that social class does. Finally, social class and the other factors, like parental attitudes, are correlated not only with educational success, but also with each other. It is that above all which makes the research results tricky to interpret, and even, as we shall see, controversial to state in any particular way.

Mackinnon, 1978

Mackinnon observes that, if these were different people, the factors might be disentangled, but this is not the situation. Middle-class children, children who do well on IQ tests and children whose parents' attitudes are favourable to education are, by and large, the same children. This makes it difficult to separate the effects of social class on attainment from the effects of the other factors.

Other sociological attempts at explanation have stressed what pupils bring to schools with them – their social class culture. Pupils from the different social classes are held to bring different language experiences, behaviours, attitudes, ideas, values and skills. When these differences are measured in some way they can then be correlated with educational life chances, to support the proposition that the experience of being brought up in a middle-class home and neighbourhood gives advantages in coping with educational institutions, as currently organized.

One such study carried out by Bernstein (1973) identified different language 'codes' adopted by working-class and middle-class children and their families. Initially these codes were referred to as 'restricted' and 'elaborated' codes, but these terms were often misunderstood and taken to suggest working-class inferiority. The terms 'dominated' and 'dominating' are thus more commonly applied in recent accounts. Bernstein provided the following examples of the speech of five-year-olds to illustrate the codes. The children are describing a series of pictures and have been asked to tell the story that goes with them:

> *Dominating (elaborated) code*
> 'Three boys are playing football and one boy kicks the ball and it goes through the window. The ball breaks the window and the boys are looking at it and a man comes out and shouts at them because they've broken the window so they run away and then the lady looks out of her window and she tells the boys off.'

> *Dominated (restricted) code*
> 'They're playing football and he kicks it and it goes through there it breaks the window and they're looking at it and he comes out and shouts at them because they've broken it so they run away and then she looks out and she tells them off.'

> Bernstein, 1973

In the second extract we need to see the pictures to understand the story: the working-class child's language is 'context dependent'. Bernstein argued that working-class children tend to assume this different relation between speech and situations. This put the working-class child at a significant disadvantage in the school where the dominating code is used and expected by the teacher. As Labov (1969) argued, this does not imply that any dominated code (e.g. working class or African-American/Caribbean) is in any meaningful way inferior to 'Standard English'. Labov demonstrated that the dominated code was actually rich in abstract concepts. As Labov suggested, we could as easily expect the school to adapt its language to the child as expect the child to adapt his or her language to the school.

Other sociological work has developed another idea: resource provision for education varies from LEA to LEA. These differences are shown in levels of spending on buildings, equipment, teachers and facilities. Educational attainment has been shown to correlate with spending levels, so the higher the resource provision, the higher the attainments and the greater the educational life chances in that area (Byrne *et al.*, 1974). It has been suggested that Alexander's (1992) study of educational provision and innovation in Leeds showed that this relationship between resources and attainment does not always hold true. The study has attracted some criticism, however (David *et al.*, 1992; Siraj-Blatchford, 1992).

The state of sociological research does not allow any final judgements to be made about these attempts at explanation. Some (e.g. the genetic explanation) seem to be more dubious than others. Other explanations (e.g. the social class language/culture differences between home and school and the resources provision approaches) may both turn out to be significant. Currently, a network of causes rather than a single cause seems to be the most plausible position. Economic deprivation is also likely to be significant. Furthermore, deprivations may be multiple rather than single. In support of this, the increasing concentration of each deprivation with lower social class provides evidence for rapidly increasing multiple deprivation.

As Skellington has noted, of all the single parents in Britain in 1987 nearly half were living in poverty:

> Children at greatest risk lived in families where there was unemployment (nearly 8 children out of every 10 in unemployed families lived in poverty) or where there was a single parent (6 children in every 10 in single-parent families lived in poverty).
>
> Skellington, 1992

Berthoud (1976) argued that it may be more appropriate to see the absence of deprivation as a privilege of the upper middle class than to view the presence of deprivation as a problem of the lower working class.

THE CONTRIBUTION OF LABELLING THEORY

As in the case of gender, discussed in the previous chapter, the contribution of labelling theory is that of generating explanations about how influences operate both inside and outside school. The proposition is that pupils in general learn a social class identity just as girls and boys learn a gender identity. The influences appear to be more complex than in the case of gender identity, because often there is a mediating concept of 'ideal pupil'. The concept of 'ideal pupil' was used by Becker (1952) in an analysis of interviews with teachers in Chicago. He concluded that the teachers in his sample were operating with a definition of the ideal pupil that included being interested in lessons, working hard in schools and being trained at home in such a way that he or she was bright and quick at school work. The techniques of these teachers, Becker argues, were able to deal effectively with such pupils, but were inadequate to cope with those deviating from the ideal pupil image. Other features in the image of ideal pupil were moral: being clean, healthy, well dressed and moderate in behaviour by exhibiting politeness and patience.

Setting and Streaming by 'Ability'

Setting and streaming provides another illustration of labelling. Children allocated to higher sets and streams tend to improve their performance, yet the performance of children of similar initial measured ability who are placed in lower sets and streams deteriorates. The validity of the initial selection appears to be confirmed by the subsequent performance of the children, and a self-fulfilling prophecy appears to be set in motion.

Further support for this example of labelling came from a study of infant teachers and the home backgrounds of their pupils (Goodacre, 1968). Infant teachers defined 'good' homes as ones that prepared the pupils socially and educationally for classroom life. As Becker had argued, the techniques of the teachers were able to deal effectively with pupils who were close to the 'ideal pupil' concept that underpinned this set of perceptions about homes and pupils. Goodacre showed that the actual performances of the pupils did not match the teachers' perceptions: working-class pupils did better on standardized tests of reading than the teachers' assessments suggested. The key element in a self-fulfilling prophecy – the false diagnosis – was thus present again.

If Bernstein's theory is correct, then false diagnosis will be systematically employed as the children continue to 'fail' assessments and tests which are inherently biased. There can be little doubt that the social class differences that begin at the earliest stages of schooling and lead to differences in educational opportunity will increase at the primary school stage.

The Labelling of Parents

The notion of teacher expectations and the typifications that are used to identify students are multifaceted. When teachers generate expectations and label their pupils in various ways this involves a complex of characteristics, such as sex, ethnicity, cognitive performance and classroom behaviour, measured against a concept of ideal pupil and perceptions related to social class. In making their categorizations, people draw information from a variety of first-hand and second-hand information. Most of the information about parents is second-hand, and is related to the mediating concept of 'good parent'.

The social class identity that a teacher gives a pupil is therefore filtered through the concepts of ideal pupil and good parent. An early study by Sharp and Green (1975) concluded that the good parent was seen as having a number of characteristics, including that of training children at home to be neat and tidy, to be able to concentrate and to be polite, yet not indulging in direct teaching, e.g. of reading, since this was the professional teacher's task.

Sharp and Green point out that the successful parents, in terms of their children's school achievement and relationship with the school, did not fully conform to this definition of good parent, because they did engage in surreptitious teaching at home. As a result, their children matched some of the features of the ideal pupil by being 'ready', learning quickly, making 'progress' and therefore 'doing well'. However, the parents were able to give the appearance of the good parent, defined, among other things, as one who did not actively teach at home. To admit this involved the risk of being labelled as interfering, as Wade (1978) signifies in a personal account: 'What a pity Richard can read ... ' (see Chapter 4 for further discussion of the labelling of parents).

Implications

One implication of all of this is that the common assertion that schools are middle-class institutions is a vast oversimplification. Labelling theory can help to tease out the complex relationships between schools, pupils, social class typifications and other features. A more accurate proposition would be that, through the operation of concepts like ideal pupil and good parent, the chances of pupils whose parents have occupations defined as middle class demonstrating the appropriate characteristics are greater than those of pupils whose parents are defined as working class. This does not eliminate the possibility of some working-class pupils and their parents matching the concepts of ideal pupil and good parent; neither does it preclude the possibility of a middle-class pupil and parent being defined as bad pupil and poor parent.

CONCLUSION

Labelling theory can be overstated in its effects: teacher expectations are often self-fulfilling rather than inevitably so. But when a particular pupil faces the power of a school staff and the backing of a school administration to persist with a categorization, the most likely outcome is that the student learns the identity being imposed. The process, as Good and Brophy (1972) outlined it, involves five stages:

1. The teacher expects specific behaviour and achievement from particular students.
2. Because of these different expectations, the teacher behaves differently towards the different students.
3. This teacher treatment tells each student what behaviour and achievement the teacher expects from him or her and affects his or her self-concept, achievement motivation and level of aspiration.
4. If this teacher treatment is consistent over time, and if the student does not actively resist or change it in some way, it will tend to shape his or her achievement and behaviour. High-expectation students will be led to achieve at high levels, while the achievement of low-expectation students will decline.
5. With time, the student's achievement and behaviour will conform more and more closely to that originally expected of him or her.

Some studies have illustrated that labels can be generated very quickly and then remain stable over months, and even over whole school careers. Rist (1977) reports how he found, during a three-year study of an elementary school in the black community of St Louis, that after only eight days of kindergarten, the teacher made permanent seating arrangements based on what she assumed were variations in academic capability. No formal evaluation of the children had taken place. The placement of the children reflected the social class distinctions in the room: the poor children from public welfare families all sat at one table, the working-class children at another and the middle class at the third. The teacher operationalized her expectations of these different groups of children in terms of her differentials of teaching time, her use of praise and control, and the extent of autonomy within the classroom. Rist showed how the initial patterns established by the kindergarten teacher came to be perpetuated year after year.

> By second grade, labels given by another teacher clearly reflected the reality each of the three groups experienced in the school. The top group was called the 'Tigers', the middle group the 'Cardinals', and the lowest group, the 'Clowns'. What had begun as a subjective evaluation and labelling by the teacher took on objective dimensions as the school proceeded to process the children on the basis of the distinctions made when they first began.
>
> Rist, 1977

When the label is a social class label, the result may be seen in the patterns of life chances given earlier. Labelling theory appears to generate some insights into what is taking place. As Hargreaves (1978) observed, secondary schools often take great public pride in the relatively small number of working-class pupils who pass through their sixth form, but the majority of working-class pupils are ignored. An important hidden curriculum message is thus conveyed:

> There is something wrong with being, and certainly with ending up as being, working class. To be working class is something unfortunate and undesirable from which any pupil with sense will seek to escape. The pupils absorb this message – which is transmitted daily through teachers' exhortations to work hard in school for the benefit it will bring – yet the vast majority of pupils from the working class do not escape their working-class fate.
>
> Hargreaves, 1978

Consequently, Hargreaves suggests, to get defined by teachers as a 'success', a working-class pupil must be on the road to becoming interpreted as middle class, but the majority of working-class pupils must bear the scars of damaged dignity. They collect the inevitable stigma of being 'failures'.

Summary

1. Whatever definition of social class is used, upper- and middle-class children tend to have 'better' educational life chances in terms of examination results and full-time further education.
2. A wide range of studies and statistical sources support the above conclusion.

3. A variety of explanations has been offered and, from psychology, theories of inheritance and of motivation have been proposed.

4. Sociological explanations stress that success and failure may be learned, or 'allocated' by the institution of the education system, or related to social class cultures, or related to resource provision.

5. A network of causes seems more plausible than a monocausal approach.

6. A contribution from labelling theory is that a social class identity is learned, and that some identities match the concept of ideal pupil better than others.

7. Those labelled as good pupils may be grouped into 'high-ability' groups and others grouped in 'low-ability' groups.

8. The first group can be shown to tend to overachieve in the sense of improving on initial performance, whereas the second tends to underachieve, by a deterioration from initial performance.

9. The concept of good parent is related to pupil success: parents become labelled and must give the appearance of not teaching at home to match the good-parent definitions in operation, while actually doing so surreptitiously.

10. Although teacher expectations mediated through the concepts of 'ideal pupil' and 'good parent' are not always self-fulfilling, the power of a school to persist with a categorization is considerable, and the most likely outcome is that the pupil learns the identity offered.

11. An influential message contained in the labelling processes that is related to social class is that to be working class, and certainly to end up there, is something unfortunate and undesirable.

Further Reading

Alexander, R. (1992) *Policy and Practice in Primary Education*. London: Routledge.

Byrne, D., Williamson, B. and Fletcher, B. (1974) *The Poverty of Education*. Oxford: Martin Robertson. The interplay of social class, region and resource provision in education is the subject of this book.

David, T., Curtis, A. and Siraj-Blatchford, I. (1992) *Effective Teaching in the Early Years*. Stoke-on-Trent: Trentham Books.

Douglas, J.W.B. (1964) *The Home and the School*. St Albans: Panther Books. Contains considerable data on social class and education.

Douglas, J.W.B., Ross, J.M. and Simpson, H.R. (1971) *All Our Future*. St Albans: Panther Books. Also contains considerable data on social class and education.

Halsey, A.H., Heath, A.F. and Ridge, J.M. (1980) *Origins and Destinations*. Oxford: Clarendon Press.

Oppenheim, C. (1990) *Poverty: The Facts*. London: The Child Poverty Action Group

Reay, D., David, M.E., and Ball, S. (2005) *Degrees of Choice: Class, Gender and Higher Education*, London: Trentham Books.

Reid, I. (1986) *The Sociology of School and Education*. London: Paul Chapman Publishing. The most prolific source of data on social class. Chapter 6 deals with education. (Anyone who cherishes the illusion that social class is no longer a feature of British life should consult this book – strongly recommended!)

Skellington, R. (1992) *'Race' in Britain Today*. London: Sage Publications in association with Open University Press.

Social Trends, **26**, 1996.

Swift, D. (1977) *Selection and Opportunity*. Milton Keynes: Open University, E207 Unit 22.

Discussion and Activities

1. An interesting simulation that could be used in a group is *Autobiography: A Look at Social Class Inequalities*, by R. Fielding and V. M. Anderson, published as a 'Briefing for Teachers' by the Association for the Teaching of the Social Sciences and available from the ATSS Resources Unit.

2. Social class emerges as an issue in relation to upper-class educational life chances in Chapter 29. It might be interesting to try to anticipate this chapter by establishing what you know and believe about this topic.

Signposts

1. Social class and gender

Consider the interplay of social class and gender. One attempt to do this is a paper by M. MacDonald (1980) 'Schooling and the Reproduction of Class and Gender Relations', in L. Barton, R. Meighan and S. Walker (eds), *Schooling, Ideology and the Curriculum*, Lewes: Falmer Press. See also Walker, S. and Barton, L. (eds) (1983) *Gender, Class and Education*, Lewes: Falmer Press.

2. Higher education

The relationship between social class and higher educational life chances is a further topic for investigation. See Reid, I. (1986) *The Sociology of School and Education*, London: Paul Chapman Publishing, Chapter 6, as a starting point.

28 'Race' and Ethnic Identity

IRAM SIRAJ-BLATCHFORD

Even though we face the difficulties of today and yesterday, I have a dream that one day my children will live in a nation where they will not be judged by the colour of their skin, but by the content of their character.

Martin Luther King Jr

INTRODUCTION AND DEFINITIONS

'Race' is a difficult subject to talk about, not least because of the contentious nature of many of the terms that are used in the discussion themselves. The word 'race' itself has an established scientific meaning: it is a biological term referring to clearly defined genetic groups. One of the problems that we currently face is due to the fact that when the majority of today's school teachers were at school they were taught that this scientific concept could be applied unproblematically to human population groups. What we now know is that the genetic variation found *within* human population groups is actually greater than the variation *between* them. There is therefore no scientific basis for defining *human* races at all. Yet nineteenth-century and early twentieth-century anthropology was dominated by a view that humans fell into three racial groupings: Negroid, Caucasoid and Mongoloid, or 'black', 'white' and 'yellow'. The belief that these groups were different in key aspects led to the ranking of them in order of superiority/inferiority, a belief developed to its logical limit in Nazi theories of the master race.

Perhaps the only reason why the term 'race' is still in use at all (even in quotes to show that it is a misnomer) is because black and ethnic minority people have chosen to hold on to it in defiance. The term 'black' certainly has this kind of history. Originally a term of abuse, the term black was first adopted by African-Americans in an effort to generate solidarity in the struggle against 'racial' prejudice in the USA. The 'Black is Beautiful' campaign of the 1960s spread throughout the world. As South African journalist Stephen Biko put it:

> Merely by describing yourself as black you have started on a road towards emancipation, you have committed yourself to fight against all forces that seek to use your blackness as a stamp that marks you as a subservient human being.

In Britain, the term black has been taken up by nearly all those groups who have suffered the common experience of racism. Black solidarity groups therefore commonly include members of South Asian, and even Far Eastern, origin. A long running debate among such groups has centred on the legitimacy of including the Irish, who have also suffered from prejudice over many generations in Britain. In the main the term is currently applied to include all the 'visible minorities', or those ethnic groups within Britain easily identifiable by the colour of their skin. It is ironic that in recent years the term has been adopted by government bodies in a much less inclusive manner in their collection of statistics. In official documents it is now common to see references to Black Caribbean and Black African categories alongside Indian, Pakistani, etc. Perhaps more worrying is the trend towards adopting the terms 'black and ethnic minority' in the so-called 'race relations' industry.

The term 'ethnic minority' also has a number of problems. It is inaccurate to begin with: the very minorities that it refers to in a British context are majorities from a global perspective. A 'minority' may be considered of marginal importance, yet in the more interdependent world of today, concepts of the global village may be more appropriate. Another problem is related to the exclusive use of the term 'ethnic' to designate or objectify minorities. In some circles the term 'ethnic' has actually become a euphemism for 'black'. This distracts attention from the fact that everyone has an ethnicity, that we are all members of ethnic groups. Everyone is brought up in a culture with particular traditions and we therefore all have an ethnic identity. If intolerance and cultural chauvinism is included as part of this culture then we need to be especially aware of it.

In the following discussion, in an effort to steer through the apparent minefield of terminology on the subject, and in the interests of literary solidarity, we will refer to those suffering the common experience of racism as 'black'. In adopting this term we are not referring to the colour of anyone's skin and so, in the interests of consistency, we will refer to the native British population (if that concept were not problematic enough in itself) as the 'ethnic majority'. This will also serve to remind some readers of their own ethnicity.

Black children represent a small proportion of the total school population yet these pupils are often concentrated in certain areas, urban areas like London, South Lancashire and the West Midlands. Estimates of the total Black population in Britain vary slightly, but the most reliable figures suggest about 2.58 million or 4.7 per cent of the total population (Labour Force Statistics 1986–8). Nearly half of this number was born in Britain. The largest single group are of Indian ethnicity, at about 30.5 per cent of the total black British population; African-Caribbeans make up about another 19 per cent and Pakistanis 16.5 per cent. The variety of other groups each make up less than 5 per cent of the total black population.

THE UNDERACHIEVEMENT OF BLACK PUPILS

The first official recognition that black children were underachieving came in 1977 when the House of Common's Select Committee on Race Relations and Immigration reported that:

as a matter of urgency the Government [should] institute a high level and independent inquiry into the causes of the underachievement of children of West Indian [African Caribbean] origin in maintained schools and the remedial action required.

The government accepted the need for inquiry and extended it to include the educational underachievement of all black children. A committee of inquiry was formed in 1979; it produced an interim report in 1981 and finally produced its report *Education for All* (The Swann Report) in 1985. The history of the two reports illustrates the political sensitivity of the issues concerned. In 1977, the House of Commons Select Committee on race relations had proposed 'as a matter of urgency' an inquiry into the causes of underachievement of children of 'West Indian' origin. The 'matter of urgency' took eight years to complete, with the dismissal of one chairperson, Lord Rampton, after the first report was published, along with the resignation of five committee members, followed later by two others, before a final report that was considered acceptable to the government of the day was produced.

One of the major limitations to early educational initiatives was that mixed comprehensive schools were considered to provide a solution to the problem in the same way that coeducational schools were seen to provide a solution to the underachievement of girls. The needs of black children and those of the underprivileged, underachieving, working-class members of the indigenous population were considered to be largely the same. The 'solution', therefore, was seen as locating the deprived areas and providing general support in various compensatory programmes. This seemed all the more plausible, since incoming ethnic minority groups often had to settle in those parts of cities that already had old school buildings, high staff turnovers and limited facilities. The inadequacies of the approach of stressing similarities with general underachievement, and largely ignoring various differences such as language, cultural identities and the prejudice related to skin colour, are the focus of several analyses of the situation (e.g. Troyna, 1978; Jeffcoate, 1979; Rex and Tomlinson, 1979; Barton and Walker, 1983; Klein, 1993).

Many mistaken assumptions were made regarding the educational expectations held by black parents and regarding the class composition of the various ethnic communities. As Nigel Harris argued in an article in the *Times Higher Education Supplement*:

> People forget that immigrants mean workers in the most energetic age groups, high-level skills and even capital. For example, a third of first-generation immigrants to Britain have a degree (compared with 12 per cent of the British-born).
>
> Harris, 1997

Look at Table 26.4 in Chapter 26 which illustrates the social class structure of the various communities. The statistics are taken from the Labour Force Survey of 1995. It is based on the occupations of people of working age and covers those people who are either in employment or who have had a job in the past eight years.

Between 1987 and 1989, the Labour Force Surveys showed that 14 per cent of black people were unemployed compared with 9 per cent of the ethnic majority. In this the young were disproportionately affected, and the figures for this age group are particularly striking. During the same period 12 per cent of ethnic majority 16- and 24-year-olds were unemployed. This can be compared with 25 per cent of African-Caribbeans, 16 per cent of Indian and 27 per cent of Pakistani and Bangladeshi young people (Oppenheim, 1990). Even when employed, black people tend to be in lower paid jobs and, as Skellington *et al.* (1992) demonstrate, Department of Employment statistics clearly show that the higher unemployment rates for black people cannot be explained by differences in qualification levels. Unemployment rates are generally higher among black people than among ethnic majority groups with the same level of qualifications:

> Racism and racial discrimination accounts for most of the discrepancies in the employment statistics for black people. Generally, the over-representation of blacks on the employment register and in low-paid jobs still prevails, and now there is consistent research data to verify this in the private as well as public sectors . . . there will no doubt be a steady growth in black businesses, but this is not going to resolve the economic crisis faced by the black community.
>
> Bhat *et al.*, 1988

The international nature of the issues raised by the presence of black children in ethnic majority schools is indicated in a survey of nearly two hundred articles on this theme published in journals from English-speaking countries worldwide conducted by Grant and Sleeter (1985). The articles included experience from Australia, Canada, England, Indonesia, Scotland, Sweden and the USA. The experience of member countries of the Council of Europe was the focus of an edition of *Forum* in 1984 entitled 'Racism and Xenophobia'. Few countries are free of conflicts related to ethnic minorities, and in some – such as Northern Ireland, Cyprus, Sri Lanka, Lebanon and the former Yugoslavia – it either is or has been the source of prolonged armed conflict.

The labour market in Britain is segregated according to both race and gender (Jenkins, 1986), and black and ethnic minority students, teachers and lecturers are underrepresented throughout our educational system. They are also disproportionately placed in low-status sets, streams and posts within school and college hierarchies (CRE, 1988; Gillborn, 1990; Siraj-Blatchford, 1991; Troyna, 1991).

THE EDUCATIONAL LIFE CHANCES OF ETHNIC MINORITY GROUPS

Some of the reasons why it is difficult to establish with any precision the educational life chances of black children have already been mentioned. First, the question of overlapping features is prominent. Some black children share the general disadvantages of members of the working classes. Many live in inner-city areas, and so share the disadvantages of a particular urban group, sometimes known as the 'new poor', often with multiple deprivations. This is a phenomenon referred to at length in Chapter 27, but as Rex and Tomlinson (1979) put it:

Apart from the problem of differences of life chances, life-styles and values between white-collar and manual workers, it now seems to be increasingly recognized that there are divisions between manual workers – between those who have job security and political and trade-union protection of their social rights on the one hand and those who live within 'a tangle of pathologies' on the other.

Second, given all the socio-economic differences referred to above, the achievement of various groups of black pupils differs. While only 21 per cent of African-Caribbean pupils gained five or more GCSEs at grade A to C in 1993, Indian children did as well as the ethnic majority, with 45 per cent achieving these grades. The Department for Education and Employment (DfEE) statistics show that in the 'Other Asian' group, which includes Chinese pupils, 51 per cent of pupils achieved the grades, yet only 23 per cent of Pakistani and Bangladeshi pupils did so.

A further difficulty is related to an assumption that underpins the concept of life chances itself. In accepting the logic of 'underachievement', the status quo is taken for granted. The questions are: What chances are there in the system as it stands? Who gets what in the present educational structure? This obscures the issue of alternatives, and these may be a crucial issue for black people, for 'getting on' at the expense of others means both adopting the dominant culture's point of view, which may be seen as corrupt, and adding to the isolation and oppression of other members of your group by distancing yourself from them. As Rex and Tomlinson argued in 1979: 'It may seem to some that to try to launch one's children into social mobility and assimilation is to connive at the oppression of one's own people.'

The regular patterns that appear in the education biographies of black pupils appear to be as follows.

1. The chances of experiencing a public school education are very small since many are located as members of the 'new poor'.
2. The chances of being allocated to an SEN school or being excluded from school are greater for black pupils than for members of the ethnic majority (Coard, 1971; Tomlinson, 1981).
3. Black pupils continue to be the victims of discrimination when applying for places in prestigious universities. As a study by the Policy Studies Institute showed in 1992: 'Black Caribbean and Pakistani applicants were still significantly less likely to have been admitted to university although Black Caribbean and Indian applicants were more likely to have been admitted to polytechnics as they were called in 1992' (CSO, 1996).
4. Black pupils are likely to be overrepresented in the bottom streams and remedial classes of secondary schools (Jeffcoate, 1977; Troyna, 1978; Ball, 1981). As Tomlinson suggests, 'ability is an ambiguous concept and school conceptions of ability can be affected by perceptions that pupils are members of particular social and ethnic groups and by the behaviour of individual pupils' (Tomlinson, 1987).
5. Black pupils tend to experience schools with a concentration of other black pupils. Describing the situation in Birmingham, Rex and Tomlinson (1979) concluded: 'Most

will go to immigrant majority schools, i.e. they will not simply be a minority presenting unusual problems against a background of white British normality. Their problems will be the problems of the school.' The finding of an Inner London Education Authority study was that 'the effect of immigrant concentration on educational performance is less important than the degree to which schools are experiencing multiple deprivation' (Little, 1975).

6. Black pupils are more likely to be suspended or expelled from school: 'ILEA figures for 1987 reveal that pupils from African-Caribbean backgrounds were heavily overrepresented among those suspended from schools: 33 per cent of pupils suspended were of African-Caribbean origin, yet African-Caribbeans were only 14 per cent of the ILEA school population. The research showed that African-Caribbean pupils were more likely than other pupils to be suspended for a single severe offence' (Skellington *et al.*, 1992).

One attempt to summarize the educational life chances of ethnic minority groups was given in Field and Hankin (1971). They suggested that immigrants and other 'out' groups in society generally benefited proportionally least from education. A few teachers chose to work in the 'twilight' zones of big cities and found it rewarding to serve among the children of immigrants, the very poor, the chronically sick and unsupported mothers. For the most part, it is difficult to attract and keep staff for schools in inner-city areas and, in addition, the buildings and equipment are often of poor quality.

Employment in Schools

In 1990 the DES reported that about 15,000 new teachers were being appointed in England and Wales each year. In 1991, 67 South Asians, 45 'black students' and 4,129 ethnic majority students were accepted into undergraduate courses in the universities and colleges of higher education (UCCA, 1992). On the one-year post-graduate certificate in education courses their were 177 South Asians, 102 'black' and 11,345 ethnic majority students admitted. In polytechnic BEd courses, 80 South Asian, 132 'black' and 8,603 ethnic majority students were admitted. This gives an overall 2.3 per cent for ethnic minority acceptance into initial teacher education (ITE) (Adelman, 1993). In many other courses for that year the acceptances of ethnic minority students reached 10 per cent. How do we account for this disparity?

A Commission for Racial Equality (1988) survey suggested that more than half of the black and ethnic minority teachers in this country experience racial discrimination, and over three-quarters feel that racial discrimination has adversely affected their careers. The research shows that the ethnic minority teachers are on lower salaries and overrepresented on the lowest rungs of the professional ladder, and that they are disproportionately concentrated in shortage subjects or where ethnic minority pupils are involved.

Further insight into the plight of black and ethnic minority teachers can be found in the reasons the Swann Report provided to explain why so few potential ethnic minority pupils aspired to be teachers. It was suggested that:

- they had experienced the racism and negative stereotyping of ethnic minority groups while at school and had no desire therefore to rejoin such an institution;
- they were disenchanted by the somewhat limited role which they felt many ethnic minority teachers were asked to play in the system – as E2L or 'mother tongue' teachers or simply as supervisors of ethnic minority pupils;
- the restricted career opportunities this presented;
- they did not regard teaching as offering good career prospects in the current economic situation, especially since they felt their own chances in the job market would be hindered by the influence of racism.

Swann Report, 1985, p. 609

Morrison and McIntyre (1976) suggested that suitably qualified candidates often chose not to enter the teaching profession owing to the perceived monotony of teachers' work, their low pay, the discipline problems and poor promotion prospects. Raminder Singh's (1988) survey of South Asian and white ethnic majority sixth-former perceptions of teaching also found that well qualified South Asian pupils cited the racism that they had experienced or witnessed among pupils and staff as a major deterrent to entering the profession.

Gender and 'Race' Research in ITE: An Apparent Contradiction

In the past, 'race' equality research in ITE tended to focus upon the differential access provided to higher education and the teaching profession, and to aspects of discrimination in course contents, teaching practice, the experiences of ethnic minority ITE students and the attitudes of their white peers. A major assumption that has informed this approach to research has been the perceived need for black and ethnic minority pupils to be given positive role models. The suggestion has also been made that the presence of black and ethnic minorities as students in ITE and as teachers in schools would have an educational influence upon their ethnic majority peers. Unfortunately, this assumed need to increase black and ethnic minority involvement in ITE in order to improve the educational achievement of black and ethnic minority pupils is clearly contradicted by realities of women's involvement in education. Women dominate the teaching profession, yet they have failed to effect radically the achievement of girls in key subject areas. The issues are more complex than they would appear at first sight (Siraj-Blatchford, 1995).

The apparent contradictions in the overrepresentation of women and the under-representation of black and ethnic minorities in education begs the question of why people choose teacher education and focuses attention upon issues of social expectations. An associated question relates to our target groups for research: are we focusing our attention on the right groups? Should we be focusing on the minority cultures or on the majority cultures?

Structured Absences

The discourses of teacher education, just as much as school curriculum, are dominated by 'technicist' concerns, to find the best means to reach pre-chosen educational ends. Mainstream research in teacher education has effectively been 'deracialized'. What we also need to recognize is that it is equally 'degendered', along with the dominant practices that it is studying. Ideology functions as much by the *structured absence* of alternative concerns as by any inclusion. The dominant research perspectives in schooling are themselves ideological and the ideology serves to provide normative consensus and socio-economic adjustment to our essentially stratified and unequal society. Despite some progress in the 1970s and early 1980s, the past ten years have seen the erosion of all official efforts to incorporate issues of gender and racial equality into ITE. The emphasis has now been firmly focused upon narrowly defined school-based competencies and the '*delivery*' of the National Curriculum.

Stasis

Menter's (1989) study of students on teaching practice focused on the triad of teacher, student and college supervisor, and described how tensions and contradictions within the triad influence students' reflective and critical development of issues of racism and sexism in schools. His findings are not encouraging. Teaching practice, he concluded,

> is characterised by 'stasis', a strong tendency for those most closely involved to avoid conflict or confrontation. Even mild appraisal of existing classroom practice is avoided. To the extent that approaches to the appraisal of practising teachers are based on similar 'supervisory' models, the implication is that the effect will not be the 'development' or 'improvement' of practice so much as the reinforcement of existing practices, whether good or bad.

Given government reforms to move ITE more firmly into schools, this stasis and reinforcement of existing practices takes on even more significance. In the short term both the training of students and those teachers designated as their mentors may be compromised. In the long term we may look forward to the further development of stasis characterizing relations at the macro level, between students, the schools and higher education institutions.

EXPLANATIONS

There have been both psychological and sociological attempts to explain the relationships outlined above. One type of psychological attempt proposes that inheritance of abilities is the major factor. As in the cases of girls and low social classes, the proposition is that inferior qualities are passed on by parents to their children. In this case the parents are said to be those belonging to distinct 'racial' groups. This approach has been at the centre of a long-standing debate about 'race' differences in intelligence, and the validity of defining 'races' at all. The logical and methodological problems are similar to those outlined earlier in the cases of gender and social class.

A National Union of Teachers report (NUT, 1978) usefully summarized the basic assumptions of this genetic approach that make it particularly suspect:

1. In biological terms the concept of 'race' is meaningless for human populations.
2. More than 94 per cent of all genetic differences between individuals that have been studied occur between individuals of the same 'race', not between 'races'.
3. Intelligence tests may give results agreeing with children's school performance, but they say nothing about any fixed 'biological potential' of the individual.
4. It is not meaningful or possible to divide a child's performance into 'genetic' or 'environmental' components.
5. The determinants of 'civilization' and the development of different human societies should be sought in social, economic and historical factors, not in biology.

It is interesting to note that Schiff and Lewontin (1986), in their celebrated critique of geneticism, argue that the greatest single source of bias in intelligence quotient (IQ) tests is in their failure to engage with practical real-life situations. In fact the only claim to validity that IQ tests have is in the correlation between their scores and subsequent success in school. We have a circular argument here. IQ testing assumes that success in schooling provides the most concrete measure of known intelligence. Yet if success in school has more to do with social conditions than with innate ability, then the IQ test becomes a measure of the effects of that instead.

An alternative set of explanations has developed the notion of cultural discontinuities, where differences in the family background and community life of black children are seen as deficits and disadvantages, e.g. inadequate linguistic stimulation in early childhood and high incidence of child-minding. One writer listed seven variations of this approach:

> A number of reasons have been offered for this different level of educational performance; they range from (1) culture shock, (2) length of separation from parents, (3) movement from a predominantly rural background to an industrial one, (4) age of the children during migration, (5) reception into an unknown ready-made family in Britain, (6) language

difficulties, (7) problems of adjustment from a poorer country to a richer and more developed one.

Chevannes, 1979

Another attempt at explanation was mentioned earlier. It is the view that the needs of black pupils and those of the underprivileged, underachieving, working-class members of the ethnic majority population are largely the same. The issue is seen as one of general disadvantage, and the concept of educational disadvantage was developed in the Plowden Report (1967), where, for example, black and ethnic majority children in the inner-city areas of cities were seen as equally deprived.

An alternative view locates the problem in the nature of contemporary British society: it has not yet become effectively multicultural, but remains essentially racist. The view that black children should be assimilated to the mainstream indigenous culture was encouraged by the Commonwealth Immigrants Advisory Council's view (1964) that the perpetration of the different values of immigrant groups could not be expected. More recently, cultural diversity and mutual tolerance have been seen as the way forward, 'as a pleasant optional extra which all sensible men will appreciate, because it adds quality to the lives of us all'. But, as Rex and Tomlinson (1979) pointed out:

> The West Indian is far from claiming an optional extra when he asks that some way be found of preserving his own cultural traditions and educating his children in them. Like black Americans, West Indians feel that they face a culture within which the achievements of white Europeans are continually asserted, while black men always appear in a degraded role. This is so deeply entrenched in our culture, according to this view, that it has become unconscious.

The consequence is that education, for black children, means having to learn to accept inferior images of themselves, their families and culture. The explanation that many black pupils underachieve because of the racist nature of British society leads to the conclusion that the children concerned are not so much failing as being failed by the nature of the current educational system. This is in line with similar explanations for the failure of girls in some subject areas and of the children of unskilled manual workers: racist, sexist and class discriminatory behaviour are all seen as stemming from the acceptance of the psychological propositions that one 'race' is superior to another, or that one sex is superior to another, or that one class is superior to another, because of some beliefs about genetic inheritance.

THE CONTRIBUTION OF INTERACTIONIST APPROACHES

Layers of Meaning and Racism

The definition of racism as 'all those theories and practices that are derived from the assumption that one ethnic group is superior to another because of genetic inheritance' seems straightforward enough. However, the manifestations of racism in a society are complicated. Racism can be proposed by any group; hence 'black' racism is as feasible as ethnic majority racism. The layers of meaning concept in interactionist sociology may help to clarify in two ways:

1. By identifying the multiple interpretation of the participants in an institution or social situation; for example, the views of a black girl arriving in British society may be shown to be quite different from those attributed to her by white members of the indigenous population (see Chevannes, 1979).
2. By analysing how racism manifests itself in different layers of social meaning and action.

Taking the latter approach, it is possible to see three layers of social meaning, distinct in some ways, but necessarily interacting in other respects:

1. The general cultural.
2. The institutional, in the case of education, schools, etc.
3. The personal.

At the general cultural layer, we are all likely to harbour a number of racial prejudices because we have been socialized into the dominant ideas, values and structures of our culture. These ideas will include notions of who counts as 'them' and not 'us', as 'foreigners', or 'immigrants'. We are also likely to harbour a few stereotypical notions regarding the expected behaviours of members of 'other' cultures. In most cultures this socialization tends to be ethnocentric, valuing the familiar culture as normally the best way of doing things and rating any alternative ways as likely to be inferior. The ethnocentric nature of history textbooks was one illustration given in the section on the hidden aspects of the official curriculum. It took hundreds of years of colonial exploitation and imperialism to construct the elaborate system of racist self-justification of late nineteenth- and early twentieth-century Britain. We should not be altogether surprised if it is taking a generation or two to dismantle it.

At the institutional layer, the notion of the teacher and pupil as victims of sets of institutional patterns to which the new arrival has to adjust has already been discussed (Chapters 2 and 3). The institutional package already in existence may include bias in selection procedures, racism in textbooks and curriculum materials, and complacency about the underachievement of black pupils.

Individual racism is perhaps easier to identify, since it leads to direct confrontations:

> Individual racism takes such forms as physical attacks and abuse directed against minority group teachers and pupils, racialist leaflets at school gates, staff prejudices, and hostile white reactions to the introduction of multiracial materials in the classroom.
>
> Jeffcoate, 1979

This analysis in terms of layers of meanings allows for some crucial contradictions in behaviour to be identified. The interactionist notion of the irony of some human action (which does not discount the maliciousness of other human behaviour) is seen in the well intentioned application of policies with unrecognized racism at their roots, which often, to the surprise of the instigators, with their lack of sociological awareness, end up as failures. To dismiss such educationalists as hypocrites is to fail to recognize the irony of human action when teachers and curriculum developers are victims of hidden bias in their well intentioned work.

However, in the case of racism, to understand is not to condone, for the consequences for the individuals and groups unfairly discriminated against are likely to be similar whether the actions were well intentioned or malicious. Therefore, those who acted in haste under the pressure of circumstances when, without adequate planning or advice, they were faced with unfamiliar problems created by the arrival of black children in classrooms can be accorded sympathetic understanding. But the outcome of many of those decisions was still racist, as the list of life chances given earlier has indicated.

Labelling Theory and Racism

Among the problems faced by black pupils in schools are those of general disadvantages of being members of the 'new poor' and the specific disadvantages of being bilingual (or multilingual) in a monolingual society, of cultural identity and racial discrimination. Labelling theory has something to contribute to the understanding of all these problems, particularly the specific ones.

Language and bilingualism

It is through the language or languages that children speak that they actually form their sense of identity, community and belonging. The way the languages that they speak are perceived also influences the way they feel about themselves. Unfortunately it is still common to find individuals working within education who view ethnic minority languages with prejudice. Such individuals typically want ethnic minority children to lose their links with their mother tongue and to assimilate with the English-speaking group. Just as there is a hierarchy of valuing some 'racial' groups more than others, there is a similar racism towards languages. Research by Rudolph Schaffer and his team (Ogilvy *et al.*, 1991) in Scotland has shown how children in multi-ethnic Scottish nurseries were treated differently, according to their ethnicity, by the nursery staff. The research reported that all the nursery staff felt they treated the children according to their individual needs. However, when the observations and video tapes of interactions between staff and children were analysed the findings were disturbing. Although the staff felt they were giving equal and caring attention to all the children, they were in reality favouring the indigenous Scottish group.

The South Asian children were reported to be receiving less attention and fewer verbal interactions, and staff used poor models of English when explaining things to them. In fact, staff often failed to attempt sustained conversations with the minority group and spoke for the children when answers were required. They resorted to a 'pidgin' English, providing a distorted version of English to the very children who most needed correct models. Research by Biggs and Edwards (1992) has provided yet another depressing reminder that children in some infant schools continue to be grossly disadvantaged by their educators. They describe their investigation of the interactions of five different teachers in multi-ethnic infant classes. As they report:

> Teachers were found to interact less frequently with Black children than White; they have fewer exchanges lasting more than thirty seconds with Black children; they also spent less time with them discussing the particular task which had been set ... It is suggested that there is an urgent need for teachers and teacher educators to look more critically at the ways in which stereotypes are mediated through language.

Early childhood teachers believe that children need to have their languages valued and their home experiences affirmed in order to feel secure enough to venture into the language and culture of their early years setting. However, staff need training, knowledge and guidance on the development of appropriate bilingual programmes.

Over 70 per cent of the world's population has more than one language, yet in British education and care settings being bilingual is still too often perceived as an aberration, or worse, as something children should grow out of. Too often bilingual children are perceived as being merely non-English speakers; they are perceived as a problem. Research directly contradicts this view, showing that supporting a child's home language aids the development of English learning and conceptual growth (Cummins, 1984; Verhallen et al., 1989; Pinsent, 1992); in other words, a strong foundation in the child's home language is a necessary prerequisite to the learning of a second or third language. Evidence from a project in Bradford (Fitzpatrick, 1987) showed, for example, that Punjabi- and English-speaking bilinguals performed better in English and other areas of the curriculum when they were given the opportunity to use their home language and to be taught using their home language simultaneously with English. Ethnic minority children should be given the opportunity to acquire English as a second (or third, or fourth) language in the most efficient and effective way, without prejudice to their home languages (Siraj-Blatchford, 1994).

Cultural identity

The conclusion of recent investigations into the self-concepts of ethnic minority pupils is that the risk of their having to accept an image of themselves as inferior as the result of schooling, among other influences, is considerable. The risk of the African Caribbean group is greater, Rex and Tomlinson argue:

> From this point of view the Asian communities must be objects of envy to the African-Caribbean. Their religious and cultural traditions and organizations are strong, and, even while their children are using school education in an instrumental way, their supplementary cultural education confirms a worthy self-image. Moreover, the host society has learned to recognize the separate Asian religions and the claim which they have to being taught in school.

Yet African-Caribbeans are expected to make no claim to have their culture taught in schools. One consequence has been a demand for Black Studies, which is not at all easily conceded:

> Multiculturalism as an optional extra is one thing. Black Studies which are based upon a refusal of the black man to be assimilated, or still worse, upon a culture of Third World revolt are quite another. As a result, the multicultural programmes which have been offered simply do not meet the needs which West Indians feel.
>
> Rex and Tomlinson, 1979

The Schools Council project Education for a Multicultural Society collected material on the cultural identities of ethnic minority pupils. Here are some examples quoted by Jeffcoate (1975) that support the proposition that images of inferiority are in evidence in schools:

> Richard is four, British and black, and he goes to nursery school. Watching television with his mother he observed that a man on the screen was black. His mother agreed and added that the man was like Richard in this respect. To her surprise Richard denied his own blackness and, in response to further questioning, the blackness of his mother and of his closest relatives. Though persuaded to agree that his mother and family were black, he persisted with the fiction of his own non-blackness. Doreen lives 20 miles away from Richard. She is also black and in her first year at secondary school. Last year at her multiracial junior school she wrote, along with the rest of her class, a piece called 'Myself'. In it she said: 'I wish that I had long hair, but I have not got long hair. I do not like myself and my writing. I do not like the colour of my eyes. I have spots on my skin which I wish that I never had ... In the future I think that I am going to turn ... black, ever so black, and ugly just like I am now, ugly.'
>
> Two hundred miles away and at about the same time, a group of three- and four-year-old white children in an all-white nursery school in a multiracial town were shown photographs of black people. The photographs were deliberately selected to portray blacks in a respectful and unstereotyped way. Yet, after three or four minutes, the children began to make derisory comments punctuated by cries of 'Ugh, blackies' and continued to do so until the teacher intervened. She was as surprised as Richard's mother had been, admitting later to having been 'bowled over' by the animosity the children had displayed. Not so one of the mothers. She had already had a similar experience with her own child, who had pointed to Pakistani customers in a shop and said: 'Oh, blackies, ugh, dirty Pakis.'

The learning of such identities can be seen as illustrations of the theories of labelling, self-fulfilling prophecies and teacher expectation effects outlined earlier. The mechanisms involved include many of the features of the hidden curriculum and the official curriculum analysed earlier.

Bias in selection procedures

There is a variety of selection procedures in schools, including selection into streams, examination and non-examination groups, remedial classes and special schooling. The list of educational life chances given earlier indicates that there is a distinct selection pattern for ethnic minority groups, and the result has been a charge of bias in the procedures. Tests of supposedly innate performance such as IQ tests have been the subject of considerable debate. The content and assumptions of such tests, as well as the statistical basis of the testing procedures, have been questioned. One writer expresses his doubt thus:

> when we administer 'a battery of attainment tests' to an immigrant child we ask him: 'How English are you?' When his performance replies: 'Not very', we say: 'You are deprived and handicapped and must have remedial treatment until we have exorcized all traces of the alien spirit from your academic behaviour.'
>
> Marsh, 1971

In the case of selection for special schools, it is frequently left to individual teachers to 'identify' possible children, using a checklist which may include items like slovenliness in appearance, attention seeking, resentfulness, argumentativeness, impudence, lack of interest in work and disobedience. Passing over difficulties such as the subjective interpretations involved (for, as Hargreaves *et al.* (1978) have shown, one teacher's 'cheek' is interpreted by another as 'lively banter'), the consequences are said to be:

> The teacher tends to pick out the most boisterous children rather than the dullest. That is why there are more boys than girls in SEN schools – and more African-Caribbeans than Asians.
>
> Lee, 1978

CONCLUSION

There appears to be a growing view that the educational policies adopted in the cases of black pupils are dubious. Williams (1979) identified three types of policy: technicist, moral and sociopolitical. The technicist approach, stressing that the existing education system was basically sound, encouraged the experts within the teaching profession to develop compensatory programmes to remedy underachievement. The moral approach implied that a new multicultural vision of society should be applied in schools in order to develop awareness, understanding and tolerance of different cultures, to replace the current racist social structures and behaviours. The sociopolitical approach also had a vision of a plural society of relatively separate but equal groups, but stressed that changes outside schools were as necessary as, if not more vital than, those inside.

The contribution of interactionist approaches in sociology and of labelling theory is to identify in some detail some of the false diagnoses that led to the adoption of the technicist approach, as well as the complexity of the consequences. In a survey of the literature on the concept of 'multicultural education' in journals written in English worldwide, Grant and Sleeter (1985) propose a typology of five competing forms of multicultural education.

Teachers as key agents of reform

Siraj-Blatchford (1995) has argued that much of the rhetoric and debates surrounding teacher education and race and gender equality in the UK has maintained that teachers have a special role and responsibility in tackling racism and sexism. It is argued that teachers need to understand the role that education plays in the process of sustaining and reproducing racism and sexism. Yet, as we have seen, there are various understandings being promoted. However, there are two broad approaches that can be identified in both the research perspectives and the forms of provision that are advocated. Multicultural/equal opportunity approaches have tended to focus upon the negative effects that education has upon the educational perfor-mance of girls in some subject areas, and on black and ethnic minority pupils in general. In contrast, anti-racist/anti-sexist approaches have more often emphasized the role that edu-cation has in reproducing structural inequality through its preferential treatment of boys and ethnic majority pupils. While some anti-racist/anti-sexist writers have drawn attention to the importance of positively influencing the socialization of future adult males and ethnic majorities as potential discriminators, others, taking a more traditional Marxist approach, emphasize the role of the state and of policy. An adequate treatment of the various con-ceptions of the state and of the neo-Gramscian approaches that have informed the emphasis upon masculinity, patriarchy, white supremacy and decolonialism is beyond the scope of this chapter.

During the 1970s and early 1980s research was focused upon the injustice of teacher stereotyping and the prejudicial treatment of ethnic minority pupils (Britain, 1976; Edwards, 1978; Rex and Tomlinson, 1979). At the same time, anti-racist perspectives were beginning to shift the emphasis beyond the adoption of policies and practices for combating racist incidents and for dealing with racial discrimination, racist abuse and name calling. The emphasis moved towards the need for *all* children to be taught about racism, even in predominantly white areas.

The dominant discourse has been firmly rooted in beliefs that multicultural education is about, and for, black and ethnic minority children. The wider context of racism in society and the role of white ethnic majority people in the production and reproduction of it has been largely ignored. It is significant in this context that Giles and Cherrington (1981) found that the main thrust for multicultural educational development was coming from those institu-tions which were situated in urban multi-ethnic conurbations.

In the same way, much of the equal opportunities provision for girls has focused on their subject choices, attitudes and the 'hidden curriculum' that has influenced them. The focus was far from anti-racist and anti-sexist in effect, and has failed to address the needs of all children.

Further Reading

Barton, L. and Walker, S. (eds) (1983) *Race, Class and Education*. Beckenham: Croom Helm.

Biggs, A. and Edwards, A. (1992) ' "I treat them all the same" – Teacher–Pupil Talk in Multi-ethnic Classrooms'. *Language and Education*, **5**, 3, 161–76.

Brown, C. and Harber, C. (eds) (1985) 'Cultural Diversity and Conflict', special edition of *Social Science Teacher*, **14**, 3.

Craft, M. (1982) *Education for Diversity: The Challenge of Cultural Pluralism*. Nottingham: School of Education, University of Nottingham.

Cherrington, D. (ed.) (1985) 'Ethnic Minorities in Education', special edition of *Educational Review*, **37**, 2.

Cummins, J. (1984) *Bilingualism and Special Education: Issues in Assessment and Pedagogy*. Clevedon: Multilingual Matters.

Fitzpatrick, F. (1987) *The Open Door*. Clevedon: Multilingual Matters.

James, A. and Jeffcoate, R. (eds) (1981) *The School in the Multicultural Society*. London: Harper and Row.

Jeffcoate, R. (1979) *Positive Image*. Richmond: Chameleon Books.

Jeffcoate, R. (1984) *Ethnic Minorities in Education*. London: Harper and Row.

Ogilvy, B., Cheyne, J. and Schaffer, R. (1991) 'Staff attitudes and perception in multicultural nursery schools', *Early Child Development and Care*, **64**.

Pinsent, P. (1992) *Language, Culture and Young Children*. London: Fulton.

Rex, J. and Tomlinson, S. (1979) *Colonial Immigrants in a British City*. London: Routledge and Kegan Paul.

Siraj-Blatchford, I. (1995) 'Racialized and Gendered Discourses in Teacher Education', in L. Dawtrey, J. Holland and M. Hammer (eds), *Equality and Inequality in Education Policy*. Clevedon: Multilingual Matters.

Tomlinson, S. (1983) *Ethnic Minorities in British Schools: A Review of the Literature 1960–82*. Aldershot: Gower.

Verhallen, M, Appel, R. and Schoonen, R. (1989) 'Language Functions in Early Childhood Education. the Cognitive–Linguistic Experiences of Bilingual and Monolingual Children', *Language and Education*, **3**, 2, 109–30.

Willey, R. (1984) *Race, Equality and Schools*. London: Methuen.

Discussion and Activities

1. Examine school textbooks for evidence of ethnic bias. A useful source-book is *Racism in Children's Books*, published by the Children's Rights Workshop.

2. Discuss the study by G. Driver, 'How West Indians Do Better at School (Especially the Girls)', *New Society*, 17 January 1980. The subsequent correspondence, lasting for several weeks, raised various points of debate and criticism about the study.

3. 'There is no one black experience in this country, no one set of parental and student aspirations. Minority groups will ask for different things of the education system at different times' (Williams, 1979). Discuss this view and its implications for schooling.

4. Make a summary of the main points of the chapter.

5. What can we learn from the pupils' perspective? See Jeffcoate in James and Jeffcoate (1981, p. 229) for one study.

Signposts

1. Multicultural society and multicultural education

As noted in the chapter these are both ambiguous ideas with competing definitions in play. However, this is not widely acknowledged, so that policies operating under the general label of 'multicultural' can actually be pulling in opposite directions. Writers addressing this issue include Grant and Sleeter (1985), contributors in Brown and Harber (1985), Burntwood in Cherrington (1985) and Mukhopaday (1984).

2. Ethnic minorities as an international experience

The cross-national aspects of ethnic minorities' experience is the focus of several sets of writings. Grant and Sleeter (1985) provide a survey and a framework for analysis, there are articles in Brown and Harber (1985) and the Council of Europe journal *Forum* has a special edition (1984) titled 'Racism and Xenophobia'. See also *The Education of Minority Groups: An Enquiry into Problems and Practices of Fifteen Countries*, Aldershot: Gower, 1984.

3. Ethnic minorities as 'other'

Most people in this country do not recognize that everyone has an ethnic identity and simply observe this phenomenon in others. Discuss the following by Neil Postman and Charles Weingartner (1971): 'it is generally assumed that people of other tribes have been victimized by indoctrination from which our tribe has remained free'. Also refer back to Chapter 23. Globally, some education systems have taught learners to 'hate the other'. A clear example was apartheid in South Africa until 1994. For further examples, see Harber, C. (2004) *Schooling as Violence*, London: Routledge Falmer, Chapter 6.

29 Other Minorities: Those with 'Special Needs'

IRAM SIRAJ-BLATCHFORD

Don't let us make imaginary evils, when you know we have so many real ones to encounter.

Oliver Goldsmith

INTRODUCTION

There are many minorities that either appear to have or lay claim to having special needs. These include travellers' children, the left-handed, commune dwellers, canal boat children, religious exclusives, high achievers (sometimes referred to as 'gifted'), mobile groups such as armed forces personnel, circus folk and other entertainers, members of the Royal Family, various kinds of physically disabled and various kinds of people identified as psychologically disabled, e.g. maladjusted.

The official use of the description 'special' refers to some of these and not others. Some of these minorities have their own school provision. Thus the children of the wealthy have access to the private school system and some religious groups (e.g. Roman Catholics, Jews, Anglicans) have schools. Some commune groups have run their own schools, such as the Bruderhof primary school of the now defunct Wheathill Bruderhof in Shropshire. Travellers, of both gypsy and tinker heritage, have been participants in experimental mobile schools housed in vans, sometimes based on voluntary provision, such as the West Midlands Travellers School, originally initiated by the Walsall Humanist Group. High achievers have a variety of special provisions, including A streams, express streams, sixth forms and the university sector as a whole, although members of pressure groups for the 'gifted' do not see these as going far enough.

When we look at the state and local education authority version of who has special needs to be catered for in terms of special education provision, the emphasis tends to be on physical and psychological disabilities, as Table 29.1 shows.

Barton and Tomlinson (1984) note that the official categories of special need (see Table

Table 29.1 Full-time pupils by category of major handicap

	At January	1973	1974	1978	1979	1980	1981	1982	1983
Blind	Boys	546	549	687	632	632	599	601	570
	Girls	464	446	506	522	494	489	479	426
Partially sighted	Boys	1 265	1 266	1 246	1 229	1 254	1 142	1 061	1 012
	Girls	762	787	830	815	810	719	670	662
Deaf	Boys	1 879	1 923	1 936	1 868	1 786	1 698	1 601	1 557
	Girls	1 549	1 574	1 541	1 462	1 460	1 359	1 266	1 166
Partially hearing	Boys	1 240	1 278	1 161	1 052	838	803	777	697
	Girls	973	978	809	811	619	584	565	515
Physically	Boys	5 606	5 930	6 975	7 140	6 901	6 663	6 525	6 316
handicapped	Girls	4 053	4 264	5 333	5 478	5 408	5 075	4 963	4 816
Delicate	Boys	3 284	3 090	2 801	2 606	2 411	2 309	2 282	2 177
	Girls	1 993	1 877	1 640	1 441	1 311	1 219	1 109	1 072
Maladjusted	Boys	7 934	8 528	10 262	10 233	10 640	10 544	10 533	10 789
	Girls	2 253	2 615	3 072	2 875	2 972	2 693	2 644	2 606
Educationally sub-normal									
Medium	Boys		31 057	33 801	34 294	33 903	34 415	34 441	34 129
Severe	Boys	45 083	14 616	12 901	13 101	13 343	13 456	13 713	13 964
Medium	Girls		20 546	21 694	21 622	21 107	21 403	21 120	20 647
Severe	Girls	31 307	10 786	9 752	9 870	10 043	10 144	10 307	10 499
Epileptic	Boys	794	851	1 115	1 138	1 021	971	878	844
	Girls	554	631	804	808	736	704	652	603
Speech defect	Boys	1 605	2 031	2 468	2 324	2 075	1 824	1 537	1 407
	Girls	779	993	1 339	1 217	1 036	867	715	625
Autistic	Boys		200	384	381	420	429	400	374
	Girls		72	147	172	192	183	180	173
Total	Boys	69 236	71 319	75 737	75 998	75 224	74 853	74 349	73 836
	Girls	44 687	45 569	47 467	47 093	46 188	45 439	44 670	43 810
	Total	113 923	116 888	123 204	123 091	121 412	120 292	119 019	117 646

From *DES Statistics of Education: Schools, 1983*, Table 20/83

29.1) combine both normative and non-normative conditions. In normative conditions there is some basis for agreement about disability or need, such as blindness, deafness or epilepsy. However, categories like 'educationally subnormal' and 'maladjusted' are non-normative, since there are no adequate measuring instruments or agreed definitions.

> In England these non-normative categories have always included the largest numbers of children in special education, and the important point is that these children are predominantly of working-class origins, and, since the settlement of West Indian (African Caribbean) immigrants, have also included large numbers of black children. Thus a major dilemma in the integration debate is that it is predominantly about the integration of children who in England were known in the 1930s as the social problem class . . . and this

raises questions about the nature of special education – how far is it education and how far is it social control?

Barton and Tomlinson, 1984

OFFICIAL CATEGORIZATIONS: WHO HAS SPECIAL NEEDS?

Even a cursory glance at the practice of special education in the UK reveals variation in organization, staffing and policies. A particular child in one LEA will be identified as special and sent to a separate school; in another LEA the same child will be catered for in a unit within a neighbourhood school; and in yet another LEA that same child may not be identified as special in the first place.

Part of the variation is historical, part is related to conceptual confusions and part is related to different pragmatic responses to the problem identified. Modern special education has its origins in the 1944 Education Act, by which local education authorities were required to make special provision for pupils who 'suffer from any disability of mind or body', either in special schools or otherwise. Ten categories of special provision were established, although with such a broad definition to work with it could have been twenty or thirty, and have covered the majority of the population. There was no clear indication of what constituted 'normal', so children defined as special in one area of the country were not necessarily so defined in another.

A further development was brought about by the 1970 Education (Disabled Children) Act, which made the local education authority responsible for those children previously catered for in hospitals. All children, regardless of the degree of disability, were entitled to receive education in schools or otherwise, as organized by the LEAs. Special schools now had a new challenge: children with multiple disabilities, some spending most of their lives in cots in hospital wards, others hyperactive and destructive, were now admitted to schools.

Some of the conceptual confusion is illustrated by the above changes. Who is normal? Who is not normal? Who is so disabled as to be unable to be in schools? These and other related questions have been given different answers at different times and in different places. The confusion is also illustrated by the steep rise in the number of pupils in special schools since 1950 (see Table 29.2).

Using the vague descriptions available, such as 'any child whose attainment falls significantly below the normal', the number of children identified as special has increased. As many as 20 per cent of the school population could be classified as special at some stage between five and 16 years, on the basis of such a description.

The pragmatic nature of the response to pupils identified as special is illustrated by the variation among LEAs. A similar child may be sent to boarding school by one, given home tuition by another and given facilities within a neighbourhood comprehensive school by another.

Table 29.2 Numbers of pupils in special schools

	1950	1975
Maladjusted		
Boys	467	10 140
Girls	120	3 421
Educationally sub-normal (mild)		
Boys	9 205	31 727
Girls	5 968	21 017

That the answer to the question of who has special needs, according to official categor-izations, is a very confused one, historically is further illustrated by the early research of Gibson and Jackson (1974) on 'mental retardation' [*sic*]. They estimate that, since the con-dition of 85 per cent of children identified as 'mentally retarded' has no precise cause (e.g. brain damage), this category may have been 'manufactured' by professional labellers such as doctors, psychiatrists and psychologists. Gibson and Jackson point out that the term 'mental retardation' is highly ambiguous, since it is employed to designate persons who in the past would have been referred to as morons, mental deficients, mental defectives, mental sub-normals or, in more general terms, the feeble-minded. However, the ambiguity of the proposed causes is even more startling: in the past over 100 'causes' of mental retardation had been specified.

From this it follows that 'mental retardation' is not a unitary disorder, in the sense that all persons who are officially thus categorized share a common condition produced by a cause that is identifiable, because the term can include:

1. Persons whose special need is marked and results from a disease of the nervous system or genetic variation.
2. Persons who suffer a fairly specific but less profoundly disabling genetic disorder (for example, Down's syndrome).
3. Persons who have no obvious physical defect and whose intellectual abilities, although inadequate for some tasks, are perfectly adequate for many others (i.e. mildly mentally retarded).

Gibson and Jackson find that the third category constitutes 85 per cent of the mentally retarded population. However, it is rarely possible to identify with any degree of certainty the precise cause of the lesser intellectual performance of those in this category. The 'professional labellers' categorize the 85 per cent with tests of dubious precision:

> While it is acknowledged that there are degrees of mental retardation of such severity that a child's intellectual impairment is undoubted, it has been argued that most mentally retarded children are 'manufactured' by those professionally engaged in the process of educational categorization. The description 'legitimate labellers' has been given to those persons (for

example, doctors, psychiatrists, psychologists and educators) who are presumed to have the necessary knowledge and skills to make a diagnosis.

Gibson and Jackson, 1974

Gibson and Jackson suggest that, as a result of their training and experience, the professional labellers develop a knowledge of trustworthy 'recipes' (i.e. sets of prescriptions to guide future professional action), and they will have a tendency, in their dealings with children referred to them, to think in terms of categories.

In this case, the appropriate 'recipe for action' for detecting and confirming the presence of mental retardation is through the use of diagnostic tests, which are dubious on three counts. First, there is an assumption that what is being examined can be measured precisely, whereas in fact this is an area in which no precision exists, except in the objectives and intentions of the labellers. Second, the diagnostic category arrived at by the labeller is rarely challenged, as it tends to be reinforced both by professional support (i.e. the labellers tend to follow occupational group conceptions) and by audience support (i.e. the labeller is presumed by their audience to have the necessary knowledge and skills to make their diagnoses). Third, spurious objectivity and precision are frequently attributed to coding schemes, checklists and written observations employed in the diagnostic process, whereas in reality these depend on rumour, gossip, instant decisions, guesswork, conversations, discrepant information and imperfect biographical stock-taking from memory.

INTEGRATION OR SEPARATION? THE LOCATION OF SPECIAL EDUCATION

One of the central issues raised by the Warnock Report (1978) was whether special education should take place in normal schools more often than it does at the moment. Part of this concern for a shift in emphasis came from the parents. The lives of children who attend special schools take on a number of characteristics. Children often have to travel some distance because the special schools are not neighbourhood schools, and this can take as much as one and a half hours a day. There is the stigma of the special bus, which may also vary in its timing and reliability, so that pupils arrive at school cold, irritable or tired, or all three. Parents may have to divide their loyalties between the local school for one or more children and the special school for another. Maintaining contact with the distant school can be difficult, and friends children make there may not live close enough to come to tea or to play with at weekends. Other parents and children in the neighbourhood, having little contact with children at the special school, are often unsympathetic and even fearful, and this can result in spiteful and tactless comments, generated by unfamiliarity, and isolation for the child concerned. Therefore, a policy of separation is seen by those involved as having negative effects on the consciousness of both the local people, who are denied familiarity with disabled children, and the parents and children identified as special.

One of the claims made for schemes such as those in the London Borough of Bromley, which provide classes in neighbourhood schools, is that the stigma, isolation and inconvenience suffered by many children categorized as special have been reduced. In Bromley, separation as a policy has been interpreted as bad for children, parents and teachers (Tuckwell and Beresford, 1978). Yet providing classes in ordinary schools does not guarantee integration, since this is an individual issue: the degree of integration achieved by a particular child will vary, but the conditions encourage rather than prevent.

Spending cuts have limited the Bromley initiatives, since it is probably more expensive to provide special classes than it is to provide special schools. Tuckwell and Beresford see the Bromley policy as more demanding for all concerned than a 'neat system of labelling and dumping'.

Support for an integration approach comes from some of those who have been on the receiving end of the separation policy. The Warnock Committee had a submission from the Association of Disabled Professionals urging 'immediate steps to ensure that many more disabled children and many more severely disabled children are integrated in ordinary schools'.

The policy of separation has been supported on several grounds. With a shortage of specialists in speech, sight, hearing and other categories of special needs, it was seen as practical to group children together to obtain the best service for them. In a neighbourhood school such children would probably end up in the remedial streams, whereas in a special school among equals they would be away from this low-status situation. Thus one function of special schools was seen as protection of the vulnerable. This was also a reflection on the neighbourhood schools, which were seen as unable to cope with special needs either in physical facilities or in providing a psychological climate of sympathy and concern to protect the vulnerable.

This raises the issue of whether the mainstream schools, to use the American term, are worth being in. One writer has argued that, unless mainstream schools adopt some of the caring approach and educational methods of the special schools for all their pupils, retaining special schools remains a plausible policy (Medlicott, 1974).

Some interested bodies advocate and adopt a dual approach. SCOPE, the society for people with cerebral palsy, has eight special schools, yet notes with approval that 50,000 pupils with cerebral palsy are 'mainstreamed', and expresses interest in the extent to which this number can be increased.

A dual policy is likely to continue for several reasons, not least because of the huge existing investment in special schools, increasing from about 600 schools in 1950 to 1,600 in 1975. A switch in emphasis may be detected if the waiting list of 12,000 names is reduced, since the largest categories represented are the 'moderately' educationally disabled and the maladjusted. These two categories are those whose validity is most frequently disputed and those which are seen as marginal, and therefore they are the most likely to be a source of candidates for integration.

One group of children that presents difficulties for the mainstreaming policy is the maladjusted. Sympathy for the physically disabled and mentally retarded can be aroused more easily than sympathy for those identified as maladjusted. Colley (1976) asks us to consider the reaction to the sight of a child walking along the railway line, putting up two fingers in a derisive gesture to the grown-ups who are trying to bring it back to safety; or the likely response to the child who deliberately lies down on the road in front of the traffic, or who steps out on to a pedestrian crossing in front of a speeding car, and who, when told that these are dangerous activities, replies that he wants to be killed. A parent may have to cope with a child who makes up its mind that it is not going to speak to any grown-up ever again, and who obstinately refuses to do so for years. A child breaking windows, throwing stones, spitting or swearing in public in the foulest possible way is likely to get a reaction of fear and disgust; to ask for help for these pupils would bring indignation. Yet children with these symptoms are disabled emotionally rather than physically.

Colley suggests that the difficulty in recognizing such children as disabled, and so in need of help, comes from the assumption made by many adults that children are good little people who are obedient, respectful and conforming – a fair assumption to make about children who are secure and who really trust and look up to adults. Colley comments further:

> But for those children who are not sure of their relationship with adults, and who have therefore taken over the organization of their own lives for themselves because they have been let down by grown-ups, it is a very dangerous assumption to make. Maladjusted children are, in my opinion, those who have had their emotional development interrupted by some experience which has been deeply hurtful to them.
>
> The more usual type of maladjusted child, in my experience as a teacher, is the aggressive and violent child. This child breaks all the rules. He cannot be educated in a normal school. He is disobedient, defiant, unruly, impossibly rude and frequently violent – damaging furniture and teachers and causing havoc in the classes. The adults are unable to cope with him. A child like this who comes to a school for maladjusted children finds himself surrounded by adults who do not panic when he insults them; who are not afraid when he is violent; who show that although they do not like his behaviour, they know he has reasons for it and that they like him. This kind of calmness in the face of all the provocation shows the child that here is a situation in which he does not have to keep up his pattern of anti-social behaviour. He has found adults who can master him, not by violence or revenge, but by acceptance. When he realizes this, his chances of recovery begin. With care and a good environment, he may recover enough to be able to function in a normal school after few years treatment.
>
> Colley, 1976. This first appeared in *New Society*, London, the weekly review
> of the social sciences.

More recently, the government White Paper of 1992, Choice and Diversity, referred to the 1981 Education Act as: 'one of the most important landmarks of education legislation this century'. It goes on to assert the commitments of government to the general principles enshrined in the 1981 Act. However, one of the main criticism(s) of the 1981 Act was that it left far too much to the goodwill of local authorities and individual teachers. Unfortunately this is still true and under the Education Reform Act of 1988 local authorities have less funding and power as resources have been allocated to individual schools under local management of schools.

Following the publication of the 1992 White Paper the government introduced the 1993 Education Act. This Act replaced the 1981 Act but embodies much of the same. The 1993 Act introduces a Code of Practice to assist schools and local authorities in the regulation of provision for special educational needs. The procedures and phases for providing for children identified as SENs, which are adopted by many local authorities, fall into the following broad categories:

1. Specifying the problem(s) clearly and recording them.
2. Identifying available resources.
3. Devising written strategies and appropriate use of resources.
4. Reviewing the effectiveness of the strategies.

THE PROCESS OF BEING LABELLED 'SPECIAL'

> We have been very successful – or lucky! – with David's early education. He could read, count, write letters, etc. and was probably more advanced academically than most of his so-called 'normal' peers. (The special needs officer and I had already disagreed about what 'peers' meant. David's attainments or potential were meaningless by the side of the fact that he had slightly slanty eyes and an indisputable 'label'! Accordingly, he 'needed to be with his peers' – and the appropriate place for him and them was in a school for the 'educationally sub-normal [severe]!').
>
> Sylvia Jeffs, who educated her son David, who has Down's syndrome, at home, quoted in
>
> Wade and Moore, 1993

Referral and Assessment

The assumption that the identification of children for special education is an objective diagnosis is rendered dubious by a study of the process involved. The most common starting point for the official process is for the headteacher to write a report. The unofficial process, however, will have begun much earlier. The headteacher will have been made aware that a child is demonstrating behaviour interpreted as undesirable from someone's point of view – teachers, parents or an educational psychologist who has performed a screening of a school-year cohort.

In the case of a teacher, the headteacher may advise alternative methods of dealing with the pupil or seek advice from the educational psychologist. The teacher may respond in various ways, including successful use of the advice, or ignoring the advice, or may be unable to act upon it. If the undesirable behaviour persists, there are several possible outcomes.

Parents of other children may complain that their children are being held back, disrupted, or otherwise affected by the pupil concerned. The headteacher then has to consider possible ways of dealing with this problem, including moving the child to another teacher, which may create tensions between teachers, or moving the pupil to another school in the area, risking the resentment of another school's staff in taking on the problems of the first school. A tempting solution is referral. Staff within the school may be protected, the special school staff are paid to receive problems, and, indeed, their jobs are secured by referrals.

Since the 1981 Education Act, in the UK parents can ask for an assessment for their child or make representations when an educational official has initiated assessment procedures. Later, parents can appeal against the verdict contained in an official Statement of Special Educational Needs.

The assessment is widely regarded as objective and reliable. However, there are doubts about the following:

1. The assessment instruments – the tests.
2. The assessment context – clinical interviewing.
3. The assumptions about the validity of educational psychology in generating adequate explanations of behaviour in educational institutions – the sociologists' preserve.
4. The pressures on educational psychologists that are occupational and political, for their position 'in the system' is far from independent – they are employees of the local education authority and, as such, are subject to wider educational and political influences.

By their actions the headteacher and the class teacher may be saying that they feel they cannot cater adequately for a particular child. The psychologist may offer to devise an alternative programme, but without control of the daily implementation much depends on the willingness and expertise of the parents or the school and therefore a programme may not be successful. One psychologist can offer to supervise only a few schemes, with up to 12,000 children within the group of schools he or she has to visit. A transfer to another 'normal' school is taken as a reflection on the school's competence, even though no criticism may have been intended. But admission to a special school is more likely to be regarded as further evidence of the severity of the child's problems, and is seldom thought to imply any criticism of the referring school.

The psychologist's own credibility may be undermined by regular requests which are seen as inappropriate or 'unrealistic', and good relationships with a school's head and staff may be jeopardized because of one child.

> We are not painting a totally black picture of any of these professional groups. Many psychologists do support children in ordinary schools on a regular basis. Many are successful in arguing for extra resources for 'supported integration' schemes. Hopefully all would take seriously the commitment to considering parents' wishes on the placement of their child.

> What needs to be emphasized, however, is that the psychologist is not an independent
> expert, equipped with magical tools, who is powerful enough to work out and win support
> for an innovative scheme for one child in the ordinary school.
>
> Goodwin, 1979

The outcome may be that in many cases pupils are designated as special for the sake of other considerations than the particular pupil's benefit – a case of the pupil as victim. An Advisory Centre for Education report concluded that there were few signs of the proposed partnership of teachers, other professionals and parents on behalf of children, but plenty of signs of the defence of vested interests (*Where?*, **196**, March 1984).

Screening and the Social Pathology Model

The idea of screening is based on a medical model. It is based on an assumption that a proportion of pupils (20 per cent in the Warnock Report) are educationally ill. The 'disability' may respond to educational treatment of an individual or group of individuals forming a ward or special provision. The emphasis is on individual children, and the causes are sought in each person's physiology or biography.

Such a model employs quasi-medical terms like examination, diagnosis, treatment and testing, and proves to be convenient for doctors, psychologists and those teachers who think in medically derived terms. Excluded by such an approach is the possibility that causes outside the biographies of the individual, such as the regime of the school, the expectations of the teachers or the ideology of education in use, may be crucial factors.

The clue to the underlying ideology of remedial education is to be found not only in its language but also in the forms of organization and methods it uses. One type of remedial provision is temporary withdrawal of pupils from the 'normal' situation, to undergo therapy often directed towards weaknesses in basic skills. The object is to return the pupil as soon as possible to what is regarded as normal schooling. The remedial teacher's success is seen, in theory, in terms of the number of pupils returned to normal classes.

The social-pathology model of educational ill-health and the screening that derives from it may have various consequences. First, labelling children as special can lead to differential teacher expectations. This affects teachers involved in remedial work and those who are not in different ways. Remedial teachers have come to see themselves as therapists, and there can be little doubt that many of them have acquired considerable expertise in the application of diagnostic approaches to the teaching of reading, drawing upon the discipline of psychology. The teachers who are not involved specifically in remedial work often have to assume that children with reading difficulties are not their concern.

> Their concept of normality involves, amongst other things, being able to meet the literacy
> demands of their fields of interest as they stand at present. That is to say, participation in a
> subject such as history requires a certain level of literacy, a level determined by the subject

itself and the media through which it is taught. Neither content nor media are regarded as open to change.

Golby and Gulliver, 1979

The outcome is that children are blamed for failing: the learning experiences are not seen as open to review. Second, screening cannot be perfect, so some pupils will be labelled incorrectly and self-fulfilling prophecies may then be set in motion.

An alternative approach is outlined by Bookbinder (1978). The Salford approach to reading has been to avoid screening and individual treatments for low achievement, and instead to redefine the problem as a teaching problem:

> Although the surveys do identify the slowest readers, we do not attempt to provide individual learning programmes for most of these children, but aim instead to improve the teachers' skills in the teaching of reading generally, so that both slower achieving and brighter children will benefit.

In 1969, more than a quarter of all infant school leavers in the largely inner-city area then covered by the authority were classified as non-readers on the Schonell Graded Word Test. For the same schools in the same area nine years later, that figure had dropped to 6 per cent.

Bookbinder proposes that these improvements in reading attainment show that it is possible to reduce significantly the number of poor achievers without resorting to expensive, time-consuming and possibly dangerous identification procedures. If a medical model of identification had been adopted the present standards would not have been achieved.

> Is it possible that a more widespread application of this kind of approach to basic areas of the curriculum could more than halve that Warnock figure of 20 per cent with special educational needs? Perhaps, then, it might make more sense to think in terms of further intervention procedures for the relatively small numbers who were still failing.

Bookbinder, 1978

STIGMA THEORY

Negative labelling of 'special', 'disabled' or 'exceptional' children has its roots in our history, myths and everyday environment. Because many of the children are cloistered away from the general public, people may have never had the chance to meet such a child and come to appreciate her or his 'normal' attributes. Many of the services and educational facilities are still run by voluntary bodies, and some of the funding depends on donations dropped in a bag at the chek-out in the local supermarket. There are plastic models of disabled children on some street corners. The image of child begging, and the constant cry to 'give a few pence', can arouse sympathy, but can also shape feelings of guilt, pity or even revulsion.

Much of our language is loaded against various minority groups. One of the definitions of 'blind' in the *Oxford English Dictionary* is 'reckless, not ruled by purpose'. The term 'spastic' is often used as an insult by 'normals'. In 1959, the Mental Health Act reclassified 'idiots' as 'severely subnormal'. The expression 'subnormal' is still widely, and officially, used today, although it can be distressing to both the parents and the child concerned.

We are all in some ways both statistical and moral deviants from the norm, because few of us can equate consistently with the average. Goffman argues that their stigma unites criminals, sexual offenders, ethnic minorities and physically disabled people. Boswell and Wingrove (1974) argue that the physically disabled are the most susceptible to being stigmatized, as their predicament removes the opportunity to control whether they deviate or not.

Goffman (1963) has an analysis of a particular type of labelling, stigma theory. Many types of labelling hold the possibility of 'reversal' or 'reform': the deviant may learn a lesson and reform. In the case of stigma, however, there is an attribute that is interpreted in a culture as deeply discrediting, and a means of reversal is not as likely. The person with a stigma is seen as not quite human, nor likely to become so. Goffman proposes three types of stigma: body deformities, personality deformities and tribal stigmas.

First, there are the various deformities. Second, there are blemishes of individual character, such as weak will, domineering or unnatural passions, treacherous and rigid beliefs, and dishonesty, these being inferred from a known record of, for example, mental disorder, imprisonment, addiction, alcoholism, homosexuality, unemployment, suicide attempts and radical political behaviour. Third, there are the tribal stigma of race, nation and religion, which can be transmitted through lineages and contaminate all members of a family or group.

The contrast, for Goffman, is between the 'stigmatized' and the 'normal'. Society generates certain definitions of what the 'normal' individual should be like, and those who fail to meet these definitions may become stigmatized. To be defined as someone with a stigma creates a problem for the person who has to respond to the situation, and for those 'normals' who act on the basis of the culturally generated definitions.

In applying Goffman's theory to special education in the USA, King (1972) notes how children judged as unable to perform 'satisfactorily' in a group of 'normals' are channelled into educational programmes that can accommodate their 'learning disabilities'. This turns out, in the case of many USA cities, to be an inflated group of black children:

> Most educators will agree that general education has failed the black ghetto child. In an effort to avoid the necessity of radically changing the general education system in the black ghetto, the educational establishment has found it expedient to turn to special education, to greatly expand the special education programs serving black children.
>
> King, 1972

Consequently a disproportionate number of black and other minority children are labelled as retarded, disturbed or delinquent. King notes that this process effectively short circuits change in the general education programme by implicating the children rather than the system.

'COOLING THE MARK OUT'

One attempt to explain the relationship between the mainstream education system and the special education sector is that of King (1972), using Goffman's (1952) concept of 'cooling out'. The idea comes from the activity of confidence tricksters. The victim of a confidence trick is the 'mark', the sucker. When a potential mark is noticed, one member of the team makes contact with and wins the confidence of the person concerned. The mark is given the chance to invest money in a get-rich-quick gambling venture apparently fixed in the investor's favour. Some money is won, so more is invested, but an 'accident' leads to the mark's losing the total investment. If the mark does not accept the loss philosophically, but threatens to call the police or complain to the press, there must be a 'cooling-out' of the mark. The 'cooler' attempts to console the mark and to define the situation in a way that makes it easier for the mark to accept the loss and become resigned to the situation. The process of cooling out the mark can be used as an analogy to educational and other processes.

The definition of 'mark' includes persons whose expectations or self-concepts have been shattered. These persons must be helped to re-accept themselves and their failure and build new self-concepts. In a situation in which a person has failed at a job, he can be offered another, perhaps lower, position, and in this way the feeling of failure is softened, the loser is pacified. Similarly, the lover may be asked to become a 'good friend', or the ageing boxer may be asked to become a trainer.

King applies the concept of 'cooling the mark out' to the relationship between general and special education. General education in the USA is supposed to be capable of teaching all children, but with inner-city black children it has failed. However, educators and their school systems can preserve their identities by cooling deviant children out. The placement will help the child, it is stated, but in fact, he is given a seemingly better placement in the hope that he will stop making a fuss. It is easier for all to 'cool out' the child, to help him and his parents to accept his failure in the regular education system, than it is to change that system for his benefit, King concludes.

Special education is part of the arrangement for cooling out students who won't conform to traditional classroom methodology, King argues, and this parallel system permits relief of institutional guilt and humiliation stemming from failure to achieve competence and effectiveness in the educational task given by society.

> Special education is helping the regular school maintain its spoiled identity when it creates special programs for the 'disruptive child', the emotionally disturbed child, or the 'mildly retarded child', most of whom happen to be black, poor, and live in the inner city.
>
> King, 1972

THE SOCIAL CONSTRUCTION OF UNDERACHIEVEMENT

One of the dangers of labelling theory is that it may lead to the individualization of blame: the labellers are then seen as the guilty ones. Chapter 3, 'Teachers as Victims', contained an attempt to avoid this false conclusion. Stigma theory in particular may set in motion a 'blame the stigmatizers' response. The thesis of this section is that labellers operate not on personal initiatives, but on socially constructed ideas fed in to their consciousness. Linking several categories of special education is the notion of underachievement. How did this notion come into being? The proposition from an interactionist perspective is that underachievement is a social construction rather than an inevitable fact of existence.

The sociology of education that developed after the 1944 Education Act tended to be of a macro-perspective, often of a structural functionalist nature, and centred on questions of the relationship between social class and academic achievement. A concern that derived from this was the 'wastage of talent', particularly of working-class children. This approach was based on several unquestioned assumptions: that schooling as currently practised was good, that selection was a prime function of education, that talent and merit could be identified objectively as traits of individuals, so that individual mobility in education demonstrated that greater equality of opportunity was being achieved. Davies (1980) argues that:

> Administrators and social scientists then were still working on the premise that school was a Good Thing; that, therefore, more schooling was a Better Thing; and that maximum identical exposure to schooling was the Best Thing.

The identification of talent would achieve 'true' mobility. There were three unquestioned assumptions:

1. That education should be about sorting and selection.
2. That definitions of 'merit' were unproblematic, objective and without class bias, with assessment of merit synonymous with competitive examinations.
3. That individual mobility through the educational system was an index of greater equality of opportunity (the more individuals were successful, the more schools were helping to combat class imbalances).

The individualization of success had as the other side of the coin the individualization of failure,

> so there was the replacement of models of genetic inheritance with social pathology models of deprivation, which further served to draw attention away from the ways in which the school itself was processing its pupils. Various sources of deprivation – cultural, social, linguistic, emotional – were identified as the sources of failure to cope with the demands of schooling. Programmes of compensation were devised to fill up the emptiness resulting from faulty socialization, restricted code use, disadvantaged social area or some combination of all three.
>
> Davies, 1980

Some critics of the compensatory approach have argued that the vessel was not actually empty, but laden with a different cultural cargo. Others have a political critique that stresses the irony of blaming the poor for their poverty: cultural deprivation suggests that the minority in question is failing rather than being failed by the mainstream society and its system of schooling.

This system of schooling is seen as suspect for a number of reasons. First, the operational definition of 'ability' is dubious. The assumption is that the facility to use symbols on paper is to be more highly regarded than skills of forming social relationships, organizing activities or skills with machinery:

> Why is the facility to manipulate other people's symbols on a piece of paper more highly regarded than the facility to form social relationships, operate a calculator, organize a trade union? In particular, why is only one continuum used to rank pupils? Given the enormous range of skills, competencies and orientations in our society, it is curious that we can glibly talk of children being 'able' and 'less able', average' and 'below average', as if all we were measuring were head size.
>
> Davies, 1980

Davies argues that the enormously misleading notion of 'general intelligence', or IQ, has a lot to answer for, as does developmental psychology, but the question is more than a matter of error. The political question is in whose interests IQ tests are legitimized. Who benefits by a school's definition of what it is to learn something? The answer is a tautology: the sorts of people who are good at IQ tests, the sorts of children who are adept at the narrow range of skills associated with school success.

Second, the operating definition of assessment is dubious. A norm-referenced examination system is designed to select successes and label others as failures. This helps to legitimize an unequal system of life chance distribution: you do not deserve many rewards because you are not very bright, as the paper-and-pencil tests have told you. 'Intelligence', then, and 'the right environment', instead of being seen as initial causal variables in educational attainment, can be interpreted as convenient labels to justify, even mask, the fact that educational practices are selective, funnelling devices rather than liberating ones.

> Examination would have little point if everyone got the same grade or even passed them; yet schools have to balance the hierarchical certification function with ideologies of equality and impartiality. The way out of the dilemma is to blame the child: to convince him, his parents, the community, that opportunities would have been there if he had not had a low IQ, was not an underachiever.
>
> Davies, 1980

The construction of underachievement is analogous to the creation of casualties as a consequence of having a war. Answering the question of why there are so many casualties by looking at the physique of the soldiers who are injured seems ridiculous. Casualties will stop when the war stops. Thus, defining certain children as failures may tell us much more about the dominant ideologies of education in schools than about the children involved.

CONCLUSION

A summary of this chapter might lead one to conclude that the contribution of the sociologist to the area of special education is to add more confusion to an already confused area, but only those who prefer misplaced certainty to constructive doubt would regard this as a bad thing. Certainly the research, as in many other areas of educational concern, is in the nature of work in progress on the reappraisal of policies which were often devised under the pressure of circumstances. Tuckwell and Beresford, writing about the reappraisal of policies in Bromley, summed up the situation in these words:

> A scheme like the Bromley one inevitably raises doubts about efficacy of our special education system, our methods of assessment and ascertainment; our teacher-education programme and our treatment of those we stigmatize as sub-normal. There are many questions to be asked: Bromley is the tip of an iceberg already too large to be ignored.

Further Reading

Barton, L. and Tomlinson, S. (eds) (1981) *Special Education: Policy, Practices and Social Issues*. London: Harper & Row.

Barton, L. and Tomlinson, S. (eds) (1984) *Special Education and Social Interests*. Beckenham: Croom Helm.

Boswell, D.M. and Wingrove, J.M. (1974) *The Handicapped Person in the Community*. London: Tavistock.

Goffman, E. (1963) *Stigma: Notes on the Management of Spoiled Identity*. Hemel Hempstead: Prentice Hall.

HMSO (1992) *Choice and Diversity: A New Framework for Schools*, Government White Paper. London: HMSO, Chapter 9.

Sewell, G. (1982) *Reshaping Remedial Education*. Beckenham: Croom Helm.

Tomlinson, S. (1982) *A Sociology of Special Education*. London: Routledge and Kegan Paul.

Wade, B. and Moore, M. (1993) *Experiencing Special Education*. Buckingham: Open University Press.

Warnock Report (1978) *Special Educational Needs*. Report of the Committee of Enquiry into the Education of Handicapped Children and Young People. Cmnd 7212. London: HMSO.

Wedell, K. (1995) *Putting the Code of Practice into Practice*. London: Institute of Education.

Discussion and Activities

1. How can we account for the differences in the figures for boys and girls given in the Table 2.2?
2. Is a sociologist justified in adding more confusion to an already confused area?
3. Make a summary of the main points of this chapter.
4. The policy of mainstreaming or integration takes it for granted that the mainstream schools are educationally sound. Do you agree?

Signposts

1. Special education and social interests

Recent writing has explored the proposition that special education is as much if not more about social interests than about individual needs or individual deficiencies, in an attempt to broaden the debate. See Barton and Tomlinson (1981, 1984) and Tomlinson (1982).

2. 1981 Education Act, England and Wales

'The 1981 Education Act promised a "joint endeavour to discover and understand" the special education needs of individual children. ACE's experience to date suggests that the idea of a "partnership" between parents and professionals was a DES fantasy, bearing little relationship to parents' real experience of dealing with their LEA' (*Where?*, **196**, March 1984). The working of this Act may become a case study in the models of 'contradictions' and 'the ironies of human action', where proposed remedies achieve the opposite effects of those intended. See ACE Special Education Handbook (1984) and 'The '81 Act: Safeguarding Your Rights', *Where?*, **196**, March 1984.

3. 1992 Government White Paper, Chapter 9

Read Chapter 9 and draw out the comparisons with the 1981 Education Act. How far can local authorities deliver adequate provision for SENs under the new funding arrangements for schools since the Education Reform Act of 1988?

4. Labelling and 'special needs'

When children rebel against imposed order, they are diagnosed as having 'attention deficit disorder' and can be prescribed powerful and potentially damaging drugs, even though the extent to which attention deficit disorder actually exists as a medical diagnosis rather than a convenient social construct to control inconvenient behaviour is a matter of controversy (see Fortune-Wood, J. (2001) *Bound to be Free*, Nottingham: Educational Heretics Press, p. 40 'From psychology to medication'.

Part Six
SIGNPOSTS TO THE NEXT LEARNING SYSTEM

I believe that the computer presence will enable us to so modify the learning environment outside the classroom that much, if not all, the knowledge schools presently try to teach with such pain and expense and such limited success will be learned, as the child learns to walk, painlessly, successfully, and without organised instruction. This obviously implies that schools, as we know them today, will have no place in the future. But it is an open question whether they will adapt by transforming themselves into something new or wither away and be replaced.

Seymour Papert, Professor of Learning Research,
Massachusetts Institute of Technology, in *Mindstorms*

Whilst my photocopying was being completed I saw a notice on the wall of the Kall Kwik Print shop. It said: 'Customised: we listen, we understand, we find the solution that's right for you'. I thought this would make a splendid slogan for the next learning system to replace the present learning system of compulsory, coercive schooling followed by the dreary steeplechase of university courses. Its slogan appears to be: 'Standardised: you listen, we only understand coercion and dominance, you accept the solution we decide.' The slogan in the shop, on the other hand, assumes that people deserve a personalised service, not a stand-ardised one.

Roland Meighan, in *Natural Parent*, July/August 2001

Almost every institution I have had contact with in my life has failed me, they have all expected me to fit them rather than they adapting to my needs and I no longer want any part in them. It's no longer to do with social capital – they could rebuild every school in the country and fund them like Eton with class sizes down to 3, and still we wouldn't send our kids...

Mike Fortune-Wood at *www.home-education.org.uk*

The nation (and its governments of either persuasion) seems to be intent on reinforcing a failing system at present ... It is no use tinkering with our 19th-century model of education. It needs to be completely re-thought and restructured. Gradual reform is unlikely to succeed. Radical change is needed.

Sir Christopher Ball, in *Natural Parent*, November/December 1999

30 Alternatives

The concept of alternatives has a complex history, not only in schooling and education, but also in medicine and other spheres of human activity. It is possible to distinguish at least five different types of interpretation in the case of schooling and education.

ALTERNATIVE SCHOOLING

One relationship that can exist among the three ideologies of education identified in Part Three is that of a struggle for supremacy. The proponents of each ideology make claims for their favoured pattern of assumptions to be the one right way and for the others to be discarded. The pattern with which we have become all too familiar in the UK is of supporters of the domination of the authoritarian approach dismissing the two non-authoritarian alternatives as 'trendy', 'permissive', 'progressive' or 'undisciplined'. This has also been the experience in communist and fascist regimes, so that one Polish professor of comparative education, Eugenia Potulicka, gave her verdict on the 1988 Education Reform Act in England and Wales as being totalitarian in style and substance, in conversations with the directors of Education Now Ltd. Her knowledge of schooling under the Nazis and then the Russian communist regime led her to a clear recognition of the signs: 'The 1988 Education Act is a very dangerous development for it has politicized schooling in the direction of fascist thinking. It is the worst development in Europe at the moment.'

Thus, a campaign in England entitled the Campaign for Real Education is, in reality, a campaign for Real Authoritarian Schooling, asserted dogmatically as the One Right 'Common-Sense' Way for everyone to learn. Evidence for this position is lacking, so insults are used to fill the gaps. A particular target is 'progressive education', and the opposite of this would appear to be 'regressive education', which is said to be superior:

> Advocates of regressive education have resorted to labelling anyone who agreed with them as a sensible person and anyone who disagreed with them in insulting terms. In one book alone, *What Is Wrong with Our Schools*, anyone who took an opposing view to that being offered was described as crazy, or brainwashed, or flashy, or new-style, or faceless facilitators, or Politically Motivated Intruders, or progressives, or child-centred activists, or wets, or hotheads, or loonies, or nihilists. The writers contributing to this book were liable to contradict each other on fundamental issues and so run the risk of having to insult each other.
>
> Meighan, 1993, p. 7

In turn, the two non-authoritarian alternatives, the autonomous and the democratic, have in the past often found agreement with each other on a complete dismissal of the authoritarian position as 'oppressive' and 'impositional'. The concept of the hidden curriculum, as outlined in Part Two, has sometimes been used for this purpose. The rival camps have then tended to set about dismissing the claims of each other and sheering off into rival splinter groups, rather than exploring ideas of cooperation and complementarity within a flexible system:

> there has generally been a refusal to join together under an umbrella philosophy that all alternatives could accept ... Without it, splinter factions surface – independent study, co-operative learning and voucher advocacy, educational futures networks.
>
> Glines, 1992

It might seem that the term 'progressive' could provide such an umbrella. Wright (1989), however, finds multiple and rival uses of the term, while Shotton (1993), having explained the ambiguity of the concept, is concerned to identify 'libertarian' as distinct.

ALTERNATIVE SCHOOLING FOR THE RICH AND POWERFUL

In the UK, there are several ways of going private, of opting out of the state system of education. A small, but growing, number of parents exercise their legal right to educate their children themselves using their home as the base, and this is facilitated by the self-help group Education Otherwise. Another small minority of parents surrender their rights almost entirely by paying for their children to go to boarding schools, where they are residential for over two-thirds of the year. A further group of parents pay for their children to attend private day-schools.

Precise figures are not easily available, but at any given time there appear to be around 4,000 schools in the private sector, and estimates of the number of children being educated at home vary between 10,000 or more families and 20,000 or more children. The proportion of the child population in the private sector lies somewhere between 5 and 10 per cent. The lack of precision is mostly to do with the constant state of flux: schools are opening and closing; some are granted official recognition, others are not; changes in government policy influence some schools to go private at particular times; the number of parents educating their children at home is changing constantly.

The categorization 'private school' covers a wide range of types. There is a broad division between boarding school and day school, although this distinction is blurred by the fact that many predominantly boarding schools have some day pupils and many predominantly day schools have a few boarders. Within each category, boarding and day, there are further variations. Most boarding schools are single-sex, but a small minority, about thirty in number, are mixed residential establishments. A larger proportion of day schools are mixed-sex. The size of school varies from establishments of five to twelve pupils to over 750. The sponsoring body may be the Licensed Victuallers, the Rudolf Steiner Foundation, the Society of Friends, the local cathedral, a famous individual (e.g. Yehudi Menuhin) or an Educational Trust. The age range varies: some schools are 8–13 preparatory schools, others exclusive to 16-year-olds and over, others 13 years and over and others span 5–18.

The differences in educational style are partly linked to features like size of school, age-span of pupils, single-sex or mixed and the characteristics of the sponsors, but other differences may be noted. The curriculum may be broad or, in the case of a crammer, be restricted almost entirely to preparation for a small range of examinations such as GCSE or A level. The educational approach may commonly be known as 'traditional' or 'progressive', both rather misleading terms, as we have seen.

Given this diversity of the private sector it is perhaps surprising that sweeping generalizations about this form of education are commonly encountered. There are some common features that can be discerned:

1   The schools are out of local education authority control – their 'recognition as efficient' is granted direct by a government department.
2.   The clientele have or obtain the economic resources to back their choice: selection is mostly by wealth, although supplementary factors, like entrance examinations, and previous contacts, like parents being old pupils of the school, may be important in particular cases.
3.   The schools are predominantly single-sex, and the major provision is for males rather than females; but this pattern is in the process of change as more and more schools find that they can only balance the books if they start to admit girls.

The Public Schools

Some of the assertions made about private education are about the public schools, perhaps a rather odd name for a group of private schools. In the absence of common agreement about the definition of a public school, they will be seen in this account as private boarding schools, mostly for boys of secondary school age, which have membership of one of three associations: the Head Masters' Conference, the Governing Bodies Association and the Association of

Governing Bodies of Girls' Public Schools. About 300 schools are included in such a category, and about 2.5 per cent of the school population attend them.

The significance of the public schools appears to be much more in what happens before the children go to school than in what happens after. Public schools recruit mostly from those born into rich homes. Most pupils are from upper-class or upper middle-class families. The pupils exit in a large proportion to Oxford and Cambridge (35 per cent) and other universities (16 per cent), and thence to elite occupations, e.g. in the civil service, law, armed forces and industry.

The educational significance of the public schools is open to considerable debate. The conclusions of Douglas (1971) were:

> The pupils at the boys' public schools, once their ability and the circumstances of their families are taken into account, are no more successful, as judged by 'O' level results and age of leaving up to 16 1/2 years, than grammar school pupils. The pupils at other independent schools (i.e. those outside the Headmasters' Conference) are considerably less successful.

A study of crammers, which are private coaching establishments operating as private sixth-form colleges for students of 16 years and above, indicated that public schools feature prominently on their rolls. For a variety of reasons these pupils left their public schools to continue their examination work at a crammer (Geddes, 1979). If the public schools really are good at academic work, Geddes reflects, why are they apparently driving many of their pupils into other institutions devoted to passing examinations?

A study by Halsey *et al.* (1980) supports the earlier study by Douglas in concluding that a lot of the supposed academic advantage turns out to be spurious, given that the public schools have able pupils from elite backgrounds with parental support and encouragement: the academic results reflect the social class background of the parents rather than anything startling about the nature of the schooling, they conclude. Glennerster and Pryke (1973) concluded that the principal commodity being purchased at a public school is not education, but privilege.

The social significance for the individuals and families concerned is clear enough. The children are being set on the road to power and influence if they end up dominating elite occupations. A study by Giddens and Stanworth (1974) showed that 70 per cent of directors in the top 50 industrial firms were old boys of public schools. Banking and insurance showed a similar pattern. In the army, 86 per cent of officers of the rank of major-general and above had been to public schools. In the legal profession, high court judges and principal judges of public school background formed over 75 per cent of the total. In 1970, 62 per cent of the civil service posts of under-secretaries and above were held by former public school boys.

The social significance for the nation is less clear. According to one view, the decline in the nation's fortunes in economic and other terms has been managed almost exclusively by the products of the public school/Oxbridge experience, and their inability to cope does no credit to either the schools or the universities concerned (see Hutton, 1995). In one form, the criticism of the 'gifted amateur', this was the conclusion of the Fulton Committee (1968) when it investigated the civil service.

Those who hold this view see a paradox between the social significance for individuals and the social significance for the nation, sometimes known as the Titanic theory of mobility: struggle to join the ruling class that is supervising the sinking and asset-stripping of the ship.

A development of this view is that the cycle of privilege perpetuated by public schools not only is undemocratic, but also perpetuates closed-society thinking in a pluralist society context, or linear thought when lateral thinking is needed. An analysis of the cycles of privilege view appears in MacDonald (1977).

Others hold that the traditional values of the public schools are the only hope for the nation, and that 'leadership' is being produced in these special institutions. Rae, former headmaster of Westminster School, writes that:

> To some they will appear havens of civilised learning and behaviour monasteries in an increasing dark age; to others a source of division and injustice in a society that badly needs to cast off its class-conscious heritage.

ALTERNATIVE SCHOOLING 'FOR THE CASUALTIES'

When the authoritarian ideology gains dominance, those learners who become recognized as failures in the system pose a problem. The temporarily defeated advocates of non-authoritarian approaches often respond to this situation by offering alternatives for the 'flawed' and 'rejected' learners of the dominant authoritarian system. This may well be done out of a real concern for a genuine problem, but the effect is to portray alternative schooling as useful as a temporary expedient to 'restore' the casualties so that they can cope with the demands of the 'real' system. The notion of 'alternatives' thus becomes marginalized. 'The greatest number of alternative programmes are focused on "at risk," dropout/pushout, teen-age pregnant minors, and other "non-conforming" youth' (Glines, 1992). Herbert Kohl expressed the same idea at the 1990 Stanford Conference when he stated: 'I do not use the term alternative education. I talk about decent education. People who call themselves "alternative" are putting themselves on the margin.'

ALTERNATIVES 'FOR EVERYONE, ALL THE TIME'

The three previous positions on alternatives are increasingly dated as a new synthesis has emerged. This can be encapsulated in the slogan of 'alternatives for everyone, all the time'. There are several influences that support the credibility of the new synthesis.

It Is Now Possible to Identify Over Thirty Different Learning Styles in Human Beings

It follows that any uniform approach is intellectual death to some, and often most, of the learners, and is therefore suspect. These learning differences fall into three broad categories: cognitive, affective and physiological. For example, some learners have a style which is typically deductive, in contrast to those whose style is usually inductive. Others learn best from material which is predominantly visual, as against others who respond best to auditory experiences. There are contrasts between impulsive learners and reflective learners. Some learn better with some background noise, others learn better in conditions of quiet. Some are early-day learners and their peak learning time is in the morning, whereas others are afternoon learners and others late-day learners. As Aviram (1992) observes:

> In sum, we have sound empirical evidence that both individuals' motivation for learning and the effectiveness of their learning processes vary with the ability of the environment to cater to their specific learning styles.

The Identification of Seven or More Different Types of Intelligence

In *The Age of Unreason*, Charles Handy (1989) notes that another way in which individuals differ is in types of intelligence. Seven types of intelligence (analytical, pattern, musical, physical, practical, intrapersonal and interpersonal) are identifiable. Only the first is given serious attention in UK schools. Handy declares:

> All the seven intelligences, and there may be more, will be needed even more in the portfolio world towards which we are inching our way. It is crazy, therefore, to use only the first of the intelligences as the criterion for further investment in any individual by society.

Handy is interpreting the ideas of Howard Gardner (1994) on multiple intelligences.

In a Complex Modern Society, All Three Behaviour Patterns and Forms of Discipline Are Needed

Effectively, educated people need the flexibility to turn to each of the three major forms of behaviour and discipline as, and when, it is appropriate. People schooled in only one form of behaviour are likely to be handicapped in the modern world: rigid forms of schooling produce rigid people, whereas flexible forms with various alternatives are needed to produce flexible people (see Meighan, 1988).

Adaptability Has Priority in a Rapidly Changing Society

There is now widespread recognition that with rapidly changing technologies, economies and lifestyles, adaptability and flexibility in learning behaviour are becoming essential require-ments. A system based on uniformity is, therefore, counter-productive (see Handy, 1989). The point is made in this proposition:

> The case for traditional education seems to me much weaker than it has been, and is getting ever weaker, and the case for an education which will give a child primarily not knowledge and certainty but resourcefulness, flexibility, curiosity, skill in learning, readiness to unlearn – the case ... grows ever stronger.
>
> Holt, 1971, p. 155

The Recognition of the Need for Lifelong Learning

The idea that essential learning is best concentrated between the ages of five and 16, and for some up to 21, has increasingly given way to the idea of the necessity of lifelong learning (Handy, 1989, 1994).

The Arrival of the Information-rich Society

When mass schooling was established, people lived in an information-poor environment. Assembling large numbers of children together in one place called a school, with teachers who had been exposed to the scarce information, made a kind of sense. Since then, radio, tele-vision, the explosion of specialist magazines, computers, videos and the like, have all provided the means of making most of the products of the knowledge explosion readily available to anyone who wants it. This is just one of the reasons why home-based education is so successful.

Democratic Schooling Has Become an International Concern

After the failure of state communism in the former USSR and Eastern Europe, the remaining choice appears to lie between fascism and democracy. Former communist states look to schools in the USA, the UK and elsewhere, hoping to find democratic models of schooling in operation, only to find to their surprise that they are usually conspicuous by their absence.

> Britain's record on educating its citizens for democracy is particularly deficient with nothing in the curriculum even approximating to the sort of political education required in a mature, modern democracy.
>
> Harber, 1995, p. 8

Harber goes on to note that the substance is not enough: it is the act of participating, and in a particular manner, that produces democratic behaviour. Authoritarian schools are not just non-democratic, they are anti-democratic. A key feature of democracy is the principle that those who are affected by a decision have the right to take part in the decision-making. This is expressed in slogans such as 'No taxation without representation!' If we apply this to schools, we get, 'No learning and therefore no curriculum without the learners having a say in the decision-making.'

In the authoritarian approach to schooling, however, there is a chronic fear of trusting students and sharing power with them. In the everyday life of schools, we find a fear of opting for the discipline of democracy. Instead teachers resort to an exclusive diet of hierarchical order and authoritarian discipline. Indeed, Carl Rogers in *Freedom to Learn in the 80s* noted that democracy and its values are actually *scorned and despised*:

> Students do not participate in choosing the goals, the curriculum, or the manner of working. These things are chosen for the students. Students have no part in the choice of teaching personnel, nor any voice in educational policy. Likewise the teachers often have no choice in choosing their administrative officers ... All this is in striking contrast to all the teaching about the virtues of democracy, the importance of the 'free world,' and the like. The political practices of the school stand in the most striking contrast to what is taught. While being taught that freedom and responsibility are the glorious features of our democracy, students are experiencing powerlessness, and as having almost no opportunity to exercise choice or carry responsibility.

The only system that is likely to meet the situation described by this new synthesis, requiring *alternatives for everyone all the time*, is a flexischooling or flexi-education approach. People persisting with an exclusively authoritarian approach can be portrayed as running the risk of consigning their children to the obsolescence of a rigid mind-set.

ALTERNATIVE FUTURES

For education in the future there are three basic options. One is to retain the present schooling system, a second is to modify the existing system and a third is to develop a completely new system. Alternative futures are concerned with the third option. The Educational Futures Project based in Sacramento, California, is under the direction of Don Glines. He distinguished clearly between the options of changing the system and developing a new one:

In the majority of states, organizations of school administrators are now urging principals to look toward the future and to become 'issue oriented'. The efforts have focused on finding answers to a multitude of problems: drugs, gangs, test scores, accountability, fiscal support, at-risk youth, limited English-speaking students, overcrowded schools, homeless children, non-college employment preparation, vigorous curriculum preparation, militant unions, non-grading, year-round education, and the affective domain.

Educational futurists state that though these concerns are of the utmost importance, and must be addressed in the real world of today, they are not the keys to tomorrow. To those envisaging the twenty-first century, there is only one overriding issue facing educators today: the transformation to communication age learning systems.

Glines, 1989

In the proposed Minnesota Experimental City, planned as a laboratory for social, technical, economic and environmental innovations, a new approach to education is proposed. The following Learning Centres are to be developed to replace schools as we currently know them:

- *Early life studios* will be designed so that parents, young children and staff members can meet regularly to create an environment that provides creative learning experiences and offers opportunities for parents and older young people and other adults to learn about the mental, emotional, physical and other needs of early childhood.
- *Stimulus studios* will be established, where there will be a constantly changing array of prompts to provoke and extend learners' perceptions and thinking, to arouse curiosity, to stimulate laughter, wonder, reverence, imagination and competence. There will be films, tapes, videos, exhibitions, books, resourceful people from the community and virtual reality experiences.
- *Gaming studios* where learning takes place by playing educational games, where there is the opportunity to take part in simulations and role-play, and where arena theatre events will be developed.
- *Project studios* will be available where learners work on real projects, such as making a video, writing a book or TV script, designing new materials and products, or planning projects to be undertaken later in the community. In the UK, Walsall Community Arts has produced a Dreaming for Real project pack which has been setting such projects in motion.
- *Learner banks* will be designed to store and loan out the tools and equipment needed by learners. A large part of the bank would store books and other material now found in conventional libraries.
- *Family life centres* where families will learn together. The centre will offer meetings, seminars, tutoring or community-centred discussions. For those who learn well some of the time in school-type settings, these will be provided here.
- *Community facilities*, such as homes, businesses, public places and sports facilities, will be available as appropriate, as part of the learning network. The network of learning centres will remain permanently fluid, open to evaluation, review and change. (See Glines and Long, 1992).

In another vision of educational futures, John Adcock (1995) tells the story of how a new system came into being in the UK:

> It is Friday, 28th December in the year 2029. The hour is 0808 EST (European Standard Time). Susan Smith checks this on her personal computer screen together with the local weather and traffic news, and her day's appointments.
>
> Susan, born in the first hour of the first year of the 21st century, is a professional personal tutor to nineteen children aged from eight to ten years.
>
> She tutors the children with their parents, or in small groups, in their homes, in her home, in community resource centres, in field stations, in museums and art galleries, in concert halls and theatres, in libraries and sports centres, and in other places where, in her professional opinion, advantage to her clients will accrue.
>
> Susan is not a teacher in the 19th or 20th century sense of the word. She does not teach in a school. There are no teachers and there are no schools. There are simply personal tutors, pupils, parents and extensive support facilities.
>
> Susan possesses for each of the children in her tutorial group a personal study programme. She devised each programme with the help of the child, her parents, and colleagues' notes on the child's earlier achievements.

The system described in Adcock's book has many features in common with the Minnesota Experimental City model of education. Adcock's later title (2000) teases out the implications for a whole new concept of the teaching profession.

Table 30.1 Assumptions of the school system and the new learning system

The school system	The new learning system
1. Learning is preparation for life so at some point learning stops and living starts.	1. Learning is life, because humans are learning animals, and while we are alive, we are learning.
2. Learning occurs mostly in school.	2. Learning occurs everywhere and anywhere.
3. Specialists are needed to impart knowledge.	3. People can direct their own learning.
4. Education takes place in a school and requires a prescribed curriculum.	4. Education is a lifelong activity that needs to be personalized using a catalogue curriculum.
5. People do not and cannot learn on their own.	5. People can learn to make decisions about what and how to learn.
6. People with a large quantity of memorized information are better people than those with less.	6. Everyone is important regardless of how much he or she has memorized.
7. Schools are needed to socialize and civilize people.	7. People are socialized and become civilized in their communities.

CONCLUSION

The assumptions on which the new system is based are different from those that underpin the school-based system. Some of them are shown in Table 30.1. In the new learning system, it is learning that is the central concern and not teaching. Every person is simultaneously a learner and a resource person for the learning of others.

Further Reading

Abbott, J. and Ryan, T. (2000) *The Unfinished Revolution*. Stafford: Network Educational Press.

Adcock, J. (1995) *In Place of Schools*. London: New Education Press.

Adcock, J. (2000) *Teaching Tomorrow*. Nottingham: Education Now.

Gardner, H. (1993) *The Unschooled Mind*. London: Fontana.

Glines, D. (1995) *Creating Alternative Futures*. Michigan: McNaughton and Gunn.

Handy, C. (1989) *The Age of Unreason*. London: Arrow Books.

Harber, C. (ed.) (1995) *Developing Democratic Education*. Ticknall: Education Now.

Meighan, R. (1995) *John Holt: Personalised Education and the Reconstruction of Schooling*. Nottingham: Educational Heretics Press.

Meighan, R. (1997) *The Next Learning System*. Nottingham: Educational Heretics Press.

Meighan, R. (2005) *Comparing Learning Systems*. Nottingham: Educational Heretics Press.

Rose, C. and Nicholl, M.J. (1997) *Accelerated Learning for the 21st Century*. New York: Delacorte Press.

Wright, N. (1989) *Assessing Radical Education*. Milton Keynes: Open University Press.

Discussion and Activities

1. Seymour Papert, in *Mindstorms*, writes: 'I believe that the computer presence will enable us to so modify the learning environment outside the classroom that much, if not all, the knowledge schools presently try to teach with such pain and expense and such limited success will be learned, as the child learns to walk, painlessly, successfully, and without organised instruction. This obviously implies that schools, as we know them today, will have no place in the future. But it is an open question whether they will adapt by transforming themselves into some-thing new or whither away and be replaced.' Are events likely to prove him wrong or right?

2. Don Glines, in *Creating Alternative Futures*, explains how he introduced 69 simultaneous changes when he was appointed to regenerate a US high school. Make a list of some of the changes you would advocate if you had a similar task.

Signposts

1. Other ideas associated with the new education system are those of the information-rich society, the catalogue curriculum, the concept of personal learning plans, the use of word recognition technology and the personal wallet computer giving instant access to information. Find out all you can about these ideas.

2. In chaos theory, predictability is not possible even though we know the variables in play, because minor fluctuations alter patterns in unforeseen ways: this is why long-range weather forecasting is so inaccurate. In MacPherson, E. (1995) 'Chaos Theory in the Curriculum', *Journal of Curriculum Studies*, **27**, 3, 263–79, *there is an attempt to show how this applies in education.*

3. More influences stimulating change
There are other influences leading to a new synthesis apart from the seven listed in this chapter. Here are two more, and you may think of, or encounter in your reading, others:

We now know much more about how the brain actually works
The new technologies allow us to watch a living brain at work. Recent studies in neurology challenge the common metaphor that the brain is like a linear computer, waiting to be programmed. Instead, the metaphors are increasingly biological. The brain is more like a flexible, self-adjusting organism that grows and reshapes itself in response to challenge, with elements that wither away through lack of use. (See Rose C. and Nicholl M.J. (1997) *Accelerated Learning for the 21st Century*. New York: Delacorte Press.)

Home-based education is blazing the trail towards the next learning system
The arrival of the information rich society is just one of the reasons why home-based education is so successful and why its practitioners out-perform schools with relative ease. During twenty years of researching home-schooling, I grew to realise that most of the features of the next learning system were being field-tested in front of my eyes. (See Meighan, R. (1997) *The Next Learning System: and why home-schoolers are trailblazers*. Nottingham: Educational Heretics Press.)

31 Anatomy of Choice in Education

Only when all parents, not just rich ones, have a truly free choice in education, when they can take their children out of a school they don't like and have a choice of many others to send them to, or the possibility of starting their own, or of educating their children outside of school altogether – only then will we teachers begin to stop being what most of us still are, and if we are honest know we are, which is jailers, babysitters, cops without uniforms, and begin to be professionals, freely exercising an important, valued, and honoured skill and art.

John Holt

Choice in education, like the concept of education itself, turns out to be complicated. It is a multidimensional issue. A number of these dimensions are considered below.

DIMENSION ONE: THE PATTERNS OF EDUCATION

In attempting to map the territory of education, it was proposed earlier that it is possible to distinguish among three major groupings of educational pattern, each having quite different logistics. A considerable amount of debate about education in the UK never actually strays out of the first group, the authoritarian, being content to contrast two and sometimes three forms of adult-imposed visions under various inaccurate and ambiguous labels, such as traditional, modern, permissive and progressive. The actual choice, as we saw, is much greater than this, and includes two other major options, the autonomous pattern and the democratic pattern.

A further option is that posed by the pattern of flexischooling (Mcighan, 1988). Here the authoritarian, democratic and autonomous patterns are all included on the premise that they all have a modest part to play in the scheme of things, provided that the overall aim of the education in question is to produce flexible people able to operate effectively under each of the three general patterns of behaviour, as circumstances indicate.

Debates in the press and on television about choice in education are, in contrast, usually very stilted and revolve around which form or sub-type of authoritarian approach is best. One sub-type favours the most rigid form, where adults simply dictate the aims, the required knowledge, the forms of assessment, the teaching and learning methods, the resources and the other aspects of any viable approach to education as analysed in Chapter 1. This is often called the 'traditional' approach, although going back to Roman and earlier times, other versions of traditional can be found.

Another variation within the authoritarian approach is the sub-type where adults make some reference to the psychology and social context of children before devising their prescriptions. Although this is often labelled the child-centred approach, this is a serious misnomer. All that adults actually do is try to observe and deduce the nature of children's development and adjust the imposed programme accordingly. The children are rarely consulted in all this, and are accorded little power of any significance in the outcome. It makes the pattern clearer if we adopt the convention of describing this approach as child-referenced: adults remain firmly in control in such an approach. Compulsion is retained as the major principle of education, even if persuasion and kindliness replace direct force as the main instruments of control.

A few parents, with enough wealth, can choose an autonomous pattern operating within a school. As we saw, this approach has a long history and has a strong claim to be called traditional too. They can choose this by buying the education provided at one of the few schools in the private sector, such as Summerhill or Sands, that operate with the idea that learners should be accorded some say, some power over the nature of their education (see Meighan, 1995a).

Some aspects of schools like Summerhill and Sands can also be described as democratic, particularly in terms of the context of learning, but less so in terms of the learning approach itself. The Sudbury Valley school in the USA goes deeper into democratic practice, in having nothing recognizable as an organized curriculum until the learners devise one (see Meighan, 1995a).

More and more parents operate autonomous forms of education by choosing the option of home-based education. Even where they begin with an authoritarian approach, they tend to evolve gradually, and sometimes quite suddenly, into more and more of a learner-managed learning approach (Meighan, 1984b). Where they work cooperatively within a family and community context or share activity with other home-based education families, they too begin to operate some aspects of a democratic approach.

It is interesting to fit the 'choice' offered by the present administration in the UK into this scene. It consists of choosing between school A, authoritarian in style, operating a National Curriculum, limited by a centrally imposed testing system and having even its methods of teaching limited by government activity, and School B, which is the same. The only distinction between the two will be that one has stolen a march, for the moment, on the others in the centrally imposed league tables. It is the Henry Ford theory of 'choice': you can have your car in any colour you wish provided that it is black. It is pseudo-choice. Flexischooling, in contrast, allows real educational choice.

DIMENSION TWO: THE SCALE OF ORGANIZATION

Apart from the pattern of education in general, there is the specific issue of the scale of the educational setting proposed. These range from the scale of the one family, choosing to operate home-based education, through the small school operating as an extended family, to the large institution operating with hundreds of families. The scale itself does not automatically tell us the pattern of education adopted. It is possible for one family or a small school to operate with the most rigid form of authoritarian education, just as it is possible for a large institution using techniques like mini-schooling or schools-within-schools to operate with democratic, autonomous or flexischooling educational patterns.

On the other hand, there are strong tendencies to be observed. Families choosing the home-based education option, even when they begin with the one authoritarian pattern, tend to diversify into the autonomous and the democratic patterns. Large schools, however, tend to show strong tendencies to develop into the more rigid form of authoritarian education. A small school can be authoritarian and adopt the very rigid form, but the tendency is for a more flexible approach to be found, especially when such schools cooperate in cluster arrangements of schools within a vicinity.

As regards choice, most parents, as recorded in public opinion surveys, would choose a small school in preference to a large one, and so would most pupils and most teachers. Only those with enough money can actually have their choice in the UK at present. All others have largeness thrust upon them, whether they like it or not, as many a village community has found when its school is closed down against its wishes, on some dubious economic grounds. There is not much evidence of real choice here. Choice in this dimension requires a variety of sizes of institution, ranging from home-based learning provision in the family, through small local learning centres, to larger institutions.

DIMENSION THREE: THE APPROPRIATE CHOOSER

There are several candidates for the role of the appropriate person to make the choices about someone's education. The first would seem to be the learners themselves. Another candidate is the parent of the learner. But then other candidates appear. Adults running industry and commerce make a claim. The government and its officers may think they are legitimate choosers regarding the education of people other than themselves. Those adults who have been trained for teaching claim that it is a matter of professional judgement.

There are severe conflicts here. In the libertarian view, the learners themselves are the key people who should exercise choice and the main people to be consulted. In the adult chauvinist view, learners, especially if they are children, have no rights in the matter and the wise, all-seeing, all-knowing adults will decide. In the authoritarian type of government view, children and most adults outside the government are all to be disregarded, and the government will impose the form of education and enforce it via its inspectors. If all these groups are actually consulted in turn, quite different prescriptions are found.

As we have seen, the parents who can actually choose express almost the opposite view about a desirable education to that which is commonly imposed. They prefer small, human-scale learning situations. Most get the opposite thrust upon them.

Since the adult chauvinist view is backed up by adults having all the power, the idea of consulting the young learners is regarded as heresy and, therefore, very little research has been conducted into their point of view. Studies like Blishen's *The School that I'd Like* are rarities. The research studies by Meighan into pupils' views of teaching and schooling were all refused research funding, since there was no official interest in what the pupils had to say, and all the studies were conducted against a background of official reluctance at best, and refusal, ridicule and opposition at worst.

The studies of the learners' viewpoint that have been conducted contain both good news and bad news. The good news is that their requests are sensible and operational. The bad news is that their vision is stagnant, for it lacks any developing vision. The young learners' preferences are for a kindly, authoritarian learning regime which allows them some involvement and some say. The reason for this modest desire with its limited vision is that they comment and reflect on the experiences they have actually had, and most of them are not able to imagine what learning of a democratic style or autonomous nature or of a flexischooling pattern might be like, and how these approaches might be an important part of their education. After all, imagination has hardly been on their educational diet: the authoritarian approach is not famed for it.

One severe problem with the adult chauvinist position adopted by people in power positions is that the adults claiming superior wisdom to the learners are the same adults who have created or sustained the world in its present state of near environmental collapse, successive wars, human rights violations and economic confusion. Then, their conduct of their own personal lives is often unimpressive. We have had to witness the spectacle of a government minister extolling the virtues of family life in major speeches and being against the 'evils' of one-parent families, while he is busy creating a one-parent family outside his marriage, all of his own. In addition, it is the 'wise' adults who have created the education system, now held to be in crisis, in the first place. Constructive doubt seems to be missing.

Despite its limitations, the community education approach has been one of the most positive on this issue, since it sees the appropriate chooser as a matter of negotiation and consultation, with parents, industry and community groups. Sometimes, the young learners, both as individuals and as democratic, cooperating groups, have been seen as having some role to play in the scheme of things, but this has not often been high on the community education agenda.

DIMENSION FOUR: STATE VERSUS PRIVATE

The relationship between state and private provision for schooling varies from country to country. In some (Denmark, for example), the private school sector exists to offer parents, teachers and learners the choice of alternative approaches by setting up small schools that are 75 per cent state-financed provided a few minimum requirements are met. The experience and practice of such schools is said to create a continuous dialogue about effective learning, which is seen, for the most part, as constructive. Thus, there is on offer a chance for parents, teachers and learners to find learning approaches appropriate to their needs from a diversity of provision, which is not determined solely by the ability to pay.

In other countries, the relationship between state and private is akin to that of educational apartheid. For example, that sector of private education in the UK confusingly known as 'the public schools' operates an exclusive set of training institutions for the males, and occasionally females, of rich and powerful families (Duane, 1991).

A second sector of 'independent private schools' offer facilities for the less wealthy and powerful who desire small class sizes, often an imitation of the public school style of training and also separation from contact with the mainstream state schools. Within this sector can be found a few schools offering an alternative educational philosophy, such as Steiner schools, or religious foundation schools such as the Quaker schools and Roman Catholic schools.

The third sector, of state schools with poorer resources and larger classes, is made available for the majority of the population who have the least financial resources. Visitors to the UK often comment on the continuing stranglehold the social class system has on the country and how this is thought to have contributed to its continuing decline. The relationship between the state and private sector clearly helps to perpetuate this structure.

There is no reason in principle why real educational choice cannot exist in a solely state-provided system, or an entirely private system, or in a mixed system organized along the lines of the Danish system. On the other hand, all these types of system are capable of preventing choice as well.

DIMENSION FIVE: APPROPRIATE LOCATIONS FOR EDUCATION

The most modern educational institution is, perhaps, the Open University. A considerable amount of the learning is located in the home and supported there by the postal service bringing the study units at regular intervals, television broadcast programmes, video recorders, audio tapes and home experimental kits. Students use other locations, such as local study centres for tutorials and seminars. They may meet in each other's homes for self-help groups. Many courses include a week's residential summer school at a suitable location.

Schooling, on the other hand, has not adapted to modern conditions in the same way. The most flexible use of locations is that of families opting for home-based education, when they regularly use the home learning station as a springboard out into learning activities in a wide variety of community locations.

The rigidity of thinking on this matter of location can be illustrated by just making the suggestion that learners might select different courses from different schools and colleges in their locality, to build into their personal learning programme, and watching the incredulous reaction that usually follows. Yet the same discomforted people would be unlikely to support the idea of being confined to doing their shopping or pursuing their leisure in one compulsory location.

Yet, in an information-rich society, learning can take place anywhere and everywhere. Developments in computer technology, such as CD-ROMs storing vast amounts of data and the Internet linking of computers across the world, have underlined this possibility. The resistance to using a variety of locations has no educational justification, so its roots must lie elsewhere. John Holt gives one reason:

> It is only in theory, today, that educational institutions serve the student; in fact, the real job of a student at any ambitious institution is, by his performance, to enhance the reputation of that institution.

He also gives a second reason:

> This task or function of schools, the custodial or jail function, the task of keeping young people out of everybody else's way, is quite obviously not a humane function. It is an expression of adults' general dislike and distrust of the young. It is and must be in conflict with the humane function of true education, of encouraging and helping human growth.

And a third:

> The channelling function, the task of separating the winners from losers, may be a needed and proper function somewhere, but it is improper and inhumane in the schools. The things we do to select a few winners defeat whatever things we do to encourage the growth of all. We cannot do both of these kinds of work at the same time, in the same place. We cannot in any true sense be in the education business and at the same time in the grading and labelling business.

Educational choice in a post-industrial society requires flexibility of learning locations to become reality.

DIMENSION SIX: THE ETHICS OF EDUCATION

The school organized by Fagin for the production of young pickpockets scores highly in educational management appraisal. It had clear aims, clear lines of communication, high levels of on-task activity and high success rates. It produced enterprising young capitalists devoted to the acquisitive values. Any report of school inspectors would have been glowing, in these respects. But it was deemed to be unethical and unlawful.

This raises the difficult question of how far freedom of choice is restricted by ethical considerations. Thus, if the UK adopted the view of the people in Denmark that single-sex educational institutions are an infringement of the UN Charter of Human Rights, we would have to admit that most of our current public figures had received an unethical form of education and that their personal mental health and their powers of judgement were open to question. Such charges have, in fact, been made from time to time. The tacit acceptance of homosexual rape in boys' boarding schools as toughening and 'making a man of him since it never did his father much harm' has been quoted as an example:

> Public schoolboys, whatever their particular school . . . had a language of their own . . . ways and attitudes which they took for granted but which were foreign to me: for instance their acceptance of sodomy as more or less normal behaviour.
>
> Malcolm Muggeridge

Cabinet ministers calmly condemning large numbers of people to poverty, unemployment, business failure and home repossessions by their policy decisions have been found to have been nicknamed 'Hitler' during their public school education because of their brutal behaviour to younger pupils, and the behaviours of the youth and the man have been held to be connected.

Support for this kind of analysis of the mental health aspects of schooling has come from Alice Miller, writing about the education of the people who became the leaders of the Third Reich under Hitler (Miller, 1987). The same detachment to initiating actions that caused others considerable suffering and often death, on the supposed grounds of necessity, was linked by Miller to the emotionally destructive effects of their education, a consistent application of the most rigid authoritarian pattern, which constituted 'the poisonous pedagogy'. Shute (1993) has described this outcome as 'compulsory schooling disease'.

It was ethical arguments that led the European Court of Human Rights to support the stance of the STOPP campaign against corporal punishment in UK schools, despite the ridicule of the British press, as an infringement of basic human rights. The Conservative government view that physically punishing children was acceptable and desirable cost taxpayers large sums of money in an unsuccessful court hearing. The verdict implied that the various governments of the UK had sanctioned a type of child abuse for centuries.

The Netherlands and Denmark both uphold the UN Charter on the issue of religious freedom and give of parents the right to have schools that respect their religious and philosophical views, supported by grants of up to 75 per cent from state funds. From this point of view, the education system of the UK is in breach of the UN Charter of Human Rights on this issue, just as it was in the case of corporal punishment, because it denies Muslims as well as followers of the Steiner educational philosophy such facilities, while permitting Christian denominational schools, Jewish schools and grant-maintained schools.

These are only some of the ethical issues that are raised. Others relate to the ageist nature of schooling: is it ethical that children should be compelled to spend 15,000 hours in the largely unrelieved company of members of their peer group whether they wish it or not?

Then there is the social class discrimination of the independent/state division which has divided the two largest political parties for years: is it ethical that some wealthy families can buy a kind of schooling, e.g. small schools and small classes, that is denied to those without money, and that results in the perpetuation of the rigid social class system that still astonishes visitors with its apartheid characteristics?

It is not the purpose of this book to resolve these issues. The aim is to provide an anatomy of the choice issues so that the debate can break out from its current limited nature. Nevertheless, the concept of flexischooling that the Education Now Cooperative has been exploring and developing does resolve some of these by allowing considerable diversity and encouraging the idea that a variety of educational ideas and experiences have a legitimate part to play in one person's educational programmes. Thus authoritarian, autonomous and democratic forms of education can all be seen as having a role to play in producing flexible people. The answer to many questions in educational debate is transformed if there is a refusal to be simplistic and propose right/wrong positions.

The key formulation in response to any such right/wrong type questions would seem to be to say, 'both probably, though not inevitably, have a modest part to play in the scheme of things', and then to begin the exploration of when and why in each case. For example:

> *Question*: Are you in favour of a centrally imposed, adult-designed British national curriculum or a learner-referenced curriculum?

> *Reply*: Both may well have some modest part to play in the scheme of things, at least as a temporary expedient, along with the other four or five types of curriculum, and we need to work out carefully what part each might play. Perhaps there are persuasive reasons for allocating as much as 25 per cent of the time to a national curriculum, even if this is only on the realistic grounds of needing to recognize that adult chauvinism is not going to disappear overnight.
>
> It is not clear, however, why this is a national curriculum and not a European or even a world or global curriculum. The adoption of a catalogue curriculum would, however, allow a wide variety of possibilities, including some 'required' items to calm the fears of those adults who are nervous about trusting the intelligence of the learners.

CONCLUSION

A consideration of these six dimensions does point to the conclusion that educational choice requires a flexible system. The purposes of such a flexible system can be held to include the following:

1. to equip individuals so that they can cope with a rapidly changing world, creatively and imaginatively, rather than with fear, obstructionism and fatalism;
2. to match the needs of a modern, living democracy for people who can operate as participating citizens exercising responsible, informed choice, and acting with all the necessary possible positive tolerance needed to make an open and diverse society work;
3. to match the wide variety of individual learning styles, learning biographies, forms of intelligence and learner aspirations;
4. to match the needs of the modern economy for flexible, capable and adaptable people.

Further Reading

Abbott, J. and Ryan, T. (2000) *The Unfinished Revolution*. Stafford: Network Educational Press.

Adcock, J. (2000) *Teaching Tomorrow*. Nottingham: Education Now.

Handy, C. (1994) *The Empty Raincoat*. London: Hutchinson.

Harber, C. (1996) *Small Schools and Democratic Practice*. Nottingham: Educational Heretics Press.

Hutton, W. (1995) *The State We're In*. London: Jonathan Cape.

Meighan, R. (1993) *Theory and Practice of Regressive Education*. Nottingham: Educational Heretics Press.

Meighan, R. (1997) *The Next Learning System*. Nottingham: Educational Heretics.

Miller, A. (1987) *For Your Own Good: Hidden Cruelty in Child-rearing and the Roots of Violence*. London: Virago.

Shotton, J. (1993) *No Master High or Low*. Bristol: Libertarian Education.

Discussion and Activities

John Holt writes in *The Underachieving School*:

> The fundamental educational problem of our time is to find ways to help children grow into adults who have no wish to do harm. We must recognise that traditional education, far from ever solving this problem, has never tried to solve it. Indeed, its efforts have, if anything, been in exactly the opposite direction. An important aim of traditional education has always been to make children into the kind of adults who were ready to hate and kill whomever their leaders might declare to be their enemies.

Does this mean that most of what is done in the name of schooling at present needs to be made illegal?

Signposts

1. Natural learning

In Thomson *et al.* (1995) *Natural Childhood*, London: Gaia Books, the idea of getting back to the natural learning styles of children and working with such styles, rather than trying to impose an artificial methodology, is explored.

See also Meighan, R. (2001) *Natural Learning and the Natural Curriculum*, Nottingham: Educational Heretics Press.

In Rose, C. and Nicholl M.J. (1997) *Accelerated Learning for the 21st Century*, New York: Delarcote Press, the implications of different learning styles, different intelligences and the new findings about the brain as an organism rather than a computer, are all worked through in terms of how these can lead to optimum or 'accelerated' learning.

2. Alternative schools

In Gribble, D. (1998) *Real Education*, Bristol: Libertarian Education, the writer describes a selection of schools that he has visited around he world that have 'non-traditional' or 'alternative' regimes. They include Summerhill and Sands (England), Tamariki (New Zealand), Sudbury Valley (USA), Mirambika (Canada), Tokyo Shure (Japan) and Hadera (Israel).

32 The Next Learning System

Much of our expenditure on teachers and plant is wasted by attempting to teach people what they do not want to learn in a situation that they would rather not be involved in.

Colin Ward

HOME-BASED EDUCATION

In the UK, the USA and elsewhere, an unusual, quiet revolution has been taking place in the form of educating children at home. At the time that the fierce debates about mainstream education have been taking place concerning the National Curriculum, testing, 'back to basics', opting out or opting in, local management of schools, etc., some families have quietly been getting on with a 'do it yourself' approach to education. In the USA, over a million families are now 'home-schoolers' as they are known across the Atlantic. In the UK, over 10,000 families, involving over 20,000 children, are estimated to be operating home based education. Thousands more are involved in Australia, New Zealand and Canada (Meighan, 1992).

This phenomenon is most accurately described as home-based education because most families use the home as a springboard into community-based activities and investigations, replacing the 'day prison' model operated by most schools. People often find this quite hard to grasp, and wonder whether such children become socially inept. The research indicates the reverse, and every study has shown that home-educated children are almost always more emotionally stable and mature, and more socially aware and competent. The reasons identified are that learning activities out in the community give children more social contacts and more varied encounters than the restricted social life on offer in the majority of schools, as well as reducing the limiting effects of the peer group dependency feature common to school-based adolescent experience (Meighan, 1995c).

People often try to generate generalizations and stereotypes about families educating in the home-based way. The only ones that the evidence supports are that: (a) they display considerable diversity in motive, methods and aims; and (b) they are remarkably successful in achieving their chosen aims (Webb, 1990).

Schools often claim that if home-based education is to be tolerable, the families should learn how to do it from the 'professionals'. The evidence, however, is that secondary schools in particular have a great deal to learn from the flexibility of these families. Thomas, for example, shows how the flexible learning methods employed by home-educators are more effective and more efficient (in Meighan, 1995c).

In 1977 the research question posed was whether the few families opting for home-based education would cope. Ten years later, the research question had changed to a consideration of why they coped so well and so easily, and outperformed schooling in almost all respects. Part of the answer emerged as follows. When schools were set up, we lived in an information-poor environment. Today we live in an information-rich environment. This is a major factor in contributing to the success of home-based education. Furthermore, schools were designed to produce rather rigid, conformist people on a production line model. Today we need flexible, adaptable people and the production line approach does not produce them. The conclusion to be drawn from the research is that until schools adapt into more flexible patterns, as some have, home-based education is the most generally effective and successful kind of education available.

FLEXITIME

For some parents and their children the best arrangement for learning is for part of the time to be at home, and for part of the time to be at school. Some flexitime arrangements are relatively easy to achieve. These are when *large blocks of time* are spent either at school or at home:

1. The whole of the primary years are devoted to home-based education, then the secondary years given over to school.
2. The reverse pattern: primary phase in school, secondary phase home-based.
3. Whole years in school, or college, and whole years home-based, as and when seen to be appropriate.
4. In the same way, whole terms are spent either in school or home-based.

The most difficult arrangement appears to be that of a *flexible week* with two or three days in school and two or three days home-based. This is commonplace in nursery schools in the UK, later in colleges at the further education phase, where flexistudy programmes are made available, and in some cases in higher education.

The position in law in the UK is that there are two *absolute* rights in education, either to educate at home or to use a school. Flexitime is a *relative* right, so that a school or local education authority can arrange this, but if permission is refused, no reason has to be given. So each arrangement has to be negotiated afresh, and parents have patiently to explain that it *is* permissible, that plenty of people *have* done it and are doing it, and that it *does* work very well if the will and the vision are there.

Strangely enough, it immediately becomes possible if parents allow their child to be labelled odd and accept a 'school phobic' label or 'school refuser' description, or some other categorization offered by the educational psychological industry. There is hypocrisy here. If it suits the needs of the school, flexitime is deemed a good thing, but if requested by the parents and children, it is deemed to be a bad idea.

In the USA, flexible week arrangements are called independent study programmes or ISPs, and are becoming more common. A specially trained member of staff negotiates the timetable with the families concerned.

At first, the idea of flexitime was described as flexischooling in the UK, but the latter notion grew in scope to cover much more than just part-time schooling, so the terms now need to be more carefully distinguished (Meighan, 1988).

SMALL SCHOOLS

Even smaller than small schools are homes, and, as the evidence shows, home-based education is currently the most effective education on offer in the UK and the USA. This lends some credibility to the claim of the advocates of small schools that it is folly to destroy them without good reason, because they *operate like extended families*.

Next, there is the *efficiency* argument. If you have one bad school of one thousand pupils, you get a thousand-person disaster. The same pupils in ten small schools would require them all to be bad to achieve the same disaster.

Third, there is the *quality of relationships* – the proposition that small is more beautiful because it is more personal and human. Large schools run the constant risk of becoming impersonal because of the logistics of their organization. Small schools can, of course, run a different risk: that of suffocation; smothering rather than mothering.

A further issue is *choice*, starting with parental choice. Those parents whose wealth allows them to choose tend to favour smallness. Those who are left often have largeness thrust upon them. Next, there is the matter of pupil choice. In a survey of pupils in schools in Britain, Canada and Australia, they were strongly in favour of small schools. Cohesiveness and satisfaction were seen as high and friction as low. Schoolchildren really liked their small schools and enjoyed being there, because they provided positive learning environments. In the same survey, the teachers in these schools responded in the same favourable way, despite identifying a few possible drawbacks.

Small schools are an international experience, for they exist in large countries and small, rich countries and poor (Harber, 1995). But although they are so common, they have both advocates and critics. Those in favour recommend their personal atmosphere and make claims for their role at the centre of a local community. Those against claim that they are expensive, having high unit costs, and that they can only offer a restricted curriculum. In the UK, administrators with the latter view have been dominant and have forced many small school closures on often unwilling populations.

MINI-SCHOOLING

Mini-schooling is a method of organizing a large school into small sub-units (Meighan and Toogood, 1992). Each sub-unit, or mini-school, has its own small team of teachers, a defined student population of about 100 pupils, some autonomy over the use of time, some resources of its own and a base area in the school. Parents could attach themselves to this base to help out with the teaching, supervision, resources production, administration, maintenance, repair and decorating.

Mini-schooling is based on the idea that inside every large and inevitably, to some degree or other, impersonal school are lots of small, personal, family-style schools waiting to be liberated. A large school becomes organized as a cluster of small learning communities or a federation of mini-schools.

From time to time, the pupils of a mini-school will visit other parts of the campus, such as a science block, even though they have a science facility within their base area, to use special facilities. Another example is a physical education block's facilities. Mini-school teachers will operate some of the time as specialist teachers in their chosen subject area with pupils other than their mini-school cohort.

Learners, teachers and parents all feel strongly identified with the mini-school with which they are involved. This has two particular benefits, the most significant being a fall in truancy rates among children and absenteeism among teachers, owing to their enjoyment of time spent at the mini-school.

Because the mini-school is a common and unifying factor, the groups of teachers and parents are more inclined to see each other as people to work with rather than rivals to fight against. This is demonstrated by increased fund-raising successes. These indicate that if they know that they will see the full benefits, people will always be willing to contribute whatever they can towards their children's education.

The ideas and principles of mini-schooling were first implemented at Madeley Court School in Telford, Shropshire, under the direction of Philip Toogood. They are currently in operation at the Stantonbury Campus, Milton Keynes, Buckinghamshire. In the USA, in 1993, the New York City Board broke up its large high schools into smaller units. By 1996, the results of this policy were already declared as better academic results, a marked reduction in violent incidents, fewer pupil pregnancies, and increased attendance rates to over 90 per cent.

SCHOOLS WITHIN SCHOOLS

'Schools within schools' is a form of mini-schooling. It is a method of organizing a large school into small sub-units. Each sub-unit, or mini-school, has its own small team of teachers, a defined student population often of about 100 pupils, some autonomy over the use of time, some resources of its own and a base area in the school. Parents can attach themselves to this base to help out, assisting with the teaching, supervision, resources production, administration, maintenance, repair and decoration.

In 'schools within schools', however, the mini-schools are deliberately organized following different philosophies to provide a range of learning choices. There may be three types on offer: an authoritarian, a democratic and an autonomous mini-school. Other choices of philosophy and practice may be offered. Learners, parents and teachers are all able to choose the style of learning that suits them and to change their choices from time to time.

It is also possible to have mixed choices; for example, to study sciences in a democratic mode, literature in an authoritarian mode and language studies in an autonomous mode. All these studies would also be available in the other modes, so that if studying science, say, in one mode is not so successful for an individual one year, he or she can try another mode in the next. Teachers are also able to operate in different styles if they so desire, either by making a change from one year to the next or by teaching two curriculum areas in two different mini-schools.

COMMUNITY EDUCATION

The Community Education Association's manifesto declares that community education:

- is a concept of education being a life-long learning process concerned with identifying and meeting the needs of individuals and their communities;
- enables people to take greater control of their own learning and to participate fully in the making of decisions which affect them and communities of which they are part;
- encourages individuals and groups to take personal and collective action and responsibility leading to a fully active society in which common effort is made to improve everyone's quality of life.

Harry Reé, in his biography of Henry Morris, writes:

> Henry Morris started Community Education. He did this in two ways. First he sketched out a new philosophy of education, and then basing his plans on that philosophy, he persuaded the Cambridgeshire County Council to build a series of Village Colleges, which were the prototype for the Community Schools which are to be found all over the country today.

The ten Village Colleges of Cambridgeshire were to be located in market towns and they would serve everyone by bringing together in one location the schools, social services, medical services, county library, careers office, agricultural education, further education, the Workers' Educational Association, the youth services, playing fields and sports facilities. The sharing of these facilities would mean that the complex served as a community centre for the neighbourhood. The antithesis of community education would appear to be the English public school. Hitler admired them as the model institution for producing the kind of people he wanted to become leaders of the Fatherland. Morris did not: 'The case against them is moral. The English nation has been riven into two nations, not on any principle based on virtue or intelligence but on money.'

USING WORK AS A RESOURCE: CITY AS SCHOOL

Established in 1972 in New York, *City as School* (CAS) was a response to the high drop-out rate of the city's other high schools. Originators Fred Koury and Richard Safran wanted to provide a school with the flexibility to meet the individual needs of its pupils far more closely than the curricula of existing schools evidently did.

A choice of around 2,500 'learning experiences' is on offer. Each has its own curriculum and a duration of 25–32 hours per week for nine weeks. The nine-week timespan is considered to be long enough to be meaningful, without becoming torturous if a student encounters problems. The curriculum is agreed upon by the students in conjunction with a resource coordinator from the CAS. When the nine-week 'mini-apprenticeship' concludes, the observations and reactions of both the curriculum provider and the student are sought.

The variety of 'learning experiences' is not just denoted by subject matter. Some units can be arranged to take place at un-school-like hours, such as weekends or evenings, which can be useful if a separate interest is to be accommodated, such as art or sport courses.

By its nature, the CAS is dependent upon what the city offers as resources and facilities. Consequently, basic reading, writing and mathematics courses for the age groups involved can be hard to find. The CAS responds by itself putting these courses in its own classrooms.

The method of meeting any needs still not met is to set up a project for the student, requiring use of the resources of the CAS as well as the city. Books, video and audio cassettes are available, as well as people. The nine-week module duration still applies. Students can join the CAS at any time of the year, owing to the relatively short nature of the 'learning experiences', compared with the common year-long school curriculum.

The flexibility of CAS, coupled with the involvement of students in the curriculum arrangement, results in a feeling for the students that they are being respected and treated as maturing adults, capable of making their own decisions and managing their own time profitably, when given the opportunity.

LEARNER-MANAGED LEARNING: THE AUTONOMOUS EDUCATION APPROACH

There is a long-standing tradition regarding autonomous learning; indeed, it is as traditional as the idea of formal instruction and probably pre-dates it. Socrates was noted for the approach of advocating that a teacher enters into an individual dialogue with each pupil. Quintillian held that Roman education should follow similar principles:

> The skilled teacher, when a pupil is entrusted to his care, will first of all seek to discover his ability and natural disposition and will next observe how the mind of his pupil is to be handled . . . for in this respect there is an unbelievable variety, and types of mind are no less numerous than types of body.

Contemporary research supports Quintillian. Human beings, adults and children alike, differ from each other in learning styles. To date, over thirty such differences have been identified.

Ironically, we live in a society that expects you to manage your own life more and more, but takes over the management of learning of most people between the ages of five and sixteen, expecting attendance for a minimum of 15,000 hours, with the centrally imposed National Curriculum transmitted to them in a 'tell them and test them' environment.

Some areas of learning are left for learners to manage for themselves, such as driving a car, coping with sexual behaviour and acquiring some skills of parenthood when children arrive. Learners managing their own learning may, mistakenly, be assumed to be solo learners. This is neither a necessary condition nor a desirable one. What distinguishes learners managing their own learning is the motivation to choose to learn and to act upon that choice effectively. Whether that learning is carried out by working alone, by working cooperatively in a group or by deciding to submit to formal instruction is not the issue. All these styles of learning can be harnessed in turn, if this is seen as appropriate, by the autonomous learners. What learners effectively managing their own learning do is to follow the essential sequence of 'plan, do, review' (Ginnis, 1992).

DEMOCRATIC EDUCATION

In democratic education, the learners as a group have the power to make some, most or even all of the key decisions, since power is shared and not appropriated in advance by a minority of one or more. Ironically, in many countries, including the UK, that sustain the illusion that they are very democratic, such educational practices are rare and meet with sustained, hostile and irrational opposition.

The autonomous and democratic approaches can complement each other, for effective democratic learning can incorporate both the solo type of learner-managed and the collective form, in interaction with each other. The group can use the device of allocating tasks to individuals, and sometimes pairs and trios, which requires them to go off and research and prepare material, activities and sessions. The results of their solo activities would then be fed back into the group programme.

What does democratic learning look like? The group learning contract described earlier in this book gives some of the flavour of it:

- We agree to accept responsibility for our course as a group.
- We agree to take an active part in the learning of the group.
- We agree to be constructively critical of our own and other people's ideas.
- We agree to plan our own programme of studies, implement it using the group members and appointed teachers as resources, and review the outcomes in order that we may learn from any limitations we identify.
- We agree to the keeping of a group logbook of work completed, planning decisions, session papers and any other appropriate documents.
- We agree to share the duties of being in the chair, the task of being meeting secretary and the roles of session organizers and contributors.
- We agree to review this contract from time to time.

Democratic practice is rarely proposed as an ideal state but, paraphrasing Winston Churchill's words, is the worst system of organization and order available – except for all the alternatives. The point is well made, perhaps, in a passage from E.M. Forster's famous essay 'What I Believe':

> Democracy is not a beloved republic really, and never will be. But it is less hateful than other contemporary forms of government, and to that extent deserves our support. It does start from the assumption that the individual is important, and that all types are needed to make a civilisation. It does not divide citizens into the bosses and the bossed – as an efficiency regime tends to do. The people I most admire are those who are sensitive and want to create something or discover something, and do not see life in terms of power, and such people get more of a chance under democracy than elsewhere. They found religions, great or small, or they produce literature and art, or they do disinterested scientific research, or they may be what is called 'ordinary people' who are creative in their private lives, bring up their children decently, for instance, or help their neighbours. All these people need to express themselves; they cannot do so unless society allows them liberty to do so, and the society which allows them most is a democracy.
>
> Democracy has another merit. It allows criticism ... That is why I believe in the press, despite all its lies and vulgarity, and why I believe in Parliament ... Whether Parliament is either a representative body or an efficient one is questionable, but I value it because it criticises and talks, and because its chatter gets widely reported.

So two cheers for Democracy: one because it admits variety and two because it permits criticism. Two cheers are quite enough: there is no occasion to give three.

It is possible to extract from the above quotations and ideas some propositions about the democratic school and democratic educational programmes. They will tend to:

1. admit variety rather than uniformity;
2. permit critical thought rather than belief;
3. operate power-sharing rather than authoritarian imposition;
4. promote flexibility rather than rigidity;
5. respect the Thirty Articles of the Universal Declaration of Human Rights rather than religious or political creeds, thus adopting the value base of equal human rights.

FLEXISCHOOLING

Flexischooling is a new blueprint for education derived from the notion that the conventional rigid model of schooling is no longer an adequate vehicle for the development of young people. The idea was developed in discussions between John Holt and Roland Meighan in 1984, during Holt's last visit to England, and not long before his death from cancer. The key idea is that: 'rigid systems produce rigid people, flexible systems produce flexible people'.

Flexischooling developed, at first, as a more open way of viewing the partnership of home, school and community. Some parents do not want to consign their children totally to an educational institution which claims to do the whole job of educating their children for them. Nor do they want to do all of it themselves in a home-based education programme, although many are forced to do so as the best option open to them. What they seek is a way of having the best of both worlds in the interests of serving their children's needs in a world of rapid change.

Flexischooling, even in its first version as flexitime, could be seen to be questioning the basic assumptions of compulsory schooling in Britain in the 1990s:

1. *There does not have to be a single location for education.* There can be several, including schools, homes, workplaces, museums and libraries.
2. *Parents are seen as having an active educational role* in cooperation and partnership with schools and as capable of building on their astonishing achievements of helping their children learn to talk, walk and develop in the first five years of life.
2. *Children can learn many things without a teacher being present.* After all, they managed to learn their mother tongue this way.
4. *Teaching is not synonymous with instructing.* 'Learning coach' activities, such as helping them to locate resources to further their own research, are types of teaching. Thus, facilitating learning is a teaching act as well as 'full frontal' instruction.

5. *Resources available at home can be utilized in educational programmes.* These include the ubiquitous TV and radio, as well as cassette recorders, video recorders and home computers.

6. *The uniqueness of individuals can be respected.* Different learning styles can be accommodated in a more flexible system.

In later expanded versions, flexischooling is seen as a much more flexible approach to education in all its dimensions, and it raises more questions still. For example, could the curriculum become a negotiated experience more than an imposed one? Could there be choice from the variety of types of curriculum available? In general, it offers the prospect of diversifying, starting from the rigid school system, without losing any positive features that can be identified.

Although flexischooling sounds futuristic, a central finding is that some of the key components are already available and operational in different schools, homes and community locations, and in various countries. It is an attempt to see how a new model of schooling can be generated out of the old to respond to the needs of a society in the throes of a communications revolution. We have a changing world. Its technologies and its cultures continue to change and become more complicated. Knowledge continues to grow and existing knowledge is shown to be partial and sometimes in error. Rigid people cannot cope: flexible people have a better chance of coping.

Behaviour in the modern world is also complex. Sometimes we need authoritarian behaviour, i.e. the types of responses and people who know when it makes sense to take orders or give them. At other times we need the self-managing skills of autonomous behaviour, and at other times the cooperative skills of democratic behaviour. The world is multidimensional. An adequate education means helping people to grow to match it. Our present school system is, for the most part, unidimensional, offering predominantly authoritarian experiences.

John Holt had a proposal about how schools could be *invitational* rather than based on conscription. It went like this:

> Why not make schools into places where children would be allowed, encouraged, and, when they asked, helped to make sense of the world around them in ways that interested them?

In flexischooling, it is proposed that we should rename such places as *learning resource centres* to avoid confusion with the 'day prison', compulsory attendance, adult-imposed curriculum model of a school.

NOTSCHOOLNET – A CASE STUDY IN PERSONALIZED LEARNING

Notschool.net is a research project run by Ultralab at Anglia Polytechnic University under the supervision of Professor Stephen Hepple. It began in the year 2000 and the director is Jean

Johnson. It devises ways of re-engaging young people in education when all else has failed and there is a broad mix of teenagers currently taking part. There are young people excluded from school, sick children, school phobics, young mothers – a range of people that conventional schooling has failed to inspire or cope with.

Others involved include:

- The Researchers – the name given to the young people in the project; their needs determine any content to be devised.
- The Tutors – they provide the researchers with learning support as needed.
- The Mentors – undergraduates or postgraduates who are paid online buddies to a group of researchers.
- The Governors – high profile people from any walk of life whose role is to provide models of success to encourage the researchers.
- The Curriculum experts – who are brought in when necessary to create online materials.

In the project, young people learn at their own pace and at a time that suits them. The starting point is to find what interests them and to focus on it, whatever it may be. They become part of a secure on-line learning community that is supportive and has an ethos of self-respect. There is no destructive criticism or blame culture. The young people grow to be proud to show their work and to share their experiences. They manage their own learning with whatever help they require being made available.

Many of the young people, though rejected by the schooling system, turn out to be high achievers within their chosen field of study. The broad and balanced curriculum idea based on endless uninvited teaching, has stifled their progress in the past and they will now happily spend hours on a subject that interests them, whether it is art, music, mathematics, ICT or anything else. Most seem quite capable of making choices about their education and are quite clear about the reasons they have difficulty with schools.

The reports from Notschool.net explain that, given the opportunity to choose their pathway in education, almost all of the young people achieve. The outcomes make it difficult to remember that we are referring to a group of people previously so disengaged from learning that Notschool.net was the last resort. Over 50% have achieved formal qualifications. Over 30% have asked to stay on. Some are now at college, others have their sights on university – a path seemingly closed to them in the past.

It seems clear that these young people needed an alternative to school in order to achieve and that given this, they can be high achievers. The comments of the young people echo this conclusion:

> It's a shame that kids have to go to the edge before they get on a programme like Notschool.net or into a special unit.

Don Glines of the Education Futures Projects, USA makes a similar point when he declares that to get to the good learning systems in the USA, you first have to be bad at the bad ones.

Bullying is a significant factor since 70% of those taking part in the project report that they were bullied by their peers in school and many of these felt bullied by the teachers as well. The figures may well be higher since this information is not deliberately sought by the project but volunteered in feedback.

The numbers of young people who opt out of the mass schooling system in the UK is currently estimated at 100,000 but the figures could easily be much higher. This figure does not include the 90,000 or more who are fortunate enough to be educated at home. Once young people reject schooling, their options are few.

As noted before, the members of the project are not called pupils, or students, or even clients, (or even curriculum study units, CSUs, as the civil servants who designed the second National Curriculum of 1988 once proposed), but are called 'researchers'. It is a significant piece of 'rebranding' that signals their switch to a form of autonomous learning.

Sources

Notschool.net by Jean Johnson in *Education Now News and Review* 36, Summer 2002.
Evaluation of the Notschool.net research project Initial Pilot by Julia Duckworth
Notschool.net Research Phase Final Report Dec 2001
See www.notschool.net

CREATING LEARNING COMMUNITIES

Creating Learning Communities: Models, Resources, and New Ways of Thinking about Teaching and Learning is the name of a book edited in 2000 by Ron Miller of the Foundation for Educational Renewal Inc. USA (ISBN 1–885580–04–5). It is in all respects a contemporary book. First, it was written and published on the Internet at *www.PathsofLearning.com*. The writers met on the Internet on a list-serve, *CCL-LLCs@onelist.com*. The common interests of the writers were the future of learning and the potential impact on society of cooperative community lifelong learning centres. These are emerging, in particular, from the rapidly growing home-schooling movement. This social phenomenon is spontaneously self-organizing without leadership, without planning, without design and (often) without being noticed. All of the educators involved, whether home-schoolers, autodidacts, cooperatives or futurists, are playing one role or another in trying to transform the learning system.

In the book, 30 leading innovators and writers from a variety of countries tackle the issue of the next learning system. These writers are agreed that our common experience tells us that all is not well with society. Today's schools teach by the mode they use – hierarchy, self-interest, authoritarianism, patriarchy, competition, materialism and survival of the fittest. Humanity looks set to destroy itself with this value system. And, as increasing number of observers, including scientists, philosophers, historians, and artists, are starting to warn us, if present trends continue, we are headed for an enormous cultural and ecological disaster.

Creating Learning Communities includes a number of inspiring case studies. There are also analyses of the age of information technology and its impact. A key section looks at the philosophical roots of the next learning system. Finally, there is a directory of information and contacts.

The writers set a challenge. Emerging is a future in which all people could learn what and when they want, regardless of age – a future where learning can be lifelong, where the old paradigms are set aside. We could be able to intellectually roam and seek out as much knowledge, information and experience as we wish, and be able to both learn and teach according to our curiosity, needs and knowledge. In most segments of society we are some distance from this future, not least because schooling, based on the 'tell them and test them' ideology, has dimmed our imagination. But here and there, in growing numbers, all around the world, people are actually living this future today.

Ron Miller draws distinctions between three general approaches. First, the transmission approach assumes that the primary purpose of education is to induct young people into the established values, beliefs and accepted knowledge of the existing society. Second, the transaction approach is more sensitive to the social context of learning. There is more room for individual differences, more respect for diverse understandings, and a concern that only a democratic community encourages dialogue and experimentation. Third, the transformation approach is more radical and proposes that to educate human beings is not merely to make them all knowledgeable, productive members of society (transmission), or an active, engaged citizen (transaction), but also to encourage each person to discover a deeper meaning for his or her life.

Miller adds a fourth possibility: self direction. This is found well expressed in the writings of John Holt and A.S. Neill. It holds that we are naturally learners, and if social institutions would stop cluttering our paths with various prejudices, agendas and bad habits, young people would follow a natural curriculum and learn throughout their lives all that is necessary to experience meaningful and productive lives. Most, if not all, of the structures of schooling – grades, lesson plans, age groupings, teaching strategies, key stages and obsessive testing – are seen as irrelevant and counter-productive.

The writers in this book have little sympathy for the existing learning system of mass, coercive schooling. Some see it as obsolete. Well, perhaps spending time in a museum of education might not be all that harmful, you might argue. But some of the writers see mass schooling as actually counter-productive in that it produces a series of bad habits, ranging from intellectual, through emotional, psychological and political, to social. Others go further and see mass, coercive schooling as infringing three and sometimes four human rights. One of these is conscription to an ageist institution. Such an imposition is justified by the dubious belief that being compelled to spend large amounts of time in the company of people chosen for you and of the same age and immaturity as yourself will somehow turn you into a mature, reflective human being. What it really does is set up the context for the tyranny of the peer group with its pressure on the inmates to conform to whatever fads and fashions grip it at any particular time, whether it be expensive trainers or expensive drugs.

The writers in this book have found common cause through the Internet. In their own communities they can often be rather lone voices for a more sane learning system. Now, they are able to avoid the mass media techniques of 'soft' censorship (for example, by systematically failing to report alternative ideas), and present their ideas direct to a worldwide audience.

PERSONALIZED LEARNING AS LEARNER-MANAGED LEARNING INSTEAD OF GOVERNMENT-DIRECTED LEARNING

The current profile of an individual's learning journey in the UK (and it is similar in many respects in most countries in the world) for the first stages of his/her life looks like this:

At one to four/five years: Home-based learning with playgroup experience and/or child-minding and nursery experience in some cases.

At four/five years: Attendance at a state school with a government-dictated curriculum, testing, and inspection with a teacher-directed learning regime, apart from small minorities who attend private schools or are home-educated by family choice.

At six years: The same

At seven years: The same

(In various European countries such as Sweden, Finland and Denmark, the expected school attendance years do not begin until eight years of age.)

At eight years: The same

At nine years: The same

At ten years: The same

At eleven years: The same

At twelve years: The same

At thirteen years: The same

At fourteen years: The same

At fifteen years: The same

At sixteen years: Some continue with the same, some leave school and go into employment.

At seventeen years: The same

At eighteen years: Almost half the population go to a university where they study a lecturer-directed learning regime with university-dictated course contents and testing. A growing minority are choosing the more learner-friendly regime of the Open University at a fraction of the debt incurred from the old-style, 'late-adolescent three-year-exile' university course.

Within this time period, some will have had some true educational experiences: 'Some true educational experiences are bound to occur in schools. They occur, however, despite and not because of school' (Everett Reimer). But, overall, none of this has much to do with personalised learning. It is people processing. It has been said that education is properly defined as 'asking questions all the time'. The profile above is based on the idea of NOT asking questions but learning the required material, and developing only the required skills, hence the description of it by Paul Goodman as 'compulsory mis-education'.

From the point of view of personalized education, what are the possible building blocks of a learner-managed education? These can be seen as 'episodes' in the learning journey and they are organized in one-year building blocks. But such episodes could be shorter – a half-year or a quarter of a year. These building blocks can be seen as the macro-level of the Catalogue Curriculum, the alternative to an imposed, dictated curriculum. (The micro-level contains the more detailed items of the content of experiences, projects, courses and, where appropriate, subjects – the whole range of all possible learning experiences available in society, including the methods of invited teaching, research, books, computers, workshops, and so on.)

Here is a list of possible 'episodes':

1. Home-based education – properly acknowledged and supported
2. Home-based education learning cooperatives
3. Weekday programmes at Community Learning Centres (schools recycled into non-ageist centres)
4. Weekend programmes at local Community Learning Centres
5. Travel and study year in the UK
6. Travel and study year in Europe
7. Travel and study year elsewhere
8. Residential college year with a sports focus (recycled residential school like the Danish EFTA Skole)
9. Residential college year with an arts focus
10. Residential college year with a music and dance focus
11. Residential college year with a rural studies and environmental focus
12. Year for exploration of the learner's locality and its learning sites
13. Joining a democratic learning cooperative based on the local community learning centre or public library
14. Joining a City as School scheme
15. Duke of Edinburgh's Award Scheme year or a Scouts, Guides or Woodcraft Folk year
16. Voluntary work in the community
17. Joining an ICT Virtual Learning community or programme such as NotSchoolNet.

I am sure readers could add further options to this list.

One learning profile, as decided by the learner in conjunction with the family and a support and advice service of a new profession of personal tutor-guides, might look like this. (Members of this new profession might be called pedagogues or 'PEDAs' for short, who would act more frequently as educational travel agents than as instructors and 'miserable rule-followers'.)

At one to five years:	Home-based learning with playgroup experience, and/or child-minding and nursery experience in some cases
At six years:	Further home-based education and involvement in a home-based education learning cooperative
At seven years:	Weekend programmes at local community learning centres with further home-based learning
At eight years:	Weekday programmes at local community learning centres
At nine years:	Year for exploration of the learner's locality and its learning sites
At ten years:	Residential college year with a rural studies and environmental focus
At eleven years:	Weekday programmes at local community learning centres
At twelve years:	Weekday programmes at local community learning centres
At thirteen years:	Residential college year with a music and dance focus
At fourteen years:	Joining a democratic learning cooperative based on the local community learning centres or public library
At fifteen years:	Joining an ICT virtual learning community scheme, e.g. NotSchoolNet
At sixteen years:	City as School scheme combined with voluntary work in the community and involvement in a community arts project
At seventeen years:	Residential college year with a sports focus with some music and dance
At eighteen years:	Travel and study year in the UK
At nineteen years:	Open University studies along with a Travel and Study year in Europe.

At the outset of such an 'episodes' scheme, many families might ask for the familiar pattern of weekday provision for many of the years. This would be available, on request, in a flexible learning system, with the pattern decided by the learners and their families in conjunction with their personal tutor. But, if the experience of the all-year-round education schemes in the USA is anything to go by, the delight of the first families to vary their pattern is catching.

The two systems outlined above produce different kinds of people. The repetitive pattern of the current model brings to mind the comment of John Holt that schooling is really a long drawn-out course in practical slavery.

The second system, the learner-managed system, is more likely to produce confident, capable researchers with the ability to cooperate with others and institutions as and when necessary. It does not look like the conventional view of a 'balanced curriculum'. But then, the 'balanced curriculum' may just be a superstition or an adult hang-up with no basis in realty. For example, Patrick Moore, the astronomer, was educated at home and did not go to university. He tells us that he chose his curriculum at the age of seven as learning to type, which he thought would be useful, by copy-typing some tomes in astronomy. This, he thought, would inform him about the subject that interested him, and would also serve as a course in improving his English. He would also spend some time on his xylophone and later the piano, developing his musical skills. This unbalanced curriculum served him well, he explains, since the central activities of his life have been astronomy, journalism and music.

In the second system, the learners manage their learning programmes by exercising choice, with support and guidance. Indeed, an alternative title for this approach could be 'Real Choice in Education'.

Personalized learning, using a system based on the learning episodes in a learning journey approach, could move us into a new, exciting and vibrant education landscape with a real professional role for the teachers as 'the guide on the side' more than 'the sage on the stage (see *www.c.person.ed.gn.apc.org* for further information about personalized learning).

CONCLUSION

From this catalogue of alternatives, a number of common themes about the next education system emerge. A key concern is how this complex system can be organized and monitored. Central ideas here are those of the personal learning plan, the catalogue curriculum and the new professional tutor described by Adcock (2000). The mechanics of monitoring are already well established, since the Open University already tracks the individual study plans of 100,000 students with the aid of a central computer modifying a TV slogan, 'We have the technology – we can track them.'

Further Reading

Adcock, J. (2000) *Teaching Tomorrow*. Nottingham: Education Now Books.

Bloomer, M., and Hodgkinson, P. (2000) 'Learning Careers' in *British Educational Research* 26, 5, pp. 583–97.

Glines, D. and Long, K. (1992) 'Transitioning Toward Educational Futures', *Phi Delta Kappan*, March.

Gray, S.L. (2004) Defining the Future: an interrogation of education and time', in *British Journal of the Sociology of Education*, 25, 3, pp. 323–4.

Harber, C. (ed.) (1995) *Developing Democratic Education*. Ticknall: Education Now Books.

Harber, C. (1995) *Small Schools and Democratic Practice*. Nottingham: Educational Heretics Press.

Holt, J. (1977) *Instead of Education*. Harmondsworth: Penguin.

Meighan, R. (1988) *Flexischooling*. Ticknall: Education Now Books.

Meighan, R. (ed.) (1992) *Learning from Home-based Education*. Ticknall: Education Now Books.

Meighan, R. (1995) *The Freethinkers' Pocket Directory to the Educational Universe*. Nottingham: Educational Heretics Press.

Meighan, R. (1997) *The Next Learning System*. Nottingham: Educational Heretics Press.

Meighan, R. (2005) *Comparing Learning Systems*, Nottingham: Educational Heretics Press.

Miller, R. (2000) *Creating Learning Communities*. New York: Foundation for Educational Renewal.

Shute, C. (1993) *Compulsory Schooling Disease*. Nottingham: Educational Heretics Press.

Discussion and Activities

Debate any of the following quotations:

> When you take the free will out of education, that turns it into schooling.
>
> John Taylor Gatto

> It is the great triumph of compulsory government monopoly mass schooling that among even the best of my fellow teachers, and among even the best of my students' parents, only a small number can imagine a different way to do things.
>
> John Taylor Gatto

> If a curriculum is to be effective … it must contain different ways of activating children, different ways of presenting sequences, different opportunities … A curriculum, in short, must contain many tracks leading to the same general goal.
>
> Jerome Bruner

> Over the past hundred years, the family has been stripped of most of its functions – as a major source of paid employment, of health-care, of welfare services or of education after the age of five. The only growth area is that of 'leisure centre', since television, video, radio and music-playing technology have been developed for home use. But in this one aspect, home-based education, the family has been striking back.
>
> Roland Meighan

Signposts

1. The catalogue curriculum

Instead of the imposed National Curriculum, I propose the idea of the catalogue curriculum of choices. Others may have used this description before, but I have not come across it. Don Glines has something similar in his 'window-shopping' approach to the curriculum, and the 'shopper's guide' for students in his *Creating Educational Futures* (1995).

The learners are offered a printed catalogue of learning opportunities, including (a) set courses, (b) ideas for making their own courses, (c) instructions as to how to set up a learning cooperative, (d) self-instructional packages and (e) lists of any available learning resources and opportunities in the community.

Because the catalogue includes pre-planned, negotiated and individual options, it serves the requirements of both the democratic and autonomous approaches, while also allowing authoritarian offers to be included. It thus serves the flexischooling synthesis, which is an attempt to incorporate the advantages of all three approaches and types of discipline.

There are several operating examples of the catalogue curriculum approach in existence, although none of them is quite as broad-ranging as I have in mind. Thus, the *City as Schools* initiative in the USA presents its students with a catalogue of hundreds of learning-at-work placements and associated college-based course options. From these, students devise personal study programmes in consultation with a tutor. A second example comes from the Duke of Edinburgh's Award Scheme, which has an extensive catalogue of ideas for the skills component. Another example is that of the Scout and Guide Movement's catalogue of badges. This particular example shows how an authoritarian approach can be dominant in a catalogue – all the badge options are pre-planned recipes for learning.

Of course, a kind of catalogue approach is common in further and higher education and adult education. The further education colleges all produce a prospectus and the Open University, the UK's most modern teaching university, is the best example of a catalogue approach to devising your own degree programme. Nursery schools use a catalogue approach because the young learners choose from a range of activities. The teachers write down the choice in their team meetings for planning purposes.

The case for the catalogue curriculum to replace any version of the imposed set curriculum, is based on the most recent research into learning. Howard Gardner identifies at least seven types of intelligence. Charles Handy suggests that there are more than this. We have known for many years that there are more than thirty learning styles in humans. The flexibility a full-blown catalogue curriculum approach implies is now widely recognized as the way forward. (From an article by Roland Meighan in *Education Now News and Review*, Autumn 1995.)

Task: Construct a catalogue curriculum to include authoritarian, autonomous and democratic sections. Would you have any required courses or structure any of the sections in any particular way? (For example, the Open University has foundation courses and two must be chosen to complete a recognized degree.)

2. Year-round education

In 'Year-Round Education' students are able to learn in any of the twelve months at will. Some of this learning will be on site and some in other locations in the community on a flexitime basis. Flexible attendance has effects on traffic congestion, on use of community facilities, on volunteering, on holiday and travel breaks, on flexible employment patterns, on staff morale and on student motivation. The culture of the school is changed from compulsory uniformity to invitational variety. Pressure on facilities is reduced if computer suites, art studios, drama studios, sports facilities are all available all year, and another result can be smaller classes and less crowding in schools. Thirty nine States in the USA have now adopted this idea in some form or other. Further information can be obtained from: Don Glines, Educational Futures Project, P.O. Box 2077, Sacramento, California, 95812, USA. Tel: 00 1 916 393 8701.

3. Cyber schools

Alberta province, Canada, already has ten cyber schools linking home-educating families with schools by computer. Seven thousand students are registered on home-based education programmes. Families may devise a learning programme of their own or they may choose to use the Alberta Distance Learning assignments, and make use of 'chat lines' with staff or for group discussions. Students can meet face-to-face with teachers every two weeks for such activities as group work, oral presentations, and tutorials. (Reported in *Education Now News and Review*, **15**, Spring 1997.)

4. Natural learning and the natural curriculum

Parents soon find out that young children are natural learners. They are like explorers or research scientists busily gathering information and making meaning of the world. Most of this learning is not the result of teaching, but rather a constant and universal learning activity, as natural as breathing. Our brains are programmed to learn unless discouraged. A healthy brain stimulates itself by interacting with what it finds interesting or challenging in the world around it. It learns from any mistakes and operates a self-correcting process.

We parents achieve the amazing feats of helping our children to talk, walk and make sense of the home and the environment in which it is set, by responding to this natural learning process. All this is achieved, with varying degrees of success, by so-called amateurs – those of us who are parents, along with other care-givers such as grandparents.

The highly sophisticated activity of parents is described as 'dovetailing' into the child's behaviour. Parents (frequently the mothers for the largest share of the time) have no predetermined plan of language teaching. We simply respond to the cues provided and give support to the next stage of learning as the child decides to encounter it. What we discover as parents is that, if supported and encouraged, children will not only begin to make sense of their world, but can also acquire the attitudes and skills necessary for successful learning throughout their lives.

However, this process of natural learning can be hindered or halted by insensitive adult interference. Sadly, the schools available to us, whether state or private, are often based on an impositional model which sooner or later causes children to lose confidence in their natural learning and its self-correcting features, and instead learn to be dependent on others to 'school' their minds. In the process, most schools manage to gradually transform learning from one of the most rewarding of all human activities into a rather dull, often boring, fragmenting, mind-shrinking, sometimes painful and soul-shrinking experience. A prize-winning New York teacher, John Taylor Gatto, describes this kind of schooling as 'training children . . . to be obedient to a script written by remote strangers . . . Education demands you write the script of your own life with the help of people who love or care about you.'

The consequence is that parents wanting an effective and morally healthy education, based on natural learning principles, for their children, are in the same position as people wanting more healthy, vegetarian or vegan diets, or non-smokers wanting clean air in public places, or investors wanting to invest their money in ethical rather than exploitative enterprises, or people wanting to save the environment from further and possibly terminal destruction. The system is not in the habit of providing any of these things, and often has a vested interest in providing the opposite. So, like the vegetarian pioneers, the non-smoking rights movement and the environmental protection groups, parents wanting education that respects natural learning principles will have to argue and organise to try to get it.

A curriculum can be defined, in simple terms, as 'a course of study'. Knowledge can be taken, for now, to be 'some kind of content that is the substance of a curriculum'. The latest research on the brain tells us that babies 'hit the ground running' as active learners. Their brains are already programmed to begin their lifelong course of study by interacting with their environment – unlike a cow, say, that is programmed to work in set routines. Indeed, one definition of what it is to be human is given in the title of a John Holt (1991) book – we are human because we are *Learning All the Time* (Ticknall: Education Now).

The 'natural' curriculum is the 'course of study' that humans develop as fast as physical and other conditions permit. So, babies accumulate knowledge through activities such as play, imitation, and interaction with any adults around. Play is best seen as children's work: one grandparent noted recently that her granddaughter, at the end of a refreshment and chat break, suddenly said, 'I must get on with my play-work now'.

The content of this natural curriculum is a set of existential questions. They include: Who am I? Who are you?

Who are they? Where do we belong? Who gets what? How do we find out? Where are we going? How am I doing? Who decides what? It is a set of questions that stays with us permanently, with the answers being reviewed constantly throughout our lives, as we assemble our tool-kit of knowledge. For example, the question 'Who am I?' will be redefined many times. As a person passes through the roles of infant, child, adolescent, young adult, single person, couple, married person, parent and older person their self-concept has to be revised.

From time to time, we may engage with those attempts at systematic bodies of knowledge called subjects, to help provide some answers to some of these questions. When young children reach five they are asking, on average, 30 questions an hour based on their natural curriculum. At this stage, one provisional answer to the question 'How do we find out?' has been gained: by achieving competence in the mother tongue. Until quite recently in human history, this natural curriculum was sufficient to keep most of us going throughout life. But then, about 150 years ago, an institution called the compulsory school was introduced, and suddenly, the natural curriculum was displaced. The natural questions became replaced by an imposed curriculum based on THEIR questions, THEIR required answers, and THEIR required assessment. The message is dramatically changed: 'Your experience, your concerns, your hopes, your fears, your desires, your interests, they count for nothing. What counts is what we are interested in, what we care about, and what we have decided you are to learn.' (From J. Holt. (1971), *The Underachieving School*, Harmondsworth: Penguin.)

George Bernard Shaw declared that 'What we want to see is the child in pursuit of knowledge, not knowledge in pursuit of the child.' I take this as a plea to return to the learner-managed 'natural' curriculum, with personal learning plans supported by adults providing a catalogue of learning possibilities. Our society has been information-rich for many years now, and we have even more possibilities than before through computer access to a kaleidoscope of websites. We have the technology and know-how: we can rebuild the natural curriculum.
(From Meighan, R. (2000) *Natural Learning and the Natural Curriculum*,
Nottingham: Educational Heretics Press.)

References

Abraham, J.H. (1966) *Sociology*. Sevenoaks: English Universities Press.

Acker, S. and Piper, D.W. (eds) (1984) *Is Higher Education Fair to Women*? Guildford: SRHE and Nelson.

Adcock, J. (1995) *In Place of Schools*. London: New Education Press.

Adelman, C. (1993) 'Access to teacher training and employment' in Verma, G. (ed.), *Inequality and Teacher Education: An International Perspective*. London: The Falmer Press.

Ainley, P. (1994) *Degrees of Difference: Higher Education in the 1990s*. London: Lawrence and Wishart.

Alexander, R. (1992) *Policy and Practice in Primary Education*. London: Routledge.

Alexander, R. (2000) *Culture and Pedagogy: International Comparisons in Primary Education*. Oxford: Blackwell.

Alexander, R., Rose, J. and Woodhead, C. (1992) *Classroom Organisation in the Primary School*. London: DES.

Allen, V. (1975) *Social Analysis*. Harlow: Longman.

Althusser, L. (1971) 'Ideology and the state' in Althusser, L., *Lenin and Philosophy and Other Essays*. London: New Left Books.

Anderson, C. and Dill, C. (2000) 'Video Games and Aggressive Thoughts', *Journal of Personality and Social Psychology*, **78**.

Apple, M. (1979) 'The production of knowledge and the production of deviance in schools' in Barton, L. and Meighan, R. (eds), *Schools, Pupils, and Deviance*. Driffield: Nafferton.

Apple, M. (1980) 'Curricular form and the logic of technical control' in Barton, L., Meighan, R. and Walker, S. (eds), *Schooling, Ideology and the Curriculum*. Lewes: Falmer.

Apple, M. (1982) *Education and Power*. Boston, MA: Routledge and Kegan Paul.

Apple, M. and Beane, J. (1999) *Democratic Schools: Lessons from the Chalkface*, Buckingham: Open University Press.

Apple, M. and Weis, L. (eds) (1983) *Ideology and Practice in Schooling*. Philadelphia: Temple University Press.

Archer, M. (1979) *The Social Origin of Educational Systems*. London: Sage.

Ashton, P., Keen, P., Davies, F. and Holley, B. (1975) *The Aims of Primary Education: A Study of Teachers' Opinions*. London: Macmillan.

Aviram, A (1992) 'Non-logocentric education', *Educational Review*, **44**, 1.

Ayers, W., Klonsky, M. and Lyon, G. (2000) *A Simple Justice: The Challenge of Small Schools*. New York: Teachers' College Press.

Bailey, D. and Hall, S. (1992) 'Critical decade: black British photography in the 80s', *Ten-8*, **2**, 3.

Baker, J. (1974) *Children in Chancery*. London: Hutchinson.

Ball, S. (1981) *Beachside Comprehensive: A Case Study of Secondary Schooling*. Cambridge: Cambridge University Press.

Ball, S. (1987) *The Micro-Politics of the School*, London: Methuen.

Ball, S. (1993) 'Education policy, power relations and teachers' work', *British Journal of Educational Studies*, **41**, 2.

Ball, S., Hull, R., Skelton, M. and Tudor, R. (1984) 'The tyranny of devil's mill: time and talk at school' in Delamont, S. (ed.), *Readings in Interaction in the Classroom*. London: Methuen.

Ball, S.J. (1999) 'Performativities and fabrications in the education economy; towards the performative society?', keynote address to the Australian Association of Research in Education, Annual Conference, Melbourne.

Banks, O. (1955) *Parity and Prestige in English Secondary Education*. London: Routledge and Kegan Paul.

Banks, O. (1968) *The Sociology of Education*. London: Batsford.

Banks, O. (1978) 'School and society' in Barton, L. and Meighan, R. (eds), *Sociological Interpretations of Schooling and Classrooms: A Reappraisal*. Driffield: Nafferton.

Barber, T.X. and Silver, H.J. (1968) 'Fact, fiction and the experimenter bias effect', *Psychological Bulletin*, Monograph Supplement, **70**, 6.

Barnes, D. (1976) *From Communication to Curriculum*. Harmondsworth: Penguin.

Barnes, D. and Shemilt, D. (1974) 'Transmission and interpretation', *Educational Review*, **26**, 3.

Barnes, D. and Todd, F. (1977) *Communication and Learning in Small Groups*. London: Routledge and Kegan Paul.

Barnes, D., Britton, J. and Rosen, H. (1969) *Language, the Learner and the School*. Harmondsworth: Penguin.

Barrett, M. (1984) *Women's Oppression Today: Problems in Marxist Feminism Analysis*. London: Verso.

Bartholomew, J. (1976) 'Schooling teachers: the myth of the liberal college' in Whitty, G. and Young, M.F.D. (eds), *Explorations in the Politics of Knowledge*. Driffield: Nafferton Books.

Barton, L. and Meighan, R. (1978) *Sociological Interpretations of Schooling and Classrooms: A Reappraisal*. Driffield: Nafferton.

Barton, L. and Meighan, R. (1979) *Schools, Pupils and Deviance*. Driffield: Nafferton.

Barton, L. and Tomlinson, S. (eds) (1981) *Special Education: Policy, Practices and Social Issues*. London: Harper and Row.

Barton, L. and Tomlinson, S. (eds) (1984) *Special Education and Social Interests*. Beckenham: Croom Helm.

Barton, L. and Walker, S. (1978) 'Sociology of education at the crossroads', *Educational Review*, **30**, 3.

Barton, L. and Walker, S. (eds) (1981) *Schools, Teachers and Teaching*. Lewes: Falmer.

Barton, L. and Walker, S. (eds) (1983) *Race, Class and Education*. Beckenham: Croom Helm.

Barton, L. and Walker, S. (eds) (1986) *Youth, Unemployment and Schooling*. Milton Keynes: Open University Press.

Barton, L., Meighan, R. and Walker, S. (1980) *Schooling, Ideology and the Curriculum*. Lewes: Falmer.

Baudrillard, J. (1994) *Simulacra and Simulation*. Ann Arbor: University of Michigan Press.

Bauman, Z. (1991) *Modernity and Ambivalence*. Cambridge: Polity Press.

Bealing, D. (1972) 'The organisation of junior school classrooms', *Educational Research*, **14**, 3.

Becker, H. (1952) 'Social class variation in the teacher–pupil relationship', *Journal of Educational Sociology*, **25**.

Becker, H. (1963) *Outsiders*. Oxford: Free Press.

Becker, H. (1968) *Making the Grade*. Chichester: Wiley.

Becker, H. (1970) *Sociological Work*. London: Aldus.

Beechey, V. (1986) (ed.) *Women in Britain Today*. Milton Keynes: Open University Press.

Bell, R. and Grant, N. (1974) *A Mythology of British Education*. St Albans: Panther.

Bellack, A., Kliebard, H., Hyman, R. and Smith, F. (1966) *The Language of the Classroom*. New York: Teachers' College Press.

Bennett, S.N. (1976) *Teaching Styles and Pupils' Progress*. London: Open Books.

Bennett, S.N. (1980) *Open Plan Schools: Teaching, Curriculum, Design*. Windsor: NFER-Nelson.

Bennett, S.N. and Jordan, J. (1975) 'A typology of teaching styles in primary schools', *British Journal of Educational Psychology*, **45**.

Berg, I. (1973) *Education and Jobs*. Harmondsworth: Penguin.

Berg, L. (1968) *Risinghill: Death of a Comprehensive School*. Harmondsworth: Penguin.

Berger, P. (1966) *Invitation to Sociology*. Harmondsworth: Penguin.

Berger, P. (1971) 'Sociology and freedom', *The American Sociologist*, **4**.

Berger, P. (1977) *Facing Up to Modernity*. Harmondsworth: Penguin.

Berger, P. and Kellner, H. (1983) *Sociology Reinterpreted*. Harmondsworth: Penguin.

Berger, P. and Luckmann, T. (1967) *The Social Construction of Reality*. Harmondsworth: Penguin.

Berlak, A.C., Berlak, H., Bagenstos, N.T. and Mikel, E.R. (1975) 'Teaching and learning in English primary schools' in Hammersley, M. and Woods, P. (eds), *The Process of Schooling*. London: Routledge and Kegan Paul.

Berliner, W. (2001) 'Gay in Silence', *Education Guardian*, 2 October.

Bernstein, B. (1967) 'Open schools, open society?', *New Society*, 14 September.

Bernstein, B. (1971) 'On the classification and framing of educational knowledge' in Young, M.F.D. (ed.), *Knowledge and Control*. London: Collier-Macmillan.

Bernstein, B. (1973) *Class, Codes and Control: Volume 1*. St Albans: Paladin.

Bernstein, B. (1975a) *Class, Codes and Control: Volume 2*. London: Routledge and Kegan Paul.

Bernstein, B. (1975b) 'The sociology of education: a brief account' in Bernstein, B., *Class, Codes and Control: Volume 2*. London: Routledge and Kegan Paul.

Bernstein, B. (1977) *Class, Codes and Control: Volume 3*. London: Routledge and Kegan Paul.

Berthoud, R. (1976) *The Disadvantages of Inequality: A Study of Social Deprivation*. London: MacDonald and James.

Best, R., Ribbins, P. and Jarvis, C. (1983) *Education and Care: The Study of a School and Its Pastoral Organisation*. London: Heinemann.

Bhat, A. *et al.* (eds) (1988) *Britain's Black Population: A new perspective*, 2nd edn. The Radical Statistics Race Group, Aldershot: Gower.

Biber, B. and Minuchin, P. (1971) 'The impact of school philosophy and practice on child development' in Silberman, M. (ed.), *The Experience of Schooling*. Eastbourne: Holt, Rinehart and Winston.

Bidwell, C.E. (1965) 'The school as a formal organization' in *Handbook of Organizations*. New York: Rand McNally.

Biggs, A.P. and Edwards, A.V., (1992) ' "I treat them all the same." Teacher–pupil talk in multi-ethnic classrooms', *Language and Education*, **5**, 3.

Black, H. and Broadfoot, P. (1982) *Keeping Track of Teaching*. London: Routledge and Kegan Paul.

Blair, T. (2002) 23 May 2002, speech on scientific research to the Royal Society, London.

Blenkin, G. and Kelly, A.V. (1981) *The Primary Classroom*. London: Harper and Row.

Blishen, E. (1969) *The School that I'd Like*. Harmondsworth: Penguin.

Blishen, E. (1973a) 'Your children on their teacher', *Where?*, **84**.

Blishen, E. (1973b) 'Why some secondary teachers are disliked', *Where?*, **86**.

Bloom, B., Englehart, M., Furst, E., Hill, W. and Krathwohl, D. (1964) *Taxonomy of Educational Objectives: The Classification of Educational Goals*. New York: McKay.

Blum, A. (1974) *Theorising*. London: Heinemann.

Blumer, H. (1962) 'Society as symbolic interaction' in Rose, A. (ed.), *Human Behaviour and Social Processes*. London: Routledge and Kegan Paul.

Blumer, M. (ed.) (1977) *Sociological Research Methods*. London: Macmillan.

Blyth, W. and Derricott, R. (1978) *The Social Significance of Middle Schools*. London: Batsford.

Blyth, W.A.L. (1985) *Development, Experience and Curriculum in Primary Education*. Beckenham: Croom Helm.

Bono, E. de (1971) *Practical Thinking*. London: Cape.

Bono, E. de (1972) *About Thinking*. London: Cape.

Boocock, S. (1972) *An Introduction to the Sociology of Learning*. Boston, MA: Houghton Mifflin.

Bookbinder, G. (1978) 'Meddling with children?', *Times Educational Supplement*, December.

Boswell, D. and Wingrove, J. (1974) *The Handicapped Person in the Community*. London: Tavistock.

Boulter, H. (1984) 'Parents and children: 100 years of the parents' National Educational Union and its world-wide education service' in Harber, C. *et al.* (eds), *Alternative Educational Futures*. London: Holt, Rinehart and Winston.

Bourdieu, P. and Passeron, J. (1977) *Reproduction in Education, Society and Culture*. London: Sage.

Bowles, S. and Gintis, H. (1976) *Schooling in Capitalist America*. London: Routledge and Kegan Paul.

Braverman, H. (1974) *Labour and Monopoly Capitalism*. London: Monthly Review Press.

Bridgeman, T. and Fox, I. (1978) 'Why people choose private schools', *New Society*, 29 June.

Brim, O.G. (1960) 'Family structure and sex-role learning by children' in Bell, N.W. and Vogel, E.F. (eds), *An Introduction to the Modern Family*. New York: Free Press.

British Humanist Association (1975) *Objective Fair and Balanced: A New Law Forum in Education*. London: BHA Publications.

Britton, J. (1971) 'What's the use? A schematic account of language functions', *Educational Review*, **23**, 3.

Broadfoot, P. (1979) *Assessment, Schools and Society*. London: Methuen.

Broadfoot, P. (1984) *Selection, Certification and Control: Social Issues in Educational Assessment*. Lewes: Falmer.

Brophy, J. (1983) 'Teacher Praise: A functional analysis', *Review of Educational Research*, **51**, 5–32.

Brown, C. (1978) 'Education otherwise: a sociological case study of one alternative to state schooling', unpublished MEd dissertation, University of Birmingham.

Brown, C. (1979) *Understanding Society*. London: John Murray.

Brown, C. and Harber, C. (1985) 'Cultural diversity and conflict', special edition of *Social Science Teacher*, **14**, 3.

Bruner, J.S. (1965) *The Process of Education*. Harmondsworth: Penguin.

Bruner, J.S. (1966) *Towards a Theory of Instruction*. Cambridge, MA: Harvard University Press.

Buckingham, D. (1993) *Reading Audiences: Young People and the Media*. Manchester: Manchester University Press.

Bull, R. and Stevens, J. (1976) 'Do we get "A" for attractiveness?', *Sesame*, December.

Burgess, R.G. (1984a) *Field Methods in the Study of Education*. Lewes: Falmer.

Burgess, R.G. (1984b) *The Research Process in Educational Settings: Ten Case Studies*. Lewes: Falmer.

Burke, C. and Grosvenor, I. (2003) *The School I'd Like*. London: Routledge Falmer.

Burns, E. (1952) *Introduction to Marxism*. London: Lawrence and Wishart.

Burrows, J. (1978) *The Middle School – High Road or Dead End?* London: Woburn Press.

Byrne, D., Williamson, B. and Fletcher, B. (1974) *The Poverty of Education*. Oxford: Martin Robertson.

Byrne, E. (1975) 'Inequality in education – discriminal resource allocation in schools?', *Educational Review*, **27**, 3.

Byrne, E. (1978) *Women and Education*. London: Tavistock.

Calvert, B. (1975) *The Role of the Pupil*. London: Routledge and Kegan Paul.

Cameron, R. (1984) 'Sharing expertise', *Where?*, **194**.

Campbell, J. (1994) 'Managing the primary curriculum: the issue of time allocation', *Education 3–13*, **22**, 1.

Cannon, C. (1964) 'Social studies in secondary schools', *Educational Review*, **7**, 1.

Carnie, F. (2003) *Alternative Approaches to Education*. London: Routledge Falmer.

Carter, B. (1993) 'Losing the common touch: a post-modern politics of the curriculum?', *Curriculum Studies*, **1**, 1.

Carter, C., Harber, C. and Serf, J. (2003) *Towards Ubuntu*, Birmingham: Birmingham Education Development Centre.

Casey, T. (1974) 'Corporal punishment', *The Schoolmaster*, November.

Cashmore, E. and Troyna, B. (1990) *Introduction to Race Relations*, 2nd edn. Lewes: Falmer Press.

Central Statistics Office: Statistics 1996, HMSO.

Chanan, G. and Gilchrist, L. (1974) *What School Is For*. London: Methuen.

Chandler, D. (1984) *Young Learners and the Microcomputer*. Milton Keynes: Open University Press.

Charkin, A., Sigler, E. and Derlega, V. (1975) 'Non-verbal mediators of teacher expectancy effects', *Journal of Personality and Social Psychology*, **30**, 1.

Cherrington, D. (1985) 'Ethnic minorities in education', special edition of *Educational Review*, **37**, 2.

Chevannes, M. (1979) 'Supplementary education – the Black Arrow Night School Project', *Social Science Teacher*, **8**, 4.

Chevannes, M. and Reeves, F. (1979) 'Footprint in the sand: black exploration of the white community' in Meighan, R. *et al.* (eds), *Perspectives on Society*. Sunbury-on-Thames: Nelson.

Children's Rights Workshop (1977) *Sexism in Children's Books*. London: Children's Rights Workshop.

Claiborn, W. (1969) 'Expectancy effects in the classroom: a failure to replicate', *Journal of Educational Psychology*, **60**.

Claxton, G. (1978) *The Little Ed Book*. London: Routledge and Kegan Paul.

Cleave, S. and Brown, S. (1991) *Early to School: Four Year Olds in Infant Classes*. London: Routledge.

Coard, B. (1971) *How the West Indian Child Is Made ESN*. London: New Beacon.

Cohen, L. (1965) 'An exploratory study of the teacher's role as perceived by headteachers, tutors, and students in a training college', unpublished MEd dissertation, University of Liverpool.

Cohen, L. and Manion, L. (1980) *Research Methods in Education*. Beckenham: Croom Helm.

Cohen, L. and Manion, L. (1981) *Perspectives on Classrooms and Schools*. London: Holt, Rinehart and Winston.

Cohen, L. and Manion, L. (1994) *Research Methods in Education*, 4th edn. London: Routledge.

Cohen, P. (1968) *Modern Social Theory*. London: Heinemann.

Colley, M. (1976) 'Another kind of handicap', *New Society*, 12 February.

Collier, G. (1983) *The Management of Peer Group Learning*. London: Society for Research into Higher Education.

Commission for Racial Equality (1988) *Ethnic Minority School Teachers*. London: CRE.

Common, J. (1951) *Kiddar's Luck*. London: Turnstile Press.

Commonwealth Immigrants Advisory Council (1964) *Third Report* (Cmnd 2458). London: HMSO.

Connell, R.W. (1985) *Teacher's Work*. London: George Allen and Unwin.

Connolly, J. (1993) 'Gender balanced geography: have we got it right yet?', *Teaching Geography*, **18**, 2.

Cookson, C. (1979) 'Parents find home help a magic ingredient', *Times Educational Supplement*, 28 December.

Cooley, C.H. (1972) *Human Nature and the Social Order*. New York: Charles Schribner.

Cooper, I. (1981) 'The politics of education and architectural design: the instructive example of British Primary Education', *British Educational Research Journal*, 7.

Cooper, I. (1982) 'The maintenance of order and the use of space in primary school buildings', *British Journal of Sociology of Education*, **3**, 3.

Cooper, R. (1965) 'The psychology of organisations', *New Society*, 22 April.

Cornbleth, C. (1984) 'Beyond hidden curriculum?', *Journal of Curriculum Studies*, **16**, 1.

Corrigan, P. (1979) *Schooling the Smash Street Kids*. London: Macmillan.

Corrigan, P. and Frith, S. (1977) 'The politics of education' in Young, M. and Whitty, G. (eds), *Society, State and Schooling*. Lewes: Falmer.

Cosin, B. (1972) *Ideology*. Milton Keynes: Open University Press.

Cosin, B., Dale, R., Esland, G. and Swift, D. (eds) (1971) *School and Society*. London: Routledge and Kegan Paul.

Coulthard, M. (1977) *An Introduction to Discourse Analysis*. Harlow: Longman.

Craft, M. (1982) *Education for Diversity: The Challenge of Cultural Pluralism*. Nottingham: School of Education, University of Nottingham.

Craft, M., Raynor, J. and Cohen, L. (1980) *Linking Home and School*. London: Harper and Row.

Crocker, A. (1988) 'Are some gifted children at risk because of their infant school experience?', *Education Today*, **38**, 3.

Cullingford, C. (1994) 'Children's response to television advertising: the magic age of 8', *Research in Education*, **51**, May.

Cummins, J. (1984) 'Bilingualism and special education: issues in assessment and pedagogy', *Multilingual Matters*, **6**.

Cuzzort, R. and King, E. (1976) *Humanity and Modern Social Thought*. Hillsdale, IL: Holt Dryden.

Cuzzort, R.P. and King, E.W. (1989) *Twentieth Century Social Thought*, 5th edn. Orlando, FL: Harcourt Brace.

Cyster, R., Clift, P.S. and Battle, S. (1983) *Parental Involvement in Primary Schools*. Windsor: NFER-Nelson.

Dahrendorf, R. (1959) *Class and Class Conflict in Industrial Society*. London: Routledge and Kegan Paul.

Dahrendorf, R. (1980) *Life Chances*. London: Weidenfeld and Nicolson.

Dale, R. (1972a) *The Context of the Classroom*. Milton Keynes: Open University Press.

Dale, R. (1972b) *The Use of Time in the School*. Milton Keynes: Open University Press.

Dale, R. (1977) 'Implications of the rediscovery of the hidden curriculum for the sociology of teaching' in Gleeson, D. (ed.), *Identity and Structure*. Driffield: Nafferton.

Dale, R. (1985) *Education and Employers' Needs*. Oxford: Pergamon.

Daly, B. (1985) *Portage: The Importance of Parents*. Windsor: NFER-Nelson.

Danziger, K. (1971) *Socialisation*. Harmondsworth: Penguin.

David, T., Curtis, A. and Siraj-Blatchford, I. (1992) *Effective Teaching in the Early Years*. Stoke-on-Trent: Trentham Books.

Davies, I. (1969) 'Education and social science', *New Society*, 8 May.

Davies, K. (1974) 'History is about chaps', *Times Educational Supplement*, 29 November.

Davies, L. (1973) 'The contribution of the secondary school to the sex typing of girls', unpublished MEd dissertation, University of Birmingham.

Davies, L. (1978) 'The view from the girls', *Educational Review*, **30**, 2.

Davies, L. (1980) 'The social construction of underachievement' in Raybould, E., Roberts, B. and Wedell, K. (eds), *Helping the Low Achiever in the Secondary School*. Educational Review Occasional Publications, No. 7.

Davies, L. (1983) 'Gender, resistance and power' in Walker, S. and Barton, L. (eds), *Gender, Class and Education*. Lewes: Falmer.

Davies, L. (1984) *Pupil Power: Deviance and Gender in School*. Lewes: Falmer.

Davies, L. (1994) *Beyond Authoritarian School Management*. Ticknall: Education Now Books.

Davies, L. and Kirkpatrick, G. (2000) *The EURIDEM Project: A Review of Pupil Democracy in Europe*. London: Children's Rights Alliance.

Davies, L. and Meighan, R. (1975) 'A review of schooling and sex roles', *Educational Review*, **27**, 3.

Dawe, A. (1970) 'The two sociologies', *British Journal of Sociology*, **21**, 2.

Deakin, M. (1973) *The Children on the Hill*. Tunbridge Wells: Abacus.

Deem, R. (1978) *Women and Schooling*. London: Routledge and Kegan Paul.

Deem, R. (1984) *Coeducation Reconsidered*. Milton Keynes: Open University Press.

Delamont, S. (1976) *Interaction in the Classroom*. London: Methuen.

Derricott, R. (1984) *Curriculum Continuity: Primary to Secondary*. Windsor: NFER-Nelson.

Derrida, J. (2003) *Structure, Sign, and Play in the Discourse of the Human Sciences*, trans. Alan Bass. London: Routledge.

DES (Department of Education and Science) (1975) *Curricular Differences Between the Sexes*. London: HMSO.

DES (1985) *Education for All*, The Swann Report. London: HMSO.

DES (1988) Education Reform Act. London: HMSO.

Dessent, T. (1984) *What Is Important about Portage?* Windsor: NFER-Nelson.

Diamond, L. (1984) 'State-supported alternative schools' in Harber, C. *et al.* (eds), *Alternative Educational Futures*. London: Holt, Rinehart and Winston.

Dore, R.P. (1976) *The Diploma Disease*. London: Allen and Unwin.

Douglas, J.W.B. (1964) *The Home and the School*. St Albans: Panther.

Douglas, J.W.B., Ross, J.M. and Simpson, H.R. (1971) *All Our Futures*. London: Peter Davies.

Dreeben, R. (1968) *On What Is Learned in School*. London: Addison Wesley.

Dreeben, R. (1976) 'The unwritten curriculum and its relation to values', *Journal of Curriculum Studies*, **8**, 2.

Driver, G. (1980) 'How West Indians do better at school', *New Society*, 17 January.

Duane, M. (1991) *Work Language and Education in the Industrial State*. London: Freedom Press.

Durkheim, E. (1956) *Education and Sociology*. New York: Free Press.

Durkheim, E. (1961) 'Moral education', quoted in Hargreaves, D., 'Durkheim, deviance and education' in Barton, L. and Meighan, R. (eds), (1979), *Schools, Pupils and Deviance*. Driffield: Nafferton.

Durkheim, E. (1968) *The Rules of Sociological Method*. New York: Free Press.

Easthope, G. (1974) *A History of Social Research Methods*. Harlow: Longman.

Easthope, G. (1980) 'Curricula are social processes' in Barton, L. *et al.* (eds), *Schooling Ideology and the Curriculum*. Lewes: Falmer.

Edwards, A.D. (1976) *Language in Culture and Class: The Sociology of Language and Education*. London: Heinemann.

Edwards, A.D. and Furlong, V.J. (1978) *The Language of Teaching: Meaning in Classroom Interaction*. London: Heinemann.

Edwards, R. (1976) 'Individual traits and organisational incentives: what makes a "good worker"?', *Journal of Human Resources*, Spring.

Edwards, V.K. (1978) 'Language attitudes and under performance in West Indian children', *Educational Review*, **30**, 1.

Eggleston, J. (1974) *Contemporary Research in the Sociology of Education*. London: Methuen.

Engels, F. (1969) *The Condition of the Working Class in England* [1844]. St Albans: Panther.

Epstein, D. (1995) 'Girls can't do bricks' in Siraj-Blatchford, I. and J. (eds), *Educating the Whole Child*. Buckingham: Open University Press.

Esland, G. (1977) *Legitimacy and Control*. Milton Keynes: Open University Press.

Etzioni, A. (1964) *Modern Organizations*. Hemel Hempstead: Prentice Hall.

Etzioni, A. (1969) *The Semi-professions and Their Organisations*. London: Collier-Macmillan.

Evans, K. (1974a) 'The head and his territory', *New Society*, 24 October.

Evans, K. (1974b) 'The spatial organisation of infants schools', *Journal of Architectural Research*, **3**, 7.

Eysenck, H. (1957) *Sense and Nonsense in Psychology*. Harmondsworth: Pelican.

Farrington, P., Pritchard, G. and Raynor, J. (1972) 'The Parkway Programme' in Raynor, J. and Harden, J. (eds), (1973), *Readings in Urban Education Volume 2: Equality and City Schools*. Milton Keynes: Open University Press.

Ferron, O. (1966) 'The test performance of coloured children', *Educational Research*, **8**, 1.

Fiddy, R. (1983) *In Place of Work: Policy and Provision for the Young Unemployed*. Lewes: Falmer

Fiddy, R. (1985) *Youth Unemployment and Training: A Collection of National Perspectives*. Lewes: Falmer.

Field, F. and Hankin, P. (1971) *Black Britons*. Oxford: Oxford University Press.

Fielding, R., Meighan, R., Rutherford, D and Sparkes, J. (1979) 'Towards Democratic Teaching and Learning' in Massey, T.P. (ed.), *Improving University Teaching*. Maryland: Maryland University Press.

Finn, D. (1983) 'A new deal for British youth?', *Social Science Teacher*, **13**, 2.

Fitzgerald, A. (1976) 'School mathematics and the requirements of industry', *Vocational Aspects of Education*, **28**.

Fitzpatrick, F. (1987) *The Open Door*. Clevedon: Multilingual Matters.

Flanders, N.E. (1970) *Analysing Teacher Behaviour*. London: Addison Wesley.

Fletcher, C., Caron, M. and Williams, W. (1985) *Schools on Trial*. Milton Keynes: Open University Press.

Floud, J. and Halsey, A.H. (eds) (1956) *Social Class and Educational Opportunity*. Milton Keynes: Open University Press.

Floud, J. and Halsey, A.H. (1961) *Education Economy and Society: a reader in the sociology of education*. Milton Keynes: Open University Press.

Flude, R. and Parrott, A. (1979) *Education and the Challenge of Change*. Milton Keynes: Open University Press.

Fortune-Wood, J. (2001) *Bound to be Free*. Nottingham: Educational Heretics Press, p. 40 'From psychology to medication'.

Fortune-Wood, M. (2005) *The Face of Home-based Education: Who, Why and How*, Nottingham: Educational Heretics Press.

Foucault, M. (1977) *Discipline and Punish*. London: Penguin Books.

Foucault, M. (1986) 'Kant on Enlightenment and Revolution', *Economy and Society*, 15, 88–96.

Fox, J. (1984) *Private School and Public Issues: The Parents' View*. London: Macmillan.

Freire, P. (1972) *Pedagogy of the Oppressed*. Harmondsworth: Penguin.

Friedman, N.L. (1967) 'Cultural deprivation: a commentary on the sociology of knowledge', *Journal of Educational Thought*, **1**, 2.

Fuchs, E. (1968) 'How teachers learn to help children fail' in Keddie, N. (ed.), (1973), *Tinker, Tailor ... The Myth of Cultural Deprivation*. Harmondsworth: Penguin.

Fulton Committee (1968) *The Civil Services Volume 1*. Report of the Committee (Cmnd 3638). London: HMSO.

Galton, M. and Simon, B. (1980) *Progress and Performance in the Primary School*. London: Routledge and Kegan Paul.

Galton, M. and Willcocks, J. (1983) *Moving from the Primary School Classroom*. London: Routledge and Kegan Paul.

Galton, M., Simon, B. and Croll, P. (1980) *Inside the Primary Classroom*. London: Routledge and Kegan Paul.

Garaundy, R. (1970) *Marxism in the Twentieth Century*. Glasgow: Collins.

Garfinkel, H. (1967) *Studies in Ethnomethodology*. Hemel Hempstead: Prentice Hall.

Garland, R. (1982) *Microcomputers and Children in the Primary School*. Lewes: Falmer.

Garwood, S.G. (1976) 'First name stereotypes as a factor in self concept and school achievement', *Journal of Educational Psychology*, **68**, 4.

Garwood, S.G. and McDavid, J.W. (1975) *Ethnic Factors in Stereotypes of Given Names*. Atlanta: Georgia State University Resources in Education ED097994.

Geddes, D. (1979) 'The crammer boom', *New Society*, 15 February.

Gerbner, G. (1980) 'The "mainstreaming" of America: violence profile no. 11', *Journal of Communication*, **30**.

German, G. (1983) 'Some thoughts on institutional racism', *Educational Journal*, November.

Gibson, D. and Jackson, R. (1974) 'Some sociological perspectives on mental retardation', *Educational Review*, **27**, 1.

Gibson, H. and Francis, L. (1993) 'The influence of age, sex, social class and religion on television viewing time and programme preferences among 11–15 year olds', *Journal of Educational Television*, **19**, 1.

Giddens, A. (1971) *Capitalism and Modern Social Theory*. New York: Cambridge University Press.

Giddens, A. (1976) *New Rules of Sociological Method*. London: Hutchinson.

Giddens, A. (1978) *Durkheim*. London: Fontana-Collins.

Giddens, A. (1979) *Central Problems in Social Theory*. London: Macmillan.

Giddens, A. (1984) *The Constitution of Society: Outline of the Theory of Structuration*. Cambridge: Polity Press.

Giddens, A. (1986) *Sociology: a brief but critical introduction*, 2nd edn. Basingstoke: Macmillan Education.

Giddens, A. (1989) *Sociology*. Cambridge: Polity Press.

Giddens, A. (1990) *The Consequences of Modernity*. Cambridge: Polity Press.

Giddens, A. (1991) *Modernity and Self-identity: Self and Society in Late Modern Age*. Cambridge: Polity Press.

Giddens, A. (1993) *Sociology*. Cambridge: Polity Press.

Giddens, A. and Stanworth, P. (eds) (1974) *Elites and Power in British Society*. Cambridge: Cambridge University Press

Giddens, A. *et al.* (1994) *The Polity Reader in Social Theory*. Cambridge: Polity Press.

Giles, H. (1971) 'Patterns of evaluation to RP, south-Welsh and Somerset-accented speech', *British Journal of Social and Clinical Psychology*, **10**.

Giles, R. and Cherrington, D. (1981) (eds) *Multicultural Education in the UK*. London: Commission for Racial Equality

Gilkes, J. (1989) *Developing Nursery Education*. Milton Keynes: Open University Press.

Gillborn, D. (1990) *'Race', Ethnicity and Education*. London: Unwin Hyman.

Ginnis, P. (1992) *Learner Managed Learning*. Ticknell: Education Now

Ginsburg, M.B., Meyenn, R., Miller, H. and Ranceford-Hadley, C. (1977) *The Role of the Middle School Teacher*. Birmingham: University of Aston.

Gintis, H. and Bowles, S. (1980) 'Contradiction and reproduction in educational theory' in Barton, L. *et al.* (eds), *Schooling, Ideology and the Curriculum*. Lewes: Falmer.

Giroux, H. (1981) *Ideology, Culture and the Process of Schooling*. Lewes: Falmer.

Giroux, H. (1983) *Theory and Resistance in Education*. South Hadley: Bergin and Garvey.

Giroux, H. (1992) *Border Crossings: Cultural Workers and the Politics of Education*. New York: Routledge.

Giroux, H. (1996) 'Hollywood, race, and the demonization of youth: the "kids" are not "alright"', *Educational Researcher*, **25**, 2.

Giroux, II. and McLaren, P. (eds) (1994) *Between Borders: Pedagogy and the Politics of Cultural Studies*. New York: Routledge.

Glaser, B.G. and Strauss, A.L. (1968) *The Discovery of Grounded Theory*. London: Weidenfeld and Nicolson.

Gleeson, D. (1983) *Youth Training and the Search for Work*. London: Routledge and Kegan Paul.

Gleeson, D. (1984) 'On the politics of youth training' in Harber, C. and Meighan, R. (eds), 'Political education in 1984', special edition of *Educational Review*, **36**, 2.

Gleeson, D. (1986) 'Privatization of industry and the neutralization of youth' in Barton, L. and Walker, S. (eds), *Youth, Unemployment and Schooling*. Milton Keynes: Open University Press.

Glennerster, H. and Pryke, R. (1973) 'The contribution of the public schools and Oxbridge' in Urry, J. and Wakeford, J. (eds), *Power in Britain*. London: Heinemann.

Glines, D. (1989) 'Can schools of today survive very far into the 21st century?', *NASSP Bulletin*, **73**, February.

Glines, D. (1992) *Educational Alternatives: Unifying a Fragmented Movement*. Sacramento, CA: Educational Futures Project.

Glines, D. (1995) *Creating Alternative Futures*. Michigan: McNaughton and Gunn.

Glines, D. and Long, K. (1992) 'Transitioning toward educational futures', *Phi Delta Kappan*, March.

Glynn, T. (1980) 'Parent–child interaction in remedial reading at home' in Clark, M. and Glynn, T. (eds), *Reading and Writing for the Child with Difficulties*. Birmingham: Educational Review Occasional Publications 8.

Goffman, E. (1952) *Encounters: Two studies in the sociology of interaction*. Indianapolis: Bobbs-Merrill.

Goffman, E. (1961) *Asylums*. Harmondsworth: Penguin.

Goffman, E. (1963) *Stigma: Notes on the Management of Spoiled Identity*. Hemel Hempstead: Prentice Hall.

Goffman, E. (1971) *The Presentation of Self in Everyday Life*. Harmondsworth: Penguin.

Golby, M. and Gulliver, J.R. (1979) 'Whose remedies, whose ills? A critical review of remedial education', *Journal of Curriculum Studies*, **11**, 2.

Goldthorpe, J.H. (1977) 'The relevance of history to sociology' in Bulmer, M. (ed.), *Sociological Research Methods*. London: Macmillan.

Gomm, R. (1978) 'Medicine' in Meighan, R., Shelton, I. and Marks, A. (eds), *Perspectives on Society*. Sunbury-on-Thames: Nelson.

Gomm, R. (1983) 'Social science teachers and the new vocationalism' special edition of *Social Science Teacher*, **13**, 2.

Good, T. and Brophy, J. (1970) 'Teacher child dyadic interactions: a new method of classroom observation', *Journal of School Psychology*, **8**, 2.

Good, T. and Brophy, J. (1972) 'Behavioural expression of teacher attitudes', *Journal of Educational Psychology*, **63**, 6.

Good, T. and Brophy, J. (1974) 'Changing teacher and student behaviour: an empirical investigation', *Journal of Educational Psychology*, **66**, 3.

Good, T. and Brophy, J. (1984) *Looking in Classrooms*. New York: Harper and Row.

Goodacre, E.J. (1968) *Teachers and Their Pupils' Home Backgrounds*. Windsor: NFER.

Goodman, P. (1971) *Compulsory Miseducation*. Harmondsworth: Penguin.

Goodson, I. (1975) 'The teachers' curriculum and the New Reformation', *Journal of Curriculum Studies*, **7**, 2.

Goodson, I. (1983) *School Subjects and Curriculum Change*. Beckenham: Croom Helm.

Goodwin, C. (1979) 'Labelling a child special', *Where?*, **147**.

Gorbutt, D. (1972) 'The new sociology of education', *Education for Teaching*, **89**.

Gould, R. (1976) 'The ecology of educational settings', *Educational Administration*, **4**, 2.

Gouldner, A.W. (1971) *The Coming of Western Sociology*. London: Heinemann.

Gow, L. and McPherson, A. (1980) *Tell Them from Me*. Aberdeen: Aberdeen University Press.

Grace, C. (1978) *Teaching, Ideology and Control*. London: Routledge and Kegan Paul.

Grace, C. (1985) 'Judging teachers: the social and political contexts of teacher evaluation', *British Journal of Sociology of Education*, **6**, 1.

Gramsci, A. (1971) *Selections from the Prison Notebooks of Antonio Gramsci* (ed. and trans. Hoare, Q. and Nowell Smith, G.). London: Lawrence and Wishart.

Grant, C. and Sleeter, C. (1985) *After the School Bell Rings*. London: Falmer Press.

Griffiths, A. and Hamilton, D. (1985) *Parent, Teacher and Child: Working Together in Children's Learning*. London: Methuen.

Grossberg, L. (1994) 'Introduction: bringin' it all back home – pedagogy and cultural studies' in Giroux, H. and McLaren, P. (eds), *Between Borders: Pedagogy and the Politics of Cultural Studies*. New York: Routledge.

Habermas, J. (1987) *The Philosophical Discourses of Modernity*. Cambridge, MA: MIT Press.

Habermas, J. (1996) *Between Facts and Norms. Contributions to a Discourse Theory of Law and Democracy*. London: Polity Press.

Hahn, C. (1974) 'Teaching about women: a review of materials', *Social Studies Journal*, January.

Hall, E.T. (1959) *The Silent Language*. New York: Doubleday.

Hall, S. (1992) 'Race, culture and communications: looking backward and forward in cultural studies', Rethinking Marxism, **5**.

Halsey, A.H. and Anderson, C. (1961) *Education, Economy and Society*. New York: Free Press.

Halsey, A.H., Health, A.F. and Ridge, J.M. (1980) *Origins and Destinations*. Oxford: Oxford University Press.

Hammersley, M. (1977a) *Teacher Perspectives*. Milton Keynes: Open University Press.

Hammersley, M. (1977b) *The Social Location of Teacher Perspectives*. Milton Keynes: Open University Press.

Hammersley, M. and Hargreaves, A. (1983) *Curriculum Practice: Some Sociological Case Studies*. Lewes: Falmer.

Hammersley, M. and Woods, P. (1976) *The Process of Schooling*. London: Routledge and Kegan Paul/ Open University Press.

Hammersley, M. and Woods, P. (1984) *Life in School: The Sociology of Pupil Culture*. Milton Keynes: Open University Press.

Handy, C. (1984) *Taken for Granted? Understanding Schools as Organisations*. York: Longman.

Handy, C. (1989) *The Age of Unreason*. London: Arrow Books.

Handy, C. (1994) *The Empty Raincoat: Making sense of the future*. London: Hutchinson.

Hannan, C., Smyth, P. and Stephenson, N. (1971) *Young Teachers and Reluctant Learners*. Harmondsworth: Penguin.

Hansen, S. and Jensen, J. (1971) *The Little Red Schoolbook*. London: Stage 1 Publications.

Hanson, D. and Herrington, M. (1976) *From College to Classroom*. London: Routledge and Kegan Paul.

Harari, H. and McDavid, J.W. (1973) 'Name stereotypes and teachers' expectations', *Journal of Educational Psychology*, **65**, 2.

Harber, C. (1984) 'Politics and political education in 1984' in Harber, C. and Meighan, R. (eds), 'Political education in 1984', special edition of *Educational Review*, **36**, 2.

Harber, C. (ed.) (1995) *Developing Democratic Education*. Ticknall: Education Now Books.

Harber, C. (1996) *Small Schools and Democratic Practice*. Nottingham: Educational Heretics Press.

Harber, C. (2004) *Schooling as Violence: How Schools Harm Pupils and Societies*. London: Routledge Falmer.

Harber, C. and Davies, L. (1997) *School Management and Effectiveness in Developing Countries*. London: Cassell.

Harber, C., Meighan, R. and Roberts, B. (1984) *Alternative Educational Futures*. London: Holt, Rinehart and Winston.

Hardy, C. (1977) 'Architects and the hidden curriculum', *Times Educational Supplement*, 22 July.

Hare, R.M. (1964) 'Adolescents into adults' in Hollins, T. (ed.), *Aims in Education*. Manchester: Manchester University Press.

Hargreaves, A. (1978) 'The significance of classroom coping strategies' in Barton, L. and Meighan, R. (eds), *Sociological Interpretations of Schooling and Classrooms*. Driffield: Nafferton.

Hargreaves, A. and Tickle, L. (1980) *Middle Schools: Origins, Ideology and Practice*. London: Harper and Row.

Hargreaves, A. et al. (1988) *Personal and Social Education: Choices and Challenges*. Oxford: Basil Blackwell.

Hargreaves, D.H. (1967) *Social Relations in a Secondary School*. London: Routledge and Kegan Paul.

Hargreaves, D.H. (1972) *Interpersonal Relations and Education*. London: Routledge and Kegan Paul.

Hargreaves, D.H. (1978a) 'The two curricula and the community', *Westminster Studies in Education*, **1**.

Hargreaves, D.H. (1978b) 'Whatever happened to symbolic interactionism?' in Barton, L. and Meighan, R. (eds), *Sociological Interpretations of Schooling and Classrooms: A Reappraisal*. Driffield: Nafferton.

Hargreaves, D.H. (1982) *The Challenge for the Comprehensive School*. London: Routledge and Kegan Paul.

Hargreaves, D.H., Hestor, S. and Mellor, F. (1975) *Deviance in Classrooms*. London: Routledge and Kegan Paul.

Harris, N. (1997) 'Over here, overworked, overlooked', *Times Higher Education Supplement*, 14 February.

Hart, R. (1992) *Children's Participation from Tokenism to Citizenship*, Innocenti Essaya, No. 4. London: UNICEF.

Hartog, P.J. and Rhodes, E.C. (1935) *An Examination of Examinations*. London: Macmillan.

Harvey, D. and Slatin, G. (1976) 'The relationships between child's SES and teacher expectations: a test of the middle class bias hypothesis', *Social Forces*, **54**, 1.

Hatch, T. (1996) 'If the "kids" are not "alright," I'm "clueless" ', *Educational Researcher*, **25**, 7.

Hatcher, R. and Shallice, J. (1983) 'The politics of anti-racist education', *Multicultural Education*, **12**, 1.

Head, D. (1974) *Free Way to Learning*. Harmondsworth: Penguin.

Head, D. (1978) 'Five years out of school', *Where?*, **135**.

Heal, C. (1995) 'Children and television', *OMEP: Current Research in Early Childhood*, **72**, Spring.

Hemming, J. (1980) *The Betrayal of Youth*. London: Marion Boyers.

Henry, J. (1963) *Culture Against Man*. Harmondsworth: Penguin.

Henry, J. (1971) *Essays on Education*. Harmondsworth: Penguin.

Hewison, J. and Tizard, B. (1980) 'Parental involvement and reading attainment', *British Journal of Educational Psychology*, **50**.

Hextall, I. (1976) 'Marking work' in Whitty, G. and Young, M.F.D. (eds), *Explorations in the Politics of School Knowledge*. Driffield: Nafferton.

Hine, R.J. (1975) 'Political bias in school physics', *Hard Cheese*, **4**, 5.

Hipkin, J. (1975) 'Time to abolish exams?', *Where?*, **109**.

Hirst, P. and Peters, R.S. (1970) *The Logic of Education*. London: Routledge.

Hobbes, T. (1951) *Leviathan*. London: Dent.

Hodge, R. and Tripp, D. (1986) *Children and Television: A Semiotic Approach*. Cambridge: Polity Press.

Hodgkinson, K. (1987) 'Eurocentric views – the hidden curriculum of humanities maps and atlases', *Multicultural Teaching*, **5**, 2.

Hoffman, M. (1975) 'Assumptions in sex education books', *Educational Review*, **27**, 3.

Hoghughi, M. (1978) *Troubled and Troublesome: Coping with Severely Disabled Children*. London: Burnett Books.

Holly, D. (1973) *Beyond Curriculum*. St Albans: Hart-Davis MacGibbon.

Holt, J. (1969) *How Children Fail*. Harmondsworth: Penguin.

Holt, J. (1971) *The Underachieving School*. Harmondsworth: Penguin.

Holt, J. (1973) *Freedom and Beyond*. Harmondsworth: Penguin.

Holt, J. (1982) *Teach Your Own*. Brightlingsea: Lighthouse Books.

Holt, M. (1984) 'The high-rise curriculum', *Times Educational Supplement*, 12 October.

Hopkins, D. (1985) *A Teacher's Guide to Classroom Research*. Milton Keynes: Open University Press.

Hopper, E. (1971a) 'A typology for the classification of educational systems' in Hopper, E. (ed.), *Readings in the Theory of Educational Systems*. London: Hutchinson.

Hopper, E. (ed.) (1971b) *Readings in the Theory of Educational Systems*. London: Hutchinson.

Horne, J. (1986) 'What's so new about the new vocationalism?' in Barton, L. and Walker, S. (eds), *Youth, Unemployment and Schooling*. Milton Keynes: Open University Press.

Horton, J. (1979) 'Time and cool people' in Rainwaer, L. (ed.), *Black Experience Soul*. New Brunswick, NJ: Transaction Books.

Hoskynss, A. (1976) 'An experiment in the teaching of physics' in Whitty, G. and Young, M.F.D. (eds), *Explorations in the Politics of School Knowledge*. Driffield: Nafferton Books.

Hoyle, E. (1969) *The Role of the Teacher*. London: Routledge and Kegan Paul.

Hoyle, E. and Bell, R. (1972) *Problems of Curriculum Innovation*. Milton Keynes: Open University Press.

Hughes, J. (1984) *The Best Years: Reflections of School Leavers in the 1980s*. Aberdeen: Aberdeen University Press.

Hughes, M.G.H., Ribbins, P. and Thomas, H. (1985) *Managing Education*. London: Holt, Rinehart and Winston.

Hull, J. (1975) *School Worship: An Obituary*. London: SCM.

Hunt, G.J.F. (1976) 'Designing instruction for individuals', *Delta*, **18**.

Hunt, P.J. (1974) 'Coping with those big questions', *Child Education*, August.

Hurman, A. (1979) *A Charter for Choice*. Windsor: NFER-Nelson.

Husen, T. (1974) *The Learning Society*. London: Methuen.

Husen, T. (1985) *The Learning Society Revisited*. Oxford: Pergamon.

Illich, I. (1971) *Deschooling Society*. Harmondsworth: Penguin.

Irigaray, L. (1982) 'This sex which is not one' in Kuhn, A. (ed.), *Women's Pictures*. Boston, MA: Routledge and Kegan Paul.

Jackson, B. (1964) *Streaming: An Educational System in Miniature*. London: Routledge and Kegan Paul.

Jackson, B. and Marsden, D. (1962) *Education and the Working Class*. London: Routledge and Kegan Paul.

Jackson, M. (1984) 'Building a bridge to nowhere ...', *Times Educational Supplement*, 14 December.

Jackson, P. (1968) *Life in Classrooms*. Eastbourne: Holt, Rinehart and Winston.

Jackson, P. (1971) 'The student's world' in Silberman, M. (ed.), *The Experience of Schooling*. Eastbourne: Holt, Rinehart and Winston.

Jackson, R.N. (1970) 'Educable mental handicap: an ecological analysis', *Scottish Educational Studies*, November.

James, A. and Jeffcoate, R. (1981) *The School in the Multicultural Society*. London: Harper & Row.

James, C. (1968) *Young Lives at Stake*. Glasgow: Collins.

Jeffcoate, R. (1975) 'Curing a social disease', *Times Educational Supplement*, 5 December.

Jeffcoate, R. (1977) 'Looking in the wrong place', *Times Educational Supplement*, 24 June.

Jeffcoate, R. (1979) *Positive Image*. Richmond: Chameleon Books.

Jeffcoate, R. (1984) *Ethnic Minorities in Britain*. London: Harper and Row.

Jenkins, C. and Sherman, B. (1979) *The Collapse of Work*. London: Eyre Methuen.

Jenkins, R. (1986) *Racism and Recruitment: Managers, Organisations and Equal Opportunity in the Labour Market*. Cambridge: Cambridge University Press.

Jensen, K. (1986) 'Work, education and democratization' in Barton, L. and Walker, S. (eds), *Youth, Unemployment and Schooling*. Milton Keynes: Open University Press.

Jensen, K. (2004) 'Agency and structure in the systematic production and reproduction of alienation in industrialized service societies: The social conditions of public service'. Paper IIS 36th World Congress and RC36 Midterm Conference, Beijing, 7–11 July 2004, published in RC36 newsletter.

Jensen, K. and Walker, S. (2000) A contribution to the mapping of alienation: Alienation and how to get rid of it'. Paper RC36's Midterm Conference, Washington, July 2000, published in RC36 newsletter.

Jensen, K. and Walker, S. (2000) 'The Modernisation of Western European States And Its Implications For Public Sector Professionals. "Getting further out of Chaos".' Conference of ISA Research Committee, Sociology of Professional Groups, RC52, Lisbon, September 2000.

Jessen, C. and Holm-Sorensen, B. (2000) 'It Isn't Real: Children, Computer Games, Violence and Reality' in C. Von Feilitzen and U. Carlsson (eds), *Children and Media Violence: Yearbook 2000, Children in the New Media Landscape*. Göteborg: UNESCO International Clearinghouse on Children and Violence on the Screen, NORDICOM, Göteborgs University.

Johnson, T.J. (1972) *Professions and Power*. London: Macmillan.

Joiner, D. (1971) 'Office territory', *New Society*, 7 October.

Jones, J. (1966) 'Family and Social Class', Policy Studies Unity, Institute of Education. University of London.

Jones, P. (1992) 'The timing of the school day', *Educational Psychology in Practice*, **8**, 2.

Karabel, J. and Halsey, A.H. (eds) (1977) *Power and Ideology in Education*. Oxford: Oxford University Press.

Kelly, A. (1976) 'Family background, subject specialization and occupational recruitment of Scottish university students', *Higher Education*, **5**, 2.

Kelly, A. (1985) 'The construction of masculine science', *British Journal of Sociology of Education*, **6**, 2.

Kelly, G.A. (1955) *The Psychology of Personal Constructs*. London: Norton.

Kemmis, S. (1983) *Curriculum Theorising: beyond reproduction theory*. London: Falmer Press.

King, E. (1972) *Educating Young Children: Sociological Interpretations*. London: William C. Brown.

King, E. (1973) 'The presentation of self in the classroom', *Educational Review*, **25**, 3.

King, R. (1980) 'Weberian perspectives and the study of education', *British Journal of Sociology of Education*, **1**, 1.

King, R. (1983) *The Sociology of School Organisation*. London: Methuen.

Kitto, D. (1981) 'Doing it their way', *Times Educational Supplement*, 10 July.

Klein, G. (1993) *Education towards Race Equality*. London: Cassell.

Knight, P. (1973) *The Successful Applicant Will Be a Man*. London: British Humanist Association.

Kohl, H. (1970) *The Open Classroom*. London: Methuen.

Kohl, H. (1971) *36 Children*. Harmondsworth: Penguin.

Kohn, A. (1993) *Punished by Rewards*. Boston, MA: Houghton Mifflin.

Komarovsky, M. (1946) 'Cultural contradictions and sex roles', *American Journal of Sociology*, **52**.

Kozol, J. (1968) *Death at an Early Age*. Harmondsworth: Penguin.

Labour Party (1972) *Discrimination Against Women*. London: Labour Party.

Labov, W. (1969) 'The logic of non-standard English' in Giglioli, P.P. (ed.), (1972), *Language and Social Context*. Harmondsworth: Penguin.

Lacey, C. (1970) *Hightown Grammar*. Manchester: Manchester University Press.

Lauwerys, J.A. and Scanlon, D.G. (1969) *World Yearbook of Education: Examination*. London: Evans.

Lawn, M. (1985) *The Politics of Teacher Unionisation*. Beckenham: Croom Helm.

Lawson, T. and Harrison, J.K. (1999) 'Individual Action Planning in Initial Teacher Training: Empowerment or Discipline?,' *British Journal of Sociology and Education* 20 (1), 89–105.

Lawton, D. (1968) *Social Class, Language and Education.* London: Routledge and Kegan Paul.

Lawton, D. (1994) *British Journal of Curriculum and Assessment,* **3,** 3.

Lee, D. and Newby, H. (1983) *The Problem of Sociology.* London: Hutchinson.

Lee, S. (1978) 'Black bitterness', *Times Educational Supplement,* 20 January.

Leinster-Mackay, D. (1984) *The Rise of the English Prep School.* Lewes: Falmer.

Lemert, E. (1951) *Social Pathology.* Maidenhead: McGraw-Hill.

Lemert, E. (1972) *Human Deviance, Social Problems and Social Control.* Hemel Hempstead: Prentice Hall.

Lewis, B. (1972) Quoted in Dale, R., *The Use of Time in the School.* Milton Keynes: Open University Press.

Lewis, D.G. (1978) *Assessment in Education.* Sevenoaks: Unibooks.

Lewis, I. and Vulliamy, G. (1980) 'Warnock or warlock? The sorcery of definitions: the limitations of the Report on Special Education', *Educational Review,* **32,** 1.

Linderoth, J. and Lantz-Andersson, A. (2002) 'Electronic Exaggerations and Virtual Worries: Mapping Research of Computer Games Relevant to the Understanding of Children's Game Play', *Contemporary Issues in Early Childhood,* **3,** 2, available online at *http://www.triangle.co.uk/ciec/content/pdfs/3/issue3_2.asp*

Lippitt, R. and White, R.K. (1958) 'An experimental study of leadership and group life' in Maccoby, E. (ed.), *Readings in Social Psychology.* Eastbourne: Holt, Rinehart and Winston.

Lister, I. (1971) 'The deschoolers', *Times Educational Supplement,* 9 July.

Lister, I. (1974) *Deschooling.* Cambridge: Cambridge University Press.

Little, A. (1975) 'The performance of children from ethnic minority backgrounds in primary schools' in Rushton, J. and Turner, J. (eds), *Education and Deprivation.* Manchester: Manchester University Press.

Lloyd, B. (1987) 'Social representations of gender', in J. Bruner and H. Haste (eds), *Making Sense: The Child's Construction of the World.* London: Routledge.

Lloyd-Smith, M. (1984) *Disrupted Schooling: The Growth of the Special Unit.* London: John Murray.

Lobban, G. (1975) 'Sex roles in reading schemes', *Educational Review,* **27,** 3.

Lyman, S.M. and Scott, M.B. (1970) *A Sociology of the Absurd.* Hemel Hempstead: Appleton Century-Crofts.

Lyon, D. (1994) *Postmodernity.* Buckingham: Open University Press.

McCarthy, C. and Apple, M. (1988) 'Race, class, and gender in American educational research: towards a nonsynchronous parallelist position' in Weis, L. (ed.), *Class, Race and Gender in American Education.* Albany: State University of New York Press.

Maccoby, E. (ed.) (1966) *The Development of Sex Differences.* London: Stanford.

MacDonald, M. (1977a) *Culture, Class and the Curriculum.* Milton Keynes: Open University Press.

MacDonald, M. (1977b) *The Education of Elites.* Milton Keynes: Open University Press.

MacDonald, M. (1977c) *The Curriculum and Cultural Reproduction.* Milton Keynes: Open University Press.

McDougall, J (2005) 'Subject Media: A Study in the Sociocultural Framing of Discourse', unpublished PhD thesis, University of Birmingham.

McGee, R. *et al.* (1977) *Sociology: An Introduction.* Eastbourne: Holt, Rinehart and Winston.

Mack, J. (1977) 'Schools for privilege', *New Society*, 7 July.

McKenzie, W. (1994) 'The Video Game as Emergent Media Form', *Media Information Australia*, **71**.

Mackinnon, D. (1978) 'Social class and educational attainment' in Swift, D. (ed.), *Selection and Opportunity*. Milton Keynes: Open University Press.

McPherson, J. (1983) *The Feral Classroom*. London: Routledge and Kegan Paul.

MacRae, D.G. (1974) *Weber*. London: Fontana.

Mahoney, P. (1985) *Schools for the Boys? Coeducation Reassessed*. London: Hutchinson/Explorations in Feminism Collective.

Maizels, J. (1970) 'How school leavers rate teachers', *New Society*, 24 September.

Maizels, J. (1971) *Adolescent Needs and the Transition from School to Work*. London: Athlone.

Makins, V. (1969) 'Child's eye view of teacher', *Times Educational Supplement*, 19 and 26 September.

Makins, V. (1984) 'Giving the customers a say', *Times Educational Supplement*, 23 November.

Marbeau, V. (1976) 'Autonomous study by pupils', *Education and Culture*, **21**.

Marsh, A. (1971) 'In a second culture', *Times Educational Supplement*, 1 June.

Marsh, C. and Stafford, K. (1984) *Curriculum: Australian practices and issues*. Sydney: McGraw-Hill.

Marsland, M. (1974) *Pastoral Care*. London: Heinemann.

Martin, B. (1952) *School Buildings*. St Albans: Crosby Lockwood.

Martin, N. (1971) 'What are they up to?' in Jones, A. and Mulford, J. (eds), *Children Using Language*. Oxford: Oxford University Press.

Martin, W. (1976) *The Negotiated Order of the School*. Toronto: Macmillan.

Marton, F., Hounsell, D. and Entwhistle, N. (1984) *The Experience of Learning*. Edinburgh: Scottish Academic Press.

Marx, K. (1958) *Selected Works*. Moscow: Progress Publishers.

Marx, K. (1969) 'The eighteenth brumaire of Louis Bonapart' in Feuer, L.S. (ed.), *Marx and Engels: Basic Writings on Politics and Philosophy*. London: Fontana.

Marx, K. (1970) 'Introduction to a critique of political economy' in Arthur, C.J. (ed.), *The German Ideology*. London: Lawrence and Wishart.

Marx, K. (1973) *Grundrisse*. Harmondsworth: Pelican.

Marx, K. (1976) *Capital, Volume I*. Harmondsworth: Penguin.

Marx, K. and Engels, F. (1967) *The Communist Manifesto*. Harmondsworth: Penguin.

Matza, D. (1964) *Delinquency and Drift*. Chichester: Wiley.

Mays, J.B. (1962) *Education and the Urban Child*. Liverpool: University of Liverpool Press.

Mead, G.H. (1934) *Mind, Self and Society*. Chicago: University of Chicago Press.

Measor, L. and Woods, P. (1984) *Changing Schools*. Milton Keynes: Open University Press.

Medlicott, P. (1974) 'Special teaching for special children', *New Society*, 3 March.

Meighan, R. (1974a) 'Children's judgements of the teaching performance of student teachers', *Educational Review*, **27**, 1.

Meighan, R. (1974b) 'The concepts of authoritarian and democratic regimes and classroom discipline', *Dudley Educational Journal*, Spring.

Meighan, R. (1975) 'Individual study-folders', *Social Science Teacher*, **5**, 2.

Meighan, R. (1977a) 'Pupils' perceptions of the classroom techniques of post-graduate student teachers', *British Journal of Teacher Education*, **37**, 2.

Meighan, R. (1977b) 'Towards a sociology of assessment', *Social Science Teacher*, **7**, 2.

Meighan, R. (1978a) 'Consultation and educational ideologies: some issues raised by research into children's judgements of teaching performance' in Barton, L. and Meighan, R. (eds), *Sociological Intepretations of Schooling and Classrooms: A Reappraisal*. Driffield: Nafferton.

Meighan, R. (1978b) 'The learners' viewpoint', *Educational Review*, **30**, 2.

Meighan, R. (1981) 'A new teaching force? Some issues raised by seeing parents as educators', *Educational Review*, **33**, 2.

Meighan, R. (1984a) 'Home-based educators and education authorities: the attempt to maintain a mythology', *Educational Studies*, **10**, 3.

Meighan, R. (1984b) 'Political consciousness and home-based education', *Educational Review*, **36**, 2.

Meighan, R. (1988) *Flexischooling*. Ticknall: Education Now Books.

Meighan, R. (ed.) (1992) *Learning from Home-based Education*. Ticknall: Education Now Books.

Meighan, R. (1993) *Theory and Practice of Regressive Education*.

Meighan, R. (1995a) *John Holt: Personalised Education and the Reconstruction of Schooling*. Nottingham: Educational Heretics Press.

Meighan, R. (1995b) *The Freethinkers' Pocket Directory to the Educational Universe*. Nottingham: Educational Heretics Press.

Meighan, R. (1997) *The Next Learning System*. Nottingham: Educational Heretics Press.

Meighan, R. (2001) *Natural Learning and the Natural Curriculum*. Nottingham: Educational Heretics Press.

Meighan, R. (2004) *Damage Limitation: trying to reduce the harm schools do to children*. Nottingham: Educational Heretics Press.

Meighan, R. (2005) *Comparing Learning Systems: The Good, the Bad, the Ugly and the Counter-productive*. Nottingham: Educational Heretics Press.

Meighan, R. and Brown, C. (1980) 'Locations of learning and ideologies of education' in Barton, L. *et al.* (eds), *Schooling, Ideology and the Curriculum*. Lewes: Falmer.

Meighan, R. and Doherty, J. (1975) 'Education and sex roles', *Educational Review*, **27**, 3.

Meighan, R. and Roberts, M. (1977) 'Autonomous study and educational ideologies: a review of some theoretical and practical issues with special reference to the Schools Council General Studies Project', *Journal of Curriculum Studies*, **11**, 1.

Meighan, R. and Toogood, P. (1992) *Anatomy of Choice in Education*. Ticknall: Education Now.

Meighan, R., Shelton, I. and Marks, A. (eds) (1979) *Perspectives on Society*. Sunbury-on-Thames: Nelson.

Meltzer, B., Petrat, J. and Reynolds, L. (1975) *Symbolic Interactionism: Genesis, Varieties and Criticisms*. London: Routledge and Kegan Paul.

Mennell, S. (1974) *Sociological Theory: Uses and Unities*. Sunbury-on-Thames: Nelson.

Menter, I. (1989) 'Teaching practice stasis: racism, sexism and school experience in initial teacher education', *British Journal of Sociology of Education*, **10**, 4.

Merton, R. (1948) *Social Theory and Social Structure*. New York: Free Press.

Meyer, P. (1972) 'School and the reproduction of the social division of labour', unpublished thesis, Harvard University.

Miles, H.B. (1969) 'Handicaps for the rat race', *Times Educational Supplement*, 22 August.

Milgram, S. (1971) *Obedience to Authority*. London: Tavistock.

Miller, A. (1987) *For Your Own Good: Hidden Cruelty in Child-rearing and the Roots of Violence*. London: Virago.

Miller, C.M.L. and Parlett, M. (1983) *Up to the Mark*. London: SRHE.

Millstein, B. (1972) *Women's Studies – Women in History*. New York: New York Board of Education.

Milner, D. (1976) 'Home-based education', *New Era*, **57**, 4.

Montemayor, R. (1974) 'Children's performance in a game and their attraction to it as a function of sex-typed labels', *Child Development*, **45**, 1.

Moody, E. (1968) 'Right in front of everybody', *New Society*, 26 December.

Moon, B. (1983) *Comprehensive Schools: Challenge and Change*. Windsor: NFER-Nelson.

Morris, T. and Morris, P. (1963) *Pentonville*. London: Routledge and Kegan Paul.

Morrison, A. and McIntyre, D. (1976) *Teachers and Teaching*. Harmondsworth: Penguin.

Moss, H.A. (1967) 'Sex, age and state as determinants of mother–infant interaction', *Merrill Palmer Quarterly*, **13**.

Mukhopadgay, A. (1984) *Assessment in a Multicultural Society*. London: Schools Council/Longman.

Mullarny, M. (1984) *Anything School Can Do You Can Do Better*. London: Marion Boyers.

Murphy, P. (1994) 'A farewell to criterion referencing?', *British Journal of Curriculum and Assessment*, **4**, 3.

Murphy, P. and Gipps, C. (1996) *Equity in the Classroom: Towards Effective Pedagogy for Girls and Boys*. Lewes: Falmer Press and UNESCO Publishing.

Murray, R. (1979) *Sociological Theories of Education*. Maidenhead: McGraw-Hill.

Musgrove, F. (1966) 'The good home' in Craft, M. (ed.), *Family, Class and Education: A Reader*. London: Longman.

Musgrove, F. and Taylor, P.H. (1969). *Society and the Teacher's Role*. London: Routledge and Kegan Paul.

Nash, R. (1972) 'History as she is writ', *New Society*, 3 August.

Nash, R. (1973) *Classroom Observed*. London: Routledge and Kegan Paul.

Nash, R. (1976) *Teacher Expectations and Pupil Learning*. London: Routledge and Kegan Paul.

National Curriculum Council (1990) *Policy to Practice*. London: DES.

National Union of Teachers (1978) *Race, Education and Intelligence*. London: NUT.

Neill, A.S. (1968) *Summerhill*. Harmondsworth: Pelican.

Newsome Report (1963) *Half Our Future*. Report of the Central Advisory Council for Education. London: HMSO.

Nightingale, C. (1974) 'What Katy didn't do', *Spare Rib*, February.

OECD, 2001: *The Well-Being of Nations*. Paris: OECD.

Ogilvy, B., Cheyne, J. and Schaffer, R. (1991) 'Staff attitudes and perception in multicultural nursery schools', *Early Child Development and Care*, **64**.

Oppenheim, C. (1990) *Poverty: The Facts*. London: Child Poverty Action Group.

Osler, A. (1995) 'Does the National Curriculum bring us any closer to a gender balanced history?', *Teaching History*, **79**, April.

Owen Cole, W. (1978) *World Faiths in Education*. London: Allen and Unwin.

Ozga, J. and Lawn, M. (1981) *Teachers' Professionalism and Class: A Study of Organised Teachers*. Lewes: Falmer Press.

Palardy, J.M. (1969) 'What teachers believe – what children achieve', *Elementary School Journal*, **69**.

Parsons, T. (1958) *Essays in Sociological Theory*. New York: Free Press.

Parsons, T. (1959) 'The school class as a social system', *Harvard Educational Review*, **29**, 4.

Parsons, T. (1964) *Social Structure and Personality*. New York: Free Press.

Patrick, J. (1973) *A Glasgow Gang Observed*. London: Eyre-Methuen.

Pearson, E. (1971) 'Informal learning', *Architectural Review*, July.

Piaget, J. (1964) 'Development and learning' in Ripple, R.E. and Rockcastle, V.N. (eds), *Piaget Rediscovered*. London: Cornell University Press.

Pidgeon, D. (1970) *Expectation and Pupil Performance*. Windsor: NFER.

Pieron, H. (1969) 'Examens et docimologie' in Lauwerys, J.A. *et al.* (eds), *World Yearbook of Education: Examinations*. London: Evans.

Pinsent, P. (ed.) (1992) *Language, Culture and Young Children*. London: Fulton.

Pitzner, E.G. (1963) 'Male and female', *Atlantic*, **221**.

Plowden Report (1967) *Children and Their Primary Schools*. Report of the Central Advisory Council for Education. London: HMSO.

Pomeroy, W.B. (1969) *Girls and Sex*. Harmondsworth: Penguin.

Portelli, J. (1993) *Journal of Curriculum Studies*, **25**, 4.

Porter, A. (1983) *Teaching Political Literacy*. London: Bedford Way Papers.

Postman, N. and Weingartner, C. (1971) *Teaching as a Subversive Activity*. Harmondsworth: Penguin.

Pring, R. (1984) *Personal and Social Education in the Curriculum*. London: Hodder and Stoughton.

Pugh, G. and De'Ath, E. (1989) *Working towards Partnership in the Early Years*. London: National Children's Bureau.

Raaheim, K. and Wankowski, J. (1981) *Helping Students to Learn at University*. London: Sigma Forlag.

Rae, J. (1979) 'Myths of the pulbic school', *Times Educational Supplement*, 28 December 1979 and 11 January 1980.

Raynor, J. (1972) *The Curriculum in England*. Milton Keynes: Open University Press.

Reading, H.F. (1977) *A Dictionary of the Social Sciences*. London: Routledge and Kegan Paul.

Reeves, F. (1976) 'Mildly radical sociology', *Social Science Teacher*, **5**, 2.

Reeves, F. (1979) 'Race and education', *Social Science Teacher*, **8**, 4.

Reeves, F. (1995) *The Modernity of Further Education*. London: Bilton College Publications and Education Now.

Reid, I. (1981) *Social Class Differences in Britain*. London: Grant McIntyre.

Reid, I. (1986) *The Sociology of School and Education*. London: Paul Chapman.

Reid, I. and Wormald, E. (1982) *Sex Differences in Britain*. London: Grant McIntyre.

Reid, W. (1972) *The Universities and the Sixth Form Curriculum*. London: Schools Council Research Studies.

Reimer, E. (1971) *School Is Dead*. Harmondsworth: Penguin.

Rendel, M. (1968) *Equality for Women*. London: Fabian Research Series 268.

Rex, J. (1961) *Key Problems of Sociological Theory*. London: Routledge and Kegan Paul.

Rex, J. and Tomlinson, S. (1979) *Colonial Immigrants in a British City: A Class Analysis*. London: Routledge and Kegan Paul.

Reynolds, D. (1976) 'The delinquent school' in Hammersley, M. *et al.* (eds), *The Process of Schooling*. London: Routledge and Kegan Paul.

Reynolds, D. and Sullivan, M. (1979) 'Bringing schools back in' in Barton, L. and Meighan, R. (eds), *Schools, Pupils and Deviance*. Driffield: Nafferton.

Reynolds, D. and Sullivan, M. (1980) 'Towards a new socialist sociology of education' in Barton, L., Meighan, R. and Walker, S. (eds), *Schooling, Ideology and the Curriculum*. Lewes: Falmer.

Reynolds, H. and Davies, L. (1977) 'Sex roles and society', *Social Science Teacher*, **6**, 4.

Richards, C. (1979) 'Belief, myth and practice' in Shaw, K. and Bloomer, M. (eds), *Innovation and Constraint*. Oxford: Pergamon.

Richards, C. (1982) *New Directions in Primary Education*. Lewes: Falmer.

Richards, C. (1984) *The Study of Primary Education: A Source Book, Volume 1*. Lewes: Falmer.

Ricks, F.A. and Pyke, S.W. (1973) 'Teacher perceptions and attitudes that foster or maintain sex role differences', *Interchange*, 4, 1.

Rist, R. (1977) 'On understanding the process of schooling: the contribution of labelling theory' in Karabel, J. and Halsey, A. (eds), *Power and Ideology in Education*. New York: Oxford University Press.

Roberts, K. (1984) *School Leavers and Their Prospects*. Milton Keynes: Open University Press.

Roberts, M. (1994) *Skills for Self-managed Learning*. Nottingham: Education Now Books.

Roberts, M.M. (1977) 'The theory and practice of independent learning', unpublished MEd dissertation, University of Birmingham.

Rock, P. (1979) 'The sociology of crime, symbolic interactionism and some problematic qualities of radical criminology' in Downes, D. and Rock, P. (eds), *Deviant Interpretations*. Oxford: Martin Robertson.

Rogers, C. (1983) *Freedom to Learn for the Eighties*. Colombus, OH: Merrill.

Rosen, H. (1972a) *Language and Class*. London: Falling Wall Press.

Rosen, H. (1972b) 'The language of textbooks' in Chashdan, A. and Grugeon, E. (eds), *Language in Education*. London: Routledge and Kegan Paul.

Rosenthal, R. (1968) 'Weighing the effect of a smile', *New Society*, 7 November.

Rosenthal, R. (1973) 'The Pygmalion effect lives', *Psychology Today*, 7.

Rosenthal, R. and Jacobson, L. (1968) *Pygmalion in the Classroom*. Eastbourne: Holt, Rinehart and Winston.

Roth, J.A. (1963) '*The study of career timetables*' in Cosin, B. *et al.* (eds), *School and Society*. London: Routledge and Kegan Paul.

Rousseau, J.J. (1883) *Emile*. Boston, MA: Heath.

Russell, B. (1916) *Principles of Social Reconstruction*. London: Unwin.

Russell, B. (1926) *On Education*. London: Unwin.

Russell, B. (1950) *Unpopular Essays*. London: Unwin.

Russell, D. (1980) *The Tamarisk Tree, Volume 2*. London: Virago.

Rutter, M., Maughan, B., Mortimor, P. and Ouston, J. (1979) *Fifteen Thousand Hours*. London: Open Books.

Said, E. (1983) *The World, the Text and the Critic*. Cambridge, MA: Harvard University Press.

Sakamoto, A. (2000) 'Video Games and Violence – Controversy and Research in Japan' in C. Von Feilitzen and U. Carlsson (eds), *Children Yearbook 2000, Children in the New Media Landscape*. Göteborg: UNESCO International Clearinghouse on Children and Violence on the Screen, NOR-DICOM, Göteborgs University.

Sarup, M. (1978) *Marxism and Education*. London: Routledge and Kegan Paul.

Sarup, M. (1996) *Identity, Culture and the Postmodern World*. Edinburgh: Edinburgh University Press.

Saussure, L. and Schulz, P. (2003) *Manipulation and Ideologies in the Twentieth Century: Discourse, Language, Mind*. University of Neuchâtel/University of Lugano.

Sawyer, W.W. (1943) *Mathematician's Delight*. Harmondsworth: Penguin.

SCAA (1996) *The Desirable Outcomes*. London: DfEE.

Scheff, I. (1966) *Being Mentally Ill*. Chicago: Aldine.

Schegloff, E. (1979) 'Repair after next turn', paper given at the BSA Language Study Group Conference, Oxford.

Schiff, M. and Lewontin, R. (1986) *Education and Class: the Irrelevance of the Genetic Studies*. Oxford: Clarendon.

School of Barbiana (1970) *Letter to a Teacher*. Harmondsworth: Penguin.

Schools Curriculum and Assessment Authority (1996) *Desirable Outcomes*. London: DfEE

Scott, J.F. (1975) *Comparability of Grade Standards in Mathematics at GCE: 'A' Level*. London: Schools Council/Evans/Methuen.

Scott, M. and Lyman, S. (1968) 'Accounts' in Manis, J. and Meltzer, B. (eds), (1976), *Symbolic Interactionism*. Boston, MA: Allyn and Bacon.

Seaborne, M. and Lowe, R. (1977) *The English School: Its Architecture and Organisation 1870–1970*. London: Routledge and Kegan Paul.

Seabrook, J. (1971) 'Dead English', *New Society*, 25 March.

Select Committee on Race Relations and Immigration (1972) *Statistics of Immigrant School Pupils*. London: HMSO.

Select Committee on Race Relations and Immigration (1973) *Education, Volumes 1–3*. London: HMSO.

Sellar, W.C. and Yeatman, R.J. (1930) *1066 and All That*. London: Methuen.

Sennett, R. and Cobb, R. (1972) *The Hidden Injuries of Class*. Cambridge: Cambridge University Press.

Sewell, G. (1982) *Reshaping Remedial Education*. Beckenham: Croom Helm.

Sharma, S. and Meighan, R. (1980) 'Schooling and sex roles: the case of GCE "O" level mathematics', *British Journal of Sociology of Education*, **1**, 2.

Sharp, R. and Green, A. (1975) *Education and Social Control*. London: Routledge and Kegan Paul.

Sharpe, S. (1976) *Just Like a Girl*. Harmondsworth: Penguin.

Shaw, B. (1934) 'Preface to Misalliance' in *Prefaces to the Plays of Bernard Shaw*. London: Constable.

Shepherd, J., Virden, P., Vulliamy, G. and Wishart, T. (1977) *Where Music?* London: Latimer.

Shipman, M. (1972) *The Limitations of Social Research*. Harlow: Longman.

Shipman, M. (ed.) (1976) *The Organisation and Impact of Social Research*. London: Routledge and Kegan Paul.

Shipman, M. (1977) *Inside a Curriculum Project*. London: Methuen.

Shotter, M (1982) *Social Accountability and Selfhood*. Oxford: Blackwell.

Shute, C. (1993) *Compulsory Schooling Disease*. Nottingham: Educational Heretics Press.

Silberman, C. (1970) *Crisis in the Classroom*. New York: Random House.

Silberman, M. (ed.) (1971) *The Experience of Schooling*. Eastbourne: Holt, Rinehart and Winston.

Silver, H. (1973) *Equal Opportunity in Education*. London: Methuen.

Simkin, J. (1976) 'What a waste', *Sesame*, April.

Sinclair, J.M. and Coulthard, R.M. (1974) *Towards an Analysis of Discourse: The English Used by Teachers and Pupils*. Oxford: Oxford University Press.

Singh, R. (1988) *Asian and White Sixth Formers' Perceptions of the Teaching Profession*. Bradford: Bradford and Ilkley Community College.

Siraj-Blatchford, I. (1991) 'A study of black students' perceptions of racism in initial teacher education', *British Education Research Journal*, **17**, 1.

Siraj-Blatchford, I. (1992) *'Race', Gender and the Education of Teachers*. Buckingham: Open University Press.

Siraj-Blatchford, I. (1993) 'Educational research and reform: some implications for the professional identity of early years teachers', *British Journal of Educational Studies*, **41**, 4.

Siraj-Blatchford, I. (1994) *The Early Years: Laying the Foundations for Racial Equality*. Stoke-on-Trent: Trentham Books.

Siraj-Blatchford, I. (1995a) 'Critical social research and the academy: the role of organic intellectuals in educational research', *British Journal of Sociology of Education*.

Siraj-Blatchford, I. (1995b) 'Racialized and gendered discourses in teacher education' in Dawtrey, L., Holland, J. and Hammer, M. (eds), *Equality and Inequality in Education Policy*. Clevedon: Multilingual Matters.

Skager, R. (1984) *Organising Schools to Encourage Self-direction in Learners*. Oxford: Pergamon.

Skellington, R. (1992) *'Race' in Britain Today*. London: Sage in association with the Open University.

Smale, M. (1974) *Trials Report (Schools Council General Studies Project)*. York: University of York.

Smith, F. (1985) *Reading*. Cambridge: Cambridge University Press.

Smith, D. (1973) *Distribution Processes and Power Relations in Educational Systems*. Milton Keynes: Open University Press.

Smith, T. (1980) *Parents and Pre-school*. London: Grant McIntyre.

Smoker, B. (1973) *A Humanist View of Women in Britain*. London: British Humanist Association.

Snow, R. (1969) 'Review of Pygmalion in the classroom', *Contemporary Psychology*, **14**, 4.

Snyder, B. (1971) *The Hidden Curriculum*. Cambridge, MA: MIT Press.

Social Security Committee (1991) *Low Income Statistics*. London: HMSO

Spender, D. (1978) 'Don't talk, listen', *Times Educational Supplement*, 3 November.

Spender, D. (1980) *Man-made Language*. London: Routledge and Kegan Paul.

Spender, D. (1982) *Invisible Women: The Schooling Scandal*. London: Writers and Readers.

Spender, D. and Sarah, E. (1980) *Learning to Lose*. London: The Women's Press.

Stanworth, M. (1983) *Gender and Schooling*. London: Hutchinson.

Stanworth, P. and Giddens, A. (eds) (1974) *Elites and Power in British Society*. Cambridge: Cambridge University Press.

Stebbins, R. (1975) *Teachers and Meaning*. Leiden: E. Brill.

Steele, F. (1973) *Physical Settings and Their Organization*. London: Addison Wesley.

Steele, J. (1973) 'Educated at home', *New Society*, 18 October.

Stenhouse, L. (1976) *An Introduction to Curriculum Research and Development*. London: Heinemann.

Stevens, C. (1984) 'All parents as a resource for education' in Harber, C. *et al.* (eds), *Alternative Educational Futures*. London: Holt, Rinehart and Winston.

Stevenson, R. and Ellsworth, J. (1991) 'Dropping out in a working class high school: adolescent voices on the decision to leave', *British Journal of Sociology of Education*, **12**, 3.

Stone, J. and Taylor, F. (1976) 'The sad tale of pupils' rights', *Where?*, **122**.

Stopes-Roe, H. (1976) 'Rethinking RE', *New Humanist*, June.

Stradling, R. (1983) *Political Education in West Germany and Britain*. London: Hansard Society.

Stubbs, M. (1976) *Language, Schools and Classrooms*. London: Methuen.

Stubbs, M. and Delamont, S. (1976) *Explorations in Classroom Observation*. Chichester: Wiley.

Sugarman, S. (1979) 'Freedom and choice for the family: how to reform the system fairly', *Where?*, **149**.

Swift, D. (1965) 'Meritocratic and social class selection at age 11', *Educational Research*, **8**, 1.

Swift, D. (1969) *The Sociology of Education*. London: Routledge and Kegan Paul.

Swift, D. (1977) *Selection and Opportunity*. Milton Keynes: Open University Press.

Sylva, K. and Siraj-Blatchford, I. (1992) 'Top-down effects of the National Curriculum on pre-school education', *International Journal of Early Childhood*.

Talbert, I. and Frase, L. (1969) *Individualized Instruction*. Columbus, OH: Merrill.

Taylor Committee Report (1977) *A New Partnership for Our Schools*. London: HMSO.

Taylor, L.C. (1971) *Resources for Learning*. Harmondsworth: Penguin.

Taylor, M. and Garson, Y. (1982) *Schooling in the Middle Years*. Trentham: Trentham Books.

Taylor, P.H.T. (1970) *How Teachers Plan Their Courses*. Windsor: NFER.

Taylor, P.H.T. (1974) *Purpose, Power and Constraint in the Primary Curriculum*. London: Macmillan.

Taylor, P.H.T., Wicksteed, D. and Hill, M. (1978) *Primary School Teachers' Attitudes to the Great Debate*. London: Primary Schools Research and Development Group.

Thomas, K. (1990) *Gender and the Subject in Higher Education*. Buckingham: SRHE and Open University Press.

Thompson, K. (1984) *Work, Employment and Unemployment*. Milton Keynes: Open University Press.

Thorndike, R.L. (1968) 'Review of Pygmalion in the classroom', *AERA Journal*, **5**, 4.

Tizard, B. and Hughes, M. (1984) *Young Children Learning*. London: Fontana.

Tizard, J., Schofield, W.N. and Hewison, J. (1982) 'Collaboration between teachers and parents in assisting children's learning', *British Journal of Educational Psychology*, **52**.

Tomlinson, S. (1981) *Educational Subnormality: A Study in Decision Making*. London: Routledge and Kegan Paul.

Tomlinson, S. (1982a) 'The educational performance of ethnic minority children' in James, A. and Jeffcoate, R. (eds), *The School in the Multicultural Society*. London: Harper and Row.

Tomlinson, S. (1982b) *A Sociology of Special Education*. London: Routledge and Kegan Paul.

Tomlinson, S. (1983) *Ethnic Minorities in British Schools: A Review of the Literature 1960–82*. Aldershot: Gower.

Tomlinson, S. (1987) 'Curriculum option choices in multi-ethnic schools' in Troyna, B. (ed.), *Racial Inequality in Education*. London: Tavistock.

Tongue, A. and Tongue, A. (1973) 'The revolution that never happened', *Times Educational Supplement*, 24 August.

Toogood, P. (1984) *The Head's Tale*. Telford: Dialogue Publications.

Toogood, P. (1991) *Small Schools*. Ticknell: Education Now Books.

Townsend, H.E.R. and Brittan, E.M. (1972) *Organisation in Multi-racial Schools*. Windsor: NFER.

Trafford, B. (1993) *Sharing Power in Schools: Raising Standards*. Ticknell: Education Now Books.

Trafford, B. (1997) *Participation, Power-sharing and School Improvement*. Nottingham: Educational Heretics Press.

Trafford, B. (2003) *School Councils, School Democracy, School Improvement*. Leicester: Secondary Heads Association.

Troyna, B. (1978) 'Race and streaming: a case study', *Educational Review*, **30**, 1.

Troyna, B. and Hatcher, R. (1992) *Racism in Children's Lives*. London: Routledge and National Children's Bureau.

Trudgill, P. (1974) *Sociolinguistics*. Harmondsworth: Penguin.

Tucker, N. (1979) 'Could do better: children reporting on teachers', *Where?*, **152**.

Tucker, N. (1980) 'Hostile reaction to student reports on teachers', *Where?*, **155**.

Tuckwell, P. and Beresford, P. (1978) *Schools for All*. London: MIND.

Turkle, S. (1995) *Life on the Screen: Identity in the Age of the Internet*. New York: Simon and Schuster.

Turner, E.S. (1964) 'Sociology examination paper', *Punch*, 2 October.

UCCA (1992) University Central Clearning House Statistics. London: HMSO.

Vallance, E. (1974) 'Hiding the hidden curriculum', *Curriculum Theory Network*, **4**, 1.

Veldman, D.J. (1970) 'Pupil evaluation of student teachers and their supervisors', *Journal of Teacher Education*, **21**.

Veldman, D.J. and Peck, R.F. (1963) 'Student teacher characteristics from the pupils' view point', *Journal of Educational Psychology*, **54**.

Verhallen, M., Appel, R. and Schoonen, R. (1989) 'Language functions in early childhood education: the cognitive linguistic experiences of bilingual and monolingual children', *Language and Education*, **3**, 2.

Vulliamy, G. (1978) 'Culture clash and school music' in Barton, L. and Meighan, R. (eds), *Sociological Interpretations of Schooling and Classrooms: A Reappraisal*. Driffield: Nafferton.

Wade, B. (1978) 'What a pity Richard can read', *Cambridge Journal*, **8**, 1.

Wade, B. (1984) *Story at Home and School*. Birmingham: Educational Review Publications.

Wade, B. and Moore, M. (1993) *Experiencing Special Education*. Buckingham: Open University Press.

Wakeford, J. (1969) *The Cloistered Elite*. London: Macmillan.

Walford, G. (1984) *British Public Schools: Policy and Practice*. Lewes: Falmer.

Walker, R. (1985) *Doing Research: A Handbook for Teachers*. London: Methuen.

Walker, S. and Barton, L. (1983) *Gender, Class and Education*. Lewes: Falmer.

Wallace, N. (1983) *Better than School*. New York: Larson.

Waller, W. (1932) *The Sociology of Teaching*. Oxford: Wiley.

Walteenspuhl, P. (1994) 'Team teaching and didactically defined spaces in school architecture: the triadic system applied to education', *Education Media International*, **31**, 2.

Wankowski, J. (1973) *Temperament, Motivation and Academic Achievement*. Birmingham: University of Birmingham Survey and Counselling Unit.

Wankowski, J. (1974) 'Teaching method and academic success in sixth form and university', *Journal of Curriculum Studies*, **6**, 1.

Wankowski, J. (1981) 'Summing up' in Raaheim, K. and Wankowski, J., *Helping Students to Learn at University*. Bergen: Sigma Forlag.

Warmsley, J. (1970) *Neill and Summerhill*. Harmondsworth: Penguin.

Warnock Report (1978) *Special Educational Needs*. Report of the Committee of Enquiry into the Education of Handicapped Children and Young People (Cmnd 7212). London: HMSO.

Watkins, J.W.N. (1973) 'Historical explanations in the social sciences' in O'Neill, J. (ed.), *Modes of Individualism and Collectivism*. London: Heinemann.

Watts, A.G. (1983) *Education, Unemployment and the Future of Work*. Milton Keynes: Open University Press.

Watts, J. (1977) *The Countesthorpe Experience*. Hemel Hempstead: George Allen and Unwin.

Watts, J. (1980) *Towards an Open School*. London: Longman.

Webb, J. (1990) *Children Learning at Home*. Lewes: Falmer Press.

Weber, M. (1964) *The Theory of Social and Economic Organization*. New York: Free Press.

Wedell, K. (1995) *Putting the Code of Practice into Practice*. London: Institute of Education.

Weightman, G. (1977) 'Sociologists observed', *New Society*, 24 March.

Weinburger, J. (1983) *Fox Hill Reading Workshop*. London: Family Service Units Publication.

Weiner, G. (1985) *Just a Bunch of Girls*. Milton Keynes: Open University Press.

Weis, L. (ed.) (1988) *Class, Race and Gender in American Education*. Albany: State University of New York Press.

Weitzman, L. (1972) 'Sex role socialization in picture books', *American Journal of Sociology*, **77**, 6.

Welgemoed, A. 'Democratising a School in South Africa', in Harber, C. (ed) (1998), *Voices for Democracy*. Nottingham: Education Now Books.

Wells, G. and Nicholls, J. (1985) *Language and Learning: An Interactional Perspective*. Lewes: Falmer.

Werthman, C. (1963) 'Delinquents in school: a test for the legitimacy of authority' in Cosin, B. *et al.* (eds), *School and Society*. London: Routledge and Kegan Paul.

Weston, P., Taylor, P.H.T. and Hurman, A. (1978) 'Clients' expectations of secondary schooling', *Educational Review*, **30**, 2.

Wexler, P. (1976) *The Sociology of Education: Beyond Equality*. Indianapolis: Bobbs-Merril.

Wexler, P. (1982) 'Structure, text, and subject: a critical sociology of school knowledge' in Apple, M. (ed.), *Cultural and Economic Reproduction in Education*. London: Routledge and Kegan Paul.

White, R. and Brockington, D. (1983) *Tales out of School*. London: Routledge and Kegan Paul.

Whittaker, P. (1993) *Managing Change in Schools*. Buckingham: Open University Press.

Whitty, G. (1977) *School Knowledge and Social Control*. Milton Keynes: Open University Press.

Whitty, G. (1978) 'School examinations and the politics of school knowledge' in Barton, I. and Meighan, R. (eds), *Sociological Interpretations of Schooling and Classrooms: Reappraisal*. Driffield: Nafferton.

Whitty, G. and Young, M.F.D. (1976) *Explorations in the Politics of School Knowledge*. Driffield: Nafferton.

Whyld, J. (1983) *Sexism in the Secondary Curriculum*. London: Harper & Row.

Whyte, J. (1986) *Getting the GIST*. Henley-on-Thames: Routledge and Kegan Paul.

Widlake, P. and Macleod, F. (1984) *Raising Standards*. Coventry: Community Education Development Centre.

Wilby, P. (1981) 'The Belfield experiment', *Sunday Times*, 29 March.

Wilkinson, A. (1975) *Language and Education*. Oxford: Oxford University Press.

Willes, M. (1983) *Children into Pupils*. London: Routledge and Kegan Paul.

Willey, R. (1984) *Race, Equality and Schools*. London: Methuen.

Williams, J. (1979) 'Perspectives on the multi-cultural curriculum', *Social Science Teacher*, **8**, 4.

Williams, J. (1987) 'The construction of women and black students as educational problems: reevaluating policy on gender and "race"' in Arnot, M and Weiner, G. (eds), *Gender and the Politics of Schooling*. London. Unwin Hyman.

Williams, R. (1961) *The Long Revolution*. Harmondsworth: Penguin.

Williams, R. (1977) *Ideology*. Milton Keynes: Open University Press.

Willis, P. (1977) *Learning to Labour*. Farnborough: Saxon House.

Willis, P. (1978) *Profane Culture*. London: Routledge and Kegan Paul.

Willis, P. (1984) 'Youth unemployment', *New Society*, 5 April and 12 April.

Wilmott, A. and Nuttall, D. (1975) *The Reliability of Examinations at 16 Plus*. London: Schools Council/ Evans/Methuen.

Wiseman, S. (1964) *Education and Environment*. Manchester: University of Manchester Press.

Wolpe, A. (1978) 'Education and the sexual division of labour' in Kuhn, A. and Wolpe, A. (eds), *Feminism and Materialism*. London: Routledge.

Woodin, M. and Lucas, C. (2004) *Green Alternatives to Globalisation: A Manifesto*. London: Pluto.

Woods, P. (1976) 'Pupils' views of school', *Educational Review*, **28**, 2.

Woods, P. (1977a) *The Ethnography of the School*. Milton Keynes: Open University Press.

Woods, P. (1977b) *The Pupil's Experience*. Milton Keynes: Open University Press.

Woods, P. (1979) *The Divided School*. London: Routledge and Kegan Paul.

Woods, P. (ed.) (1980a) *Pupil Strategies*. Beckenham: Croom Helm.

Woods, P. (ed.) (1980b) *Teacher Strategies*. Beckenham: Croom Helm.

Woods, P. (1983) *Sociology and the School*. London: Routledge and Kegan Paul.

Worsley, P. (1973) 'The state of theory and the status of theory', *Sociology*, **8**, 1.

Wragg, T. (1984), 'Education for the twenty-first century' in Harber, C. *et al.* (eds), *Alternative Educational Futures*. London: Holt, Rinehart and Winston.

Wright, N. (1989) *Assessing Radical Education*. Milton Keynes: Open University Press.

Wright Mills, C. (1959) *The Sociological Imagination*. Oxford: Oxford University Press.

Wrong, D. (1961), 'The oversocialized view of man in modern sociology', *American Journal of Sociology*, **26**.

Wynn, B. (1977) 'Aspects of the teaching of domestic subjects', unpublished MA dissertation, University of London.

Young, M.F.D. (ed.) (1971) *Knowledge and Control*. London: Collier-Macmillan.

Young, M.F.D. (1976) 'The schooling of science' in Whitty, G. and Young, M.F.D., *Explorations in the Politics of School Knowledge*. Driffield: Nafferton.

Young, M.F.D. and Whitty, G. (eds) (1977) *Society, State and Schooling*. Lewes: Falmer.

Zifferblatt, S. (1975) 'Architecture and human behaviour', unpublished paper, Stanford University.

Index of Subjects

Index of Names

Abraham, J.H. 3
Adcock, J. 450, 477
Ainley, P. 349
Alexander,R. 99, 104
Allen, V. 214
Apple, M 77, 88, 84
  and McCarthy, C. 84
  and Weis, L. 86
Aspen, P. 346
Aviram, A. 446

Bailey, D., and Hall, S. 352
Baker, K. 389
Baldero, J. 263, 265
Ball, C. 40, 440
Ball, S. 360, 407
Banks, O. 294
Barber, T.X. and Silver, H.J. 166
Barnes, D. 131, 132, 173, 187, 189, 190
  and Shemilt, D. 185, 186, 187, 218, 236
Barrett, M. 85, 86
Barthelomew, J. 263
Barton, L.
  and Tomlinson, S. 421
  and Walker, S. 29, 246, 353, 405,
Bauman, Z. 348
Bealing, D. 96
Becker, H. 24, 161, 164, 198, 305, 338, 368, 369, 397,
Bell, R. and Hoyle, E. 257
Bellack, A. 188
Bennett, S.N. and Jornan, J. 221
Beresford, P and Tuckwell, P. 426, 436
Berger, P. 3, 7, 8, 9, 34, 285, 302,
and Luckmann, T. 174, 303
Berliner, W. 80

Bernstein, B. 78, 84, 176, 177, 178, 179, 180, 191,
  330, 331, 396, 398
Berthoud, R. 397
Bhat, A. 406
Biber, B. and Minuchin, P. 153
Bidwell, C.E. 148
Biggs, A.P. and Edwards, A.V. 415
Biko, S. 403
Blair, A. 359
Blishen, E. 18, 19, 20, 21, 23, 25, 101
Bloom, E. 40, 197
Blum, A. 298
Blumer, H. 304
Bonner, S. 264
Bookbinder, G 431.
Boswell, D. and Wingrove, J. 432
Bourdieu,P. 78, 84
  and Passeron, J. 84
Bowles, S. and Gintis, H. 326, 328, 329, 330, 331,
  332
Braverman, H. 326, 327
Britton, J. 184,
Broadfoot, P. 194
Brockington, D. and White, R. 18
Brophy, J. and Goode, T. 168
Browne, L. 264, 267
Bruner, J.S. 478
Buckingham, D 69.
Bull, R. and Steven, J. 160
Burgess, R.G. 341
Burke,C, and Grosvenor, I. 20, 91
Burnham, J.R. and Hartshough, D.M. 163
Burns, E. 324
Byrne, D. 376

Callaghan, J. 16